CW00621553

EXPLORE
HISTORIC
AUSTRALIA

EXPLORE HISTO

Your Guide to Austr

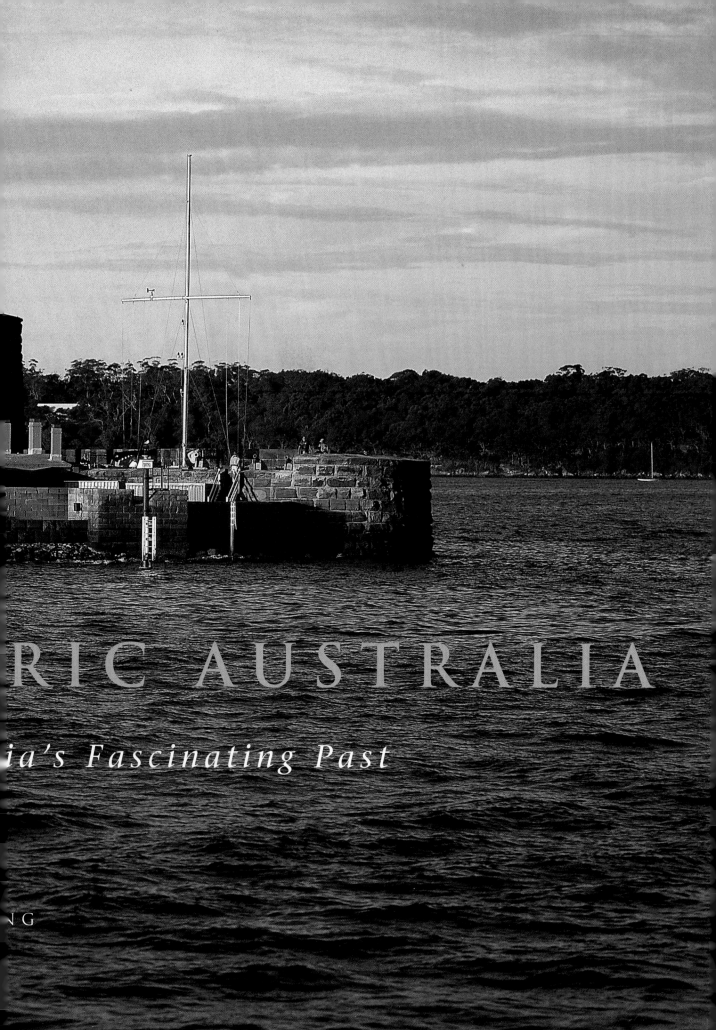

RIC AUSTRALIA

ia's Fascinating Past

CONTENTS

Miss Traill's House, Bathurst, New South Wales

CONTENTS

Rippon Lea, Melbourne, Victoria

HOW TO USE THIS BOOK

EXPLORE HISTORIC AUSTRALIA is divided into State chapters featuring the following sections:

1. STATE INTRODUCTION

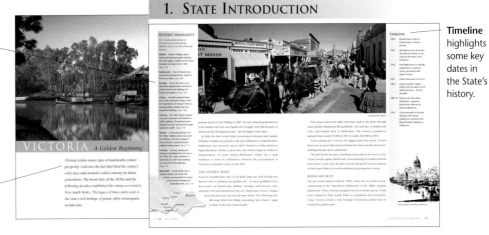

Historic Highlights
summary lists towns of historical significance in the State that appear as double-page features.

Timeline highlights some key dates in the State's history.

Introduction provides an overview of the State's history.

2. CAPITAL CITY INTRODUCTION

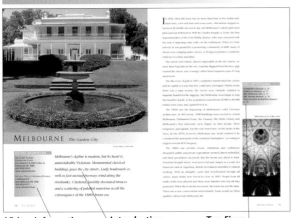

Visitor Information with contact details.

Introduction to the history of the capital city.

Top Fives are the must-see sights in each capital.

3. INNER CAPITAL CITY

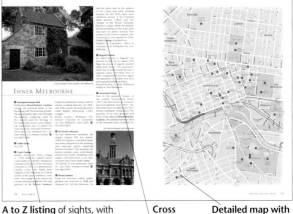

A to Z listing of sights, with practical information – addresses, opening details and phone numbers.

Cross references are in bold.

Detailed map with numbered sights locates A to Z entries in the inner city.

4. AROUND THE CAPITAL CITY

Map References to road atlas section.

A to Z listing of sights, with practical information – addresses, opening details and phone numbers.

Area map with numbered sights relates to the A to Z listing around the capital city.

5. A FEATURED WALK IN THE CAPITAL CITY

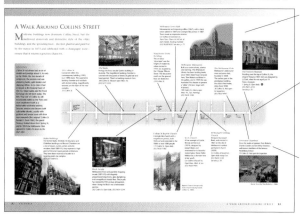

Walking feature provides a more in-depth look at an area of special historic interest close to the city.

Places of interest marked on the map allow a self-guided tour.

Informative entries on individual sights, most illustrated with recent photos or historic material.

SPECIAL NOTES

Some properties mentioned are not open to the public. Visitors are reminded to respect private property. Some major properties, public and private, are open on a limited basis, sometimes just once or twice a year. Check with the local Visitor Information. Opening times do change and some venues close. Regional museums in particular are often staffed by volunteers and their hours vary. The opening hours listed do not apply to public holidays unless specifically stated. We recommend you ring ahead to check current opening times.

6. THE STATE FROM A TO Z

A to Z listing of historic towns with a brief history of the town, visitor information and contact details.

In the Area offers information on sights near the town.

Map References to road atlas section.

7. HISTORIC HIGHLIGHTS

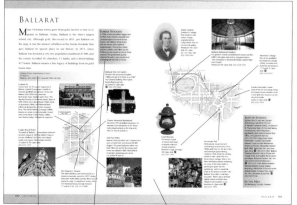

Visitor Information and contact details.

History panels provide additional background information.

Historic Highlights look at some of the State's most interesting historic towns. Most sights are illustrated, some with historic images.

8. ROAD ATLAS

Road Atlas section at the back of the book provides complete coverage of each State.

All towns marked with a 🏛 symbol on the road maps have an entry in the A to Z section.

9. INDEX

This extensive section contains over 10 000 text and map references. It includes town names mentioned in the text and on the maps. Every major historic sight is listed, as well as significant natural features. *See p.382.*

TEXT SYMBOLS

🛈	Visitor Information
NT	Property owned or managed by the National Trust of Australia
Ⓢ	Fee charged for entry

INTRODUCTION

ANCIENT CONTINENT, ANCIENT CULTURE

Australia is an ancient land, its geological history reaching back millions of years, its landscape a blend of often startling landforms, arid desert, pockets of dense forest and sweeping coastlines.

That unique physical heritage is intimately linked to Australia's Aboriginal people, who have called this land home for more than 40 000 years. Their lives, their culture and history are inextricably tied to the land. Their history has been passed from generation to generation through rich oral traditions, recounting through legend and mythology their spiritual beliefs and how the landscape was formed.

Aboriginal shields, South Australian Museum

The natural history and the Aboriginal history of Australia are largely outside the scope of this book, which deals mainly with the built environment, and with history from European settlement to the early twentieth century. However, there are tangible signs of the Aboriginal occupation of this country over millennia. Most impressive are the magnificent rock-art galleries that can be found, especially in the northern parts of Australia. In some cases, in the so-called 'contact art', the coming of white settlers, with sailing ships, guns and horses, is recorded. Although many Aboriginal sites of historic significance are sacred sites and not open to the general public, some of the rock-art galleries, and major sites such as those at Uluru and Kata-Tjuta, which are accessible to the public, are included.

SINCE 1788

Against this ancient background is Australia's modern history, a mere 200 years of occupation, migration and expansion. Although the Dutch, the Portuguese, possibly the Spanish and certainly the French sailed along our shores in the 1600s and 1700s, it was the British who finally settled here. They claimed the land, initially as a penal settlement to cater for the overflow from British gaols, hoisting the Union Jack at Sydney Cove in 1788. But somehow, the gaol 'beyond the seas' turned into a colony, and not much more than a century later – when the colonies formed a federation – into a nation.

Portrait of Capt. Cook by John Webber, National Portrait Gallery, Canberra

BUILDING OUR HERITAGE

Sturdy convict-built structures from those penal days – from windmills and bridges, to churches and barracks offer a fascinating link with that era. Many historic buildings across the country reflect our British heritage, the way the colonials established themselves always with an eye on England. Some of our finest nineteenth-century buildings are government buildings – the regal abodes of governors, courthouses, houses of parliament, grand treasuries – that emulated those of the 'mother country'.

Squatters, in their relentless search for new lands, helped pioneer the bush, living first in slab huts or rudimentary houses and later in spacious homesteads. Some of these pioneers became landed gentry, erecting 'palaces in paddocks'. Often the outbuildings, such as shearing sheds, coach-houses and stables, have their own unique stories to tell.

Gold, a recurring theme in Australia's nineteenth-century history, brought immense wealth and left a remarkable architectural legacy. Extravagant bank buildings, imposing mansions and isolated ghost towns are all testimony to those heady days.

SHAPING OUR CULTURE

The coming together of people from many nations is an integral part of our history. In South Australia, German migrants brought their culture, traditions and building styles to the Adelaide Hills and Barossa Valley. Elsewhere, Cornish miners built as they had done in their homelands. A Chinese joss house in Bendigo, a tin mosque in Kalgoorlie, Japanese gravestones in Broome – across the country are signs of cultures that have helped shape Australia.

Until late in the twentieth century, virtually all migrants arrived by sea, and Australia has a strong maritime history – shipwrecks, sailing ships and steamers, ports and bond stores, custom houses, lighthouses and fortifications are evidence of that tradition.

Australia's modern history may be short, but it is a surprisingly rich and varied tapestry of events, people and places, with much to explore and much to teach us about our past – and our future.

Argyle Stores, The Rocks, New South Wales

Government House by George William Evans, 1805, Parramatta, New South Wales

Japanese gravestone, Broome, Western Australia

NEW SOUTH WALES

New South Wales began as a penal colony; a thousand or so recalcitrant convicts and reluctant soldiers dumped on the shores of Sydney Cove. It's unlikely that any amongst those of the First Fleet could have guessed on that day in January 1788, when the Union Jack was unfurled on such foreign land, that this was the birth of a new nation.

irth of a Nation

Sydney Harbour Bridge and The Rocks

For these earliest settlers the most urgent need was for food and shelter, and the first tentative steps into the inland were in search of fertile land for crops and materials for building. Survival was a struggle, and few of these men and women were committed to the task of colonising.

When Governor Macquarie arrived in 1809, New South Wales was still a convict outpost. But Macquarie had a vision of grander things and set to work initiating public works and fine buildings.

The original inhabitants, such as the Aboriginal Eora people around Sydney, were pushed further from their lands as the British established

HISTORIC HIGHLIGHTS

For a look around some of New South Wales' most interesting historic towns, see the following entries.

Armidale   A university town on the New England plateau, in a wealthy pastoral district, noted for its fine cathedrals and elegant Victorian buildings. *See p. 40*

Bathurst   Australia's oldest inland town boasts generous, wide streets and a rich architectural heritage, from early colonial cottages to a splendid courthouse. *See p. 42*

Berrima   This delightful village is a remarkable legacy of colonial times. Handsomely restored colonial Georgian buildings include Australia's oldest gaol. *See p. 44*

Broken Hill   The epitome of a mining town, in a desert landscape. This is the birthplace of BHP, and a town whose mining and union heritage is of national significance. *See p. 46*

Goulburn   A major provincial city, surrounded by prosperous farming country, Goulburn dates back to 1828. *See p. 48*

Parramatta   The site of the colony's first land grant, the first successful 'farm', the country's oldest farmhouse, and the first cemetery. *See p. 50*

Windsor   Settled in 1810, Windsor has a wealth of early colonial buildings including convict architect Francis Greenway's masterpiece, St Matthew's Church. *See p. 52*

themselves and moved inland. They suffered from introduced disease, lack of food as their hunting grounds were taken, and then finally at gunpoint as settlers took the land for themselves.

EARLY EXPLORATION

European settlement was confined to a coastal strip until 1813, when explorers Blaxland, Wentworth and Lawson finally crossed the Blue Mountains, opening the way for expansion to the west. Other explorers – such as John Oxley, Charles Sturt and Major Sir Thomas Mitchell – were also gradually mapping the country, and close behind were the squatters and pastoralists, eager for new lands.

In the 1850s gold was discovered by Edward Hargraves in Summerhill Creek, near Bathurst. Its immediate effects were disruptive, as people downed tools to head for the diggings, but soon its benefits began to filter through society. Capital and labour boosted the economy. Markets grew, settlement spread, building boomed and the colony prospered. Other wealth lay below the surface – coal near Newcastle and Wollongong, silver–lead–zinc ore around Broken Hill.

Silverton ghost town

TIMELINE

1788   The First Fleet – 11 ships in all – arrives at Botany Bay. Capt. Arthur Phillip is appointed Governor-in-Chief of NSW.

1791   The first land grant is made in Australia – Experiment Farm granted to James Ruse.

1793   The first free settlers reach New South Wales.

1851   Gold is discovered near Bathurst by Edward Hargraves, sparking the State's first gold rush.

1883   Charles Rasp registers the first mineral claim at what becomes Broken Hill.

1889   Sir Henry Parkes, NSW Premier, makes a passionate call for federation.

1901   The Commonwealth of Australia is proclaimed in a ceremony at Centennial Park, Sydney.

1932   Sydney Harbour Bridge is officially opened.

BOOM AND BUST

The 1870s and 1880s were boom years. Roads were improved and thousands of kilometres of railway line linked the bush with towns and ports. The cry to 'unlock the land' forced the government to make more land available – the colony's coffers swelled as both small farmers and squatters purchased properties. The 1890s, however, saw the first Depression. Farming the land proved to be tough – droughts, plagues of rabbits, over-grazing and low prices affected those in the country. Things weren't much better in the cities, with many businesses (including banks) failing, many people out of work and even evicted from their houses.

NEW SOUTH WALES LEADS THE WAY

By the turn of the century, however, a new sense of optimism was in place. After years of discussion the six colonies agreed to form a federation and on 1 January 1901 became states of the Commonwealth of Australia. New South Wales, especially buoyant, had overshadowed its gold-rich rival Victoria and was the country's most prosperous state.

King Street, Sydney, 1886

THE HYDE PARK BARRACKS

SYDNEY *Harbourside City*

Hyde Park Barracks

VISITOR INFORMATION

SYDNEY VISITOR INFORMATION CENTRE
106 George St, The Rocks
Sydney NSW 2000
13 20 77
www.visitnsw.com.au

NATIONAL TRUST OF AUSTRALIA (NSW)
Observatory Hill, The Rocks
Sydney NSW 2000
(02) 9258 0123
www.nsw.nationaltrust.org.au

Sydney is Australia's oldest, largest and most spectacular city. From a tiny, squalid prison – scarcely more than 1000 people huddled around Sydney Cove – it has grown into a thriving metropolis in just over 200 years. Amidst its towering skyscrapers are fascinating signs of its colonial heritage.

Governor Phillip, in charge of the motley crew that made up the First Fleet in 1788, declared Port Jackson 'the finest harbour in the world'. Its sweeping bays and swelling headlands are still dramatically beautiful and amongst its greatest assets. Dense modern development, the majestic arch of the Harbour Bridge and the soaring sails of the Opera House serve only to enhance it.

When the first reluctant marines and convicts arrived in January 1788, they set to work at once: 'in one place a party cutting down the woods; a second setting up a blacksmith's forge; a third, dragging along a load of stones or provisions; here an officer pitching his marquee'.

Captain Cook's glowing reports about the fertile soils, the 'Woods and Lawns', the pastures where cattle could graze all year, had raised high expectations. The reality was something else. With few tools and little experience, the settlers made do with primitive wattle-and-daub huts, many of them so flimsy that they were washed away in the first heavy shower. Governor Phillip's house was a prefabricated affair of canvas and timber, 'neither wind nor weatherproof'.

When Lachlan Macquarie arrived to take up his post as Governor in 1809, he found a town 'cobbled up by amateurs', a higgledy-piggledy settlement in disorder and disarray. He laid down rules for the width of streets, introduced building regulations and commissioned buildings that were, and still are, inspiring. Aided by emancipist architect Francis Greenway, Macquarie had laid the foundations for a fine city by the time he returned to England in 1821.

FIVE TOP HISTORIC HOUSES

Elizabeth Bay House, *p. 12*
Experiment Farm Cottage, *p. 51*
Old Government House, *p. 50*
Rouse Hill Estate, *p. 15*
Vaucluse House, *p. 15*

By the 1870s Sydney was prospering, the capital of a rapidly expanding colony that had experienced the tumult and the wealth of gold. Rows of small workmen's cottages were strung up and down the hilly inner-city streets. Elsewhere, more elaborate and extravagant Victorian-era buildings began to emerge on the skyline, in complete contrast to the existing restrained Colonial Georgian architecture, some of it dating back to convict days.

Grand banks, classical edifices, Gothic cathedrals and, most grandiose of all, the profusely ornamented town hall were the order of the day. Until after World War II these buildings dominated Sydney. Now, soaring skyscrapers tower above all else, but much remains to reveal Sydney's origins, from the humble cottages of the historic Rocks area to Georgian mansions and splendid civic buildings in the mellow Sydney sandstone.

Government House

Admiralty House, Kirribilli

INNER SYDNEY

1 Admiralty House
One of Sydney's classic waterside mansions, formal in appearance and grand in scale, in a superlative setting on a grassy headland with sweeping harbour views. The original single-storey house (1842) was enlarged into a two-storey, late-Victorian residence by 1892 and purchased about this time for the British Naval Commander in Australia. It is an imposing sight from the harbour waters. Since 1913 this has been the Sydney residence of Australia's Governors-General.
Kirribilli Ave, Kirribilli. Open on special occasions only (advertised in press, or check with Visitor Information).

2 Art Gallery of NSW
The Classical Revival edifice (1885–1909) stands solitary, looking across the green slope of The Domain. The sandstone facade features a massive Ionic portico and wall carvings of figures from Classical antiquity; inside, much of the building is modern. The gallery, established in 1874, has a distinguished collection of Australian artwork, including some of Australia's finest colonial paintings and extensive exhibits of Aboriginal and Torres Strait Islander art.
Art Gallery Rd, The Domain, City. Open daily. (02) 9225 1744.

3 Australian Museum
Australia's largest natural history collection is housed in a grandiose Classical sandstone building (1846–1910). The south wing (1902–07) is notable for its Roman coffered ceilings and decorative columns. The museum, founded in 1827, has a brilliant collection, presented in a scholarly and engaging manner. Environmental and cultural heritage are explored and the Djamu ('I am here') Gallery features an excellent display of indigenous arts from Australia and the Pacific.
68 College St, City. Open daily. Ⓢ (02) 9320 6000.

4 Australian National Maritime Museum
A fascinating look at how the sea has shaped Australia and our coastal culture. Our maritime history is explored through the waves of migration, from 50 000 years ago to the convict-era, post-war migrants and refugee 'boat people'. There's also a fleet of mostly operational craft, including a racing yacht, a pearling lugger, a Vietnamese refugee boat and – the most popular exhibits – the naval destroyer HMAS *Vampire* and the submarine HMAS *Onslow*. State-of-the-art displays and on-board tours of vessels bring the history to life.
2 Murray St, Darling Harbour. Open daily. Ⓢ (02) 9552 7777.

5 Cadman's Cottage
Sydney's oldest surviving house, a sturdy, four-room, rubble sandstone dwelling built 1815–16 as a boatmen's barracks. John Cadman, a former convict, and coxswain of government boats, lived in the cottage until 1845. The cottage, originally right on the beach, was left landlocked by the construction of Circular Quay. It now serves as the information centre for Sydney Harbour National Park.
110 George St, The Rocks. Open daily. (02) 9247 5033.
See also A Walk Around The Rocks p. 16

6 Customs House
One of the most significant buildings in the history of European settlement in Australia, on the site where the First Fleet marines are said to have hoisted the British flag in January 1788. The customs house has evolved over 150 years into an impressive five-storey building, looking across the original 'Sydney Cove'. Its modest, two-storey Greek Revival beginnings (1844) were transformed in 1885–87 into a

Australian National Maritime Museum, Darling Harbour

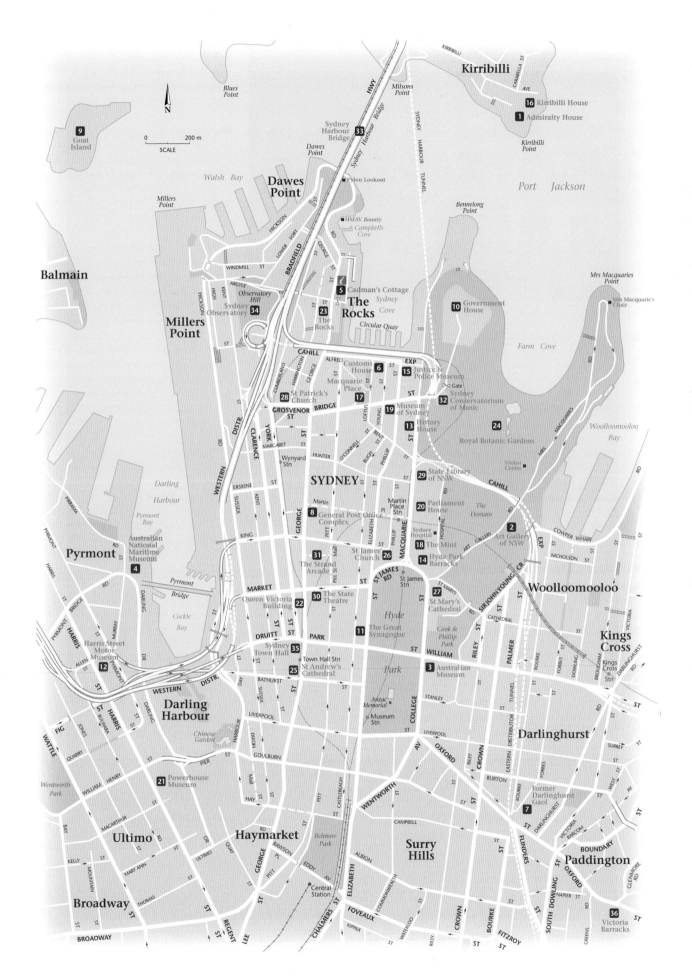

Kirribilli

16 Kirribilli House
1 Admiralty House

Kirribilli Point

Blues Point

Milsons Point

9 Goat Island

N

0   200 m
SCALE

Port Jackson

Walsh Bay

Dawes Point

33 Sydney Harbour Bridge

Dawes Point

■ Pylon Lookout

■ HMAV Bounty
Campbells Cove

Bennelong Point

Mrs Macquaries Point

■ Mrs Macquarie's Chair

Balmain

Millers Point

Millers Point

Observatory Hill
34 Sydney Observatory

23 The Rocks

5 Cadman's Cottage

The Rocks

Sydney Cove

Circular Quay

10 Government House

Farm Cove

Woolloomooloo Bay

28 St Patrick's Church

6 Customs House
15 Justice & Police Museum

17 Macquarie Place

32 Sydney Conservatorium of Music

■ Gate

19 Museum of Sydney

13 History House

Royal Botanic Gardens

24

SYDNEY

Wynyard Stn

8 General Post Office Complex

29 State Library of NSW

20 Parliament House

The Domain

■ Visitor Centre

2 Art Gallery of NSW

Woolloomooloo

Darling Harbour

Pyrmont Bay

Pyrmont

4 Australian National Maritime Museum

Pyrmont Bridge

Cockle Bay

Martin Place Stn

Martin Place

Sydney Hospital
■ Hospital

18 The Mint

14 Hyde Park Barracks

31 The Strand Arcade

26 St James' Church

St James Stn

27 St Mary's Cathedral

Kings Cross

Kings Cross Stn

12 Harris Street Motor Museum

22 Queen Victoria Building

30 The State Theatre

35 Sydney Town Hall

25 St Andrew's Cathedral

Town Hall Stn

11 The Great Synagogue

Hyde Park

3 Australian Museum

Museum Stn

■ Anzac Memorial

7 Former Darlinghurst Gaol

Darlinghurst

Wentworth Park

Ultimo

21 Powerhouse Museum

Chinese Garden

Darling Harbour

Haymarket

Belmore Park

Surry Hills

Paddington

36 Victoria Barracks

Broadway

Central Station

Government House

three-storey Italianate palazzo. In 1895–1903 French Classical elements were added. Note the polished granite columns and beautifully sculpted coat-of-arms above the entrance. Dramatically refurbished, with soaring glass atrium, shops and cafes, it is also a venue for cultural events.
31 Alfred St, Circular Quay, City. Open daily. (02) 9247 2285.

◼ Former Darlinghurst Gaol
The first large gaol in the colony and Australia's largest 19th-century walled prison. Francis Greenway chose the site under directions from Gov. Macquarie. Convicts erected the massive, forbidding stone wall (1822–24), most of which is still intact. Mortimer Lewis designed the gaol, with cell blocks radiating from a fine central building (originally a circular chapel, now a library), topped by a lantern. Work started in 1835 but, beset by financial difficulties, was only completed 50 years later. The gaol became a technical college and art school in 1921, and is now part of the Sydney Institute.
Forbes St, Darlinghurst. Grounds open daily. (02) 9252 3366.

◼ General Post Office Complex
Dominating Martin Pl. is this huge Classical Revival building (1874) designed by Colonial Architect James Barnet and modelled on the lines of an Italian Renaissance palazzo, with lengthy colonnaded arcades, carved capitals, a many-layered clock tower and ornamental carvings. Amidst a public furore Barnet was requested to

remove the 'grotesque carvings', but they can still be seen. Now converted to a hotel, office and retail complex.
Cnr Martin Pl. & George St, City (between Pitt & George sts). Open daily.

◼ Goat Island
A long, colourful and sometimes grisly history links Goat Island to Sydney's colonial days. Convict-built structures from the 1830s include a powder magazine (1836–38) and an extensive wharf, a barracks, kitchen, sentry post, cooperage and well-designed sandstone soldiers' quarters (1839), with six verandah columns carved from single pieces of stone. During the 1860s more than 7000 barrels of explosives were in storage on the island. In 1900, the island was used briefly as a quarantine zone during the outbreak of bubonic plague.
Sydney Harbour. NPWS. Tours depart from Cadman's Cottage Fri.–Mon. Booking essential. $ (02) 9247 5033.

◼ Government House
A 'mini-castle', this two-storey Gothic Revival house (1837–45) with turrets, crenellated battlements and Gothic arches, surrounded by formal grounds within the lush **Royal Botanic Gardens**, was built in the colonial era and was used as the official residence of the governor of NSW until the 1990s. Late 19th-century and early 20th-century furnishings in the State Rooms reflect the varied tastes of the vice-regal occupants.
Macquarie St, City. Open Fri.–Sun. Guided tours only. Grounds open daily. (02) 9931 5222.

◼ The Great Synagogue
A focal point for Sydney's Jewish community since it was consecrated in 1878, this magnificent synagogue features a carved sandstone facade and a grand internal space. A sound and light show (30 min) is followed by a tour of the Rosenblum Museum.
187A Elizabeth St, City (enter from 166 Castlereagh St). Sound & light show Tues. & Thurs. at 12 noon. Booking essential. (02) 9267 2477.

◼ Harris Street Motor Museum
Vintage and veteran vehicles of all description provide an extraordinary view of the fads and fashions (and follies) of the motoring world. From grand touring vehicles to a T-model truck, from steam cars to slot cars, a Goggomobile and a black State Hearse. Motorcycles and a mass of memorabilia are also displayed.
320 Harris St, Pyrmont. Open Wed.–Sun., daily during school hols. $ (02) 9552 3375.

◼ History House
Tucked between tall office buildings, this four-storey sandstone terrace (1872) is one of Sydney's few 19th-century townhouses. The filigree iron lacework (an 1880s addition) and elaborate roofscape reflect the Victorian passion for detail. Inside, carved cedar joinery and moulded ceiling decorations provide a showcase for the Royal Historical Society of Australia's fine furnishings. There is also a library.
133 Macquarie St, City. Library and office open Mon.–Fri. Tours of the reception rooms on request. (02) 9247 8001.

◼ Hyde Park Barracks
Gov. Macquarie was so pleased with the design of this building, convict architect Francis Greenway's first major commission (1817–19), that he granted Greenway an absolute pardon. The simple, elegantly proportioned, sandstock-brick barracks was built by convict labour. Up to 1000 convicts, who had formerly roamed the streets, were crammed into the spartan dormitories at night. In 1848 the barracks became an immigration depot, and was later used as an asylum for destitute women, then as law offices and courts. Now a museum, it has exhibits documenting the building's history, including a re-creation of

Convict costume, Hyde Park Barracks

its 1820s' convict days, and excellent social history exhibitions.
Macquarie St, City. Open daily. $ (02) 9223 8922.

[15] Justice and Police Museum
The world of cops, crooks and criminals comes to life behind the heavy sandstone walls and spiked gates of this former water-police court. The Water Police, established in 1830, was formed to prevent smuggling, which was rife, and to stop convicts from stowing aboard ships in port. The 1856 building, restored to its 1890s character, exhibits bushranger Capt. Moonlite's death mask, mug shots of Sydney's early criminals, a bleak corridor of cells, forensic evidence from notorious crimes and various other spine-chilling exhibits.
Cnr Albert & Phillip sts, Circular Quay, City. Open Sat.–Sun., & Sat.–Thurs. during Jan. $ (02) 9252 1144.

[16] Kirribilli House
A simple but romantic single-storey Gothic Revival house (1854–55) with steep gables and panoramic views of Sydney Harbour. It is linked to **Admiralty House**. This is the Sydney residence of Australia's prime minister.
Kirribilli Ave, Kirribilli. Not open for inspection.

[17] Macquarie Place
Relics from the first decades of colonial settlement are found in this small, leafy square, once part of the gardens of Sydney's first Government House. The hand-hewn stone Obelisk (1818), designed by Francis Greenway, was the point from which all roads and distances in the colony were measured. Close by are the anchor and cannon from HMS *Sirius*, the warship that accompanied the First Fleet.
Bridge & Loftus sts, City.

[18] The Mint
Sydney's oldest surviving public building, built as a hospital by convicts (1811–16) and financed by three wily citizens in exchange for a monopoly on selling rum, granted by Gov. Macquarie. The project was fraught with difficulties, and Macquarie severely reprimanded, but three two-storey, verandahed buildings were completed, thereafter commonly known as the 'Rum Hospital'. The central section, demolished in 1879, was later replaced by the present Sydney Hospital. The south wing, The Mint, has been a medical store, a military hospital and part of the Royal Mint. Now used as a conference centre.
10 Macquarie St, City. Not open for inspection.

[19] Museum of Sydney
Located on the site of Sydney's first Government House, built by Gov. Arthur Phillip in 1788. This intriguing purpose-built museum focuses on Sydney history, with a particular emphasis on colonial life 1788–1850, including Aboriginal culture and issues. In 1983, archaeologists unearthed the footings of the original Government House, demolished in 1846, which can be viewed through glass panels in the floor. Governors' records, artifacts and furnishings from the first Government House are also displayed. There are regularly changing exhibitions. Highly recommended.
Cnr Phillip & Bridge sts, City. Open daily. $ (02) 9251 5988.

[20] Parliament House
Consisting of the northern wing of the notorious Rum Hospital (see **The Mint**), with the addition of an 1843 Italianate Gothic section and a prefabricated iron chamber (originally intended as a church for the Victorian gold town of Bendigo) tacked on in 1856, this has been the home of the NSW State Parliament since 1829. It is an integral part of NSW's heritage. There is a parliamentary museum, the Jubilee Room, in the former library.
Macquarie St, City. Visitors' gallery and museum open Mon.–Fri. Guided tours (booking essential). (02) 9230 2111.

[21] Powerhouse Museum
This museum houses part of the huge and diverse collection of the Museum of Applied Arts and Sciences, which began in the 1870s in the extravagant Garden Palace exhibition building. The building was destroyed by fire in 1882 just three years after being built. (The original gates can still be seen in Macquarie St, outside the **Royal Botanic Gardens**.) Among the exhibits are the first locomotive to

Library, Parliament House

Queen Victoria Building

run on Sydney's railways (1855), and the fragile canvas-and-wood Bleriot monoplane, flown by Maurice Guillaux in 1914 on the first Melbourne–Sydney airmail flight. The flight took 9 hours and 33 minutes.
500 Harris St, Ultimo. Open daily. Free guided tours twice daily. Ⓢ (02) 9217 0111.

22 Queen Victoria Building
The extravagant, multi-domed Queen Victoria Building (1893–98), known generally as the QVB, has had a chequered career as everything from a winery to an air-raid shelter but has been restored to its regal splendour. Magnificent stained glass, tiled floors and cedar joinery form a glittering backdrop to its many specialist shops and cafes.
George St, City. Open daily.

23 The Rocks
See p. 16

24 Royal Botanic Gardens
A lush, quiet retreat curving around the harbour front near prestigious Macquarie St, and the site of the colony's first farm in 1788. Seeds and plants brought by Gov. Phillip from Rio de Janeiro and the Cape of Good Hope were cultivated in an attempt to feed the struggling colony. After 1816 the area was developed as botanic gardens and 'pleasure grounds'. Today, the 25-ha gardens, dotted with fascinating buildings, fountains and statuary, embrace a whole range of landscaping tastes. A path (signposted) leads to Mrs Macquarie's Chair, a rustic carved and inscribed stone seat (1816) from which Gov. Macquarie's wife Elizabeth enjoyed the harbour views.
Mrs Macquaries Rd, City. Open daily. Free guided walks depart daily at 10.30 a.m. from Visitor Centre. (02) 9231 8111 or (02) 9231 8125.

25 St Andrew's Cathedral
The oldest cathedral in Australia was consecrated in 1868. It is a harmonious and well-proportioned example of Gothic Revival architecture, its stone walls weathered to a warm golden brown. Recent painstaking restoration has greatly enhanced the interior.
Cnr George & Bathurst sts, City. Open daily. Tours Mon.–Fri. & Sun. Ⓢ (02) 9265 1661.

26 St James' Church
Substantially but sympathetically altered over the years, Sydney's oldest church (1820–24), and one of Australia's finest colonial churches, still reflects the sophisticated design of architect Francis Greenway. The rectangular sandstock-brick form, basically Georgian in concept, has Doric porticos and a central tower with a copper-sheathed spire. St James' was built on an axis with the **Hyde Park Barracks** and court buildings as part of Greenway's vision of a grand townscape.
King St, City. Open daily. Tours Mon. & Wed. or by appt. Ⓢ (donation for tours). (02) 9232 3022.

27 St Mary's Cathedral
William Wardell, who designed St Patrick's Cathedral in Melbourne, also designed this Gothic Revival cathedral (1868–1928). The sandstone exterior is impressive, although the spires Wardell intended were only completed in 2000. The soaring internal space is filled with golden light from the amber clerestory windows. This is the third Catholic church built on the site. Gov. Macquarie laid the foundation stone of the first in 1821, on the earliest land grant to the Catholic Church in Australia.
Cnr College St & St Marys Rd, City. Open daily. Tours Sun. or by appt. Ⓢ (donation for tours). (02) 9220 0400.

28 St Patrick's Church
Sydney's oldest surviving Catholic church, consecrated in 1844. The colony's first official Catholic mass was said in The Rocks area in 1803.
Cnr Grosvenor & Harrington sts, City. Open daily. (02) 9247 3525.

29 State Library of NSW
Started as a subscription library in 1826, the library moved into its own premises in 1845 but, 'hopelessly in debt', was bought by the NSW government, who opened it as the Free Public Library in 1869. This is Australia's oldest public library. The building, commenced in 1906, features a massive Ionic portico (1939–42). The magnificent bronze entrance doors depict Aboriginal people, Australian navigators and explorers. A marble floor mosaic of the 1644 map of explorer Abel Tasman and superb stained glass dominate the vestibule. The State Library includes the unsurpassed Mitchell Library of Australiana books, documents, maps and historical artwork. The newest wing was opened in 1988.
Cnr Macquarie St & Shakespeare Pl., City. Reference Library open daily. Mitchell Library Mon.–Sat. Free tours Tues. & Thurs. (02) 9273 1414.

30 The State Theatre
Hailed as 'a veritable symphony in steel and stone' when it opened in 1929, the opulent theatre is a lavish blend of Empire Style, Gothic, Italian and Art Deco, but pure Hollywood in concept and scale. The auditorium seats more than 2000. The interior is

The Strand Arcade

rich with gold and red, mosaic flooring and gleaming marble, brass and bronze doors and crystal chandeliers, including the *pièce de résistance* – a glittering 20 000-piece chandelier. Now a concert venue and theatre.
49 Market St, City. Open Mon.–Sat. (limited access during performances). Ⓢ *(02) 9373 6660.*

31 The Strand Arcade

An excellent example of late-Victorian extravagance, built in 1891 between George and Pitt sts, with three levels, filigree ironwork balustrades, mosaic flooring and elegantly trussed skylighting. The Strand is the last arcade of this size and splendour in Australia.
408 George St. Open daily. (02) 9232 4199.

32 Sydney Conservatorium of Music

In 1817 Gov. Macquarie requested a 'commodious castellated house' as the new Government House. Francis Greenway designed a remarkable towered and turreted stables complex (1821) as the first stage, although lack of funds meant the house itself was not begun until 1837. The stables were later converted to become the state conservatorium (1908–15) and the courtyard was roofed to create a concert hall. Flanked by towering palms, the building presents an arresting sight on the edge of the **Royal Botanic Gardens**. The building has recently been restored.
Macquarie St, City. Open by appt only. Lunchtime concerts every Wed. during term. (02) 9351 1222.

33 Sydney Harbour Bridge

One of the world's largest single-span steel arch bridges, a triumph of engineering and construction in its day and an icon on the Sydney skyline, opened in 1932. The arch spans 503 m and the total bridge stretches 1149 m. The bridge took 1400 men nine years to build and 16 workers died during the construction. A display about the bridge's history can be viewed in the Chamber Area, 70 steps up from the pylon entrance. Higher still is a dramatic lookout. For the intrepid, 'Bridgeclimb' runs small group adventure climbs across the arch.
Harbour Bridge, Pylon Lookout, access via Bridge Stairs, Cumberland St, The
Rocks. Open daily. Ⓢ *Bridgeclimb (02) 9247 3408.*
See also A Walk Around The Rocks p. 16

34 Sydney Observatory

A splendid copper-domed building (1856–57), with a square tower, built on the highest point in The Rocks. For over a century the time-ball on the tower was dropped at 1 p.m. to signal the precise time. The building, used as an astronomical observatory from the late 1880s, is now an astronomy museum. One interesting exhibition, 'Cadi Eora Birrung', tells how some Aboriginal Dreamtime stories relate to constellations.
Observatory Hill, Watson Rd, Millers Point. Open daily. Also evening viewings (booking essential). Ⓢ *(02) 9217 0485. See also A Walk Around The Rocks p. 16*

35 Sydney Town Hall

The Duke of Edinburgh laid the foundation stone in 1868, but a number of architects were involved before the final monumental and extravagant French Renaissance building was completed in 1889. Its grandiose, lavish facades, with columns and soaring towers culminating in a turret, declaimed Sydney's vision of its own importance. The flamboyance and rich decoration continue inside. The magnificent timber-panelled concert hall has an 8000-pipe organ.
George St, City. Open daily. (02) 9265 9766. Tours Mon.–Fri. booking essential. (02) 8223 3815.

36 Victoria Barracks

The largest, best-preserved colonial Georgian complex in Australia, built

Sydney Observatory, Millers Point

by convict labour (1841–47), and combining military precision with the symmetry of Georgian architecture. The lengthy main block provided accommodation for a British regiment of 800 men. The guardhouse has been manned 24 hours a day since 1848. Victoria Barracks is still used by the military, and includes a military heritage museum.
Oxford St, Paddington. Army band performs 10 a.m. each Thurs., followed by a tour of the barracks. Museum open Thurs. & Sun. Ⓢ *(02) 9339 3000.*

Also of interest

For those keen to re-live history, sail Sydney Harbour aboard a replica of Capt. Bligh's ill-fated tall ship, HMAV *Bounty*. Cruises depart several times daily.
Campbells Cove, The Rocks. Booking essential. Ⓢ *(02) 9247 1789.*

Victoria Barracks, Paddington

Fort Denison, Sydney Harbour

AROUND SYDNEY

◼ Aboriginal Sites
Aboriginal people have left many signs of their occupation of the Sydney area over the last 20 000 years, with rock engravings, art sites, shell middens and other archaeological evidence. There are more than 5500 known rock art sites and 2000 middens. All are protected by the National Parks and Wildlife Service (NPWS).
NPWS Information Centre, 102 George St, The Rocks. (02) 9253 4600 or Infoline (NSW callers only) 1300 361 967.

❶ Bare Island Fort
Map ref. 291 Q8

A well-preserved and formidable-looking concrete fort (1881–85) stands on this small island, named by Capt. James Cook in 1770. A number of forts were built, as colonists feared foreign invasion. Access to the fort was originally by flying fox. The bridge to the island was constructed in 1887.
Accessible by walkway from Anzac Pde, La Perouse. Open Sat.–Sun. $ (02) 9311 3379.

❷ Captain Cook's Landing Place
Map ref. 291 P8

The site of the first recorded landing on the east coast of Australia, at Botany Bay, where James Cook, and botanists Daniel Solander and Joseph Banks came ashore in 1770. Now part of Botany Bay National Park. A 'Discovery Centre' provides background information on this historic area.
Cape Solander Dr., Kurnell. Open daily. $ (02) 9542 0648.

❸ Centennial Park
Map ref. 287 O12, 291 Q2

Gov. Macquarie set aside this area as a common for the people of Sydney in 1820. A ceremony held here on 1 January 1901 officially established the Commonwealth of Australia, and a Federation Monument of polished granite, with six sides representing the six States, was erected that year to commemorate the event. A sweeping circular drive, palm trees, sprawling fig trees, formal flower gardens, fields of native grasses and the reflective waters of nine lakes give Centennial Park a distinctive character.

Oxford St & Alison Rd, Centennial Park. Open daily. (02) 9339 6699.

❹ Don Bank Museum
Map ref. 287 M8

A vertical slab cottage, the oldest section c. 1854, typical of early colonial construction, but gradually extended over the years. Shuttered french windows open on to the verandah, and several rooms have cedar joinery. The Victorian-style garden includes a magnificent *Magnolia grandiflora*.
Napier St, North Sydney. House open Wed. & Sun. afternoons. Garden open daily. $ (02) 9955 6279.

❺ Elizabeth Bay House
Map ref. 287 N10

This elegant, two-storey Greek Revival villa is one of the finest colonial mansions in Australia. The inspired design of John Verge was completed in 1839 for the Colonial Secretary, Alexander Macleay. A magnificent cantilevered stone staircase sweeps from the oval entrance hall to the galleried balcony, the whole crowned by a domed lantern. The house originally stood on 20 ha of land granted to Macleay by Gov. Darling and formal gardens reached down to the waterfront. Restoration by the Historic Houses Trust has been scholarly, and the house is filled with treasures from the colonial era. Regular exhibitions are held here.
7 Onslow Ave, Elizabeth Bay. Open Tues.–Sun. & most pub hols. Guided tours. $ (02) 9356 3022.

Elizabeth Bay House

6 Fort Denison

Map ref. 287 N9

The stone fort was built on a rocky island in Port Jackson, and was once known as Pinchgut – a name reputedly bestowed by convicts confined to the island on meagre bread and water rations. The term also has a nautical meaning (where a channel narrows) and, though less romantic, this may be the derivation. The body of murderer Francis Morgan was hung from the fort's gibbet in 1796, and left as a macabre warning to arriving convicts. The 'whimsical, gingerbread fortress' (1840–57) was constructed when there was fear of a Russian invasion. The superb Martello tower, the only one in Australia, is one of the best examples in the world. Well worth visiting.

Sydney Harbour. NPWS. Tours depart daily from **Cadman's Cottage.** *Booking essential.* Ⓢ *(02) 9247 5033.*

7 Juniper Hall

Map ref. 287 N11, 291 P1

The oldest surviving mansion from the Macquarie era, and one of the oldest houses in Sydney, is a grand two-storey Georgian residence (1824), built by emancipist 'gin king' Robert Cooper, who arrived in the colony in 1813. Cooper, variously engaged as a gin-distiller, architect, builder, cedar-cutter and publican, built the house for his third wife and 14 children (he went on to have another 14). Juniper Hall occupies an entire city block. The grand fanlight, fluted columns and harmonious proportions are hallmarks of the colonial Georgian houses of the well-to-do. After many years of neglect it has been well restored by the National Trust and is now used as private offices.

Cnr Oxford & Ormond sts, Paddington. Not open for inspection.

8 Ku-ring-gai Chase National Park

Map ref. 288 H8, 293 L7

Dedicated in 1894, the extensive park (over 15 000 ha) contains much evidence of Aboriginal occupation, including rock engravings and cave paintings (the Basin Track is worth exploring for Aboriginal art). Much of the park is densely wooded and it takes in the intricate, deeply indented coastline of Broken Bay and spectacular views of Pittwater. The park's Kalkari Discovery Centre

Rock carvings, Ku-ring-gai Chase National Park

arranges heritage walks, bushwalks and visits to Aboriginal sites.

Bobbin Head Rd, Turramurra. Open daily. (02) 9472 8949 or Infoline (NSW callers only) 1300 361 967. Kalkari Discovery Centre, Ku-ring-gai Chase Rd. Tours. (02) 9472 9300 or (02) 9457 9853.

9 Lindesay

Map ref. 287 O10

The first house on 'Mr Darling's Point' was the romantic mansion Lindesay, built in 1834 with a harbour view for the Colonial Treasurer, Campbell Riddell. It is a curious blend of Gothic inspiration and classic Georgian style, with lofty gables, a battlemented parapet, soaring octagonal chimneys and delicately glazed Gothic windows. Marble fireplaces, period wallpapers and the formal interiors evoke the atmosphere of more gracious days. The basement, once service quarters, is a network of cool, stone-walled

rooms with deep casement windows. Surveyor-General Major Sir Thomas Mitchell bought the residence in 1841, and there have been several other distinguished residents.
1 Carthona Ave, Darling Pt. Open for special exhibitions, recitals and an annual antique fair (usually Mar.–April). (02) 9363 2401. NT.

[10] Lyndhurst
Map ref. 287 L10

An outstanding two-storey Regency mansion (1833–36) designed by architect John Verge for Dr J Bowman, Principal Surgeon of Sydney Hospital and a son-in-law of John Macarthur. Sumptuously furnished, in its heyday, this 'genteel marine residence' was a venue for Sydney's colonial elite. By the 1840s, however, the Bowmans were bankrupt. Lyndhurst's fortunes plummeted too. It was saved from demolition in the 1970s and is now the Historic Houses Trust's Conservation Resource Centre. It has a research library and artifact reference collection related to domestic design and building conservation.
61 Darghan St, Glebe. Resource Centre open Mon.–Fri. by appt. (02) 9692 8366.

[11] Macleay Museum
Map ref. 287 L11, 291 O1

This remarkable natural history collection, started in 1780 by Alexander Macleay, the first Colonial Secretary, and continued by his son and nephew, was given to Sydney University in 1873. It encompasses one of the world's oldest and most extensive collections of anthropological and ethnographic artifacts from Australia and the South Pacific, as well as more than half a million insects, rare, exotic and extinct birds and animals, scientific instruments and historic photos.
Cnr Gosper La. & Science Rd, **University of Sydney**. *Open Mon.–Fri. Tours by appt. $ (tours only). (02) 9351 2274.*

Nutcote, Neutral Bay

Macquarie Lighthouse, Watsons Bay

[12] Macquarie Lighthouse
Map ref. 287 Q9

Francis Greenway designed the first permanent navigational aid on the Australian coast. The original lighthouse, built in 1817 on the south head of Port Jackson, was fitted with a whale-oil beam lantern. The stone used proved to be unsatisfactory, as Greenway had predicted it would, and the building was structurally faulty. By the 1880s it had to be replaced. James Barnet designed almost an exact copy of Greenway's structure. The new lighthouse (1883) operated on electricity.
Old South Head Rd, Watsons Bay. Not open for inspection.

[13] Nutcote
Map ref. 287 N8

Australia's much-loved children's author, May Gibbs, the creator of such famous characters as Snugglepot and Cuddlepie, as well as banksia men and bush babies, lived in this charming Mediterranean-style house (1925) for 44 years. Nutcote, with its stuccoed walls and blue-green shutters, is surrounded by terraced and cottage gardens. It is now a house museum, restored and furnished as it would have been in the 1930s.
5 Wallaringa Ave, Neutral Bay. Open limited hours Wed.–Sun., guided tours only. $ (02) 9953 4453.

[14] Parramatta
Map ref. 286 C6

See Historic Highlights, p. 50

15 Quarantine Station
Map ref. 287 Q6

The quarantine station, founded in 1832 at North Head, provided Sydney residents with protection for more than 150 years from contagious disease such as smallpox, bubonic plague and cholera. The haunting (some say haunted) settlement encompasses abandoned streets, more than 60 buildings, including a hospital and mortuary, cemeteries and spectacular views across the harbour. Over 1500 rock engravings tell the stories of the ships and the isolation of people quarantined. This is now part of Sydney Harbour National Park. Tours, including evening 'ghost walks', leave from Manly Wharf.
North Head Scenic Dr., Manly. Tours Mon., Wed. & Fri.–Sun. Booking essential. $ *(02) 9247 5033.*

16 Rouse Hill Estate
Map ref. 293 K7

An extraordinary homestead, once the heart of a 480-ha property taken up by free settler Richard Rouse in 1813, and occupied by six generations of the family. The substantial convict-built Georgian house and the 20 or so outbuildings – from a rustic slab piggery to an architect-designed 1875 brick stable – record the lives of the Rouse family through 180 years. The exterior, interior and the furnishings are fragile but remain remarkably intact. The garden is one of the earliest surviving gardens in Australia. Managed by the Historic Houses Trust of NSW.
Guntawong Rd (off Windsor Rd), Rouse Hill. Guided tours only, Thurs. & Sat.–Sun. Booking recommended. $ *(02) 9627 6777.*

17 Royal National Park
Map ref. 290 G12, 293 L9

Dedicated in 1879, this is the second oldest national park in the world (Yellowstone in the USA being the oldest). This remarkable 16 009-ha park is just 32 km south of Sydney. At Audley, an original dance hall and picnic pavilion from the park's Victorian era have been restored. Original carriageways, and even some ornamental trees, can be seen, although much of the park retains its wild and natural beauty. Aboriginal people of the Dharawal culture lived

Vaucluse House

in this district for thousands of years and there are many relics and rock-art sites within the bush landscape. Aboriginal Discovery Rangers take guided tours of rock engravings and explain the indigenous heritage of the area.
Farnell Ave, off Princes Hwy, 32 km s. Open daily. (02) 9542 0648 or Infoline (NSW callers only) 1300 361 967. For rock engraving tour booking (02) 9542 0649.

18 University of Sydney
Map ref. 287 L11, 291 N1

The oldest university in Australia (established c. 1850) is dominated by dramatic Gothic Revival and Elizabethan edifices ranged across the clipped, green lawns, and was inspired by the medieval colleges of Oxford and the Houses of Parliament in Westminster. The first buildings, designed by Colonial Architect Edmund Blacket, were begun in 1854. The Great Hall, Blacket's finest work, is superb, with the beamed ceiling embellished by angels carved from cedar. The Nicholson Museum of Antiquities is an archaeological museum founded in 1860 (ground floor, Old Fisher Library, 1906–10). *See also* **Macleay Museum**.

Parramatta Rd, Glebe. Grounds open daily (02) 9351 2222. Guided tours by appt. $ *(tours). Booking (02) 9351 2274.*

19 Vaucluse House
Map ref. 287 P9

William Charles Wentworth – explorer, reformer, politician and philanthropist – bought a 'snug cottage' in 1827 and began work on his 'elegant chateau'. The romantic, rambling mansion we see today, largely completed by c. 1850, was home to Wentworth, his wife and 10 children. From the front elevation Vaucluse looks like a small, castellated villa, but behind it rises to three storeys, with a turreted stair hall and a network of fine stone buildings facing the courtyard. Many of the furnishings belonged originally to the Wentworths including the carved oak dining furniture. The magnificent gardens sweep down to the harbourside in the grand landscape tradition and have been restored to their 19th-century character. Vaucluse is managed by the Historic Houses Trust.
Cnr Olola Ave & Wentworth Rd, Vaucluse. House open Tues.–Sun. Grounds open daily. $ *(02) 9388 7922.*

A WALK AROUND THE ROCKS

Sydney's oldest area, The Rocks, clings to its colonial character, as it does to the rugged sandstone cliffs around the edge of Sydney Cove. A surprising jumble of tiny cottages, stone bond stores, old-time port pubs and elegant nineteenth-century townhouses line its often chaotic maze of streets. Its maritime traditions are strong and it offers a unique insight into Sydney's beginnings. Recent decades have seen it gradually restored, and today the area is a favourite with Sydneysiders and visitors alike.

The Hero of Waterloo Hotel
One of the oldest surviving (1843–44) and one of the most colourful of The Rocks' many hostelries. A tunnel beneath the pub was apparently used for smuggling, including transporting unwilling, often drunken sailors onto waiting ships. The corner pub is virtually unchanged outside. Tours available.
81–83 Lower Fort St, Millers Point. Open daily. (02) 9252 4553.

The Rocks Sydney Visitor Information Centre
106 George St
(02) 9255 1788

Holy Trinity (Garrison Church)
Established in 1840 for the military stationed nearby and still retaining regimental plaques. In its early days the windows were of oiled canvas. The rich stained-glass window was donated in 1860 by philanthropist Dr James Mitchell, whose son endowed the **State Library of NSW** with the collection that forms the basis of the renowned Mitchell Library.
Argyle Pl., Millers Point. Open daily. (02) 9247 2664.

Argyle Place
Chosen by Gov. Macquarie in 1810 and named after his birthplace in Scotland. It retains a 19th-century village character – stone and iron fences, a sculpted stone drinking fountain (1869) and elegant gas lamps.

Lord Nelson Brewery Hotel
Believed to be the oldest hotel in Sydney, this three-storey waterfront pub opened in 1842.
19 Kent St. Open daily. (02) 9251 4044.

HISTORY

Capt. Arthur Phillip sailed into Sydney Cove at the head of the First Fleet in 1788. Almost immediately, convicts were sent ashore to clear the land for tents and huts. Most of these were built along the western shores of the cove, with its rocky sandstone outcrops, which soon became known as 'The Rocks'. From shanty town to bustling port and a stop-over for rum-soaked sailors, The Rocks became one of Sydney's most crowded but colourful inner city precincts. It has witnessed bubonic plague and dire poverty, neglect and the onslaught of wreckers' hammers, but many buildings have survived to recall its unique role in Australia's history.

Argyle Cut
A remarkable engineering feat, a passage hacked through the sandstone, at first by convicts using primitive tools, to allow easier access from Sydney Cove to Millers Point and Darling Harbour. Construction began in the 1830s.
Argyle St.

Agar Steps
Picturesque stone steps, partly carved from the bedrock, winding from Kent St to Observatory Hill, lined by Victorian terrace houses (1870s–80s).
Kent St.

National Trust Centre, SH Ervin Gallery
This building incorporates the remains of Gov. Macquarie's 1815 military hospital. For more than 120 years the highly regarded Fort Street School was based here. The 1850 wing with bowed walls (nicknamed 'the bulge' by students) is now home to the SH Ervin Gallery, specialising in Australian art. The National Trust (NSW) headquarters, a gift shop and small cafe are also here.
Observatory Hill, Watson Rd. Gallery, gift shop & cafe open Tues.–Sun. National Trust Centre open Mon.–Fri. (S) (gallery). (02) 9258 0123. NT.

Colonial House Museum

The museum occupies two floors in a four-storey house and has domestic rooms furnished as they would have been in the 19th century. There are more than 100 photographs and etchings of early Sydney.
53 Lower Fort St, Dawes Point. Open daily. Ⓢ *(02) 9247 6008.*

Sydney Harbour Bridge

One of Australia's icons, the Bridge looms large on the edge of The Rocks. Built in 1923–32, it is one of the world's largest single-span bridges. Climb the Pylon Lookout's 200 steps for sensational views.
See also p. 11.

Campbells Cove

The boarding point for the magnificent replica of Capt. Bligh's tall ship, HMAV *Bounty. See also p. 11.*

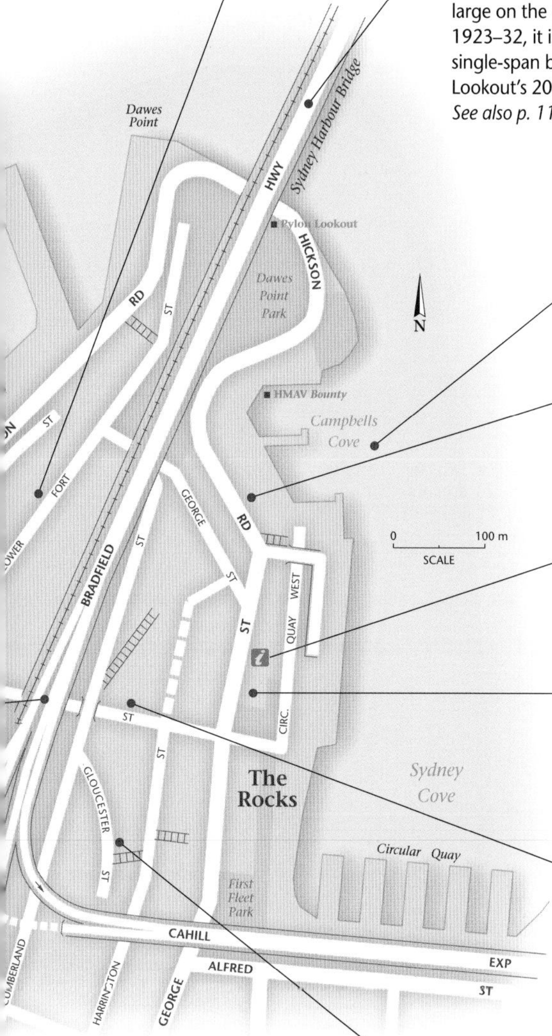

Campbell's Storehouse

A splendid line of three-storey bond stores (1838–61), with skilful stonework and a sawtooth roofline, built by Robert Campbell, the first substantial merchant and later one of the wealthiest men in the colony. The stores now house a complex of restaurants.
9–27 Circular Quay West. Open daily.

Sailors' Home

Established in 1864 so that sailors could doss down somewhere other than a brothel or rowdy inn when their ships were in port. Now Visitor Information, with museum-style displays about The Rocks.
106 George St. Open daily. (02) 9255 1788.

Cadman's Cottage

Sydney's oldest surviving house, built in 1815–16 as a boatmen's barracks. John Cadman, a former convict, lived in the cottage until 1845. Now the information centre for Sydney Harbour National Park.
110 George St. Open daily. (02) 9247 5033. See also p. 6.

Argyle Stores

One of the earliest bond stores, the first section built by convicts in 1828 as a house for Capt. Piper, and later owned by well-known emancipist businesswoman Mary Reibey. Today shops and restaurants open onto the courtyard's worn cobblestones.
16–20 Argyle St. Open daily.

Sydney Observatory

After 125 years as an astronomical observatory this distinctive colonial structure (c. 1856) is now an astronomy museum.
Observatory Hill, Watson Rd, Millers Point. Open daily. Ⓢ *(02) 9217 0485. See also p. 11.*

Susannah Place

A terrace of four houses (1844), including the original basement kitchens and backyard privies from those early days. Continuously occupied from the 1840s to the 1990s, and now part of a fascinating museum of domestic life in The Rocks. A corner store, re-created to capture the era around 1900, sells old-fashioned goods.
58–64 Gloucester St. Open Sat.–Sun. & daily in Jan. Ⓢ *(museum). (02) 9241 1893.*

Dawes Point

HWY

Sydney Harbour Bridge

Pylon Lookout

Dawes Point Park

HICKSON

RD

ST

N

HMAV *Bounty*

Campbells Cove

GEORGE

ST

RD

QUAY WEST

0   100 m
SCALE

ST

CIRC.

FORT

ST

BRADFIELD

ST

The Rocks

Sydney Cove

Circular   Quay

First Fleet Park

ST

GLOUCESTER

ST

CAHILL

ALFRED

EXP

ST

CUMBERLAND

HARRINGTON

GEORGE

NEW SOUTH WALES FROM A TO Z

Railway Station, Albury

ALBURY
Map ref. 299 Q13, 319 P4, 320 C1

The city of Albury, on the northern banks of the Murray River, began as a popular meeting place for drovers and stockmen after explorers Hume and Hovell crossed the river near here in 1824 and opened up the region. Robert Brown first settled in the area that was to become known as Albury in 1836. The city is a major regional centre, closely linked with Wodonga on the Victorian side of the Murray.

Albury Regional Museum Originally the Turk's Head Inn, a sandstock-brick hotel (1860s) with a reputation last century as the most popular pub in town. Now a local history museum. *Australia Park, Wodonga Pl. Open daily. (02) 6021 4550.*

ALSO OF INTEREST Albury Regional Art Gallery, in the splendid, lavishly ornamented Edwardian town hall (1907); its collection features some fine early Australian paintings. *546 Dean St. Open daily. (02) 6023 8187.* The Hovell Tree is a river gum blazed by William Hovell, who, with explorer Hamilton Hume, discovered the Murray River in

1824. *Near junction of Hume St & Wodonga Pl.* The grandiose Italianate railway station (1881), is built of bricks believed to have been imported from Belgium, with a massive clock tower. *Railway Pl., at top of Smollett St.* The courthouse (1860), (not open for inspection), post office (1878) with cupola and weathervane crowning the clock tower, and the former town hall (now the Regional Art Gallery, see left) form a notable Victorian streetscape. *All Dean St.* The Botanical Gardens (1877), with a 1890 bandstand, are a peaceful oasis. The PS

Cumberoona, a replica of an 1886 paddle-steamer, takes cruises (with a commentary) along the mighty Murray, leaving from Noreuil Park. The cruising season is usually late Sept.–April. $ *(02) 6041 5558.*

IN THE AREA Mungabareena Reserve: this 42-ha reserve was once used as a meeting place by many Aboriginal tribes before they headed to the high country to feast on Bogong moths. Mungabareena is an Aboriginal word that is believed to mean 'women talking'. There are several scar trees and river red gums that are up to 800 years old. There's also a Wiradjuri walkabout track. A festival celebrating Aboriginal culture is held here on the last weekend of Nov. *Off Borella Rd, opp. Albury Airport.* The award-winning Jindera Pioneer Museum has a general store (1864), a residence (c. 1905) furnished in period style, a slab hut and other pioneer relics. *16 km N, Urana Rd, Jindera. Open Tues.–Sun. (02) 6026 3622.* 🄸 *Lincoln Causeway; (02) 6041 3875, freecall 1800 800 743. Website: www. albury.wodonga.com See also Beechworth, Rutherglen, Yackandandah (all Vic.); Holbrook, Yass (NSW)*

ARMIDALE
Map ref. 295 L9

See Historic Highlights, p. 40

BATHURST
Map ref. 292 H6

See Historic Highlights, p. 42

BERRIMA
Map ref. 293 J10, 300 I3

See Historic Highlights, p. 44

BERRY
Map ref. 293 K11, 300 I4

This pretty township, with its English oak, elm and beech trees, was known originally as Broughton's Creek. It took its current name in 1888 from the district's first resident, industrious Scotsman and ship's surgeon Alexander Berry, who settled near the Shoalhaven River in 1822. **Berry Historical Museum** Located in the former ES&A Bank (1886), a single-storey brick building with a curious stepped facade. *135 Queen St. Open Sat.–Sun., pub hols & daily during school hols. (02) 4464 3097.*

IN THE AREA At Shoalhaven Heads on the coast, Coolangatta Estate Winery includes a unique complex of small, convict-built buildings, mainly 1820s–30s, erected for Shoalhaven's first settler, Alexander Berry, and now used for accommodation. *1335 Bolong Rd, Shoalhaven Heads. Open daily. (02) 4448 7131.* 🄸 *Cnr Princes Hwy & Pleasant Way, Nowra; (02) 4421 0778, freecall 1800 024 261. Website: www. shoalhaven.nsw.gov.au See also Nowra*

BLUE MOUNTAINS
Map ref. 293 J7

See Faulconbridge, Katoomba, Leura

BOURKE
Map ref. 297 N5

Bourke prides itself on being the 'gateway to the real outback' and it is still something of a frontier town. Since 1862 the town has been the centre of a pastoral industry that thrives in searing summer temperatures on the red saltbush plains. The township, on the floodplains of the Darling River, is surprisingly green, watered by the Bourke Weir since 1892. In its heyday as a river port in the 1870s–90s, bullock and camel wagons brought the district's vast wool clip to be loaded on steamers and shipped down the Darling.

OF INTEREST The well-restored Lands Department Building (1898). *Mitchell St. Not open for inspection.* The substantial courthouse (1875–77) has a crown on the spire, indicating that it's a Maritime Court, the furthest inland in the country. *3 Oxley St. Not open for inspection.* A plaque on the post office (1880s), also in Oxley St, records the height of the treacherous 1890 flood waters. Henry Lawson is said to have written some stories at the Carriers' Arms Hotel, a Cobb & Co. depot in the 1800s (he also reputedly slept in the town park). *Mitchell St. Not open for inspection.* Paddle-steamers and bullock wagons brought the steel for the North Bourke Bridge (1883), which spans the Darling River. Bourke Cemetery has the graves of several Afghan camel drivers. *Cobar Rd.*

IN THE AREA A 'hypothetical replica' of the original, very basic 1830s 'Fort Bourke' stockade, after which the town was named, is a minor tourist attraction. *20 km SW. Open daily.* At Brewarrina, traditional Aboriginal stone fish traps can still be seen in the Barwon River. *90 km E via Kamilaroi Hwy.* Nearby the Aboriginal Cultural Museum features Aboriginal artifacts, a scale model of the fish traps, a section relating to the Brewarrina Aboriginal Mission, and many photographs. *Cnr Bathurst & Darling sts, Brewarrina. Open Mon.–Fri., Sat. mornings; also Sat.–Sun. afternoons by appt.* $ *(02) 6839 2868.* The Settlers Museum documents European settlement and town life in the 1800s. *Bathurst St, Brewarrina. Ring for opening times.* $ *(02) 6839 2126.* 🄸 *Old Railway Station, Anson St; (02) 6872 2280. Website: www. outbackonline.net Shire Offices, Bathurst St, Brewarrina; (02) 6839 2106. See also Cobar*

BRAIDWOOD
Map ref. 292 H13, 300 G6

Braidwood began in the 1830s as a pastoral centre for the big grazing properties in the southern highlands. It boomed when gold was found nearby in 1851, flourished, then faded. It has a rich architectural heritage and a peaceful, rural atmosphere. Braidwood has been classified as an historic town by the National Trust.

Bedervale John Coghill, a retired Scottish sea captain, commissioned fashionable architect Capt. John Verge to design this Georgian country residence (1836–40). It is mostly single storey, built of brick, then stuccoed and lined to resemble stone, and dominated by a massive roof. Inside, the glow of polished cedar joinery and elegant Victorian furnishings give an air of refined gentility. *3 km S. Monkittee St. Guided tours only, 1st Sun. of the month (Sept.–May) or by appt.* $ *(02) 4842 2421. NT.*

ALSO OF INTEREST Braidwood Museum is housed in the Old Royal Hotel (1845–46) with small-paned windows. Exhibits recall Braidwood's pioneer and gold days. Pick up walking tour brochures from here. *Wallace St. Open Fri.–Mon., daily in school hols.* $ *(02) 4842 2310.* Buildings of Georgian origin and the more elaborate Victorian style, generous streets and aged trees merge into a delightful country townscape. The Braidwood Hotel (1859), open daily, (02) 4842 2529;

the neo-Classical courthouse (1900), not open for inspection; St Bede's Catholic Church (1859), open daily, (02) 4842 2444; several verandahed shops and former banks give Wallace St its character. St Andrew's Anglican Church (1881), with a robust tower, stands in Elrington St. *Open daily. (02) 4884 4363.* Other streets have their own surprises, from huge old mills to tiny cottages.

National Theatre, Wallace St; (02) 4842 1144. Website: www.tourism.braidwood.net.au

BROKEN HILL Map ref. 296 B12

See Historic Highlights, p. 46

CAMDEN Map ref. 293 K8, 300 I1

Pioneer John Macarthur settled in the Camden district, then known as Cowpasture Plains, on his land grant of around 2000 ha in 1805. Macarthur and his wife, Elizabeth, began the pioneering sheep-breeding work that became the basis of Australia's fine-wool industry. Australia's wine industry also had its beginnings here, thanks to the Macarthurs. Despite being on the edges of Sydney's suburban sprawl, the township of Camden, founded in 1840, retains something of its rural origins.

Belgenny Farm Part of the historic Camden Park estate (see following), 'the birthplace of Australia's agriculture'. The Macarthurs didn't just breed sheep – they were the first to plant tobacco in Australia, grew vines and made wine (90 000 litres in 1829), and introduced mechanical irrigation to the country. The cluster of convict-built farm buildings, mainly constructed of ironbark, reflect more than 170 years of rural heritage. Descendants of the Macarthurs' original merino sheep flock, Clydesdale horses, demonstrations of early Australian rural skills and historic re-enactments are additional attractions. John and Elizabeth Macarthur are buried in the family graveyard on the property. *Elizabeth Macarthur Ave. Open regularly for guided tours (ring for times). Twilight tours held 1st Fri. of each month. Booking essential. $ (02) 4655 9651.*

Camden Park An elegant Regency mansion (1835), commissioned by John Macarthur and designed by architect John Verge, Camden Park stands at the heart of a 19th-century garden and the oldest sheep stud in Australia. An imposing colonnaded verandah graces one facade of the homestead. Inside, it is a showcase of colonial craftsmanship, with finely worked cedar and treasured family heirlooms. Camden Park, still owned by the Macarthur family, is one of the most important historic houses in Australia. *Off Elizabeth Macarthur Ave. Open for guided tours only, one weekend in Sept. $ (02) 4655 8466.*

ALSO OF INTEREST One of Australia's finest early Gothic Revival churches (1840s), St John the Evangelist, a mellowed, reddish sandstock-brick building with a towering needle spire (dramatically floodlit at night). John Macarthur himself chose the site and donated the land, and his sons contributed substantially to the cost. *Menangle Rd. Open Tues. & Fri., 10 a.m.–3 p.m., & for Sun. services. Tours by appt. $ (donation, for tours). (02) 4655 1675.* John St has many architectural treasures: the graceful CBC Bank (now National Australia Bank) with intricately worked iron balconies (note the Queen Victoria medallions in the gates), opened for business in 1878; Dr Crookston's House, at no. 75, is a magnificent two-storey residence (c. 1870) built originally for the manager of Camden Park, not open for inspection; the foundation stone for the Gothic Revival St Paul's Catholic Church was laid in 1859 and the church still holds regular services; nearby is the 1857 courthouse and, next door, the 1878 police station, again on land donated by the Macarthur family. *All John St.* Further along, the romantic Macaria (c. 1842), the epitome of a Gothic Revival cottage, is now the home of Camden Council (not open for inspection), while Camden Museum is in an extension (1900) which is part of the former School of Arts (1866). *40 John St. Open Thurs.–Sun.* The museum organises tours of the town and nearby district. *$ (for tours). (02) 4655 9210.* Beautiful Macarthur Park, with a lovely rotunda (1913), is on land donated by the Macarthur family. *Cnr Menangle Rd & Park St.* Some of the many historic homes in the area have annual open days.

IN THE AREA Wivenhoe, a Regency country house, was built c. 1837 on land granted to the Rev. Cowper in 1812. The classical design by John Verge features a Doric colonnaded verandah. The 1834 stables house the Wivenhoe Art Craft Workshop and Gallery. *Cnr Kirkham La. & Macquarie Grove Rd, Kirkham. Open daily except Thurs. (02) 4655 6061. For details about the house phone (02) 4655 7481 9 a.m.–4 p.m., Mon.–Fri.* Gledswood Farm includes a spacious, colonial stone-rubble homestead (c. 1827–55), its long verandah draped in wisteria. The oldest part was convict-built for pioneer James Chisholm. There's a winery in the sandstone coach-house (c. 1810), shearing demonstrations, hand-milking and more. *10 km NE via Camden Valley Way, Catherine Field. Open daily. $ (02) 9606 5111.* Historic Cobbitty, settled in 1812, one of the most picturesque hamlets in NSW, has several classified buildings. *7 km N via Macquarie Grove Rd.* The towered mansion Studley Park (c. 1889), the zenith of Victorian residential splendour, is owned by the Camden Golf Club. *4 km NE Lodges Rd, Narellan. Open to the public about twice a year. $ (donation). (02) 4646 1203.* Kirkham Stables is an imposing two-storey Georgian stone stables, built c. 1816 by explorer John Oxley. *Kirkham La., Kirkham. Not open for inspection.* St Mary's Towers (formerly Parkhall) is a grand Gothic Revival country residence, begun in 1842 by Surveyor-General Sir Thomas Mitchell. *15 km S. Douglas Park Dr., Douglas Park. Open by appt only. $ (donation). (02) 4630 9232.* Struggletown Fine Arts complex in Narellan is in an 1840s cottage with slab walls and rammed-earth floors. *Cnr Sharman Close & Stewart St, Narellan. Open Wed.–Sun. (02) 4647 1911.*

Oxley Cottage, Camden Valley Way; (02) 4658 1370.
See also Campbelltown, Picton

CAMPBELLTOWN Map ref. 293 K8

Gov. Macquarie, on his second visit to the Cumberland Plains district in 1820, founded this village, naming it Campbelltown 'in honour of Mrs Macquarie's maiden name'. In recent years the once quiet village has become a satellite city of Sydney.

Tucked within this urban sprawl are signs of pioneer settlement.

Glenalvon Michael Byrne, a publican and son of an Irish political exile, built this two-storey colonial Georgian townhouse (1839), with stone-flagged verandah, cedar staircase, marble hall, and stone and marble fireplaces. Now owned by Campbelltown Council, which plans to restore the building. *8 Lithgow St.*

ALSO OF INTEREST St Peter's Anglican Church, a sandstock brick Georgian church (c. 1823) on a site chosen by Gov. Macquarie. *Cordeaux St. Open daily.* Ⓢ *(donation). (02) 4625 1041.* Old St John the Evangelist Church (1825–41), Australia's oldest Catholic church. *Cnr Sturt & George sts. Self-guided tours by appt. (02) 4625 8044.* A cluster of stone and brick houses in Queen St, nos 284–98, date from the 1830s–40s. There are outstanding heritage properties in Campbelltown and the immediate vicinity. Some have annual open days.

IN THE AREA The historic village of Menangle. *9 km sw.*

🄸 *Art Gallery Rd; (02) 4645 8921.* Website: www.mycommunity.com.au/campbelltown
See also Camden

CANDELO
Map ref. 300 G10, 321 P6

Located peacefully in the dairy country of south-east NSW is the historic village of Candelo, with its simple verandahed timber buildings.

Kameruka Estate was established in the 1840s, later taken over by the Tooth family of Tooth Brewery fame. Sir Robert Tooth bought the property in 1857 and gradually extended it into an English village, complete with cottages, school, church, store and post office for the tenant farmers. Kameruka is one of Australia's oldest, and certainly most interesting, dairy properties. The beautiful grounds are entered through a Dutch-gabled gatehouse with a four-storey clock tower (1911). *Candelo–Bega Rd. Group booking only, by appt.* Ⓢ *(02) 6493 2205.*

🄸 *Gipps St, Bega; (02) 6492 2045.* Website: www.sapphirecoast.com.au

CANOWINDRA
Map ref. 292 E7

Verandahed shops and grander pubs and banks line Canowindra's crooked main street, little changed since it grew up along the old bullock wagon road in the mid-1800s, more than 300 km west of Sydney. The town boomed in 1910 when the railway came through. In 1863, bushranger Ben Hall and his gang herded the entire town – 40 locals including the policeman – into Robinson's Hotel for a compulsory three-day party. Robinson's is gone (the Royal Hotel has occupied the site since 1910), but the legend lives on.

OF INTEREST Canowindra (pronounced Can-oun-dra) has some classic 19th- and early 20th-century architecture. The main street and its buildings have been classified by the National Trust. Canowindra District and Historical Museum preserves and houses the town's history. *Memorial Park, Gaskill St. Open 11 a.m.–noon daily or by appt.* Ⓢ *(02) 6344 1534.* Fish fossils more than 350 million years old were discovered 11 km sw of town. The Age of Fishes Museum has natural and geological history displays. You can also book to go on a 'fossil dig'. *Gaskill St. Open daily.* Ⓢ *(02) 6344 1008.*

🄸 *Canowindra Newsagency, 45 Gaskill St; (02) 6344 1618.*
See also Cowra

CARCOAR
Map ref. 292 G7

Carcoar has a decidedly English air, cradled in a small valley, cloaked in green, with the oak-lined Belubula

Carcoar Courthouse

River meandering by. Thomas Icely took up the first land grant in this district west of the Blue Mountains in 1831. By 1839 the town was proclaimed. Carcoar went down in history when John Gilbert and John O'Meally (later members of bushranger Ben Hall's gang) held up the town's Commercial Bank in the first daylight bank robbery, in 1863. The town is classified by the National Trust.

Courthouse Carcoar's second courthouse (1882), designed by Colonial Architect James Barnet, has an Italianate tower, clustered columns and hand-forged ironwork. Fine cedar joinery and an elaborate painted frieze distinguish the interior. *Not open for inspection.* In one wing there is a craft and pottery shop. *Belubula St. Open Sat.–Sun., pub hols & most school hols, or by appt. (02) 6367 3138.*

ALSO OF INTEREST The town's name is possibly derived from the Gundungura people's word for kookaburra, 'cahcoah'. Belubula St, the serpentine main street, has many historical gems including Daylesford (1863), now a private residence. *Not open for inspection.* The Firearms Technology Museum is in the old CBC bank building (1877). *Open by appt. (02) 6367 3154.* Enterprise Stores, an old-fashioned general store, is also the town's Visitor Information. *Open daily. (02) 6367 3085.* At the northern end, the slim, shingled tower of St Paul's watches over the town. The

church was built in 1845–48, the tower and spire added almost 30 years later. *Belubula St. Open daily. (02) 6368 2065.* The modest St James' Presbyterian Church (1861), in a gentle hillside setting in Icely St, was built by the Rev. James Adam, known as the Apostle of the Saddle because of his horseback journeys to carry the Word to far-flung parishioners. *Open by appt.* [$] *(donation). (02) 6368 2432.* The Church of the Immaculate Conception (1870), also on a hill, has an unusual stone bell-tower with a spire. The Angelus bells ring at noon and 6 p.m. daily. *Coombing St. Open daily. (02) 6367 3058.* Many pockets of Carcoar reveal its long history – slab fences, quaint cottages, rustic stone barns. Walking tours are run by the Carcoar Historical Society. [$] *(02) 6367 3085.*
IN THE AREA Coombing Park, originally owned by Thomas Icely, where an elegant Federation house (1900) replaced Icely's 1830s' cottage. A shearing shed (1830s) and stables (1848) here (both convict-built) are well preserved. The house has been converted into a guesthouse. *4 km SW, Mid Western Hwy, between Carcoar & Mandurama. Guided tours available. (02) 6367 3021.*
ℹ *Enterprise Stores, Belubula St; (02) 6367 3085.*

CENTRAL TILBA

Map ref. 300 H9, 321 R3

Clustered on a steep hill, with rugged Mt Dromedary looming up behind, the timber buildings of this unique village were built in the 1880s–90s. Gold was mined in the hills in the 1860s, but the lush land has been dairying country ever since. Remarkably well preserved, Central Tilba is classified by the National Trust.
OF INTEREST The Dromedary Hotel, which began life in the 1890s as The Palace, a two-storey pub with scalloped bargeboards, provides views of the township from its old-fashioned verandah. *Open daily.* Stroll down Bate St: most of the quaint weatherboard buildings are now tearooms, craft shops and galleries where local artists sell their works. The ABC Cheese Factory has produced cheese on site in Bate St since 1891. *Open daily. (02) 4473 7387.*

Central Tilba

ℹ *Bates General Store and Post Office, Bate St; (02) 4473 7290.*

CESSNOCK

Map ref. 293 M4

Cessnock lies in the rich and diverse rural landscape of the Hunter Valley. The town, settled in the 1850s, grew slowly at first, then expanded rapidly after the first coal mine opened in 1891. It is still an industrial city. The rolling hills of nearby Pokolbin are renowned for their fine wines; many vineyards date back to the 1800s.
IN THE AREA Following are just some of the Hunter Valley's historic vineyards – Visitor Information provides excellent guides and maps for wineries. Drayton's Family Wines date from 1859. *Oakey Creek Rd. Open daily. Guided tours by appt.* [$] *(includes wine tasting). (02) 4998 7513.* Lindeman Hunter River Winery was established by Dr Henry Lindeman, who planted his first vines at Cawarra in 1843. They were destroyed by bushfires in 1851, but through successful cattle- and horse-breeding he earned enough money to redevelop his vineyard. *McDonalds Rd. Cellar door open daily. (02) 4998 7501.* Tyrrell's Vineyards was established by a nephew of the first Bishop of Newcastle, Edward Tyrrell, who produced his first wine in 1864. A slab hut from the vineyard's fledgling days still stands. *Broke Rd. Open Mon.–Sat. Tours daily. (02) 4998 7509.* Tulloch Wines was established in 1895. *Debeyers Rd. Open daily. (02) 4998 7503.* Wyndham Estate is one of Australia's oldest wine companies, established by George Wyndham in 1828. His Georgian house (1838) still stands on the estate. *25 km N. 700 Dalwood Rd, Dalwood, via Branxton. House open for groups by appt.* [$] *(02) 4938 3374. Winery open daily. Tours daily. (02) 4938 3444.*
ℹ *Turner Park, Abedare Rd; (02) 4990 4477.* Website: www.winecountry.com.au
See also Maitland

COBAR

Map ref. 297 N10

The first copper-mining leases were granted in 1870, and the population of this isolated town on the dusty, red plains of the northern outback peaked at 10 000 in the early 1900s. The main mine closed in 1920, and the town languished until a new mining boom started in the 1960s – it continues to flourish.
The Great Cobar Heritage Centre An extensive, informative museum – one of the best rural museums in the State – documenting the district's unique industrial, pastoral, Aboriginal and social history, in the rather grand, two-storey, red-brick former Mines Office (1910). A walkway provides access to the original Great Cobar open-cut mine. *Barrier Hwy. Open daily.* [$] *(02) 6836 2448.*
ALSO OF INTEREST The impressively long iron-lacework balcony of the Great Western Hotel (1898). *Marshall St. Open daily. (02) 6836 2503.* Two-storey

courthouse (1887) and police station (1886), both in Barton St (not open for inspection), and the railway station (1892) all point to Cobar's 19th-century importance and wealth. IN THE AREA Aboriginal paintings in three sandstone shelters at Mt Grenfell, by the Wongaibon people, are amongst the most significant in the State. *40 km W, Barrier Hwy, then 32 km N, past Mt Grenfell Homestead.* Check with National Parks and Wildlife Service, 19 Barton St, Cobar, for leaflets and directions. *(02) 6836 2692.*
The Great Cobar Outback Heritage Centre, Barrier Hwy; (02) 6836 2448.

COOMA
Map ref. 300 E9, 321 M3

Settlers arrived in the district known as the Monaro (a corruption of the Aboriginal Maneroo, meaning 'tree-less plain') in 1827, and the village of Cooma was gazetted by 1849. The discovery of gold at nearby Kiandra in 1859 hastened the town's growth. A century later, in the 1950s, Cooma was hailed as the country's most cosmopolitan town as migrants flooded in to work on the Snowy River Scheme.
OF INTEREST Lambie St is Cooma's pride – a streetscape that echoes the past, with more than 10 buildings classified by the National Trust. The town's oldest licensed pub still trading is the splendid Royal Hotel, which opened for business in 1858. *Cnr Lambie & Sharp sts. Open daily. (02) 6452 2132.* The courthouse (1887) has a stately portico with a bold coat-of-arms, and Cooma Gaol (begun in 1872) presents a forbidding facade to Vale St. Both were designed by Colonial Architect James Barnet. *Not open for inspection.* Close by is Cooma's substantial granite post office (1879). Christ Church, dating from 1845, is the Monaro's oldest church. *Myalla Rd. Church not open for inspection; grounds and cemetery open.* The first service at St Paul's Church, Commissioner St, was held in 1872. *Open daily. (02) 6452 1544.* The Lord Raglan Inn (1854) was Cooma's first licensed hostelry, a typical colonial inn of stone and pit-sawn timber with a low verandah. Now an art and craft gallery. *9–11 Lambie St. Open Wed.–Sun.* Ⓢ *(donation). (02) 6452 3377.*

IN THE AREA South of Cooma is the pioneering village of Nimmitabel, first settled around 1840 and a graceful survivor of busier days. Notable is the round, three-storey Geldmacher's flour mill (1865–75) built by a German settler and originally fitted with sails. *42 km S via Monaro Hwy. Not open for inspection.*
119 Sharp St; (02) 6450 1742, freecall 1800 636 525. Website: www. coomavc.com.au
See also Canberra (ACT)

COROWA
Map ref. 299 O13, 319 M3

Corowa has earned its place in history as the birthplace of Federation. Sited on the NSW–Vic. border, liable to tariffs from both colonies, it was in the town's interests to lobby for free trade. The Border Federation League, founded in Corowa, demanded action and their meeting at Corowa in 1893 helped re-ignite the call for Federation. OF INTEREST The Federation Museum, in a 1915 hall built for the Border Brass Band, documents the Federation movement, and also covers the district's local and indigenous history. *Queen St. Open Sat.–Sun. afternoons or by appt.* Ⓢ *(02) 6033 1568.* The wide main street, Sanger St, is lined with a group of late-Victorian buildings, notably grand banks, a generous selection of hotels and the original 1880 post office (still operating). During the 1893 Federation Conference politicians banqueted at the Globe Hotel (1860s). *Open daily. (02) 6033 1026.* The Corowa Railway Station was built (1890s) for the Culcairn–Corowa railway line. Tom Roberts visited nearby Brockelsby station woolshed in 1889 when painting his famous *Shearing the Rams.*
IN THE AREA Vines were first planted in this district in the early 1850s. All Saints Estate at Wahgunyah, established in 1864, won Australia's first international wine medal in Vienna in 1873. The winery's substantial 1878 red-brick 'castle' was built over the original cellars. *5 km SE. Open daily. (02) 6033 1922.*
88 Sanger St; (02) 6033 3221.

COWRA
Map ref. 292 F8

In 1944, as World War II was nearing its end, more than a thousand Japanese prisoners-of-war made a desperate bid to escape from their internment camp near this country town in NSW's Central Tablelands. More than 200 Japanese and four Australian soldiers died in the tragic struggle. The town has since formed strong links with the Japanese, and the international peace movement.
OF INTEREST Visitor Information features a short free film about the Japanese breakout. A walk around town reveals several fine heritage buildings, such as the Gothic St Raphael's Church (1861) in Lachlan St. *Open daily. (02) 6342 1369.* Also notable are the courthouse (1879) in Kendal St (not open for inspection) and the 1861 former mill, now The Mill Winery. *6 Vaux St. Open daily. (02) 6341 4141.*
IN THE AREA The extensive Cowra Fun Museum, an interactive museum mainly focusing on rural and rail history with surprisingly diverse exhibits, from tanks, jeeps and bayonets to petrol bowsers, and the largest HO model train layout in the world. *4 km E. Sydney Rd (Mid Western Hwy). Open daily.* Ⓢ *(02) 6342 2666.* At Gooloogong stands one of the country's oldest dwellings, the convict-built Croote Cottage (c. 1827). The four-roomed pisé (rammed earth) cottage has been in the one family for more than 150 years. Australia's first Catholic bishop, John Pody, said Mass in the cottage and bushranger Ben Hall is said to have raided the house. *35 km NW. Open by appt only.* Ⓢ *(02) 6344 8381.* The small, old gold town of Grenfell, where poet and author Henry Lawson was born in 1867. *50 km W.*
Olympic Park, Mid Western Hwy; (02) 6342 4333. Website: www.cowra.org
See also Canowindra

DUBBO
Map ref. 292 E2

Old Dubbo Gaol Grim reminders of punishment in the restored gaol (c. 1870) include the gruesome 'hangman's kit' and the original gallows, last used in 1904. *Macquarie St. Open daily.* Ⓢ *(02) 6882 8122.*
ALSO OF INTEREST Don't miss Dubbo's most imposing building, the Classical Revival courthouse (1885–89), designed by Colonial Architect James Barnet. *Not open for inspection.* Holy Trinity Anglican Church (1875–76) in the Early English style, is by another

Norman Lindsay's studio, Faulconbridge

distinguished Australian architect, Edmund Blacket. The lovely stone font inside was also designed by Blacket. *Brisbane St. Open daily. (02) 6884 4990.* Opposite, the Commercial Hotel, built in 1859, is the town's oldest remaining building.

IN THE AREA On the banks of the Macquarie River, Dundullimal Homestead is a colonial slab-timber house, built by John Maughan c. 1840 on his extensive sheep station. Historic photos capture the property's past and a working blacksmith, saddler and other activities bring the farm to life. *7 km s. Obley Rd, via Newell Hwy. Open daily. Guided tours by appt.* Ⓢ *(02) 6884 9984. NT.*

🄸 *Cnr Newell Hwy (Erskine St) & Macquarie St; (02) 6884 1422.* Website: www.dubbotourism.com.au

FAULCONBRIDGE   Map ref. 293 O12

Henry Parkes, the 'father of Federation' and five times premier of NSW, moved to this district in the Blue Mountains in the 1870s. In fact, the town is named after his property Faulconbridge. Artist and author Norman Lindsay is the town's other famous son.

Norman Lindsay Gallery and Museum Norman Lindsay lived in this sandstone house (1890s) 1912–69. Distinguishing features are the colonnaded verandah and a pergola heavy with masses of wisteria. Lindsay's studio remains as he left it – easels, books, props and the typewriter he used for 40 years. Etchings, paintings,

ships' models and books, puppets from his classic children's tale, *The Magic Pudding* (1918) and more fill the house. The garden – a vivid expression of Lindsay's talents – is well endowed with statues, fountains and urns. *14 Norman Lindsay Cres. Open daily.* Ⓢ *(02) 4751 1067. NT.*

ALSO OF INTEREST Sir Henry Parkes (1815–96) is buried in the Faulconbridge Cemetery.

🄸 *Three Sisters, Echo Point Rd, Echo Point; 1300 653 408.* Website: www.bluemountainstourism.org.au *See also Katoomba, Leura*

FORBES   Map ref. 292 D6

Forbes (originally known as Blackridge) was established on the Lachlan River in the early 1800s, but flourished with the discovery of gold in the 1860s. Infamous bushranger Ben Hall, who hid out in the district's rugged bush between daring raids, is buried in the local cemetery.

Forbes Museum Displays relate to Ben Hall, gold-rush days, colonial and indigenous history. Some fascinating photos. *11 Cross St. Open limited hours, afternoons only.* Ⓢ *(02) 6851 6600.*

Lachlan Vintage Village On the old Lachlan goldfields, visitors can stroll the dusty streets past slab huts, miners' cottages and old-fashioned shops, reliving the gold era 1860–1900. A smithy works in a rustic workshop, and various goldmining methods are demonstrated, such as the giant Cornish horse-powered

whim, originally used to haul gold ore from the gullies. The village is spread over 20 ha. *Newell Hwy. Open daily.* Ⓢ *(02) 6852 2655.*

ALSO OF INTEREST Forbes has a rich architectural heritage, with buildings carefully maintained and many classified on the National Estate Register. Significant in Lachlan St are the post office (1879–81) and town hall (1890–91) – both featuring grand three-storey towers. The Albion Hotel (one of 10 hotels in town); established in 1861, partly rebuilt in 1889–91 after a fire, was for many years a Cobb & Co. depot, and has tunnels below that were used to ferry gold safely to and from the banks. Visitors can tour some of the tunnels that have not been sealed. *Open daily.* Ⓢ *(02) 6851 1881.* St John's Anglican Church (1874–77) had a timber-shingled roof until the 1930s. *Court St. Open daily. (02) 6851 1544.*

🄸 *Old Railway Station, Union St; (02) 6852 4155.*

GILGANDRA   Map ref. 294 D13

This small town in the central west of NSW is famed as the home of the Coo-ee March. The first of these patriotic marches left Gilgandra in 1915 on a 500-km walk to Sydney, to recruit soldiers for WW I.

OF INTEREST The Cultural Heritage Museum features memorabilia from the Coo-ee March. *Newell Hwy. Open daily.* Ⓢ *(02) 6747 2045.* The Rural Museum features antique farm machinery, shearers' cottages, an old gaol and old school. *Newell Hwy. Open Sat.–Sun. & school hols or by appt.* Ⓢ *(02) 6847 0806.* The Hitchen House Museum has memorabilia from the Boer War, both world wars and Vietnam. *Miller St. Open Sat.–Sun., school hols or by appt. (02) 6847 0889.*

🄸 *Cultural Heritage Museum, Coo-ee March Memorial Park, Newell Hwy; (02) 6847 2045.*

GLEN INNES   Map ref. 295 L6

Glen Innes, a town with strong Celtic associations, lies at the heart of the magnificent New England tablelands in northern NSW. Two stockmen, Chandler and Duval, opened up the district as cattle country in the 1830s. Legend has it that their long beards earned the region its title 'Land of the Beardies'. The bushranger Capt. Thunderbolt stood trial in the town's first courthouse.

Land of the Beardies History House Museum One of the State's largest country museums, with an authentic century-old slab cottage, Victorian parlour, colonial furnishings and machinery, depicting rural life in the 1900s. The main museum is in the town's original 1877 hospital, set in spacious grounds. *Cnr Ferguson & West sts. Open Mon.–Fri. & Sat.–Sun. afternoons.* Ⓢ *(02) 6732 1035.*

ALSO OF INTEREST Grey St is notable for its Federation-era buildings, a number of them handsomely restored. Sir Henry Parkes laid the foundation stone for the profusely ornamented town hall in 1875. Also in Grey St is the prominent but sombre courthouse (1874). *Not open for inspection.* Further along is the Great Central Hotel (1874) a typical country pub, built on the first land auctioned after the official town survey in 1851. *Cnr Grey & Meade sts. Open daily. (02) 6732 3107.*

IN THE AREA The Emmaville Mining Museum. *40 km NW. Open Fri.–Mon. or by appt.* Ⓢ *(donation). (02) 6734 7025.* Amidst magnificent mountain scenery is a 20-m road tunnel hewn from rock by convicts c. 1860s that is unique in Australia. *35 km E on Gwydir Hwy, then 64 km SE on Old Grafton Rd (unsealed).*

🛈 *152 Church St (New England Hwy); (02) 6732 2397.* Website: www. gleninnestourism.com
See also Armidale, Inverell

GOSFORD
Map ref. 293 L6

Henry Kendall Cottage & Historical Museum Poet Henry Kendall lived with the Fagan family from 1874 to 1875 in this convict-built stone cottage (c. 1838), licensed at one time as the Red Cow Inn. Displays include the original treadle lathe of James Dunlop (the first Superintendent of the Government Observatory at Parramatta in 1830). The cottage and museum display relics related to local history. *Henry Kendall St. Open Wed., Sat.–Sun., pub & school hols, or by appt.* Ⓢ *(02) 4325 2270.*

IN THE AREA Old Sydney Town is an imaginative re-creation of Sydney Cove, from 1788–c. 1810. Rudimentary buildings stand in a bush setting and a throng of people in period costume re-enact the chores of daily life in the colony as well as lively court scenes, duels and even floggings. Bullock drays rumble past, 'redcoats' order convicts to work and the inns serve food. The town is the result of meticulous research from this crucial phase in Australia's European settlement. *6 km w. Old Pacific Hwy, Somersby. Open daily.* Ⓢ *(02) 4340 1104.* Bulgandry Aboriginal engravings, figurative drawings etched into the rock by the Guringai people, can be seen in Brisbane Water National Park. *7 km SW, off Woy Woy Rd. Open daily. (02) 4324 4911.*

🛈 *200 Mann St; (02) 4385 4430.* Website: www.cctourism.com.au

GOULBURN
Map ref. 292 H11, 300 G3

See Historic Highlights, p. 48

GRAFTON
Map ref. 295 P6

Grafton straddles a horseshoe bend of the Clarence River, shaded by avenues of jacarandas and surrounded by fertile river plains. Cedar-getters settled this district of northern NSW in the 1830s, followed closely by pastoralists. Gold finds in the upper Clarence boosted growth in the 1850s, and by the 1880s this was a thriving, prosperous river port. The port closed long ago, but Grafton has continued to prosper.

Schaeffer House A residence built c. 1900 by architect F Schaeffer as his own home, with rooms furnished in late-Victorian and Edwardian style and historical displays. *190 Fitzroy St. Open Sun., Tues.–Thurs. afternoons.* Ⓢ *(02) 6642 5212.*

ALSO OF INTEREST Grafton's late 19th-century prosperity is evident in its handsome civic buildings. Clustered around Victoria St are the town's first courthouse (1877–80), police station (1861) and post office (1878) – all designed by Colonial Architect James Barnet. The courthouse is impressive with its stone-flagged and colonnaded verandah. *Not open for inspection.* In Victoria St (cnr Duke St) Christ Church Cathedral (1881), designed by J Horbury Hunt, is built in a salmon-coloured brick. *Open daily. Tours on Tues. (02) 6642 2844.* Further along Victoria St is the Post Office Hotel (1876), still serving customers and looking very much a true country pub. *Open daily. (02) 6642 2199.* The grandiose CBC Bank (1876), in Princes St, adds a formal note to the streetscape. Grafton's domestic architecture illustrates a wealth of styles, many adapted to the subtropical climate with shutters, louvres and deep eaves. Heritage walking and driving tours recommended. There are also significant heritage buildings to see in South Grafton. Susan Island in the Clarence River, a haven for birdlife and a popular picnic spot, was named after the first vessel to enter the Clarence in 1838.

IN THE AREA The village of Ulmarra, a busy river port during the 19th century, classified by the National Trust. *15 km NE on Pacific Hwy.*

🛈 *Cnr Pacific Hwy & Spring St, South Grafton; (02) 6642 4677.* Website: www.tropicalnsw.com.au

GRIFFITH
Map ref. 299 N7

The countryside here was dismissed by early explorers such as Surveyor-General John Oxley in 1817 and later Charles Sturt as 'barren and 'inhospitable'. Irrigation, however, has allowed farming to flourish and this busy Riverina town owes its prosperity to agriculture. The town plan by Walter Burley Griffin echoes that of Griffin's Canberra master plan, with circles and curves, but was less strictly adhered to by the locals.

Griffith Pioneer Park Museum Natural bushland surrounds the 40 historic buildings and replicas moved to this site. Byna Homestead (1879), a shingle cottage, church, smokehouse, coach-house of river gum slabs and other structures reflect pioneer ingenuity and determination. *Scenic Hill, Airport Rd. Open daily.* Ⓢ *(02) 6962 4196.*

🛈 *Cnr Banna & Jondaryan aves; (02) 6962 4145.*

GULGONG
Map ref. 292 H3

Narrow winding streets and tiny timber cottages hint at this town's hurried beginnings. After Tom Saunders' gold strike in 1870, word spread like wildfire. Gulgong sprang up around the diggings, and by 1872 up to 30 000 people milled about the

Henry Lawson Centre, Gulgong

countryside. But by the 1880s hopes were fading, the population dwindling. Now, the days when the town hummed with activity are a distant memory. Poet and author Henry Lawson spent part of his childhood in the district.

Gulgong Pioneers Museum Award-winning museum in the old Times Bakery (1872–73) houses a diverse collection, notably a Cobb & Co. coach, several rooms of Victoriana and photographs from the renowned Holtermann collection, a unique record depicting goldfield life in NSW in the 1870s. *73 Herbert St. Open daily.* $ *(02) 6374 1513.*

Also of interest This is one of Australia's best preserved gold towns. Small in scale, with quaint cottages, verandahed shops and Mayne St meandering through the town. Hitching posts, horse troughs and weathered hoardings recall its heyday. More than 100 buildings have been classified by the National Trust. The Prince of Wales Opera House (1871), where performers were once showered with gold nuggets, still comes to life with music hall and drama performances on special occasions. *10 Mayne St. Open by appt.* $ *(02) 6374 2199.* Henry Lawson Centre is a treasure trove of information about Lawson and also his mother, pioneer feminist publisher Louisa Lawson. *147 Mayne St. Open limited hours daily.* $ *(02) 6374 2049.* TA Browne, author of the classic *Robbery Under Arms*, under the pen name Rolf Boldrewood, was the police magistrate here in the 1870s.

[i] *109 Herbert St; (02) 6374 1202* Website: www.mudgee-gulgong.org

Gundagai

Map ref. 292 D12, 300 B5

At the foot of Mt Parnassus, near the Murrumbidgee River, Gundagai has been celebrated in song and verse and known for the legendary 'Dog on the Tucker Box'. The first settlement at Five Mile Creek was swept away in the great flood of 1852, when it is believed 83 people perished. A local Aboriginal man from the Wiradjuri tribe, Yarri, saved many lives and there are several memorials to his bravery. In the 1860s and 1890s gold fever set the town buzzing and attracted bushrangers such as the notorious Ben Hall and Capt. Moonlite. Gundagai is a busy country town with some fine heritage architecture.

Gabriel Gallery A memorable collection of photographs, the work of eminent physician Dr CL Gabriel, whose acute observation has left an irreplaceable record of 19th-century provincial life. Henry Lawson and Banjo Paterson memorabilia are also displayed. *1st floor, Butcher & Roberts Store, Sheridan St. Open Mon.–Fri. & Sat. mornings, or by appt. (02) 6944 1722.*

Also of interest The two-storeyed, verandahed Family Hotel (1858) was at one time an agent for Cobb & Co. *213 Sheridan St. Open daily. (02) 6944 1019.* Adjacent is the splendid CBC Bank (1879). Further along, set back from the street and approached by steps, is the monumental Classical courthouse (1859). *Not open for inspection.* St Patrick's Church (1885). *Cnr Homer & Sheridan sts. Open daily. (02) 6944 1029.* St John's Anglican Church (1861) is classified by the National Trust. *Otway St. Open for services and generally on Sat., or by appt. (02) 6944 1063.* The Historical Museum has guns reputedly owned by Ben Hall and Capt. Moonlite, wagons, machinery, gold scales and even a saddlecloth worn by racing legend Phar Lap. *Homer St. Open Mon.–Sat. mornings & Sun. afternoons. (02) 6944 1995.* Gundagai Visitor Information has historic photos and walking tour brochures. You can walk across the impressive Prince Alfred Bridge, which spans the Murrumbidgee and is the longest timber viaduct in Australia. The central iron section was built in 1869 and the timber approaches in 1896. Adjacent is the historic railway bridge, opened 1903.

In the area 'Five miles from Gundagai' is the Dog on the Tucker Box (1932), a monument to teamsters and their faithful dogs. It stands at the original site of Gundagai before the 1852 flood. *8 km N.*

[i] *249 Sheridan St; (02) 6944 1341.* Website: www.gundagaishire.nsw.gov.au

Hartley

Map ref. 293 M11

The historic village of Hartley, at the foot of the Victoria Pass, was one of the first settlements on the road to Bathurst. It became an important stop for settlers moving west of the Blue Mountains after the first road was finished in 1814, but was bypassed by the railway later that century. Today, a cluster of carefully preserved buildings evokes a mid-19th-century character in this historic site.

Hartley Courthouse Believed to be the first courthouse west of the Blue Mountains, designed by Mortimer Lewis and built by convicts, opened in 1837. Its fine proportions are enhanced by the golden sandstone. The authentic 1840s furnishings have been retained. *Great Western Hwy. Open daily. Tours by appt.* Ⓢ *(02) 6355 2117.*

ALSO OF INTEREST Trahlee (1845), a colonial stone house with steep roof; the old sandstone post office (1846); the former Royal Hotel (1846); St Bernard's Church, built in 1842 from local rock and pit-sawn timbers for the many Irish Catholic settlers; the adjacent presbytery (c. 1852) has carved stone window surrounds, French doors and cedar joinery. *All Old Great Western Hwy. Not open for inspection.* St John the Evangelist Church (1858–59) is open once a month for Sun. service. *(02) 4787 8127.* The town of Hartley is under the care of the National Parks and Wildlife Service (NSW).

IN THE AREA The former Collits' Inn (c. 1823), Hartley Vale Rd, Hartley Vale, is now a delightful B&B. There are remnants of the original Pass of Victoria road, with its 1832 convict-built bridge.

🛈 *Farmers Inn, Great Western Hwy; (02) 6355 2117.*
See also Lithgow

HAY
Map ref. 299 K8

On the edge of the Murrumbidgee River, surrounded by the harsh saltbush plains of the Riverina, lies the small but busy town of Hay. Squatters ran sheep in the district from the 1840s. By the 1850s a punt crossed the river and a hotel catered to thirsty stockmen; the town was gazetted in 1859. Cobb & Co. had a major base here 1862–96, including a coach-building factory.

Hay Gaol Museum A substantial, typical country town gaol (1879) of the Victorian era, closed in 1915. It served as a maternity hospital 1921–30 and during WW II was a prisoner-of-war (POW) detention centre. Now a museum with local memorabilia. *Church St. Open daily.* Ⓢ *(02) 6993 2167.*

Bishop's Lodge Museum An unusual, corrugated-iron Victorian villa (1888), built for Sydney Linton, the first Anglican bishop of the Riverina. Restored and surrounded by a charming 19th-century garden. *Moama St. Open Sat. afternoons for guided tours & by appt.* Ⓢ *(02) 6993 1974.*

ALSO OF INTEREST The restored 1886

Witcombe Fountain, Hay

'Sunbeam' Cobb & Co. coach, which serviced the Deniliquin–Wilcannia line in its heyday, and was used in the film *Mad Dog Morgan* in 1975. *Moppett St.* The 1892 courthouse with its deep, arcaded verandahs. *Moppett St. Not open for inspection.* The elaborate cast-iron drinking fountain was donated by Hay's first mayor, John Witcombe. *Cnr Lachlan & Moppett sts.* St Andrew's Presbyterian Church (1872) is probably the town's oldest building. *Open for services once a month. Bank St.* The scale and detail of the restored Victorian railway station (1882) hint at Hay's importance at the time of its construction. Train

services stopped in 1983. A train carriage at the station has an interpretive centre on Hay's POW internment camp. *Murray St. Open Mon.–Sat.* Ⓢ *(donation). (02) 6993 2112.*

IN THE AREA Sturt's Marked Tree, carved by explorer Charles Sturt in 1829. *About 5 km E, Mid Western Hwy.*
🛈 *407 Moppett St; (02) 6993 4045.*

HILL END
Map ref. 292 G5

Hill End, amid the rugged mountain and gorge country of the Central Tablelands, was a fabulously rich gold-boom town. In 1872 the district had a population of 30 000 and 50 hotels, whilst Hill End's nearly 2 km of shops catered to every whim. In 1872 the largest specimen of reef gold that had ever been found, 'Holtermann's Nugget', containing 93 kg of gold, was uncovered. In that week, 700 kg of gold were trucked out of Hill End. By 1874, gold yields were dwindling and the diggers were moving on, leaving Hill End to slowly disappear. Today there are more memories than buildings.

OF INTEREST The National Parks and Wildlife Service Centre, the Hill End Museum and Visitor Information are located in Hill End's restored hospital (1873). *High St.* Fascinating photos from the Holtermann collection taken during the gold days chronicle the town's golden past. *High St. Open Tues.–Sun. (02) 6337 8206.* Henry Stuart's Great Western Store (1870s)

Hill End

is again in business. *Tambaroora St. (02) 6337 8377.* The Royal Hotel (1872), the only pub left, still has shades of its Victorian character. *Beyers Ave. Open daily. (02) 6337 8261.* St Paul's Presbyterian Church dates from 1872. *Open for service once a month. (02) 6337 8251.* Craigmoor House is a restored 1875 homestead. *Beyers Ave. Open by appt for guided tours only. Check with Visitor Information.* $ Tin shanties, ramshackle cottages, slab huts, rusting machinery and overgrown shafts dot the landscape. A signposted walk to Bald Hill starting from the post office, cnr Church & Tambaroora sts, leads to the restored Bald Hill mine (regular tours – contact Henry Stuart's Great Western Store for bookings, (02) 6337 8377). The town is classified by the National Trust and is under the care of the National Parks and Wildlife Service (NSW).

[i] *High St; (02) 6337 8206.*

See also Bathurst, Mudgee

HUNTER VALLEY

Map ref. 293 L4

See Cessnock, Maitland, Morpeth, Newcastle

INVERELL

Map ref. 295 K6

Scotsman Alexander Campbell established Inverell station in the New England district in the 1830s. The town itself grew up around 1850, although it was the discovery of minerals and gems in the area, most notably sapphires, that has kept Inverell a busy and prosperous town.

Pioneer Village, Inverell

OF INTEREST The Pioneer Village includes authentic buildings from around 1840 to 1920. Especially interesting are the Grove homestead (1840), a village church, the pit-sawn timber Paddy's Pub (1874), which once stood on the road to Bundarra, and a fully equipped farrier's shop. *Tingha Rd. Open Tues.–Sun.* $ *(02) 6722 1717.* At Inverell Visitor Information the Mining Museum has historic photos that conjure the district's often tough early mining days. *Campbell St. Open Mon.–Fri. & Sat. mornings.* The town's pride is the surprisingly grand courthouse (1886). *Otho St. Not open for inspection.* It's worth a detour to see the lovely Gothic Revival St Augustine's Anglican Church (c. 1890), from the distinctive architectural hand of Canadian architect J Horbury Hunt. *Rivers St. Open for tours by appt. (02) 6722 3179.*

IN THE AREA At the Draught Horse Centre traditional draught horse breeds are paraded twice daily and harnesses and memorabilia displayed. *Open Thurs.–Mon., daily in school hols. Guided tours only.* $ *(02) 6722 1461.*

[i] *Water Towers, Campbell St; (02) 6722 1693, (02) 6728 8161.* Website: www.inverell-online.com.au

See also Glen Innes

JUNEE

Map ref. 292 C11, 299 R9, 300 A4

Squatters took up land in this part of southern NSW around the 1840s, and one of the earliest stations was known as 'Jewnee'. The present town grew up in the late 1870s, after the arrival of the railway line, and for many years was a major rail centre. Junee has an undeniable charm, with its verandahed shops and vast country pubs lining the wide streets.

Monte Christo Homestead An elegant, two-storey Victorian brick residence (1884), with wide balconies fringed with iron lacework. Painstakingly restored, fully furnished in the lavish late-Victorian fashion, with notable collections of glass and silverware. The original 1876 homestead (later used as servants' quarters), stables, horse-drawn vehicles and a working wheelwright's shop are also here. *Off Potts Dr. Open daily. Guided tours only for residence.* $ *(02) 6924 1637.*

ALSO OF INTEREST The Railway Roundhouse Museum has a massive 32-metre train turntable, working steam crane, locomotives and much more – a must for rail enthusiasts. *Harold St. Tours Tues. & Thurs. 2.30 p.m.; Sat.–Sun. & pub hols 10.30 a.m. & 2.30 p.m.* $ *(02) 6924 2909.* You can't miss the massive 1896 Loftus Hotel (now a B&B) – it occupies an entire city block. *Humphrey St. (02) 6924 1511.* Also the eye-catching Commercial Hotel (c. 1915), Lorne St, or the Junee Hotel (1912), Seignior St. *All open daily.* The 1881 railway station is impressive. *Main St.* Nearby is the Heritage Railway Cafe, in the original railway refreshments room (1900), still rather grand with its cast-iron columns, lofty ceilings and polished-oak counters. Visitor Information is also here. The small Junee Historic Museum is opposite Memorial Park. *Peel St. Open afternoons Wed., Sat. & pub hols or by appt.* $ *(02) 6924 2185.*

[i] *Railway Square; (02) 6924 2522.*

KATOOMBA

Map ref. 293 N13

High in the spectacular Blue Mountains, Katoomba has been a popular resort for well over a century. In the late 1870s the gentry journeyed from Sydney aboard Cobb & Co. coaches. The opening of the rail line in the 1880s increased the resort's popularity, especially in the summer, when the mountains were a cool retreat. The name Katoomba is said to be derived from the Aboriginal word 'kedumba', meaning 'shiny, falling waters'.

Scenic Railway Built in 1878 by J North, founder of Katoomba Coalary Ltd, to bring out coal and transport miners from the valley. The incredibly steep descent, reputedly the steepest incline railway in the world, passes through a beautiful tree-clad gorge into the Jamison Valley. *1 Violet St. Open daily.* $ *(02) 4782 2699.*

ALSO OF INTEREST Many guest houses and hotels have been returned to their former grandeur, and many houses have found a new life as B&Bs. Don't miss the marvellous Carrington Hotel (1882), with lofty ceilings, sparkling leadlight and a reputation for old-world splendour. The Duke and Duchess of York were entertained here in 1927. *10–15 Katoomba St. Open daily. (02) 4782 1111.* The Paragon Restaurant, the epitome of

1930s Art Deco cafe style, is also justifiably well known. *65 Katoomba St. Open daily. (02) 4782 2928.* The stunning view from Echo Point includes the rock formation known as The Three Sisters. According to one Aboriginal legend, three beautiful giant sisters, members of a local tribe, were turned to stone to prevent them marrying three warrior brothers from another tribe. Nobody has been able to break the spell and bring them back to life. Evidence of Aboriginal occupation in the Blue Mountains dates back at least 14 000 years.

IN THE AREA Horseshoe Bridge (1833), on the Mitchell Pass Rd at Lapstone, was the first solid stone bridge built on the Australian mainland. *45 km E.* The little village of Blackheath, the lovely gardens at **Leura** and Norman Lindsay's house at **Faulconbridge** are close by.

🛈 *Three Sisters, Echo Point Rd, Echo Point; 1300 653 408.* Website: www.bluemountainstourism.org.au *See also Hartley, Lithgow*

KEMPSEY
Map ref. 295 O11

This district was first settled by cedar-cutters after 'red gold' in the 1820s. Kempsey, established in 1836, became a busy river port in the late 1800s as steamers plied the Macleay River ferrying timber and local produce.

Macleay River Historical Society's Museum This small, award-winning museum is housed in the Kempsey Cultural Centre. It explores the district's traditional Aboriginal heritage as well as more recent European history. A collection of glass negative prints from the late 1800s to mid-1900s capture Kempsey's history. *Pacific Hwy. Open daily.* Ⓢ *(02) 6562 7572.*

ALSO OF INTEREST The elaborate High Victorian post office (1879–80), in Smith St, is noteworthy. Architecturally, most of the historic buildings are in West Kempsey.

IN THE AREA On a rocky headland overlooking the Pacific Ocean stand the massive fortress walls and abandoned buildings of Trial Bay Gaol. The granite penitentiary (1877–86) housed men working on a breakwater for the bay, but was abandoned in 1903. It was also used as an internment camp for Germans living

Monte Christo Homestead, Junee

in Australia 1915–18. A restored wing has a museum and historic photographs. *35 km NE. Arakoon State Recreation Area. Museum open daily.* Ⓢ *(02) 6566 6168.*

🛈 *Cultural Centre, Pacific Hwy; (02) 6563 1555, freecall 1800 642 480.* Website: www.kempsey.midcoast.com.au *See also Port Macquarie, Wauchope*

KIAMA
Map ref. 293 K10

Towering Norfolk pines, church steeples, fine 19th-century civic buildings and small cottages create an attractive townscape in this coastal town, first settled in the 1820s. Shipping timber for the lucrative cedar trade kept the port busy during the 19th century. The first recorded sighting of the town's famous 'blowhole' was made by explorer George Bass, who sheltered in the bay in 1796.

Gerringong Heritage Centre Displays dedicated to pioneers, including aviator Kingsford Smith. *10 Blackwood St. Open Sat.–Sun. afternoons.* Ⓢ *(02) 4234 1964.*

Pilot's Cottage Museum A neat country cottage, erected in 1880–81 as a pilot's office and home. Now a local history museum with some great photos. *Blowhole Point. Open Fri.–Mon.* Ⓢ *(02) 4232 1001.*

ALSO OF INTEREST The Terrace is a rare example of a weatherboard terrace, built c. 1885 for local quarry workers. The quaint quarrymen's cottages now

house craft shops, galleries and restaurants. *Collins St. Open daily.* Hartwell House (c. 1858) a spacious, early Victorian country residence, with stone-flagged verandah and outbuildings. *Hartwell Cres. Not open for inspection.* The Coach House Gallery, in an old coach-house on the Hartwell House property. *Farmer St. Open Sat.–Sun., pub & school hols. (02) 4232 3420.* Kiama has a surprising number of interesting private and public historic buildings. Kiama Lighthouse, at Blowhole Point, began operating in 1887. *Not open for inspection.* Looking across Storm Bay, Christ Church is a small Gothic Revival church, built 1858 (but altered twice since then). Note the unusual blue windows with the HMS *Kiama* design. *Not open for inspection.* In the graveyard lies John Gower, a marine from the First Fleet.

IN THE AREA At Rose Valley, Gerringong is Alne Bank (1851), an elegant, two-storey house in the late colonial Georgian tradition, built and still owned by the Hindmarsh family and set amidst an old-world garden. *10 km S. Off Princes Hwy. Open by appt.* Ⓢ *(02) 4234 1468.* Inland is the pretty village of Jamberoo, surrounded by dairy country, in an area settled by Europeans in the 1820s. *10 km W.*

🛈 *Blowhole Point Rd; (02) 4232 3322, freecall 1800 803 897.* Website: www. kiama.com.au *See also Wollongong*

Leura

Map ref. 293 N13

A small village in the Blue Mountains, settled in the late 1800s and noted for its gardens.

Everglades Gardens A garden of spectacular beauty high in the Blue Mountains. The gardens, and house, were designed during the 1930s–40s, by Paul Sorensen. Secluded corners contrast with magnificent panoramas of the Jamison Valley below and the Blue Mountains beyond. A sandstone arch, the original facade of Sydney's London Chartered Bank of Australia (1866), adds an opulent note to an outdoor theatre. *37 Everglades Ave. Garden & house open daily.* $ *(02) 4784 1938. NT.*

ℹ *Three Sisters, Echo Point Rd, Echo Point; 1300 653 408.* Website: www.bluemountainstourism.org.au

Lismore

Map ref. 295 Q3, 365 Q12

Lismore was settled by cedar-getters who came to the district in the 1840s. It has a charming setting, circled by hills, near a branch of the Richmond River known as Wilsons River. The town, the largest on the north coast, is 30 km inland.

Richmond River Historical Museum Exhibits include some beautiful colonial furniture crafted from the local cedar, and historic photos. *165 Molesworth St. Open Mon.–Thurs.* $ *(02) 6621 9993.*

ALSO OF INTEREST Lismore has a distinctive Art Nouveau post office (c. 1897), impressive Classical Revival courthouse (c. 1883) and several fine churches including St Carthage's Catholic Cathedral (1892–1906), which has fine woodwork and stained glass. *Leycester St. Open daily.* $ *(donation). (02) 6621 2271.* The official opening of Fawcett's Bridge in 1884 had such a poor turnout that a second opening was scheduled with a public holiday to encourage attendance.

IN THE AREA In Tucki Tucki, past Wyrallah, is a traditional Aboriginal bora ring, where a cleared area (22 m in diameter) forms a ceremonial site at the Tucki Tucki Cemetery. *12 km SE.* Red cedar was once loaded onto sailing ships at the coastal resort of Ballina. *33 km E.* In the 1860s, a gold rush followed the discovery of gold in beach sand near the mouth of the Richmond River.

ℹ *Cnr Bruxner Hwy & Molesworth St; (02) 6622 0122, 1300 369 795.* Website: www.liscity.nsw.gov.au

Lithgow

Map ref. 293 L10

Lithgow lies in the western foothills of the Blue Mountains. The construction of a railway line into the valley in the 1860s ensured Lithgow's future. The town has been an important coalmining centre since 1869, and Australia's first steel industry was established here in 1900.

Eskbank House Thomas Brown, who founded Lithgow's coal industry, had this colonial Georgian sandstone cottage built c. 1842. The furnished house retains its covered courtyard (added in 1925), original stables, blacksmith's shop and garden-house in the grounds. *Cnr Inch & Bennett sts. Open Thurs.–Mon.* $ *(02) 6351 3557.*

Small Arms Museum A unique and extensive collection of weapons, many manufactured in this factory; memorabilia and historic photos. *Methven St. Open Sat.–Sun., pub & school hols, or by appt.* $ *(02) 6351 4452.*

ALSO OF INTEREST In Blast Furnace Park stand the eerie ruins of the old blast furnaces (1875–1930), with a network of buildings, tunnels and foundations. *Inch St. Open daily.* State Mine Heritage Park and Railway contains mining and railway memorabilia. *State Line Gully Rd. Open for tours Sat.–Sun. & pub hols.* $ *(02) 6353 1513.* The brick flues and warehouses of the old Lithgow Pottery (1876–98) stand silently. The former coach-house is now artists' studios. *Silcock St. Open daily. (02) 6351 4483.* Visitor Information is in the former Bowenfels railway station, a handsome sandstone structure, opened in 1869 to coincide with the arrival of the Zig Zag rail line. Historic photos document the district's history. Lithgow Heritage Tours arrange guided tours. *Cooerwull Rd.* $ *(02) 6351 4848.*

IN THE AREA The Zig Zag Railway is a section of the Great Western Railway, comprising lofty stone viaducts, a tunnel and a track laid in a zigzag pattern to enable trains to descend the sharp 70-m drop from Clarence to the Lithgow Valley. Opened in 1869, it was a spectacular engineering feat for its time. Steam locomotives take tourists along the restored line, affording spectacular views of the ruggedly beautiful valley. *10 km E, via Bells Line of Rd. Trips daily.* $ *Timetable information (02) 6351 4826 or (02) 6353 1795.*

ℹ *1 Cooerwull Rd; (02) 6353 1859.* Website: www.lisp.com.au/~lithtour

See also Faulconbridge, Hartley, Katoomba, Leura

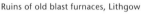

Ruins of old blast furnaces, Lithgow

Cedar-getters explored the lower Hunter Valley district as early as 1804, and by the 1820s a small town had emerged. Maitland's prosperity is amply reflected in the splendid civic and domestic architecture that remains from the 1800s. Coalmining in the early 1900s brought further wealth.

Grossmann House A two-storey Victorian gentleman's residence (now a folk museum) built in 1870 by Isaac Beckett and architecturally identical to his business partner's house, Brough House, next door. Furnished in the style of a well-to-do 19th-century merchant family. *Church St. Open Sat.–Sun. afternoons or by appt.* Ⓢ *(02) 4933 6452. NT.*

Maitland City Art Gallery At Brough House, a Victorian townhouse (c. 1870s) built by merchant Samuel Owen. (See Grossmann House, above.) *Church St. Open daily.* Ⓢ *(02) 4933 1657.*

Maitland Gaol A remarkably preserved colonial gaol, designed by architect Mortimer Lewis and completed 1848. The monumental sandstone building served as a prison until 1998. *John St, East Maitland. Open for tours, including evening tours. (02) 4936 6610.*

ALSO OF INTEREST Maitland's curving High St, with its rich legacy of commercial and civic buildings, and Regent St, with some of the city's finest domestic architecture, have both been classified by the National Trust. Typical of the civic buildings is the lavishly arcaded Italianate post office (1881). One of the town's grandest residences is the towered, boom-style mansion Cintra (1880s). Tall gates open on to a curved carriage driveway and spacious grounds. *34 Regent St. Not open for inspection.* Another display of affluence is the late-Victorian mansion Anambah House (1889), set in a wonderful National Trust-classified garden. *Open for group tours only. Contact Visitor Information, 1300 653 320.* Gothic St Mary's Anglican Church (1867) was designed by Edmund Blacket. Its spire, added in 1885, dominates the city skyline. *Church St. Open daily. (02) 4933 5302.* At St Peter's Church of England (1886), also designed by Blacket,

Tocal Homestead, near Maitland

note the beautifully carved marble pulpit. *William St. Open daily. (02) 4934 5303.*

IN THE AREA At Oakhampton, the Walka Waterworks Complex, constructed 1879–85 as part of the original water supply system for Newcastle, supplied the Hunter Valley 1887–1929. The extensive complex is distinguished by its elegant Italianate design. *3 km N of West Maitland. Open daily.* Ⓢ 15 km N, at Paterson, Tocal is one of Australia's finest collections of heritage farm buildings, including a splendid 1841 homestead and a barn designed by Edmund Blacket (c. 1850). Now part of CB Alexander Agricultural College. *Special open days are held during the year. Freecall 1800 025 520.* Ⓢ

ℹ *Ministers Park, cnr New England Hwy & High St; (02) 4933 2611, 1300 652 320. Website: www. maitlandtourism.nsw.gov.au See also Cessnock, Morpeth*

MITTAGONG   Map ref. 293 J10, 300 I2

Mittagong is the 'gateway to the southern highlands', an area dotted with historic towns such as Bowral, **Berrima**, Moss Vale and smaller hamlets. Colonial sandstone buildings, old inns and grand houses are set in picturesque countryside. Australia's first iron-ore smelting works was established here in 1848.

IN THE AREA Bartholomew Rush's handsome, two-storey colonial Georgian coaching inn (1845), the Prince Albert Hotel, now Poplars Restaurant. *4 km N. Old Hume Hwy. Open Fri.–Sat. evenings & Sun. for lunch. Tours by appt. (02) 4889 4240.*

ℹ *62–70 Main St; (02) 4871 2888.* Website: www.southcoast.com.au/ *See also Berrima*

MORPETH   Map ref. 293 M4

Sturdy buildings of mellowed stonework and wood weathered to silver grey, mature trees and the pretty riverside setting create the unique character of this former river port. This was the Hunter Valley's major port from around 1832 to 1890. It has a legacy of interesting heritage properties and is listed on the National Estate Register.

OF INTEREST The splendid old courthouse (1862) is now the Morpeth Museum. *Swan St. Open Tues., Fri.–Sun. or by appt.* Ⓢ *(02) 4934 4301.* The solid old bond stores (c. 1850) with cantilevered verandahs are near the bridge. *Not open for inspection.* Closebourne House, an extensive two-storey sandstone Georgian house built in 1826 by Lt Edward Charles Close, who founded the town, is one of Australia's oldest residences. *Morpeth Rd.* The sandstone Church of St James (1837–40), is noteworthy for a beautiful carved stone pulpit (1864) and a stone lychgate. *19 Tank St. Open daily.* Ⓢ *(donation). (02) 4933 6218.* Many buildings have found new life as antique and craft shops, tearooms and B&Bs. *Historic guided tours available by appt.* Ⓢ *(02) 4934 5660.*

IN THE AREA Wallalong House, one of the Hunter Valley's most historic properties, a colonial homestead (c. 1840) with wine cellar, original stables, and lovely garden with magnificent trees. *3 km NE. End of Morpeth St, Wallalong. Open for guided tours by appt only. (02) 4930 5114.*

🖪 *Ministers Park, cnr New England Hwy & High St, Maitland; (02) 4933 2611, 1300 652 320. Website: www. maitlandtourism.nsw.gov.au*
See also Maitland

MUDGEE
Map ref. 292 H3

The Mudgee district was settled in the 1820s, although the 'Village of Mudgee' was not gazetted until 1838. Robert Hoddle, who laid out Melbourne's early street pattern, planned the town. Mudgee nestles in an upland valley of the Cudgegong River and, with its fertile soils, has a long tradition of vine growing. As a centre for the surrounding goldfields in the mid-1800s, especially **Gulgong** and **Hill End**, Mudgee acquired some solid buildings from that era.

Colonial Inn Museum (the former West End Hotel) is an 1856 hostelry with rooms furnished in Victorian style, and some fascinating historic photos. *Market St. Open Sat.–Sun., pub & school hols.* Ⓢ *(02) 6372 3078.*

ALSO OF INTEREST More than 25 buildings are listed by the National Trust. The post office, one of the first major country post offices in NSW, the police station and the courthouse date from the early 1860s. *All Market St. Not open for inspection.* Pretty Robertson Park, opposite, was the site of Mudgee's first market place. The attractive rotunda was erected in 1903. The rather elegant railway station (1883–84) shows the influence of the French Empire style, and has fine cedar work in the former waiting-room. It now houses an art and craft store. *Cnr Church & Inglis sts. Open daily. (02) 6372 2822.* Sandstone St Mary's Catholic Church (1873) has a graceful tower and spire (1911). *Cnr Market & Church sts. Open daily. (02) 6372 2122.* The church's presbytery (1851) is the longest continually occupied building in Mudgee. There

are about 20 wineries in the area – a few, such as Platts Wines and Craigmoor, have historic links. Ask at Visitor Information for directions.
🖪 *84 Market St; (02) 6372 1020.* Website: www.mudgee-gulgong.org
See also Gulgong, Hill End

NEWCASTLE
Map ref. 293 N4

Newcastle is a major industrial city, the second largest city in NSW and one of the busiest ports in Australia. The area was settled in 1800, a penal settlement was established in 1804, and coalmining began soon after. The town expanded after it became the main port for the busy Hunter River district in the mid-1800s. In recent years Newcastle has restored many of its significant heritage buildings.

Fort Scratchley Historical Society and Military Museum A formidable military fortification erected in 1880–86, when authorities feared a Russian invasion of this strategic coal port. The fort was maintained and finally came under attack from Japanese submarines in 1942, when retaliatory shots were fired. Its prominent site on Flagstaff Hill offers exceptional views of the city and out to sea. Military relics, a maze of tunnels and gun emplacements are features. *Fort*

Dr. Open Tues.–Sun. Ⓢ *(for tunnel tours). (02) 4929 3066.*

Newcastle Regional Maritime Museum Around 5000 artifacts and archives, including model boats, historic lifeboat, colonial paintings and an original Rocket Cart used in beach rescues. Part of Fort Scratchely. *Fort Dr. Open Tues.–Fri.; Sat.–Sun. & pub hols, noon–4 p.m. (02) 4929 2588.*

Newcastle Regional Museum An extensive collection, housed in the former Tooth's Brewery building, where the oldest wing dates from 1876. Exhibits cover the district's industrial, technological and social history. Recommended. *787 Hunter St. Open Tues.–Sun. & daily in school hols. (02) 4974 1400.*

ALSO OF INTEREST In inner Newcastle there are more than 100 buildings of historic significance. Of particular note are the splendid Italianate customs house (1876–77), designed by James Barnet, now the Customs House Hotel, Watt St, (02) 4925 2585, and, opposite, the monumental railway station (1878), believed to have been built of imported Dutch bricks. The courthouse (1890), the elaborate court chambers (1898) (neither open for inspection) and the grand, arcaded Italianate post office, opened in 1903 and still serving its original

Customs House Hotel, Newcastle

purpose, are all imposing. *All Bolton St.* Behind the court chambers, Rose Cottage (1828) is the city's oldest surviving building. *Not open for inspection.* Newcastle Regional Art Gallery is renowned for its collection of Australian art, including outstanding 19th-century works. *Laman St. Open Tues.–Sun. (02) 4974 5100.* Christ Church Cathedral (1892), designed by J Horbury Hunt, dominates the skyline. Inside are superb religious artworks. Visitors can climb the tower. *Church St. Open daily.* $ *(02) 4929 2052.* A road leads through King Edward Park to Bogey Hole, which was cut into the rock ledge, probably by convicts c. 1819–22, for the personal bathing pleasure of Major Morisset, Newcastle's Military Commandant. It became a public pool in 1863. *South Newcastle Beach. Open daily.* The obelisk (1850) in the park marks the site of Newcastle's first windmill (1820). The obelisk was used as a navigational aid for ships. Pick up brochures for the Shipwreck Walk along the foreshore, the Town Walk and the signposted Newcastle East Heritage Walk from Visitor Information.

IN THE AREA The Hunter Valley, with its many vineyards and historic towns, lies in the hinterland.

🛈 *363 Hunter Street; (02) 4974 2999, freecall 1800 654 558.* Website: www.newcastletourism.com
See also Stroud

NOWRA
Map ref. 293 K11, 300 I4

Cedar-getters in the district were floating logs from the dense rainforest down the Shoalhaven River in the early 1800s. The township itself grew up around 1850 as an agricultural centre for the surrounding farmlands.

Meroogal This picturesque two-storey timber Gothic-style house (1885), in its attractive garden, was lived in by four generations of women. The house, virtually untouched, is an intriguing and rare glimpse into a lifestyle now past. Meroogal is managed by the Historic Houses Trust of NSW. *Open Sat.–Sun. for guided tours. Cnr West & Worrigee sts.* $ *(02) 4421 8150.*

ALSO OF INTEREST Nowra Museum is in the old police station (1901). *Cnr*

Meroogal, Nowra

Kinghorne & Plunkett sts. Open Mon., Wed., Fri., Sat.–Sun. & pub hols. $ *(02) 4421 2021.* St Andrew's Presbyterian Church (1873–75) was designed by J Horbury Hunt, noted for his powerful and unusual designs. *3 Shoalhaven St. Open Sun. for services.*

IN THE AREA The historic sandstone homestead Bundanon (c. 1866), which was the home and studio of famous landscape painter Arthur Boyd, was donated to the Australian people, along with its 400-ha property, by the artist and his wife. *30 km w, well signposted. Open Sun. Pre-purchased tickets only, from Shoalhaven Visitor Information.* $ Adjacent to the HMAS *Albatross* naval base, Australia's Museum of Flight presents an impressive display, including vintage aircraft, historic photos. *8 km sw. Open daily.* $ *(02) 4424 1920.*

🛈 *Cnr Princes Hwy & Pleasant Way; (02) 4421 0778, freecall 1800 024 261.* Website: www.shoalhaven.nsw.gov.au
See also Berry

O'CONNELL
Map ref. 292 H6

The first route west of the Blue Mountains passed through this pretty valley, and the village of O'Connell that grew up was a popular stopping place for travellers in the early 1800s. A gold rush in the 1850s brought a flurry of activity, but since then the town has been almost forgotten. It has been classified by the National Trust.

OF INTEREST The handsome St Thomas'

Anglican Church (1865), with a stone font and fine cedar pews. Services held once a month. *Beaconsfield Rd. (02) 6332 4606.* The steep-gabled brick school in Blackmill La. (1870) continues to operate as the town's school. The small timber school (1840s) and the former St Francis' Church, whose dignified steeple has watched over the village since 1867, are now part of a B&B. *O'Connell Rd. Guided tours by appt. (02) 6337 5773.* An old hotel is still in business, and small cottages are sheltered by huge, old trees. Lindlegreen, one of the first houses in the valley, was the town's first school, store and post office. *Cnr O'Connell & Beaconsfield rds. Tours by appt. (02) 6337 5773.*

🛈 *137–139 Oberon St, Oberon; (02) 6336 0666.*
See also Bathurst

ORANGE
Map ref. 292 G6

The discovery of gold at Ophir in 1851, the first payable gold strike in Australia, gave a boost to the infant town of Orange, in the State's central west. Since then the district's fertile countryside has ensured the town's continued prosperity. The town's most famous son is the poet AB 'Banjo' Paterson (of 'Man from Snowy River' fame), born here in 1864.

OF INTEREST Stately homes, graceful churches, well-established parks and conservative public buildings give Orange a look of solid respectability.

Of special note are the grand court-house (1882–83), Lords Pl., not open for inspection, the almost equally grand post office, officially opened in 1880, Summer St. Both were designed by James Barnet. St Joseph's Church, opened 1871, was finally completed in 1899. *Cnr Hill & Byng sts. Open daily. (02) 6362 2378.* The Victorian Gothic Revival Holy Trinity Church (1879). *Open daily. (02) 6362 1623.* The rectory dates from 1856. *Not open for inspection.* Cook Park is shaded by trees planted in the 1880s and has an octagonal bandstand (1908) with the original gas light fittings. *Summer St.*

IN THE AREA Australia's first goldfield (1851) at Ophir is now a flora and fauna reserve. The pebbly, shaded creek is popular with fossickers, but scattered relics are the only signs of the vanished town. *27 km N. Open daily. (02) 6361 5226.* Molong, dating back to 1845, has a museum in an old inn (1856). *35 km NW. Cnr Riddell & Edward sts. Open Sun. afternoons & by appt.* $ *(02) 6366 8270.* Lucknow was the site of one of Australia's earliest gold strikes. One of the old mines still operating is Gunnadoo Gold Mine. *10 km SE. Off Millers Crossing Trk, Doctors Hill. Gold panning and tours for groups by appt. Open daily.* $ *(02) 6366 0445.*

🛈 *Civic Sq., Byng St; (02) 6361 5226.* Website: www.orange.nsw.gov.au
See also Bathurst, Carcoar

PARKES
Map ref. 292 D5

Squatters began taking up land in the area in the 1850s, but the discovery of gold brought diggers flocking to the district in the 1860s and 1870s. The village that grew up, originally known as Bushmans, was renamed after Sir Henry Parkes, who visited the prosperous goldfield in 1873, whilst he was governor of NSW. Such was the town's enthusiasm for Parkes that the residents even renamed the main street after his wife, Clarinda.

OF INTEREST Bushman's Hill Reserve contains relics of the old Bushman's mine and information about the area's traditional Aboriginal inhabitants, the Wiradjuri people, and their culture. Pioneer Park Museum has Sir Henry Parkes memorabilia and a replica of the cottage, in Coventry,

England, where Parkes was born. There is also vintage agricultural machinery. *Peak Hill Rd. Open daily.* $ *(02) 6862 3509.* For motoring enthusiasts, the Parkes Motor Museum displays vintage vehicles. *Open daily. Cnr Bogan & Dalton sts.* $ *(02) 6862 1975.*

🛈 *Kelly Reserve, Newell Hwy; (02) 6862 4365.* Website: www.parkes.nsw.gov.au

PARRAMATTA
Map ref. 286 C6, 293 L7

See Historic Highlights, p. 50

PICTON
Map ref. 293 K9, 300 I2

A peaceful rural atmosphere pervades the old town of Picton, built on a site chosen by Gov. Macquarie in 1820 and first settled in 1822. The town, south of Sydney, is well endowed with early colonial buildings.

George IV Inn Built around 1819, and licensed since c. 1839, this rambling stone inn, with broad sweeping verandahs and stables facing the courtyard, is one of the oldest inns in NSW. *Argyle St. Open daily. (02) 4677 1415.*

Razorback Inn Built (1840s) as a convict overseer's residence, this two-storey stone building, although altered, still typifies colonial Georgian architecture. Now Oliver's Restaurant. *Hume Hwy, near Brookside Bridge. Open Thurs.–Sat. evenings. (02) 4677 1379.*

St Mark's Anglican Church Work began on this modest stone church, designed

by Edmund Blacket, in 1850, but was delayed when workmen abandoned their tools to head for the gold diggings. *Menangle St West. Open Sun.* $ *(donation). (02) 4677 2047.*

ALSO OF INTEREST The CBC Bank (1885) with pointed Gothic arch windows. The original stables at the rear house a craft shop. *Argyle St.* Opposite is the towered post office (1892), now the town's Visitor Information. The Imperial Hotel was called the Terminus when first licensed in 1863 – the same year the railway came to town. *Menangle St. Open daily. (02) 4677 1441.* Two men lost their lives building the massive stone viaduct, with its five arches, over the steep Stonequarry Creek Gorge, next to the station, in 1862–67. Victoria Bridge (1897) is classified by the National Trust. Anthill Golf Club is housed in the old Jarvisfield mansion (1864). *Hume Hwy. (02) 4677 1512.* Tours of the mansion, and other historic tours are available. $ *(02) 4677 2044.*

IN THE AREA Rail Transport Museum, acclaimed as one of the country's best such museums, features 60 locomotives and runs regular tourist trips on the old Picton–Mittagong Loop Line (first opened 1867). *7 km SW. Barbour Rd, Thirlmere. Open daily.* $ *(02) 4681 8001.*

🛈 *Cnr Argyle & Menangle sts; (02) 4677 3962.*

POKOLBIN
Map ref. 293 L4

See Cessnock

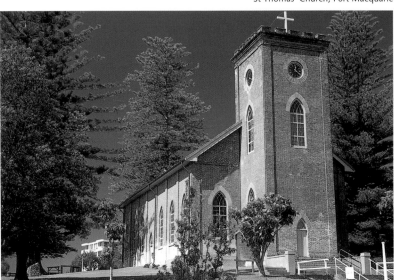
St Thomas' Church, Port Macquarie

PORT MACQUARIE Map ref. 295 P12

Port Macquarie, on the north coast, is one of NSW's oldest towns, serving as a penal settlement 1821–30. It remained under military rule until 1847 when it was opened to free settlement. The town languished for many years, a sleepy fishing village, but is now a popular tourist and retirement destination.

Roto House An excellent example of a late Victorian country house. Built of red mahogany in 1890, it has 10 rooms and a generous encircling verandah. *Roto Pl. Open daily.* $ *(donation). (02) 6584 2180.*

Port Macquarie Museum An award-winning museum, part of which is housed in a convict-built 1830s store. Relics of the convict era, colonial crafts, farm equipment and period costumes are displayed. *22 Clarence St. Open Mon.–Sat. & Sun afternoons.* $ *(02) 6583 1108.*

Port Macquarie Historic Courthouse Opposite the museum (see above), flanked by tall Norfolk pines, is the simple but handsome courthouse (1869), designed by Colonial Architect James Barnet. *Cnr Clarence & Hay sts. Open Mon.–Sat.* $ *(02) 6584 1818.*

St Thomas' Church Gov. Macquarie chose the site for this small Georgian brick church, the third oldest church in Australia. It was built by convicts in 1824–28, with all the nails and spikes forged by female convicts. Capt. Rolland, the Commandant who supervised the building, was buried beneath the front pews, allegedly in the hope that convicts would not touch a grave on consecrated ground. The chapel (1821) in the grounds was originally a dispensary for the garrison hospital. *Cnr William & Hay sts. Open Mon.–Fri.* $ *(02) 6584 1033.*

ALSO OF INTEREST Flagstaff Maritime Museum displays shipwreck relics and historic photos of ships that have plied this coast. *6 William St. Open Mon.–Sat.* $ *(02) 6583 1866.* The cemetery has the weathered tombstones of convicts and colonial settlers. *End of Horton St.* Tacking Point Lighthouse (1879), off Pacific Dr., is the third oldest on the Australian coast. *Not open for inspection.* Matthew Flinders named the point when he was 'tacking' up the coast in his sloop *Investigator,* in 1802, on his circumnavigation of the continent.

[i] *Cnr Clarence & Hay sts; (02) 6583 1293, freecall 1800 025 935.* Website: www.portmacquarieinfo.com.au

See also Wauchope

RICHMOND Map ref. 293 Q11

Despite the encroachments of suburban Sydney, a sense of history lingers on in the heart of Richmond, one of Australia's oldest towns. Richmond was one of the 'five Macquarie towns', chosen by Gov. Macquarie in the early 1800s. Its colonial origins are evident in its Georgian-style architecture and a leafy park in the town centre, once the village common.

OF INTEREST The most interesting streets to explore are Windsor St, Kurrajong Rd and Francis St. The elegant country mansion Hobartville (c. 1828) was the scene of some of Richmond's busy social life, with parties, balls and 'Pic Nics'. It was built for magistrate William Cox, who opened a bank branch at the house in 1817 for 'the savings of the industrious poor'. *End of Chapel St (best viewed from Kurrajong Rd). Not open for inspection.* The former farmhouse Josieville, almost French Provincial in style, stands on a prominent corner. It was built for former convict Joseph Onus. The ground floor was built in the late 1830s. *2 Chapel St. Not open for inspection.* St Peter's Church (1837–41) features a timber spire and dark cedar woodwork inside. The neighbouring graveyard, older than the church, has the weathered headstones of many early pioneers. *384 Windsor St. Open daily for services or by appt. (02) 4578 3832.* The two-storey, Georgian townhouse, Toxana (c. 1840), was built by William Bowman, politician and a member of a distinguished pioneering family. There is now an art gallery in the basement. *159 Windsor St. Open Thurs. & Sat. or by appt. (02) 4578 2770.* Hawkesbury Agricultural College opened in 1891. The extensive timber stable complex (1896–97) is now offices. The college is now the Richmond campus of the University of Western Sydney. There is usually an annual open day in Aug. *(02) 4570 1333.*

IN THE AREA The sleepy settlement at Pitt Town, another of the 'five Macquarie towns', has retained vestiges of its colonial origins. *12 km E.* At Ebenezer, Australia's oldest surviving church, the Presbyterian (now Uniting) Church (c. 1807–09), and the oldest surviving school building (1817) overlook the Hawkesbury River. *20 km NE. Open daily. (02) 4579 9350.*

[i] *Bicentenary Park, Ham Common, Clarendon; (02) 4588 5895.* Website: www.hawkesburyvalley.com

See also Rouse Hill Estate, p. 15, Wilberforce, Windsor

SPRINGWOOD Map ref. 293 P12

See Faulconbridge

STROUD Map ref. 293 N3

This tiny town north of Newcastle, nestled in the quiet Karuah Valley, has a history stretching back to the colony's convict days. The township was established in 1826 and by 1851 was being described as 'decidedly one of the finest villages . . . in the colony'. The farming didn't prove quite as fine and Stroud remains much as it was more than a century ago.

OF INTEREST Pick up a heritage trail brochure which details Stroud's architectural legacy from its earliest days, including some beautiful 1830s buildings. The modest courthouse (1878) houses the Stroud Historical Society's headquarters. *Cowper St. Open limited hours Wed.* $ *(02) 4994 5400.* St John's Anglican Church, built by convicts in 1833, with lovely stained-glass windows, remains largely unaltered. *Cowper St. Open daily.* $ *(donation). (02) 4994 5193.* Silo Hill is so-called because of the eight underground silos built by convicts in 1841 to store grain and protect it from weevils. The colonial Georgian two-storey Schoolhouse Museum (1830), previously known as Quambi House, contains the original school room, schoolmaster's quarters and two bedrooms, with Victorian and Edwardian furnishings. *Open Sun. afternoons or by appt.* $ *(02) 4994 5400.* Stroud House (1828, extended 1832), a restrained colonial residence, is also from Stroud's earliest days. *Cowper St. Not open for inspection.* Stroud Historical Society organises historic tours. *By appt.* $ *(02) 4994 5400.*

[i] *Stroud Newsagency, Cowper St; (02) 4994 5117.*

See pp. 4–17

TAMWORTH   Map ref. 295 J11

Surveyor-General John Oxley praised the Peel Valley's 'luxuriant country' when he passed through the district in 1818. Tamworth was gazetted in 1850 and pastoral and agricultural farming have grown steadily.

Calala Cottage This Victorian cottage, built in 1875, was home to Tamworth's first mayor, Philip King, who was the grandson of Gov. King. In the grounds are an authentic slab shepherd's hut with a bark roof (1836–40), smithy's workshop and a folk museum. *142 Denison St. Guided tours only, Tues.–Fri. afternoons & Sat.–Sun. $ (02) 6765 7492.*

Powerstation Museum In 1888 Tamworth became Australia's first town to have electric street lighting. The museum celebrates the 'city of light' with exhibits of electrical equipment and appliances. *Cnr Peel & Darling sts. Open Tues.–Fri. mornings. $ (02) 6766 8324.*

ALSO OF INTEREST The grand, arcaded post office (c. 1883–86) is a major focus in the town's streetscape. There are a number of other substantial 19th-century civic buildings. Follow the signposted heritage walk or pick up a heritage walk brochure. *Cnr Peel & Murray sts; (02) 6755 4300.* Website: www. tamworthonline.com.au

TENTERFIELD Map ref. 295 M4, 365 N13

Tenterfield, which sits high on the New England plateau, was gazetted in 1851. It was in Tenterfield in 1889 that Sir Henry Parkes, when premier of NSW, made his famous call for the colonies to become a federation.

Sir Henry Parkes Memorial School of Arts Former school of arts (1876–84), where Parkes delivered his famous Tenterfield Speech, the call for unity that led to the Federation movement. Now a museum, theatre and public library. A fine portrait of Parkes by painter Julian Ashton hangs here. *Cnr Manners & Rouse sts. Open Mon.–Fri. (02) 6736 1454. NT.*

Centenary Cottage Stone cottage (c. 1871) with local history displays, including a gallery dedicated to Sir Harry Chauval, a foundation member of the Australian Light Horse Regiment (which had its beginnings in Tenterfield). *Logan St. Open Wed.–Sun., pub hols and daily during school hols. $ (02) 6736 2844.*

OF INTEREST The poet 'Banjo' Paterson married Bessie Walker in 1903 in the timber Presbyterian Church (1884). *Logan St. Open by appt. Check with Visitor Information or (02) 6736 1534.* Pioneer craftsmanship is evident in St Mary's Church (c. 1870), the town's first Catholic church. *Miles St. Open for services or by appt. (02) 6736 1810.* Visitors are welcome at Tenterfield Saddlery (established 1870) to watch the saddler at work in the classified former bank building (1860). *High St. Open daily. $ (02) 6736 1478.* Lord Carrington officially opened the Victorian railway station at a gala celebration in 1886. It is now a museum with photos and railway memorabilia. *Logan St. Open Wed.–Sun. & pub hols. $ (02) 6736 2223.* Stannum House, an elegant late-Victorian Italianate villa (1888), was a military hospital during WW II. It is now a restaurant and B&B. *114–116 Rouse St. Tours by appt. $ (02) 6736 3770.*

IN THE AREA Bushranger Thunderbolt is said to have holed up in the local area. There are Aboriginal sacred sites within the Woolool Reserve, Boonoo Boonoo National Park and Bald Rock National Park. Ask at Visitor Information for details or arrange guided tour through Woolool Woolool Aboriginal tours. *(02) 6736 3209.* *157 Rouse St (cnr Miles St) (New England Hwy); (02) 6736 1082.* Website: www.tenterfield.com

WAGGA WAGGA   Map ref. 292 B12

Wagga Wagga (Aboriginal for 'many crows') has grown steadily since the first settlers arrived in 1832. The city, the largest in the Riverina district, has grand-scale civic architecture, wide tree-lined streets and some notably fine ecclesiastical buildings.

Museum of the Riverina The emphasis is on pioneer life in the Riverina. Yallowin Hut (1834) originally stood in the now flooded Tumut Valley. *Open Tues.–Sun. (02) 6925 2934.*

ALSO OF INTEREST The towered, Edwardian courthouse (1901) with campanile, clock tower and a flourish of iron work, the former post office (1886–88) and CBC Bank (1885). *All Fitzmaurice St. Not open for inspection.* St Andrew's Church (1869) and the Manse or minister's house (1890). *Church St. Church open for services or by appt. (02) 6921 2317.* St Michael's Catholic Cathedral was started in 1885, but extended into a cathedral in the 1920s. *Church St. Open daily. (02) 6921 2164.* A cannon used in the Lambing Flat riots (see **Young**) stands in shady Collins Park (1880s). Ask at Visitor Information about the Wiradjuri Walking

Main street, Tenterfield

Track – it covers 30 km but there are many short sections. It incorporates historic viaducts and the botanic gardens.

IN THE AREA The historic goldmining town of Adelong. *90 km E.*

🛈 *Cnr Tarcutta & Morrow sts; (02) 6926 9621.* Website: www.wagga. nsw.gov.au/tourism
See also Junee

WAUCHOPE   Map ref. 295 O12

Wauchope (pronounced 'war-hope') spreads out near the Hastings River on NSW's north coast, in an agricultural district noted from colonial times for its superb timber country.

Timbertown Pioneer Village A recreated pioneer town of the late 1880s, situated in 35 ha of bushland. A steam train wends its way through the countryside, a bullock team is harnessed for work and a Cobb & Co. coach provides transport, whilst a smith, printer, cooper and others demonstrate their 19th-century trades. A steam sawmill, schoolhouse and general store are other attractions. *2 km W via Oxley Hwy. Open daily. Ⓢ (for rides). (02) 6585 2322.*

ALSO OF INTEREST The Wauchope and District Historical Society, adjacent to the Pioneer Village (see above). *Oxley Hwy. Open by appt. Ⓢ (donation). (02) 6585 3473.*

🛈 *High St; (02) 6586 4055.*

WENTWORTH   Map ref. 298 D6, 316 F2

Explorer Charles Sturt discovered the junction of the Murray and Darling rivers in 1830, and it soon became an important camp for overlanders. A site was surveyed, and named Wentworth in 1859. By the 1890s bullock, camel and donkey wagons were hauling in the huge wool clip of south-west NSW to one of Australia's busiest river ports. Wentworth is now a quiet holiday town.

Old Wentworth Gaol Over a million bricks, bluestone from Malmsbury (Vic.) and Welsh slate brought to the colony as ship's ballast were used to build the gaol (1879). A stretching rack and whipping stool are amongst the grimmer displays. *Beverley St. Open daily. Ⓢ (03) 5027 3337.*

ALSO OF INTEREST Darling St has a peaceful, unhurried character, with

Lake Mungo National Park, near Wentworth

verandahed shops, pubs and shady trees, watched over by the graceful spire of St John's Anglican Church (1871). *Open for tours by appt. Ⓢ (donation). (03) 5023 1037.* The attractive courthouse (1880), not open for inspection, was built to replace a rustic slab courthouse, which now stands in Fotherby Park. PS *Ruby* (early 1900s), one of the last steamers on the river, is also in the park, dry-docked near the Darling Bridge. Lawns lead down to the creaking old timber wharves in Wharf St. Wentworth Pioneer Museum contains an eclectic display, from fossil remnants of extinct Australian megafauna to old machinery. *117 Beverley St. Open daily. Ⓢ (02) 5027 3160.* Sturt's Tree, marked by the famous explorer in 1830, can be seen in the caravan park. *Darling St (s end).*

IN THE AREA Aboriginal heritage in the district is especially rich and includes the World Heritage-listed Mungo National Park. Archaeologically fascinating, this unique landscape reveals evidence of Aboriginal occupation over 40 000 years. Guided tours provide a fascinating insight into that past. *130 km NE. Check with Harry Nanya Outback Tours, Sandwych St. Open Mon.–Sat. Ⓢ (03) 5027 2076.*

🛈 *28 Darling St; (03) 5027 3624.* Website: www.walkabout.com.au

WILBERFORCE   Map ref. 293 R11

Wilberforce is one of the five towns Gov. Macquarie declared in the Hawkesbury Valley in 1810. For more than 200 years market gardens here have supplied food to Sydney.

Hawkesbury Heritage Farm The major attraction is Rose Cottage, built 1811 by Thomas Rose, one of the colony's first free settlers. An 1840s slab cottage and a church of Huon pine (c. 1860) have been moved to the site. There are also shops, a shearing shed, a saddlery, horse-drawn vehicles – all set in 13 ha of parkland on the banks of the Hawkesbury River. *Rose St. Open Thurs.–Sun. or by appt. Ⓢ (02) 4575 1457.*

ALSO OF INTEREST St John's Anglican Church is a rustic stone church (c. 1859) with an unusual vertical stone sundial. *Macquarie Rd. Open by appt. (02) 4575 1417.* The adjacent school is a large, sandstock-brick Georgian building (c. 1819–20). One of its pupils went on to become the bushranger Capt. Thunderbolt. *Not open for inspection.*

IN THE AREA At Ebenezer, in a pretty setting above the Hawkesbury, is Australia's oldest church still in use. Built c. 1807–09 by Scottish farmers, it looks like a crofter's cottage with a neat porch. A pioneer graveyard adjoins the church. *8 km NE. Coromandel Rd. Open daily. (02) 4579 9350.* The village of Wisemans Ferry overlooks a sharp bend of the Hawkesbury, where Solomon Wiseman ran his ferry service in the early 1800s. *50 km NE.* Part of the Great North Rd built by convict chain gangs in the 1830s can still be seen, the stonework remarkably intact.

🛈 *Bicentenary Park, Ham Common, Clarendon; (02) 4588 5895.* Website: www.hawkesburyvalley.com
See also Richmond, Windsor

Cooma Cottage, Yass

WINDSOR
Map ref. 293 Q12

See Historic Highlights, p. 52

WOLLONGONG
Map ref. 293 K10

Wollongong is one of Australia's biggest cities, a major industrial centre and international shipping port. The earliest settlement was established near Lake Illawarra about 1815. Agriculture and farming, and later coalmining and heavy industry, have driven the city's constant expansion. **Illawarra Historical Society Museum** Located in the former post office (1882–92). Some rooms are furnished to capture the building's pre-Federation domestic style and there are museum exhibits. *11 Market St. Open Thurs., Sat.–Sun. & pub hol afternoons. Ⓢ (02) 4228 7770.* ALSO OF INTEREST Few buildings remain from the 19th century. One of the most notable is St Michael's Church (1859), designed by respected ecclesiastical architect Edmund Blacket, strategically sited on a hill. *Church St. Open daily. Ⓢ (donation). (02) 4228 9132.* Market Square, opposite the museum, retains early lampposts, bandstand and avenue of spreading fig trees. Belmore Basin Lighthouse is an iron lighthouse (1872) reputedly watched over by the spirit of a harbour pilot drowned in 1867. *Wollongong Boat Harbour. Not open for inspection.* The Wollongong City Art Gallery's major collection includes some fine colonial paintings of the region. *Cnr Kembla & Burelli sts. Open Tues.–Sun. & pub hols. (02) 4228 7500.* Illawarra Motoring Museum conjures up more leisurely days with its vintage vehicles and memorabilia. *634 Northcliffe Dr., Kembla Grange. Open Wed.–Sun. Ⓢ (02) 4272 2086.* IN THE AREA The village of Mount Kembla, the scene of Australia's worst mining disaster in 1902, when 95 men were killed, remains little changed in the last century. *11 km w.* A vintage train climbs the Illawarra escarpment, on the 'Cockatoo Run', every Sun. and Wed. Train departs Sydney and stops at Wollongong, Thirroul, Unanderra, Robertson and the historic town of Moss Vale. A commentary is provided. *Booking essential. Ⓢ 1300 653 801.* 🅘 *Cnr Kembla & Crown sts; freecall 1800 240 737.* Website: www.tourismwollongong.com

YASS
Map ref. 292 F11, 300 D4

Famous explorer Hamilton Hume discovered the Yass district in 1821 and later settled there. Set in undulating countryside renowned for its fine-wool sheep, Yass possesses a grand streetscape with a wealth of prestigious 19th-century buildings. **Cooma Cottage** A delightful, weatherboard cottage, the front section dating from 1835, a fine example of colonial architecture, with a rustic portico across the back, brick stables and coach-house. One of the oldest houses in NSW, it was home to explorer Hamilton Hume for more than 40 years. The cottage has delicately paned french doors, a verandah and handsome cedar joinery. The house overlooks a bend in the Yass River lined with peppercorns and gums. *4 km E via Yass Valley Way. Open Wed.–Mon. Ⓢ (02) 6226 1470. NT.* ALSO OF INTEREST Formal Classical buildings, old-fashioned country pubs and broad, shady verandahs line the main street (once on the main Sydney–Melbourne hwy). Of particular note are the impressive courthouse (1879), set in landscaped grounds, not open for inspection, the c. 1872 CBC Bank (note the original hitching rails), the Italianate post office (c. 1884), still operating, and the Bank of NSW (1885). *All Comur St.* St Clement's Anglican Church (1847–50) designed by architect Edmund Blacket, has a tall, shingled spire and five bells, inscribed 'We sing the Lord's song in a Strange Land'. *Church St. Open for guided tours by appt. (02) 6226 1089.* At the Railway Museum see antique rolling stock in the historic (1891) station building and Australia's shortest railway platform. *Cargo St. Open Sun. afternoons. Ⓢ (02) 6226 2169.* Hamilton Hume Historical Museum includes historic photos and a scale model of the town's main street in the 1890s. *Comur St. Open Sat.–Sun. by appt. Ⓢ (02) 6226 2557.* Yass and District Historical Society run guided tours for groups. *By appt. Ⓢ (02) 6226 2557.* 🅘 *Coronation Park, Comur St; (02) 6226 2557.*

YOUNG
Map ref. 292 D9, 300 C2

Young, originally known as Lambing Flat, was the site of the violent Lambing Flat riots in 1861, when the local gold miners determined to drive the Chinese from the diggings. After months of tension and strife, several thousand miners attacked the Chinese and burnt their possessions. The Riot Act was read, police reinforcements called in and, finally, the Royal Artillery summoned. The Chinese Immigration Restriction Act – a precursor to the White Australia Policy – was passed in November 1861, largely as a result of the riots. OF INTEREST Lambing Flat Folk Museum has the famous Roll Up Flag carried by miners during the 1861 riots on display. *Campbell St. Open daily. Ⓢ (02) 6382 2248.* 🅘 *2 Short St; (02) 6382 3394.* Website: www.young.nsw.gov.au

HISTORIC HIGHLIGHTS

Old Government House, Parramatta

E xploring some of New South Wales' historic towns sheds light on various phases in our history – from earliest colonial days at Parramatta to the gold rushes near Bathurst, and from Francis Greenway's renowned Georgian architecture at Windsor to the heavy mining and union history at Broken Hill.

ARMIDALE

Etruscan boar vase c. 500 B.C.

Armidale is a city of Victorian grace and charm, set high on the spectacular New England plateau. The first pastoral station in the area was taken up in 1835 and the fine grazing land was soon attracting many squatters. In 1839, the Commissioner of Crown Land, George James MacDonald, called the area Armidale. The township was gazetted in 1849. By early this century two exceptionally fine cathedrals had been built and several secondary schools opened. These, together with the University of New England, earned the city a reputation as a city of refinement and a seat of learning, which it still retains to this day.

Museum of Antiquities
A unique collection of archaeological artifacts from ancient civilisations dating as far back as 100 000 B.C.
Faculty of Arts building, Arts Rd, University of New England. Open Mon.–Fri. (02) 6773 3333.

Armidale Visitor Information Centre
82 Marsh St
(02) 6772 4655, freecall 1800 627 736
Website: www.new-england.org/armidale

St Peter's Anglican Cathedral
One of Australia's most distinctive churches, designed by J Horbury Hunt and opened for worship in 1875. The brickwork is exceptional – many varieties of brick were moulded specifically for this cathedral.
Dangar St. Open daily. (02) 6772 2269.

Cathedral of St Mary & St Joseph
Piercing the skyline is the soaring spire of this impressive cathedral, completed c. 1912.
Cnr Dangar & Barney sts. Open daily. (02) 6772 4971.

IN THE AREA
In **HILLGROVE**, an old gold ghost town, the Hillgrove Rural Life and Industry Museum has some marvellous photographs of the boom era 1890–1910. *31 km E. Open Fri.–Mon. & pub hols or by appt. $ (donation). (02) 6778 1189.*
At the small town of **URALLA** there are signs of goldmining and, in the old cemetery, the grave of the notorious bushranger Capt. Thunderbolt. The three-storey McCrossin's Mill Museum has paintings depicting Capt. Thunderbolt's life and exhibits related to Chinese goldmining at Rocky River. *22 km sw. Open daily. $ (02) 6778 3022.*
DEEARGEE (part of the former Gostwyck Station) is one of New England's oldest stations. The tiered, circular woolshed (c. 1872), willow-lined creek and small, vine-covered church give it a special charm. *11 km E of Uralla. Not open for inspection, but visible from the road. Uralla Visitor Information, 104 Bridge St, Uralla. (02) 6778 4496.*

Saumarez Homestead
Set in formal gardens, this homestead (1888–1906) was built on one of the district's oldest properties by the White family, a distinguished Australian pioneering family, whose best-known member is Nobel prize-winning author Patrick White. Saumarez provides a fine record of Victorian–Edwardian life, containing all the homestead's original furnishings.
5 km sw on New England Hwy. Guided tours of house daily from 1 Sept–15 June. Booking recommended. $ (02) 6772 3616. NT.

New England Regional Art Museum
Exhibits include the renowned Howard Hinton collection of Australian artworks, covering the period 1833–1950s. Also located here is the fascinating Museum of Printing (MOP), tracing the development of the printing industry in Australia.
Kentucky St. Open daily. (MOP open Thurs.–Sun. afternoons only $) (02) 6772 5255.

Ploughing at Hinton, Roland Wakelin, 1945

Booloominbah

Architect J Horbury Hunt designed the vast, 45-room brick mansion Booloominbah (an Aboriginal word meaning 'home of the native apple trees') for pastoralist FR White. It was completed in 1888 in the Queen Anne style. Dark oak panelling and beautiful pictorial stained glass enrich the interior. Surrounded by lovely gardens, it is now part of the University of New England.
Off Queen Elizabeth Dr. then Elm Ave. Open daily. Ⓢ *(donation). (02) 6773 3050.*

Armidale Courthouse

A formal 1860 building with grand portico, lovely iron gates and a squat clock tower, added in the 1870s.
Cnr Beardy St (The Mall) & Faulkner St. Not open for inspection.

Armidale City Heritage Trolley

A commentary during the two-hour tour outlines the town's history and points out places of historic and cultural interest.

🚋 *Tours daily. Booking recommended.* Ⓢ *(donation). Freecall 1800 627 736.*

Heritage Precinct

The conservation area around Beardy and Faulkner streets contains a wealth of heritage architecture.

Imperial Hotel

This eye-catching hotel (c. 1890) curves around the corner of Beardy and Faulkner sts, its extravagant parapet and lacework balconies (the longest in NSW) adding a Victorian flourish to the centre of town.
Cnr Beardy St (East Mall) & Faulkner St. Open daily. (02) 6772 2405.

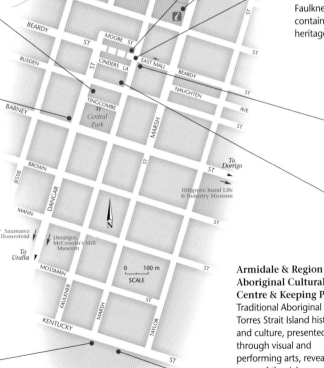

Armidale & Region Aboriginal Cultural Centre & Keeping Place

Traditional Aboriginal and Torres Strait Island history and culture, presented through visual and performing arts, reveal some of the richness of indigenous history in the region.
Kentucky St. Open Mon.–Sat. Ⓢ *(donation). (02) 6771 1249.*

Armidale Folk Museum

Housed in the former Literary Institute, the oldest wing of which dates back to 1863. A fine regional folk museum, with 19th-century furnishings, horse-drawn vehicles and more.
Cnr Rusden & Faulkner sts. Open afternoons. Ⓢ *(donation). (02) 6770 3536. NT.*

BATHURST

Bathurst is Australia's oldest inland settlement, a town of wide streets – 'wide enough for a bullock team to turn', as Governor Lachlan Macquarie had dictated – with English shade trees and Victorian buildings of mellowed brick attesting to its nineteenth-century prosperity. Macquarie himself chose the site in 1815. After a slow beginning, the discovery of Australia's first payable gold at nearby Ophir in 1851 dramatically boosted Bathurst's fortunes and future. When the gold yields dwindled, Bathurst's progress continued, its economy by then firmly based on the prosperity of the excellent surrounding pastoral lands.

Bathurst Visitor Information Centre
28 William St
(02) 6332 1444
Website: www.bathurst.nsw.gov.au

Bathurst Courthouse
Bathurst's pride is the magnificent courthouse complex (1877–80), designed by Colonial Architect James Barnet. The courthouse is the central building, with massive dome and lengthy colonnaded verandahs. The dainty bell-turret and clock were added in 1883.
Russell St. Open Mon.–Fri. (when court is not in session).

Bathurst, 1880s

Bathurst Gaol
The monumental entrance to this still operational gaol (1886) provides a grim warning to passers-by of the consequences of crime. The finely worked stone facade features a keystone with a lion's head holding a symbolic key.
Browning St. Not open for inspection.

Bathurst Historical Museum
The local historical society houses its extensive archives in the east wing of the courthouse building.
Russell St. Open Tues.–Wed., Sat.–Sun., pub & school hols. $ (02) 6332 4755.

Machattie Park
Bathurst's gaol stood on this site until the citizens' sensibility was offended by having a prison so close to the town centre. Dr R Machattie, several times mayor of Bathurst, was a key figure in lobbying for a park. The elegant rotunda was installed in 1890.
Bounded by George, Keppel & William sts.

ALSO OF INTEREST

James Rutherford established Cobb & Co.'s headquarters here in 1862 and later claimed 'people whopped and cheered at the prospect of good, speedy times ahead'. The building is long gone. *Cnr William & Howick sts.* Bathurst possesses a rich variety of architectural styles and a fine legacy of historic buildings, from cottages to affluent residences, exceptionally fine civic buildings and several distinguished churches. Bathurst Visitor Information has excellent walking and driving tours of the area.

Bathurst Goldfields
A re-creation of a goldfield, with demonstrations of the various mining methods, such as shaft sinking and crushing ore. Hopefuls can try their hand at gold-panning.
428 Conrod Straight, Mount Panorama. Guided tours only, Mon.–Fri. $ (02) 6332 2022.

Miss Traill's House

This colonial Georgian house, in an old-world garden of daisies and roses, is time-worn but scarcely changed since it was built in 1845. Miss Traill, who lived here 1931–76, was a descendant of Bathurst pioneers. Family furnishings and memorabilia fill the house.
1321 Russell St. Open for tours Tues.–Sat. afternoons & Sun. Ⓢ *(02) 6332 4232. NT.*

Abercrombie House

A huge, 52-room baronial mansion (1870–78), built from rock-faced granite. Its mass of Flemish gable-ends, turrets and spires create a distinctive silhouette. The lavish interior features 30 fireplaces and seven staircases. Built by James Stewart, whose family were among Bathurst's pioneer settlers.
7.5 km NW on Ophir Rd. Guided tours only, Sun. at 3 p.m. (closed Aug.). Visitors advised to check first. Ⓢ *(02) 6331 4929.*

Old Government House

Gov. Macquarie stayed for a short time in this small sandstock-brick building (c. 1819) in 1821, thus earning the cottage its title. It is typically early colonial in style.
Rear of 1 George St. Open Sun. afternoons & by appt. Ⓢ *(02) 6332 4755.*

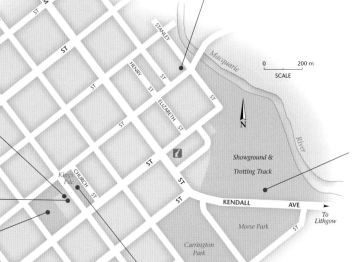

Showground Pavilions

Several of these unusual pavilions date from the 1880s. One pavilion, built of portable timber panels and highlighted by decorative timberwork known as 'carpenter's Gothic', was transported from Ashfield, NSW, in the 1890s. Note the carved eaves, fretwork bargeboards and detailed fanlights.
Kendall Ave. Can be viewed from outside any time, open during shows.

Chifley Home

This modest Victorian timber house (1880s) was home to one of Australia's best-known political figures, Ben Chifley, prime minister 1945–49.
10 Busby St. Ⓢ *Open Tues.–Sun.*

William George Evans Statue

In 1813, Deputy Surveyor WG Evans was the first European to reach this point. Evans proclaimed the countryside west of the Blue Mountains 'the handsomest country I ever saw . . . a fine rich plain of land.'
Kings Pde.

IN THE AREA

The old diggings at **OPHIR** are now within a flora and fauna reserve. There are few signs of the original town, but Summer Hill Creek is popular with fossickers. *40 km NW.* Other old gold towns are close at hand: Rockley, built around a village green, the little settlement of O'Connell, sleepy Sofala, Millthorpe and the near-ghost town of Hill End.
CARCOAR, with church steeples and its winding main street, is one of the State's most delightful country towns. *55 km SW on Mid Western Hwy. See also p. 21.*

BERRIMA

The village of Berrima is renowned for its country charm and its distinctive Georgian buildings. Explorer Dr Charles Throsby and nine other 'Free Persons' took up land here in the early 1800s and in 1829 Major Mitchell chose a 'fine romantic part of the river' as the town site. A gaol and an elegant court-house soon appeared, and a cluster of inns and hostelries vied for passing trade. But the district court was moved to Goulburn in 1850, the railway line bypassed Berrima in the 1860s, and people began to move away. More than a century later, conservationists saved many heritage buildings and today the small town is a unique legacy from colonial days.

Berrima Visitor Information Centre
Berrima Courthouse Museum
Cnr Wilshire & Argyle sts
(02) 4877 1505
Website: www.highlandsnsw.com.au

Bull's Head Fountain
On the north wall of the gaol, the fountain allowed run-off water from the roof to drain into a trough for horses. The bull's head is a fine piece of cast-iron work (1877).
Argyle St.

Gaol
Work on the gaol began in 1834. When completed in 1839, authorities considered it 'the finest and most commodious building of the kind in the colony' (prisoners weren't quite so impressed). The building was extended in 1865–66. It was used as an internment camp during WW I. The flawless stonework, arched entrance and cedar doors create an imposing sight. It is now a training centre.
Argyle St. Not open for inspection.

Surveyor General Inn
Convict-built of sandstone and sandstock bricks in 1834 for James Harper. First licensed in 1835, and the oldest continuously licensed inn in Australia.
Old Hume Hwy. Open daily.
(02) 4877 1226.

Berrima House
One of Berrima's first houses (c. 1835). Legend has it that bushranger Ben Hall once slept on the verandah.
Jellore St. Not open for inspection.

Berrima District Historical Society Museum
Items of historical interest dating back to the early 1800s, and an exhibition titled 'Berrima – To Federation and Beyond'.
Market Pl. Open Sat.–Sun., pub & school hols or by appt.
$ *(02) 4877 1130.*

Whitehorse Inn
This early colonial hostelry, established in 1832 and first known as Oldbury's Inn, is now a restaurant and motel.
Market Pl. Restaurant open daily.
(02) 4877 1204.

ALSO OF INTEREST
Ask at the Courthouse Museum about the excellent guided tours of the town or pick up a brochure. *(02) 4877 1505.* Berrima is well known for its many B&Bs and accommodation in historic old inns and houses.

St Francis Xavier Catholic Church
Dates from 1851. A convict stockade was originally on this site.
Old Hume Hwy. Open for services only.

Berrima Courthouse Museum

Berrima's splendid golden sandstone courthouse (1838), designed by architect Mortimer Lewis, was built using stone hewn from the riverbanks. The cedar doors are shaped from solid planks and the interiors are impressive. The colony's first trial by jury took place here in 1841. Museum tours include a fascinating audio-visual presentation. The Visitor Information is also here. *Cnr Argyle & Wilshire sts. Open daily.* $ *(02) 4877 1505.*

Old Breen's Inn

Weathered steps lead from the highway, and a quaint dormer window breaks the steep roofline of this picturesque old inn, built c. 1858. Now a restaurant. *Old Hume Hwy. Open Tues.–Sun. for lunch & dinner. (02) 4877 1977.*

Harper's Mansion

Fine sandstock-brick Georgian house (c. 1834), on a rise overlooking the town, was built for James Harper, the son of convicts. It remained in the Harper family for three generations. Harper also built the Surveyor General Inn. *Wilkinson St. Not open for inspection.*

Berrima Galleries

A former coaching inn, which went by the name of Taylor's Crown Inn, this two-storey, mellow red-brick Georgian building (c. 1840) is now an arts and craft shop. *Old Hume Hwy. Open daily. (02) 4877 1333.*

Old Bakery Tearooms

The single-storey bake-house, now tearooms, is behind the two-storey neat sandstone cottage that once was the baker's residence (both c. 1850s). You can still see the old ovens. *Cnr Old Hume Hwy & Wingecarribee St. Open daily. (02) 4877 1343.*

Holy Trinity Anglican Church

A small provincial church (c. 1849), near the town common, designed by eminent architect Edmund Blacket. The stained-glass windows, from Cornwall, are much older than the church. *Argyle St. Open daily.*

Map labels

WILKINSON ST · HUME HWY · To Sydney · OXLEY ST · ST · WILSHIRE ST · ARGYLE · OLD · WINGECARRIBEE ST · 0 100 m SCALE · N · JELLORE ST · HWY · MARKET · ST · PL · ARGYLE ST · Wingecarribee River · HUME · OLD · To Goulburn · OLDBURY ST · Throsby Park · To Moss Vale

Magistrate's House

Sheltering beneath a sweeping roof and verandah and facing the pine-studded village green, the house was built in the 1830s by JJ Higgins, a shopkeeper and postmaster, and leased to a police magistrate. The garden's walnut trees were planted in 1880. *Market Pl. Not open for inspection.*

Market Place Park

Berrima's village green, or common, the first land surveyed in the town in 1831. Stones around the edge of the park are said to be from the Lennox Bridge (1836).

A Throsby family portrait, c. 1860s

In the Area

THROSBY PARK, on the outskirts of Moss Vale, in Robertson Rd, is a handsome, single-storey stone farmhouse built c. 1834 by Charles Throsby, a nephew of Dr Charles Throsby, whose original exploration party south of Sydney in 1818 discovered the Berrima district. Dr Throsby received the land as a grant from Gov. Macquarie. This is one of the oldest farms in the district and is administered by the National Parks and Wildlife Service. *Open during History Week in April and Heritage Week in Sept. 8 km s.* $ *(02) 4877 7244.*

BROKEN HILL

The countryside around Broken Hill is red, dusty and barren, but the silver–lead–zinc mines in the Barrier Mountains are the world's richest. German-born boundary rider Charles Rasp discovered the ore body in 1883 and, despite the isolation and harsh conditions, a town sprang up almost immediately. Major developments in mining technology and the history of the union movement have been closely allied to Broken Hill. Today it's a thriving outback town, with a heritage of national significance and many signs of its nineteenth-century beginnings.

Broken Hill Visitor Information Centre
Cnr Blende & Bromide sts
(08) 8087 6077
Website: www.murrayoutback.org.au

Trades Hall
The union movement has always been a force in Broken Hill, its history often marked by bitter disputes and prolonged strikes. The elaborate, late-Victorian building (1898, extended 1904) shows that the organisation was well funded from its early days.
Cnr Blende & Sulphide sts. Not open for inspection. (08) 8087 5258.

Railway Station, c. 1900

Railway, Mineral & Train Museum
Sulphide Street Railway Station, built by a private tramway company 1904–05, is now a transport museum. A narrow-gauge line linking the 'Silver City' and South Australia ran 1888–1970, carrying nearly 3 million passengers and almost 43 million tonnes of ore concentrates.
Cnr Bromide & Blende sts. Open daily. $ (08) 8088 4660.

Mural of BHP workers by Napier Waller, 1930s

The Big Australian
The top of the ore body stood out like a jagged ridge against the undulating countryside and was known by pastoralists as 'the broken hill'. BHP (Broken Hill Proprietary Co. Ltd) was founded here in 1885. Mining is now on the decline, but BHP has become one of Australia's largest corporations.

Palace Hotel
An impressive three-storey building, opened as the Coffee Palace in 1889, but coffee didn't sufficiently slake the miners' thirsts and the unprofitable business became a licensed hotel in 1892. It's still a pub today.
Argent St. Open daily. (08) 8088 1699.

SILVERTON

The once thriving town of Silverton, settled before Broken Hill, is now a ghost town, but worth the visit. Films such as *Mad Max 2*, *A Town Like Alice* and *Priscilla Queen of the Desert* have been filmed here. The much-photographed pub (1880), still serving refreshments, is something of an outback icon. The Silverton Gaol (1889) is now a museum. *Open daily. (08) 8088 5317.* The former school building in town (1887) is now used by the Broken Hill Historical Society. *Not open for inspection. 27 km NW.*

Geo Centre
Originally built (1890) as a bond store and offices for the SA Brewing Company. Now an interpretive centre and museum, with displays focusing on Broken Hill's unique geology and mining history.
Cnr Bromide & Crystal sts. Open daily. $ (08) 8087 6538.

Royal Flying Doctor Service
This unique Australian service, set up in 1928, has a small museum at the Broken Hill base.
5 km s. Broken Hill Airport. Open daily. $ (08) 8080 1777.

Afghan Mosque

A modest, corrugated-iron structure, built in 1891 by Moslem cameleers. It stands on the site of the former camp where the drivers loaded their camel teams in the town's earliest days.

Cnr Williams & Buck sts. Open Sun. afternoons or by appt. (S) *(donation). (08) 8088 1713.*

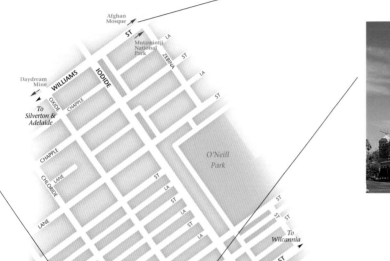

Post Office

Another Victorian-era building (1892) which testifies to the city's early prosperity. It was designed by Colonial Architect James Barnet. *Argent St.*

Line of Lode Visitors Centre & Museum

Surface tours of the South Mine and an outstanding mining history collection in the museum.

260 Eyre St. Two 2-hour tours daily. (S) *(08) 8088 6000.*

Town Hall

Splendid town hall (1890) with multi-level tower topped by a delicate cupola, epitomises Broken Hill's 19th-century vision of a grand future. The main hall has been demolished, but the ornate facade remains.
Argent St.

IN THE AREA

The historic **DAYDREAM MINE**, dating back to 1882, where you can view the original smelter and township, and tour the mine. *28 km NW. Open daily. Regular tours.* (S) *(08) 8088 5682.*
MUTAWINTJI NATIONAL PARK in the Bynguano Ranges is rich in cultural and ceremonial significance for Aboriginal people of western NSW. It contains one of the best collections of Aboriginal relics and paintings in NSW, with over 300 recorded archaeological sites, dating from 8000 years ago. Tours by Mutawintji Heritage Tours. *130 km NE, via Silver City Hwy, then E. Guided tours Wed. & Sat.* (S) *(08) 8088 7000.*

GOULBURN

Goulburn is one of Australia's oldest inland towns, on the main Melbourne–Sydney route, in a district renowned for the superior quality of its wool and its long-established farming properties. In 1828 a plan for the 'township of Goulburn Plains' was drawn up and the next decades were years of pastoral expansion and growth. Gold, discovered at Braidwood in the 1850s, brought wealth, and then in 1869 the railway line arrived from Sydney. Today Goulburn is a busy and modern country town, but its history is rich, and the observant eye will detect much of interest, including many signs of its colonial origins.

Goulburn Visitor Information Centre
201 Sloane St
(02) 4823 4492
Website: www.goulburn.nsw.gov.au

St Saviour's Anglican Cathedral
A fine example of the work of architect Edmund Blacket, who also designed the magnificent early buildings at Sydney University. The sandstone building was erected in 1874–88 but the tower was finally added a century later.
Bourke St. Open daily. $ *(for tours).*
(02) 4821 2206.

Former Fire Station
Designed by EC Manfred, who also designed the Old Town Hall, the station (1880) features a quaint bell.
11 Montague St. Not open for inspection.

Post Office
The most prominent building in the main thoroughfare, a grand Italianate structure with arcading and a tower, designed by James Barnet in 1880–81.
Auburn St.

Goulburn, 1896

Old Town Hall
An unusual building of red brick (1889) with a carved shell motif highlighting the Dutch gable, and a small, curved balcony.
Auburn St. Not open for inspection.

ALSO OF INTEREST
The stately bluestone Bishopthorpe Manor (1870), home to the first bishop of the Diocese of Goulburn, is now a country guesthouse. *Bishopthorpe La. Open daily. (02) 4822 1570.* Visitors to the Hillstead property, in Garroorigang Rd, will find the South Hill Homestead, a homestead mansion (1860–70), now a B&B, and the 19th-century School – an 1880s schoolroom offering a nostalgic view of Victorian-era schooling. *Separate tours for children and adults available by appt.* $ *(02) 4821 9591.*

Testimonial, NSW Government Railways, 1892

Goulburn Rail Heritage Centre
Century-old rail workshop with veteran locomotives and rolling stock.
Braidwood Rd. Open for tours limited hrs Mon.–Fri., daily Sat.–Sun. Closed 2nd & 4th Thurs. of month. $ *(02) 4822 5721.*

Goulburn Historic Waterworks Museum

The steam pumping engine and boilers for Goulburn's original water supply, still in working order, are housed in this handsome brick building (1883).

Wollondilly River, overlooking Marsden Weir. Open for tours by appt only. Bookings essential. (02) 4823 4448.

Stables at Riversdale

Riversdale

Built by former convict John Richards in 1838 as the Victoria Inn. By the 1850s it had become a school, and in 1875 it was bought by Edward Twynam, the Surveyor-General, and stayed in his family for almost a century. Riversdale is Georgian in style, and is furnished with some notable colonial pieces. Also on the property is Garrison Cottage, Goulburn's oldest house.

Maud St. Open for tours by appt only. Ⓢ
(02) 4821 4741 or (02) 4821 9591. NT.

St Clair Cottage

Goulburn's first architect, Scotsman James Sinclair, lived in this single-storey townhouse (c. 1845) with its fine cedar panelling. The cottage now houses the Goulburn District Historical Society's museum and archives.

318 Sloane St. Open Sat.–Sun. afternoon or by appt.
Ⓢ *(02) 4821 1156.*

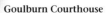

Goulburn Courthouse

Distinguished by its grandeur and scale, with its copper dome topped by a crown, and a keystone depicting Queen Victoria. When it was opened in 1887, Chief Justice Sir Frederick Darley declared it 'amongst the best in Her Majesty's Dominions'.

Montague St. Guided tours for groups by appt.

Goulburn Brewery

Probably the oldest surviving brewery–flour mill complex in NSW. It was designed by architect Francis Greenway, and built 1833–36. It includes a three-storey mill building, stables, a brewer's cottage and a castellated brewing tower. Now a boutique brewery with a restaurant and gallery. The brewer's cottage and stables are now a motel.

Bungonia Rd. Open daily. Guided tours on Sun. or by appt. Ⓢ
(02) 4821 6071.

Garroorigang House

Originally the Mulwaree Inn (1857), and a popular stop on the route to Braidwood. In 1868 Samuel Belcher converted it into a boys' school, which it remained until the 1880s. Some rooms are furnished in the ornate late-Victorian style and there's a schoolroom display.

Braidwood Rd. Open daily for guided tours. B&B accommodation. Ⓢ *(02) 4822 1912.*

PARRAMATTA

Although a city in its own right, Parramatta is a Sydney suburb – hectic, commercialised, constantly growing. It is justifiably proud of being the second settlement on the mainland, in an area discovered by Governor Phillip in 1788 and laid out as a town in 1790. John Macarthur, the pioneer of Australia's merino wool industry, was granted land here in 1793. His house, Elizabeth Farm, is the oldest in Australia. A number of other properties are also of national significance in the history of European settlement in this country.

Parramatta Heritage & Visitors Information Centre
346A Church St
(02) 9683 6922
Website: www.parracity.nsw.gov.au

Parramatta Park
On land set aside by Gov. Phillip in 1788 as a government farm. It later became the Governor's Domain, and was declared a public park in 1858. Within the Dairy Precinct is a small cottage (1796–1800), converted to a government dairy by Gov. Macquarie c.1815. Perhaps the most striking structure in the 86-ha park is the 1885 Tudor Gatehouse (not open for inspection).
O'Connell St. Vehicle access via Pitt St. Gardens open daily. (02) 8833 5000.

Government House by George William Evans, 1805

Old Government House
The oldest public building on the Australian mainland sits in refined splendour overlooking Parramatta Park. A house built in 1799 for Gov. Hunter was enlarged in 1815 for Gov. Macquarie, resulting in the spacious, elegant, Georgian building. This was the official residence until Government House in Sydney was finished in 1845. The colonial and Georgian furnishings, all pre-1850, are outstanding. The flagged courtyard leads to the willow-lined banks of the Parramatta River. Lunch and coffee are served on the verandah.
Parramatta Park. Open daily for tours. $ *(02) 9635 8149. NT.*

St John's Cemetery
Australia's oldest cemetery. It contains the oldest undisturbed marked grave of a European settler, that of Henry Dodd (1790), Gov. Phillip's faithful servant. Some of those who arrived on the First Fleet, and some notable pioneers, are buried here. The wall, constructed using hand-made bricks (1821–25) was built by convicts.
O'Connell St. Open at all times.

St John's Cathedral
The first church consecrated in the colony was begun on this site in 1802. Macquarie's aide-de-camp, John Watts, designed the four-storey, copper-spired twin towers (c. 1820), and the central section dates from 1855.
Church St. Open for services or by appt. (02) 9635 5904.

Linden House (Lancers Memorial Museum)
This sandstone house was built in Macquarie St, Parramatta, in 1828 to house a domestic arts school founded by Gov. Darling's wife. In 1964 it was moved stone by stone 600 m to the Lancer Barracks' grounds and is now a regimental museum.
Cnr Smith & Station sts. Open Sun. $ *041 488 6461.*

Lancer Barracks by Eirene Mort, 1934

Parramatta River by Danny Eastwood, 2000

Parramatta Heritage & Visitors Information Centre

Audio-visual displays on Parramatta's history, a list of sites of historic significance, walking trail brochures. You can also book for tours and there's a family history library.
346A Church St. Open daily. (02) 9683 6922.

Harrisford

This colonial Georgian house (1823–28) was the birthplace of Australia's oldest independent school. The prestigious King's School, established in 1831, leased the house from 1832–35.
182 George St. Not open for inspection.

Hambledon Cottage

John Macarthur built this stuccoed brick cottage (early 1820s) on Elizabeth Farm for his children's governess. It has the sweeping colonial roof, shuttered windows and stone-flagged verandah of the era.
63 Hassall St, Harris Park (access via Gregory Pl.). Open for tours only, Wed.–Thurs., Sat.–Sun. or by appt. ⓢ (02) 9635 6924.

Elizabeth Macarthur, early 1800s

Elizabeth Farm

Probably the most historic house in Australia, begun in 1793 by John Macarthur and named after his wife, Elizabeth, who played a key role in managing the family's affairs. Although modest, the original four-room cottage was larger than nearby Government House. Macarthur had it extended c. 1826–28 into 'an elegant and commodious residence'. By 1834, at the time of Macarthur's death, Elizabeth Farm was a distinguished country residence. The Macarthur family sold the property in 1881.
70 Alice St, Rosehill. Open daily. ⓢ (02) 9635 9488.

Lancer Barracks

The oldest military barracks on the mainland, established by Gov. Macquarie in 1820 and still used by the military. John Watts, Gov. Macquarie's aide-de-camp, designed the complex of buildings (c. 1820–28). Only two of the original three buildings survive.
Cnr Smith & Station sts. Grounds open for inspection, buildings not open. (02) 9635 7822.

Experiment Farm Cottage

A handsome, single-storey colonial bungalow (early 1830s) stands on land granted to James Ruse in 1792, the first land grant made in the colony. Gov. Phillip placed Ruse, a Cornish transportee, on part of the land and promised him a grant of 12 ha if he could support himself there. The experiment being successful, Ruse was granted 'Experiment Farm'. Surgeon John Harris bought the property in 1793 and later built the present colonial bungalow.
9 Ruse St, Harris Park. Open Tues.–Sun. & most pub hols. ⓢ (02) 9635 5655. NT.

WINDSOR

Windsor is sited on a ridge above a sweep of the mighty Hawkesbury River, surrounded by fertile flood plains. It is graced by probably the finest church built in colonial Australia, the beautiful Saint Matthew's Church, and possesses the first major courthouse built outside Sydney. Both buildings were designed by renowned colonial architect – and convict – Francis Greenway. Windsor also boasts the oldest inn, the oldest rectory and one of the oldest public squares in the country, as well as classic colonial Georgian and mid-Victorian buildings.

Windsor Visitor Information Centre
Hawkesbury Museum, 7 Thompson Sq.
(02) 4577 2310
Website: www.hawkesburyvalley.com

The Doctor's House
A red-brick and sandstone terrace of two houses (1837). The first doctor in residence appears to have been Dr Day. Thomas Fiaschi, an Italian surgeon, moved here in 1877. Fiaschi was also a noted vigneron, who established a successful winery, Tizzana, at Sackville Reach.
3 Thompson Sq. Guided tours by appt. (02) 4577 8088.

Hawkesbury Museum & Visitor Information
In the 1840s Edward Coffee ran the Daniel O'Connell Inn in this elegant two-storey building, which now houses a museum. Its collection includes Aboriginal artifacts and documents the history of European settlement in the valley.
7 Thompson Sq. Open daily. Ⓢ *(02) 4577 2310.*

Thompson Square
In 1811 Gov. Lachlan Macquarie named this square in memory of Andrew Thompson, variously described as 'that most respectable and Opulent Free Settler' and as an artful 'knave'. Thompson, a former convict, became a magistrate and was one of the district's first settlers.

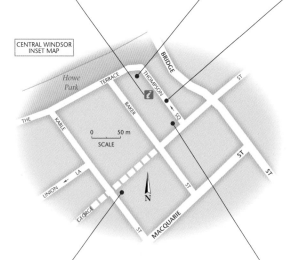

CENTRAL WINDSOR INSET MAP

Howe Park

0   50 m
SCALE

N

Governor Macquarie,
c. 1805

HISTORY

In the first years of settlement, the infant colony at Port Jackson came perilously close to starvation, and there were tentative forays into the hinterland in search of farming land. In 1789 Gov. Phillip and a small party sailed up the Hawkesbury, where the fertile flood plains of the magnificent Hawkesbury River valley were a welcome and promising sight. The first colonists settled in the district in 1794. Within a decade the area had a reputation as the 'granary of the colony', though floods were a persistent problem. When Gov. Macquarie toured the district in 1810, he chose sites above the flood level for the 'five Macquarie towns': Windsor, Richmond, Wilberforce, Pitt Town and Castlereagh.

The Linden on George (Loder House)
A Georgian townhouse, built in 1834 as a residence for explorer and innkeeper George Loder. The date of the building is incised in the keystone above the elegant fanlight. Now a restaurant.
126 George St. Open Wed.–Sun. for lunch & Fri.–Sat. for dinner. (02) 4577 3324.

Macquarie Arms Hotel
The oldest surviving inn in the country, built in 1815 on a land grant given to former convict Richard Fitzgerald by Gov. Macquarie 'on the express condition of his building immediately thereon a handsome commodious inn of brick or stone'. Largely altered, but the original entrance door and fanlight remain.
99 George St. Open daily. (02) 4577 3322.

St Matthew's Anglican Church

This beautiful brick church (1817–20) is widely acknowledged as architect Francis Greenway's masterpiece. It was built by convicts and consecrated by pioneer cleric, Rev. Samuel Marsden. In Windsor's early days, regiments stationed in the town marched to St Matthew's accompanied by the regimental band. The adjacent graveyard is older than the church. *Moses St. Open daily. (02) 4577 3193.*

St Matthew's Rectory

Built in 1825, a perfect complement to Greenway's handsome church and the oldest continuously occupied rectory in Australia. *Moses St. Not open for inspection.*

Architectural drawings, 1912

Courthouse

A Georgian sandstock-brick building (c. 1822), designed by Francis Greenway, who designed some of the infant colony's finest buildings. The finely proportioned interior is fitted with cedar furnishings. Restored and still in use as a courthouse. *Cnr Court & North sts. Open for tours by appt. (02) 4577 3023.*

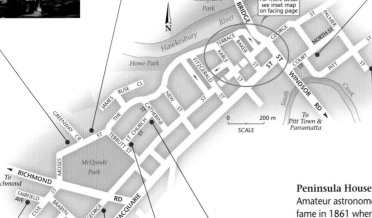

Peninsula House & John Tebbutt Observatories

Amateur astronomer John Tebbutt achieved international fame in 1861 when he discovered the Great Comet (subsequently named after him). He built the two observatories that stand in the grounds of this house, the small one in 1863, the larger in 1879. Tebbutt is portrayed on the $100 note. The observatories are used as a reception venue. *Palmer St. Not open for inspection.*

Fairfield House

Built by William Cox in 1831–33 and extended into a Victorian mansion in the 1880s, it can be seen from Richmond Rd. *Fairfield Ave. Not open for inspection.*

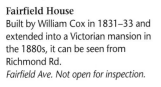

Old General Store

One of Windsor's most interesting shop buildings, erected in 1897 by a former sailor. Finely sculpted stone carvings of recumbent figures with various nautical symbols grace the facade. Now an antique store. *394 George St.*

Former Bell Inn

A colonial inn (1845) with stone-paved verandah, scalloped timber valance and a bevelled corner entrance. Now a residence. *2 Little Church St. Not open for inspection.*

St Matthew's Catholic Church

Dates from 1840. *Tebbutt St. Open for services or by appt. (02) 4577 2310.*

IN THE AREA

Historic **TIZZANA** winery. *15 km N. 518 Tizzana Rd, Sackville Reach. (02) 4579 1150.* The picturesque settlement of Pitt Town. *10 km NE. See also Richmond, Wilberforce*

AUSTRALIAN CAPIT

The Australian Capital Territory is well endowed with natural forest and the contrast of rolling countryside and rugged landscape. It reaches north to the rich wool-growing country around Yass and Goulburn, west to the Brindabella Range and south to the spectacular Australian Alps. The ACT was created in 1911 to house the national capital, Canberra.

TERRITORY *A Grand Vision*

Old Parliament House, Parkes

The European history of the district extends back to the 1820s, when explorer Dr Charles Throsby reported glowingly that 'the country is well-watered with extensive meadows of rich land'. JJ Moore took up the first land grant in 1824, naming his station Canberry, or 'meeting place'. Sydney merchant Robert Campbell sent his overseer James Ainslie to claim a grant soon after. Campbell's homestead, named Duntroon after a family castle in Scotland, is today part of the prestigious Royal Military College.

CANBERRA *The National Capital*

Blundells' Farm House, Parkes

VISITOR INFORMATION

CANBERRA VISITORS CENTRE
330 Northbourne Ave
Dickson ACT 2602
(02) 6205 0044
www.canberratourism.com.au

NATIONAL TRUST OF AUSTRALIA (ACT)
2 Light St, Griffith ACT 2603
(02) 6239 5222
www.nationaltrust.org.au

When the Commonwealth of Australia was formed in 1901, it was agreed that the seat of government was to be on neutral ground due to intense Sydney–Melbourne rivalry. In 1908 the southern tablelands of New South Wales were chosen as the site. Chicago architect Walter Burley Griffin won an international design competition with his innovative city plan.

Burley Griffin was a young American and an associate of renowned architect Frank Lloyd Wright. His plan showed a city laid out in a series of circles and rectangles, echoing the natural amphitheatre formed by Mount Ainslie, Black Mountain and Pleasant Hill.

Although Griffin won the prize, his plan had its detractors. Many thought his vision was too extravagant and it looked likely it would be compromised. But eventually, in 1913, Griffin was appointed Federal Capital Director of Design and work proceeded. Before long World War I had started to drain the country's resources, and Griffin was forced to continue with a limited budget.

One of the criticisms of Griffin's plan was its generous scale, wide streets and boulevards. One wit described it 'as a good sheep paddock spoiled'. Yet the scale of the city has allowed Canberra to grow as a modern metropolis.

It was not until 1923 that work started on the 'provisional' Parliament House – the very reason that the city was to exist. Until 1927, the parliament convened in Melbourne, before taking up residence in the building now known as 'Old Parliament House'.

When parliament was held in the new premises for the first time in 1972, Canberra had a population of just 7000. Although public servants moved to the administrative capital – many of them reluctantly – the population grew slowly. The Depression of the late 1920s and early '30s and then World War II hindered progress. It was not until the 1950s that the city's development finally gained momentum.

Today Canberra is streamlined and modern, a tribute to Walter Burley Griffin's vision. It has become something of a showcase for architecturally imposing buildings, from the widely acclaimed new Parliament House, which finally opened in 1988, to the dramatic new National Museum overlooking Lake Burley Griffin. But the past has its place too, and historic buildings are carefully preserved, from modest cottages and well-to-do estates of the 1800s to the elegant Art Deco style of the 1920s and '30s when modern Canberra had its beginnings.

Although the name Canberra is said to be from an Aboriginal word meaning 'meeting place', it is only in more recent decades that the long Aboriginal history related to the area has been more fully acknowledged. The Ngunnawal people are the traditional owners and their rock-art sites in Namadji National Park are a tangible reminder of another aspect of Canberra's history.

TIMELINE

1824 JJ Moore takes up the first land grant, and names his station 'Canberry'.

1901 Commonwealth of Australia is formed. Interstate rivalries mean a neutral seat of government must be found.

1908 Tablelands of southern New South Wales chosen as the capital site.

1911 American architect Walter Burley Griffin wins an international competition to design the capital.

1913 Parliamentarians travel to Canberra for the official opening ceremony. The Governor-General's wife, Lady Denman, formally names the city Canberra.

1927 Australian parliament convenes in Canberra for the first time. Dame Nellie Melba sings the national anthem and the Duke of York officially opens the 'provisional' Parliament House.

1988 Opening of the new Parliament House coincides with the Bicentennial celebrations.

Senate Chamber, Old Parliament House, Parkes

INNER CANBERRA

1 Australian War Memorial
See A Walk Around the Australian War Memorial, p. 64

2 Blundells' Farm House
Robert Campbell of Duntroon had this small, rubble-stone cottage built for his head ploughman, William Ginn, c. 1858. Flora and George Blundell – Campbell's bullock driver – later took up residence and lived here for nearly 60 years, raising their eight children and adding extra slab-timber rooms (1888). The Oldfield family then lived here for around 25 years. The cottage, overlooking Lake Burley Griffin, is authentically furnished as a memorial to the early settlers on the Limestone Plains.
Wendouree Dr. (entry off Constitution Ave), Parkes. Open Tues.–Sun. Tours available. $ *(02) 6273 2667.*

3 National Archives
'The memory of the nation' is housed in Canberra's first GPO (1927), an elegant Art Deco building. Records here dating back to Federation include government records, personal papers of prime ministers, military dossiers, lighthouse plans, theatrical scripts, historic photos, and much more. Many exhibits are displayed in the galleries. One of the most impressive is the Royal Commission of Assent, signed by Queen Victoria, giving Royal Assent to the Bill creating the Commonwealth of Australia. Amateur and professional historians can research in the Orientation Centre.
Queen Victoria Tce, Parkes. Open daily. $ *(02) 6212 3600.*

4 National Capital Exhibition
An extensive exhibition covering the history, design and development of the nation's capital through rare photos, maps, models for the original design competition, audio-visual displays, and a laser show.
Regatta Point. Open daily. Tours available. $ *(02) 6257 1068.*

5 National Gallery of Australia
The Gallery's collection includes important Aboriginal and Torres Strait Islander art, both traditional and more recent. The Gallery also has a world-class art research library which includes 19th-century art catalogues and periodicals and a unique collection of historic archives and ephemera.
Parkes Pl. East, Parkes. Open daily. (02) 6240 6502; reference desk (02) 6240 6530.

6 National Library of Australia
Established in 1941, the Library moved to the present building, with streamlined, five-storey columns faced with Italian Carrara marble, in 1968. It contains an immense collection, strongly emphasising Australian history and culture. There are more than 6 million books, an historical collection of 5000 films, rare books, maps, documents, photographs and paintings. Among the library's treasures are Capt. Cook's handwritten journal from his 1768–71 *Endeavour* voyage (a facsimile is on display). There are changing exhibitions, films and behind-the-scenes' tours.
Parkes Pl. West (near Commonwealth Ave Bridge), Parkes. Open daily & Mon.–Thurs. evenings. (02) 6262 1111.

7 National Museum of Australia
In a spectacular modern building on the edge of Lake Burley Griffin, the new museum explores the history of Australia based on the main themes of Land, Nation and People. It surveys the many cultural identities of the people who have created the

Royal Commission of Assent, National Archives, Parkes

Convict uniform, National Museum, Acton Peninsula

nation, the heritage and spiritual life of Aboriginal and Torres Strait Islander people, and recounts moving stories 'from the emotional heartland of Australia'.
Acton Peninsula. Open daily. Tours available. $ (02) 6208 5000.

National Portrait Gallery
See Old Parliament House

8 Old Parliament House

A splendid 1920s two-storey white stucco brick building, home to Australia's federal parliament from 1927, when it was officially opened by the Duke of York (later King George V), until 1988. (From Federation in 1901 until 1927 the federal parliament convened in Melbourne.) Of particular note are Kings Hall, with its native timber parquetry floors, fine timber craftsmanship, historic chambers and the rose gardens. Excellent guided tours provide a fascinating glimpse of the political intrigues that took place here over 60 years. The sound and light show *Order! Order!* in the House of Representatives' chamber brings the chamber to life. The refurbished public spaces now house the **National Portrait Gallery**, with an historically and artistically significant collection. A recent major acquisition is the famous 19th-century portrait of Capt. James Cook (valued at $5 million) by John Webber. A fascinating glimpse of the faces of Australia. Highly recommended.
King George Tce, Parkes. Open daily. Tours available. $ (02) 6270 8222.

9 Parliament House

Opened in 1988, this vast, architecturally dramatic building, directly behind Old Parliament House and emerging from Capital Hill, is designed as an integral part of the site and surroundings. Australian materials and finishes predominate and many works of art have been commissioned specifically. One of the most important is the mosaic design by Papunya artist Michael Nelson Tjakamarra, which represents the gatherings of Aboriginal people for important ceremonies. The Senate and House of Representatives are furnished in traditional green and red, but the new shades used echo the natural tones of the Australian landscape. Guided tours every 30 minutes.
Capital Circle, Capital Hill. Open daily. (02) 6277 5399.

Portrait of Capt. James Cook by John Webber

10 St John the Baptist Anglican Church

St John's has the peaceful air of an English village church, its pale stone tower and shingled spire rising amongst the pines, oak and elm trees. Robert Campbell of Duntroon initiated the building of the sandstone and granite church (1841). The original unstable tower, struck by lightning, was replaced in 1864 and the slender spire added in 1878. Above the altar, one of the earliest stained-glass windows in Australia is engraved with the Campbell family motto 'Work with all your might'. Many pioneers and figures linked with the nation's political history lie in the graveyard. The earliest recorded burial was in 1838.
Cnr Constitution Ave & Anzac Pde, Reid. Open daily. $ (02) 6248 8399.

11 St John's Schoolhouse Museum

The district's first schoolhouse (early 1840s), its only school for 35 years and one of Canberra's oldest buildings. A trim little bluestone building with shingled roof and tiny shuttered windows, it was repaired and enlarged after a fire in 1864, and continued in use until 1907. Displays re-create a colonial classroom.
Cnr Constitution Ave & Anzac Pde, Reid. Open Wed. & Sat.–Sun. $ (02) 6249 6839.

12 ScreenSound Australia

Film and sound treasures – from rare recordings and historic film footage, to costumes and props – make the National Film and Sound Archive a particularly engaging venue. There are interactive displays, film screenings and a specialist library. Regular tours and live presentations on the history of film and sound. The Archive is in an extremely elegant Art Deco building (1929–30), in pale Hawkesbury sandstone, which features finely executed, decorative Australiana motifs, such as frilled lizards on door surrounds and goannas on capitals.
McCoy Cirt, Acton. Open daily. (02) 6248 2000.

St John the Baptist Anglican Church, Reid

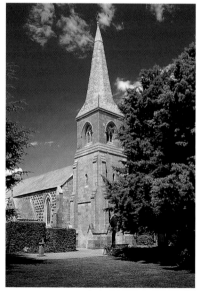

All Saints' Church, Ainslie

AROUND CANBERRA

1 All Saints' Church
Map ref. 300 H8

This remarkable church began life in 1868 as Number One Mortuary Station at Rookwood Cemetery in outer Sydney. Trains with coffins and mourners steamed into the unique sandstone station, designed with an elaborate Venetian Gothic ceiling adorned with angels and cherubs. The church-like station fell into disuse when cars gradually replaced trains. The imaginative Rev. EG Buckle, however, bought it for £100 in 1957. Every stone was numbered, the structure dismantled and moved in 83 semi-trailer loads to Canberra, re-erected, and then consecrated in 1959.
Cowper St, Ainslie. Open daily. $ (donation). (02) 6248 7420.

2 Calthorpes' House
Map ref. 300 G12, 301 E3

A 1920s Californian bungalow with a touch of Spanish Mission, this family house captures perfectly the era of Canberra's early years. HED Calthorpe was a senior public official and his family was prominent in Canberra's early days. The Calthorpes lived here for more than 70 years. The house has remained virtually unchanged since it was built and has a remarkable collection of domestic appliances and ephemera. Original furnishings include a pianola and there's even an air-raid shelter. The spacious garden is also typical of its era.
24 Mugga Way, Red Hill. Open Tues.–Thurs. & Sat.–Sun. Tours available weekdays. $ (02) 6295 1945.

3 Canberra Bicycle Museum
Map ref. 300 H7

Just a small selection, around 60, of the more than 700 cycles that the museum owns, are displayed in this quirky but fun museum. Cycles from all eras, from boneshakers and penny-farthings to military cycles, can be seen. As well, the collection encompasses cycling magazines, photos, posters and more.
Canberra Tradesman's Union Club, Badham St, Dickson. Open daily. (02) 6248 0999.

4 Cuppacumbalong
Map ref. 299 E7

Leopold de Salis, an hereditary Count of the Holy Roman Empire, bought this property on the banks of the Murrumbidgee River in 1855. The original dwelling was destroyed by fire before World War II, but several members of the family, including Leopold de Salis, are buried in a nearby graveyard surrounded by a small, white marble wall. The homestead (1923) is now a craft gallery and restaurant. Parts of the garden date back to 1886.
Naas Rd, via Tharwa. Open Wed.–Sun. & pub hols. $ Gallery (02) 6237 5116.

5 Lanyon
Map ref. 299 E7

A fine country homestead set in rich grasslands above the tree-fringed banks of the Murrumbidgee River. The station was named after John Lanyon, one of the original owners, who took up the land with James Wright in 1835. Scotsman Andrew Cunningham bought Lanyon about 1849 and built the main homestead (1859–60) of stucco stone rubble,

Calthorpes' House, Red Hill

Lanyon homestead, Tharwa

with delicately paned french doors opening onto the generous verandah. The fine joinery includes full-length shutters cut from solid cedar panels. Mrs Cunningham maintained the refinements of English country living, and 'for more than half a century, this home had a reputation for everything that was beautiful'. Elegant furnishings and liveried groomsmen were part of Lanyon's lifestyle. Outbuildings clustered around the courtyard include a stout-walled stone building with tiny windows and a quaint belltower (pre-1841), the old kitchen with its head-skimming verandah, a stone stable with a honeycombed floor of sawn logs, and a rustic dairy built of log slabs joined entirely without nails. The main house was extended in 1905 in the fashionable Edwardian style. Rooms have been elegantly restored and furnished. There's a cafe and guided tours are available. Near the entrance is the (Sidney) Nolan Gallery.

Tharwa Dr., via Tharwa. Open Tues.–Sun. & most pub hols. Tours available. Ⓢ *(02) 6237 5136.*

6 Mugga Mugga
Map ref. 301 G5

Surrounded by a small pocket of grazing land, just south of Canberra, on land taken up in the 1830s, a shepherds' cottage is one of Canberra's earliest historic sites. Mugga Mugga is a reminder of the rural workers who farmed the district long before a national capital was considered. The rubble-walled cottage (c. 1870s), built by professional stonemasons from the Duntroon estate, still has the original timber roofing shingles beneath the corrugated iron. A slab kitchen dates from c. 1850s. Some of the furniture and memorabilia belongs to the Curley family, which has been associated with Mugga Mugga since the 1860s. The house has been carefully preserved and is furnished in modest style.

Narrabundah La. (off Mugga La.), Symonston. Open 1st Sun. afternoon of each month. Ⓢ *(02) 6239 5607.*

7 Royal Australian Mint
Map ref. 300 F12, 301 D2

When the mint opened in 1965, it was the first mint in Australia not to be a branch of the Royal Mint in London. Exhibitions document the history of Australia's currency and include Gov. Macquarie's 'holey dollar' currency. When the colony ran short of coins in 1813, Macquarie had holes cut out of Spanish dollars, so that each coin became two coins. The 'outer' ring was the 'holey dollar' and the centre was the lesser-valued 'dump'. *Denison St, Deakin. Open daily. (02) 6202 6819.*

8 Royal Military College, Duntroon
Map ref. 300 I11, 301 H1

At the heart of Australia's most renowned military academy is Canberra's most historic homestead, Duntroon House. Robert Campbell, a well-established Sydney merchant, chose 'Limestone Plains' as part of a government grant, and named his new station Duntroon, after a family castle in Scotland. He built a single-storey, colonial-style, verandahed house in 1833, and his fourth son, George, added the romantic Gothic Revival two-storey wing c. 1862. The magnificent garden (including a traditional maze) dates from this era, and the outbuildings,

Mugga Mugga, Symonston

To Bywong

Belconnen

CANBERRA

Ainslie

Weston

Woden

Queanbeyan

To Bungendore

Wannaissa

Hume

Tuggeranong

Tharwa

N

SCALE

0   5 km

such as the bluestone apple shed (1840s), the dairy (pre-1835) and the woolshed (c. 1840), are picturesque reminders of Duntroon's colonial beginnings. The Military College was established here in 1910. Today the main homestead is the officers' mess; other buildings have been added over the years. In the grounds of the college stands Changi Chapel. This rudimentary structure was the place of worship for those interned at Changi prisoner-of-war camp in Singapore during World War II. The building was reassembled and dedicated to all Australian prisoners of war. It is open daily.
Morshead Dr. or Fairbairn Ave, Duntroon. Grounds open daily. Duntroon House open once a year, in Oct. $ (02) 6265 9241.

9 Tuggeranong Homestead
Map ref. 301 E10

This homestead dates back to the 1830s and has a rich social and cultural history. The original land grant was made in 1827, and by the 1840s this was one of the largest farms in the district. By the 1890s 50 000 sheep were being shorn on the property each year. From 1919 until 1925, Dr Charles Bean (*see A Walk Around the Australian War Memorial, p. 64*) and his team were based at Tuggeranong whilst they wrote the official history of World War I. Today, the homestead is set on 31 ha. The main house has been restored and its 10 rooms are filled with period furniture. Outbuildings include a century-old schoolhouse, maid's quarters, two woolsheds and a stone barn, built some time before 1840 by convict labour. The homestead is used for cultural events, conferences and other functions and there is a cafe.
Johnson Dr., Richardson. Open Sat.–Sun. (02) 6292 8888.

10 Yarralumla Government House
Map ref. 300 E10, 301 C1

In 1881 Frederick Campbell, grandson of Robert Campbell of Duntroon, bought Yarralumla, established in 1828, and built a palatial three-storey mansion (1891). The Commonwealth acquired the property in 1913, and the Duke and Duchess of York stayed at Yarralumla when they officially opened the first parliament in Canberra in 1927. Since then it has been the residence of Australia's Governor-Generals. There are fine views of the house and gardens from the lookout on Lady Denman Dr.
Dunrossil Dr., Yarralumla. House open for guided tours at least twice a year. $ (02) 6283 3533. Tours of the garden every Thurs., visitors meet at Southern Cross Yacht Club, Alexandrina Dr., Lotus Bay, Yarralumla. Ticket includes a 30-min cruise to Government House. $ (02) 6273 1784.

In the area
The historic village of Bungendore was settled in the 1830s and retains some authentic buildings around the village green. *35 km E on Kings Hwy.* Bywong Gold Mining Town, set in natural bushland, is a re-created 1890s gold mining camp capturing the harsh existence and pioneering spirit of early settlers. Gold was mined here briefly in the late 1800s and some authentic shafts and workings remain. There are demonstrations of blacksmithing and wheelwrighting, and the chance to pan for gold. *28 km NE, 35 Bywong Town Rd, Bywong. Open daily. $ (02) 6236 9183.*

Duntroon House, Royal Military College

A Walk Around the Australian War Memoria

The colossal, pale stone Byzantine-style Memorial stands solemnly at the foot of Mount Ainslie, its entrance flanked by medieval stone lions from Belgium. The stark building is symbolic, but it is more than that, for its vast national collection conjures the heroism and the tragedy of Australia's involvement in world wars, conflict and peacekeeping in many parts of the world. The Memorial closes daily to the haunting sounds of the Last Post.

Visitor Information Centre
Anzac Pde, Campbell. Open daily except Christmas Day
(02) 6243 4211
Website: www.awm.gov.au

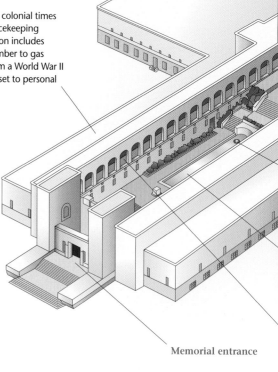

World War I Gallery
The defeat at Gallipoli was a defining moment in Australia's history. From the bloodshed and sacrifice emerged the legend of the ANZAC – the Australian (and New Zealand) troops' bravery captured the heart of the nation. Many of the War Memorial's most poignant images and stories are in this gallery.

The Galleries
The galleries cover all eras, from colonial times and both world wars to the peacekeeping forces in East Timor. The collection includes everything from a Lancaster bomber to gas masks worn in the Gulf War, from a World War II prisoner-of-war miniature radio set to personal letters and diaries.

History
CEW Bean, Australia's official World War I historian, conceived the idea of a national war collection and the Memorial is the splendid realisation of that concept. It was built between 1934 and 1941, but has been substantially extended since then. The copper-covered dome is over the Hall of Memory.

CEW Bean by George Lambert, 1924

Charles Bean
CEW Bean was Official War Correspondent to the AIF (Australian Imperial Forces) during World War I, and reported from the front-line at Anzac Cove and the Western Front. He was appointed War Historian in 1919.

Memorial entrance

Hall of Memory

Three huge stained-glass windows and a mosaic containing more than 6 million tiny glass fragments, designed and built by Napier Waller, dominate the Hall of Memory. Napier Waller was himself a war veteran, who lost his right arm in 1917 during World War I. After returning to Australia, he learnt to paint with his left hand and mastered mosaics and mural painting.

Stained glass

The 15 stained-glass panels in the Hall of Memory celebrate the 'resource', 'candour', 'devotion', 'curiosity' and 'independence' of Australians at war. They depict service men and women from World War I.

Sculpture Garden

Peter Corlett's sculpture *Simpson and his Donkey, 1915* is a tribute to the camaraderie of Australia's servicemen and women.

ANZAC Hall

An extensive new gallery to display such icons of the collection as the Japanese midget submarine recovered from Sydney Harbour in 1942, a rare World War I Mark IV tank, and the Avro Lancaster bomber 'G for George'.

Tomb of the Unknown Soldier

The tomb symbolises all Australians who have died serving their country at war.

Victoria Cross (VC)

The highest award for acts of bravery in wartime, instituted by Queen Victoria and first awarded for the Crimean War (1854). The medals are cast from a cannon captured during the Crimean War. The War Memorial displays 57 VCs along with other medals in the Hall of Valour.

World War II Gallery

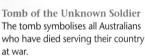

Eternal Flame

The Pool of Reflection

A place for quiet reflection, containing the Eternal Flame and bordered by rosemary plants to symbolise remembrance.

of Honour

Pool of Reflection in the central court is flanked by
ters containing the bronze Roll of Honour – more
102 000 dead, listed without rank or
nction – the human toll of war.

Commemorative area

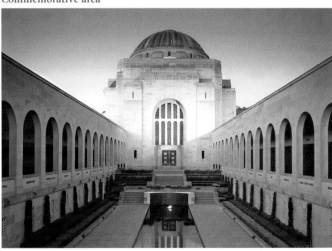

VICTORIA *A Golden Beginning*

Victoria retains many signs of nineteenth-century prosperity. Gold was the fuel that fired the colony's early days and ensured a solid economy for future generations. The boom time of the 1850s and the following decades established the colony as a rival to New South Wales. The legacy of those early years is the state's rich heritage of grand, often extravagant, architecture.

The wharf at Echuca

Victoria was born as squatters searched for new pastoral lands, a spontaneous movement by settlers from Van Diemen's Land (now Tasmania) and New South Wales. In 1834, Edward Henty, impressed by reports of whalers and sealers, sailed across Bass Strait and established himself at Portland Bay.

Major Sir Thomas Mitchell's enthusiastic reports on the rich Western districts, 'Australia Felix', encouraged a rush of squatters after his 1836 exploration. Meanwhile, in 1835, rivals John Batman and John Pascoe Fawkner and their parties had already staked claims around the Port Phillip district. Batman had requested a land grant to

HISTORIC HIGHLIGHTS

For a look around some of Victoria's most interesting historic towns, see the following entries.

Ballarat Miners' cottages, grand hotels and impressive public buildings. The gold diggers' rebellion at the Eureka Stockade took place here in 1854. *See p. 102*

Beechworth One of Victoria's best-preserved small gold towns, nestled in the Ovens Valley. *See p. 104*

Bendigo One of the State's most important regional cities, noted for its grand Victorian-era buildings and picturesque gardens. *See p. 106*

Echuca Australia's greatest inland port in the nineteenth century. There are magnificent old red-gum wharves, vintage paddle-wheelers and some wonderful buildings. *See p. 108*

Geelong The State's largest regional city, and a major port with handsome public buildings. The gold and wool shipped from here last century brought significant wealth. *See p. 110*

Maldon A fascinating glimpse into the 1800s. Maldon retains many gold-era buildings, from tiny cottages to shops and pubs, spread along the original winding streets. *See p. 112*

Portland Farming, whaling and shipping of gold kept the town busy in the 1840s–50s. Today, Portland is a substantial city, with many buildings surviving from those early days. *See p. 114*

Queenscliff A small seaside town, a popular holiday resort in the 19th century, now known for its cottages and impressive Victorian and Edwardian hotels. *See p. 116*

pasture stock in Port Phillip in 1827. He was refused permission so took matters into his own hands and 'bought' 240 000 hectares of land from the Aboriginal people – the floodgates were open.

In 1836 the New South Wales Government relented and Captain William Lonsdale was posted to the new settlement as Administrator. Melbourne was surveyed, and in 1839 Charles La Trobe arrived as Superintendent. Within a short time, the settlers began to lobby for independence. It seems Sydney–Melbourne rivalry has a long tradition. A week of celebrations followed the proclamation of Victoria as a separate colony in July 1851.

THE GOLDEN YEARS

Scarcely a month later, the cry of 'gold' rang out, and Victoria was thrown into a turbulent but golden era. As more goldfields were discovered – at Buninyong, Ballarat, Bendigo and beyond – men downed tools and abandoned the city. Businesses closed, cottages were deserted and even schools were silent. The following year, 300 ships filled Port Phillip, unloading 'new chums' , eager to share in the new-found wealth.

Sovereign Hill, Ballarat

Newcomers and locals alike tried their luck in the bush, though many quickly abandoned the goldfields – hot and dry, or muddy and cold – and headed back to Melbourne. The colony's population jumped from around 70 000 in 1851 to nearly 200 000 in 1853.

Towns sprang up to service the diggers and their needs. At first these were no more than tents and bark huts, but as money flowed in, buildings became more substantial.

The gold boom became a building boom and at the heart of the colony was the capital, Melbourne, demonstrating its wealth in bricks and mortar. In just a few decades Victoria had grown from an outpost of New South Wales to a well-established and prosperous colony.

BOOM AND BUST

The good times lasted until the 1890s, when the economic boom, culminating in the 'Marvellous Melbourne' of the 1880s, crashed disastrously. When Victoria emerged from its economic gloom, it had been eclipsed by New South Wales in population and prosperity. Today, Victoria retains a fine heritage of Victorian architecture to recall those golden years.

Royal Exhibition Building, Melbourne

Como House, South Yarra

MELBOURNE *The Garden City*

VISITOR INFORMATION

MELBOURNE TOURISM
INFORMATION CENTRE
Cnr Swanston & Little Collins sts
Melbourne VIC 3000
(03) 9658 9955
www.visitvictoria.com

NATIONAL TRUST OF AUSTRALIA (VICTORIA)
4 Parliament Pl.
East Melbourne VIC 3002
(03) 9654 4711
www.nattrust.com.au

Melbourne's skyline is modern, but its heart is unmistakably Victorian. Monumental classical buildings grace the city streets. Leafy boulevards as well as fast-moving freeways wind along the riverbanks. Clustered, lavishly decorated terraces and a scattering of palatial mansions recall the extravagance of the 1880s boom era.

In 1836, when the town was no more than four or five wattle-and-daub huts, a few turf huts and some tents, officialdom stepped in. Surveyor RJ Hoddle was sent to lay out Melbourne's orderly grid street plan and was followed in 1839 by Charles Joseph La Trobe, the first Superintendent of the Port Phillip district, who was entrusted with the task of imposing some order on the settlement. When La Trobe arrived, he was greeted by a pioneering community of 6000, many of whom were camping under canvas, or living in primitive conditions without even basic amenities.

The streets were rutted, almost impassable in the dry season, no more than bog holes in the wet. Laundry flapped from the trees, pigs roamed the streets, and crossing Collins Street required a pair of 'long mud-boots'.

The discovery of gold in 1851 completely transformed the colony and its capital in a way that few could have envisaged. Within weeks there was a mass exodus; the streets were virtually emptied as hopefuls headed for the diggings. But Melbourne soon began to reap the benefits of gold, as the population soared from 20 000 to 80 000 within a few years, and capital flowed in.

The 1850s saw the beginning of Melbourne's solid Victorian architecture. In 1853 alone, 1000 buildings were erected in central Melbourne. Parliament House, the Treasury, the Public Library and Melbourne's first university were begun in that decade. More temporary, and squalid, was the vast 'tent town' on the banks of the Yarra. By the 1870s, however, Melbourne was 'justly entitled to be considered the metropolis of the Southern Hemisphere', according to English novelist REN Twopeny.

The 1880s saw another boom. Optimism and confidence abounded, public and private expenditure seemed almost unbridled, and land speculation increased. But the boom was about to bust. Perennial drought struck, wool prices fell and, largely as a result of a financial crash in Argentina, British investment dwindled to almost nothing. With an almighty crash that reverberated through all classes, many banks were forced to close in 1893. People from all walks of life were affected and there were families who lost all they possessed. When the economy recovered, the town was not the same. There was a new conservatism and restraint. Some would say these qualities still pervade Melbourne life.

FIVE TOP MUSEUMS

Immigration Museum p. 74
Melbourne Museum p. 75
Old Melbourne Gaol p. 75
Old Treasury Museum p. 76
Polly Woodside & Maritime Museum p. 76

1890s dome at 333 Collins Street

Cook's Cottage, Fitzroy Gardens, East Melbourne

INNER MELBOURNE

1 Aboriginal Heritage Walk
Melbourne's **Royal Botanic Gardens** occupy the ancestral lands of the Bunurong and Woiwurrung people. Aboriginal guides take tours through the gardens, exploring some of the customs and the heritage of the traditional owners, and explaining traditional uses of plants for food, medicine, tools and ceremony.
Observatory Gate, Birdwood Ave, City. Tours Thurs., Fri., booking essential. (S) *(03) 9252 2300.*

2 Collins Street
See p. 82

3 Cook's Cottage
Quaint stone and brick cottage (c. 1755) built by Captain James Cook's father in Yorkshire. Shipped to Australia at the time of the Victorian centenary in 1934, to commemorate Captain Cook, who sailed from England in the *Endeavour* in 1768 in search of the 'great southern continent'. The cottage is now clad in ivy creeper and surrounded by the lush greenery of the **Fitzroy Gardens**.

Inside the diminutive house, with its narrow creaking staircase, are 18th- and 19th-century furnishings and a small display illustrating Cook's voyages.
Fitzroy Gardens, Wellington Pde, between Clarendon & Lansdowne sts, East Melbourne. Open daily. (S) *(03) 9419 4677.*

4 Fire Services Museum
An East Melbourne landmark, the elegant Eastern Hill Fire Station (1892–93) features a red-brick Italianate tower designed for fire-spotting, and stuccoed panels depicting firemen's helmets. The museum collection includes some meticulously restored fire trucks, including a fire engine converted from a car once owned by diva Dame Nellie Melba.
39 Gisborne St, East Melbourne. Open Fri., Sun. Tours, booking essential. (S) *(03) 9662 2907.*

5 Fitzroy Gardens
Land for Victoria's oldest public gardens was reserved in 1848 and designed by LaTrobe Bateman. He had the paths laid in the pattern of the Union Jack with winding avenues. By the 1870s there were numerous statues, a Neo-Classical band pavilion (1862) and the 'Temple of the Winds' Rotunda. Sinclair's Cottage (1864) the delightful brick building on the main path was built for James Sinclair, first curator of the Fitzroy Gardens. The Conservatory was opened in 1930. **Cook's Cottage** is located here.
Bounded by Lansdowne, Albert & Clarendon sts & Wellington Pde, East Melbourne.

6 Flagstaff Gardens
So called because a flagstaff was erected on this site to signal with flags the arrival of eagerly awaited ships from 'home'. The announcement that Victoria would become a separate colony was made here in 1851. A huge bonfire was lit to signal the separation, six rockets were fired and a general holiday declared.
Bounded by King, La Trobe, William & Dudley sts, West Melbourne.

7 Government House
One of the grandest houses in the country, Government House (1871) has been home to Victoria's governors-general since 1873. The tall white tower is a distinctive Melbourne landmark, rising above the greenery of its own grounds and those of the adjacent **Royal Botanic Gardens**. The palatial mansion, built in the Italianate style, contains the

Fire Services Museum, East Melbourne

Parkville

University of Melbourne

35

Carlton

Fitzroy

North Melbourne

Carlton Gardens

Melbourne Museum **12**

Royal Exhibition Building **27**

Carlton Gardens

West Melbourne

Queen Victoria Market **23**

Melbourne City Baths **10**

Old Melbourne Gaol **16**

National Gallery of Victoria on Russell

Fire Services Museum **4**

St James' Old Cathedral **28**

Flagstaff Gardens **6**

Melbourne Central Stn

State Library **33**

15

Museum of Chinese Australian History **14**

Parliament House

St Patrick's Cathedral **30**

Tasma Terrace **34**

Fitzroy Gardens **5**

East Melbourne

Princess Theatre **22** **19**
Parl't Stn

Windsor Hotel **37**

Stamford Fountain

Old Treasury Museum **18**

Treasury Gardens

Cook's Cottage **3**

MELBOURNE

GPO

Royal Arcade **25**

Melbourne Town Hall **13**

Burke & Wills Monument

St Michael's Uniting Church

Scots Church **29**

Regent Theatre **24**

Collins Street **2**

Spencer Street Station

Immigration Museum **8**

St Paul's Cathedral **31**

Federation Square

Flinders Street Railway Station

Birrarung Marr

Jolimont
Jolimont Stn

Yarra Park

Australian Gallery of Sport & Olympic Museum, MCC Cricket Museum

Melbourne Cricket Ground **11**

RIVER

YARRA

Batman Park

Alexandra Gardens

Queen Victoria Gardens

Victorian Arts Centre

Southbank

0   200 m
SCALE

N

Polly Woodside & Melbourne Maritime Museum **20**

Kings Domain

Domain

Victoria Barracks **36**

Gate

Government House **7**

Old Observatory **17**
Aboriginal Heritage Walk **1**

26

Royal Botanic Gardens

32

Shrine of Remembrance

La Trobe's Cottage **9**

South Melbourne

Portable Iron Houses **21**

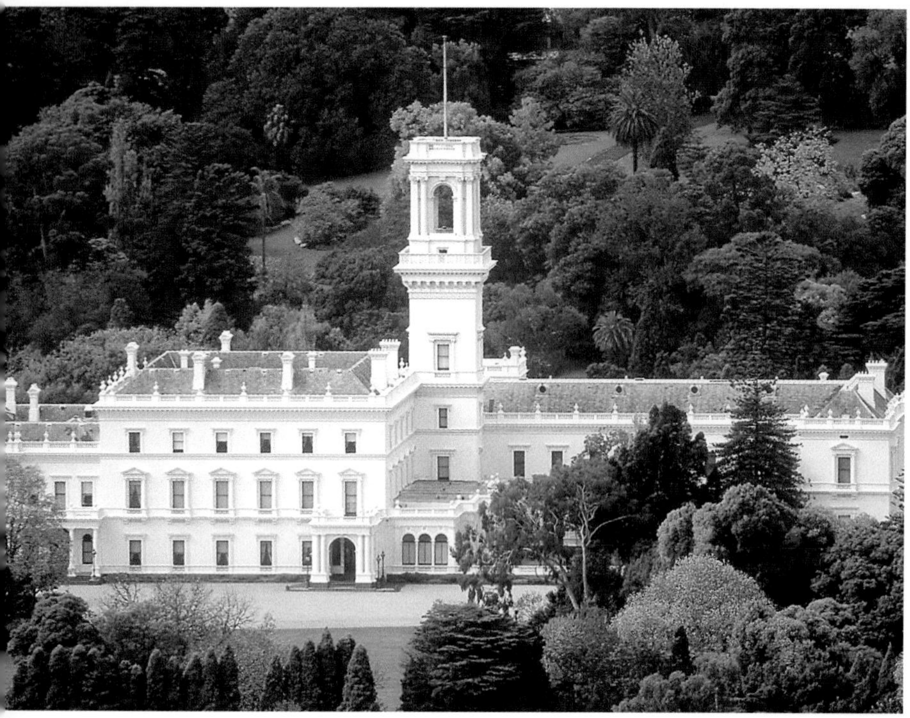

Government House

State apartments and offices, and the Vice-Regal residence. The State Ballroom, with its magnificent chandeliers, is larger than the ballroom at Buckingham Palace. An outstanding collection of locally made 18th- and early 19th-century furniture is displayed and used throughout the house. The National Trust organises combined tours of **La Trobe's Cottage** and Government House. Tours leave from La Trobe's Cottage; places limited.
Government House Dr., City. Guided tours only, Mon., Wed., Sat., booking essential. $ *(03) 9654 4711.*

[8] Immigration Museum

The Old Customs House (1873–76), an imposing, three-storey Classical building, designed by JJ Clark, is close to where Melbourne's first European settlers camped in 1835. The first Customs House was a tent pitched on the Yarra banks, followed by a 'shabby, leaky, comfortless weatherboard cabin'. The present building is one of the last links with the city's rich maritime history. Recently restored, it has been transformed into an outstanding museum imaginatively documenting the history of the state's immigration and celebrating the cultural diversity of the immigrants who have shaped Australia.
400 Flinders St, City. Open daily. $ *(for upstairs galleries only). (03) 9927 2700.*

[9] La Trobe's Cottage – First Government House

In 1839, Charles Joseph La Trobe erected this small, prefabricated timber cottage on several hectares east of the city, naming his new home Jolimont. La Trobe was Superintendent of Port Phillip and later Victoria's first Lt-Governor (1851–54). His house, 'merely a small wooden cottage but elegantly furnished and standing in spacious grounds' was the State's first Government House. It was moved to its present site and has been restored and furnished with many of La Trobe's original possessions.
Cnr Dallas Brooks Dr. & Birdwood Ave, City. Open Mon., Wed., Sat., Sun. Tours available. $ *(03) 9654 5528.*

[10] Melbourne City Baths

This exuberant red-brick and cream stucco building was opened in 1904 on a site occupied by the City Baths since 1858. The original 1850s building offered basic washing facilities for early residents, most of whom had no running water. This pavilion-style structure, reminiscent of the British Raj style of architecture, was modelled on 19th-century English public baths. The facade has been restored and the interior renovated as a swimming pool and health centre.
Cnr Swanston & Victoria sts, City. Open daily. (03) 9663 5888.

[11] Melbourne Cricket Ground

This was the site of the first international cricket match between England and Victoria (1862), the first Australia–England Test cricket match (1877) and the main venue for the 1956 Olympic Games. The Australian Gallery of Sport and Olympic Museum, and the MCC Cricket Museum are also located here.
Cnr Jolimont St & Jolimont Tce, Jolimont. Open daily. Entrance fee includes 1-hour guided tour of the ground and cricket museum, entry to the Australian Gallery of Sport and Olympic Museum. $ *(03) 9657 8879.*

Melbourne Town Hall

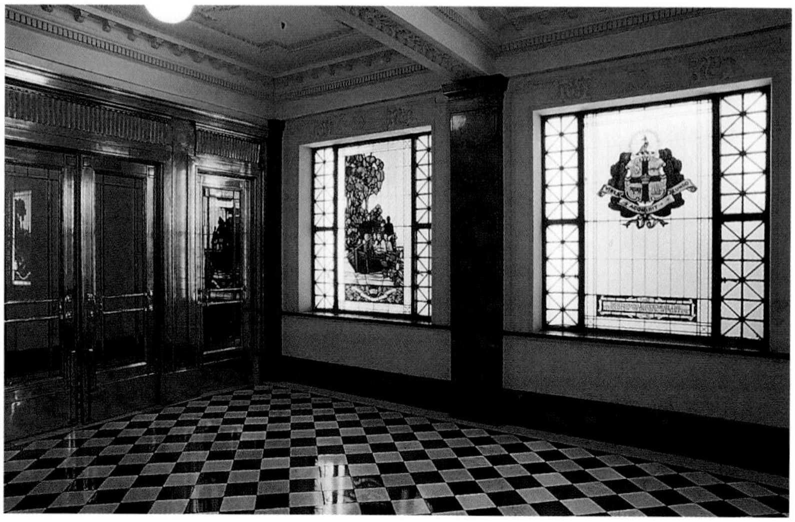

12 Melbourne Museum

At the heart of Melbourne's dynamic new museum, opened in 2000, is Bunjilaka, the Aboriginal Centre, documenting the history of one of the oldest living cultures in the world. Bunjilaka, created in consultation with Indigenous people, provides an insight into the culture of Australia's Aboriginal people, especially the Kooris of south-eastern Australia. An exhibition gallery, 'Kalaya' the performance space, an elders' meeting room and a keeping place – where Aboriginal people can view in private, stored items of cultural significance – are all part of the Centre. The new Museum also has outstanding social and natural history collections. Racing icon Phar Lap remains a star attraction. The Children's Museum provides interactive exhibitions. The museum is next to the historic **Royal Exhibition Building**.

Carlton Gardens, between Rathdowne & Nicholson sts, Carlton. Ⓢ *(03) 8341 7777.*

13 Melbourne Town Hall

Melbourne's Town Hall (1870) was built to reflect Victoria's growing prosperity and grand vision of itself as 'Marvellous Melbourne'. Prince Albert, Duke of Edinburgh, laid the foundation stone in 1867. The tower was built in 1869 and the grand portico added in 1887. Fire destroyed much of the main hall in 1925 but the subsequent rebuilding and the restoration in recent years reveal impressive public rooms highlighted by distinctive Australian motifs. The building features murals by artist Napier Waller, stained-glass windows, chandeliers and ornate plaster ceilings. Dame Nellie Melba made her debut in the Town Hall in 1884.

Cnr Collins & Swanston sts, City. Tours Tues.–Thurs., & 3rd Sat. of each month, booking essential. Ⓢ *(03) 9658 9658. See also A Walk Around Collins Street, p. 82*

14 Museum of Chinese Australian History

Located in the heart of Chinatown, in a three-storey building dating back to 1895, the museum contains some intricately worked Chinese costumes, bound-feet slippers, Chinese cabinets and historic photos of Melbourne's Chinese community. The 'goldfields' display gives a Chinese perspective. Chinatown heritage walking tours can be arranged at the museum.

22 Cohen Place, City. Open daily. Ⓢ *(03) 9662 2888.*

15 National Gallery of Victoria on Russell

Whilst the National Gallery's premises on St Kilda Rd are extended, more than 700 works from the collection have been moved to the Gallery's original home, the old Museum building in Russell St. The National Gallery is the oldest public gallery in Australia, established in 1861. The buoyant economy of

Museum of Chinese Australian History

the gold era and the enormously generous Felton Bequest, a donation to the gallery in 1904, helped the establishment of a rich and diverse collection. The former museum building's magnificent 19th-century rooms, handsomely renovated, provide an excellent foil to both European and Australian masterpieces. The Gallery will be exhibiting at Russell St until 2003.

Cnr Russell & La Trobe sts, City. Open daily. (03) 9208 0222.

16 Old Melbourne Gaol

'Like a gaunt spectre', the Old Melbourne Gaol rose gradually on the Melbourne skyline from 1841 until 1862. Monumental, splendidly proportioned, designed to impress the viewer and defy escape, the formidable edifice was built of bluestone with sandstone dressings. Much has been demolished, but the three-tiered cell block that remains, with its tiny, dark cells, death masks and prison paraphernalia, is a chilling reminder of penal life and punishment in the 19th century. In all, 135 executions took place here, including the hanging of legendary bushranger Ned Kelly. Tours available, including somewhat spooky evening tours.

Russell St, between La Trobe & Victoria sts, City. Open daily. Ⓢ *(03) 9663 7228.*

17 Old Observatory

See Royal Botanic Gardens

Old Melbourne Gaol

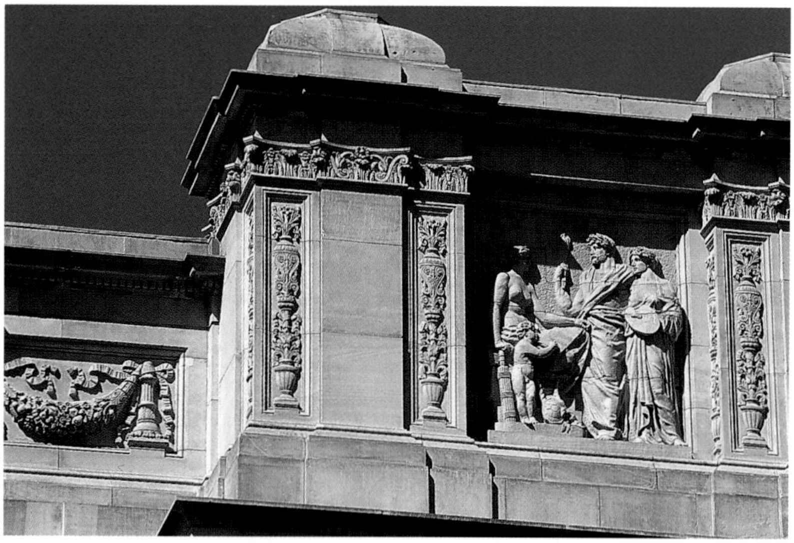

Parliament House

[18] Old Treasury Museum

At the top end of Collins St is the elegant Old Treasury. The handsomely proportioned building, in the Renaissance Revival style, features fine timber joinery in its grand rooms. The Treasury was built on the proceeds of the gold rush, and generous vaults, now part of the permanent exhibition, were included to house the gold. The Treasury also has some fascinating photos of Melbourne in the mid-1800s, as well as changing exhibitions.
Spring St (top of Collins St), City. Open daily. Tours available, booking essential. $ *(03) 9651 2233.*
See also A Walk Around Collins St, p. 82

[19] Parliament House

Magnificently sited in Spring St at the top end of Bourke St, Parliament House (1856–1930) is a superb example of 19th-century civil architecture. The original grandiose plans 'for a building of colossal proportions' included a dome, which has never been built. The classical facade has a huge Doric colonnade and sculpted allegorical figures representing Science, Art, Agriculture and Commerce. The interiors are lavishly decorated, from the tiled floor of the vestibule to the magnificent vaulted ceilings of the Legislative Chambers. This was the seat of the Commonwealth Government from Federation in 1901 until 1927 when the Parliament moved to Canberra.
Spring Street, City. Open Mon.–Fri. (when Parliament not sitting). Tours, booking recommended. (03) 9651 8568.

[20] *Polly Woodside* & Melbourne Maritime Museum

Declared the 'prettiest vessel ever launched in Belfast', the deep-water, barque-rigged *Polly Woodside* set sail in 1885. She was a work ship, highly seaworthy, without any frills, and performed admirably on the South American run – out with coal, home with nitrates, rounding the treacherous Horn 16 times. When acquired by the National Trust in 1968, the ship was a rusting, filthy coal hulk. Now restored, she stands proudly at the old Duke's and Orr's dry dock, one of the last original sailing ships afloat in the world, and the showpiece of the Melbourne Maritime Museum. Exhibits are on display in 1930s cargo sheds.
Lorimer St, Southbank. Open daily. Tours, booking essential. $ *(03) 9699 9760. NT.*

[21] Portable Iron Houses

In 1853 the *Illustrated London News* was writing of 'towns of iron houses to shelter the hordes of emigrants to the newly discovered lands of gold'. From the 1830s, prefabricated or 'portable' houses, first of timber and later of iron, were shipped to the far-flung colonies. By the 1850s demand was intense, and these houses, often no more than boxes – and hot boxes at that – began to replace the tent towns on the diggings. Their popularity was short-lived, however, and they were soon replaced by more conventional and congenial houses. These three examples – austerely simple, iron-framed, clad with corrugated iron – were each inhabited for over 120 years.
399 Coventry St, South Melbourne. Open first Sun. of month afternoons; closed Dec. 4–first Sun. in Feb. Tours available, booking essential. $ *(03) 9822 4369. NT.*

[22] Princess Theatre

The theatrical facade of the Princess Theatre (1886), influenced by the flamboyance of the French Baroque, matches the grandeur of the nearby **Windsor Hotel** and the impressive scale of **Parliament House.** Trumpeting angels and pavilions with lacy coronets festoon the roof. The theatre opened with a performance of *The Mikado*. The interiors, remodelled in 1922, included a sliding roof which could be rolled back on balmy evenings (no longer in use). There is said to be a resident ghost.
163 Spring St, City. Tours, booking essential. $ *(03) 9299 9850.*

[23] Queen Victoria Market

Extensive, busy and often boisterous covered market selling fresh food, flowers and other goods. It started life in three open-ended sheds on the corner of Elizabeth and Victoria sts in March 1878, although the land had been used as an animal and hay market from 1859. Part of the market is built on the site of the Old Cemetery (1837–86), where more than 100 000

The restored old sailing vessel, *Polly Woodside*, at Southbank

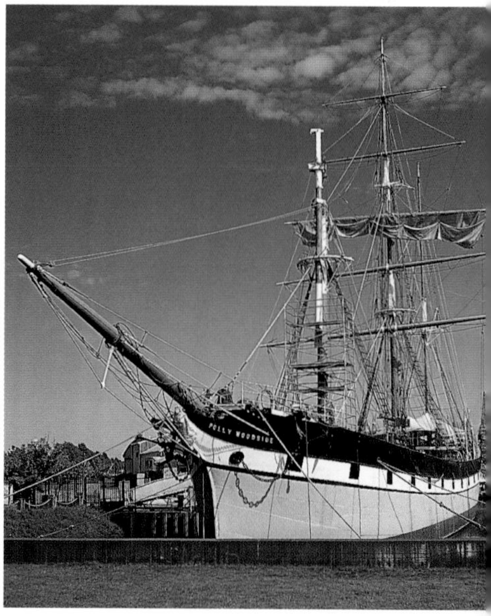

people were buried (the remains were removed before the market was opened). The Meat Market facade (1884) facing Elizabeth St features farm animal mouldings.

513 Elizabeth St, West Melbourne. Open Tues. & Thurs.–Sun. Heritage tours available. Ⓢ (for tours only). (03) 9320 5822.

24 Regent Theatre

The Regent Theatre and the Plaza Ballroom below, which opened in Collins St in 1929, epitomised the glamour of Hollywood. A riot of Spanish–Hollywood decor and lavish ornamentation – no surface was left unembellished – the 'Palace of Dreams' quickly found a place in Melburnians' hearts. The Regent was for live shows and musicals, whilst the Plaza, originally a ballroom, was soon converted to a cinema to provide a venue for the increasingly successful 'talkies'. After being closed for almost three decades, and narrowly escaping demolition, the Regent has been magnificently restored and is back in business.

191 Collins St, City. Tours when no performances, booking essential. Ⓢ (03) 9299 9850.

25 Royal Arcade

The bustling, ornate Victorian-era Royal Arcade, linking Bourke and Little Collins sts, officially opened in 1870 and is the oldest retail arcade in Australia. Its best-known feature, Gog and Magog, standing guard on either side of Gaunt's clock, was installed in 1892. The boldly carved and richly coloured figures, supposedly the last survivors of a rare race of giants, are based on an English model.

Between Bourke & Little Collins sts, City.

26 Royal Botanic Gardens

A magnificent landscaped garden covering 38 ha, incorporating ornamental lakes, sweeping lawns, exotic and native trees (around 12 000 plant species) and numerous pergolas, arbours and pavilions. The site was chosen by Charles La Trobe in 1846. Government Botanist Baron von Mueller was appointed director of the Gardens in 1857, although it was not until William Guilfoyle took over in 1873 that the garden began to take its present shape. Under his

Regent Theatre

direction (1875–77) more than 2300 trees (some 10 m tall) were transplanted. His vision and landscaping skills produced one of the world's finest botanic gardens. The Old Melbourne Observatory, and several other astronomical buildings, built in the Italianate style between 1861 and 1902, are at the garden's Birdwood Ave entrance. Tours, including evening tours of the Observatory and viewing of the night sky through the 1869 'Great Melbourne Telescope'.

Birdwood Ave, City. Open daily. Tours available, booking essential. Ⓢ (for tours only). (03) 9252 2300.
See also Aboriginal Heritage Walk

27 Royal Exhibition Building

This monumental structure, designed by Joseph Reed, was built by David Mitchell, Dame Nellie Melba's father. It was part of a complex of buildings for the 1880 International Exhibition, which was attended by a million people. The slate-covered dome, modelled on the cathedral in Florence, rises 60 m, and pavilion towers flank the entrances. The first Commonwealth Parliament opened here in 1901. The

building has been painstakingly restored and is now linked to the **Melbourne Museum**.

Nicholson St, Carlton. Open during major exhibitions. Ⓢ (03) 9270 5000.

28 St James' Old Cathedral

St James', the 'Pioneers' Church', is Melbourne's oldest building. The foundation stone was laid in 1839 and the first service held here in 1842, but the building was only completed in 1847. It was originally on the corner of William and Little Collins sts, but was moved (stone by stone) to its present site in 1914. One of the only colonial Georgian churches in Australia, it is built of bluestone and sandstone with a domed tower. Capt. William Lonsdale was influential in the decision to erect the church, and John Batman (one of Melbourne's co-founders) who donated £50, was one of the first subscribers. The 800-year-old marble baptismal font came from St Katherine's Abbey, London, and the English bell chimes were hung in 1853. The church is an outstanding pioneer relic.

Cnr Batman & King sts, West Melbourne. Open daily. Ⓢ (03) 9321 6133.

St Paul's Cathedral

29 St Michael's Uniting Church

Designed by architect Joseph Reed, who designed the **State Library**, **Royal Exhibition Building** and **Rippon Lea**, and built in 1867. The rich polychromatic brickwork, arcades and splendid eye-catching campanile all show Reed's affection for northern Italian architecture. The church contrasts markedly with the pale Early Gothic form of the Scots Church (1873), also designed by Reed, which stands on the opposite corner. Inside, it features a curved gallery and is gracefully proportioned, spacious and light filled. Melbourne's earliest permanent church was built on this site in 1839. *Cnr Collins & Russell sts, City. Open daily, except Sat. (03) 9654 5120.*
See also A Walk Around Collins Street p. 82

30 St Patrick's Cathedral

With its soaring spires and sombre bluestone, this is one of the finest Gothic Revival cathedrals in the world. A masterly example of architect William Wardell's talents, it is the largest cathedral in Australia. It was begun in 1858, the spires added in 1937–39. The bronze cross on the main spire was donated by the Republic of Ireland and the interior, flooded with golden light from the amber glass windows, has a massive open-timbered ceiling with carved angels. Free guided tours available. *Cathedral Pl., East Melbourne. Open daily. (03) 9662 2233.*

31 St Paul's Cathedral

A wonderful piece of Gothic Revival architecture, St Paul's Anglican Cathedral (1880–91) is an intrinsic part of Melbourne's skyline and streetscape, located on one of the city's busiest intersections. Eminent English architect William Butterfield carried out the original design, although Joseph Reed later worked on the project, and the spires, added in 1926–31, were designed by Sydney architect John Barr. The interior is awesome in scale, splendidly proportioned. The magnificent pulpit, carved on site from Tasmanian blackwood, took seven men five months to complete. St Paul's is built on the site where Melbourne's first official church service took place, in 1836. *Cnr Swanston & Flinders sts, City. Open daily.* Ⓢ *(03) 9650 3791.*

32 Shrine of Remembrance

This imposing stone monument, combining Egyptian and Greek motifs, and commenced in 1927, is a memorial to those Victorian soldiers who have died at war for their country. At exactly 11 a.m. on Armistice Day, 11 November, a shaft of sunlight illuminates the Stone of Remembrance in the inner sanctuary. An Eternal Flame burns in the front court. *St Kilda Rd, City. Open daily. (03) 9654 8415.*

33 State Library

Joseph Reed's prize-winning Neo-Classical design was the result of a competition held in 1854. Building began soon after, but the Corinthian portico, first-floor Reading Room and elegant Queens Hall were not completed until 1870. The vast dome (1911) that crowns the main reading room, designed by Sir John Monash, was impressive but impractical – amongst other problems, the skylights leaked – and the dome was eventually sheathed in copper. Recent restoration work includes reinstating the skylights, to create the spectacular La Trobe Reading Room, and introducing public gallery spaces around the dome. These galleries will exhibit works from the library's collection that highlight Victoria's history. The original library opened in 1856 with 3846 volumes; the collection now exceeds 1.5 million books as well as providing a multimedia centre. Building works are expected to be completed in 2003. *382 Swanston St, City. Open daily, plus Mon.–Thurs. evenings. Tours available. (03) 9669 9810.*

34 Tasma Terrace

An excellent example of well-to-do, late 19th-century terrace housing. Merchant George Nipper, the original owner of the **Windsor Hotel**, had three of the houses erected in 1878; Joseph Thompson added four more in 1886–87. Inside, fine proportions, rich wallpaper, warm colours and elegant drapery provide a fitting headquarters for the National Trust (Vic.). There is a small bookshop and the Tasma Cafe is open to the public. No tours available.

4 Parliament Pl., East Melbourne. (03) 9654 4711.

35 University of Melbourne

Construction of the cloistered, ivy-clad walls of the Gothic quadrangle at the heart of the university was begun in 1854, the year after the university was founded. Trinity College, the oldest residential college, was founded in 1872 in a fine Gothic building, notable for its beautiful windows. The distinctive, almost-medieval looking Newman College (1915–17) was designed by Walter Burley Griffin, who designed the city of Canberra. Tours of Newman are available, bookings essential.

Grattan St, Parkville. Open daily. 1800 801 662.

36 Victoria Barracks

A complex of sturdy, mainly bluestone buildings built 1856–72, which has been occupied by the military for over 140 years. The buildings include the three-storey Renaissance Revival A Block, where the official War Cabinet convened during World War II. There is an exhibition of memorabilia and photos from that era. A heritage display can be viewed in the original guard house and cells.

256–310 St Kilda Rd, Southbank. Guided tours only, Wed. & Sun. (03) 9282 5999.

37 Hotel Windsor

Spring Street's 'grand old lady' is the last of Australia's great 19th-century hotels. Built by merchant George Nipper, it opened officially as The Grand in 1883. Later in the 1880s, when James Munro took over, it was extended, equipped with electric bells, 'speaking tubes' and other essentials and became the Temperance Coffee Palace. After a chequered career, the hotel has been restored, both within and without, to her former glory. The sumptuous dining room, one of the most beautiful in the country, has rare domed lights glazed with stained glass, and 24-carat gold leaf emphasises the intricate mouldings. There are some fine paintings by classic Australian artists in the foyers. No guided tours available.

115 Spring St, City. (03) 9633 6000.

Victorian-era light fitting outside Parliament House

Also of interest

The domed Flinders St Railway Station complex (completed 1901–10), *cnr Flinders & Swanston sts*, was the winning design in a competition. Trains have been pulling into this site since 1854. The GPO (1867), *cnr Bourke & Elizabeth sts*, is built in the Renaissance style; the third storey and clock tower were added in the 1880s. There are plans to convert the building to a five-star hotel. The Burke and Wills Monument (1860) is now located in the City Square, *cnr Swanston & Collins sts*. It was the first large-scale bronze to be cast in Australia. Burke and Wills' failed expedition to find a route to northern Australia roused massive public sympathy. The fine bluestone Stanford Fountain (1870), next to the Old Treasury, was carved over four years, by a young sculptor, William Stanford, whilst he was serving a sentence in Pentridge Gaol. The Johnson Collection, housed in an historic East Melbourne terrace, originally built in 1853 as two houses, is an eclectic and intriguing collection of late Georgian and Regency furnishings and fine arts. *East Melbourne. Open by appt only Mon.–Fri.* Ⓢ *(03) 9416 2515. NT.*

Hotel Windsor entrance

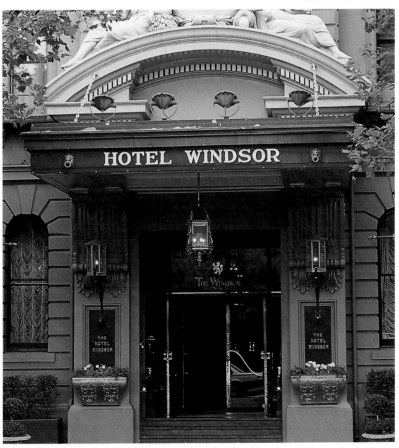

Puffing Billy, Belgrave

AROUND MELBOURNE

1 Como House
Map ref. 304 I11, 306 C4

Como's restrained elegance, an unusual blend of Australian Regency and Italianate design, complements its fine furnishings, many of which have been in the house for well over a century. EE Williams built the first permanent residence here in 1847. The young FG Dalgety owned the house briefly but found it 'devilishly dull stuck out there alone' and in 1854 sold it to John (later 'Como') Brown who extended the house and established a formal garden. Wealthy pastoralist Charles Armytage bought Como in 1864 and it remained in the Armytage family for 95 years. A grand, two-storey mansion, Como was renowned for its lavish entertainment – glittering chandeliers, gilt-edged mirrors and mellow polished woods recall those gracious days. The kitchen wing, c. 1840s, is the oldest section, and the outbuildings include coach-house and stables.
Cnr Williams Rd & Lechlade Ave, South Yarra. Open daily. Tours available. $ *(03) 9827 2500. NT.*

2 Enterprize
Map ref. 304 E13

A full-scale replica of the 27-m, square-rigged tops'l schooner *Enterprize*, which brought the first English settlers from Tasmania to Port Phillip in 1835. John Pascoe Fawkner purchased the ship to undertake the expedition, but was forced to remain in Tasmania by his creditors. The replica was built traditionally using Australian and New Zealand timber, much of it recycled, including 100-year-old ironbark wharf timbers. The sails are hand-sewn from flax cloth imported from Scotland and the rigging is woven from natural fibre hemp. The ship takes regular sailing trips on Port Phillip.
Gem Pier, Williamstown. Open Sat.–Sun. Tours available. $ *(03) 9397 3477.*

3 Labassa
Map ref. 304 I13, 306 C6

An elaborate mansion, inspired by the French Renaissance style, completed in 1890 for investor Alexander Robertson and befitting the extravagant mood of boom Melbourne at that period. A rare *trompe-l'oeil* ceiling looks down on the magnificent staircase. Labassa's sumptuous interiors, with fine wallpapers, superb stencilling, unusual polychromatic schemes and decorated columns and cornices, make it a masterpiece of the late Victorian era.
2 Manor Gve, Caulfield. Open last Sun of month; closed Dec. Tours available. $ *(03) 9527 6295. NT.*

4 Point Cook
Map ref. 308 G12

Birthplace of the RAAF, founded during World War I. At Point Cook is the RAAF Museum. The Heritage Gallery explores the evolution of aircraft including fragile biplanes and wartime workhorses, as well as the stories of the daring men who flew them. View the fleet of meticulously maintained aircraft, including planes undergoing major restoration.
10 km SE of Werribee. Open Tues.–Sun. & pub hols. $ *(donation). (03) 9256 1300.*

5 Puffing Billy
Map ref. 307 P8

Meticulously restored, narrow-gauge steam engine, which winds its way 24 km through heavily wooded hills and valleys and across a magnificent curved trestle bridge, to the terminus at Gembrook.
Departs from Belgrave daily (except days of total fire ban). $ *For timetable (03) 9754 6800.*

6 Rippon Lea
Map ref. 306 B6

At the end of a curving shaded driveway, at the heart of Australia's finest existing 19th-century urban garden, lies Rippon Lea, with its elegant porte-cochère, glass conservatory and loggia'd tower. The 33-room mansion was built (1860s–80s) for politician and business magnate Frederick Sargood. The rich, polychromatic brickwork highlights architect Joseph Reed's bold use of the Romanesque style. The front drawing room, restored to its opulent, late-Victorian splendour, re-creates the room as it was when photographed c. 1902. In contrast, the dining room, ballroom and swimming pool, added in the 1930s, splendidly conjure the Hollywood vogue of that era. In the grand English manner, the gardens (now reduced to 5.6 ha) feature vast lawns, extensive flower gardens, a lake with islands, bridges, pavilions and look-out tower. The massive fernery, with luxuriant undergrowth and soaring palms, is cool and inviting.

192 Hotham St, Elsternwick. Open daily. Tours available. Ⓢ *(03) 9523 6095. NT.*

7 Schwerkolt Cottage Museum
Map ref. 305 Q10, 307 J3

The three-roomed pioneer stone cottage, built by German settler August Schwerkolt in 1864, is furnished in period style. Outbuildings include a replica of the original smokehouse, a barn, cellar and a rustic stone building, which contains a local history museum.

Deep Creek Rd, Mitcham. Open Sat.–Sun., pub hol afternoons. Ⓢ *(03) 9262 6333.*

8 Spotswood Pumping Station (at Scienceworks)
Map ref. 304 E11

Melbourne's rapid growth in the 1800s meant that 'Marvellous Melbourne' soon became Smelly Melbourne. The lack of proper sewerage and the vile refuse spilling into the rivers were contributing to the rising death rate – not to mention the tremendous stench. A central system was planned, and work started in 1894 on the grand pumping station, built in the French Classical Revival style, with an elegant, mansard-towered roofline. With its massive steam pumping engines, it was a key component of Melbourne's sewerage system until the 1960s. The machinery can be seen in motion daily except Sat.

Scienceworks Museum, Douglas Pde, Spotswood. Tours daily. Ⓢ *(03) 9392 4800.*

9 Werribee Park Mansion
Map ref. 308 C12

Scotsmen Thomas and Andrew Chirnside built a pastoral empire in the district, which they crowned in 1875 with this 'palace in a paddock'. Victoria's finest colonial homestead epitomises the grand lifestyle of the 19th-century pastoral princes. The tower and balconies of the 60-room Italianate mansion afford panoramic views of the formal garden, planned by William Guilfoyle, and the pastoral country beyond. Inside, sweeping staircases and spacious

Rippon Lea, Elsternwick

rooms resplendent with fine paintings and European furniture (much of it commissioned), glittering gilt mirrors and crystal chandeliers, evoke an era and lifestyle gone forever. The servants' wing gives an insight into life 'downstairs'. The original cottage and small farm buildings recall humble beginnings. There are 10 ha of splendid formal gardens, regular exhibitions, tours of the garden, farm, mansion and tower.

K Rd, Werribee. Open daily. Ⓢ *13 1963 or (03) 9741 2444.*

10 Woodlands Historic Park
Map ref. 304 C1

These grassy slopes and woodland, with beautiful river red gums, a winding creek and panoramic views from Gellibrand Hill, have been used for grazing since the 1840s. The restored historic Woodlands Homestead is a rare surviving prefabricated timber structure brought to Australia from England by WP Greene in 1842. He and his family moved into the house in 1843. A barn, also used as a coach-house and shearing shed, was built in 1845 and the house has been extended several times.

Access to park via Somerton Rd, Oaklands Junction. Park open daily. Access to Woodlands Homestead via Oaklands Rd. Open (afternoons only) Wed., Sat.–Sun. & pub hols. Tours available. 13 1963.

A Walk Around Collins Street

Multi-rise buildings now dominate Collins Street, but the mellowed stonework and distinctive style of the older buildings, and the spreading trees – the first planted and paid for by the mayor in 1873 and celebrated with a champagne toast – ensure that it retains a gracious character.

History

Collins St has always had an air of wealth and prestige about it. As early as the 1840s, the first decade of settlement, the western end was attracting banks, gold dealers and shipping offices. In no time it had emerged as the financial heart of the city. Major banks and the Stock Exchange are still there today. The hilly 'Top End' of Collins St, still occasionally hailed as the 'Paris end', soon established itself as a fashionable residential address. Doctors, dentists and lawyers built substantial abodes, usually with gardens and several even with their own vineyards (the original 'Collins St farmers'). From 1862, the grand Treasury looked down from Spring St, and in 1858 the Melbourne Club opened its Collins St doors to the city's elite.

ANZ Bank
Perhaps the finest secular Gothic building in Australia. The magnificent banking chamber is covered with thousands of sheets of gold leaf and hand painted. There's a banking museum here. *380 Collins St. Museum open Mon.–Fri. (03) 9273 5555.*

333 Collins St
Contained within this contemporary building (1991) is an 1890s bank. The superlative banking chamber and vestibule with domed ceiling, magnificently restored, are the foyer of the new complex. *333 Collins St.*

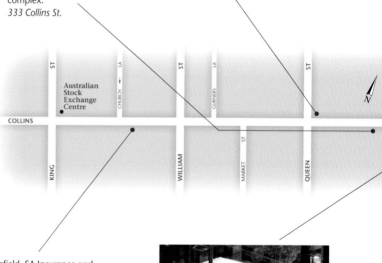

Rialto Buildings
The former Rialto, Winfield, SA Insurance and Olderfleet buildings and Record Chambers are a riot of towers, turrets, arches and attic windows. Built 1889–93, they represent a high point of Victoria's boom-period architecture. They have been retained as facades to a towering multi-rise complex. *475–503 Collins St.*

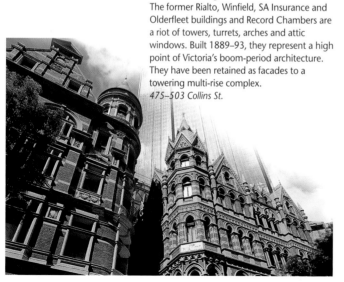

Block Arcade
Melbourne's finest and grandest shopping arcade (1891–93) with elegantly proportioned shop fronts, glass skylighting and a magnificent mosaic floor. The arcade has retained its 19th-century atmosphere, when 'doing the Block' was a fashionable pastime. *282 Collins St. Open daily. (03) 9654 5244.*

Melbourne Town Hall
Monumental and imposing edifice (1867), with a clock tower added in 1869 and a temple-like portico in 1887. Tours reveal an impressive interior.
Cnr Collins & Swanston sts.
Tours Tues.–Thurs. & 3rd Sat. of each month, booking essential.
(03) 9658 9658. See also p. 75

Manchester Unity Building
This art deco 'skyscraper' was the height of modernity when erected in 1931–32, inspired by the Chicago Tribune Tower. The decorative motifs on the ground floor are distinctive.
220 Collins St.

Melbourne Athenaeum
Built as a centre of arts, science and learning. The Athenaeum Library has been lending books since 1842. Mark Twain lectured here, Tom Roberts exhibited in the gallery, and in 1929 this was Australia's first theatre to present a 'talkie' (*The Jazz Singer* with Al Jolson).
188 Collins St. Library open Mon.–Fri., Sat. mornings.
(03) 9650 3100.

The Melbourne Club
Melbourne's oldest and most exclusive club, founded in 1838. The earliest part of the prestigious building, the club's third home, dates from 1858.
36 Collins St. Not open for inspection.
(03) 9650 4941.

Old Treasury Museum
Presiding over the top of Collins St, the elegant Treasury (1857–62) was designed by J J Clark, when he was aged just 19. Now a museum.
1 Spring St. Open daily. Ⓢ
(03) 9651 2233.
See also p. 76

[Map of Collins Street showing: Australia on Collins; SWANSTON ST; Regent Theatre; RUSSELL ST; Grand Hyatt Melbourne; GEORGE PDE; ALFRED PL; EXHIBITION ST; Collins Place; Hotel Sofitel; SPRING ST; MACARTHUR ST. Scale 0–100 m.]

Collins St Baptist Church
A temple-like church with a magnificent portico, built 1845–62 and extended in the 1860s to seat 1000 people.
174 Collins St. Open daily.
(03) 9650 1180.

Scots Church
A fine example of Gothic Revival architecture (1874), designed by Joseph Reed, and renowned for its beautiful stained glass. Dame Nellie Melba was a chorister here in her youth.
Cnr Collins & Russell sts.
Open Mon.–Wed. & Sun.
(03) 9650 9904.

St Michael's Uniting Church
Designed by Joseph Reed, and erected in 1867 on the site of Melbourne's earliest permanent church (1839).
Cnr Collins & Russell sts.
Open daily except Sat.
(03) 9654 5120.
See also p. 78

Grosvenor Chambers
Once the studio of painters Tom Roberts, Charles Conder and Sir Arthur Streeton, well-known members of the famous Heidelberg School.
19 Collins St. Not open for inspection.

Baptist Church (foreground), Scots Church (background), Collins St, 1880s

Bourke Street by Tom Roberts, c.1886

VICTORIA FROM A TO Z

Chateau Tahbilk, Tabilk

ARARAT

Map ref. 313 K2, 315 K13

In 1841 the first settler in this area, Horatio Wills, named the mountain from which he surveyed the surrounding pastoral country, Mt Ararat. The town itself dates from 1857, when a group of Chinese overlanding to the Victorian diggings discovered gold in the area. One of Australia's earliest and best-known wine regions, Great Western, is close by. The first vines in the district were planted by French settlers Jean-Pierre Trouette and Emile Blampied in 1863.

J-Ward (Old Ararat Gaol) Part of the former Ararat Gaol and institution for the criminally insane, J-Ward is a substantial two-storey bluestone building. Tours show a glimpse of what life was like behind the walls. There's also a museum. *Girdlestone St. Open daily. Tours available.* Ⓢ *(03) 5352 3621.*

ALSO OF INTEREST Ararat Gallery is located in the imposing red-brick and stucco town hall building (1898), which has paired columns, slate-tiled mansard roof and an ornate central clock tower. *Vincent St. Open Mon.–Fri. and pub hols.* Ⓢ *(donation). (03) 5352 2836.*

Langi Morgala Museum in the bluestone woolstore (1874) contains pioneering relics and Aboriginal artifacts from the region. *Queen St. Open Sat.–Sun. afternoons. Tours available.* Ⓢ *(03) 5352 3117.* There are several mid-Victorian public buildings, notably the bluestone post office (1862), courthouse (1866–67) and shire hall (1871) – all in Barkly St. Gum San Chinese Heritage Centre is a modern museum commemorating the role of the Chinese miners in founding Ararat. *Lambert St. Open daily.* Ⓢ *(03) 5352 1078.*

In the area Best's Wines began on the edges of the Concongella Creek by pioneer vigneron Joseph Henry Best and his family in 1866. The Thompson family took over in 1920 and are still the proprietors. The winery is now state-of-the-art but visitors can inspect the original 1860s underground cellar; the sales area is in the original stables, built 1870. *17 km NW, 1 km off hwy, Stawell side of Great Western. Open daily. (03) 5352 2096.* Seppelt Great Western winery. Joseph Best planted vines here in 1865 and began the underground tunnel cellars, hewn from soft granite. Hans Irvine bought the vineyard in 1888, extended the cellars and won prizes after importing French winemakers and equipment. Seppelt took over in 1918 and are today well known for the sparkling and table wines produced here. The cellars, known as 'The Drives', were dug by goldminers during the 1860s and 1870s. They provide 2.5 km of rack space and have been listed on the National Estate Register. *16 km NW on Moyston Rd. Open daily. Tours Mon.–Sat. & Sun. on pub & school hols. $ (for tours). (03) 5361 2239.*

ℹ *Old Railway Station, 91 High St; freecall 1800 657 158.* Website: www.ararat.asn.au

AVOCA Map ref. 315 M12

The Surveyor-General, Major Thomas Mitchell, named this district in 1836, but the little township on the banks of the Avoca River, at the edge of the gentle Pyrenees, owes its existence to the discovery of gold in the area in 1852.

Of interest The Avoca and District Historical Society is in the town's small brick courthouse (1859), one of the earliest in the state. *Open Sun. (03) 5465 3265.* There is also a solid bluestone gaol (1867) and the brick powder magazine (1860) used to store gunpowder for blasting during the gold era. *Open by appt. (03) 5465 3265.* Lalor's Pharmacy, believed to be the oldest pharmacy in Victoria still operating on its original site, began in 1854 and is still in business. *Open Sun.*

ℹ *120 High St; (03) 5465 3767.*

See also Maryborough

BAIRNSDALE Map ref. 311 P4, 320 F13

The original inhabitants of the district were the Brabralung clan, a tribe of East Gippsland's Kurnai Aboriginal people. A cattle run was established in the district by Europeans in 1842, but the town grew up after gold brought an influx of miners in the 1850s. Grain growing in the 1870s and 1880s was followed by dairying in the 1890s and many of the public buildings date back to then.

Krowathunkooloong is an Aboriginal 'keeping place' with information and artifacts related to the history, heritage and culture of East Gippsland Koories. While there, ask about the Bataluk Cultural Trail. This records various sites from Sale to Cape Conran, linked to local Koorie history, following routes these people have travelled for more than 18 000 years. *Dalmahoy St. Open Mon.–Fri. Tours available. $ (03) 5152 1891.*

Also of interest Don't miss the Bairnsdale courthouse (1893), an extravagant design featuring a Rapunzel-like round tower, arches, gables, tall mullioned chimneys and carvings of Australian flora and fauna in local stone. *Nicholson St. Not open for inspection.* East Gippsland Historical Museum in Delvine Hall, a former secondary college (1891), documents local history. *Macarthur St. Open Wed., Thurs., Sun. afternoons. Tours available, booking essential. $ (03) 5152 6363.* St Mary's Church (1913) has a ceiling and part of its walls covered with murals painted by Italian artist Frank Floreani. *Main St. Open daily.*

ℹ *240 Main St; (03) 5152 3444.*

BALLARAT Map ref. 313 O3, 318 A13

See Historic Highlights, p. 102

BEECHWORTH Map ref. 319 O6, 320 A3

See Historic Highlights, p. 104

BELLARINE PENINSULA Map ref. 310 B7

See Portarlington, Queenscliff

BENALLA Map ref. 319 K7

Scene of the 'Faithfull Massacre' in 1838, when between eight and 13 drovers overlanding sheep to Port Phillip were killed by Aboriginal people protecting their land. It's believed one Aborigine was killed, but reprisals lasted many years, with up to a hundred Aboriginal people eventually dying. This is Ned Kelly country – the Commercial Hotel was headquarters for the 'Kelly Hunt' in 1878.

Of interest Benalla Art Gallery has some excellent Australian colonial paintings. *Bridge St. Open daily. (03) 5762 3027.* Old courthouse, built in 1864, with a distinctive two-storey facade added in 1888. Various members of the Kelly family stood trial here, including Ned, aged just 14 years. The Museum Complex houses the Benalla and District Historical Society. The Pioneer

Great Western Cellars, Ararat

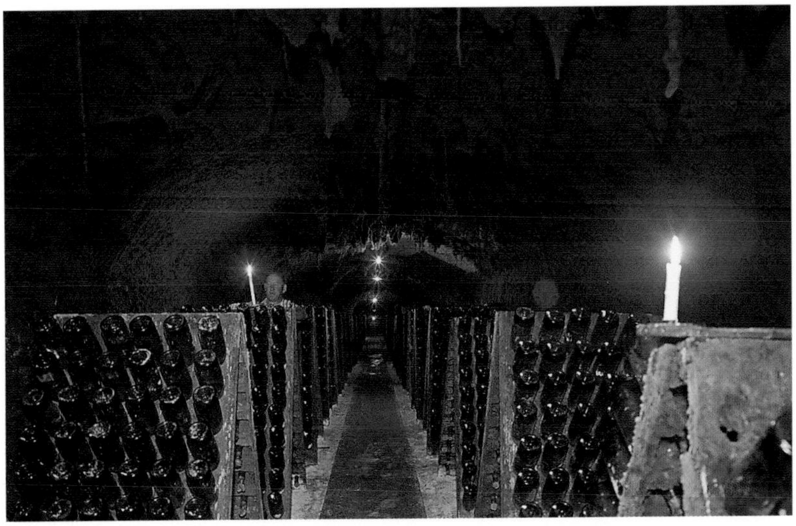

Museum (with some wonderful period costumes) is in the former Mechanics Institute (1869). *Mair St. Open daily.* Ⓢ *(03) 5762 1749.*

IN THE AREA Brown Brothers Vineyard, at Milawa, has been run by the Brown family since they opened it in 1889 and you can see some of the old wine-making equipment. The barn, built by the original family, is still standing. *50 km E. Open daily. (03) 5720 5500.*

🛈 *14 Mair St; (03) 5762 1749.*

BENDIGO Map ref. 315 Q10, 318 C8

See Historic Highlights, p. 106

BUNINYONG Map ref. 313 O4

Victoria's first inland town (1842) and the site of one of Australia's earliest gold rushes in the 1850s. The spacious main street suggests visions of a great future, but wealthier fields soon overtook Buninyong.

OF INTEREST Buninyong Post Office (1873) was in use as a post office for well over a century. *Learmonth St.* The rather grand, Gothic-inspired Crown Hotel, which lords it over the small, verandahed shopfronts opposite, replaced a colonial wooden pub on the same site. *Warrenheip St. Open daily.* The Public Library-Mechanics Institute (1861) has a hand-crafted Oregon timber facade. *Warrenheip St. Open Sun. afternoons.* In Learmonth St the splendid town hall with mansard-roofed clock tower (1886) has been well restored. The Buninyong and District Historical Society open the old courthouse in the town hall to the public on Sun. afternoons. *(03) 5431 7618.*

IN THE AREA Lal Lal blast furnace, next to the Lal Lal Reservoir (between Elaine and Buninyong): the unique ruins of a blast furnace and smelting works (1875–85), one of the country's most significant industrial remains. Much of the wrought iron for which **Ballarat** is famous was smelted here. *Falls Rd. Open daily.*

🛈 *Old Library, Warrenheip St; (03) 5341 7618.*

See also Ballarat

BURRAMINE Map ref. 319 K3

See Yarrawonga

CAMPERDOWN Map ref. 313 L8

Century-old elms, wide streets and conservative, mostly red-brick buildings, give Camperdown a solid, old-fashioned air.

OF INTEREST The mansard-roofed clock tower, erected in 1896 in memory of Thomas Manifold, whose family settled the district in 1838, the polychromatic brickwork of the courthouse (1886–87) and the Historical Society Museum (1896) (open Tues., Fri., Sun. afternoons. Ⓢ (03) 5593 1883) all in Manifold St.

IN THE AREA Purrumbete is an exceptional 28-room bluestone mansion, on a property owned by the Manifold family for over 120 years. The modest dwelling built on the district's first pastoral run in 1842 was extended in 1901 in the Art Nouveau style. There are carved panels by Robert Prenzell and murals by romantic painter Walter Withers. The sumptuously panelled hall has a medieval minstrels gallery and the formal gardens are impressive. *9 km E. Not open for inspection.*

🛈 *Old Courthouse, Manifold St; (03) 5593 3390.*

CAPE SCHANCK Map ref. 310 C9

Cape Schanck Lightstation This traditional stone lighthouse has provided a beacon on the often wild and windy coast since 1859. Towering 21 m above Cape Schanck it marks the eastern approach to Port Phillip bay. Climb to the top of the lighthouse for a stunning view across Bushrangers Bay and out to sea. There's also a small museum, and the keepers' residences are rented out. *Cape Schanck Rd. Open daily. Guided tours.* Ⓢ *(03) 5988 6184.*

🛈 *359b Point Nepean Rd, Dromana; (03) 5987 3078, freecall 1800 804 009.*

See also Sorrento, Portsea

CASTERTON Map ref. 312 C4

Captivated by the beauty of this district, the explorer Major Thomas Mitchell called it 'Australia Felix' when he passed through in the 1830s. Casterton – the name means 'walled city' – is hemmed in by volcanic tableland.

IN THE AREA Scottish perseverance and the iron will of John George

Robertson created Warrock Homestead, a self-sufficient complex of more than 50 buildings. Mostly from sawn timber, they spread across the Western District hills and gullies in a sea of gum trees. Erected between 1840 and the mid-1860s, the buildings are linked by their neat regularity, pitched roofs, louvred ventilators, timber finials and fretted bargeboards. A rambling homestead, woolshed, dog house, smoke-house, killing sheds, stables and smithy shop are just part of this 'town in miniature'. The Robertsons owned and occupied Warrock until the 1980s. *29 km N on Warrock Rd. Open daily. Tours available.* Ⓢ *(03) 5582 4222.*

🛈 *Shiels Tce; (03) 5581 2070.*

CASTLEMAINE Map ref. 315 Q11, 318 C10

Gold was discovered here in 1851. By 1852, 25 000 people swarmed over the low hills around Castlemaine, the heart of the Mt Alexander field, one of the world's richest alluvial goldfields. Within ten years 90 tonnes of gold had been extracted; within 20 years the fields were worked out. Most of Castlemaine's important buildings date from that first golden decade.

Buda A distinctive single-storey residence, built by a retired Indian Army colonel in 1857. It was bought by the noted Hungarian silversmith Ernest Leviny and extended in the 1890s. A giant cypress hedge, a curious greenhouse and an aviary are features of the 19th-century garden. *Hunter St. Open Wed.–Sun. or by appt.* Ⓢ *(03) 5472 1032.*

Castlemaine Market An impressive design built in stone and brick with bold rendering, and opened in 1862. The facade has an elegant portico, flanked by windows with classical pediments. Wrought-iron gates are cast in an elaborate Greek acanthus pattern, and Ceres, the Roman goddess of the harvest, presides over the entrance. The light, airy interior now houses a craft and antiques market. Also home to the town's Visitor Information. *Mostyn St. Open daily.*

Old Castlemaine Gaol After 130 years of greeting 'Her Majesty's guests', the extensive and historic old gaol (1861) has been restored and turned into

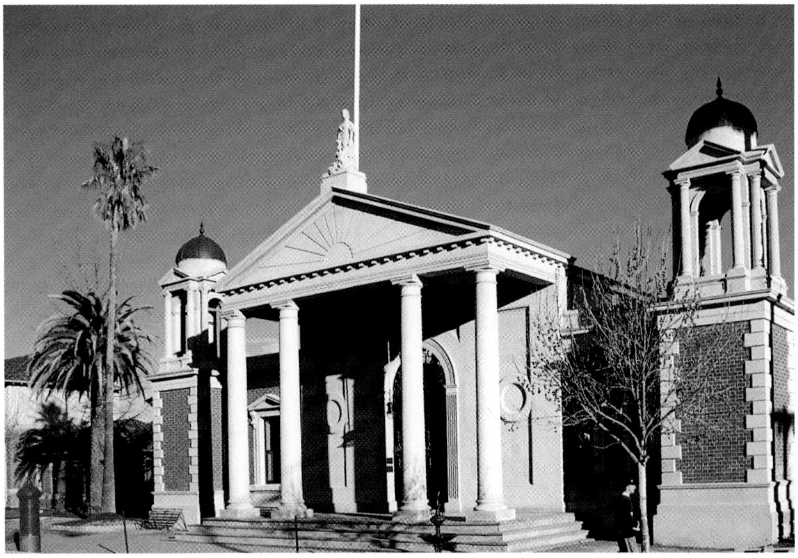

Castlemaine Market

friendlier accommodation. *Bowden St. Open daily.* $ *(03) 5470 5311.*

Also of interest Castlemaine Art Gallery and Historical Museum contains a significant collection of works by the marvellous goldfields artist ST Gill, Tom Roberts, Fred McCubbin and other colonial painters. *Lyttleton St. Open daily.* $ *(03) 5472 2292.* The former Imperial Hotel with french doors, quaint dormer windows along the mansard roofline, and an iron-crested lookout (1861) has a French-colonial character. *Lyttleton St. Not open for inspection.* Also in Lyttleton St are the monumental town hall (1898) and Italianate law courts (1878). *Not open for inspection.* The towered Italianate post office (1875) and the Classical Revival Bank of NSW (1854) are both in Barker St. The Botanic Gardens (1856) were planned with the assistance of famed botanist Baron von Mueller. *Open daily.*

ℹ *Old Market, Mostyn St; (03) 5470 6200, freecall 1800 171 888.* Website: www.mountalexander.vic.gov.au/tourism

See also Bendigo, Creswick, Maldon

CHILTERN Map ref. 299 P13, 319 O4, 320 A2

This tiny town in north-eastern Victoria began life as Black Dog Creek and saw Victoria's last great gold rush begin in the late 1850s. Its small-scale architecture, low verandahs and quiet streets preserve the atmosphere of a 19th-century country town.

Athenaeum Museum Originally library, council chambers and town hall (1866). Now displays a library of rare 19th-century books, photographs, paintings and goldfields artifacts. *Conness St. Open Sat.–Sun., pub hols. (03) 5726 1467.*

Dow's Pharmacy (1868) Original 19th-century shop fittings, old-fashioned pharmaceutical equipment and apothecary jars conjure another era. Dow's ran from 1830–1968. *Conness St. Open Sat.–Sun. afternoons, pub hol afternoons & by appt.* $ *(03) 5726 1597. NT.*

Federal Standard Printing Office This single-room, red-brick building with buttressing piers (1859) was home to Chiltern's *Federal Standard* newspaper for over a century. At one time several goldfields papers were printed on the steam-driven press, still in working order. The press is believed to be one of the oldest in Australia. *Main St. Open 2nd weekend of each month. (03) 5726 8258. NT.*

Old Grapevine Hotel Built in 1866 to replace the original Star Hotel. The grapevine (1867) in the courtyard is said to be one of the world's largest. A theatre attached to the hotel was the busy venue for plays, vaudeville, dances and public meetings during the gold rush. *Conness St. Open daily. (03) 5726 1395.*

Lake View Homestead Amid the old-fashioned country scents of lilac and roses stands the simple colonial house where Henry Handel Richardson (her real name was Ethel Florence Richardson) spent two years of her childhood. The house (under the name Barambogie) is vividly described in her masterly trilogy *The Fortunes of Richard Mahony.* Lake View (c. 1870) is red brick with an encircling verandah 'where we could be sure of finding shade and space'. Furnishings capture the atmosphere of the 1870s. *Victoria St. Open Sat.–Sun. afternoons, pub & school hols.* $ *(03) 5726 1317. NT.*

Also of interest Railway station (1875), courthouse (1865), post office (1863) and more. Chiltern has plenty to explore at a leisurely pace. Excellent walking tour brochures are available. Also guided tours from the museum. *Booking essential. (03) 5726 1467.*

ℹ *30 Main Street; (03) 5726 1611.*

See also Beechworth, Rutherglen

CHURCHILL ISLAND Map ref. 310 E9

Historic island just 57 ha in area, discovered by explorer and former naval surgeon George Bass in 1798. In 1801, Lt James Grant, RN, of the *Lady Nelson,* built a cottage here and planted crops, establishing Victoria's first European settlement. John Rogers, who settled on the island in the early 1860s, built two small cottages, the island's oldest remaining buildings. Well-known Melbourne businessman Samuel Amess bought the island in 1872 and built a weatherboard homestead, Amess House, which still stands. Amess planted the huge spreading Norfolk pine in 1872, and several gnarled fruit trees remain from the orchard he started in the 1880s. Now a National Park. *Open daily.* $ *(03) 5956 7214.*

ℹ *Phillip Island Rd, Newhaven; (03) 5956 7447.*

CLUNES Map ref. 313 Q2, 315 Q13, 318 A11

Cradled in a deep river valley, surrounded by trees, Clunes was the site of Victoria's first gold strike, in 1851. Today, it's a sleepy town with a surprising number of dignified, two-storey sandstone buildings, substantial churches and modest, verandahed shops.

Of interest Architecturally significant town hall and courthouse (1872–73), St Thomas Aquinas Catholic Church (1872) and the romantic presbytery (c. 1904), all in Bailey St. The grandiose two-storey Italianate post office (1872) is now a bookshop. The Uniting Church was built in 1862. Victoria Park, stretching along the river banks, is graced by century-old silver poplars and elms. Pick up a walking tour brochure from Clunes Arts & Historic Centre, at the Clunes Museum, located in a bluestone and brick building (1868). *36 Fraser St. Open Sat.–Sun., pub & school hols.* $ *(03) 5434 3592.*

Bailey St; (03) 5345 3896.

CORINELLA
Map ref. 310 F8

One of Victoria's earliest British settlements took place at Corinella in 1826, when Capt. Wright established a military outpost here for 15 months following fear of a French 'invasion'. A cairn marking the site is signposted.

Phillip Island Rd, Newhaven; (03) 5956 7447.

CORRYONG
Map ref. 300 B8, 320 G2

Corryong lies amid towering mountains on the edge of the high plains cattle country in north-eastern Victoria. This is the home of the legendary horseman Jack Riley, immortalised in Banjo Paterson's classic ballad *The Man from Snowy River.*

OF INTEREST Man from Snowy River Museum contains early skiing equipment, pioneer relics and a replica of Riley's primitive hut. *Hanson St. Open daily.* $ *(02) 6076 1114.* Riley's grave (1854), in the Corryong Cemetery. *Pioneer Ave.*

IN THE AREA Old goldfields diggings, historic cattlemen's huts and small picturesque towns steeped in the history of the area.

50 Hanson St; (02) 6076 2277.

CRESWICK
Map ref. 313 O2, 315 O13, 318 A12

The Creswick brothers settled here in 1842, but it was the discovery of a spectacularly rich alluvial goldfield in 1852 that gave rise to a boom town servicing a population of more than 25 000. In all, 11 tonnes of gold were washed from the Madame Berry Mine, just one of the underground 'rivers of gold'.

OF INTEREST Creswick Historical Museum, situated in the grand former town hall (1876) is worth visiting even if only to see the magnificent winding staircase and beautifully carved stone pillars. *70 Albert St. Open Sun. & pub hols.* $ *(03) 5345 2329.* The sturdy two-storey former Bank of NSW (1861) is now a B&B. The single-storey wing (1873) was reputedly added to store gold bullion. St John's Church (1861) and adjacent Gothic Revival rectory (not open for inspection).

IN THE AREA The countryside is scarred by giant mullock heaps, gullies and other evidence of mining. Australasia No. 2 Mine (1877–82) was the scene of Australia's worst gold-mining disaster, when 22 men drowned. *4 km NW.*

Raglan St; (03) 5345 1114.
See also Daylesford, Smeaton

DAYLESFORD
Map ref. 313 Q2, 315 Q13, 318 B12

A former gold town, now – with Hepburn Springs – a popular mineral springs resort, surrounded by heavily wooded hills.

Convent Gallery Adjacent to the Botanic Gardens and housed in a former girls' convent school, an imposing building on the slope of Wombat Hill. Part of the convent was built (1860s) as a residence for the Gold Commissioner, and known as 'Blarney Castle'. The restored chapel, original cells used by the nuns, stained-glass windows and picturesque views from the tower are highlights. *Cnr Hill & Daly sts. Open daily.* $ *(03) 5348 3211.*

ALSO OF INTEREST Botanic Gardens, established 1861, include majestic cedars, elms and oaks, many on the National Register of Significant Trees. *Open daily.* Daylesford Historic and Cultural Museum, Daly St, in the former School of Mines (1890) has historic photos and significant collection of Koorie artifacts. *Open Sat.–Sun., pub & school hols.* $ *(03) 5348 1453.* Central Highlands Tourist Railway runs fully restored diesel railmotors from the Daylesford Station (c. 1884) in Raglan St. *Sun. only. (03) 5348 3503 or (03) 5348 1759.* The small but elegant Romanesque courthouse (1863), and towered Italianate post office

(1867). Christ Church has splendid cedar fittings. Visit St Peter's Catholic Church (1863) to see its skilful carvings of the 12 apostles. Pick up a walking tour brochure from Visitor Information. The district celebrates its strong Swiss–Italian heritage in an annual 'festa'.

Vincent St; (03) 5348 1339.
See also Hepburn Springs

DUNOLLY
Map ref. 315 O10

A placid town with leafy kurrajongs shading the mellowed, 19th-century buildings in the main street, called Broadway. More large gold nuggets were found in and around this town than anywhere else in Australia – 126 in Dunolly alone. In 1869 the biggest nugget ever found, the 'Welcome Stranger' (a hefty 66 kg), was found at Moliagul, 15 km north.

OF INTEREST A stroll through town is a step back in time – courthouse (1862), the original lock-up (1862) and stables (1863), Royal Hotel (1896), post and telegraph office (1872), town hall (1884), St John's Church (1866–69) and St Mary's Catholic Church (1869–71), with its single spire and gabled porch. The Dunolly courthouse (now the Visitor Information) has a hand-carved cedar interior and historical display. *Cnr Bull & Market sts. Open Fri.–Mon. (03) 5468 1032.* Goldfields & Historical Arts Society. *Broadway. Open Sat.–Sun. (03) 5460 4511.*

Cnr Bull & Market sts; (03) 5468 1032.
See also Maldon, Maryborough

ECHUCA
Map ref. 299 K13, 318 E4

See Historic Highlights, p. 108

GEELONG
Map ref. 310 A6, 313 R7

See Historic Highlights, p. 110

GLENROWAN
Map ref. 319 M6

The infamous Ned Kelly was ambushed by police and shot it out here in 1880. He was subsequently tried for murder and hanged in the old Melbourne Gaol. Whether he was an outlaw or a hero is still debated. His life and times are well documented in Glenrowan.

OF INTEREST A marker indicates the site of Kelly's last stand, in Siege St. Ned Kelly Memorial Museum & Homestead is worth visiting (it's also the Visitor Information). *Open daily.* Ⓢ *(03) 5766 2448.* Cobb & Co. Museum. *Open daily.* Ⓢ *(03) 5766 2409.* Kellyland contains a computerised video theatre. *Open daily.* Ⓢ *(03) 5766 2367.* **ⓘ** *Kate's Cottage, Gladstone St (Old Hume Hwy); (03) 5766 2448.*

HALLS GAP Map ref. 312 I1, 314 I12

Wrapped around by the rocky grandeur of the Grampian Mountains, traditionally known as Gariwerd by the local Aboriginal people, this tiny town is a good base from which to experience the ancient landscape.
Brambuk Aboriginal Cultural Centre The Centre helps visitors explore the rich culture and history of the Koorie communities in south-west Victoria. Signs of their history and occupation of the land, such as ancient rock-art sites, oven mounds and tool making, are a reminder of just how short European history is in this country. Archaeologists estimate Aboriginal people have been living in this region for at least 5000 years. Tours to historic rock-art sites. *Grampians Tourist Rd. Open daily.* Ⓢ *(03) 5356 4452.*
ⓘ *Dunkeld Rd; (03) 5356 4616. 50–52 Western Hwy, Stawell; (03) 5358 2314, freecall 1800 246 880.* Website: www.ngshire.vic.gov.au

HAMILTON Map ref. 312 F5

This is the heart of huge pastoral runs, many settled from the late 1830s by Scottish migrants, and home of the Western District 'squattocracy'. Hamilton has been called 'the wool capital of the world'.
Big Woolbales A display based in several outsize 'wool bales' explains the history and process of wool growing, the district's most important farming industry. *Coleraine Rd. Open daily.* Ⓢ *(03) 5571 2810.*
Botanic Gardens Established 1870, and redesigned by William Guilfoyle in 1881, these exemplify formal Victorian garden design with mature European trees, an historic band rotunda and fine fountain. *Cnr Thompson & French sts. Open daily. Freecall 1800 807 056.*
ALSO OF INTEREST Hamilton Art Gallery has a significant collection. *Brown St. Open daily. Tours available.* Ⓢ *(donation). (03) 5573 0460.* Sir Reginald Ansett Transport Museum centres around the original hangar for Ansett Airlines, started by 'Sir Reg'. *Ballarat Rd. Open daily.* Ⓢ *(03) 5571 2767.* Hamilton History Centre in the former Mechanics Institute (1859). *43 Gray St. Open Sun.–Sat. (03) 5572 4933.* Pastoral Museum exhibits include Old Lutheran church (1861), smithy shop, horse-drawn vehicles, agricultural equipment and other pioneer relics. *Ballarat Rd. Open last Sat. of each month & one weekend in Mar. & Oct.* Ⓢ *(03) 5572 2373 or (03) 5571 2586.* Gray St has some fine buildings and residences. Visit leafy Church Hill to see St Andrew's Church (1909), a local landmark with its massive spire. Pick up a walking tour brochure from Visitor Information in Lonsdale St.
IN THE AREA Some wonderful historic homesteads and gardens, built on the wealth of wool – some are B&Bs, others offer garden and/or homestead tours, usually by appt only. Inquire at the Visitor Information. Notable is Narrapumelap, an exotic French Gothic homestead (1873) with a tower, gatehouse, magnificent elm-lined driveway and elegant garden. *55 km E, Narrapumelap Rd, Wickliffe. Open for groups of eight or more, by appt only.* Ⓢ *(03) 5350 3220.* Glenisla, first settled in 1842 and one of the state's oldest-established stations, has a sandstone homestead (1873), flagged courtyard and timber-slab stables. Now a B&B. *65 km N, Henty Hwy, Glenisla. (03) 5380 1532.* At the nearby town of Dunkeld, settled in the 1830s, visit the historic Royal Mail Hotel (with a streamlined modern wing), in Parker St, and the local history museum. *27 km E.*
ⓘ *Lonsdale St; (03) 5572 3746, freecall 1800 807 056.* Website: www.sthgrampians.vic.gov.au
See also Casterton

Convent Gallery, Daylesford

Heritage Village, Coal Creek, Korumburra

HARROW Map ref. 312 D1, 314 D12

Tracing its beginnings to 1836, Harrow is possibly Victoria's oldest inland town (Kilmore makes the same claim).

OF INTEREST The Hermitage Hotel has been an intrinsic part of Harrow's history. Built by 1854, and altered in the 1890s (the original shingles can be seen under the roof) it is still in business. *Blair St. Open daily. (03) 5588 1209.* Log lock-up, (c. 1859), a primitive gaol of stacked, rough-hewn logs, with a log ceiling and slits for windows. *Blair St. Open daily.*

Hermitage Hotel, Blair St; (03) 5588 1209, for local brochures.

HEPBURN Map ref. 313 Q2, 315 Q13, 318 B12 SPRINGS

A mineral springs and spa centre, just 3 km from **Daylesford**, where mineral waters have been bottled since 1850. The district's Italian and Swiss–Italian populations – more than 20 000 in the 1850s and 1860s – have left their mark on the architecture and gardens.

OF INTEREST The original spa complex was built in 1895 and you can still sample mineral water from old hand-pumps. The modern spa complex, with its hydrotherapy and mud baths, and the Edwardian pavilion (1908) are in Hepburn Springs Reserve. *Open daily.* The Old Macaroni Factory, built of handmade bricks by the Lucini

brothers in 1859, would not look out of place in northern Italy. Inside, the decorations depicting Italian and Swiss scenes, hand-painted before 1866, have been restored. *Open to the public four times a year.* $ *(03) 9457 7035.* Historic guesthouses in the area have evocative names like the 'Bellinzona' and the 'Locarno Grande'.

Vincent St; (03) 5348 1339.
See also Daylesford

HORSHAM Map ref. 314 G9

Horsham is surrounded by the rich wheat- and wool-growing country of the Wimmera, almost 300 km northwest of Melbourne. In 1842 James Darlot, the district's first European settler, established his Brighton run on both sides of the Wimmera River. In 1849 George Langlands set up a humble store and post office near the corner of present-day Darlot and Hamilton sts. Horsham developed after the area was opened up in the 1870s.

OF INTEREST The well-established Botanic Gardens, Firebrace St, designed in the 1870s by William Guilfoyle, the noted curator of the Melbourne Botanical Gardens. The Historical Society, in the former Mechanics Institute building, has photos and local history documents. *33 Pynsent St. Open Tues.–Wed. afternoons. (03) 5382 2573.*

20 O'Callaghans Pde; (03) 5382 1832, freecall 1800 633 218.
See also Halls Gap, Stawell, Warracknabeal

JEPARIT Map ref. 314 F6

Sir Robert Menzies, one of Australia's longest serving prime ministers, was born in 1894 in this tiny Wimmera town.

Wimmera-Mallee Pioneer Museum Of special interest in the 4 ha museum is the Albacutya homestead complex of three buildings (1840s–70s), moved here from John Coppock's station, 30 km away, which demonstrate early building techniques. Authentic blacksmith's shop, church, vintage machinery and other displays. *Dimboola Rd. Open daily.* $ *(03) 5397 2101.*

Wimmera-Mallee Pioneer Museum, Dimboola Rd; (03) 5397 2101.

KORUMBURRA Map ref. 310 H8

Coal Creek Heritage Village Established on the site of the original Coal Creek Mine (1890s), this unique village recreates the daily life of coal miners and their families last century. A smithy shop, original wattle-and-daub cottage (c. 1840s) and well-stocked general store are highlights. In all, more than 30 historic buildings, and an authentic mine with a timber poppet head, are set in rolling countryside near a small creek. Visitors can take a guided tour into an original mine. *Cnr South Gippsland Hwy & Silkstone Rd. Open daily.* $ *(03) 5655 1811.*

Cnr South Gippsland Hwy & Silkstone Rd; (03) 5655 2233, freecall 1800 630 704.

KYNETON Map ref. 313 R1, 315 R12, 318 D11

Once the very heart of Victoria's wheat district, Kyneton is surrounded by massive hills and several huge bluestone mills near swift-flowing streams. During the 1850s and '60s, Piper Street reverberated with the sound of thousands of diggers and loads of supplies en route to the goldfields. Superseded as a main thoroughfare more than a century ago, the street and vicinity retain some of their 19th-century character.

Kyneton Museum in a handsome colonial Georgian bluestone building (1855), formerly the Bank of NSW and bank residence, and the oldest bank building in Vic. Visitors can see the original loft, coach-house, drop-log settlers' cottage (1842), carriages in the courtyard, and more. Worth visiting. *67 Piper St. Open Sat.–Sun. (03) 5422 1228.*

ALSO OF INTEREST GW Willis Steam Mill is an 1862 flour mill of bluestone and timber. *Piper St. Not open for inspection.* Courthouse (1856), Hutton St; post office (1870), cnr Jennings & Mollison sts; two-storey bluestone Royal George Hotel (1852), Piper St, still serving thirsty travellers and locals; and the impressive bluestone hospital (1854–56) extended 1861, with elegant cast-iron lacework verandah (1910). *Simpson St. Not open for inspection.* St Paul's Church (1855) is very fine and the rectory (1851), with its sweeping iron roof, is one of Kyneton's oldest houses. *Yaldwin St.*

IN THE AREA South along the Calder Hwy, a huge old bluestone mill (1859) on the Campaspe River and a tantalising glimpse of an 1850s two-storey farmhouse, Skelsmergh Hall. *Not open for inspection.*

🅸 *Jean Haynes Playground, High St; (03) 5422 6110.* Website: www. macedon-ranges.vic. gov.au

LANGWARRIN
Map ref. 309 D11

Mulberry Hill An American-colonial style weatherboard house (1926) with curved balcony and views across Western Port bay. Of historical interest as the home of artist and former Director of the National Gallery of Victoria, Sir Daryl Lindsay and his wife Joan (Lady) Lindsay, author of the well-known novel *Picnic at Hanging Rock.* The house, bequeathed to the National Trust by the Lindsays, has some fine Georgian furnishings and original artwork. *Golf Links Rd. Open Sun. afternoons, closed July.* 🅢 *(03) 5971 4138. NT.*

🅸 *359b Pt Nepean Rd, Dromana; (03) 5987 3078, freecall 1800 804 009.*

McCRAE
Map ref. 310 C8

McCrae Homestead A small, early colonial timber-slab cottage built on a run taken up by Scottish lawyer Andrew McCrae in 1843. His wife Georgiana drew the plans, and her detailed sketches and diary entries were used to authentically restore

the house to the period 1844–51, when the McCraes lived there with their eight children. Although rustic (Georgiana recorded seeing 'long lines of actual landscape' through the drop-slab walls), with shingled roof and rough-hewn posts, there are touches of refinement, such as the delicate casement windows. Many original furnishings and paintings brought from Scotland remain. The reconstructed kitchen and museum help to convey the family's mid-Victorian lifestyle. *11 Beverley Rd. Open daily.* 🅢 *(03) 5981 2866. NT.*

🅸 *359b Pt Nepean Rd, Dromana; (03) 5987 3078, freecall 1800 804 009.*

MALDON
Map ref. 315 P11, 318 B10

See Historic Highlights, p. 112

MARYBOROUGH
Map ref. 315 O11

The grand public buildings that remain in this quiet town hint at the golden future Maryborough saw for itself after gold was found in 1854.

Civic Square Group On the site of the original government camp, a fine cluster of Italianate buildings – post office, town hall, municipal offices (all 1877) and courthouse (1892) – face a small square in the European tradition. Even the belltower on the fire station (adjacent) is impressive in its size and handsome detailing. The fire station (1861), in Neil St, is now an art gallery. *Open Sun.–Fri.* 🅢 *(donation). (03) 5460 4588.*

ALSO OF INTEREST The grandiose, red-brick railway station (1890) with its bold stucco trimming, Flemish gables, clock tower, enormous platform and massive portico, today houses a gallery and antique shop. *Station St. Open daily. (03) 5461 4683.* Tiny, stone Worsley Cottage (1894) is now the Historical Society Museum. *3 Palmerston St. Open Sun.* 🅢 *(03) 5461 2800 or (03) 5464 7225.*

🅸 *Railway Station Complex, Station St; (03) 5460 4511, freecall 1800 356 511. See also Castlemaine, Clunes, Dunolly, Maldon*

MELBOURNE
Map ref. 304 G10, 306 A3, 310 D4

See pp. 70–83

MILDURA
Map ref. 298 D7, 316 G3

Canadian brothers George and William Benjamin Chaffey, invited to Australia by Premier Alfred Deakin in 1885, introduced irrigation to this parched region, transforming what had been a vast, dusty-red sheep station into excellent agricultural land.

Rio Vista WB Chaffey had this distinctive two-storey residence built in the early Federation style in 1890, using local bricks, jarrah and cedar timbers delivered by paddle-steamer. Rio Vista, featuring an open balcony and encircling verandah, is furnished and used as a museum, and is part of the Mildura Arts Centre Complex. *199 Cureton Ave. Open daily. Tours on request.* 🅢 *(03) 5023 3733.*

ALSO OF INTEREST The Grand Hotel opened in 1890 as the Mildura Coffee Palace, but didn't stay dry for long, becoming a licensed hotel in 1891. Substantially altered, but retaining a little of its former grandeur. *7th St. Open daily. (03) 5023 0511.* Riverboats, such as the steam-driven PS *Melbourne*, ply the Murray. *Mildura Wharf. Cruises daily. (03) 5023 2200.* Alfred Deakin Centre documents Mildura's history (Visitor Information also here). *Deakin Ave. Open daily. (03) 5021 4424.* Langtree Hall Museum (1889), Mildura's original public hall, has historic displays. *Walnut Ave. Open Tues.–Sun. (03) 5021 3090.* Psyche Bend Pumping Station, part of the original irrigation system. *Kings Billabong (end of 11th St). Special running days held during the year. Open Tues.–Thurs., Sun.* 🅢 Old Mildura Homestead, re-creation of Mildura's first house (c. 1847) a slab-and-log construction. *Cureton Ave. Open daily.* 🅢 *(donation). (03) 5023 3733.*

IN THE AREA 'Big Lizzie' (1915) at Red Cliffs is the biggest traction engine ever built in Australia. Australia's largest soldier-settlement took place in this district in 1920. The lunar landscape of the World Heritage-listed Mungo National Park, and proof of Aboriginal occupation dating back 40 000 years.

🅸 *Alfred Deakin Centre, 180–190 Deakin Ave; (03) 5021 4424, freecall 1800 039 043. See also Wentworth (NSW)*

MOE

Map ref. 311 J7

Gippsland Heritage Park Pioneer village notable for several authentic early settlers' buildings. 'Loren' is a rare, prefabricated iron building, imported in 1853–54, the great era of 'portable' houses in Victoria. The old Bushy Park homestead was built of pit-sawn red-gum timber over 120 years ago for Angus McMillan, credited with the discovery of Gippsland. A miner's bark hut, a weatherboard school (1889), the 1863 Cobb & Co. Coach Inn (still licensed) and restored horse-drawn vehicles are among the sights re-creating a typical Gippsland rural town from days gone by. *Princes Hwy. Open daily.* $ *(03) 5127 3082.*
ℹ *Gippsland Heritage Park, Lloyd St; (03) 5127 3082.*

MORNINGTON PENINSULA

Map ref. 310 C8

See McCrae, Mount Martha, Portsea, Sorrento

MOUNT MARTHA

Map ref. 310 D7

The Briars Historic Park One of the Mornington Peninsula's oldest pastoral stations, this small, colonial farmstead in a rural setting has been carefully farmed since AB Balcombe acquired the land in 1843. The front section of the house (c. 1863) of handmade bricks, shelters beneath a wide return verandah with creeper twining around timber posts. The oldest timber wing was started in 1846 and probably completed in 1850. The rare and exquisitely fine Napoleonic artifacts collection was begun by AB Balcombe's father. The 225 ha property features wetlands and walks through natural woodland. *Nepean Hwy, Mt Martha. Open daily.* $ *(03) 5974 3686.*
ℹ *359b Point Nepean Rd, Dromana; (03) 5971 4138, freecall 1800 809 009.*

OMEO

Map ref. 300 A12, 320 F8

Nestled in a valley, tucked away in the heart of the high country, Omeo takes its name from a station settled by squatters in the 1830s. Alluvial gold saw the area flourish briefly in the 1850s.

OF INTEREST The state school (1866), the red-brick corner post office (1890s) and the ornate courthouse (1892) are still in use. The Golden Age Hotel (1940s) is the fifth hotel on this site. The original 1858 gaol *(not open for inspection)*, a log lock-up built of roughly squared hardwood logs, stacked 12 high, with an iron bar grille door and slits for windows, looks primitive but secure. It is part of Omeo's Historical Park. *Great Alpine Rd.* $ The Omeo Courthouse is still operating.
ℹ *German Cuckoo Clock Shop, Day Ave (Great Alpine Rd); (03) 5159 1552.*
Website: www.omeo.net/region

'Loren', Gippsland Heritage Park, Moe

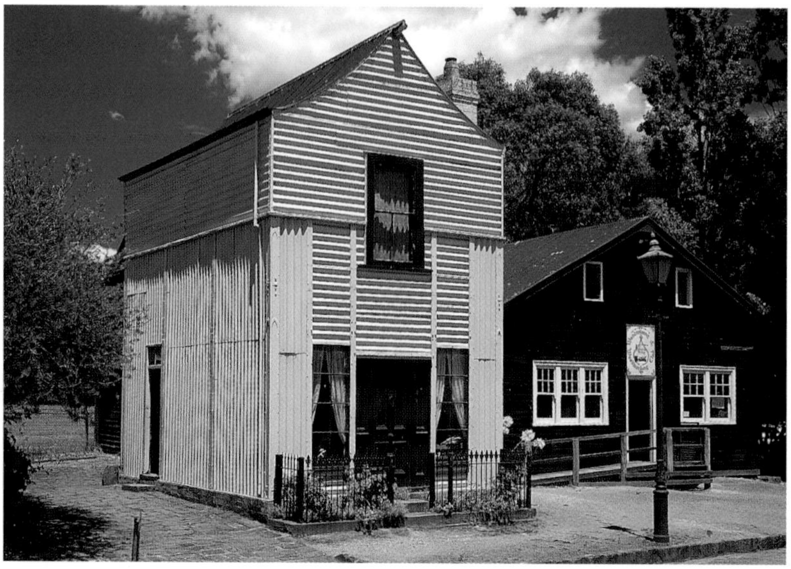

POINT LONSDALE

Map ref. 310 B7

OF INTEREST The original wooden lighthouse (1863) was replaced by a stone lighthouse in 1902. It overlooks The Rip (the treacherous waters between here and Point Nepean) and has seen shipwrecks and tragedy. *Tours Sun. or by arrangement. Booking essential.* $ *0419 513 007.* Buckley's Cave: William Buckley, the 'wild, white man', was an escaped convict who lived with Aboriginal people for 32 years, possibly spending some time in this cave at the base of Point Lonsdale lighthouse. He was found by John Batman's party in the 1830s and granted a pardon. The expression 'You've got two chances, Buckley's or none' refers to Buckley's luck in surviving.

PORT ALBERT

Map ref. 311 L10

Gippsland's first town, and port of entry, once saw sailing ships from Europe, China and America and thousands of eager miners arriving, headed for the goldfields at **Walhalla**, **Omeo** and beyond. Millions of ounces of gold were shipped out. These days Port Albert is a tranquil fishing village.

Maritime Museum in the former Bank of Victoria (1861), which once held gold from the flourishing local diggings. Historic photos, navigation equipment and maritime memorabilia. *Tarraville Rd. Open pub & summer school hols.* $ *(03) 5183 2206 or (03) 5182 5264.*

ALSO OF INTEREST Port Albert Hotel, one of the State's oldest licensed hotels (1842), was originally a prefabricated timber structure. The oldest section remaining dates from 1858. *Wharf St. (03) 5183 2212.*

IN THE AREA In Tarraville, Christ Church, a drop-slab timber church (c. 1856), built without nails, with decorative woodwork and a miniature belltower, is one of the State's oldest.
ℹ *The Court House, Rodgers St, Yarram; (03) 5182 6553.*

PORT CAMPBELL

Map ref. 313 K11

A sleepy fishing village on Victoria's rugged, often wild 'shipwreck' coast. It was named after Capt. Campbell who was in charge of the whaling station at Port Fairy in the 1840s, and sometimes sheltered in this small harbour.

Loch Ard Shipwreck Museum Fascinating artifacts, memorabilia and photos linked to shipwrecks on this coast between 1878–91, including the *Loch Ard* (1878) when 52 lives were lost, leaving just two teenage survivors. *Lord St. Open daily.* Ⓢ *(03) 5598 6463.*

ALSO OF INTEREST Historical Hall. *Lord St. Open daily in Jan. or contact Visitor Information.* Follow the signposted 'discovery walk' linking historic places. Historic Shipwrecks Trail marks the site of 25 wrecks along the coast – plaques along the cliff-top tell the tragic stories.

IN THE AREA Glenample Homestead (1866–69), on one of the district's earliest pastoral runs (1840s), sheltered the Loch Ard survivors. *12 km E on Great Ocean Rd. Open daily during school hols & Sat.–Sun. For other times contact Visitor Information.* Ⓢ *(03) 5598 6089.* Cape Otway Lightstation, the oldest lighthouse tower on the Australian mainland, which has guided ships through the narrow western entrance to Bass Strait since 1848. Visitors can stay in the lighthouse keepers' original sandstone residences. *Otway Lighthouse Rd (off Great Ocean Rd). Open daily.* Ⓢ *(03) 5237 9240.*

🖼 *26 Morris St; (03) 5598 6089.* Website: www.greatoceanrd.org.au

PORT FAIRY

Map ref. 312 G9

Mellowed by the salty winds that blow in off the harbour, its streets lined with tiny stone cottages and Norfolk pines, Port Fairy is a seaside village with a long maritime tradition. Whalers and sealers frequented these waters even before Capt. James Wishart named the harbour after his vessel the *Fairy*, in 1810. In the 1850s, Belfast (as it was known) was a major port of entry, and wool and gold were shipped out. But other ports provided better shelter and by the 1860s the town's growth had ground to a halt.

Caledonian Inn This early colonial seaport hotel of bluestone was left unfinished when workers abandoned tools to head for the Ballarat

Moyne River, Port Fairy

gold diggings. *Cnr Bank & James sts. Open daily. (03) 5568 1044.*

Former Merrijig Inn (c. 1841). Once one of Belfast's premier hotels, used for meetings of the Hunt and Race Club and, at one stage, as a police barracks. Now a boutique hotel. *Cnr Gipps & Campbell sts. (03) 5568 2324.*

Mott's Cottage Timber and stone cottage, one of Port Fairy's oldest, believed to have been built for two of Capt. Wishart's sailors, Mott and Stevenson. It was built in stages (1845–90), and the central stone section, with walls a sturdy 45 cm thick, was possibly by a Devon stonemason. *5 Sackville St. Open Wed., Sat.–Sun. Tours available.* Ⓢ *(donation). (03) 5568 2632. NT.*

Port Fairy History Centre Housed in the stately, Palladian-style bluestone courthouse (1859–60), originally intended for sittings of the Supreme Court. *Near cnr Gipps & Campbell sts. Open Wed., Sat.–Sun. & daily in Vic. school hols. (03) 5568 2263.*

Seacombe House Built 1847 by Capt. James Saunders. In its heyday, it was the venue for such 'Unprecedented Attractions' as the Ethiopian Serenaders. Now a motel and restaurant. *Cnr Sackville & Cox sts. (03) 5568 1082.*

OF INTEREST Make time to look around the old wharf area. Captain Mills's Cottage is a somewhat ramshackle timber and stone cottage (1850s) possibly including Charles Mills's original hut (1840s). *Not open for inspection.* Author Rolf Boldrewood,

in his well-known *Old Melbourne Memories*, records staying at wealthy merchant William Rutledge's residence 'Emoh' (1840s). *8 Cox St. Not open for inspection.* Star of the West Hotel was built in 1856 by John Walwyn Taylor, a West Indian Negro. *Cnr Sackville & Bank sts. Open daily. (03) 5568 1715.* Former office of the Port Fairy *Gazette*, one of Australia's oldest newspapers, started in 1864 and still published weekly. Now a cafe and shop. *Sackville St.* The bluestone lighthouse (1859) on the eastern end of Griffiths Island, reached across the footbridge. *Not open for inspection.* Port Fairy Historic Lifeboat Station. *Griffiths St. Open Sun. afternoons on long weekends & daily in Jan. Tours available.* Ⓢ *(03) 5568 2682.* Both the lookout and flagstaff at the Fort and Battery Hill, date from the settlement's early days. The guns were installed in 1885 and there's an 1860s powder magazine. *Battery Lane. Open daily.* St Patrick's, a Gothic Revival church (1859). Note the unusual stone roof guttering with gargoyle water spills. *Yambuk Rd. Princes Hwy. Open daily. Tours available. (03) 5568 1734.* More than 50 buildings are classified by the National Trust. A signposted 'history walk' starts from the historic Lecture Hall in Sackville St or walking tour brochures are available from Visitor Information.

IN THE AREA Port Fairy is part of the 'shipwreck coast'. Follow the 'shipwreck walk' just over 2 km, from the

surf club to the mouth of the Moyne River, where ships such as the barque *Socrates* (1843) and brig *Essington* (1852) met their untimely end. 🛈 *22 Bank St; (03) 5568 2682.*
See also Hamilton, Portland, Warrnambool

PORTARLINGTON   Map ref. 310 B6

Portarlington Mill One of Victoria's earliest flour mills (1857), four storeys high, built of sandstone from the nearby cliff, on land that may once have been an Aboriginal corroboree ground. The mill flourished whilst Bellarine Peninsula was the 'granary of the colony', but success was short-lived, and by 1874 it had closed. Exhibitions explore the area's local history and the history of the mill. *Turner Crt. Open (Sept.–May) Sun.; (Jan.) Wed., Sat.–Sun.* Ⓢ *(03) 5259 3847. NT.* 🛈 *Cnr Grubb Rd & Bellarine Peninsula Hwy, Wallington; (03) 5250 2669.*

PORTLAND   Map ref. 312 D9

See Historic Highlights, p. 114

PORTSEA   Map ref. 310 B8

Former Quarantine Station These barracks-style, rendered limestone buildings with timber verandah-balconies (1850s) were part of the quarantine station, important in protecting the colony from infectious diseases such as cholera, typhoid, smallpox and leprosy. Guided tours provide an insight into how the station operated. *Pt Nepean. Tours Sat.–Sun., pub &. school hols. Booking essential.* Ⓢ *(03) 5984 3606.*
Point Nepean Fortifications Overlooking Port Phillip heads, the army constructed a labyrinth of turrets, forts and lookouts to guard this coast against invasion. Until 1988, information about this military defence outpost was highly classified – now it's possible to explore the fortifications. Displays and soundtracks explain the history. *Pt Nepean Rd. Open daily. (03) 5984 4276.*
🛈 *359b Point Nepean Rd, Dromana; (03) 5987 3078, freecall 1800 804 009.*

QUEENSCLIFF   Map ref. 310 B7

See Historic Highlights, p. 116

RAINBOW   Map ref. 298 D13, 314 F4

A small town in the Mallee district of north-western Victoria. John Coppock settled on the district's first land grant, at Albacutya station, in 1847–48. The Wotjobaluk people originally occupied the area, and the name Albacutya is said to be the word for 'where the quandongs grow'. Quandongs are a sweet fruit known as good bush food, eaten by Aboriginal people and early settlers.
Yurunga Homestead A gracious Edwardian house (1909–10) with patterned slate roof, brick and limestone walls and a generous encircling verandah providing protection from the district's harsh summer climate. A special underground room was built to provide relief from heatwaves. Wunderlich pressed-metal ceilings, period tiles and glasswork embellish the interiors, and cellars extend beneath the house. *Cnr Gray & Cust sts. Open Sun. afternoons.* Ⓢ *(03) 5295 1373.*
🛈 *Shell Service Station, cnr Federal & Tavern sts; (03) 5395 1026.*

RUTHERGLEN   Map ref. 299 O13, 319 N4

Settled by pastoralists in the 1830s and almost overrun by gold diggers in the 1850s, Rutherglen is the centre of one of the most important wine areas in Victoria. Phylloxera devastated many vineyards here in the 1890s, as it did vineyards elsewhere in Victoria.
All Saints Estate The vineyard was established in 1864 by former ferry-master GS Smith and remained in the Sutherland-Smith family for several generations. A fortress-like castellated and towered wall surrounds the winery building (c. 1880). There are extensive cellars and what is believed to be the largest oak wine storage in Australia. In 1873, the winery won the first gold medal ever awarded to an Australian wine at the Vienna International Exhibition. There is also a winemaking museum, old winemaking machinery and the original Chinese dormitory has been restored. *8 km NW, 1 km E of Wahgunyah. Open daily. (02) 6033 1922.*
Campbells Winery Fascinating vintage wine-making equipment. *Murray Valley Hwy. Open daily. (02) 6032 9458.*
Fairfield Vineyard Established by George Francis Morris in 1859. Some

of the original equipment is still used to make wine today. The superb Italian Victorian mansion with a strong Italian influence and almost equally impressive cellar building (1889) have been restored. *13 km E on Murray Valley Hwy. Open Mon.–Sat. Mansion open on special occasions. (02) 6032 9381.*
Gehrig Estate Winery is the oldest continuously operating winery in the State, established in 1858. Fifth-generation Brian Gehrig is the winemaker. The distinctive Barnawartha House (1870) features a three-storey belltower. *25 km SE on Murray Valley Hwy. Open daily. (02) 6026 7296.*
Mount Prior Vineyards & Cellars Established in 1874, overlooking the Murray River. The handsome red-brick Victorian homestead has accommodation and a grand restaurant. *14 km NE, Gooramadda Rd then Howlong Rd. Open daily. (02) 6026 5591.*
🛈 *Cnr Drummond & Main sts; (02) 6032 9166.*
See also Beechworth, Chiltern, Yarrawonga

ST ARNAUD   Map ref. 315 L9

An old gold-mining town, St Arnaud retains a solid, Victorian-era character, especially in its main streetscape, Napier St, which is classified by the National Trust. Mining remained important to the town for many years, but unlike many gold towns, St Arnaud also developed as a centre for the agricultural community. By the time gold supplies faded, the town was well established and continued to prosper quietly.
OF INTEREST A wealth of historic buildings including several balconied, two-storied hotels, with lavish iron lacework. Don't miss the original police lock-up (1862). The Historical Society Museum in St Arnaud's first fire station (1883) is being refurbished. The old post office (1866) now a B&B, with a gallery and tea rooms, is in Napier St. *Open daily.* Ⓢ The elegant botanic gardens, Queen Mary Gardens (1884), contain an ornamental lake, once a watering hole used by bullock teams. *Open daily.*
IN THE AREA The vast Tottington Woolshed (1840s), an outstanding vertical-slab woolshed, weathered to silver grey and dappled with light

from magnificent overhanging gums. On private property but visible from the road. *24 km s on Stawell Rd. Not open for inspection.*

🄸 *Old Post Office, 2 Napier St; (03) 5495 2313.*

SALE
Map ref. 311 N6

Sale began life as a maritime port for the agricultural hinterland, but progressed rapidly after the gold strike in **Omeo** in 1851, being located on the busy goldfields route from **Port Albert**, and at the head of the railway line to Melbourne.

OF INTEREST The historic swing bridge (1883), which pivoted on a central pier to allow ships to pass either side. In its heyday, it opened up to 20 times a day to allow paddle-steamers into the port. *5 km N on Sth Gippsland Hwy.* Our Lady of Sion Convent (1892–1901) a stately three-storey, Gothic Revival convent and chapel. *York St. Not open for inspection.* The Criterion Hotel (1865) is Gippsland's oldest hotel. The intricate iron lace-work verandah was added in the late 1800s. *Cnr York & MacAlister sts. Open daily.* A heritage trail brochure identifies Sale's architectural heritage.

🄸 *8 Foster St (Princes Hwy); (03) 5144 1108.* Website: www.sale3850.com

SMEATON
Map ref. 313 P2, 315 P13, 318 A12

Anderson's Mill The grand scale of Anderson's bluestone mill (1861) says much about the flourishing grain industry in this district in the 1800s. Located in a pretty valley, near the swift-flowing Birch Creek that once turned its magnificent water wheel, the mill, its chimney and associated buildings comprise a fascinating and extensive 19th-century industrial complex. Designed by Scotsman John Anderson and owned and operated by the Anderson family for its entire working life, almost 100 years. Visitors are welcome to use the grounds at any time. *2.5 km SE, off Daylesford Rd. Open Sun. afternoons. Tours available.* Ⓢ *(donation). 13 1963.*

🄸 *Vincent St, Daylesford; (03) 5348 1339.*

See also Clunes, Creswick, Daylesford, Hepburn Springs

Coolart Homestead, Somers

SOMERS
Map ref. 310 D8

Coolart Homestead & Reserve A late-Victorian mansion (1890s), earlier farmhouse and outbuildings on a property first taken up by Alfred Meyrick in 1840. The name Coolart is from the Aboriginal word for 'sandy point'. The mansion was built by the Grimwade family. Period photos capture the Grimwades' prosperous and refined lifestyle here early last century. Outbuildings, such as the smokehouse and buttery, are of handmade brick. The property contains an extensive waterbird lagoon, ibis rookery and observation hides. *Lord Somers Rd. Open daily.* Ⓢ *(03) 5983 1333.*

SORRENTO
Map ref. 310 B8

In 1803, Sorrento was the site of the first, unsuccessful attempt at colonisation in Victoria, led by Lt-Col. David Collins. The town has been a holiday resort since the 1870s, when steam ships plied between here and **Queenscliff**, on the other side of the bay. In the 1890s, steam trams and a horse tram ran from the pier to the back beach. Most of the town's historic buildings use the pale, local limestone.

First Settlement Site The graves of some of Collins's settlement party are in a wooded grove overlooking Sullivan Bay. There are signs of the settlement and also of Aboriginal occupation. The first recorded European birth, marriage and death took place here. *Point Nepean Rd. Open Sat.–Sun., pub hols & Vic. school hols.* Ⓢ *(donation). (03) 5986 8987 or 13 1963.*

Nepean Historical Society Museum & Heritage Gallery, housed in the former mechanics institute (1876–77) is an excellent local museum. A tour includes access to Watts Cottage, a tiny 1869 wattle-and-daub cottage. *Cnr Melbourne & Ocean Beach rds. Open Sat.–Sun. afternoons, pub hols & school hols.* Ⓢ *(03) 5984 0255.*

IN THE AREA The unusual and romantic Gothic Revival bluestone homestead, Heronswood (1871) at Dromana, overlooks Port Phillip. Now part of a nursery and garden club. The cottage gardens are magnificent. *Latrobe Pde, Dromana. Gardens open Mon.–Fri. House open twice a year; once in Feb. & on Melbourne Cup Day, Nov. (03) 5987 1877. See also Cape Schanck, Mount Martha, Portsea, Somers*

🄸 *St Albans Way (near Sorrento Aquarium); (03) 5984 5678.* Website: www.travelbook.com.au

STAWELL
Map ref. 315 J11

Stawell is another Victorian town that owes its existence to gold, discovered here in 1853 on what was part of the Concongella sheep run. The alluvial gold finds, spectacular but short-lived, were replaced by quartz reef mining, which lasted for 60 years. In recent years, however, there has been

Bunjil's Shelter, Stawell

a resurgence and Victoria's largest-producing gold mine is now in Stawell. The famous Stawell Gift, a foot race, was first raced in 1878, to entertain the local miners.

Central Park The Stawell Gift has been raced at this venue since 1898 and the Hall of Fame located here has memorabilia and items related to the race's 120-year history. There's a splendid Victorian grandstand, still in use. *Lower Main St. Park open at all times. Hall of Fame open daily.* Ⓢ *(03) 5358 1326.*

Also of interest Pleasant Creek Courthouse Museum (1860), contains historic photos (offering a wonderful glimpse of Stawell's early days), 1800s costumes and gold-rush relics. *Western Hwy. Open Wed.–Thurs., Sun. (03) 5358 2784.* The former station (1877) is now the Railway Station Gallery. *Open Thurs.–Sun. and pub hols. (03) 5358 2330.* Be sure to wait at the town hall (1872), Main St, to see the sculpture of two bronze gold diggers at work, which appears in the clock tower on the hour. The handsome, two-storey post office (1874–75) is also in Main St. The slender spire of St Matthew's Church (1868) dominates the town's skyline. *Scallan St. Open daily.* Stawell is definitely worth exploring on foot – fine churches, public buildings and gracious and modest private residences line the wide streets. Visitor Information is in the former shire office (1866).

In the area Bunjil's Shelter, a cave containing a rare rock painting of Bunjil, an important Aboriginal spirit figure. Archaeologists estimate the area was in use 5000 years ago. *11 km s, signposted on the Pomonal Rd, then a 45-minute walk to the site in the Black Ranges.*

🛈 *50–52 Western Hwy; (03) 5358 2314, freecall 1800 246 880.* Website: www. ngshire.vic.gov.au
See also Ararat, Halls Gap, St Arnaud

STEIGLITZ   Map ref. 313 Q5

Steiglitz Historic Park Contains intriguing remnants of a major gold centre that flourished from the 1850s–70s, but dwindled by 1900, then gradually faded to almost nothing. The red-brick courthouse (1875), the town's second, is now a park information centre. A self-guided walk starts from there. Explore the remains of streets, buildings such as the old school, timber churches, and signs of mining activity, surrounded by bushland and seasonal wildflowers. *Adjoins Brisbane Ranges NP. Park open at all times. Courthouse open Sun. & pub hols. Guided tours by appt. (03) 5284 1230 or 13 1963.*

🛈 *Old Courthouse, Stawell St; (03) 5284 1230 (open Sun., pub hols only).*

SUNBURY   Map ref. 310 B2, 318 E13

Emu Bottom Homestead Believed to be the oldest homestead in Victoria, a low-slung vernacular stone building with shingled roof and skillion verandahs on sapling posts, begun by pioneer George Evans in 1836. Post-and-rail fences and various outbuildings (some reconstructed) contribute to its colonial appearance. The homestead is now a reception centre. Sunday luncheons are served in the woolshed (1854), which was built on the property Runnymede near Hamilton by Chinese on the way to the goldfields, and moved to the homestead in 1970. *Racecourse Rd. Open for country-style lunches on Sun. Bookings essential. (03) 9744 1222.*

Rupertswood A magnificent mansion with a tall tower culminating in a steep mansard roof, the whole building lavishly decorated with Gothic detailing. Built 1874–76 for pastoralist Sir William Clark at a cost of £25,000. Rupertswood reverberated for many years with the sound of extravagant house parties, balls and hunt's meets. The house once had its own railway siding. Extensive gardens, an elaborate lodge and magnificent gates. It is also the birthplace of cricket's famous 'Ashes'. Now a reception centre. *Macedon St. Open once a year. Also limited tours for groups, bookings essential.* Ⓢ *(03) 9744 2467.*

In the area Vines were planted in the district as early as the 1860s and several vineyards have historic links. Craiglee Vineyard is in a substantial bluestone building (1868) which was part of the original winery established on the banks of Jackson's Creek in 1863. *Sunbury Rd. Open Sun. (03) 9744 4489.* Opposite is Goona Warra Winery where the vineyard was set up in 1863 by an early state premier. The new vineyard uses the original bluestone rubble cottage (1860s). *Sunbury Rd. Open daily & for Sun. lunch. (03) 9740 7766.* Andraos Brothers' Olde Winilba Vineyard was Sunbury's first vineyard, established in the early 1860s, and re-established in 1989. The early, bluestone winery is again in use. *Open Sat.–Sun. & pub hols. 150 Vineyard Road (03) 9740 9703.*

🛈 *43 Macedon St; (03) 9744 2291.*

SWAN HILL   Map ref. 298 H11, 317 N11

Swan Hill, on the banks of the Murray, was a busy river port in the 1800s. Explorer Major Thomas Mitchell named the town after a restless night here in 1836, disturbed by a flock of noisy swans. The imposing lift-span bridge (1896), crossing into NSW, was built to allow paddle-steamers through.

Swan Hill Pioneer Settlement An evocative re-creation of a late 19th-century river port (1860s–90s) built around the grand old paddle-steamer PS *Gem* (1876) on the banks of the Little Murray. Vernacular buildings, including a mallee-root stable, drop-log cabin and portable iron house. Demonstrations of traditional skills and crafts create the ambience of a small pioneer town. There are nightly 'sound and light' tours and daily cruises aboard the PS *Pyap* to the historic Murray Downs Homestead (1840s). *Horseshoe Bend. Open daily.* $ *(03) 5032 1093.*

Murray Downs Homestead Part of the area's first pastoral station, established 1839, with fortress-like, Italianate homestead (c. 1866), complete with original furnishings and surrounded by a magnificent formal English garden. In its heyday there was a bakery and blacksmith and regular church services on the property. Cottages provide accommodation, afternoon teas available. *Moulamein Hwy, 1.5 km from Swan Hill. Open daily except Fri. Closed part of Dec. & Feb. Ring before travelling to the homestead.* $ *(03) 5032 1225.*

ALSO OF INTEREST The Burke and Wills tree, Curlewis St, a massive Moreton Bay fig planted before the ill-fated explorers set off from here for the Gulf of Carpentaria, in 1860.

IN THE AREA Tyntynder Homestead built on an isolated Murray Valley station of 777 sq km in 1846 by Andrew and Peter Beveridge. Originally a pine log cabin with hides for doors, but later veneered with handmade bricks and a shingle roof was added. At one time, 34 000 sheep grazed the scrubby land and wool, tallow and hides were loaded on steamers on the river frontage. There are original squatter furnishings and a museum. Now owned by the local Aboriginal community whose guided tours also explain their history in the area. *16 km N, Murray Valley Hwy, Beverford. Open Vic. school & pub hols or by appt.* $ *(03) 5037 6380 or (03) 5030 2754.* At Lake Boga is the Flying Boat Museum in a secret communications bunker on the original RAAF Depot site, where flying boats were serviced during World War II. *16 km S, Murray Valley Hwy. Open daily.* $ *(03) 5037 2850.*

[i] *306 Campbell St; (03) 5032 3033, freecall 1800 625 373.*

TABILK

Map ref. 318 G9

Tahbilk Winery & Vineyard Idyllically sited on the banks of the Goulburn River, Chateau Tahbilk is one of Australia's oldest wineries. An Englishman, JP Bear, planted the first vines here in 1860. Historic buildings include the rustic stone and timber winery with its unusual tiered belfry. Huge timber vats and early winemaking equipment can be seen in the underground cellars (1860, extended 1875). In 1890 phylloxera destroyed most of the vines, but a few original, gnarled shiraz plantings remain. With shady mulberry trees, the grounds are perfect for a picnic. *Off Goulburn Valley Hwy, 8 km SW of Nagambie. Open daily. (03) 5794 2555.*

[i] *145 High St, Nagambie; (03) 5794 2647, freecall 1800 444 647.* Website: mcmedia.com.au/nagambie

WALHALLA

Map ref. 311 K5

This tiny town is tucked away in a deep valley in south-east Gippsland. Relics preserved from its gold-boom days include the Long Tunnel mine, once Victoria's richest single gold mine, which yielded 13.7 tonnes of gold between 1865 and 1991. Walhalla's heyday was 1880–95, but the gold petered out, the main mines closed, and the population dwindled to almost nothing. Yet Walhalla's isolation has preserved signs of its past and its remarkably strong community character.

OF INTEREST At Long Tunnel Extended Gold Mine, the shaft is 1 km deep, and the tunnel extends 8.5 km. *Main Rd. Open most weekdays, Sat.–Sun. & pub hols for tours. (03) 5165 6242.* Post and Telegraph Office Museum has remarkable photos of the town's golden days. *Main Rd. Open daily. Freecall 1800 621 409.*

ALSO OF INTEREST The Fire Station (1901), straddling Stringer's Creek, houses restored fire equipment. *Open daily.* $ *(donation).* Verandahed shops in the crooked 'wild west' main street have been restored and house art and craft shops. The Old Bakery (1865) is the town's oldest remaining building. Windsor House (1878), Walhalla's only brick dwelling, built by J Gloz using 90 000 handmade bricks, has been restored. *Not open for inspection.* Don't miss the cricket ground, carved from the top of a mountain, reached by a steep 200-m climb. The band rotunda is a quaint Victorian structure (1896), where the Mountaineer Brass Band once entertained the locals. The cemetery, surveyed in 1872, is studded with huge, sombre pines. Some graves are dug vertically into the steep slope. Walhalla's narrow-gauge railway has

Walhalla

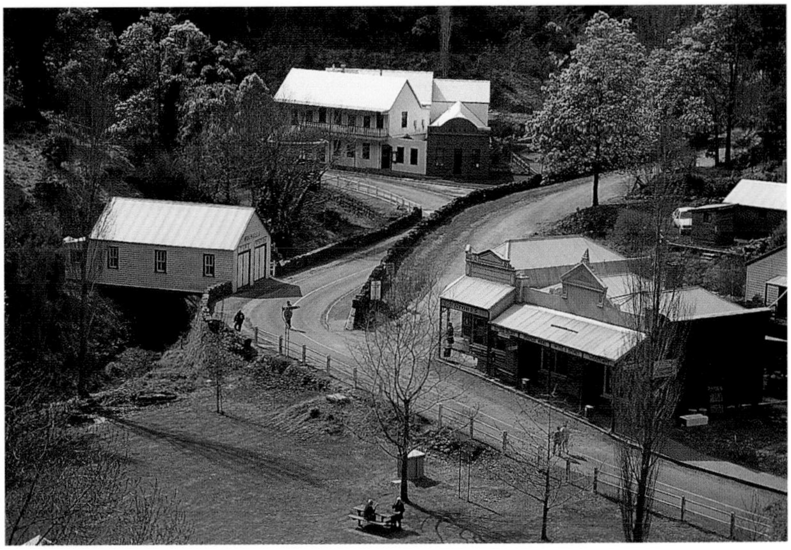

been reconstructed for special trips and again clings to its narrow ledge as it winds its way up the steep Stringer's Creek Gorge. *Open Sat.–Sun. & pub hols.* $ *(03) 9513 3669.*

IN THE AREA Interesting old town sites dot the region – Red Jacket, Jericho and Poverty Point, to name a few.

🏛 *Southside Central, Princes Hwy, Traralgon; (03) 5174 3199, freecall 1800 621 409.*

See also Bairnsdale, Moe

WANGARATTA Map ref. 319 M6

In 1836 George Faithfull established Wangaratta pastoral station (the name means 'where the cormorant sits') near the Ovens River. About 20 years later, the town of Wangaratta grew up nearby, at the junction of the Ovens and King rivers, the only crossing en route to the lucrative Ovens goldfields.

OF INTEREST St Patrick's Catholic Church, cnr Ford & Murphy sts, the first stage (1865–71) designed by architect William Wardell (who also designed St Patrick's Cathedral in Melbourne). The former ANZ Bank (1875), Reid St, with its Doric porch, is one of Wangaratta's oldest buildings (now offices, not open for inspection). The grave of notorious bushranger Daniel 'Mad Dog' Morgan is in the Wangaratta Cemetery. *Tone Rd (Hume Hwy).*

IN THE AREA Wangaratta Airworld Aviation Museum has an impressive display of vintage aircraft, mostly maintained in flying order. *Wangaratta Airport, Greta Rd. Open daily.* $ *(03) 5721 8788.* The tiny old gold town of Eldorado, where gold was still being dredged up until the 1950s. A small museum has a wealth of local history. *20 km NE. Open Sun., pub & school hols.* $ *(03) 5725 1789.*

🏛 *Cnr Tone Rd and Handley St; (03) 5721 5711.*

See also Beechworth, Chiltern, Glenrowan, Yackandandah

WARRACKNABEAL Map ref. 314 H6

Founded on the banks of the Yarriambiack Creek in the 1860s, Warracknabeal is closely associated with the development of the golden Wimmera wheatlands. The name is from an Aboriginal word meaning 'place of the big red gums shading the watercourse'.

Wheatlands Agricultural Museum has a unique collection of agricultural machinery, including a replica of the log smithy in which Hugh McKay built the revolutionary horse-drawn stripper harvester. *Henty Hwy. Open daily. (03) 5398 1901.*

ALSO OF INTEREST The Historical Centre, housed in the residence of the former State Savings Bank (1909) contains a pharmaceutical collection from Woolcott's Pharmacy, which ran from 1885–1975, plus 19th-century furnishings and household items.

Scott St. Open Sun.–Fri. afternoons. (03) 5398 1182 or (03) 5390 4236. The sturdy log lock-up (1872), Devereux St; the Commercial Hotel (1870, extended 1891) a typical late-Victorian pub with iron lacework, and Warracknabeal Hotel (c. 1890) with Art Nouveau leadlight framing the arched doorway, both Scott St, both still open for business.

🏛 *Scott St; (03) 5398 1632.*

WARRNAMBOOL Map ref. 312 I9

In the 1840s, Warrnambool, on the State's south-western coast, was a whaling and sealing port. More than 100 ships have been wrecked along this sometimes treacherous coast. Today the city is a flourishing coastal resort with a fine legacy of 19th-century provincial architecture.

Flagstaff Hill Maritime Village Re-created maritime village depicting port life from around 1850–1900, in the days of sailing ships. Includes authentic sailing vessels, the 1854 Middle Island lighthouse (moved here in 1871 from offshore), and a shipwreck museum. Stella Maris Tearooms has a colonial atmosphere; there's a ship's chandler, a sailmaker and rigger's loft, shipwrights at work using traditional skills and more. The fortifications and cannon date from 1887, when Australians feared a Russian invasion. *Merri St. Open daily. Tours available.* $ *(03) 5564 7841.*

ALSO OF INTEREST The picturesque, century-old Proudfoot's Boathouse, on the Hopkins River, is now a restaurant and reception centre. *Open daily. 2 Simpson St. (03) 5561 5055.* Wollaston Bridge (1890), Wollaston Rd, classified by the National Trust, uses suspension cables from Melbourne's early cable trams. The particularly fine Botanic Gardens, designed by William Guilfoyle in 1879, are worth exploring. *Cnr Cockman & Queen sts. Open daily.* History House, in a small stone cottage (1876) exhibits photographs, early records of the town and district. *Gilles St. Open 1st Sun. of each month & Mon. afternoons.* $ *(03) 5562 6940.* Pick up a heritage walk brochure from Visitor Information. Liebig, Timor and Fairy streets are most notable and part of a heritage conservation area.

IN THE AREA Thunder Point area has layers of Aboriginal midden deposits,

Proudfoot's Boathouse, Warrnambool

revealing shells, seeds and bone fragments, confirming that indigenous people were living in this coastal area at least 4000 years ago. *2 km SW.* Nearby is the possible site of the Mahogany Ship, one of more than a hundred ships wrecked 80 km east or west of Warrnambool in the 1800s. The ship was sighted in 1836 but by 1880 had 'vanished'. Mystery and legend surround its origins and whereabouts and both amateur and more serious searches continue. Some historians believe if it was recovered it would prove that this coast was first sighted by the Portuguese in 1522. *10 km W, off Princes Hwy.*
🛈 *600 Raglan Pde; (03) 5564 7837.*

Barwon Park, Winchelsea

WEDDERBURN   Map ref. 315 N7

This small country town was once one of the country's richest surface goldfields. A local shepherd stumbled on the first find in 1852 and valuable nuggets are still found in and around the town. (In 1980 a nugget weighing an astonishing 27.2 kg, reputedly sold for US$1 million, was found close by.)

OF INTEREST The Coach House Museum is in an old store (1864) furnished and stocked as it might have been around 1910. Historic photos, memorabilia, a blacksmith's display and an outbuilding housing carts and buggies. *51 High St. Open Tues.–Sun.* 💲 *(03) 5494 3342.* In High St: the old Methodist (now Uniting) Church with its modest tower (1866); the Australasia bank building (1875); the old Commercial Hotel (1898) and former Royal Hotel (1867). In Wilson St: the sandstone Holy Trinity Anglican Church (1866), the Presbyterian Church (1868) and Church of Christ (1872).

IN THE AREA Old ore-crushing battery in the Hard Hill Tourist Area. *W off the hwy at Tantalla St, then signposted.* Christmas Reef Gold Mine, a small-scale, working goldmine, provides an opportunity to see mining at first hand. The tunnels here were blasted and dug by hand. *4 km E, on Boort Rd. Open daily.* 💲 *(03) 5494 3620 (AH).* At Camp Kooyoora, Aboriginal heritage trail walks point out rock shelters, canoe trees and wells. Cabins available. *14 km SE off Calder Hwy.* 💲 *(03) 5438 3057 (for guided tours).*

🛈 *Wedderburn Shire Offices, High St; (03) 5494 1200.*

WINCHELSEA   Map ref. 313 P8

Winchelsea grew up in the 1840s on the banks of the Barwon River, around the Barwon Hotel, a popular stop for coaches and wagons en route from the port of **Geelong** to the Western District pastoral stations.

Barwon Park This 42-room bluestone mansion looms up suddenly in the flat landscape, bereft of formal gardens or shady trees. The house was conceived and built on a grand scale for pastoralist Thomas Austin, his wife and 11 children in 1869. It features a delicate lacework portico and a gracious sweep of verandah. At the heart of the building is a magnificent oak and cedar staircase. Thomas Austin's best-known import was 10 pairs of rabbits, which flourished with abandon – the district's many kilometres of stone fences testify to the damaging results. *Inverleigh Rd, off Princes Hwy. Open Wed. & Sun. afternoons.* 💲 *(03) 5267 2209 or (03) 5267 2230. NT.*

ALSO OF INTEREST Barwon Bridge, a triple-arched bluestone bridge, officially opened in 1867 by Prince Alfred, Duke of Edinburgh.
🛈 *Old Shire Art Gallery, Princes Hwy; (03) 5267 2769.*

WONTHAGGI   Map ref. 310 G10

Coal was essential for industry and transport in the 19th and early 20th centuries. Following a miners' strike

in NSW in 1909, the mine at Wonthaggi stepped up production. More than 750 miners and other workers lived in tents before permanent buildings were erected. Almost 17 million tonnes of black coal was extracted over 59 years. The last mine closed in 1968.

State Coal Mine There are seven historic mine sites including tunnels, brick power houses, remnants of machinery, the remains of stables for pit ponies and buildings. Underground tours of mine shafts (walk down and return by coal skip to the surface), led by a former miner, reveal how tough working conditions were. It's no surprise many lives were lost. There's also a small museum. *Garden St. Open daily.* 💲 *(03) 5672 3053 or 13 1963.*
🛈 *Watts St; (03) 5672 2484.*

WOODEND   Map ref. 310 A1, 313 R2, 318 D12

This small historic town on the Calder Freeway was a staging post en route to and from the goldfields, and a popular hangout for bushrangers.

IN THE AREA 8 km N (signposted), on the edge of the 'Black Forest', is the famous Hanging Rock, the setting for the book and film *Picnic at Hanging Rock*. Rising abruptly from the undulating landscape, the volcanic formation has been the backdrop to picnics since the 1880s. Hanging Rock is a sacred site of the Wurrundjeri Aboriginal tribe. Don't miss the magnificent five-arched bluestone viaduct (1859) outside Malmsbury (24 km N) or the town's picturesque botanical gardens (1865), on the edge of the Coliban River.

ℹ *High St; (03) 5427 2033.* Website: www.macedon-ranges.vic. gov.au

YACKANDANDAH
Map ref. 319 P5, 320 B3

A small but impressive survivor of the gold rush, nestled in a valley, with spreading shade trees and a picturesque main streetscape of verandahed shops and well-preserved public buildings. The district was first settled about 1837, and Yackandandah grew up at the heart of the central north-east goldfields country. Many buildings and the main part of the town are classified by the National Trust.

OF INTEREST Stroll along the curved High St to see the primary school, built in 1862 but extended twice (not open for inspection); the double-fronted post office (1863), still in business; the former Athenaeum (1878) originally 'the social and intellectual centre of town' with its reading rooms and its serious Greek Revival facade (now Visitor Information); and the Historical Society Museum in the former Bank of Victoria (1860), with period furnishings. *High St. Open Sun. & daily in Vic. school hols. Tours available.* Ⓢ *(02) 6027 1320.* Many shops and cafes are in restored buildings. Stop at the Yackandandah Bakery for bread from the old wood-fired Scotch oven. The handsome single-arched bluestone bridge (1859–60), Wodonga Rd, was built when the town was on the main Sydney-to-Melbourne route.

IN THE AREA Cemetery, established 1859, has beautifully worked timber gates, and Chinese graves. Indigo Valley, with its rushing streams and old diggings, still yields the occasional speck of gold to the diligent or just plain lucky.

ℹ *The Athenaeum, High St; (02) 6027 1988.*

YARRA GLEN
Map ref. 310 E3

This small town, at the centre of one of the state's earliest settled districts, is surrounded by the magnificent vineyards and many wineries of the Yarra Valley. There's a rich history of

Gulf Station, Yarra Glen

vine growing and winemaking here. The first grapes were planted in the valley in 1838 and the wine industry boomed in the 1800s. There's been a resurgence of that tradition in the last few decades.

Gulf Station A unique complex of weathered, rustic timber buildings just north of Yarra Glen, established by Scottish pastoralist William Bell in the 1850s. The homestead (1860s–early 1900s) is joined by a covered walkway to the original slab house, and there are several rudimentary timber buildings with adzed slabs, split palings and peeled-log posts. Original farm implements, household items and farm animals depict 19th-century farm life. The cottage garden is fragrant with authentic plants from the period. Special historical 'theme' days bring Gulf Station to life. *Melba Hwy. Open Wed.–Sun. & pub hols. Tours available.* Ⓢ *(03) 9730 1286. NT.*

ALSO OF INTEREST At Coldstream, prominently positioned but hidden behind a massive cypress hedge, is Coombe Cottage, an elegant, spacious and light country house created by Dame Nellie Melba. Melba bought the house in 1909 for herself and the house remains in the family. The magnificent rambling garden of more than 2 ha was designed by William Guilfoyle. *Melba & Maroondah hwys junction. Open once a year. Contact Museum of Lilydale.* Ⓢ *(03) 9739 7230.* Dominating the town is the truly grand Yarra Glen Grand hotel (1888), a towered and balconied building, restored to its Victorian-era

splendour. *19 Bell St. Open daily. (03) 9730 1230.* Not far from town is Chateau Yering Historic House (1854), a luxurious private hotel and restaurant, where an original winery building (c. 1850) is also open as a cellar bar and restaurant. *Melba Hwy. Open daily. (03) 9237 3333.*

IN THE AREA At Wandin, Mont De Lacey, an historic home of handmade bricks (1882) with an outdoor split-slab timber kitchen (1880s), museum, St Mary's Chapel (1920s), formal garden, and a tearoom in the original 1920s milking shed. *Wellington Rd, Wandin Nth. Open Wed.–Sun. & pub hols. (03) 5964 2088.*

ℹ *Old Courthouse, Harker St, Healesville; (03) 5962 2600.*

YARRAWONGA
Map ref. 299 N13, 319 K3

IN THE AREA Burramine homestead, established 1842 by Elizabeth Hume, sister-in-law of the explorer Hamilton Hume, who overlanded with her family from Gunning, NSW. One of the country's earliest and most intact colonial homesteads, it is a house of considerable charm, built of handmade bricks, with walls up to 50 cm thick, and a narrow verandah. The design was originally intended for use in India. A windowless room at the centre of the house was to serve as a 'fortress'. The garden, overlooking the river flats, is particularly pretty. Devonshire teas are served. *15 km w on Murray Valley Hwy, Burramine. Open Thurs.–Mon.* Ⓢ *(03) 5748 4321.*

ℹ *Irvine Pde; (03) 5744 1989.*

HISTORIC HIGHLIGHTS

Ovens Goldfield Hospital facade, Beechworth

Many of Victoria's historic towns grew up in the heady days of the nineteenth-century gold boom. Some have gone on to become major regional cities, whilst others provide a glimpse into the past, their winding main streets and buildings having scarcely changed in more than a century. But there are other aspects of Victoria's history to explore – from the wonderful old riverport town of Echuca, to the seaport of Portland, site of Victoria's first permanent European settlement.

BALLARAT

Many Victorian towns grew from gold, but few so fast or so grand as Ballarat. Today, Ballarat is the State's largest inland city. Although gold, discovered in 1851, put Ballarat on the map, it was the miners' rebellion at the Eureka Stockade that gave Ballarat its special place in our history. In 1871, when Ballarat was declared a city, the population numbered 47 000, and the census recorded 56 churches, 11 banks, and a thirst-slaking 477 hotels. Ballarat retains a fine legacy of buildings from its gold boom days.

Ballarat Visitor Information Centre
39 Sturt St
Website: (03) 5320 5741, freecall 1800 648 450

EUREKA STOCKADE
In 1854, armed and defiant diggers led by Peter Lalor erected a stockade and protested against the harsh licence system, the military's brutal tactics and the miners' lack of political representation. Twenty-four miners and four soldiers were killed, but the Melbourne jury would not convict those arrested. The government quickly reformed its policy, reducing fees and extending the franchise to miners.

Lydiard St
Named after the first police magistrate in Ballarat, Lydiard St possesses a wealth of Victorian goldfields architecture. At the old Ballarat Gaol (1856–62), notorious bushranger Capt. Starlight spent time. The dignified facades of the former banks: Bank of NSW (1862), the Colonial Bank (1860), Bank of Australasia (1864), and National Bank (1862) all designed by architect Leonard Terry. The former Mining Exchange (1888) features an ornate curved verandah. Grand, three-storey Reids' Coffee Palace (1886), now Tawana Lodge. *Not open for inspection.*

Ballarat Fine Art Gallery
Victoria's first provincial art gallery (1884) and one of its finest, in an 1887 neo-Classical building. The original Eureka flag hangs here.
40 Lydiard St. Open daily.
ⓢ *(03) 5331 5622.*

Craig's Royal Hotel
'The pride of Ballarat' – a marvellous Italianate structure, begun in 1859 by Walter Craig on the site of Ballarat's first hotel, has lodged royalty and rogues. Handsomely restored.
10 Lydiard St Sth. Open daily.
(03) 5331 1377.

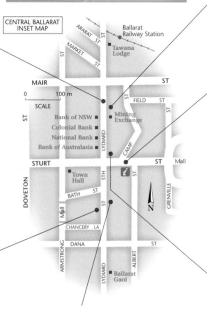

Titanic Memorial Bandstand
Erected in 1915 by Ballarat bandsmen 'in memory of the bandsmen of the *Titanic*' (who played valiantly as the ship sank).
Near cnr Sturt & Lydiard sts.

Old Post Office
Ballarat's first post office was 'a tattered tent, open at both ends' and serviced 20 000 diggers. This grand Italianate edifice was built 1863–64, and the five-storey clock tower was added in 1885. Now Ballarat University's performing arts centre.
Cnr Lydiard & Sturt sts.

Her Majesty's Theatre
The oldest building used continuously as a theatre in Australia, opened in 1875. Gladys Moncrieff, Nellie Melba and Roy Rene have all graced its stage. A magnificent venue, with a rich theatrical history, lovingly restored.
17 Lydiard St Sth. (03) 5333 5800.

Adam Lindsay Gordon's Cottage

Poet Gordon's neat timber cottage, originally behind Craig's Hotel. Now an art and craft gallery. *Wendouree Pde. Open daily Oct.–April; Sat.–Sun. May–Sept.* (03) 5320 7444.

Ballarat Botanical Gardens

The gardens include a prefabricated statuary pavilion (1887) with glass walls and an octagonal lantern. The centrepiece is the beautiful Italian marble *Flight from Pompeii*. *Wendouree Pde. Open daily.* (03) 5320 7444.

Montrose Cottage

One of the goldfields' first masonry cottages (1856), furnished with authentic period pieces. *111 Eureka St. Open daily.* Ⓢ (03) 5332 2554.

Eureka Stockade Centre

State-of-the-art technology brings the historic Eureka rebellion to life in this sleek new museum, on the site of the battle. *Eureka St. Open daily.* Ⓢ (03) 5333 1854.

Gold Museum

The history of gold, its 'power and magic'. A valuable collection, cleverly presented. *Bradshaw St (opp. Sovereign Hill). Open daily.* Ⓢ (03) 5331 1944.

Sovereign Hill

Meticulously researched and entertaining reconstruction of an 1850s gold town on the site of the old Sovereign Quartz Mining company. Walk along the winding streets or take a jerky ride on a horse-drawn carriage. Dine in the New York Bakery before embarking on a tour of the mine shafts or panning for gold. Visit the apothecary, watch a vaudeville show or the presses at work in the *Ballarat Times* office. A full day's excursion. There's also a dramatic nightly sound-and-light show 'Blood on the Southern Cross'. *Bradshaw St. Open daily.* Ⓢ (03) 5331 1944.

ALSO OF INTEREST

Explore Sturt St, with the Classical Revival town hall (1870–72) and St Patrick's Cathedral (1863), cnr Dawson St. The Eureka Trail, a 3.5-km trail linking historical sites, with interpretive signboards, starts from the former Post Office, cnr Lydiard & Sturt sts. *(03) 5333 1854.* Maps from Visitor Information. Golden City Paddle-steamer Cruise on Lake Wendouree aboard a 110-year-old paddle-steamer built 1885. *Open most Sat.–Sun. from Sept.–May.* Ⓢ *(03) 5333 7822.* Ballarat Tramway Museum: ride a 70-year-old vintage tram, and explore the museum and depot. *Botanical Gardens. Sat.–Sun., most pub & school hol afternoons.* Ⓢ *(03) 5334 1580.* Ballarat Aviation Museum features a large display, including a World War II German rocket. *Ballarat Airport, Sunraysia Hwy. Open Sat.–Sun. afternoons & pub hols.* Ⓢ *(03) 5339 5106.*

IN THE AREA

See Buninyong, Creswick, Smeaton

BEECHWORTH

Nestled in the rolling hills of the Ovens Valley at the foot of the Alps, Beechworth seems almost suspended in time. The wide streets are dappled with light from beautiful old trees and graced by early Victorian buildings, more than 30 of them classified by the National Trust. Gold was discovered near Spring Creek in 1852 and the rush was on. By 1866 the diggings had yielded more than 115 tonnes of gold, but the heydays and the drama were short lived and Beechworth settled down to the quiet existence it still enjoys today.

Beechworth Visitor Information Centre
Ford St
(03) 5728 3233

Toy horse and cart c.1860

Burke Memorial Museum
Named in honour of the ill-fated explorer, Capt. Robert O'Hara Burke, who was in charge of the local police 1854–58. The museum, added to the library (built 1857) in 1863, is one of the State's best regional museums, exhibiting natural history items from the 1860s, an Aboriginal collection (purchased in 1868), fascinating Chinese artifacts, Victorian-era children's toys, historic photos and more. Highly recommended.
Loch St. Open daily.
Ⓢ *(03) 5728 1420.*

Panel from Chinese temple c.186

Ovens Goldfield Hospital facade
A wonderful Classical facade (1854–57) in the local golden granite shows the optimism of the 1850s, but is all that remains of what was once considered the State's finest hospital. *Church St.*

Aboriginal shield c.1850

Star Hotel
The first Star Hotel on the site included a theatre, but saw plenty of real-life drama as well, in those heady gold days. The current 'Star' was erected in 1864. Shops now occupy the ground floor.
Ford St.

Tanswell's Commercial Hotel
At the peak of the gold rush, the district hummed with more than 50 000 people, and 61 hotels catered for the thirsty throng. The 1850s timber hostelry on this site was replaced in 1873 by Thomas Tanswell's more prestigious establishment. It's still in business.
Ford St. Open daily.
(03) 5728 1480.

Newtown Bridge
Spanning Spring Creek, this graceful stone bridge, erected by Scottish stonemasons in 1874, is close to the site of the district's first gold strike.

ALSO OF INTEREST
Beechworth is one of only two towns in Victoria classified by the National Trust as 'Notable' (Maldon is the other). There are several dignified bank buildings and fine churches, such as Christ Church (1858, extended 1864), cnr Ford & Church sts, and St Andrew's Uniting Church (1857), cnr Ford & Williams sts. Many historic buildings are now shops, cafes and B&Bs. The Old Priory (1886), a former convent, provides unusual accommodation and a reception centre. *8 Priory La. (03) 5728 1024.* Visitor Information, in the old Shire Hall (1888) has plenty of local knowledge.
Open daily.

BEECHWORTH'S ARCHITECTURE
Beechworth started as a tent town, but timber soon replaced canvas and was itself replaced by fine public buildings of honey-coloured granite, handsome shops and hotels. A separate town was laid out for the Chinese population.

Murray Breweries and Museum
The museum, in an 1865-brewery building, has horse-drawn carriages and historic brewing equipment, plus some old-fashioned beverages for sale.
29 Last St. Open daily. (03) 5728 1304.

Golden Horseshoe Monument
Commemorates the wildest day in Beechworth's history, in 1855, during the state's first parliamentary elections, when the diggers' candidate, Daniel Cameron, rode into town on a horse shod with gold, 'and free beer was the order of the day'.
Cnr Gorge & Sydney rds.

Beechworth Cemetery & Chinese Burning Towers
Twin ceremonial towers, an altar and small row of headstones are the sole legacy of the many Chinese who worked the Ovens goldfields.
Beechworth Cemetery, enter from Balaclava Rd. (03) 5728 3233.

Powder Magazine
Surrounded by a forbidding granite fence, this buttressed granite room (1859–60) was built to house the gunpowder and gelignite required for deep-shaft mining.
Skidmore Rd, Beechworth Historic Park. Open for group bookings by appt. $ *(03) 5726 8258. NT.*

Town Hall Gardens
Famous botanist Baron Ferdinand von Mueller donated trees when this formal public garden was established in 1875.
Williams St.

Beechworth Gaol (HM Training Prison)
The massive, pale granite walls of the prison twice held Ned Kelly. Built to last in 1859, with round sentry towers, it replaced a wooden stockade. The gaol is still operating.
Williams St. Not open for inspection.

Ned Kelly's Cell
The grim cell beneath the town hall where the legendary bushranger was detained after his conviction in 1880.
Ford St. Open daily.

Beechworth Historic Courthouse
Ned Kelly and other less famous bushrangers stood trial in this solid granite courthouse (1857). Now a museum with the original courthouse fittings.
94 Ford St. Open Sun.–Fri. $
(03) 5728 2721.

Post Office
A substantial Italianate building (1870) with clock-and-bell tower at the main intersection. In front stands an iron pedestal drinking fountain with distinctive lions' head spouts.
Cnr Ford & Camp sts.

IN THE AREA
BEECHWORTH HISTORIC PARK 5 km NW of town are 20 km of walking tracks within this park. Here you can explore old goldfields, such as Woolshed Falls, which yielded fabulous amounts of alluvial gold in the 1800s. *Off Sydney Rd. 13 1963.*
ELDORADO, a former gold town, is of note. *30 km NW.*
See also Chiltern, Rutherglen, Yackandandah

BENDIGO

Bendigo's exuberant high-Victorian buildings, with their mass of detail and richly encrusted facades, seem to embody all the aspirations and vast civic pride of the late nineteenth century. Gold was discovered here in 1851 and within a year more than 675 kg had been extracted. By the 1860s, poppet heads littered the landscape as miners tapped the incredibly rich quartz reefs. In 1871, with a population of 18 000, 'Sandhurst' – 'the great quartzopolis' – was declared a city. It was renamed Bendigo in 1891 and is today one of Victoria's most important provincial cities.

Bendigo Visitor Information Centre
Old Post Office, 51–67 Pall Mall
(03) 5444 4445
Website: www.bendigotourism.com

Alexandra Fountain
The focal point of Charing Cross is the Alexandra Fountain (c. 1881), with nymphs and seahorses, modelled from 20 tonnes of Harcourt granite.

Shamrock Hotel, c.1908

Sacred Heart Cathedral
A magnificent Gothic Revival church, begun in 1887, with the pale elegant spire finally added almost a century later, in 1977. The carved eagle lectern in the sanctuary was donated by gold millionaire George Lansell, who built the lavish mansion, Fortuna Villa. A small tour brochure is available at the church.
Wattle St. Open daily.
Ⓢ *(donation). (03) 5443 4400.*

CHINESE ON THE GOLDFIELDS

The Chinese played a significant role in goldfields life here as elsewhere in Victoria. Their foreign ways and industrious habits were feared, however, and they were forced to pay a special residence tax (£1 per annum) which financed government 'Protectors for the Chinese'. In 1854 there were 3000 'celestials' on the Bendigo diggings and in 1861 Cobb & Co. ran a coach service especially for Chinese between Bendigo and Guildford, where the largest Chinese camp was to be found.

Central Deborah Gold Mine
Bendigo's last deep-reef mine, sunk in 1909. Now fully restored, with the poppet head towering 20 m above ground, it is a constant reminder of Bendigo's beginnings. Visitors can plunge 30 storeys below ground in a miner's cage for a tour; pan for gold or inspect the old-time machinery.
76 Violet St. Open daily. Guided tours only.
Ⓢ *(03) 5443 8322.*

Golden Dragon Museum & Chinese Garden

Chinese memorabilia and an exhibition devoted to the role the Chinese have played in Bendigo's history, from the 1850s to today.

5–11 Bridge St. Open daily.
Ⓢ *(03) 5441 5044.*

Chinese Joss House

The 'Big Gold Mountain Temple' is a small, handmade brick and timber joss house (1860s), painted red, the traditional Chinese colour of strength. Inside, there are lavishly embroidered banners, commemorative tablets, early photographs of the temple and Chinese dignitaries.

Finn St, Emu Point. Open daily.
Ⓢ *(03) 5442 1685. NT.*

Bendigo Law Courts

Bendigo Art Gallery

One of Victoria's oldest provincial galleries has an outstanding collection including many early, lyrical paintings by colonial artist Louis Buvelot.

View St. Open daily. Tours available.
(03) 5443 4991.

Pall Mall

Bendigo's main boulevard has some of Australia's grandest high-Victorian buildings. The massive Italianate post office (1883–87) is now the Visitor Information (open daily). The law courts (1892–96) feature elaborate facades, an elegant French mansard roofscape and a splendid interior, renowned as one of the State's finest.

Not open for inspection.

Town Hall

In 1885, an eclectic design combining grand Italian Renaissance and a smattering of French influence transformed the modest 1859 town hall. Lavishly decorated inside and out.

Hargreaves St.

IN THE AREA

BENDIGO POTTERY, established by enterprising Scotsman DG Guthrie in 1858, produces handmade domestic pottery, fired in the original 1860s kilns. The brick stables have been converted into a function centre. An interesting museum houses old kilns and pottery equipment dating back to the 1870s.
6 km NE at Epsom. Open daily. Tours Mon.–Fri. Ⓢ *(for museum).*
(03) 5448 4104.

CAMPASPE RUN RURAL DISCOVERY CENTRE Focuses on the heritage of the grain and wool industries, early rural lifestyle and local Koorie culture. *47 km NE. Railway Pl. Elmore. Open daily. Tours available.* Ⓢ
(03) 5432 6646.

HARTLAND'S EUCALYPTUS DISTILLERY & HISTORIC FARM, established 1890 in the dense mallee scrub, is a traditional eucalyptus distillery. Visitors can see the distillery, the founders' old hut and relics of the district's early days.
Hartland's Rd, Huntly Nth. Open daily.
Ⓢ *(03) 5448 8227.*
See also Castlemaine, Maldon

Shamrock Hotel

The epitome of gold-boom architecture, four flamboyant storeys high. Built in 1897 at a cost of £25 000, it boasted 100 rooms 'with the electric light and the electric bell', marble staircases, mosaic floors and a pneumatic lift. Restored, the hotel offers gracious accommodation and a grand dining room. People are welcome to have a look around the hotel.

Cnr Pall Mall & Williamson St. Open daily.

ECHUCA

Memories of the riverboat days, when Echuca was Australia's greatest inland port, linger on in this busy town on the banks of the Murray and Campaspe rivers. Sometime-convict Henry Hopwood started an inn and ferry service here in the 1850s. By 1864 Echuca was the focus for a vast network linking three colonies by rail, road and river. But the railways replaced paddle-steamers, and by the 1890s Echuca's colourful days as a riverport were gone. Not forever, though, for restored paddle-steamers, the fascinating port and historic buildings today provide a living link with the past.

Echuca Visitor Information Centre
2 Heygarth St
(03) 5480 7555
Website: www.echucamoama.com

Echuca Historical Society Museum
River charts, documents and remarkable early photos, in the former police stables and lock-up (1867).
High St. Open daily.
$ *(03) 5480 1325.*

World in Wax Museum
There are 59 historic and famous wax characters in the museum including former Australian prime ministers John Gorton and Bob Hawke and opera singer Dame Nellie Melba.
High St. Open daily. $ *(03) 5482 3630.*

Star Hotel
Former pub, and later sly-grog shop, whose illicit drinkers escaped via an underground tunnel. Now a cafe and bar.
Murray Espl.

Shackell's Bonded Store
A vestige of the days when states were rivals and interstate duty was payable. The building (1859, extended 1865) now houses Sharp's Magic Movie House and Penny Arcade and is the booking office for the PS *Canberra*.
Murray Espl. Open daily.

ALSO OF INTEREST
Wander around the port area to soak up the ambience – there are shipwrights at work, blacksmiths and, of course, riverboat captains. In High St, plenty of shops and tearooms are in historic buildings. You can even take a horse-and-carriage tour. Pick up a walking tour brochure from Visitor Information so you don't miss sights such as the handsome courthouse (c. 1880) (above), one of Echuca's last 19th-century public buildings. *Dickson St (not open for inspection).*

Sharp's Magic Movie House & Penny Arcade
A nostalgic look at old-time entertainment – frivolous and fun with comedy classics, swashbuckling heroes, peepshows and penny arcade games. Rare archival footage of Echuca's history.
Murray Espl. Open daily. $ *(03) 5482 2361.*

PS *Canberra*

Take a boat trip back in time. PS *Canberra*, built at Goolwa in South Australia, has been cruising down the mighty Murray since 1912, first as a fishing vessel, then general cargo container. In more recent years it has carried over 1.5 million passengers. *Bookings at Shackell's Bonded Store, Murray Espl. Cruises daily.* Ⓢ *(03) 5482 2711.*

Bridge Hotel

Entrepreneur Henry Hopwood (right) built this fine two-storey hotel (1858) using bricks from his own brickworks, overlooking the approach to his pontoon on the Campaspe and his busy punt on the Murray – an excellent location ensuring a steady stream of thirsty patrons. Now a restaurant and cafe. *Hopwood Pl. Open daily (closed Mon.–Tues. in winter). (03) 5482 2247.*

Henry Hopwood

Paddle-steamers

PS *Adelaide* built in Echuca in 1866, PS *Pevensey* (1911) and PS *Alexander Arbuthnot* (1923) are genuine paddle-steamers that ply the river. *Echuca Wharf. Five cruises daily.* Ⓢ *(03) 5482 4248.*

Port of Echuca

At the heart of the port are the massive, creaking timbers of the red-gum wharf (1865–67) now weathered grey and a fraction of their former length (they once stretched more than a kilometre). They were built on three levels to accommodate the river's changing levels. Fascinating to step through the gates and see paddle-steamers chugging in to dock.

Echuca wharf, 1874

Steampacket Inn

Has been providing a bed for weary travellers since 1860. *Murray Espl. (03) 5428 3411.*

Iron Bridge

The historic bridge that crosses the Murray into Moama (Echuca's twin city in NSW) was erected in 1875.

Old Town Hall

Designed by WC Vahland, who later designed some of Bendigo's most grandiose edifices. This simple building (1868) is now the Echuca Library. *High St. Open daily. (03) 5482 1997.*

IN THE AREA

The BARMAH FOREST, with its 500-year-old river red gums and World Heritage-listed wetlands, is of special importance to the original inhabitants of this district, the Yorta Yorta people. The Dharnya Centre explores the Aboriginal history and culture of the area. *35 km NE. Barmah State Park & Forest. Open daily. (03) 5869 3302.* The town of ROCHESTER has some charming early buildings and a marked historic trail. *35 km S.*

GEELONG

Geelong stretches around Corio Bay – called Jillong by the traditional Aboriginal inhabitants, 'place of a sea bird over the white cliffs'. The first settlers came from Van Diemen's Land in 1836–37. Within two years the first inn licence was granted, a mail service to Melbourne had started, the *Geelong Advertiser* was founded and the first wool shipment was sent to London. Geelong became a major wool-selling centre and port. In the two years after gold was discovered near Ballarat in 1851, Geelong's population almost tripled. Private and public buildings and giant woolstores grew up around the port. Today Geelong is the largest provincial city in Victoria.

Geelong Visitor Information Centre
Geelong National Wool Museum, 26 Moorabool St
(03) 5222 2900, freecall 1800 620 888
Website: www.greatoceanrd.org.au

The Heights
A 14-room prefabricated timber house, imported from Germany in 1855. In the courtyard and garden a stone water-tower, hand water-pump, bluestone and timber stables, coach-house and dovecote recall a bygone era.
Aphrasia St, Newtown. Open Wed.–Sun. & pub hols. Ⓢ *(03) 5221 3510. NT.*

Steampacket Gardens
A favourite area for strolling since the 1800s, originally reclaimed from the sea, and in recent times extended. Just to the north-west is Cunningham Pier, and along the foreshore about 100 bollards have been painted to depict historic characters.

Geelong Art Gallery
Established in 1896, noted for its fine collection of colonial and Heidelberg School paintings, including Fred McCubbin's poignant *A Bush Burial* (1890), which has been in the collection since 1900.
Little Malop St. Open daily. (03) 5229 3645.

Customs House
One of the finest 19th-century public buildings in the State (1856), Classical in design, and faced in Barrabool sandstone. It overlooks the new Customs Park and the Bay.
Brougham St. Not open for inspection.

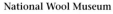

CENTRAL GEELONG
INSET MAP

Town Hall
Imposing, Classical design dominated by a lofty colonnaded portico. The oldest wing dates from 1856.
Cnr Gheringhap & Little Malop sts. Not open for inspection.

National Wool Museum
Award-winning museum, and an innovative look at the history, people and culture of the wool industry. Housed in the splendid old three-storey bluestone Dennys Lascelles woolstore (1872), which has been a landmark in Geelong for well over a century.
Cnr Moorabool & Brougham sts. Open daily. Tours available. Ⓢ *(03) 5227 0701.*

Woolstores
In Geelong's hectic wool-shipping heyday, Brougham and Corio sts were the commercial hub and several massive woolstores remain from that era.
Brougham & Corio sts.

Osborne House Naval & Maritime Museum

Osborne House (1858) is a conservative, two-storey bluestone townhouse with Doric columns and a bullnose verandah with superb bayside views. The rather grand stables at the rear house a maritime museum focusing on the port of Geelong.
Swinburne St, Nth Geelong. Open Mon., Wed., Fri.–Sun. Ⓢ *(03) 5277 2260.*

Corio Villa

A delightfully pretty, highly decorative house, the pinnacle of prefabricated domestic architecture in Australia, shipped from Scotland in 1855.
Eastern Beach. Private property. Not open for inspection.

Botanic Gardens

Established in 1851 near Limeburners Point. Wonderful vistas, formal paths, and some magnificent century-old trees shade the gardens. Don't miss the cabmen's shelter, built for waiting carriage-drivers, or the small historic glass house. The first customs house (1838) is in the gardens.
Eastern Park. Open daily. Tours available. (03) 5227 0387.

Old Geelong Gaol

Large, bleak and forbidding, this building was erected (1849–64) by convicts who slept in hulks on Corio Bay. In use as a prison until 1991, it provides a fascinating if grim picture of life behind bars. Tours explore the watchtowers, kitchen, the unheated, unsewered cells and a re-created gallows setting depicting the gaol's first hanging (1863).
Cnr Myers & Swanston sts. Open Sat.–Sun., pub & school hols. Ⓢ *(03) 5221 8292.*

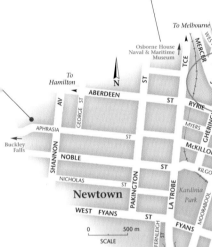

Barwon Grange

Built c. 1856 for merchant shipowner JP O'Brien, it is a picturesque house with steep gables, attic dormers and elegant bay windows. Meticulously restored and elegantly furnished. The gardens sweep down to the banks of the Barwon River.
Fernleigh St, Newtown. Open Wed., Sat.–Sun. from Sept.–Apr. Ⓢ *(03) 5221 3906. NT.*

Christ Church by ST Gill, 1850s

Christ Church

One of the state's oldest churches (1843–47), designed by distinguished architect Edmund Blacket, with a squat tower and imported stained-glass windows.
Cnr Moorabool & McKillop sts. Open daily. Tours available. (03) 5221 4507.

ALSO OF INTEREST

More than 100 buildings in Geelong are classified by the National Trust. Pick up walking tour brochures from Visitor Information. The 'Industrial Heritage Track' booklet details the bridges, aqueducts and historic industrial features, such as mills and tanneries, along the Barwon River. The huge old bluestone mill at Buckley Falls, Fyansford, is especially worth seeing.
MYSTERY AND HISTORY WALKING TOURS Guides in period costumes lead visitors through Geelong's historic streets.
Evening tours. Booking essential. Ⓢ *((03) 5243 9391.*

IN THE AREA

See Portarlington, Queenscliff, Steiglitz, Winchelsea

MALDON

At the foot of Mt Tarrengower lies the picturesque township of Maldon, with its Victorian facades, spreading trees and broad verandahs shading the flagged paths of its curving main street. The National Trust has declared Maldon 'a notable town'. The first gold rushes were for alluvial gold in 1851, but it was the incredible wealth of the quartz reefs that made this field so important – an estimated 62 tonnes of gold were extracted. By the 1860s, public buildings were appearing and Victorian-era town trappings proclaimed Maldon's importance. After the 1890s, however, gold yields dwindled and so too did the population.

Maldon Visitor Information Centre
High St
(03) 5475 2569

Maldon Hospital
Designed by David Drape and, although described by a contemporary as 'Tipperary Greek', a fine Classical Revival building (1860–62).
Cnr Adair St & Chapel St Nth.
Not open for inspection.

Holy Trinity Anglican Church
Built 1862–89 and designed by local architect David Drape, who also designed the hospital, the Royal Hotel and the Beehive Chimney. The exquisite stained glass was painted by John L Lyon and the interior joinery is particularly fine for a country church.
High St. Open daily. (03) 5475 2569.

IN THE AREA

PORCUPINE TOWNSHIP An authentic-looking re-creation of an 1850s gold-rush settlement, comprising rough slab, shingle and mud-brick buildings, set in rugged bush, on the site of the original 'Porcupine diggings' (another early name for Maldon). Characters in period costume add to the atmosphere. *2.5 km NE. Cnr Maldon–Bendigo & Allans rds. Open daily. Tours available.*
Ⓢ *(03) 5475 1000.*
CARMAN'S TUNNEL was driven through solid rock (1882–84) by the Great International Quartz Mining Co No Liability in the search for gold. Candlelight tours along the 570-m tunnel reveal the quartz reefs, mine tracks and trucks and original 1800s timbering. Easily accessible and well worth visiting. *2.7 km S, off Parkin's Reef Rd. Open Sat., Sun., pub hols & daily in school hols. Weekday tours by appt.*
Ⓢ *(03) 5475 2667.*
At **PARKIN'S REEF** are the crumbling remains of the old slate roasting ovens, where quartz was burnt before crushing. **MALDON'S PIONEER CEMETERY** has a small Chinese ceremonial funeral oven, caretaker's cottage (1866) and rotunda (1900). The first burial took place here in 1857. *6 km NW.*

Ethel (Henry Handel) Richardson

Old Post Office
The childhood home of Ethel Richardson (pen name Henry Handel Richardson), whose mother was postmistress here. Richardson's novel *Myself When Young* is an evocative account of her childhood days in Maldon.
High St. Post office open Mon.–Fri.

Old Courthouse
Maldon's oldest public building (1861) in its original form.
Fountain St. Not open for inspection.

Maldon Museum
Originally the Maldon market (1859–60) but outshone by Castlemaine's grand market, it soon became the headquarters of the 'Literary and Scientific Institute of Maldon' and later shire offices. The museum focuses on domestic and mining memorabilia. Behind the Museum is the old fire station (1870) not open for inspection.
Cnr Fountain & High sts. Open daily, afternoons. (03) 5475 2569.

Penny School

Built of local stone with small-paned windows, warm-red brick porches and a delightful timber bellcote. The original 1856 school was largely blown away by a 'tempest' in 1857. The tower and porches were rebuilt using the original brick (1862). Children paid a penny a day to attend school.
Cnr Camp & Church sts. Not open for inspection. NT.

Penny School, early 1870s

Railway Station & Steam Railway

In its heyday, the handsome railway station (1884) saw three trains a day steaming in from Melbourne. Steam-hauled tourist trains now run one-hour return trips to Muckleford Forest. Two vintage steam engines are also stationed here.
Hornsby St. Trains run Sun., Wed., pub hols & daily 26 Dec.–11 Jan.
Ⓢ *(03) 5475 2966.*

Beehive Chimney

Standing at 24 m high, though originally taller, the chimney was built for the successful mine of the same name and is now the last of its type in Victoria.
Main St. Open daily.

Domestic architecture

Maldon's domestic architecture is eclectic and basically small-scale, like the town itself. A number of houses have survived from the boom days. Noteworthy are Thomas Vivian's House (1862), 50 High St, with its highlighted serrated brickwork, and Lauriston House, also in High St, faced with Malmsbury bluestone and reported to be 'the best house in town' when it was built in 1866 for RD Oswald, Maldon's most successful miner. *Not open for inspection.*

Kangaroo Hotel

This neatly tuck-pointed red-brick hotel (c. 1860) was once a staging post for Cobb & Co. coaches, and is still a pub.
Cnr High & Fountain sts. Open daily (03) 5475 2214.

Kangaroo Hotel, c. 1883

Maldon Hotel

A rather grand element in Maldon's main streetscape – a two-storey hotel (c. 1890), with verandah and balcony.
Main St. Open daily. (03) 5475 2231.

ALSO OF INTEREST

Definitely pick up one of the excellent walking tour brochures at Visitor Information. Lots of accommodation, tearooms and other shops keep Maldon's historic buildings alive. The Tasmanian gum trees that shade the main street were planted in 1867. Maldon's outskirts are as rewarding as the town centre, with cottages and mining relics. From Mt Tarrengower you can more easily appreciate Maldon's architectural harmony.

PORTLAND

Whalers and sealers sailed frequently into Portland Bay in the early 1800s. But it is Edward Henty who established Victoria's first permanent settlement here in 1834. Wool and agricultural exports and migrants en route to the goldfields brought wealth to the young seaport. By the 1850s, broad streets and sturdy bluestone buildings proclaimed the town's burgeoning importance. But the gold rush subsided, other ports developed, and migrants and money moved to the capital cities. Portland grew slowly but steadily. Today its deep-water harbour and modern industry have ensured its future, but the vestiges of its youthful heyday remain in its outstanding architectural heritage.

Portland Maritime Discovery and Visitors Centre
Lee Breakwater Rd
(03) 5523 2671, freecall 1800 035 567

HISTORIC PORTLAND
Portland is rich in architectural gems – more than 200 buildings are classified by the National Trust. Near the waterfront, Bentinck, Cliff, Glenelg, Gawler, Julia and Henty streets all have heritage buildings.

IN THE AREA
CAPE NELSON LIGHTHOUSE, 11 km SW, built in 1883 of local stone on a rugged promontory, provides unique accommodation in caretaker's cottage. For tours, check with Portland Visitor Information.
WHALERS BLUFF LIGHTHOUSE, 1.5 km N, was originally built on the town's Battery Point, but relocated stone by stone to its current position in 1889. Not open for inspection, but the reserve is accessible. At Heywood, WINDA MARA, an Aboriginal interpretive centre, explains local Koorie history and culture and can arrange tours to Lake Condah, the only place in Australia where Aboriginal people built shelters of stone and where the relics of fish traps exist. 26 km N. Scott St, Heywood. Open Mon.–Fri.
Ⓢ (03) 5527 2051.
See also Casterton, Hamilton, Port Fairy, Warrnambool

Edward Henty

Whalers Bluff Lighthouse

Old Bond Store
Part of Stephen Henty's bluestone woolstore (c. 1850 possibly the oldest warehouse in the State. Now a restaurant.
6 Julia St.
(03) 5523 7100.

Sandilands
Dignified two-storey house (1850s) thought to have been built as a doctor's residence. Now an elegant restaurant, Selwyns of Sandilands.
33 Percy St. Open Mon.–Sat. for dinner.
(03) 5523 3319.

Mac's Hotel Bentinck
Overlooking the historic waterfront, this massive three-storey stone pub was established in 1856. The lacework verandahs add a late-Victorian flourish. Refurbished and offering accommodation.
Cnr Gawler & Bentinck sts. Open daily.
(03) 5523 2188.

Portland Powerhouse Car Museum
Vintage, veteran and classic vehicles, early petrol bowsers and other motoring memorabilia.
Cnr Glenelg & Percy sts. Open daily. Ⓢ
(03) 5523 5795.

Steam Packet Inn
Samuel Hutchinson had the prefabricated Tasmanian timber building erected on land bought at Portland Bay's first land sales in 1850. In its day, it has been the Star Hotel, police barracks, a 'house of ill fame' and a private house. One of the state's oldest buildings (c. 1842).
33 Bentinck St. Open Sat.–Sun.
Ⓢ (donation) (03) 5521 7496. NT.

All Saints Catholic Church
Blessed Mary MacKillop, who established Australia's first religious order, lived and taught in Portland 1862–64, and was sacristan at All Saints (built 1857–62). *Henty St. Open daily.* Ⓢ *(03) 5523 1046.*

Lookout Tower Museum
A 1930s water-tower, converted to a lookout (with fantastic views) and a small museum dedicated to Portland's role in World War II. *Wade St. Open daily.* Ⓢ *(03) 5523 3938.*

Portland Maritime Discovery Centre
Sleek vessel-like shapes of the ultra-modern Maritime Centre house fascinating maritime artifacts including the focal exhibit, the historic 1850s Portland Lifeboat, which was used in the dramatic rescue of 19 survivors from the *Admella* shipwreck in 1859. Visitor Information and other historic displays also located here. *Lee Breakwater Rd. Open daily. Tours available.* Ⓢ *(03) 5523 2671.*

Customs House
Raised single-storey bluestone customs house (1849–50), a scene of intense activity during Portland's youthful heyday, still serving its original purpose. *Cliff St. Open daily.*

Lookout Tower Museum

SL Patterson Berth

Portland Bay

0   200 m
SCALE

N

Fawthrop Lagoon

Henty Park

Botanic Gardens

Winda Mara

To Heywood

Cape Nelson Lightstation

TYERS ST
HENTY ST
JULIA ST
PERCY ST
AWLER ST
PALMER ST
HURD ST
GLENELG
BENTINCK ST
BREAKWATER
LEE
CLIFF ST
RD
BARTON ST
ANDERSON RD
QUAY RD
No. 2 RB
PACKET PL
MADEIRA
VICTORIA ST
VICTORIA PDE
WELLINGTON RD
BANCROFT
CANAL
HENTY HWY
KALINA CT
KUNARA CR
CAPE NELSON RD
CT

History House
Excellent local museum and historical research centre in the sombre bluestone former town hall (1863–64). *Cliff St. Open daily.* Ⓢ *(03) 5522 2266.*

Burswood Homestead
A single-storey, Regency-style bluestone mansion (1853) built for Portland's founding father, Edward Henty, set in magnificent formal gardens. Henty shipped the frame, 18 000 hardwood shingles and 2500 bricks from Tasmania. Now a luxury B&B. *15 Cape Nelson Rd. House not open for inspection. Gardens open daily Sept.–May.* Ⓢ *(03) 5523 4686.*

Cottage in the Gardens
A quaint two-storey bluestone cottage (1858) built for William Allit, who laid out the Portland Gardens (1857). Illegal Chinese immigrants were paid to help with the labour. Furnished in mid-Victorian style. *Botanic Gardens, Cliff St. Gardens open daily. Cottage open Wed. & Sun. afternoons, daily in Jan.* Ⓢ *(donation) (03) 5523 3820.*

Courthouse
Victoria's oldest surviving courthouse (1853), designed by Henry Ginn. Classical in style and austere, but the fine stonework is a tribute to the skilled masons. Visitors are welcome to sit in the public gallery during court hearings. *Cliff St. Limited opening during court hearings.*

Portland Battery
The fort and gun emplacements were built overlooking Portland Bay in 1889, when a Russian invasion was feared. One of the cannons was built in England in 1811. You can view the powder magazine and lamp chamber. *Victoria Pde. Open Sun., pub hol afternoons.* Ⓢ *(donation) (03) 5523 2450.*

ALSO OF INTEREST
Historic shipwreck trail (brochures from Visitor Information). Portland Cable Trams: grip car and saloon car are being restored for tours of the port area.

QUEENSCLIFF

The Grand Hotel, 1883

This small traditional seaside resort on the Bellarine Peninsula was proclaimed a town in 1853. The sturdy fortifications attest to the intense fear of invasion prevalent in Australia in the 1880s. Splendid Victorian and Edwardian hotels and stately Norfolk pines recall a time when steam trains brought holiday-makers to promenade in this 'Queen of the watering places' and to take pleasure excursions aboard the grand old paddle-steamers. Small neat cottages line the streets. Paradoxically, although the town name is spelt Queenscliff, the borough it lies in is Queenscliffe.

Queenscliff Visitor Information Centre
55 Hesse St
(03) 5258 4843

Vue Grand Hotel

Grand indeed, built 1881–82 to replace a wooden hotel on the site. Originally a three-storey Victorian building known as The Grand Hotel, but after the central section was gutted by fire in 1927 it was partly rebuilt, emerging with a more solid, 1920s-style tower and detailing.
46 Hesse St. Open daily. Guided tours by appt.
(03) 5258 1544.

Queenscliffe Historical Museum

A small but fascinating collection – including shipwreck relics and more than 6000 photos – traces the dramas, the fads and fashions of the seaside resort's life. Definitely worth a visit.
Hesse St (next to post office). Open daily, afternoons.
(03) 5258 2511.

Lathamstowe

A towered mansion (1882–83) built for Edward Latham, founder of Carlton Brewery, and donated to the Anglican Church who used it as a seaside residence for many years. Now a luxury B&B.
44 Gellibrand St. Guided tours by appt. $
(03) 5258 4110.

ALSO OF INTEREST

Queenscliff is well endowed with hotels and churches, as well as small timber cottages. Ask at the Queenscliffe Historical Museum about guided tours – the guides have some fascinating local yarns. A regular car-and-passenger ferry service crosses the Bay to SORRENTO daily.
$ *(03) 5258 3244.*
There's also a passenger-only ferry to Sorrento and PORTSEA.
$ *(03) 5984 1602.*

Fort Queenscliff

Australia's largest, best-preserved fort, finished in 1885, with castellated keep, dry moat, massive guns and other fort trappings. Inside, the lighthouse keepers' quarters (1863) and stone telegraph station (1856) are interesting. The first cannons were installed in 1859 because of fears of invasion by the Russians, Germans or French. There were also concerns that gold, waiting to be shipped overseas, might be stolen by invaders. Award-winning military museum in underground rooms.
King St. Tours daily. $ *(03) 5258 0730.*

St George the Martyr Anglican Church
Built 1863–66 from local limestone, with a remarkably steep, slate-clad roof and square tower (1877).
Cnr Hobson & Mercer sts. Open daily. (03) 5258 1532.

Bellarine Peninsula Railway
Vintage steam and diesel trains leave on the narrow-gauge line from the restored timber station on local trips.
Symonds St. Trips Sun. & most pub hols; extra trips during Christmas hols and Tues. & Thurs. in school hols. $ *(03) 5258 2069, 1900 931 452.*

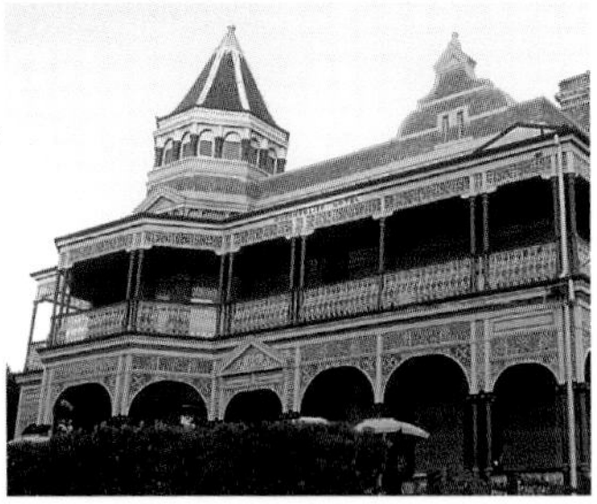

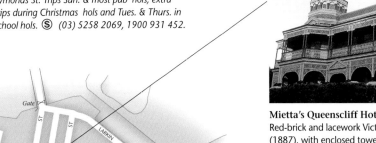

Mietta's Queenscliff Hotel
Red-brick and lacework Victorian hotel (1887), with enclosed tower, two-storey bay windows and Flemish gables. Elegantly restored and furnished to capture the late-Victorian era.
16 Gellibrand St. Open daily. (03) 5258 1066.

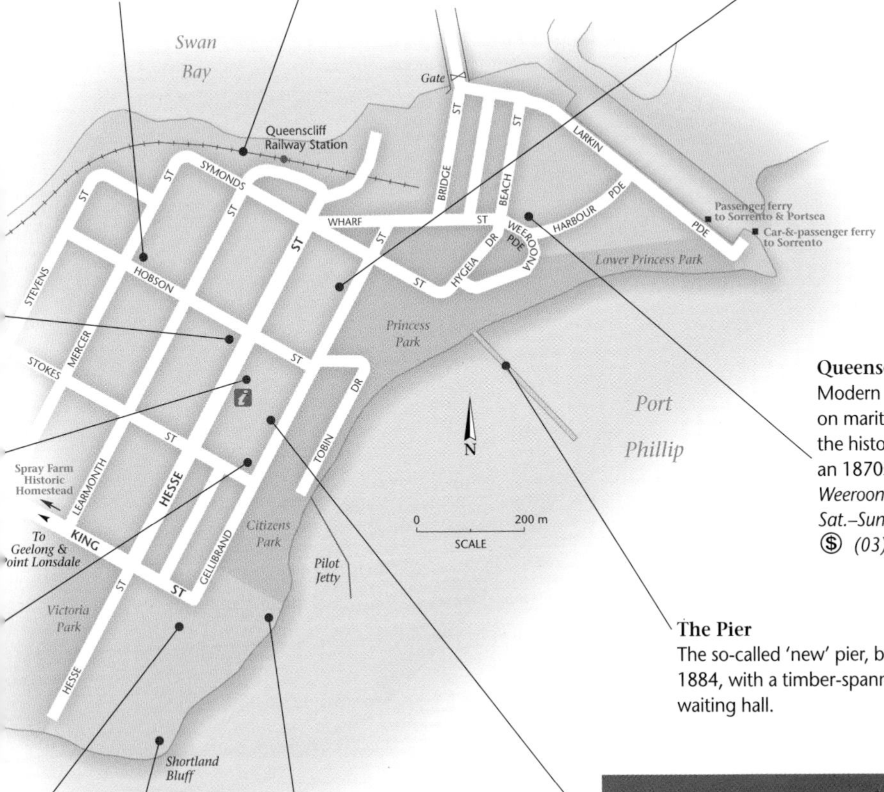

Swan Bay
Gate
Queenscliff Railway Station
SYMONDS
ST
WHARF
BRIDGE ST
BEACH ST
LARKIN PDE
HARBOUR PDE
WEEROONA PDE
HYGEIA DR
HOBSON ST
STEVENS ST
MERCER
STOKES ST
LEARMONTH
HESSE ST
KING ST
GELLIBRAND ST
TOBIN DR
Passenger ferry to Sorrento & Portsea
Car-&-passenger ferry to Sorrento
Lower Princess Park
Princess Park
Port Phillip
N
0
200 m
SCALE
Spray Farm Historic Homestead
To Geelong & Point Lonsdale
Citizens Park
Pilot Jetty
Victoria Park
Shortland Bluff

Queenscliffe Maritime Museum
Modern museum with a special focus on maritime rescue. Exhibits include the historic 'Queenscliffe' lifeboat and an 1870s fisherman's cottage.
Weeroona Pde. Open daily Mon.–Fri. & Sat.–Sun. afternoons. Tours by appt. $ *(03) 5258 3440.*

The Pier
The so-called 'new' pier, built 1884, with a timber-spanned waiting hall.

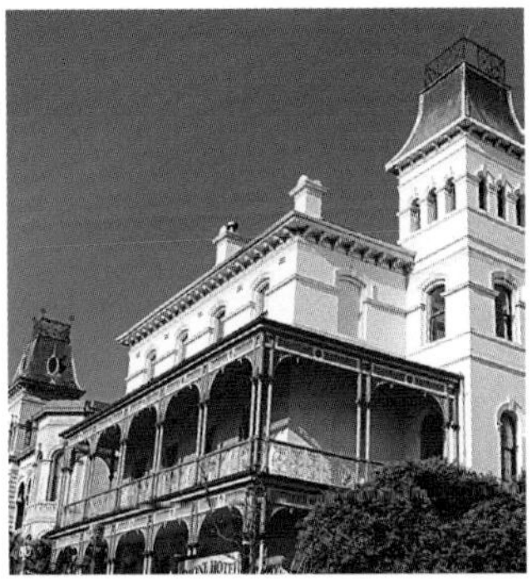

Ozone Hotel
Three-storey hotel (1881–82) whose tower affords wonderful views of the town and bay. Built for George Baillieu and renamed Ozone after a paddle-steamer.
42 Gellibrand St. Open daily. (03) 5258 1011.

Black Lighthouse
The only 'black' lighthouse in Australia, built of bluestone in Scotland, the numbered stones then dismantled and re-erected here in 1862.
Gellibrand St. Inspection part of fort tour.

White Lighthouse
Built 1892 and, in conjunction with the black lighthouse, used to guide ships through the Heads.
Not open for inspection.

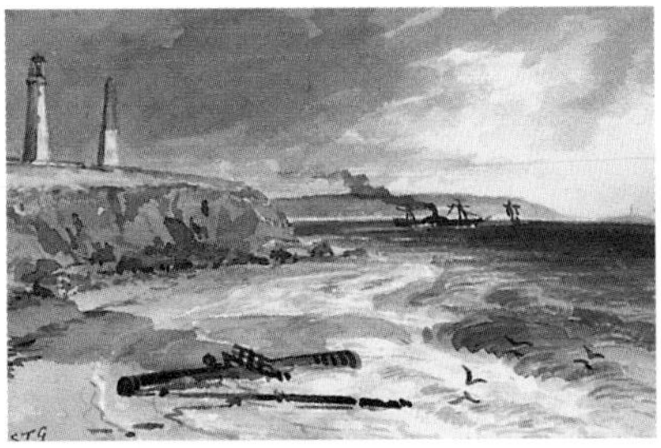

Queenscliff Lighthouse by ST Gill, c. 1864

In the Area
The handsome **Spray Farm Historic Homestead** (c. 1851) contains an art gallery and has magnificent formal gardens. The Gothic stables (c. 1875) house a wine-tasting area and restaurant.
2275 Portarlington Rd, Bellarine. Open Sat.–Sun. & pub hols. Booking essential for restaurant. (03) 5251 3176.
See also Geelong, Portarlington

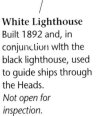

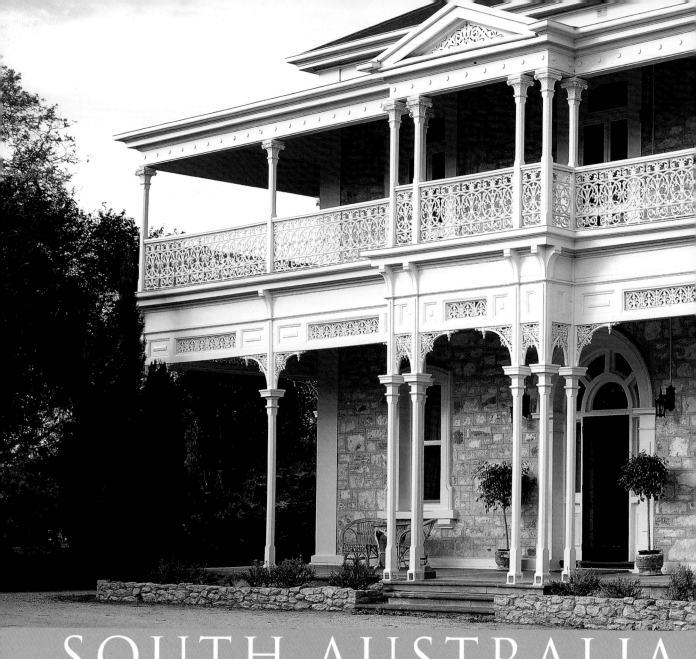

SOUTH AUSTRALIA

Much of South Australia's history is revealed in its architecture, from the humble stone dwellings of colonial days to the Cornish-style mining structures of the 'Copper Triangle' and the distinctive buildings erected by German Lutherans in the Adelaide Hills and Barossa Valley. There are, too, many Aboriginal sites of considerable heritage significance.

Padthaway Estate

The colony was founded in 1836 by members of the South Australian Company, fired by Edward Gibbon Wakefield's theory of systematic colonisation. Land would be sold at a 'sufficient price' and funds used to assist free immigrants, thus providing a plentiful labour force and creating 'so many extensions of our old society'. These extensions, however, were to be marked by order, to be free of penury and blessed by sunshine. In fact, South Australia's infant years were marked by chaos, disagreement, dissension and even bankruptcy.

HISTORIC HIGHLIGHTS

For a look around some of South Australia's most interesting historic towns, see the pages listed below.

Burra   Former copper-mining town of distinctively Celtic character, a legacy of the Cornish, Welsh and Scottish miners who flocked there from the 1840s until the mine's demise in the 1870s. The dramatic landscape is scattered with mine buildings and history lingers on in the many stone cottages and mining relics. *See p. 150*

Gawler   SA's first country town and a major stopping place on the busy route north. Planned by Surveyor-General Col. Light, Gawler has spacious parklands, church squares and many fine heritage buildings. *See p. 152*

Hahndorf   Australia's oldest German-settled town (settled in 1839), this is a delightful village in the Adelaide Hills, still proudly European in culture and atmosphere. Enjoy a German-style cake and coffee from one of the traditional bakeries. *See p. 154*

Robe   Once a thriving wool port, historic Robe is now a small but flourishing fishing town and holiday destination. Many of the original cottages, inns and larger houses, built from the local stone, are still standing. Call in at the old Customs House to learn more about Robe's colourful history. *See p. 156*

A CHAOTIC START

South Australia's first years were especially difficult. Disgruntled settlers camped in squalor at Holdfast Bay (now Glenelg) while Colonel Light hurriedly chose a site for the capital. Governor Hindmarsh arrived aboard HMS *Buffalo* on 28 December 1836, anxious to get the colony under way, and within hours of his arrival read the proclamation declaring South Australia a British province. 'A dozen or so drunken marines . . . discharged several muskets', a rather grim feast was consumed, and then it was on with business.

South Australia's colonists were determined to make it their home, and even the simplest colonial buildings convey this sense of permanence. Among the earliest migrants were German settlers, in some cases fleeing religious persecution in their homeland. With their steadfast faith and stalwart belief in hard work, they brought their traditional Germanic building styles, which are still to be seen in the Adelaide Hills, and in the Barossa Valley, where they are framed by another legacy, row upon row of lovingly tended vines.

General store, Mintaro

COPPER BRINGS MINERS

Lack of finance and lack of labour were ongoing problems for the infant colony and its capital. A turning point, however, was the discovery of copper deposits at Kapunda in 1842 and at Burra in 1845. The influx of migrants and the wealth that came from the mines helped set the colony on its feet financially. It also attracted thousands of Welsh and Cornish miners, who built in the English West Country fashion. Neat stone cottages along meandering streets and enduring mine buildings survive as testimony to their craftsmanship.

Sometimes settlement pushed beyond reasonable bounds. Abandoned stone homesteads in the ruggedly beautiful Flinders Ranges are a reminder of the pioneers who hoped to farm the Outback.

ADELAIDE

Adelaide has its own story to tell, from the Regency elegance of Ayers House and the magnificent university buildings along North Terrace to tiny workers' cottages and traditional Victorian-era pubs.

TIMELINE

1836 The colony of SA is founded for free settlers by the privately owned SA Company. Col. William Light chooses the site for Adelaide.

1838 Prussian Lutheran migrants arrive in the colony and settle in the village they name Hahndorf.

1840s Rich copper deposits, discovered at Kapunda and Burra, boost the colony's flagging economy.

1850s Thousands of Chinese land at Robe and overland to the Victorian goldfields to avoid that State's poll tax.

1862 John Stuart is the first explorer to successfully cross the continent from south to north, travelling from Adelaide to Darwin.

1874 The University of Adelaide is established. Benefactors include wealthy pastoralist Thomas Elder.

1894 SA becomes the first colony to give women the vote.

1901 The Commonwealth of Australia is declared, with SA one of the six new States.

Rundle Street, Adelaide

ADELAIDE *A Vision Splendid*

Ayers Historic House Museum

VISITOR INFORMATION

SA TRAVEL CENTRE
1 King William St
Adelaide SA 5000
(08) 8303 2033
www.visit.adelaide.on.net

SA TOURISM COMMISSION
www.southaustralia.com

NATIONAL TRUST OF SA
2/27 Leigh St
Adelaide SA 5000
(08) 8212 1133
www.nationaltrustsa.org.au

Adelaide is a city of considerable grace and charm, circled by parkland, cut into orderly grids by grand boulevards and endowed with spacious squares. The residential areas of North Adelaide are set apart from the city's heart by the gently curving River Torrens. Colonel William Light, the city's renowned designer, would no doubt be well pleased.

South Australia was founded in 1836 by high-minded men with noble plans, based on Edward Gibbon Wakefield's theory of systematic colonisation by free settlers. The intention was to establish a 'wealthy, civilised society', free from the taint of convicts. All would be organisation, order, calm and dignity.

Calm and dignified was hardly how the first arrivals felt as they struggled ashore. Settlers huddled in canvas, mud or pug huts or rough timber shanties (though timber was scarce). The Governor himself lived in a mud hut, put together haphazardly, without even a chimney, by sailors who believed they could 'rig up a house' and would brook no interference. It was soon realised that this free settlement, unlike New South Wales, had no convicts to assist in the arduous but essential tasks of clearing the land and building roads and bridges. The River Torrens provided the water supply, but it was soon 'in a wretched state, perfectly disgusting, the essence of all sorts of nastiness and filth'.

Adelaide was fortunate, however, to have a man of vision in Surveyor-General Colonel Light. Having been forced to choose the site for the capital in a rush, he proceeded to plan a city of graciously wide streets, with generous parks and gardens spread along the banks of the winding River Torrens.

The discovery of copper deposits at Kapunda in 1842 and at Burra in 1845 brought migrants and money to the young colony and business to its capital. The discovery of gold in Victoria in 1851 proved initially an immense drain on South Australia's labour resources, but most of the miners eventually returned, often bringing considerable wealth with them, which was reflected in new buildings and shops.

By the 1870s Adelaide was beginning to take shape. The grand town hall and the towered post office, facing each other across King William Street, the impressive St Peter's Cathedral, and university buildings along North Terrace were just some of the major buildings that gave Adelaide a look of solid respectability. Since then the city has grown slowly but steadily. Light's original plan has stood up well to the test of time. There are many elegant stone buildings, and the successful and prestigious Adelaide Arts Festival, held every two years, might well symbolise the 'civilised society' the colony's founding fathers dreamed of so many years ago.

FIVE TOP MUSEUMS

Art Gallery of SA, *p. 124*
Ayers Historic House Museum, *p. 124*
SA Museum, *p. 127*
SA Maritime Museum, *p. 131*
Tandanya National Aboriginal Cultural Institute, *p. 127*

Light's Vision sculpture, North Adelaide

Old Palm House, Botanic Gardens

INNER ADELAIDE

1 Adelaide Botanic Gardens
An ordered 19th-century landscape in the European style, founded in 1855. The avenue of grand Moreton Bay figs leading north from the Main Lake was planted in 1866. The Old Palm House, a marvellous Victorian glasshouse imported from Germany and opened to the public in 1877, has been restored. The construction techniques were advanced for their time, and the hanging glass walls and octagonal clerestory add to the illusion of airy lightness. The herbarium, known as the Museum of Economic Botany (1881), is also of heritage significance. The superb iron gates facing North Tce were cast in 1880 in the UK. The vast Bicentennial Conservatory was opened in 1989.
North Tce, City. Gardens & Old Palm House open daily. Guided walks, booking (08) 8226 8803. (08) 8222 9311.

2 Adelaide Gaol
The gaol complex, built in 1841, was used for its original purpose until 1988. In the early days, hangings were held outside its imposing front gates. Enduring graffiti on the cell walls, and exhibits such as manacles, cat-o'-nine-tails and a hangman's noose are vivid reminders of the harsh realities of prison life. The last hanging at the gaol was in 1964.
18 Gaol Rd, Thebarton. Open Mon.–Fri., Sun. $ (08) 8231 4062.

3 Adelaide Town Hall
Adelaide City Council bought the land in 1841 but there were insufficient funds to start the building until 1863. Noted architect EW Wright was responsible for the prize-winning Palladian design. He showed his love of all things Italian by including carved keystones of artists such as Donatello and Michelangelo, though patriotically added Queen Victoria and her consort Prince Albert.
King William St, City. Auditorium & 1st floor open Mon.–Fri. Tours of council chambers Mon. or by appt. (08) 8203 7203.

4 Adelaide University
The university was incorporated in 1874 following gifts from leading citizens, including successful pastoralist Thomas Elder. The oldest original structure is the Mitchell Building (1881). Neighbouring Elder Hall (1900), also in the Gothic Revival style, houses the Conservatorium of Music. Bonython Hall (1933), with its facade of limestone quarried at Murray Bridge, was designed by Walter Bagot. The Museum of Classical Archaeology (1879) is noted for its exceptional collection of Egyptian, Etruscan and Greek relics.
North Tce, City. Free guided tours. (08) 8303 5800.

5 Art Gallery of SA
The gallery was established in 1881 and the Elder Wing, the original building, opened in 1900. The stunning new West Wing (1996) doubled the gallery's size. Of particular interest are the Australian colonial paintings, including fine works by Glover, Tom Roberts and Arthur Streeton. Aboriginal art, notably major works from the Western Desert School, are on permanent display.
North Tce, City. Open daily. $ (for special exhibitions). (08) 8207 7000.

6 Ayers Historic House Museum
One of the finest examples of colonial Regency architecture in Australia, this was the home for over 40 years of Sir Henry Ayers, mining baron and seven times Premier of SA. The original cottage (1855) was gradually extended into a fine mansion of about 40 rooms. The ceilings, cornices, stencilled wallpapers and trompe l'oeil

Art Gallery of South Australia

work of the ballroom and the State dining-room are exquisite. The old stables and coach-house is now the Henry Brassiere and Wine Bar.
288 North Tce, City. Open Tues.–Sun. and pub hols. Ⓢ (08) 8223 1234. NT.

7 Botanic Hotel

This exuberant three-storey bluestone hotel was built in 1876–77 on a prominent corner overlooking the leafy Botanic Gardens. The stepped-back verandahs, a style found in both Adelaide and Brisbane, were added later, probably early 20th century. The hotel was a popular starting point for picnics in the Mt Lofty Ranges in the late 1800s. The building was originally a temperance hotel. The ground floor is now a restaurant, bar and cafe.
309 North Tce, City. Open daily. (08) 8227 0799.

8 Carclew

An extravagant, idiosyncratic mansion with a circular tower, on land bought in 1837 for 12 shillings in the first town land sales in Adelaide. Hugh Dixon built Carclew in 1897 and it was owned by the well-known Bonython family for 60 years. It is now the Carclew Youth Performing Arts Centre. Visitors can stroll around the gardens and view the foyer.
11 Jeffcott St, North Adelaide. Open Mon.–Fri. & Sat. morning. (08) 8267 5111.

9 Edmund Wright House

EW Wright, one of Australia's foremost colonial architects, designed this lavish edifice in 1875–78 for the Bank of SA. The facade is enriched with particularly fine carvings, and the interiors are sumptuous. Renowned Scottish sculptor W Maxwell travelled to Australia specifically to carve three keystones on the Gilbert Pl. facade. Elegantly refurbished, it is now the headquarters of the History Trust of SA.
59 King William St, City. Open Mon.–Fri. Ⓢ (08) 8226 8555.

10 Elder Park Rotunda

A graceful Victorian addition to riverside Elder Park, the octagonal rotunda with tendrils of iron lacework and a domed roof was donated by philanthropist Sir Thomas Elder. It was manufactured in Glasgow and erected in 1882.
Elder Park, King William Rd, City.

11 Former Mounted Police Barracks

The original barracks (1851) for Adelaide's mounted police – one of the city's earliest surviving public buildings. It was from the slate-roofed, limestone armoury (1853) next door that SA's contingent for the Boer War was despatched in 1899.
Kintore Ave, City. Not open for inspection.

12 General Post Office

The Duke of Edinburgh laid the foundation stone for this stately sandstone building, designed by EW

Wright and EJ Woods, in 1867. For some years a canvas imitation of a clock-face adorned the massive Victoria Tower, but in 1876 a real timepiece was installed. For a period, a flag was hoisted by day and a red light lit on the flagstaff at night to signal the arrival of English mail at Cape Borda. The main hall has been faithfully restored and the post office is still located here.
141 King William St, City.

13 Holy Trinity Church

SA's first Anglican church, its foundation stone laid by Gov. Hindmarsh in 1838. The inaugural service was held by the Colonial Chaplain, the Rev. CB Howard, on 1 January 1837 beneath a ship's sail fastened to a tree. The clock, installed in 1838, was made by Vulliamy, clockmaker to King William IV. The church was enlarged in 1845 and 1888.
87 North Tce, City. Open daily. (08) 8213 7300.

14 Lion Hotel

One of North Adelaide's most popular pubs, it began in the 1850s as the Lion Brewery. The handsome bluestone building, which features stepped-back verandahs, has been renovated extensively.
163 Melbourne St, North Adelaide. Open daily. (08) 8367 0222.

15 Migration Museum

Located in the restored former poorhouse (1852–1918) known as the Destitute Asylum, it has changing exhibitions and events that vividly bring to life SA's rich cultural diversity. The museum actively encourages the involvement of community groups.
82 Kintore Ave, City. Open daily afternoons. (08) 8207 7570.

16 Parliament House

A conservative design, but nonetheless acknowledged as one of Adelaide's most imposing public buildings. Constructed from Kapunda marble on a base of granite from Victor Harbor, it was built in two stages, 1883–89 and 1936–39. It is dominated by a monumental Corinthian portico. Carved portraits on keystones depict parliamentary dignitaries. The stone lion next to the main steps, presented to Parliament in

Carclew, North Adelaide

Aboriginal shields, South Australian Museum

1939, was originally at Westminster in London.
Cnr North Tce & King William Rd, City. Guided tours only, at 10 a.m. & 2 p.m. on non-sitting days. (08) 8237 9100.

17 St Francis Xavier's Cathedral
This monumental Gothic Revival church, the oldest section dating from 1856–58, is the focus of Roman Catholic worship in Adelaide. It was designed and constructed in three stages over 70 years, and with the involvement of several architects.
Wakefield St, City. Open daily. (08) 8210 8123.

18 St Peter's Cathedral
A dominant Gothic Revival edifice, erected 1869–1904, magnificently sited between the city centre and North Adelaide. The twin spires with minarets and the exceptionally fine lantern tower were consecrated in 1902. Richly coloured stained glass floods the lofty interior with jewel-like light.
Cnr Pennington Tce & King William Rd, North Adelaide. Open daily. Tours Wed. & most Sun. (08) 8267 4551.

19 SA Museum
This museum has the distinction of containing the world's largest collection of Aboriginal items, as well as outstanding relics from Ancient Egypt and the Pacific region. The Australian Aboriginal Cultures Gallery, planned in consultation with Aboriginal communities, features state-of-the-art displays and technologies. Completed in 1914, the French-influenced building was designed to match the Jervois Wing of the adjacent State Library.
North Tce, City. Open daily. (08) 8207 7500.

20 SA Police Museum
The museum, which focuses on law and order (or disorder, as was often the case) in colonial times, is in the Police Barracks. It houses photographs, memorabilia and a small police transport display.
Police Barracks, cnr Gaol & Port rds, Thebarton. Open by appt. (08) 8207 4099.

21 State Library of SA
The State Library is made up of the neo-Classical Revival building (c. 1850s), the French Renaissance Jervois Wing (1880s) and the 1960s Baystan building. The library contains more than 200 000 volumes and features the historic Mortlock Collection of South Australiana. The Bradman Collection of cricketing memorabilia is another feature. 'White Gloves' tours, where visitors can handle some of the library's treasures, are available. The SA Royal Geographical Society's (RGS) collection, also located in the building, includes intriguing relics, such as colonial explorer John McKinlay's trusty whisky flask. The library is undergoing major redevelopment, expected to be completed in 2003.
North Tce, City. Open daily. RGS collection open Mon. afternoons, Tues. & Thurs. Ⓢ (for White Gloves tour). (08) 8207 7200.

22 Tandanya National Aboriginal Cultural Institute
Located in the city's original electricity powerhouse, Tandanya, the first substantial national institute dedicated to Aboriginal culture, is owned and managed by Aboriginal people. It is an innovative and influential force in the sometimes controversial world of indigenous art. The heritage-classified building (1912–13) features a lofty main gallery, theatre, and smaller spaces used as workshops, galleries and performance venues. The name Tandanya, 'place of the red kangaroo', comes from the local Kaurna language.
253 Grenfell St, City. Open daily. Ⓢ (08) 8224 3200.

South Australian Museum

Carrick Hill, Springfield

AROUND ADELAIDE

1 Angove's Pty Ltd
Map ref. 325 P9

Dr William Thomas Angove began planting vines on his Tea Tree Gully property in 1886. His first wines were used for medicinal purposes for his patients. The original cellars, used to fortify wine, are open for inspection and wine-tastings.
1320 North East Rd, Tea Tree Gully. Open Mon.–Fri. (08) 8264 2366.

2 Carrick Hill
Map ref. 323 K9

An English manorhouse (1939), home of retailer Sir Edward Heyward and his wife Lady Ursula, who bequeathed the property to the people of SA. It boasts a particularly fine collection of Australian, English and French paintings, as well as some rare and beautiful furniture. The formal gardens, quintessentially English in style are in contrast to the Australian bush surrounds. They contain more than 2000 rose bushes.
46 Carrick Hill Dr., Springfield. Open Wed.–Sun. & most pub hols. ⓢ (08) 8379 3886.

3 Fort Glanville
Map ref. 324 A12

SA's first military fortification, built 1878–80 in response to widespread fear of Russian invasion but never called upon to fire a single defensive shot. The fort is a notable example of a 19th-century coastal battery. A steam train runs between Semaphore and the fort on open days.
359 Military Rd, Semaphore South. Open afternoons, 1st & 3rd Sun. of the month during Sept.–May, & Australia Day. ⓢ (08) 8242 1978.

4 Glenelg
Map ref. 322 C10, 327 K9, 336 B2, 337 A10

SA's first colonists landed here in 1836. On 28 December of that year, Gov. Hindmarsh read the proclamation declaring SA a British province, beside a gum tree that still stands in MacFarlane St, Glenelg North. The grandiose town hall (1875) dominates Moseley Sq. Restored trams run from Victoria Sq. in Adelaide to Jetty Rd, providing a nostalgic journey to this favoured watering hole for the genteel in the late 1800s.

5 HMS *Buffalo*
Map ref. 322 C9

A replica of the ship in which the first European settlers (including Hindmarsh, the first Governor) arrived in SA in 1836. The boat was built on-site to the original Admiralty plans. Now a restaurant.
Patawalonga Boat Haven, Adelphi Tce, Glenelg North. Open for dinner nightly and for lunch Fri. & Sun. (08) 8294 7000.

6 Largs Pier Hotel/Motel
Map ref. 324 B10

A grand three-storey hotel (1883), one of Adelaide's best in its day, its colonnaded verandahs curving decorously around a corner. The rooms – at the time, the last word in modernity and comfort – boasted hot, cold and seawater taps. The splendour of the 19th-century interiors is still evident. Accommodation available.
198 The Esplanade, Largs Bay. (08) 8449 5666.

7 Marble Hill
Map ref. 323 R5

Majestic ruins of a romantic, towered Gothic Revival mansion built and furnished (1878–79) at a cost of £38,900 as the Governor's summer residence. Lord and Lady Tennyson stayed there 1889–1902, Lady Tennyson being delighted by the 'wild, fearsome hills, valleys and sea'. Other visitors were less impressed, deterred not least by the long, hot haul up from Adelaide, the isolation and fear of bushfires. The residence was gutted by bushfire in 1955.

HMS *Buffalo*, Glenelg North

The tower, outbuildings and some rooms were restored in the 1970s. The property is now managed by the Friends of Marble Hill and the stables have been converted into tearooms.

Marble Hill Rd, Ashton. Open 2nd Sun. of each month. Ⓢ *(08) 8390 1884.*

8 North Adelaide
Map ref. 322 H4

Grand stone houses and rows of neat cottages flank North Adelaide's orderly streets, which are divided by parks and squares as Col. Light planned. There are old pubs, and boutiques, restaurants and cafes in historic buildings. An evocative bronze statue of Light stands at Light's Vision, Montefiore Hill. A leaflet outlining significant sites is available from the National Trust. *(08) 8212 1133.*

9 Old Government House
Map ref. 323 L12

Once known as 'The Rest', this was the summer residence of SA's governors until the more opulent Marble Hill was completed. Built 1858–60, the villa has a ballroom and – surely unique in Adelaide at the time – an indoor plunge pool. The restored buildings are set amidst a period garden. The complex is in Belair National Park (dedicated 1891), Australia's second national park.

Belair National Park, Belair. Park open daily. House open Sun. & pub hol afternoons. Ⓢ *(08) 8278 5477.*

10 Penfolds Magill Estate
Map ref. 323 M5

Dr Christopher Rawson Penfold founded the family wine-making business here in 1844. The estate still produces table and fortified wines. The revered Grange Hermitage red was produced at the estate until about 1974. It is now made in the Barossa Valley. There are tours of the historic vintage and maturation cellars, wine tastings and an award-winning restaurant.

78 Penfold Rd, Magill. Open daily. Ⓢ *(08) 8301 5569.*

11 Port Adelaide
Map ref. 324 C11, 327 K9, 336 B1, 337 A8

See A Walk Around Port Adelaide, p. 130.

12 SA Aviation Museum
Map ref. 324 C10

Pays tribute to the pioneers, heroes and technology of Australian aviation. There is memorabilia from both world wars, and a substantial collection of engines, missiles and restored aircraft, including a C-47 Dakota, a Canberra bomber, and a World War II Avro Anson.

Ocean Steamers Rd, Port Adelaide. Open daily. Ⓢ *(08) 8240 1230.*

See also A Walk Around Port Adelaide, p. 131.

13 Sturt House
Map ref. 322 C3

Known as 'The Grange', this modest red-brick house was built in 1840 for explorer and administrator Charles Sturt, who lived there until he returned to England in 1853. The house looks much as it was in Sturt's time, with many of the elegant furnishings donated by his family.

Cnr Jelly St & Nepean Dr., Grange. Guided tours only, Fri.–Sun. afternoons or by appt. Ⓢ *(08) 8356 8185.*

Sturt House, Grange

A WALK AROUND PORT ADELAIDE

Adelaide's old port still smacks of its salty, colourful past. Lying on the Port Adelaide River, a wide inlet of Gulf St Vincent, it was established in 1840 only a few years after South Australia was settled. By the 1880s it was the main gateway to the colony, and its commercial hub, boasting many fine buildings.

Port Adelaide Visitor Information Centre
66 Commercial Rd
(08) 8447 4788
Website: www.portenf.sa.gov.au

Waterfront & Port Adelaide Lighthouse
There is a distinctly nautical atmosphere along the wharf, which forms part of the **SA Maritime Museum**. Steam tug *Yelta*, MV *Nelcebee* (1883) and other boats are berthed here. The lighthouse (1869) stood on South Neptune Island 1901–85 and was moved here in 1986. A climb to the top affords panoramic views of Adelaide and the Mt Lofty Ranges.

Self-portrait by Col. William Light

Customs House & former Port Adelaide Institute Building
The Customs House (1879) on the northern side of the building, deemed by its own architect to be 'somewhat pretentious', was intended as a landmark for approaching ships. The building on the south side (1876–77) was home for 80 years to the Port Adelaide Institute, which helped nurture the colony's cultural development. *56 Commercial Rd. Not open for inspection.*

HISTORY

Col. Light's first site for the Port of Adelaide was an unfortunate choice. As sailors carried their passengers ashore through the shallow, mosquito-infested mangrove swamps, it quickly gained the title Port Misery. But like Light himself, settlers had visions of a grand future, and thousands journeyed along the new road to Port Adelaide in 1840 to see Gov. Gawler officially open a new wharf and sheds. The port grew rapidly, reflecting Adelaide's prosperity. Sailing ships and later steamships docked. By the 1850s, the railway linked the port with Adelaide and by the 1870s stately banks and bond stores lined the streets – many 19th-century buildings remain.

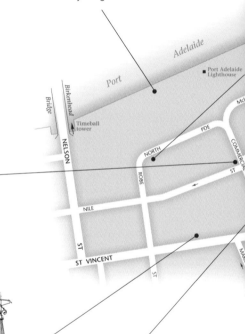

Town Hall
Built in 1866 and extended in 1884. Next door, a humbler bluestone cottage (1884) was the port's first casualty hospital. *St Vincent St. Not open for inspection.*

Police Station & Courthouse
An elegant but sturdy complex built for rowdy times. Plans for the police station (1860) were reputedly for a building in India, but arrived in Adelaide instead. The courthouse (1882) is now home to the Port Adelaide Visitor Information Centre. *66 Commercial Rd.*

Port Dock Brewery Hotel
Opened as the Dock Hotel in 1855, it was de-licensed in 1909 thanks to teetotaller Rev. John Kirby's crusade to close as many hotels as possible in the port area. It later became a renowned bordello. Now a 'boutique brewery'.
10 Todd St. Open daily. Free guided tours. (08) 8240 0187.

Falie
This historic sailing ship, built in Holland in 1919, sailed to SA in 1923. She was the last of the traditional SA trading ketches. Now converted to a first-class charter vessel, taking regular cruises.
Bookings 27 North Pde (08) 8341 2004.

SA Maritime Museum
A superb full-scale replica of an early sailing ketch, and re-creations of both port life and 3rd-class sea travel in times past, are among the displays. The handsome two-storey freestone bond store (c. 1850), built for Elders & Co., houses the museum.
126 Lipson St. Open daily. Ⓢ
(08) 8207 6255.

Sailmakers Building
Originally the centre of a sailmaking business, this 1864 building features a brick ground floor and an upper storey of corrugated iron. Now a tearoom.
117 Lipson St.

SA Aviation Museum
Celebrating Australia's pioneering and wartime aviation history and achievements.
Ocean Steamers Rd. Open daily. Ⓢ *(08) 8240 1230.*
See also p. 129

Port Admiral Hotel
Port Adelaide's oldest building (1841). First licensed in 1849, the hotel is on Black Diamond Cnr, named after the Black Diamond shipping line, which transported coal to the colony.
Cnr Commercial Rd & St Vincent St. Open daily. (08) 8447 1708.

Port Dock Station Railway Museum
The museum includes the original goods shed (1856) built for the British Empire's first government-owned steam railway. There is an eclectic display of locomotives, carriages, steam and diesel trains.
Lipson St. Open daily. Ⓢ *(08) 8341 1690.*

ALSO OF INTEREST
Nelson, St Vincent and Todd sts, with McLaren Pde, mark the boundaries of the first heritage conservation area to be declared in SA. Stroll down Lipson St for a true taste of Port Adelaide's colonial flavour. You'll see the impressive ANZ Bank (1859), the Bank of Adelaide (1885), and the tiny McLachlan building, which housed the Bank of Adelaide prior to 1885. The stone timeball tower (1874) in nearby Semaphore dropped a black ball daily at 1 p.m., so ships could set their chronometers precisely.

SOUTH AUSTRALIA FROM A TO Z

Angaston Town Hall

ADELAIDE Map ref. 322 I5, 327 K9, 337 B10

See p. 122

ANGASTON Map ref. 327 M8, 337 G4

Angaston, in the heart of the Barossa Valley, was settled by 1841 and named after enterprising English-man George Fife Angas, one of SA's founding fathers, who assisted many German migrants to settle in the Barossa Valley. The curving main street, lined by century-old Moreton Bay fig trees, has several fine historic buildings that reflect the town's dual English and German heritage.

A & H Doddridge Blacksmith Shop Forge and shop dating back to the 1870s, still houses many original tools and equipment. *19 Murray St. Open daily.* Ⓢ *(donation). (08) 8564 2021.*

Saltram Wine Estates Established by Englishman William Salter, who planted the first vines in 1859 and by 1882 was successfully exporting wine. Mamre Brook House, the property's first residence, was built 1844. The winery building dates from 1859 and the cellar door is in part of the original winery. *1 km E on Angaston–Nuriootpa Rd. Open daily. (08) 8564 3355.*

ALSO OF INTEREST Pick up a heritage walk leaflet from the town's Visitor Information and explore Angaston's distinctive architectural heritage. Stop at Angaston Abbey, an antique shop, in the restored old sandstone Methodist Church (1863). *18 Murray St. Open daily. (08) 8564 2648.* Several restored buildings offer accommo-dation, from the humble 1860s settler's home Fig Tree Cottage to more substantial residences. The quaint Strathlyn Coach House

(1906), set in an almond orchard and surrounded by vineyards, now provides B&B accommodation. *Angaston–Nuriootpa Rd. (08) 8564 2430.*

IN THE AREA Collingrove Homestead is a rambling single-storey house of 22 rooms, built in 1856 for pastoralist and parliamentarian John Howard Angas, son of SA's founder, George Fife Angas. Pale grey slate walls, cool verandahs and louvred shutters offer respite from the district's harsh summers. Stables, coach-house and workshops are joined to the house by verandahs. The homestead is meticulously maintained, and is now a museum with B&B accommodation in the old servants' quarters. *6 km s on Angaston–Eden Valley Rd. Open daily.* Ⓢ *(08) 8564 2061. NT.* Australia's oldest family-owned wine-making estate, the Yalumba Wine Company, lies just south of Angaston. It was established in 1849 by Englishman and former brewer Samuel Smith, who worked as a gardener by day and planted the vines by moonlight. He expanded the estate with £300 he made on the Victorian goldfields. Most of the facade of the grand blue marble winery was built by his son in 1907, although part of the building is older. *1.6 km s on Angaston–Eden Valley Rd. Open Mon.–Sat., Sun. afternoons. (08) 8561 3200.* Henschke and Co. is another family winery, started by Johann Henschke, who produced his first commercial vintage in 1868. The old cellar has walls of pug, clay and field stones. *11 km E then 5 km N. Henschke Rd, Keyneton. Open Mon.–Fri., also Sat. mornings. (08) 8564 8223.* The tall gum trees outside St Peter's Church (1866) in Keyneton held the German church bell when it was first brought here in 1874.

🅘 *Angaston Country Gift Store, 49b Murray St; (08) 8564 2713.*
See also Lyndoch, Nuriootpa, Springton, Tanunda

ARKAROOLA

Map ref. 329 M3

Arkaroola Wilderness Sanctuary Resort This remote, privately owned 610 sq km resort, more than 600 km north of Adelaide, is in the spectacular northern Flinders Ranges. Geologically the area dates back about 2 billion years, taking in breathtaking scenery and unique flora and fauna.

Copper mining began in this minerals-rich district in 1865, but abandoned mines and scattered relics of European settlement tell of shattered hopes. Tours explain the history, geology and Aboriginal culture. *(08) 8648 4848, freecall 1800 676 042.*

IN THE AREA Ruins of old copper mines and the strangely isolated Bolla Bollana smelter (1890s), a domed Cornish-style furnace. *8 km NE.* The Paralana hot springs are thought to be the last sign of volcanic activity in Australia. *27 km NE. Gammon Ranges NP (08) 8648 4829.*

AUBURN

Map ref. 327 L6

Auburn's position on the busy 'copper road' between **Burra** and Port Wakefield ensured a steady income from the 1840s as bullock wagons pulled through the town on the long haul south. After 1850 the town became a prosperous commercial centre. Today it is noted for its handsome stone architecture, pleasing streetscapes and mature trees – and as the birthplace of poet, humorist and creator of *The Sentimental Bloke*, CJ Dennis, in 1876. Auburn lies 110 km N of Adelaide.

OF INTEREST The main thoroughfare from early days, the heritage precinct of St Vincent St, boasts several fine buildings, among them the former Mechanics Institute (1859), now Wild Olive Cottage, a B&B, (08) 8277 8177; finely proportioned post office (1862) and Gothic-style St John's Church

(1862). *Open by appt. Contact Visitor Information.* The old courthouse and police station (begun 1859), solidly built of local stone and combining slate, pitch and cobble paving, now houses a National Trust museum. *St Vincent St. Open Thurs.–Sun., pub & school hols.* Ⓢ *(donation). (08) 8849 2262.* The handsomely restored railway station, opened 1918, is home to Mt Horrocks Wines and has a restaurant. *Curling St. Open Sat.–Sun. & pub hols. (08) 8849 2243.* Stables (1850) behind the Rising Sun Hotel, once the telegraph station, received the first messages sent by Charles Todd on the Overland Telegraph in 1872. Now a boutique hotel. *Main North Rd. Open daily. (08) 8849 2015.*
🅘 *St Vincent St; (08) 8849 2020.*
See also Clare

BAROSSA VALLEY

Map ref. 337 E4

See Angaston, Bethany, Lyndoch, Nuriootpa, Springton, Tanunda

BEACHPORT

Map ref. 336 F11

A whaling station was established on the shores of Rivoli Bay in the 1830s, though the township was not officially gazetted until 1878. Beachport, 385 km SE of Adelaide, is now a fishing centre and holiday resort.

Boandik Cultural Centre Home to one of Australia's largest private collections of Aboriginal artifacts, amassed over a lifetime by local pastoralist Tom McCourt (1917–81). Located in the renovated former Beachport

Collingrove Homestead, Angaston

schoolhouse (c. 1888). *McCourt St. Open Sun. afternoons (May–Nov.); Thurs.–Sun. (Dec.); daily (Jan.–Feb.) Guided tours only.* Ⓢ *(08) 8735 8208.*

Old Wool and Grain Store National Trust museum of local history, with a focus on whaling and shipping, housed in the two-storey limestone former warehouse and residence (note the delicate cantilevered balcony). It was built in 1879, when Beachport was a busy wool and grain port. A rail line once ran direct from the warehouse to the jetty at the port. *Railway Tce. Open Sun. & pub hol afternoons, or by appt.* Ⓢ *(08) 8735 8013.*

In the area A large midden at Three Mile Rocks, within the Beachport Conservation Park, attests to a long Aboriginal tradition of shellfishing and is one of several such sites in the area. *About 2 km N. Open daily. Access by 4-wheel drive only.*

🛈 *Millicent Rd; (08) 8735 8029.*
See also Millicent, Robe

BETHANY

Map ref. 337 F5

The first major German settlement in the Barossa Valley, founded by Lutheran dissidents in 1842 and laid out in the Silesian-village style known as *Hufendorf*, where properties are neatly aligned along the road. Several very early cottages have survived.

Of interest The spire of the Herberge Christi Lutheran church (1883) still rises above the landscape and Bethany's pioneer cemetery has many German headstones and stories of hardship to tell. *Open for services or by appt. (08) 8563 2089 or (08) 8563 3748.* The Landhaus, a stone and mud cottage built as a shepherd's hut c. 1848. The rooms feature mud and straw ceilings crossed by rough-hewn timber beams. *Bethany Rd. (08) 8563 2191.*

🛈 *66 Murray St, Tanunda; (08) 8563 0600, freecall 1800 812 662.* Website: www.southaustralia.com
See also Lyndoch, Tanunda

BIRDWOOD

Map ref. 327 L9, 337 F8

A small settlement in the Adelaide Hills, once a milling centre for locally grown wheat.

National Motor Museum Set in 8 ha centred around historic Birdwood Mill, built in 1852 by pioneer Murray paddle-steamer captain William

Randell. It offers a remarkable array of historic motorcycles and cars, with excellent interpretive displays. The mill houses a huge collection of colonial gadgetry and other Australiana. *Shannon St. Open daily.* Ⓢ *(08) 8568 5006.*

🛈 *The Top of the Torrens Gallery, Shannon St; (08) 8568 6677.*

BURRA

Map ref. 327 L5

See Historic Highlights, p. 150

CLARE

Map ref. 327 L5

Edward Gleeson, who settled in this picturesque valley in 1840, chose the town site and named it after his birthplace, County Clare in Ireland. The district's first vines were reputedly planted for explorer John Horrocks in 1842. Today Clare is at the centre of one of the state's premier wine-growing regions. The National Trust has listed more than 30 buildings, as well as the town's magnificent avenue of century-old oak trees.

Old Police Station Museum The town's first public building (1850), with unusual gabled porch: Gleeson was first Stipendiary Magistrate. Now a NT museum documenting Clare's social, agricultural and wine-growing past. *Neagles Rock Rd. Open Sat.–Sun., pub & school hols or by appt.* Ⓢ *(08) 8842 2376. NT.*

Wolta Wolta Homestead Characteristic SA colonial stone villa built by successful pastoralist John Hope in stages

from 1846. Some of the fine antique furnishings were brought by Hope from Ireland for the house. *West Tce. Open limited hours Sun. or by appt. Guided tours only.* Ⓢ *(08) 8842 3656.*

Also of interest Some of the older wineries have interesting histories. Knappstein Enterprise Wines, in the old Clare Brewery complex (1878). *2 Pioneer Ave. Open daily. (08) 8842 2096.* Leasingham Wines, established in 1893. *7 Dominic St. Open daily. (08) 8842 2555.*

In the area Sevenhill Cellars, the district's oldest winery, was established by Austrian Jesuit priests in 1851, and is still run by the Jesuits. Sacramental wines and table wines are also made and sold. The cellars are open to the public, as is the associated Church of St Aloysius (1864–75). *6 km S, then 1 km E. College Rd, Sevenhill. Open Mon.–Sat. (08) 8843 4222.* Quelltaler Wines: The first vines were planted in 1850 and the oldest building dates back to 1863. This fine stone and gabled winery continues to use the original Mintaro slate fermenting tanks. *15 km S, then 1 km E. Quelltaler Rd, off Main North Rd, Watervale. Open daily. (08) 8843 0003.* The Hawker family's Bungaree Station (1840s) is still a leading merino stud and offers accommodation. The property includes a Gothic-style church of mellowed stone, St Michael's. *12 km N, on the Port Pirie Rd. (08) 8842 2677.* On the highway near Andrews lies Geralka Rural Farm, a Clydesdale horse stud with historic farm buildings and vintage machinery. *25 km N*

Bungaree Station, near Clare

on Jamestown Rd. Guided tours only,
1.30 p.m. Sun. (except Feb.) & pub hols.
ⓢ (08) 8845 8081.
🄸 Town Hall, 229 Main North
Rd; (08) 8842 2131. Website: www.
classiccountry.org.au/clare.html
See also Mintaro

FLINDERS RANGES Map ref. 329 K8

*See Arkaroola, Melrose, Port Augusta,
Quorn, Wilpena*

GAWLER Map ref. 327 L8, 337 D5

See Historic Highlights, p. 152

GLENCOE Map ref. 336 H11

See Millicent

GOOLWA Map ref. 327 L11, 336 C3

Goolwa, on the last bend of the
Murray before it reaches the sea, was
a key river port from the 1850s to the
1880s. When Australia's first public
railway – a horse-drawn railway –
opened in 1854, cargo was shipped
down the Murray to Goolwa, then
carted to Port Elliot for export.
But with the advent of steam trains
the town's commercial importance
diminished. Today Goolwa is a
popular resort.
**Signal Point River Murray Interpretive
Centre** Celebrates the Murray River
via the culture of the area's original
inhabitants, the Ngarrindjeri people,
the colourful early days of river travel,
and the story of Goolwa itself. *Goolwa
Wharf. Open daily. (08) 8555 3488.*
ALSO OF INTEREST The Railway Superintendent's Cottage is Goolwa's oldest
house, a limestone building (1852)
overlooking the railway and wharves,
and distinguished by an unusual
vaulted roof. *Laurie La. Open by
appt.* ⓢ *(donation). (08) 8555 2221.*
National Trust Museum, housed in
the old blacksmithy (1870s), focuses
on the histories of Goolwa and
Hindmarsh Island. Diverse exhibits
include Australia's first motorised
caravan. *Porter St. Open Tues.–Thurs.;
Sat.–Sun. afternoons; most pub hols
& daily during school hols.* ⓢ *(08)
8555 2221.* In the broad main
street, Cadell St, you can see the
Goolwa Hotel (1853), crowned by
a figurehead salvaged from the

Kanyaka Station homestead ruins, Hawker

Mozambique, which was wrecked off
the coast in 1854 (open daily, (08)
8555 2012), and Australia's oldest
railway coach. The restored Corio
Hotel, with lengthy verandahed
facade, was first licensed in 1857.
*Railway Tce. Open daily. (08) 8555
2011.* In Goolwa Tce, visitors will find
the post office (1857). The limestone
police station (1859) and courthouse
(1867) house the South Coast
Regional Art Centre. *Open daily. (08)
8555 1500.* The steam-driven Cockle
Train runs along the old railway line
between Goolwa and **Victor Harbor**.
*Sun., pub hols & SA school hols. Tickets
from Goolwa, Victor Harbor railway
stations.* ⓢ *(08) 8391 1223.*
🄸 *Signal Point River Murray Interpretive
Centre, Goolwa Wharf; (08) 8555 3488.*
Website: www.alexandrina.sa.gov.au
See also Victor Harbor

HAHNDORF Map ref. 327 L9, 337 D11

See Historic Highlights, p. 154

HAWKER Map ref. 329 K9

In the semi-arid central Flinders
Ranges, more than 370 km N of
Adelaide, this isolated railway town,
surveyed in 1880, became the centre
of a large wheat-growing area until
drought devastated several of the
largest holdings.
OF INTEREST History lingers on in the
substantial 19th-century structures
such as the railway station (1880),
the Hawker Hotel (formerly the
Royal) and the original post office,

both dating from 1882. *Elder Tce*. The
stone buttresses of the extensive
Hookina railway bridge (also 1880),
which was washed away by flood in
1955, can still be seen.
IN THE AREA Several historic cemeteries
reveal the hardship of life on the
edge of the outback. About 28 km SW
lie clusters of ruins – ravaged stone
walls, crumbling chimneys, and steps
that lead nowhere – the remains of
Kanyaka Station homestead, a farm
that once covered almost 1000 sq km
and supported 70 families. This was
one of the great colonial sheep
stations, established in 1851 by Hugh
Proby, son of a British earl, when he
was just 24 years old. He drowned a
year later, and the property was completely abandoned by 1888.
🄸 *Cnr Wilpena & Cradock rds;
(08) 8648 4014.* Website: www.hawker.
mtx.net

INNAMINCKA Map ref. 331 Q7, 329 H10

Remote outpost at the end of the
rugged Strzelecki Track, near the
Qld border, about 1065 km NE of
Adelaide. It was a police interstate
customs depot (from 1882), and then
a police camp and drovers' stopping
place until Federation in 1901.
Explorer Charles Sturt passed
through in 1845 and Burke and
Wills' epic 1860–61 expedition
ended here in tragedy. Now a stopping place for Outback tourists. The
name is said to be a corruption of the
Aboriginal 'Yidniminckanie'.
OF INTEREST The former Australian

Inland Mission building (1927), now local headquarters for the National Parks and Wildlife Service. Memorials record where Burke and Wills died; another marks where the expedition's only survivor, John King, was found living with Aboriginal people several months later. About 25 km E of Innamincka, across the border in Qld, on the edge of Cooper Creek, is the 'Dig Tree' where provisions for the hapless explorers were buried. The 50 000 ha Innamincka Historic Reserve is rich in Aboriginal relics and rock carvings. ℹ *South Tce; (08) 8675 9901.*

KADINA

Map ref. 326 I6

Kadina was founded in 1861 after the discovery of vast amounts of copper ore at nearby **Wallaroo**. With **Moonta** and Wallaroo, it became known as 'the Copper Triangle', or 'Little Cornwall'. Thousands of Cornish miners flocked to the region, bringing their mining skills, traditional building styles and culture. The mines closed in the 1930s owing to falling world prices for copper, but the district still celebrates its Cornish heritage. Today, Kadina is the largest town on the Yorke Peninsula.

Matta House and Heritage Museum Matta House was built in 1863 for the manager of Wallaroo's Matta mine. Exhibits include agricultural and mining machinery, SA's largest printing museum, a forge, and a photographic display. *1.5 km S, off Kadina–Moonta Rd. Open Wed., Sat.–Sun. afternoons; extended hours for pub & school hols.* $ *(08) 8821 2721. NT.*

Traditional Cornish costume, Kadina

Wallaroo Mine Site The crumbling remains of the hugely productive mine, which once yielded several hundred tonnes of ore a week. The signposted relics include Harvey's Engine House (1876), a towering stone pumping station, the first of eight such structures and now the sole survivor. *1.5 km SW on Matta Rd.*

ALSO OF INTEREST Banking and Currency Museum, in the town's oldest surviving bank (1873), has an engaging collection of different currencies, and old banking paraphernalia. *3 Graves St. Open Mon.–Thurs., Sun.; closed June. (08) 8821 2906.* A heritage trail covers more than 30 historic sites and structures, such as the restored rotunda (1897) in Victoria Sq., which is still used by the Kadina Wallaroo Moonta Band. The monumental town hall, facing the square, began life as a reading room in 1880. *Not open for inspection.* Historic hotels, include the Wombat (1862) in Taylor St (open daily, (08) 8821 1108) and the Royal Exchange (1873). The latter hotel, previously known as The Exchange, was dubbed 'royal' after the Duke of Clarence stayed there in 1880. *Cnr Graves & Digby sts.* When Gov. Jervois was opening the railway station in Frances Tce in 1878, the platform on which he and other officials were standing collapsed amidst a sea of bunting. The Kernewek Lowender, a festival of all things Cornish, is held in May in odd-numbered years. For details contact the Town Hall, Wallaroo. *(08) 8823 3333.*

ℹ *Old Moonta Railway Station, Kadina Rd, Moonta; (08) 8825 1891.* Website: www.classiccountry.org.au/kadina.html

See also Moonta, Wallaroo

KANGAROO ISLAND

Map ref. 326 F11

The island was a base for sealers and whalers from 1802. In 1836, SA colonists set up camp for several months on the shores of Nepean Bay in the NE, near the present town of Kingscote, whilst Col. William Light chose a site for the capital of the new colony. Penneshaw is another of the island's towns. Kangaroo Island is 120 km SW of Adelaide.

Cape Borda Lighthouse (1858), at the NW end of the island, is an unusual, squat structure – just two storeys. Nearby, a small red cannon originally fired to warn ships of impending danger, is now fired daily. Accommodation available in the lightkeepers' cottages and huts. *Tours daily.* $ *(08) 8559 7235. For accommodation, (08) 8559 3257.*

Hope Cottage Museum With Faith (now gone) and Charity (privately owned), this is one of three identical stone cottages built c. 1859 by the Calnan brothers with profits made on the Victorian goldfields. Amongst the exhibits is the reconstructed stone top of SA's first lighthouse (at Cape Willoughby, 1852), replaced in the 1970s. *Centenary Ave, Kingscote. Open daily, 1–4 p.m.* $ *(08) 8553 2308. NT.*

ALSO OF INTEREST The well-preserved Kingscote Old Pioneer Cemetery is SA's oldest. The state's first introduced fruit tree, the 'Old Mulberry Tree', planted in 1836 by one of the founding settlers, is still producing fruit. A nearby cairn marks the site of the island's first settlement. *Reeves Pt, Kingscote.* Penneshaw Maritime and Folk Museum displays local history in the former Hog Bay School (1922) with maritime and shipwreck relics. An old grinding mill is a vestige of the town's early pottery industry. *Howard Dr., Penneshaw. Open Wed.–Sun. 3–5 p.m. or by appt.* $ *(08) 8553 1070 or (08) 8553 1109. NT.*

ℹ *Howard Dr., Penneshaw; (08) 8553 1185.* Website: www.tourkangarooisland.com.au

KAPUNDA

Map ref. 327 L7, 337 E3

Nestled in the rolling farmland of the northern Mt Lofty Ranges, about 80 km N of Adelaide, Kapunda was Australia's first mining town. It was officially 'discovered' in 1842 and was laid out in 1845, a year after graziers Frederick Dutton and Charles Bagot discovered copper and opened the Great Kapunda Mine. Falling copper prices caused the mines to close in 1878 but more than 50 buildings listed by the National Trust reflect a prosperous past. Kapunda is a service town for surrounding farmlands.

Cape Borda Lighthouse, Kangaroo Island

Bagot's Fortune A display in the old printing office (1866) where the *Kapunda Herald* was published 1864–1950. It vividly re-creates many aspects of mining history and the lives of miners. *5 Hill St. Open afternoons (daily Sept.–May; Sat.–Sun., pub & school hols June–Aug.) or by appt.* Ⓢ *(08) 8566 2286.*

Kapunda Museum The grand, Romanesque, former Baptist Church (1866) flanked by two towers houses an eclectic collection of historic memorabilia. *11 Hill St. Open daily afternoons or by appt.* Ⓢ *(08) 8566 2286.*

Mine, Lookout and Chimney Historic precinct encompassing the main open-cut mine and the tall chimney (1850) used as an air shaft for the mine that still stands sentry above it. A lookout affords clear views of the mine site and workings, all easily identified via descriptive displays and old photographs. *Jackson St.*

ALSO OF INTEREST The town's historic buildings mirror the community's diverse Cornish, Welsh, Irish and German origins. Excellent heritage trail maps are available free from Visitor Information. Mine Square Cottage (1846), of local stone and with a simple earth floor, is the only survivor of 18 cottages originally built by the mining company for its employees. *Cnr Mine & Mugg sts. Not open for inspection.* Early hotels include the Clare Castle (1859). *Main St. Open daily. (08) 8566 2103.* The Duke of York (in 1867) and the Prince of Wales (in 1900) dined at the North

Kapunda Hotel (1849 but with later additions) and cattle baron Sidney Kidman held regular horse sales behind the hotel in the early 1900s. Kidman's horses were shipped to the Indian Army and bought for the legendary Australian Light Horse Brigade. *Main St. Open daily. (08) 8566 2205.* William Oldham, the first manager of the stone and stucco National Bank (1862), also in Main St, was kept busy, being in addition mine manager and a minister of the Congregational Union Chapel (1858) in Chapel St. *Neither building open for inspection.*

IN THE AREA Anlaby Station, settled 1839, home of the pioneering Dutton family and once at the heart of a 65 000 ha (now 107 ha) property. Enjoy the magnificent stone homestead (1857), fine gardens and carriage collection. Now a luxury B&B. *7 km NE on Anlaby Rd. Open for tours Sat.–Sun. or by appt.* Ⓢ *(08) 8566 2465.*

ℹ *Soldiers Memorial Hall, Hill St; (08) 8566 2902. Website: www.kaptour.mtx.net*
See also Gawler

KINGSCOTE
Map ref. 326 I12

See Kangaroo Island

KINGSTON S.E.
Map ref. 336 F8

A farming and fishing resort, almost 300 km SE of Adelaide, and the first town south of the fascinating coastal

lagoon system known as the Coorong.
Cape Jaffa Lighthouse Steel-framed and timber lighthouse 33 m tall, erected 1870–72 on hazardous Margaret Brock Reef at nearby Cape Jaffa and distinguished as Australia's only offshore lighthouse with a keeper's residence. It was dismantled and rebuilt at Kingston in 1974. The lighthouse is floodlit every night. *Marine Pde. Open school hol afternoons or by appt.* Ⓢ *(08) 8767 2114. NT.*

ALSO OF INTEREST Kingston Pioneer Museum, a local history and maritime museum in the old general store, part of which dates back to the 1870s. *Cooke St. Open afternoons during pub & school hols.* Ⓢ *(08) 8767 2114. NT.* The elegant Old Kingston Bank (1867), is now tearooms. *Open by appt. 40 Holland St. (08) 8767 2559.*

ℹ *The Big Lobster, Princes Hwy; (08) 8767 2555.*
See also Robe

LOBETHAL
Map ref. 327 L9, 336 C1, 337 E9

One of SA's earliest communities, founded in 1841 by German settlers, in a pretty wooded valley in the Adelaide Hills.

OF INTEREST Lobethal Archives and Historical Museum documents the interwoven histories of the district's German and English settlers, with pioneer memorabilia and archives. The tiny, thatch-roofed pug cottage (1845) that was once the Lutheran College and seminary is located within the museum. *Main St. Open Sun. afternoons or by appt.* Ⓢ *(08) 8389 6343.* Adjacent is the Lutheran Church (1845–47), the oldest of its kind still open in Australia. *Main St. Guided tours only.* Ⓢ *(08) 8389 6343.* The National Costume Museum showcases the history of South Australian fashion with a wonderful and well-presented array of period costumes and accessories, from 1812 up to today. *Cnr Lobethal Rd & Main St. Open Tues.–Sun. or by appt.* Ⓢ *(08) 8389 6157.* The Motorcycle and Heritage Museum is also worth a visit. It has more than 100 motorcycles on display including one built in 1910. *Main St (next to Costume Museum). Open daily.* Ⓢ *(08) 8389 5734.*

ℹ *Main St; (08) 8389 6996.*

LOXTON

Map ref. 327 Q7

Loxton Historical Village Re-creation of an early farming town, recording the history and struggles of pioneer farmers in the late 19th century. Combines original structures with replicas of old cottages, shops and farm buildings from the Riverland district. There is a rudimentary pine and pug hut like one built by pioneer settler William Loxton, shaded by a pepper tree that he planted. A stone chapel, railway station, bakery, saddlery, newspaper office and the old lock-up line the dusty streets. *River Dr. Open daily.* Ⓢ *(08) 8584 71941.*
🅘 *Bookpurnong Tce; (08) 8584 7919.*

LYNDOCH

Map ref. 327 L8, 337 E6

A small village cradled in a gentle vale of the Barossa Valley, Lyndoch was settled in the early 1840s and is one of the state's oldest towns. Some fine early buildings have survived, as have a number of vineyards established in the 19th century.
OF INTEREST The two-storey Lyndoch Hotel (1869) is built of local ironstone. *Gilbert St. Open daily. (08) 8524 4211.*
IN THE AREA On the Tanunda Rd is Holy Trinity Church, consecrated in 1861. *1 km N.* The Barossa Valley's first commercial vineyard had its beginnings in 1847 when Bavarian immigrant Johann Gramp planted his vines near Jacob's Creek. The vineyard was producing wine by 1850 and today Orlando Wines is one of the country's best-known wineries. The cellar door is housed in the original Rowland Flat schoolhouse (c. 1850s). *5 km NE. Barossa Valley Way, Rowland Flat. Open daily. (08) 8521 3140.*
🅘 *66 Murray St, Tanunda; (08) 8563 0600, freecall 1800 812 662.* Website: www.barossa-region.org
See also Tanunda

McLAREN VALE

Map ref. 327 K10, 336 B2, 337 A13

This town has been the heart of the beautiful Southern Vales winegrowing region since the 1840s. The district boasts more than 60 wineries, including historic vineyards such as Hardy's, founded in 1853.
Hardy's Tintara Winery is a large complex

Old grapevine, McLaren Vale

right in the town, centred around the old McLaren Vale flour mill. The vineyard, established in 1838, was bought by Thomas Hardy in 1853 and by the late 1800s Hardy was shipping red wine and port to London. A grand old Moreton Bay fig tree on the property (planted around 150 years ago and believed to be one of the oldest Moreton Bay trees in SA) is classified for its heritage significance. *202 Main Rd. Open daily. (08) 8323 9185.*
ALSO OF INTEREST At Wirra Wirra Vineyard you can taste wines in the restored 1894 cellars. *McMurtrie Rd. Open daily. (08) 8329 4701.* Edwards and Chaffey Winery (previously known as Seaview, founded 1850) is an historic complex with a tasting room notable for its finely carved wine vats. *Chaffeys Rd. Open Mon.–Sat., Sun. afternoons. (08) 8323 8250.* The Barn (c. 1870), an old coach depot and once a stopping place for bullock teams hauling wheat from Encounter Bay, is now a gallery and restaurant. *Cnr Chalk Hill & Main rds. Open daily for lunch and dinner. (08) 8323 8618.* The McLaren Vale Hotel (1857) was at one time owned by vigneron Thomas Hardy, who insisted that a room be kept free for him at all times. *208 Main Rd. Open daily. (08) 8323 8208.*
IN THE AREA Historic Salopian Inn, first licensed in 1851, is now a restaurant. *1 km s. Cnr Willunga & McMurtrie rds. Open Thurs.–Tues. (08) 8323 8769.* At Coriole Vineyards the 1860

complex includes a fine stone barn. *5 km N. Chaffeys Rd. Open daily. (08) 8323 8305.* Cellar sales at Chapel Hill Winery are based in a small former chapel (1865). *6 km N. Chapel Hill Rd. Open daily. (08) 8323 8429.* On a bend of the Onkaparinga River is the tiny township of Old Noarlunga, founded in 1841. The towered Church of St Philip and St James (1850) overlooks the town from a nearby hill. *4 km NW. Church Hill Rd, Old Noarlunga. (08) 8323 0194.*
🅘 *Main Rd (opp. Caffrey Rd intersection); (08) 8323 9944, freecall 1800 628 410.* Website: www. visitorcentre.com.au
See also Reynella, Willunga

MANNUM

Map ref. 327 M9, 337 I9

Mannum, on the banks of the Murray River, is proud of its colourful riverboat heritage. This is the birthplace of the Murray's first paddle-steamer, the little *Mary Ann*, built at Gumeracha by Capt. William Randell and carted by bullock dray to Mannum for her maiden trip in 1853. It was also home to pioneer inventors David and John Shearer, blacksmiths by trade, who constructed Australia's first steam car, which spluttered to a start (fired by local mallee roots) in 1899. (The car is now in the National Motor Museum, **Birdwood**.)
PS *Marion* Sturdy river trader, built in 1897, which plied the Murray for over 50 years, restored and now a

living museum used for passenger cruises. *Arnold Park, Randell St. Open daily.* Ⓢ *(08) 8569 1303.*

ALSO OF INTEREST The Mannum Dock Museum of River History has displays featuring the history of the river – including the boiler of the PS *Mary Ann* – the local Aboriginal people, early river explorers and some early local industries, such as shearing. *6 Randell St. Open daily.* Ⓢ *(08) 8569 2733.* A replica of the small whale boat rowed down the Murrumbidgee to the Murray by explorer Charles Sturt in 1830 can be found at the Mary Ann Reserve. Historic buildings line Randell St, including several associated with Capt. Randell's family.

🆔 *Arnold Park, Randell St; (08) 8569 1303.*

MARREE
Map ref. 328 I1, 330 I13

A tiny outpost at the junction of the Birdsville and Oodnadatta tracks, on the edge of the desert Outback. The district, long crossed by Aboriginal trade routes, became a depot for camel trains carting wool and supplies in the 1800s and still has old date palms planted by the Afghan drivers.

OF INTEREST An excellent Aboriginal heritage museum in the Arabunna Aboriginal Community Centre. *Railway Tce. Open Mon.–Fri.* Ⓢ *(donation). (08) 8675 8351.* The quirky old truck in Museum Park was used by outback postman EG ('Tom') Kruse to deliver mail along the Birdsville Track for many years. A reconstructed mosque commemorates the region's Afghan heritage. Rusting relics of old railway vehicles, and forsaken corrugated iron houses, recall busier days.

IN THE AREA At Curdimurka Siding, remains of the original Ghan railway line, which passed through Marree until re-routed in 1980, with abandoned railway workers' cottages and associated structures. *About 90 km w, via Oodnadatta Trk.* To the north is Australia's largest lake, the saltpan Lake Eyre, named after explorer Edward Eyre who reached the lake in 1840. *100 km N, Lake Eyre National Park.*

🆔 *Marree Outback Roadhouse and General Store, Oodnadatta Track; (08) 8675 8360.*

🆔 *Flinders & Outback Tourism Centre, 41 Flinders Tce, Port Augusta;* *(08) 8641 0793, freecall 1800 633 060.* Website: www.southaustralia.com

MELROSE
Map ref. 327 J2, 329 J12

At the foot of Mt Remarkable lies the oldest town in the Flinders Ranges, settled in the 1840s and for several decades the social, commercial and judicial centre of SA's far north.

Melrose Courthouse & Police Station Museum Until 1881 this isolated complex (1862) was headquarters of the Northern Police Division, a precinct extending north to the Timor Sea. Behind the formal Victorian building are cells (1874), stables and exercise yard. *Stuart St. Open Wed.–Mon. afternoons.* Ⓢ *(08) 8666 2141. NT.*

ALSO OF INTEREST The North Star Hotel, first licensed in 1854, is now in an 1881 building. *Nott St. Open daily. (08) 8666 2110.* The Mt Remarkable Hotel remains virtually unaltered since 1857. *Stuart St. Open daily. (08) 8666 2119.* The post office (1866) and the school (1879), both Stuart St. The massive, gaunt shell of the five-storey Jacka Brewery, built as a flour mill in 1878 in Brewery Rd. Old cottages, such as the pug and pine Keating Cottage (c. 1859) in Survey Rd. *Not open for inspection.*

🆔 *Melrose Caravan Park, Joes Rd; (08) 8666 2060.* Website: www.mtr. sa.gov.au

MILLICENT
Map ref. 336 G11

Pastoral, timber and retail centre on the spectacular Limestone Coast, also known locally as the 'Shipwreck Coast' for the numerous shipping losses in treacherous nearby waters.

Millicent Museum Records the district's history and culture, including that of the traditional Boandik owners, with artifacts and replicas of local rock art. Amongst the extensive collection of restored horse-drawn vehicles is a gloomily ornate hearse complete with casket. The Maritime Room concentrates on tales and relics of local shipwrecks. Visitor Information is also here. *1 Mt Gambier Rd. Open daily.* Ⓢ *(08) 8733 3205.*

IN THE AREA All that remains of the vast Glencoe station is its splendid stone shearing shed (1856–63). Edward and Robert Leake established the property in 1844 and by 1856 it had 33 000 sheep, 6000 cattle and 250 horses. The woolshed boasts hand-adzed blackwood columns and beams: on its completion in 1863, there was a celebratory ball for 200 guests. The building is one of the country's finest examples of early rural architecture. *37 km SE. Open by appt. Key from Glencoe General Store, Main Rd, Glencoe.* Ⓢ *(08) 8739 4320. NT.*

See also Mount Gambier, Robe

🆔 *1 Mt Gambier Rd; (08) 8733 3205.*

MINTARO
Map ref. 327 L5

Mintaro developed first in the 1840s as a stop for bullockies and muleteers carting copper from **Burra** to the southern ports. A vast slate deposit discovered in the 1850s has since provided materials for billiards tables around the world as well as many of the town's buildings. Located in the eastern Clare Valley, the picturesque town has been declared a state heritage area.

OF INTEREST Many of Mintaro's well-preserved buildings, both domestic and public, are identified in a heritage trail leaflet, available from Visitor Information. Several offer accommodation, such as the historic Mintaro Mews, a former granary and stables (1850s), which also now houses a restaurant. *Burra St. Restaurant open for dinner Fri.–Sun. (08) 8843 9001.* The Magpie and Stump Hotel (licensed 1851) was one of several popular watering holes for passing bullock teamsters (and remains a favourite with travellers). The original baker's oven at the rear is still in use, though nowadays it produces pizzas. *Burra St. Open daily. (08) 8843 9014.*

IN THE AREA Mintaro Slate Quarry is still operating. *1.5 km w. Open Mon.–Fri. (08) 8843 9077.* Martindale Hall, a splendid Georgian mansion built of local freestone for Edmund Bowman in 1879, epitomises the princely lifestyle of the district's early pastoralists. Pheasants roamed the grounds and hunt club meets were held here. The interiors are magnificent, especially the lofty, galleried hall lit by a glass-domed ceiling. Sold to the Mortlock family in 1891, the property was eventually bequeathed to the people of SA. The 1970s classic *Picnic at Hanging Rock* was filmed here.

Martindale Hall, Mintaro

Accommodation available. *2 km E on Manoora Rd. Open daily afternoons.* Ⓢ *(08) 8843 9088.* The Polish Hill River church, built in the 1870s, is still used by the local Polish community. The neighbouring Pikes Polish Hill River Estate sells its wines from a restored 19th-century shearing shed built by Polish settlers. *Polish Hill River Rd, Sevenhill. Open daily. (08) 8843 4370.*

🄸 *Town Hall, 229 Main North Rd, Clare; (08) 8842 2131.* Website: www. classiccountry.org.au/mintaro.html *See also Clare*

MOONTA
Map ref. 326 I6

Cornish miners flocked to the district after shepherd Paddy Ryan discovered copper on WW Hughes' Wallaroo sheep run in 1861. The population reached about 12 000 by 1875 and Moonta, with **Kadina** and **Wallaroo**, became known as 'Little Cornwall'. The town still has strong links with the past and a fascinating Cornish heritage.

Moonta Mines Heritage Area Encompasses the original mine site, Cornish cottages, church, and ruins of the mine offices and workings. *2 km SE.* Highlights include ruins of the Hughes Pumping House, built of fossilised limestone (small shell fossils are still visible), which operated day and night from 1865 to 1923 without a major breakdown. *Verran Tce.* The impressive Mines Museum in the gabled former public school (1878) reveals much about both the lives of miners and the town's Cornish

heritage, and has an extensive local history resource centre. *Verran Tce. Open Wed., Fri.–Sun. afternoons; daily during pub & school hols.* Ⓢ *(08) 8825 2152.* A traditional whitewashed miner's cottage (1870), built of clay, limestone and mud bricks, one of few to survive, is furnished to reflect the miners' lifestyle. *Vercoe St. Open Wed., Sat.–Sun. afternoons; pub & school hols.* A narrow-gauge tourist railway winds among the scattered mine relics. *Verran Tce. Departs hourly, Sat.–Sun. & pub hol afternoons.* Ⓢ

ALSO OF INTEREST More than 30 buildings in Moonta have been listed by the National Trust. The Cornwall Hotel and the Royal Hotel, both in Ryan St, and Moonta Hotel, George St, all date from the mid 1860s, the first boom years, and are all still serving customers daily. By the 1870s the town had more than 14 Methodist churches, several of which still stand: the Wesley Moonta Mines Methodist Church (1865) has a magnificent 600-pipe organ (installed 1888). *Milne St. Open daily afternoons.* Ⓢ *(donation).* The ornate Freemasons Hall (1875) is the oldest such building in Australia. *Blanche Tce.*

IN THE AREA Fascinating underground tours are available of the Wheal (Cornish for 'mine') Hughes Mine. *3 km N on Wallaroo Rd. Tours at 1 p.m. daily.* Ⓢ *(08) 8825 1891.*

🄸 *Old Moonta Railway Station, Kadina Rd; (08) 8825 1891.* Website: www. classiccountry.org.au/moonta.html *See also Kadina, Wallaroo*

MORGAN
Map ref. 327 N6

Located on the banks of the Murray River, Morgan once hummed with activity, being a major rail centre and the State's second-busiest inland port. Now the town is a quiet holiday resort, but still retains signs of its colourful heritage.

Port of Morgan Wharf A vibrant precinct dating from 1877 and rich in reminders of the town's riverboat days – when steamers had to queue for a docking berth.

ALSO OF INTEREST Stroll along Railway Tce to see the imposing Customs House and courthouse (1878) near the station. The old 'Nor West Bend' railway station, now the Morgan Historic Museum, features riverboat and farming exhibits, and an impressive range of horse-drawn vehicles. *Open Tues., Sat.–Sun. or by appt.* Ⓢ *(08) 8540 2565 or (08) 8540 2130.* SA's oldest surviving paddle-wheel boat, the PW *Mayflower* (1884), moored nearby, takes river cruises by appt. Ⓢ *0407 818 829.*

🄸 *Morgan Roadhouse, Fourth St; (08) 8540 2205.* Website: www.riverland. net.au/~morgansa/

MORPHETT VALE
Map ref. 337 A12

See Reynella

MOUNT GAMBIER
Map ref. 336 H12

A sprawling city on the slopes of an extinct volcano that was sighted and named by Lt James Grant in 1800. The district was originally inhabited by the Boandik people: many rock engravings have survived in underground caves, and thousands of 'finger lines' and other markings have also been documented. The town was started as a private venture by Hastings Cunningham in 1854, although the Henty family from Victoria built the first dwelling, in 1841.

Blue Lake The Old Pumping Station (1884), constructed from local dolomite, now houses the station offices and a museum. There are tours on the hour, including a twilight tour in Nov.–Jan. Ⓢ *(08) 8723 1199.*

Lady Nelson Discovery Centre Intriguing historical and geological exhibits, and interactive displays. Features include a full-size replica of Lt Grant's boat, HMS *Lady Nelson*, a 'cave walk', and aspects of the district's Aboriginal history. *Jubilee Hwy East. Open daily.* $ *(08) 8724 9750.*

Mount Gambier Historic Courthouse Elegant building of pink dolomite (1865), where in times past a typical cautionary sentence was 18 months gaol and 20 cuts with 'the cat' for forging a £2 cheque. Now an engaging museum of legal and local history. *42A Bay Rd. Open daily. Tours by appt.* $ *(08) 8725 7011. NT.*

Also of interest Mount Gambier's architecture is distinguished by the use of unusually hued local limestone, freestone and dolomite. The imposing town hall (1882) with clock and tower added 1883, and King's Theatre (1906), dominate Commercial St East. The Jens Town Hall Hotel (1884), cnr Commercial St East & Watson Tce, is open daily, (08) 8725 0188, as is the Mount Gambier Hotel (1862), Commercial St West, (08) 8725 0611. Both hotels have been extended over the years. So have several of the town's churches, notably Christ Church (erected 1865) in Bay Rd, open for services & by appt, (08) 8723 1353, and St Andrew's Uniting Church (1871) in Elizabeth St, also open for services & by appt, (08) 8725 2501. St Paul's, in a prominent hilltop position, was built 1884–85, succeeding the original Catholic church, a canvas-lined log hut. *Penola Rd. Open daily. (08) 8725 6566.* The battlemented Centenary Tower on the summit of Mt Gambier, built

1900–04, honours Grant's sighting of the mount a century earlier – the lookout is open when the flag is flying. $ *(08) 8723 2351.* In the beautiful old stone King's Theatre, the regional Riddoch Art Gallery collection includes colonial paintings and contemporary Aboriginal art. *6–10 Commercial St East. (08) 8723 9566.* The former Institute building (c. 1887) is now a gallery, focusing on local artists. *20 Commercial St East. Open daily. (08) 8725 1788.*

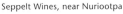 *Lady Nelson Visitor and Discovery Centre, Jubilee Hwy East; (08) 8724 9750.* Website: www.mountgambiertourism.com.au *See also Millicent, Penola, Port MacDonnell*

NARACOORTE

Map ref. 336 H9

This quiet country town began life in the 1840s as a privately owned settlement, known as Mosquito Plain. During the 1850s it expanded as it found itself a stopping place on the overland route taken by Chinese landing in SA to avoid the Victorian landing tax. The town was renamed Kingcraig in 1860 when the government township of Naracoorte was surveyed next to it.

Of interest The award-winning Sheep's Back, a wool museum in a three-storey limestone flour mill (1870), focuses on the history of sheep and wool in this pastoral district. Visitor Information is also here. *MacDonnell St. Open daily.* $ *(08)*

8762 1518. NT. The Gothic Revival St Andrew's Church (1874) is open for services. *Laurie Cres. (08) 8762 2303.* In pretty De Garis Pl., the handsome former Commercial Bank (1884), noted for its fine ironwork fence. *Not open for inspection.* The oldest section of the Commercial Hotel dates from 1861. *Robertson St. Open daily. (08) 8762 2100.*

In the area The towered Italianate mansion Struan House, built 1872–75 for pastoralist John Robertson, is typical of the stately homesteads established by pioneer landholders. Their properties were often vast – Robertson at one stage owned 50 580 ha. Leased by a government department, but visitors can look at the house. *15 km s on Penola Rd. Open Mon.–Fri. Tours by appt.* $ *(for tours). (08) 8762 9100.* At Naracoorte Caves Conservation Park, the Wonambi Fossil Centre has a unique simulated habitat of 200 000 years ago, with recreations of megafauna. Exceptional fossil displays and guided tours of caves available in this World Heritage area. *12 km SE. Hynam–Caves Rd. Open daily.* $ *(08) 8762 2340.*

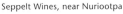 *Sheep's Back Museum, MacDonnell St; (08) 8762 1518, freecall 1800 244 421. See also Padthaway, Penola*

NURIOOTPA

Map ref. 327 M8, 337 F4

Nuriootpa grew up around William Coulthard's red-gum-slab hotel, opened in 1843, to serve bullockies and others moving between **Kapunda** and **Burra** and the south. Carefully tended vineyards have spread out from this busy Barossa Valley town for well over a century and today it is the commercial centre of the famed wine region.

In the area Seppelt Wines at Seppeltsfield was founded in 1851 by Silesian migrant Joseph Seppelt. The three-storey bluestone winery building begun in 1867 (completed by Joseph's son Benno in 1878) is the heart of a superbly maintained complex, approached via a 2-km palm-lined avenue. The family mausoleum, like the avenue, dates from the 1920s. *10 km W. Seppeltsfield Rd. Open daily. Tours available. (08) 8568 6200.* The charming nearby hamlet of Marananga, also first settled by Silesians, has several restored cottages and outbuildings, a winery and several B&Bs. The small

Seppelt Wines, near Nuriootpa

but very fine St Michael's Church opens for services only. Luhrs Cottage, nestled in an old-fashioned garden, was built in 1848 by the district's first schoolteacher. Furnishings are in the traditional German settlers' style. The cottage's detached kitchen (1880) is set up as a schoolroom with period furniture, German copy books and readers. The cellar below is also open for inspection. *3 km NE. Light Pass Rd, Light Pass. Open daily.* Ⓢ *(donation). (08) 8562 1407.* Two historic Lutheran churches, the Strait Gate Lutheran Church in Light Pass Rd and the Immanuel Lutheran Church in Immanuel Way, can be viewed from outside. ℹ *Barossa Wine and Visitor Information Centre, 66 Murray St, Tanunda; (08) 8563 0600, freecall 1800 812 662.* Website: www.barossa-region.org *See also Angaston, Tanunda*

OLD NOARLUNGA Map ref. 327 K10, 336 B2, 337 A12

See McLaren Vale

PADTHAWAY Map ref. 336 H7

Padthaway Estate A patchwork of vineyards and grassy plains with towering gum trees surround this gracious residence, built by the pioneering Lawson family in 1882. The family's original modest, six-room stone cottage (c. 1840s) is a reminder of the pioneer lifestyle. The homestead now offers fine accommodation. There is a restaurant (dinner only, booking essential) and, in the historic woolshed, a winery. The cellar door, found in the lovely old stables (c. 1850s), a forge and overseer's room are clustered around a courtyard. *Riddoch Hwy. Open daily. (08) 8765 5039.*

PENNESHAW Map ref. 327 J12

See Kangaroo Island

PENOLA Map ref. 312 A3, 336 H10

A pastoral settlement from 1850, original home of the Josephite teaching order founded in the 1860s by Blessed Mary MacKillop and Father Julian Tenison Woods, and heart of the rich Coonawarra wine-growing district since the 1890s.
The John Riddoch Interpretive Centre In

the old Mechanics Institute and Public Library (1869), it presents the history of Penola. It was named for district pioneer John Riddoch, who initiated wine-growing in the Coonawarra and in 1890 established a winery that became the famed Wynns Coonawarra Estate. The Penola and Coonawarra Visitor Information is also here. *27 Arthur St. Open daily. (08) 8737 2855.*

Petticoat Lane The town's oldest precinct, lined with charming, carefully preserved stone and timber cottages. They include the rudimentary slab and hewn timber Sharam Cottage, built by bootmaker Christopher Sharam in 1850 and thought to be the town's first house. *Open daily. (08) 8737 2884.* Gammon Cottage (1860s) features distinctive pressed-metal tiles. *Open Mon., Wed.–Sun. (08) 8737 2111.*

The Woods–MacKillop Schoolhouse was established in 1867 by Blessed Mary MacKillop and scientist Father Julian Tenison Woods as a school for all children, regardless of income. The stone building features a re-created 1860s classroom. *Cnr Petticoat La. & Portland St.* Blessed Mary MacKillop was beatified in 1995, the penultimate step towards sainthood. Next to the school is the Mary MacKillop Interpretive Centre with local history displays and information about the two pioneers. *Portland St. Both open daily.* Ⓢ *(08) 8737 2092.*

ALSO OF INTEREST McAdam Slab Hut (1840s), another rare example of the

early technique of vertical slab construction, is one of the State's oldest houses. *Cameron St, in Penola High School grounds. Open at all times. NT.* Ulva Cottage (1850s) was built by Penola's founder, Alexander Cameron, for his daughter and her husband. Now a B&B. *Bowden St.* The site of Blessed Mary MacKillop's original Josephite school (1866), a converted stable, is now the Mary MacKillop Memorial Park. *Cnr Bowden & Queen sts.* The two-storey balconied Royal Oak Hotel, built by Alexander Cameron in 1872, is the grandest building in town. *Church St. Open daily. (08) 8737 2322.*

IN THE AREA Yallum Park, a splendid sandstone mansion (1878–80), built for pioneer vigneron John Riddoch and one of the best-preserved Victorian residences in Australia. The interiors are notable for their soaring 4.5-metre ceilings, exquisite William Morris wallpapers (53 designs), Italian marble mantlepieces and hand-painted door panels. The property was originally settled by the Austin brothers in the 1840s. Two small cottages, Austin House (1840s) and Gordon House (named for poet Adam Lindsay Gordon, who often stayed here in the 1860s), form a courtyard behind the main residence. Other illustrious guests included English novelist Anthony Trollope and British royalty. *8 km SW on Millicent Rd. Open by appt.* Ⓢ *(08) 8737 2435.* More than 20 vineyards line the famed 20-km strip of rich red soil (*terra rossa*) N of

Sharam Cottage, Penola

Penola, known as Coonawarra, first recognised for its grape-growing potential by John Riddoch. Wynns Coonawarra Estate (1896) is the oldest operating winery in the Coonawarra; its historic gabled buildings are familiar to many from the company's wine labels. *Memorial Dr. Open daily. (08) 8736 3266.* Though much more recent, S. Kidman Wines stands within one of the Kidman family's original properties, Limestone Ridge. The 1850s stables, shearers' quarters and woolshed are still in use. *Riddoch Hwy. Open daily. (08) 8736 5071.*

[i] *The John Riddoch Interpretative Centre, 27 Arthur St; (08) 8737 2855.*
See also Naracoorte

Yallum Park, Penola

PETERBOROUGH

Map ref. 327 L2, 329 L13

Settled in the 1870s to service the rural hinterland, Peterborough (known as Petersburg until 1917) was reached by the railway in 1881 and eventually became the main town on the Broken Hill–Port Pirie line.

Steamtown Run by the town's Railway Preservation Society, this working museum contains a remarkable collection of rolling stock and four steam vehicles. Guided tours available. *Main St.* $ *(donation). (08) 8651 3355.* Relive the steam era with a ride on the narrow-gauge track (between Peterborough and Orroroo or Eurelia, and back) on long weekends April–Oct. *Booking (08) 8651 3566 or Visitor Information.* $

Also of interest Rann's Museum presents a steam engine, farm engines (some dating back to 1903) and other historic items. *142–44 Moscow St. Open daily. (08) 8651 2969.* A walk along Main St takes in many of the town's historic buildings, such as the Peterborough Hotel-Motel built in 1880–81, with a second storey added ten years later (open daily, (08) 8651 2006) and the spacious old town hall (1894). *Not open for inspection.* St Peter's Lutheran Church (1885), in Railway Tce, is now a private residence. *Not open for inspection.* The Gothic-style St Anacletus' Catholic Church was built in two stages (1890, 1916–17). *Railway Tce. Open for services or by appt for guided tours.* $ *(donation). (08) 8651 2008.* Around the corner in Tripney Ave is SA's only government-owned gold battery, used to treat ore found by prospectors. It opened in 1897 and is still operating. *Tours only, by appt. Contact Visitor Information (details below).* St Cecilia's (1912–13) is a 20-room mansion of mellow sandstone, originally a Catholic bishop's palace and later a convent and boarding school. Now restored, it offers accommodation and 'murder mystery' banquets. *Callary St. Open by appt. (08) 8651 3246.*

In the area The tiny town of Terowie retains many historic buildings from its days as a bustling railway town in the 1880s. *24 km SE.* At Ketchowla Historic Reserve, striking Aboriginal engravings are scattered among the rocky outcrops. In style and subject – geometric patterns and animal and bird tracks – they are characteristic of rock art in northern SA. *41 km NE. Near Nackara on Barrier Hwy.*

[i] *Main St; (08) 8651 2708.*

PORT AUGUSTA

Map ref. 328 H11

On the northern tip of Spencer Gulf, Port Augusta is just over 300 km N of Adelaide. The town was named in 1852 by AL Elder after Lady Augusta Young, but the earliest plan of the town in existence is dated 18 July 1854. Port Augusta has since serviced the small towns and sprawling sheep stations of the SA Outback.

Homestead Park Pioneer Museum Showpiece is a large pine-log homestead (c. 1868), moved from historic Yudnappinna sheep station 160 km N. Other highlights are the forge and a steam engine. *Elsie St. Open daily.* $ *(08) 8642 2035.*

Wadlata Outback Centre An impressive array of hands-on displays bring to life the history and culture of SA's vast outback region over 15 million years. Don't miss the video presentations of Dreaming stories, and colourful tales of pioneer explorers and settlers. Wadlata is an Aboriginal word meaning 'teach' or 'communicate'. *41 Flinders Tce. Open daily.* $ *(08) 8642 4511.*

Also of interest The foundation stone of the rather grand town hall was laid in 1886 though the official opening was not until 1887. *54 Commercial Rd.* The Curdnatta Art Gallery is in the original railway station. *105 Commercial Rd. Open Mon.–Sat. (08) 8641 0195.* Kapunda marble features in the courthouse (1884) facing Gladstone Sq. and the Soldiers Memorial Rotunda (1923) in Gladstone Sq. St Augustine's Church (1882) is noted for its beautiful stained glass. *Church St. (08) 8642 2487.* A well-known landmark, the town's first water tower (1882), is now a lookout offering excellent views. *Mitchell Tce.*

In the area A beautiful drive NE through the Pichi Richi Pass takes you to **Quorn**.

41 Flinders Tce; (08) 8641 0793, freecall 1800 633 060. Website: www. flinders.outback.on.net
See also Melrose

PORT LINCOLN   Map ref. 326 D8

Overlooking the brilliant blue waters of Boston Bay on the Eyre Peninsula, and named by Matthew Flinders in 1802. The site was considered for SA's capital, but the idea was abandoned due to the town's lack of fresh water and the dry hinterland. Settled in 1839, the town developed as a rural centre for the peninsula's sheep and grain farms and as a popular resort.

OF INTEREST The limestone Mill Cottage, built in 1866 by the Bishop family, and occupied by the family for more than a century, is now a museum. It displays local history artifacts, photographs and family memorabilia. *20 Flinders Hwy, Flinders Park. Open Tues.–Sun. or by appt.* $ *(08) 8682 4650. NT.* Settlers Cottage Museum, in Flinders Park, is also devoted to local history. There is a photographic display and memorabilia. *Open Sun. afternoons Sept.–June. (08) 8682 3975.* Axel Stenross Maritime Museum, centred around the workshop of Stenross, a local Finnish-born boat-builder, features maritime photographs, historic artifacts, a surviving slipway and blacksmithy. *1 km N on Lincoln Hwy. Open Tues., Thurs., Sun. afternoons; Sat. afternoons in summer. Guided tours only.* $ *(08) 8682 2963.* The Old Mill in Dorset Pl. was built as a flour mill in 1846 but never operational. *Not open for inspection.*

IN THE AREA Day tours to historic Boston Island (5 km offshore), a working sheep station which includes an 1840s slab hut and a restored cottage (1860s). *Limited accommodation available. For tour times, contact Visitor Information.* Mikkira Station, one of the oldest sheep properties on the peninsula, with restored 1840s pioneer homestead and rustic outbuildings. *Fishery Bay Rd. Camping available. Key and permits from Visitor Information.* Koppio Smithy Museum, an agricultural museum centred around a pine-log cottage (1890) and quaint corrugated-iron smithy (1903). Be sure to visit the Women's Pioneer Room, filled with

Dingley Dell, Port MacDonnell

vintage, non-labour-saving domestic appliances. There's also a Barbed Wire and Fencing Display. *40 km N via Cummins Rd (signposted). Open Tues.–Sun., pub & school hols. (08) 8684 4243. NT.* At the summit of Stamford Hill, in the northern part of Lincoln National Park, an obelisk erected in 1844 commemorates Matthew Flinders' discovery of the port. The views from here are stunning. *20 km SE.* $ *To enter the southern part of park, visitors must obtain a pass from National Parks & Wildlife Service or Visitor Information. Limit of 15 cars (4-wheel drive only) a day.* Whaling flourished briefly in the mid-1800s, and relics of the old whaling station can be seen at Sleaford Bay, along the ruggedly beautiful coastal area known as Whalers Way. *32 km SW.*

3 Adelaide Pl.; (08) 8683 3544. Website: www.portlincoln.net/touristinfo

PORT MACDONNELL   Map ref. 336 H13

This peaceful village on the SE coast, 467 km from Adelaide, was the second largest trading port in SA during the 1860s and 1870s. Today fishing vessels cluster round the historic jetty (1861) that was once the docking place for clippers loading with grain and wool.

Dingley Dell Tiny, picturesque home of poet, horseman and politician Adam Lindsay Gordon and his wife, 1864–67. Although legend has it that Gordon won the cottage from its owner in a card game, he actually purchased the two-year-old house for 150 pounds. Set in a 6-ha conservation park (ideal for a picnic), the restored and furnished cottage provides a glimpse of Gordon's modest lifestyle. *2 km W, signposted. Open daily or by appt. Guided tours only.* $ *(08) 8738 2221. NT.*

Port MacDonnell & District Maritime Museum Small but remarkably informative local history and maritime museum in the old council chambers, an attractive late-19th century rubble-stone building. A map, detailing the 30 shipwrecks along the often treacherous south-east coast, can also be viewed. *Meylin St. Open Wed., Fri., Sun. & some pub hol afternoons, or by appt.* $ *(08) 8738 7259 or (08) 8738 2177.*

ALSO OF INTEREST The substantial and elegant former Customs House (1862–75), built of local stone and incorporating, among others, the town's police station and cells, courthouse, telegraph station and customs room. A foreshore landmark, it now offers 5-star accommodation. *Cnr Charles St & The Parade. 0408 799 727.* Foundations of the original Northumberland Bay lighthouse (1859), which was built too close to the crumbling cliff edge and eventually collapsed. It was replaced in 1882 by the present lighthouse (not open for inspection), sited 400 m further east. There are magnificent views from the boardwalk approach.

District Council of Grant, 5 Charles St; (08) 8739 2576. Website: www. dcgrant.sa.gov.au
See also Mount Gambier, Robe

PORT PIRIE
Map ref. 327 J3, 328 I13

Named after schooner *John Pirie*, the first vessel to navigate the swampy tidal river on the east coast of Spencer Gulf in 1845. The town was surveyed in 1871 and BHP's smelting works opened in 1889. Since then, as the port closest to the rich silver, lead and zinc mines at Broken Hill, Port Pirie has had a largely industrial history.

OF INTEREST The former railway station (1902) is a wonderful Victorian Pavilion-style domed building. Adjacent are the former customs house (1882) and the old police station (1892), Ellen St, retains some of its late 19th-century character. The Portside Tavern opened in 1877 as the Royal Exchange. Once the town's grandest watering hole, it included a banquet room and rooftop observatory. *96 Ellen St.* The Family Hotel (1904) is also eye-catching with its flourish of lacework balconies. *134 Ellen St.* The anchor of the *John Pirie*, lost off Aldinga in the 1840s, can be seen in Memorial Park. *Norman St.*

◪ *Regional Tourism and Arts Centre, 3 Mary Elie St; (08) 8633 0439, freecall 1800 000 424.*

See also Port Augusta

QUORN
Map ref. 328 I10

An historic old railway town nestled in the Flinders Ranges at the northern end of the Pichi Richi Railway Pass. It was established in 1879 as a stop on the narrow-gauge Great Northern line, which was built by Chinese labourers and British stonemasons. Stone cottages with high-pitched roofs line the leafy side streets.

Pichi Richi Railway Steam trains plied the Pichi Richi line between Port Augusta and Quorn 1879–1956. Restored trains again travel through the picturesque Pichi Richi Pass (a 4-hour return trip between Quorn and Stirling North; 2.5–3 hours return between Quorn and Woolshed Flat) between April and Nov. The limestone railway station (1915) has distinctive curved gables and cast-iron detailing. *Railway Stn. Trains run most Sat.–Sun. & pub hols.* ⓢ *Timetable (08) 8395 2566.*

ALSO OF INTEREST A heritage trail includes the fine town hall (1891) and several historic churches. Four substantial hotels – the Austral and Transcontinental (both 1878), Grand Junction and Criterion (both 1890) – were built side by side, their names (slightly grander than the reality) reflecting Quorn's railway origins. John Dunn built the Old Mill, a three-storey flour mill (1879) during the peak of the district's wheat boom. Droughts in the 1880s crushed hopes of permanent wheat farming so far inland. Now a restaurant, gallery and museum, with accommodation. *2 Railway Tce. Open daily. (08) 8648 6016.*

IN THE AREA The evocative stone ruins of Kanyaka Station homestead. *42 km NE.*

◪ *3 Seventh St; (08) 8648 6419.* Website: www.flindersrangescouncil.sa. gov.au

See also Hawker

RENMARK
Map ref. 327 Q6

Australia's oldest irrigation settlement, begun by the Canadian Chaffey brothers near the Murray River in 1887. Their ambitious scheme foundered in the 1890s but the project was later accomplished by the Renmark Irrigation Trust.

Olivewood Charles Chaffey's verandahed log home (c. 1889) is set among fragrant citrus and olive trees, which testify to the ultimate success of the irrigation scheme. Now a museum dedicated to Murray irrigation and its pioneers. An exceptional collection of historic photos is also archived here. *Cnr Renmark Ave & 21st St. Open Mon., Thurs.–Sun.; Tues. afternoons.* ⓢ *(08) 8586 6175. NT.*

ALSO OF INTEREST Renmark Irrigation Trust Office (1888–93) was the Chaffey brothers' first office. In front stands an irrigation pump designed by George Chaffey, built in the UK c. 1890. *149 Murray Ave.* A big old hand-operated wine press (early 1900s) can be seen in Renmark Ave. The restored PS *Industry*, a 1911 steam-powered paddle-wheeler moored on the river, is now a museum. River cruises available. *84 Murray Ave. Open daily. (08) 8586 6704.*

◪ *84 Murray Ave; (08) 8586 6704.*

See also Loxton

REYNELLA
Map ref. 337 B11

Chateau Reynella One of SA's oldest and architecturally most interesting wineries. John Reynell planted his first vines here in 1838, from cuttings given to him by NSW pioneer William Macarthur. The picturesque complex includes underground cellars (1840s), the original stone cottage (c. 1854), cellars and charming homestead (both 1890s). *Reynell Rd. Open daily. (08) 8381 2266.*

IN THE AREA At Morphett Vale, St Mary's Church is the oldest Catholic church in SA, built in 1846. *4 km SW. Main South Rd.* St Hilary's Anglican Church (1855) was originally the town's police station and courthouse. John Knox Church was built the same year. *Both William St. Not open for inspection.*

◪ *McLaren Vale and Fleurieu Visitor Centre, Main Rd, McLaren Vale; (08) 8323 9944.* Website: www. visitorcentre.com.au

Pichi Richi Railway, Quorn

ROBE

Map ref. 336 F9

See Historic Highlights, p. 156

SPRINGTON

Map ref. 327 M8, 337 G7

The district around Springton, known at first as South Rhine, was settled by Scottish and English farmers in the 1850s. Prussian German settlers arrived soon after and vines have been grown in the region for well over a century.

OF INTEREST The Herbig Tree: a huge, gnarled, hollow gum tree in which Springton pioneer Johann Friedrich Herbig and later his family lived 1855–60. *Main St.*
See also Angaston

STRATHALBYN

Map ref. 327 L10, 337 E13

Scottish settlers led by Dr John Rankine took up land in 1839 and the town developed near the meandering Angas River. The lush green town common, European trees and sturdy but restrained architecture are tangible links with the town's Scottish heritage.

OF INTEREST National Trust museum in the old sandstone and rubble police station (1858) and courthouse (c. 1867). The police station incorporates three cells and furnished former residence. *1 Rankine St. Open Sat.– Sun., school & pub hols.* Ⓢ *(08) 8536 2478.* NT. The town's oldest building is the Terminus Hotel (first a home, licensed as a hotel in 1840, then rebuilt after a fire in 1868) which catered for travellers on the Goolwa–Strathalbyn tramway. To save weary travellers a walk, the line was extended to the hotel in 1874. *17 Rankine St.* London House, built as a general store in 1867, has an unusual concave verandah. Hill & Co. ran a coaching service to Adelaide from the stables behind. Now an antique shop. *7 High St. Open daily. (08) 8536 3903.* St Andrew's Church (commenced in 1840), with its noble tower and slender spire, is an elegant town feature. *Alfred Pl.* The Old Provincial Gas Co. (1868) supplied the town's street lighting from 1875. *South Tce. Not open for inspection.* Buildings dating back to the mid 1800s include the four-storey Angas Flour Mill (1849, extended 1869, now abandoned) in Commercial Rd and the Robin

Hood Hotel in High St, opened in 1855 (Strathalbyn's first agricultural show was held in its yard a year later). A decorative cantilevered balcony graces the facade of Argus House (1867–68), one-time office of the *Southern Argus*, SA's first country newspaper. Now an arts and crafts shop. *Commercial Rd. (08) 8536 3236.*

IN THE AREA Bleasdale Vineyards at Langhorne Creek, founded in 1850 by Frank Potts, a former midshipman who came to Australia in 1836 aboard HMS *Buffalo*, which also brought SA's first governor, Sir John Hindmarsh. The cellars house original red-gum wine vats and a massive red-gum grape press (1890) crafted by Potts. *15 km SE on Wellington Rd. Open Mon.–Sat.; Sun. afternoons. (08) 8537 3001.* In the historic old copper-mining town of Callington is Lavandula, a magnificent lavender and rose garden. At its heart is an elegant 1867 bluestone and sandstone building, once Callington's police station. The original stables and cells can also be viewed. *22 km NE. Open Thurs.–Sun. (Aug.–May); Sat.–Sun. (June–July).* Ⓢ *(08) 8538 5138.*
🚉 *Railway Stn, South Tce; (08) 8536 3212.*
See also Goolwa

TANUNDA

Map ref. 327 L8, 337 F5

The Germanic origins of this Barossa Valley town, settled in the 1840s, are mirrored in its architecture, fine Lutheran churches, German-style bakeries and food shops, and the long tradition of viticulture that has helped shape its history.

Barossa Historical Museum Fascinating folk museum in the dignified, two-storey former post office (1865), containing 19th-century Prussian costumes, and household and agricultural implements. *47 Murray St. Open daily afternoons. (08) 8562 2566.*
Churches The Lutheran faith was a cornerstone of Tanunda's pioneer lifestyle. Pioneer pastor Augustus Kavel is buried in the cemetery of the Langmeil Lutheran Church (1888). *Murray St.* The orb on the 26-m spire of Tabor Lutheran Church (1849, but rebuilt 1871) is a repository for church records. Langmeil Lutheran Church (1888) is approached through a narrow avenue of cypress trees. *Both Murray St.*
Goat Square The market place around

which Tanunda developed is now a modern crossroads, but still ringed by 1860s stone cottages. The town's hand-operated water-pump still stands. *Cnr John & Maria sts.*

ALSO OF INTEREST Auricht's Printing Office (1855), named for the Lutheran pastor who produced Tanunda's first German newspaper – now Tanunda Cellars. *4 Murray St.* Despite neglect, the Classical facade of the former courthouse (1866) is still very fine. *MacDonnell St. Not open for inspection.* Small cottages along the side-streets are an essential part of Tanunda's character.

IN THE AREA Langmeil Winery, named after the town's original 1840s riverside settlement, includes some original buildings of local stone. *1 km N. Para Rd. Open daily. (08) 8563 2595.* Lawley Farm Cottage provides old-world accommodation in restored 1850s cottages set amidst orchards and mature native trees. *3 km S. Krondorf Rd. (08) 8563 2141.* The magnificent, two-storey bluestone Chateau Tanunda winery (1890), a fine legacy of the winery's early days, have been restored. The towering chimney served the distillery's original steam boiler. Cellar-door tastings and sales within the heritage-listed

Langmeil Lutheran Church, Tanunda

building. *1 km SE. 9 Basedow Rd. Open daily. (08) 8563 3888.* Peter Lehmann Wines is a modern winery but cellar-door sales are from an historic 1850s winery building. *1 km N. Para Rd. Open daily. (08) 8563 2500.*
ℹ *Barossa Wine and Visitor Centre, 66–68 Murray St; (08) 8563 0600.* Website: www.barossa-region.org
See also Angaston, Bethany, Lyndoch, Nuriootpa

VICTOR HARBOR

Map ref. 327 L11, 336 B4

Victor Harbor, 83 km S of Adelaide, overlooking Encounter Bay on the Fleurieu Peninsula, started life in the 1830s as a whaling and sealing depot. SA's first export of whale oil, in 150 barrels, left Encounter Bay in 1837.

Cockle Train Beachside steam-train trip along line originally constructed (1854) for a horse-drawn train between Goolwa and Port Elliot, extended to Victor Harbor in the 1860s. The train's curious name refers to the large cockles to be found along Goolwa's broad, sandy beaches. *Railway Station. Operates 2–3 times a day on Sun., pub & school hols.* $ *(08) 8231 4366 or (08) 8552 2782.*

Encounter Coast Discovery Centre & National Trust Museum The Centre's audio-visual displays encompass the district's Aboriginal, whaling and railway history. Also part of the complex is the old customs house and stationmaster's residence (1866), with history exhibits and some fine historic photographs presented by the National Trust. *2 Flinders Pde. Open daily afternoons & by appt. (08) 8552 2059 or (08) 8552 5388. NT.*

Horse-drawn Tramway Take a nostalgic trip across the Causeway, which was extended to Granite Island in 1875. The trams, pulled by Clydesdales, began service in 1894, when a return trip cost threepence. They were replaced by a motor train in the 1950s, but horses were reintroduced in 1986. *The Causeway. Operates daily, dep. every 40 min.* $ *(08) 8552 5738.*

ALSO OF INTEREST The Whale Centre, with fascinating displays about whales and local whaling history. *Railway Tce. Open daily.* $ *(08) 8552 5644.* Stately Mt Breckan homestead, built 1879–81 for merchant and pastoralist Alexander Hay. In its heyday, peacocks strolled the grounds and the Hay family, with 32 servants, spent each summer there. Restored to its former grandeur, it is now a reception centre. *2127 Renown Ave. Only open to groups of 20 or more, by appt. (08) 8552 8900.* The mansion Adare (1891–93), built for the Cudmore family around a much earlier cottage which had belonged to Gov. John Hindmarsh. Now a conference centre with accommodation. *Wattle Dr. (08) 8552 1657.* Whaling Memorial, on the site of the town's first whaling station, established in 1837. *Grantly Ave.* St Augustine's Church (1869) was built in the Norman style beside the original limestone church. *Burke St.*

Horse-drawn tram, Victor Harbor

IN THE AREA The old town of Port Elliot has some historic buildings from its busy days as a sea port in the 1800s, when it was linked to Victor Harbor by horse-drawn tramway. *5 km NE.*
ℹ *Foreshore, adjacent to The Causeway; (08) 8552 5738.* Website: www.tourismvictorharbor.com.au
See also Goolwa

WALLAROO

Map ref. 326 I6

One of the trio of copper towns, with **Moonta** and **Kadina**, which attracted thousands of Cornish miners and became known as 'Little Cornwall'. Wallaroo was the main smelter and port for SA's lucrative 'copper coast'. Wallaroo is 160 km NW of Adelaide.

Hughes Chimney Stack Monumental square chimney (1861) soaring 36.5 m, the only remnant of the town's three copper-smelting stacks and used until quite recently as a navigation marker for ships. Named for WW Hughes, local pastoralist and copper magnate, whose vast wealth eventually helped found Adelaide University. *Foreshore (on private property).*

Heritage & Nautical Museum Housed in Wallaroo's first post office, a substantial 1865 limestone structure. Displays highlight the romantic days of sailing ships and the history of the copper industry. *Cnr Owen Tce & Emu St. Open Wed., pub & school hols; also Thurs. & Sat.–Sun. afternoons.* $ *(08) 8823 3015. NT.*

ALSO OF INTEREST Heritage walks take in some fine buildings, including several elegant 19th-century residences lining Lydia Cres., and the former customs house (1862). *Not open for inspection.* Churches and hotels sprang up in the 1860s: the Methodist Church (1863) in Stirling Tce and St Mary's Anglican Church (1864) in High St (not open for inspection); the Weeroona Hotel (1861) in John Tce and the Prince Edward (1864) Hotel in Hughes St. Take a 40-km train ride on the Wallaroo–Kadina–Bute Tourist Railway to the small inland township of Bute. *Railway Yards. (08) 8823 3111. Timetable (08) 8825 3496.* The Kernewek Lowender is a traditional Cornish festival held in 'Little Cornwall' in May of odd-numbered years. *(08) 8823 3333.*
ℹ *Town Hall, Irwin St; (08) 8823 2023.* Website: www.yorkepeninsula.com.au
See also Kadina, Moonta

WHYALLA Map ref. 326 I2, 328 H13

The area, first named Hummock Hill by Matthew Flinders in 1802, was settled by pastoralists from the 1860s. BHP acquired mining leases in the nearby Middleback Range in 1900, and the town developed after a railway was constructed (1901) to replace the bullock drays carrying ore from Iron Knob. Now SA's largest provincial city, Whyalla has been a company town for much of its history.

Whyalla Maritime Museum Dramatic centrepiece is the land-locked 650-tonne corvette HMAS *Whyalla*, the first ship (1941) built at the Whyalla shipyards and which saw service during World War II. Exhibits chart the city's WW II naval history, BHP shipbuilding, maritime heritage and nautical history of the upper Spencer Gulf. *Lincoln Hwy. Open daily, with regular ship tours.* Ⓢ *(08) 8645 8900.*

ALSO OF INTEREST At Mt Laura Homestead Museum, the 1920s house, once the homestead for a surrounding sheep station (now suburbia) has historic artifacts and photographs. Other features include the Telecommunications Museum and a sprawling railway shed which houses over 60 engines. *Ekblom St. Open daily.* Ⓢ *(08) 8645 3565. NT.*

IN THE AREA On the foreshore at Pt Bonython is the Pt Lowly lighthouse, built in 1883 and Whyalla's oldest building. Accommodation is available in the heritage-listed lighthouse-keepers' cottages. *24 km E, 2 km past the Santos distillation plant. (08) 8645 0436.*

ℹ️ *Lincoln Hwy; (08) 8645 7900, freecall 1800 088 589.*

WILLUNGA Map ref. 327 K10, 337 B13

One of the state's oldest country settlements, just 40 km S of Adelaide in the McLaren Vale region of the Fleurieu Peninsula. The district's early wealth was founded on quarrying slate and wheat growing, but the wheat industry failed in the 1870s and the demand for building slate dwindled in the 1890s. The small township, now an almond-growing centre, retains many historically significant buildings from its early days.

Old Courthouse & Police Station Museum Built (c. 1858–63) of sandy coloured local stone with neat red-brick detailing. The cells feature slate flagstones and vaulted ceilings and the exercise yard is cobbled with stones carted by dray from Sellicks Beach, 12 km away. *High St. Open Tues.; also Sat.–Sun. & pub hol afternoons and by appt. (08) 8556 2195. NT.*

ALSO OF INTEREST The Bassett School Museum, a simple, slate-roofed stone building housing a local history collection. Opened by James Bassett in 1847, it was a boys' school until 1874 and later used as council chambers. *St Lukes St. Open by appt. (08) 8556 2195. NT.* St Stephens Anglican Church (1884), has a bell cast 300 years ago. *St Andrews Tce.* Beside the Uniting Church (1895), St Judes St, there are beautifully carved slate tombstones. The Willunga Hotel combines the original hotel, a single-storey cottage and a former shop (all c. 1870). *3–5 High St. Open daily. (08) 8556 2135.*

ℹ️ *Main Rd, McLaren Vale; (08)*

8323 9944. Website: www.visitorcentre.com.au
See also McLaren Vale

WILPENA POUND Map ref. 329 K7

Spectacular natural amphitheatre in the central Flinders Ranges, more than 400 km N of Adelaide, rimmed by jagged, towering peaks and entered almost theatrically via a narrow gorge. Discovered by Europeans in 1850s, the Pound was deemed impossible to cultivate but was at one time used for grazing sheep and horses. Rich in history and pre-history as well as scenic grandeur.

OF INTEREST Hawker farmer John Hill and his family leased the Pound in 1899 and defied all odds by growing wheat there. Their small stone homestead (1904) still stands, and derelict farm artifacts are sometimes encountered in this extraordinary landscape. The family abandoned the farm c. 1914, when floods destroyed the log road, the only way into the Pound. Accessible via a two-hr walk through Pound Gap.

IN THE AREA 16 km N, off the main road to Blinman, on the edge of a tree-lined creek bed, the evocative ruins of 1851 Appealinna homestead. John Wills established the station, which once supported 40 families, keeping cattle and over 2000 goats, whose feral descendants cause immense problems for the area's delicately balanced ecology. At Arkaroo Rock, 15 km S, on the slopes of Rawnsley Bluff and at Sacred Canyon there are fine Aboriginal rock carvings and ochre and charcoal drawings depicting bird and snake tracks, and geometric designs. Tours available. *(08) 8648 0004.* Also on the road south is Rawnsley Park Station. The early stone house was replaced by the present homestead in 1915. Now a tourist park with accommodation. *Wilpena Rd. (08) 8648 0030.* Not far away is one of the region's earliest pastoral leases, Arkaba Woolshed, established in 1851 and still a working sheep station. Cottage accommodation available. *20 km N of Hawker on Wilpena Rd. (08) 8648 4217.*

ℹ️ *Wilpena Pound Tourist Resort; (08) 8648 0004.* Website: www.wilpenapound.on.net
See also Hawker

Willunga

HISTORIC HIGHLIGHTS

Old Customs House Museum, Robe

Two of South Australia's most interesting historic towns are Hahndorf and Burra, fascinating because of their strong cultural heritage, which can still be seen in the distinctive architecture and customs that recall their past. Handsome civic buildings from the 1900s line Gawler's main street, a reminder of the days when it was a major market centre for the northern region. And in the south is the small, sleepy town of Robe, where vestiges of its era as a bustling port are found.

BURRA

GAWLER

ADELAIDE HAHNDORF

ROBE

BURRA

Trim Cornish cottages line Burra's winding streets, and gaunt enginehouses, tall chimneys and stone footings are scattered across the rounded hills. This heritage mining town bears many traces of its industrial past and of the Anglo-Celtic migrants who worked its copper mines for three decades. Between 1845 and 1877 the Burra Burra mine produced 50 000 tonnes of copper ore worth almost £5 million, by which time the town was well-established and prosperous. Today its social and industrial past is revealed in over 40 heritage sites.

Burra Visitor Information Centre
2 Market Sq.
(08) 8892 2154
Website: www.weblogic.com.au/burra/

A symbol of the Cornish miners on one of the mine chimneys

Unicorn Brewery Cellars

One of several breweries, the Unicorn operated 1873–1902. Much of the original complex was demolished in 1911, but the manager's residence has been converted into cottages. The original maze of underground tunnels and cellars is open to the public.
Bridge Tce. Entry via Burra Passport key. Ⓢ
(08) 8892 2154.

Burra Art Gallery

Housed in the old Post and Telegraph building (1861), this gallery houses works by local and national artists, and travelling exhibitions.
Market St. Open daily afternoons.
(08) 8892 2411.

CENTRAL BURRA
INSET MAP

Paxton Square Cottages

Between 1849 and 1852 the SA Mining Association built a terrace of 33 stone cottages to entice miners away from the creek-side dwellings. Miners preferred their rent-free dugouts, but eventually the company threatened not to employ any 'dugout dwellers'. The renovated cottages now offer accommodation. No. 11, 'Malowen Lowarth', leased by the National Trust, is furnished in period style.
Paxton Tce, Kingston St and Bridge Tce.
Accommodation (08) 8892 2622. No. 11 open for tours Sat.–Sun. & pub hols. Ⓢ
(08) 8892 2154.

THE BURRA PASSPORT

Burra is a State Heritage Area and a signposted 11 km heritage trail takes in more than 40 of the town's historic highlights. With a 'Burra Passport' (purchased from Visitor Information) you receive a key which lets you into eight of the towns locked heritage sites, and use of a guide book.
Visitor Information. Ⓢ *(08) 8892 2154.*

Market Square

During the mining era, hundreds of miners gathered on pay day, jostling in front of the Miners' Arms Hotel (now gone) to watch fist fights and Cornish wrestling. On winter evenings a blunderbuss was fired to signal closing time for the shops.

Market Square Museum

Located in a former tailor's shop and dwelling (1880) this re-creates a 1900-era general store and family home.
Market Sq. Open afternoons Sat.–Sun. & pub hols. (08) 8892 2154.

Redruth Gaol
The state's first gaol (1856) outside Adelaide, and for some time known as Perry's Hotel in honour of the gaoler, Mr Perry. It closed as a gaol in 1894. The 1980 film *Breaker Morant* was filmed here.
Tregony St. Entry via Burra Passport key.
Ⓢ *(08) 8892 2154. NT.*

Hampton Village
Romantic ruins of one of Burra's original settlements. The walled English-style village of 30 cottages and a chapel was laid out in 1857.

Smelting Paddocks
A copper smelting works from 1849 to 1860, it comprised 25 furnaces, residential and office buildings, stables and smithies. Over 150 tonnes of wood were used daily to fire the furnaces.
Smelts Rd. Entry via Burra Passport key. Ⓢ *(08) 8892 2154.*

St Mary's Church
An Anglican church (1879) on land made available by the SA Mining Association on condition that the church could be demolished, if necessary, to allow mining.
Market St. Open daily. (08) 8892 2393.

Police Lockup & Stables
Erected in 1847, this was the town's prison until Redruth Gaol was built.
Cnr Ludgvan & Tregony sts. Entry via Burra Passport key.
Ⓢ *(08) 8892 2154. NT.*

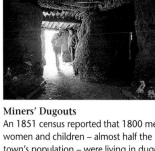

Burra Community School
This fine stone school epitomises Burra's optimism, but by the time it opened in 1878, prepared for 800 primary pupils, the main copper mine had already closed. Burra's community library is now here.
Bridge Tce (access from Smelts Rd). Open Mon.–Fri. (08) 8892 2007.

Bon Accord Mine Complex
Burra's third mine was built in 1846 but closed after three years. The town's water supply was pumped from the main mine shaft from 1908–1966. The complex includes a mining museum with a viewing platform above the mine shaft, and a working forge. The original mine manager's residence (1859) is now the Bon Accord Cottage (B&B).
Cnr West & Linkson sts. Open Sat.–Sun. & some weekdays. Guided tours only.
Ⓢ *(08) 8892 2056 or Visitor Information (08) 8892 2154. B&B (08) 8892 2154. NT.*

Morphett's Enginehouse Museum
The museum incorporates Australia's oldest mining building, an 1847 powder magazine, as well as mining relics. Morphett's enginehouse (1858) has been restored.
Burra Mine Open Air Museum. w off Market St.
Ⓢ *For opening hours, contact (08) 8892 2154.*

Miners' Dugouts
An 1851 census reported that 1800 men, women and children – almost half the town's population – were living in dugouts in the clay banks of Burra Creek. Some of these dwellings were no more than caves – others had such luxuries as glazed windows. All of them were unsanitary, typhus and smallpox being rife. Floods destroyed most of the dugouts in the 1850s, but two survived.
Blyth St. Entry via Burra Passport key. Ⓢ *(08) 8892 2154.*

In the Area
See Clare, Kapunda

GAWLER

In 1837, just a year after the founding of Adelaide, Surveyor-General Colonel William Light chose the site for Gawler, 'bounded by rivers, backed by hills'. He had high hopes for the town's future, predicting that it would become the gateway to the north, as indeed it did – a steady stream of traffic has passed along the main street since the town's earliest days. Light surveyed and planned the town, endowing it with spacious parklands, church squares, a market place and a sense of order, from all of which it still benefits.

Gawler Visitor Information Centre
2 Lyndoch Rd
(08) 8522 6814
Website: www.gawler.sa.gov.au

Gawler Library
The former Gawler Institute building (1870), now the public library, has an iron balustrade cast in Gawler from the first iron ore smelted in SA at the Phoenix Foundry. Don't miss the library's lofty reading room.
Open Mon., Wed., Thurs.–Sat.
(08) 8522 9213.

Murray Street,1878

Murray Street
This main thoroughfare boasts substantial public and commercial buildings, such as the post office (1866) and stately town hall (1878), with garlanded urns and formal pediment. Symbolic of Gawler's 19th-century prosperity are the dignified Italianate ANZ Bank (1873), the more showy National Bank (1881) and the Bank of South Australia (completed 1911).

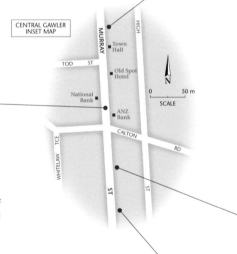

CENTRAL GAWLER INSET MAP

Town Hall
Old Spot Hotel
National Bank
ANZ Bank
TOD ST
MURRAY
HIGH
CALTON RD
WHITELAW TCE
ST
ST
N
0   50 m
SCALE

Coat of Arms
Gawler adopted Gov. Gawler's family coat of arms. Its motto translates 'without labour there is no reward'.

HISTORIC PUBS

Murray Street's constant passing trade ensured a plentiful supply of hotels, among them the Old Spot (1839), on the site of the town's first pub. The two-storeyed and balconied Kingsford (1858, originally called the Globe Inn), with its flourish of iron lacework, was headquarters for some time to the town's eccentric Humbug Society. The Society produced the satirical pamphlet *The Bunyip*. First issued in1863, it became more serious over time, chronicling local events, and is still published weekly.
Murray St.

Old Telegraph Station Museum
Gawler's oldest surviving public building (1863) is now a folk museum, furnished in period style.
59 Murray St. Open Sun. afternoons & by appt.
Ⓢ *(08) 8522 5557. NT.*

Gawler Post Office
The towered post office dates from 1866.
Murray St.

St Peter and St Paul's Church

Church Hill heritage area
There are five churches on peaceful Church Hill, including the splendid St George's Anglican Church, Cowan St, where the foundation stone was laid in 1858 (the tower was not finished until 1909); and St Peter and St Paul's Catholic Church (1897) with its imposing towers.

Old Bushman Hotel
Victorian hotel (1870s) of limestone rubble with cast-iron lacework balcony. Built on the site of an earlier hotel, a humbler 1840s wattle-and-daub structure.
9 Cowan St. Open daily. (08) 8522 1001.

Phoenix Foundry
The town's first engineering foundry, owned by James Martin & Co., produced farm machinery and hundreds of railway locomotives and wagons – in its heyday, at the turn of the century, it employed over 800 people.
King St. Not open for inspection.

McKinlay Memorial
Dedicated to explorer, pastoralist and Gawler resident 'Big John' McKinlay (1819–72). He was one of the men to find the bodies of ill-fated explorers Burke and Wills. The memorial (1875) features a finely carved keystone depicting McKinlay's head.
Murray St, opp. Cowan St.

John McKinlay

Orleana Square
The square was named by Col. Light after the sailing ship HMS *Orleana*, which arrived in the colony in 1839, bringing several pioneering Gawler families. Distinctive houses in a blend of architectural styles surround the square.

Craiglee
The original Irish owner, Dr Popham, built the mansion in 1858. He allegedly fired a cannon when the coach carrying mail from England arrived. The coach-house and the old bakehouse have been converted into a B&B.
25 High St. (08) 8523 2300.

Para Para Mansion
Magnificent 23-room stone mansion, with substantial stone outbuildings, built in 1851–62 on 180 ha for thriving local miller Walter Duffield. At one time there were vineyards, orange groves and a renowned garden. In its heyday, Para Para was the scene of lavish parties, and Prince Albert, the Duke of Edinburgh, was amongst the guests.
Penrith Ave, West Gawler. Not open for inspection, but visible from Penrith Ave.

Gawler Mill
The grand four-storey former Union Mill (1855) was one of several flour mills that prospered in Gawler in the 1860s–70s. Now a restaurant.
1 Julian Tce. (08) 8522 3633.

Dead Man's Pass
Legend has it that Col. Light and his surveyor Finniss found the body of a man lying in the hollow of a gum tree at the South Para River crossing in 1837. The site has had this name ever since. Now part of Clonlea Park.
South end of Murray St.

Map labels
To Nuriootpa
Essex Park
MAIN NORTH RD
KING ST
EDITH ST
WARREN ST
VICTORIA TCE
HOWARD ST
JERNINGHAM ST
CAMERON TCE
QUEEN ST
THOMAS TCE
PORTER TCE
PARNELL SQ
NIXON TCE
St Peter & St Paul's Catholic Church
COWAN ST
ORLEANA
St George's Anglican Church
COWAN ST
COWAN SQ
MOORE ST
REID ST
Gawler Central Railway Station
MURRAY ST
UNION ST
HORROCKS PL
To Lyndoch
HIGH ST
FINNISS ST
JACOB ST
DUNDAS ST
PATERSON ST
TOD ST
SCHEIBENER TCE
South Para
CALTON RD
For more detail see inset map on facing page
KING ST
WHITELAW TCE
EIGHTH ST
TENTH ST
TWELFTH ST
Para Para Mansion
BRIDGE ST
Kingsford Hotel
Bank of SA
JULIAN ST
MURRAY ST STH
SEVENTH ST
FOURTH ST
0   100 m
SCALE
AYERS ST
COOMBS TCE
GAWLER TCE
River
Clonlea Park
To Adelaide
N

HAHNDORF

Hahndorf is Australia's first, and best-known, German-settled town. A hardy band of Prussian Lutherans arrived in South Australia in 1838 aboard the *Zebra*. The ship's Danish captain, Dirk Hahn, became their benefactor and they named their town after him – Hahndorf or 'Hahn's village'. The settlers brought with them their religious faith, their culture and their customs. Using traditional building methods, they constructed German-style, half-timbered cottages, barns, mills and shops which still contribute much to the charm of this beautiful valley in the Adelaide Hills.

Hahndorf Visitor Information Centre
41 Main St
(08) 8388 1185
Website: www.visitadelaidehills.com.au

Hahndorf Old Mill
Two-storey former flour mill, rebuilt by FW Wittwer in 1853 after flood and fire damage. When flour milling became less profitable, the Wittwers turned to crushing bark, metals and even bones to make fertiliser. The mill closed as a flour mill in 1923. Though much altered internally, it retains a 19th-century character. Now a restaurant.
98 Main St. Open daily for lunch and dinner. (08) 8388 7255.

Haebich's Cottage
Hahndorf's first blacksmith, August Haebich, built this half-timbered cottage in the mid-1850s. Adjacent are the Haebich family's original smithy and shop, now an art and craft gallery. The cottage has a German-style gabled roof, but the shady verandah is a concession to the Australian climate. Now a B&B.
75 Main St. Open daily. (08) 8388 7247.

German Arms Hotel
Sergeant Lubasch, a Battle of Waterloo hero, opened the original German Arms, a small country inn, in 1839 at 80 Main St. This two-storey, verandahed hotel was built in 1861 by publican Robert Hunt, and the licence from the original hotel was transferred to the new building a year later.
69 Main St. Open daily. (08) 8388 7013.

IN THE AREA
Off the main roads around Hahndorf are farmlets tucked into pretty valleys, old-fashioned shops and winding streets. Typical is the township of BRIDGEWATER, which grew up in the 1850s around the water-powered flour mill built beside the swift-flowing creek. The mill has been restored and is Petaluma Wines' cellar door complex, while the huge old water wheel now turns on the terrace of their restaurant. *6 km w.* Almost hidden in the hills is the hamlet of ALDGATE, dating back to the 1860s. *8 km w.* The pretty town of STIRLING traces its beginnings to the 1850s. *10 km w.* MOUNT BARKER is the largest town in the hills, its handsome Victorian buildings attesting to steady growth last century. *7 km SE.*

Old mill wheel, Bridgewater

Old German Shop
A two-storey shop (c. 1850s) placed sideways to the street, in the central European fashion. The steep, half-hipped roof and delicate upstairs casement windows are original. The first recorded proprietor was a watchmaker, August Christoph. Now tearooms.
51 Main St. Open daily.

The Cedars

Built in 1858, 'The Cedars' was home to renowned landscape artist Sir Hans Heysen from 1912 to 1968. Still owned by his family, it contains many of the original furnishings as well as a number of Heysen's paintings. The single-storey sandstone studio with timber ceiling (1912) is maintained in its original condition.
Heysen Rd. Open Mon.–Fri., Sun. Ⓢ
(08) 8388 7277.

Portrait of Sir Hans Heysen by Joshua Smith, 1968

St Michael's Lutheran Church

Work on St Michael's began in 1859. Most of the gravestones have been removed from the adjacent cemetery, but some with Gothic German inscriptions have survived.
Church St. Services Sun. & open by appt. (08) 8388 1225.

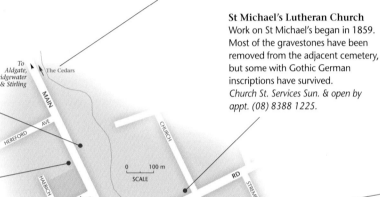

Hahndorf Academy

The Academy, established in 1857, was one of South Australia's first boarding schools for boys. The towered, two-storey stone building was completed by 1875. It now contains an art gallery, studios and the town's German Migration Museum. The 1857 cottage next door is a souvenir shop.
68 Main St. Open Mon.–Sat. (08) 8388 7250.

Former Australian Arms Inn

A half-timbered cottage of red gum, wattle and daub, with a steeply pitched, half-hipped roof in the German style. First licensed in 1854, it is now a leathersmith and gallery.
46 Main St.

Nixon's Mill

Stone mill built on Hahndorf's windiest hill in 1842 by surveyor FR Nixon. An early employee, FW Wittwer, later bought the mill but eventually moved his business to the two-storey flour mill that still dominates the main street. The mill has been damaged by bushfire and partly restored.
3 km S, on Mt Barker Rd. Not open for inspection.

Paechtown

A farming settlement created by Johann Georg Paech and his three sons in the 1840s, tucked amidst the trees on the town outskirts. They built four half-timbered houses with outbuildings. Three of the farmhouses were destroyed by bushfire in the 1980s, though one has since been rebuilt.
Paechtown Rd. Not open for inspection.

AMBLESIDE

Anti-German sentiment during World War I made life difficult for people so closely tied to their German origins. Hahndorf's name was changed to Ambleside, and a number of citizens anglicised their surnames.

ROBE

Robe's modest stone cottages and quiet streets belie its colourful past. During the mid-1800s Robe, on the sheltered waters of Guichen Bay, was one of the busiest ports in the young colony of South Australia. Irish and Scottish settlers poured in. Sailing ships were loaded with wool, horses bound for India, and other cargo from as far east as Victoria's Mallee district. Robe thrived until the 1870s but it was bypassed by the new rail network, other ports opened, and Robe slipped into a peaceful life as a small country town, fishing port and holiday resort.

Robe Visitor Information Centre
Mundy Tce
(08) 8768 2465
Website: www.robe.sa.gov.au

Cape Dombey Obelisk
Visible from 15 km out to sea, this distinctive red-and-white striped obelisk (1855) originally housed rockets that carried lines to ships in distress. *Cape Dombey.*

Old Telegraph Station
The site of Robe's first post office, which opened in 1849. Overland telegraph transmission, linking Adelaide and Melbourne, began from here in 1858. *Mundy Tce. Not open for inspection.*

Old Customs House Museum
The sturdy limestone customs house (1863) in Royal Circus, overlooking Lake Butler, was the office of Robe's first harbourmaster and customs collector. *Royal Circus. Open Tues. & Sat. afternoons; daily during Jan.* $ *(08) 8768 2419. NT.*

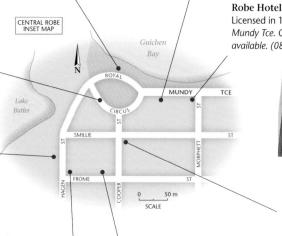

Robe Hotel, 186

Robe Hotel
Licensed in 1848 and trading ever since. *Mundy Tce. Open daily. Accommodation available. (08) 8768 2077.*

Royal Circus
The 19th-century heart of Robe, known as 'the Roundabout of the Teamsters', as rowdy bullockies could load their huge wagons without needing to back or turn. Few buildings are left in this once bustling area.

CENTRAL ROBE INSET MAP

Guichen Bay

Lake Butler

ROYAL
CIRCUS
ST
SMILLIE
MUNDY   TCE
MORPHETT ST
ST
HAGEN ST
FROME
COOPER ST
ST
N

0   50 m
SCALE

St Mary's Star of the Sea Church
Robe's first church, built 1868–69. During the 1870s the Sisters of St Joseph, founded by Blessed Mary MacKillop, used the two-roomed building as a convent and school. *Hagen St. Mass held twice a month. Open by appt. (08) 8733 3530.*

Ormerod Cottages
George Ormerod built this terrace of little stone cottages c. 1863. Gov. Sir James Ferguson's staff stayed here when he was holidaying at Karatta House. *Cnr Smillie & Cooper sts. Not open for inspection.*

CHINA SHIPS

In the 1850s 'China ships' dropped anchor at Robe, and in all as many as 16 000 Chinese disembarked, then headed overland to the gold diggings, thus avoiding Victoria's poll tax of a hefty £10 per head.

Robe House
The town's first house (1847) and until 1869 the home of the region's Government Resident. The elegant stone residence now provides B&B and holiday accommodation. Guided tours by appt. *1a Hagen St. Open daily. (08) 8768 2770.*

Old Courthouse & Police Station
The town's first police station (1847) and courthouse (1848). The two-storey stable block (1858) at the rear was for the mounted police. Now an antiques store. *Frome St.*

Old Gaol

The gaol (1861) was only ever half-completed, and finally closed in 1881. The walls were partly rebuilt in 1995 and reveal the floor plan of the various prison buildings. The ruins can be visited.
Obelisk Rd, Cape Dombey.

Caledonian Inn

A romantic, ivy-clad limestone inn (1859) with several rooms overlooking Guichen Bay. There are teak doors salvaged from the Dutch ship *Koning Willem II*, which was wrecked off the coast in 1856. Poet Adam Lindsay Gordon convalesced here in the 1860s after a riding accident, and later married the innkeeper's niece Maggie Park. Accommodation available.
Victoria St. Open daily. (08) 8768 2029.

Library & Interpretive Centre

The library (1868) has some excellent historical records and photos. Pick up a walking tour brochure here.
Mundy Tce. Open daily. (08) 8768 2465.

Adam Lindsay Gordon on his horse 'Outlaw', 1863

Lakeside

Grand 17-room residence overlooking Lake Fellmongery, built by Englishman GA Danby in 1882. Danby had already inherited and dissipated two fortunes. He reputedly chartered a ship to bring oak and teak, artworks and fine china from Europe for Lakeside.
Main Rd. Not open for inspection.

Karatta House

Pastoralist Henry Jones built this two-storey stone mansion overlooking Lake Butler and Guichen Bay in 1857. It was used as a summer residence by Gov. Sir James Ferguson during the 1870s, when guests were entertained with kangaroo hunts, dances and concerts, and the mansion became known locally as the 'governor's house'.
Karatta Rd. Not open for inspection.

Moorakyne

Prominent Robe merchant George Ormerod built this gracious Victorian house c. 1856 and lived there until his death in 1872. Note the pretty scalloped valances.
Between Sturt & O'Halloran sts. Not open for inspection.

Bush Inn Craft Centre

One of several roadside inns which sprang up to cater for the bullock teamsters frequenting the port. The inn, built and licensed in the 1850s, remained (under various names) a popular watering hole for bullockies until the 1880s. Today it is an arts and crafts centre.
Millicent Rd. Open Tues. (08) 8768 6298.

WESTERN AUSTRAL

Western Australia's history is long, colourful and varied. Ancient sites show evidence of Aboriginal occupation dating back 40 000 years or more. Historic shipwrecks litter the treacherous coast. Convict buildings recall transportation. There are signs of whaling in the south, pearling in the north, colonial homesteads and old gold towns, where untold wealth was won from isolated goldfields.

The Old Farm, Strawberry Hill, Albany

Early Days

The Dutch are known to have landed on the west coast of Australia en route to Batavia as early as the 1600s. In 1688, Englishman William Dampier stepped ashore near present-day Cygnet Bay, but it was not until the nineteenth century that the British decided to claim the land for themselves. In 1826, to forestall possible French invasion, the British sent a garrison of soldiers under Major Edmund Lockyer to King George Sound, on the southern coast, where Albany stands today.

Soon after, in 1828, impressed by Captain James Stirling's enthusiastic report on the Swan River area, the British government ordered

HISTORIC HIGHLIGHTS

For a look around some of
Western Australia's most
interesting historic towns,
see the following entries.

Albany   The site of the State's first
European settlement, in 1826,
overlooking the magnificent Princess
Royal Harbour. The city boasts many
heritage buildings and an old whaling
station. *See p. 182*

Broome   Once 'the pearling capital
of the world', this small isolated town
has a fascinating past. Despite
tropical weather and wartime
bombing, several historic buildings
remain. *See p. 184*

Fremantle   Settled by the British
in 1829, Perth's port retains a
remarkable heritage of convict-built
structures, a wealth of Victorian and
Edwardian hotels, shipping and
maritime buildings. *See p. 186*

Kalgoorlie–Boulder   Founded in
1895, Kalgoorlie continues to prosper
from gold and has maintained its
heritage of grand, boom-style
architecture in the harsh Outback
environment. *See p. 188*

York   The State's oldest inland town,
with a fine legacy of colonial and
Victorian-era architecture. Classic
churches, museums, the old gaol, and
the splendid town hall are just a few
of the sights. *See p. 190*

that a warship be dispatched 'without the smallest loss of time' to
claim the land. On 2 May 1829 Captain Fremantle formally annexed
the whole west coast of New Holland for the British Crown.

A FREE COLONY

Stirling was appointed the first Governor, and arrived in June 1829.
He chose the site for Perth and established Fremantle as the port of
the new Swan River Colony.

Although Britain sent some officials and troops, this was to be a self-
supporting colony of free, independent settlers. Despite the generous
land grants, much of the land was poor quality and many settlers had
never farmed, let alone pioneered unknown country. Beset by a lack of
capital, food and labour, the colony battled to survive.

ABORIGINAL RESISTANCE

Right from the start, relationships with the Indigenous people were
poor, especially in the south-west. Although early on the Aboriginal
tribes formed groups to defend themselves, they were soon pushed
away from their traditional lands, usually with fatal results.

Courthouse, Broome

CONVICTS ARRIVE

Eventually the colonists agreed that, in exchange for additional funds, British convicts could be sent. Despite misgivings by many, the almost 10 000 male convicts who arrived between 1850 and 1868 facilitated public works, created larger markets and brought British money into the colony. A number of the buildings erected to house and administer the convicts remain as a legacy of those days. Some of these buildings, remarkably well preserved, are now open to the public.

THE GOLDEN YEARS

Colonising such a vast state was a slow, arduous process. Pastoralists in search of new land pioneered the north-west of the State in the 1860s and the Kimberley in the 1870s. But it was the discovery of gold in the 1880s and 1890s that set the colony firmly on its feet. Within a decade the population trebled, reaching 101 000 by 1895. Grand buildings were erected, major public works initiated and transport extended. By the time of Federation, Western Australia faced the twentieth century in a buoyant mood, its most arduous pioneering work behind it.

TIMELINE

1826 Major Edmund Lockyer, with soldiers and convicts, establishes a British settlement on the site of Albany.

1829 The British claim the entire west coast of the continent. Capt. (later Gov.) James Stirling establishes a settlement on the present site of Perth (the Swan River Colony).

1850 Transportation of convicts to WA begins.

1868 The last shipment of convicts to Australia arrives in WA.

1877 Perth is linked to the eastern colonies for the first time by telegraph.

1885 The State's first gold rush starts after gold is found at Halls Creek.

1890 Responsible government is granted to WA.

1901 The Commonwealth of Australia is declared, with WA one of the six new States.

Streetscape, Perth, 1890s

PERTH *Swan River Settlement*

Old Observatory, West Perth

VISITOR INFORMATION

PERTH VISITOR CENTRE
Cnr Forrest Pl. & Wellington St
Perth WA 6000
(08) 9483 1111 or 1300 361 351
www.westernaustralia.net

NATIONAL TRUST OF AUSTRALIA (WA)
Old Observatory, 4 Havelock St
West Perth WA 6005
(08) 9321 6088
www.ntwa.com.au

Perth is a modern city, yet tucked amidst the gleaming skyscrapers and landscaped gardens are surprising treasures from the past. Sited on a curve of the Swan River, colonised by free settlers, the town struggled in its early days. But convict labour in the 1850s, and the gold rushes of the 1890s, brought wealth that helped firmly establish the city.

The Swan River Colony, as it was known for fifty years, was established in 1829. When the future Governor, Captain James Stirling, arrived in June 1829 aboard the *Parmelia*, he chose two town sites. Fremantle, at the mouth of the river, was to be the colony's port. The other site, some kilometres up river, which was to be the colony's administrative centre, he named Perth, in honour of the British Colonial Secretary, Sir George Murray, Member for Perth, Scotland.

The Swan River Colony was the first British colony in Australia that comprised only free settlers. The settlers began to arrive soon after Stirling's official party, but instead of the promised – or expected – land of milk and honey, they found poor-quality soil, a lack of fresh food and contaminated drinking water. The allocation of land grants had not been finalised, so people huddled in improvised huts and shelters. When the settlers did receive their grants, many of them were unequal to the task of farming the difficult land.

The colony struggled on until 1850 when, at the colonists' request, transportation was introduced. This provided vital labour, introduced considerably more British funds into the colony and enabled much-needed public works programmes to be carried out.

Convicts were soon put to work in Perth and the results of their labour can still be seen in a number of fine buildings, such as the imposing Government House and Perth's distinctive Town Hall. By the time transportation ceased in 1868, again at the colonists' request, Perth looked considerably more substantial.

The discovery of gold in the 1890s was a major impetus to development and growth of the capital. The population increased dramatically and money poured into government coffers.

Perth became a thriving commercial and political capital. It was the centre of the vast new railway network stretching to the Outback and a vital link in the State's communications system. Many of the earlier colonial buildings were demolished to make way for new buildings, often built in the latest, most ostentatious styles.

The grand architecture symbolised the prosperity and buoyant optimism of those years. It is ironic that many of these buildings were replaced during another mining boom, that of the 1960s, when the discovery of huge quantities of iron ore, nickel, bauxite and other minerals saw a later generation again display its prosperity and good fortune in bricks and mortar.

FIVE TOP MUSEUMS

Berndt Museum of Anthropology, *p. 168*
His Majesty's Theatre, Museum of Performing Arts, *p. 164*
Museum of Childhood, *p. 169*
Perth Fire Station Museum, *p. 167*
WA Museum, *p. 167*

His Majesty's Theatre

Government House

INNER PERTH

1 Barracks Archway

This splendid Tudor, four-storey, arched gateway is all that remains of the Pensioners' Barracks (1863), which were built to house soldiers of the Enrolled Pensioner Forces. These soldiers had stayed on after the removal of regular British troops in 1868. The building was constructed by convict labour and demolished in the 1960s to make way for the Mitchell Freeway.
St Georges Tce, City.

2 Central Government Buildings

A harmonious complex of buildings (1874–1905) located near the original core of Perth. The interpretation of the Classical Revival style shows the talents of Colonial Architects RR Jewell and GT Poole. With their rose-coloured brickwork, elaborate stucco decoration and projecting colonnaded balconies, these offices are among Perth's most distinguished buildings. The GPO was here until 1923 and a plaque on the east corner marks the point from which all distances are measured in WA.

Cnr St Georges Tce & Cathedral Ave, City. Not open for inspection.

3 The Cloisters

A two-storey former school building (1858) erected by Bishop Hale, Perth's first bishop, to provide a classical education for the sons of Perth's elite. This was the earliest secondary boys' school in the colony and the first enrolment was 23 students. With its cloistered arcades it echoed traditional British halls of learning. The school closed in 1872 and the building has served many purposes since. It is now used as offices.
220 St Georges Tce, City. Not open for inspection.

4 Constitutional Centre of WA

The superbly restored, heritage-listed Old Hale School (1914) is now a venue for exploring the constitutional basis of Australia's government and federalism, with a special focus on the history of political development in WA, from colonisation in 1829. The building is close to Parliament House.
Cnr Parliament Pl. & Havelock St, West Perth. Open Mon.–Fri.; also some Sun. (08) 9222 6922.

5 Government House

The governor's residence (1860–64) is perhaps Perth's most unusual heritage building. Whilst most of the city's early colonial buildings were functional, even austere, Government House provided a romantic silhouette, being built in the Gothic style with arches, towers and turrets. The work was carried out by convicts. There was a public outcry at the excessive cost and the amount of convict labour required, and more fuss still in 1864 when a storm blew down the chimneys over the drawing room of the new building. Government House remains largely unchanged externally and is set in particularly fine 19th-century gardens.
St Georges Tce, City. Open about three times a year, advertised in local press. See also A Walk Around Central Perth, p.171

6 His Majesty's Theatre

Australia's first steel and concrete building, His Majesty's opened in 1904 with a spectacular production of *The Forty Thieves*. The theatre was built at a time when the State's economy was buoyed by the gold boom, and the building reflects this prosperity. The four-storey facade is theatrically enlivened by pilasters, garlands, pediments and crouching lions. The original interior featured four artificial waterfalls and the roof was designed to slide back on balmy evenings so that theatregoers could sit

Barracks Archway

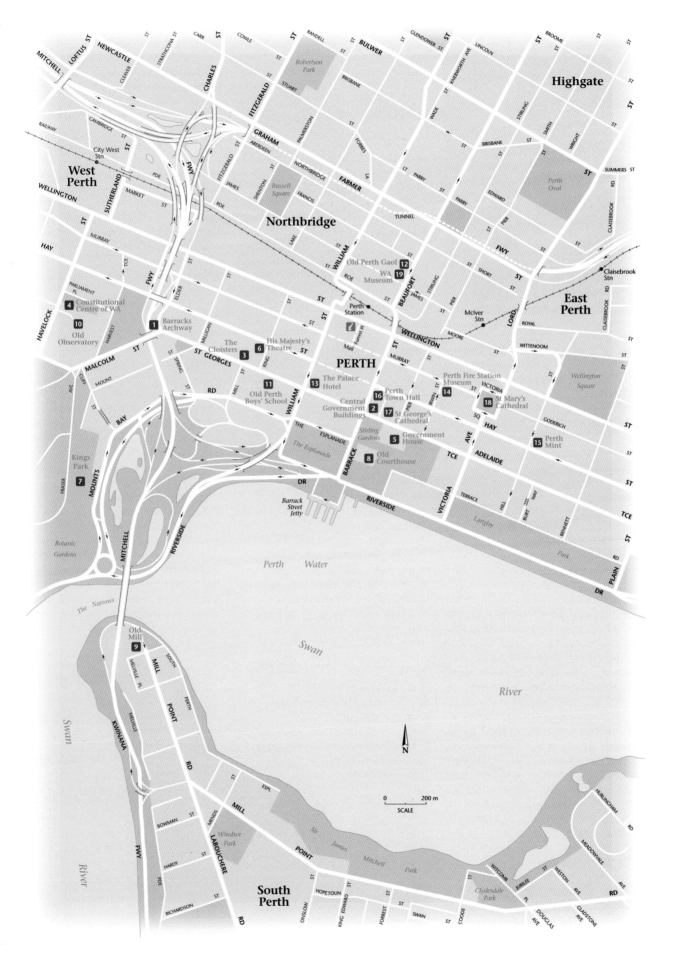

Old Mill, South Perth

under the stars. Renovation and restoration has seen substantial changes but the restored interiors still capture the lavish Edwardian decor of the theatre's heyday. The recently opened Museum of Performing Arts within the building houses an extensive collection of photographs, programmes, press clippings, scripts and magnificent costumes from every genre of the performing arts.
Cnr King & Hay sts, City. Open Mon.–Fri. Tours available. Ⓢ *(08) 9265 0900.*

7 Kings Park

In 1831, just two years after the colony was founded, John Septimus Roe, the colony's first Surveyor-General, had chosen Mt Eliza, now within the park, as land for public purposes. In 1872, 172 ha of bushland was set aside as parkland, and became known as Perth Park. By 1901 the area had been extended and renamed Kings Park. Today, the beautiful parkland covers 404 ha, much of it natural bushland, and includes a botanic garden of native wildflowers, walking trails, rotundas and statuary. There are guided tours of the park and botanic gardens.
Fraser Ave, West Perth. Open daily. (08) 9480 3659.

8 Old Courthouse

The City of Perth's oldest remaining public building (1836) is a rare surviving gem from colonial times. In its early days, as well as being a courthouse, it was used for religious worship, as a meeting place, a theatre and concert hall. The building is now part of the Francis Burt Law Education Centre.
Stirling Gardens, cnr St Georges Tce & Barrack St, City. Open Mon.–Fri. Tours available. (08) 9325 4787. See also A Walk Around Central Perth, p. 170

9 Old Mill (Shenton's Mill)

Picturesque, whitewashed stone mill, built for millwright WK Shenton. The foundation stone was laid by Gov. Stirling in 1835. The mill was driven by sails and used to grind grain for flour for the infant colony. Poorly sited, however, it proved inefficient and closed in 1859. The little mill cottage adjacent has colonial furnishings, and the surrounding grounds contain various relics, including horse-drawn carriages.
Near Narrows Bridge, Mill Point Rd, South Perth. Open daily. Tours available. Ⓢ *(08) 9367 5788. NT.*

10 Old Observatory

A fine Victorian building, constructed in 1897 as residence and office for WA's first government astronomer, WE Cooke. Prestigiously located, with a commanding view of the Swan River, the elegant building was designed by the Colonial Architect, GT Poole. The observatory section was dismantled many years ago and the telescope moved. The residence is now headquarters of the National Trust (WA).
4 Havelock St, West Perth. Tours by appt. (08) 9321 6088. NT.

11 Old Perth Boys' School

This quaint school building was erected in the ecclesiastical Early Gothic Revival style in 1853, probably to the design of William Sanford, Colonial Secretary and amateur architect. The church-like appearance was further accented by a spire and belltower, which have since been removed. The original building, with its small windows, was apparently dark and stuffy, but it was later expanded. The sandstone used in the construction was ferried up the Swan River from Rocky Bay, near Fremantle. There is a cafe here.
139 St Georges Tce, City. Open Mon.–Fri. NT.

12 Old Perth Gaol

An exceptionally fine example of colonial architecture, built in 1854 in the restrained colonial Georgian style to the design of Colonial Architect RR Jewell and used as Perth's prison until 1888. Numerous executions took place in the grounds until residents complained. Now part of the **WA Museum**.
Francis St, City. Open daily. (08) 9427 2700.

13 The Palace Hotel

A grand three-storey facade is all that remains of this once impressive pub on a prominent city corner. When it opened in 1895 the Palace Hotel epitomised the State's gold-boom grandeur. A multi-storey building now towers behind the facade.
Cnr St Georges Tce & William St, City.

Perth Mint

14 Perth Fire Station Museum

For almost 80 years this was Perth's No. 1 Fire Station. Perth's first ambulance service also operated from here, at the turn of the 20th century. The striking building, with its distinctive rusticated limestone facade, now houses a museum on the history of firefighting in Perth and WA. Exhibits include some intriguing firefighting apparatus. There is also a fire safety centre in the station.
Cnr Murray & Irwin sts, City. Open Mon.–Fri. (08) 9323 9353.

15 Perth Mint

The Mint was established in 1899 as a branch of the London Royal Mint (amazingly, it remained a branch of the British mint until 1970, when the Union Jack was lowered and it became the Perth Mint). Gold from WA's lucrative goldfields was refined and sovereigns and half-sovereigns produced here. After Federation, Australian currency was struck. Limited edition proof coins are still produced, making this Australia's oldest operating mint. There are displays of historic and rare coins, regular tours and gold-pouring demonstrations every hour. The landmark building (1899), handsomely proportioned and finely detailed, is listed on the National Estate Register. It is faced with limestone, some of it from

Katta Djinoong Gallery, Western Australian Museum

Rottnest Island. The Mint shop is in the lavish surrounds of the original Bullion Receiving Room.
310 Hay St, City. Open Mon.–Fri. & Sat.–Sun. mornings. $ (08) 9421 7277. See also A Walk Around Central Perth, p. 171

16 Perth Town Hall

A most unusual colonial building, partly Gothic Revival, partly French in inspiration, with towers and turrets culminating in a great clock tower with an iron-crested lookout. One of Perth's oldest buildings, it was constructed by convicts in 1867–70. The Flemish brickwork is accented by white stucco decoration. For many years the tower bells were used to raise the alarm in the event of a fire. The building is no longer used for administrative purposes but is open for functions and special occasions. It has recently been restored.
Cnr Hay & Barrack sts, City. See also A Walk Around Central Perth, p. 170

17 St George's Cathedral

Architect Edmund Blacket, considered the pre-eminent architect of his day in New South Wales, designed this very fine Victorian Gothic Revival church (1879–88), although he never visited Perth. Local bricks, jarrah and limestone, and bluestone from Melbourne, were used in the construction. The original tall tower that Blacket envisaged was not built, but a crenellated bell-tower, a memorial to Queen Victoria, was added in 1902 to the design of the leading

Perth Town Hall

Perth architect J Talbot Hobbs.
38 St Georges Tce, City. Open daily. (08) 9325 5766. See also A Walk Around Central Perth, p. 171

18 St Mary's Cathedral

St Mary's was built to plans by the prolific English architect Augustus Pugin, whose designs included the Houses of Parliament in Westminster, London. Benedictine monks built the cathedral themselves, walking more than 9 km a day from their lodgings in Subiaco and completing the cathedral in two years. It was substantially extended in the 1920s.
Victoria Sq., City. Open daily. (08) 9223 1351. See also A Walk Around Central Perth, p. 171

19 WA Museum

This fine museum is housed in a group of contemporary and historic buildings, including Hackett Hall (1908), which was originally built as a library. **Old Perth Gaol** is also part of the complex. The collection explores the State's pre-history in its dinosaur gallery, as well as its natural science, social history and architectural history. Of special note is the extensive collection related to the history and culture of Aboriginal people. *Katta Djinoong*, 'First Peoples of Western Australia', is a wonderful new gallery that provides an overview of the lives and culture of Aboriginal people in Western Australia over the past 60 000 years.
Perth Cultural Centre, Francis St, City. Open daily. (08) 9427 2700.

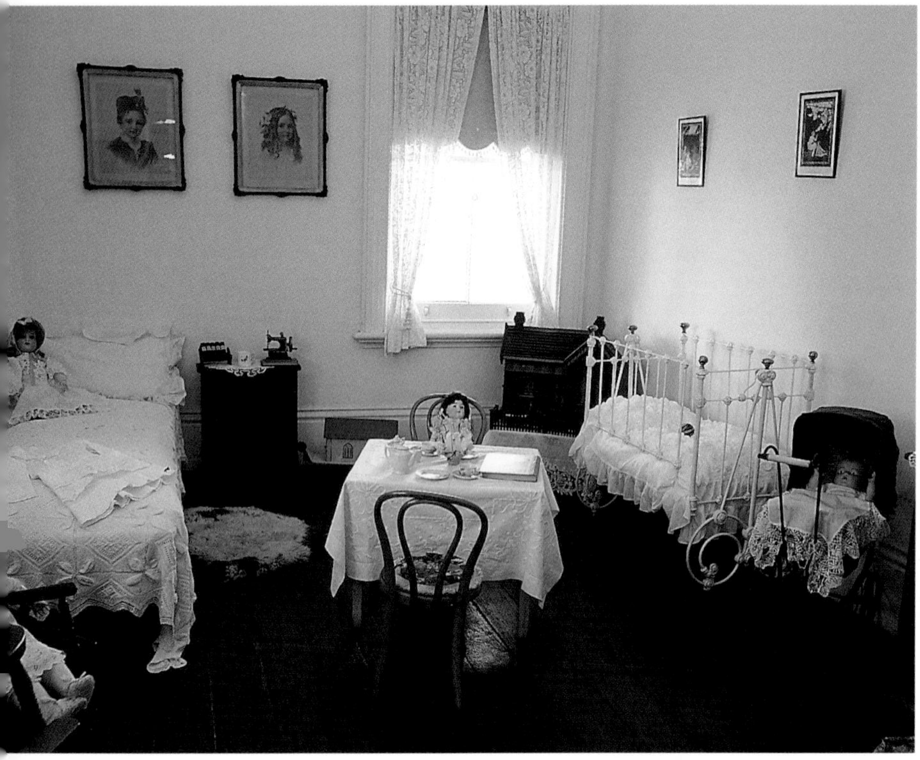

Nursery at Woodbridge House, West Midland

Around Perth

[1] Aviation Heritage Museum

Map ref. 338 H10

This outstanding museum features more than 30 military and civil aircraft, models and other aviation memorabilia. The collection includes such classics as a Tiger Moth, a Lancaster bomber, and a Supermarine Spitfire. There is also an aviation library and photographic display.
Bull Creek Dr., Bull Creek. Open daily. $ *(08) 9311 4470.*

[2] Berndt Museum of Anthropology

Map ref. 338 F5

An exceptional collection of Aboriginal art and culture, based around the collection bequeathed by Australia's distinguished anthropologists Prof. Ronald Berndt and Dr Catherine Berndt. As well as artifacts and works of art, the collection includes rare photos, documents, and sound recordings. It provides a small insight into the rich and varied culture of Aboriginal Australia.
University of WA, Hackett Dr., Crawley. Open Mon. & Wed. afternoons & Fri. 10 a.m.–2 p.m. (08) 9380 2854.

[3] Freshwater Bay School (Claremont Museum)

Map ref. 338 D6

When the first ships bringing convicts from Ireland arrived in 1853, a permanent convict depot was established at Freshwater Bay (now Claremont Park). One of Perth's oldest surviving buildings (1861–62), this limestone structure was built as a school for the children of Pensioner Guards (who watched over convict labourers) and other local residents. Now it is a local history museum, including shops and a schoolroom. The Claremont heritage walk is well worth while.
66 Victoria Ave, Claremont. Open Mon.–Fri. afternoons. $ *(08) 9285 4345.*

[4] Gallop House

Map ref. 338 E6

A well-known local landmark, a two-storey limestone house (1870s), overlooking the Swan River, with a stairway leading down to the riverbank.
Birdwood Pde, Dalkeith. Open Sun. afternoons. $ *(08) 9386 4363.*

[5] Guildford

Map ref. 341 O9

Guildford was one of the first three settlements in the Swan River Colony, established in 1829 as a market town and inland port at the meeting of the Swan and Helena rivers. Although now a suburb of Perth, it retains much of its turn-of-the-century character. The former convict commissariat store (1854), with shuttered windows, is now the Garrick Theatre. *Meadow St. Not open for inspection.* Next to the old gaol is the former courthouse, which opened with a celebratory ball in 1867. *Cnr Meadow & Swan sts. Not open for inspection.* The church-like Mechanics Institute, the district's first public hall in 1865, still serves the community. *20 Meadow St.* Neat St Matthew's (1873), a modest brick church with lancet windows, is the focus of attractive Stirling Sq. On a much grander scale are the Italianate post office (1898) at 24 Stirling St, and the Guildford Hotel (1886, extended 1899), at 161 James St. Whiteman's Abroad Gallery & Restaurant is located in a grand Edwardian residence (1895), which was a private museum for 40 years. The fully restored, National Trust-classified coach-house (1855) now offers accommodation. Also on site is the Flemish-bond building known as Jane's Cottage (1860). *34 Johnson St. Gallery, cottage & restaurant open Wed.–Sun. (08) 9379 2990.* Padbury's Colonial Stores and Residence (1869) houses a gift shop, an antique shop and a cafe. *112 Terrace Rd. Open Tues.–Sun. (08) 9379 1234.*
See also Guildford Museum, Rose & Crown Hotel, Woodbridge House

[6] Guildford Museum

Map ref. 341 O10

This museum is housed in the former gaol, a sturdy 1840s structure of handmade bricks, with walls up to almost 2 m thick in places. Managed by the Swan Guildford Historical Society, the collection focuses on the town's colonial days.
Cnr Swan & Meadow sts, Guildford. Open Sun. afternoons Mar.–Dec. $ *(08) 9279 1248.*

[7] Houghton Wines

Map ref. 341 P7

Set in vineyards with rows of gnarled vines, the winery includes an 1863

homestead and cellars noted for their large 19th-century wooden casks. A small museum chronicles historic wine-making techniques. Colonial Surgeon Dr John Ferguson, who bought the property in 1859, established the vineyards and winery, today one of the State's best known. River cruises run along the Swan River from Perth to Houghton Wines.
Dale Rd, Middle Swan. Open daily. (08) 9274 5100.

8 Kalamunda History Village
Map ref. 342 D4

A folk museum centred around the old railway station, with original buildings, such as cottages and a schoolhouse from Kalamunda's pioneer days in the late 1800s.
56 Railway Rd, Kalamunda. Open Mon.–Thurs., Sat.; also Sun. afternoons. $ *(08) 9293 1371.*

9 Museum of Childhood
Map ref. 338 D6

A trip down memory lane – and beyond – for adults, and a wonderful introduction to the toys, costumes, nursery and schoolroom furnishings from the Victorian and Edwardian eras up to the present day.
Edith Cowan University, Bay Rd, Claremont. Open Mon.–Fri.; closed 16 Dec.–18 Jan. $ *(08) 9442 1373.*

10 Rose & Crown Hotel
Map ref. 341 O10

A country inn, built 1840, then rebuilt in the 1850s when Guildford was a busy town servicing Perth and the Avon Valley farmlands. The old camel stables (1880s) at the back

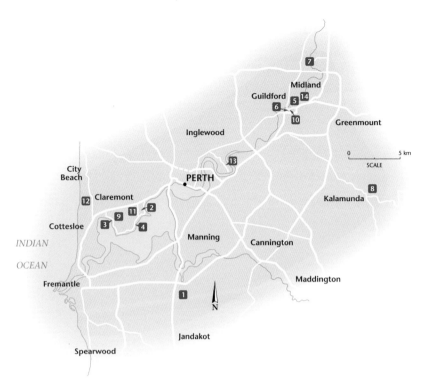

feature Dutch gables. Boutique beers (brewed on site) are served in the historic underground bar.
105 Swan St, Guildford. (08) 9279 8444.

11 Stirling House
Map ref. 338 F5

Headquarters of the Royal WA Historical Society, containing unique relics such as the sewing table of Lady Ellen Stirling, wife of the first WA Governor, and a 'Cottage' piano made in Leipzig by Zimmerman Bros in 1887. Period costumes are also displayed. The Society maintains a research library, photographic archive, documents and mementoes. There is a library, bookshop, and reading room.
49 Broadway, Nedlands. Open Mon.–Fri. (08) 9386 3841.

12 Tom Collins House
Map ref. 338 B5

A modest weatherboard house (1907) built by Joseph Furphy, author (under the pseudonym Tom Collins) of the Australian classic *Such Is Life*. The house, classified by the National Trust, has been moved to the leafy environs of Allean Park. It contains Furphy's antiquated typewriter and original manuscripts. It is now a writers' centre.
Cnr Wood St & Kirkwood Rd, Swanbourne. Open Mon. & Thurs. afternoons. (08) 9384 4771.

13 Tranby House
Map ref. 339 K2

A rambling vernacular farmhouse (c. 1839) with rough, stuccoed walls and a sweeping roof, shaded by century-old oaks. Joseph Hardey, a Lincolnshire farmer, and his wife, Ann, arrived in 1830 aboard the brig *Tranby*. Within weeks of moving into their 'Peninsula farm', the first of their six children had been born and Hardey had begun to sow crops. The colonial furnishings reflect the Hardeys' simple, pioneering lifestyle.
Johnson Rd, Maylands. Open Tues.–Sun. Closed July. $ *(08) 9272 2630. NT.*

14 Woodbridge House
Map ref. 341 P9

Stately, warm red-brick, late-Victorian mansion (1885), on land originally settled by WA's first Governor, Capt. James Stirling. It was built at a cost of £5000 by Charles Harper, explorer, MP and influential proprietor of the *West Australian* newspaper. Guildford Grammar School began in this building, and Woodbridge Preparatory School occupied the premises for 20 years. It has been furnished as an elegant period home; there are tearooms in the former stables. River cruises run from Perth to Woodbridge.
Ford St, West Midland. Open afternoons, closed Wed. $ *(08) 9274 2432. NT.*

Houghton Wines, Middle Swan

A WALK AROUND CENTRAL PERTH

Ǥt Georges Terrace, at first called Front Street, was part of the original town plan for the young Swan River Colony. Hay Street (originally Middle Street) and Murray Street also date from those earliest days. Soaring skyscrapers create Perth's skyline today, but within the heart of the city are some outstanding heritage buildings that recall the city's colonial beginnings.

Perth Visitor Centre
Cnr Forrest Pl. & Wellington St
Perth WA 6000
(08) 9483 1111 or 1300 361 351
www.westernaustralia.net

Perth Town Hall
A distinctive landmark, built in 1867–70. In 1875, after his epic overland expedition from South Australia, explorer Ernest Giles housed his party and their camels in the building's ground-floor market area.
Cnr Barrack & Hay sts.
(08) 9461 3333. See also p. 1

The Town Hall, Perth by TS Henry, 1914

Alexander Forrest Statue
Alexander Forrest was mayor of Perth, but he and his brother John are best known as explorers. In the 1870s Alexander mapped the Fitzroy River, and explored the isolated Kimberley region. The statue, by Pietro Porcelli, was unveiled in 1903.
Cnr Barrack St & St Georges Tce.

HISTORY
Although the Swan River Colony was planned, when the first settlers arrived in 1829 no surveying had been carried out. Officials quickly started reserving land for government and religious purposes. 'High ground' was saved for government offices and Government House. A small hill site was set aside for the Anglican Cathedral (later given to the Catholic Church). At first, buildings were modest. After 1850, when Britain supplied extra funds and convict labour, however, more substantial – even grand – buildings were erected. At one time, many fine residential mansions graced St Georges Tce, but with the gold boom of the 1890s, houses were replaced by offices. In the second half of the 20th century, wealth from minerals funded a new building boom.

The Weld Club
This exclusive men's club was founded in 1871 and named after WA Governor Sir Frederick Weld. Well-to-do members met to discuss business and politics informally and read the latest local and imported newspapers. The club moved to these premises in 1892.
Cnr Barrack St & The Esplanade.
Not open for inspection.
(08) 9325 2677.

Stirling Gardens
A small oasis in the city, opened as the city's botanic gardens in 1845 and named after the first governor, Sir James Stirling.
Cnr St Georges Tce & Barrack St.
Open at all times.

Old Courthouse
The city of Perth's oldest surviving public building, bu in 1836–37 by Henry Reveley
Stirling Gardens, cnr St George Tce & Barrack St. Open Mon.–
(08) 9325 4787. See also p. 1

St George's Cathedral

Gothic Revival in style, the cathedral replaced an 1840s church on the site. The interior is noteworthy for its warm rose-coloured brickwork and the beautiful wrought-iron chancel screen.
38 St Georges Tce. Open daily.
(08) 9325 5766. See also p. 167

Murray Street Precinct

Murray Street was one of Perth's first streets, in Surveyor-General John Septimus Roe's original 1838 town plan. This area has been classified by the National Trust and listed on the National Estate Register for its historic significance. Most of the area's buildings are dated between 1890 and 1914, when the State's economy was buoyed by gold.

Victoria Ave, 1880s, with St Mary's Cathedral on the right, Bishop's Palace on the left

St Mary's Cathedral

St Mary's Cathedral (1865) is on land set aside in the town's first plan as 'Church Square'. It was originally intended for the Anglican Church but was passed to the Catholic community when the area was deemed too far from the centre of Perth.
Victoria Sq. Open daily.
(08) 9223 1351. See also p. 167

Bishop's Palace

The Benedictine monks who built St Mary's Cathedral also erected this building in the late 1850s. In the 1920s it was extended in the grand Italianate style, with columns massed across the front.
Victoria Sq. Not open for inspection.

Adelaide Terrace

Like St Georges Terrace, this street was once lined with grand residences belonging to Perth's elite families.

St George's Hall Facade

A Classical facade is all that remains of WA's first theatre, built in 1879. The design was by Henry Prinsep.
508 Hay St.

Perth Mint

A splendid, solid building (1899) with rusticated limestone facade. In its early days gold from WA's flourishing goldfields was refined here. The building now includes a museum and visitors can see gold being poured in the melting house.
310 Hay St. Open daily Mon.–Fri. & Sat.–Sun. mornings. Regular tours. Ⓢ (08) 9421 7277. See also p. 167

The Deanery

A handsome, two-storey *cottage ornée*-style building, with multi-gabled roof and carved valances, 1859.
Cnr St Georges Tce & Pier St. Not open for inspection.

Government House

Official residence of the Governor of WA, a romantic Gothic mansion (1860–64), with arches and arcades, towers, turrets and mullioned windows, set in fine gardens.
St Georges Tce. Open about three times a year. See also p. 164

Old Courthouse, 1836–37

WESTERN AUSTRALIA FROM A TO Z

Schoolhouse, Wonnerup, near Busselton

ALBANY
Map ref. 342 H13, 344 E12

See Historic Highlights, p. 182

AUGUSTA
Map ref. 342 B11, 344 B11

Overlooking the tranquil Hardy Inlet, near Cape Leeuwin, the tiny town of Augusta lies about 320 km south of Perth. It was one of WA's earliest European settlements, founded in 1830 by families such as the Molloys, the Bussells and the Turners, whose names have become part of the State's history. OF INTEREST The Augusta Historical

Museum focuses on pioneering and timber-getting history. *Blackwood Ave. Open limited hours daily (longer in school hols).* Ⓢ *(08) 9758 1948.*
IN THE AREA Cape Leeuwin Lighthouse (1895) is on the most south-westerly tip of the continent. It's a steep climb up the stairs, but offers stunning views of the rugged coastline, where the Indian and Southern oceans meet. It is one of the State's best spots for whale-watching. *8 km s, Leeuwin–Naturaliste NP, Leeuwin Rd. Open daily.* Ⓢ *(08) 9758 1920.*
🄸 *70 Blackwood Ave; (08) 9758 0166.*

Website: www.margaretriverwa.com
See also Margaret River

AUSTRALIND
Map ref. 342 C8, 344 C10

Australind was the scene of an ambitious but ill-fated settlement programme undertaken by the Western Australian Company in 1841 on the eastern shores of the Leschenault Estuary. A vast estate was divided into small farms, and 500 British settlers arrived, but the soil was poor and the settlement, planned as a vital trade link between

Australia and India (hence the name Austral-Ind), was soon abandoned.

OF INTEREST St Nicholas' Church, reputedly the State's smallest, was built in 1841 as a residence. *Paris Rd. Not open for inspection.* Henton Cottage (c. 1841) opposite, once the Prince of Wales Hotel, is now an art and craft gallery. *Paris Rd. Open daily. (08) 9796 0102.*

IN THE AREA The Yarloop Workshops is an engineering museum on the site of the area's first mill (1895). *47 km NE, Railway Pde, Yarloop. Open daily.* $ *(08) 9733 5368.*

[i] *Henton Cottage, Paris Rd; (08) 9796 0102.*

See also Bunbury

BEVERLEY

Map ref. 342 F4, 344 D8

The small township of Beverley, on the banks of the Avon River, east of Perth, dates from 1838.

OF INTEREST The Aeronautical Museum houses WA's first privately built aircraft, assembled in the 1930s, and photos of the State's early aviation history. *139 Vincent St. Open daily.* $ *(08) 9646 1555.* Dead Finish Museum, built as a hotel in 1872, is one of Beverley's oldest buildings. *Hunt Rd. Open Sun. afternoons Mar.–Nov.* $ *(08) 9646 1149.*

IN THE AREA Avondale Discovery Farm includes an 1850s homestead set in a gracious garden and an extensive collection of vintage and other farm machinery still in use. The magnificent Clydesdale horses, traditional farm animals, are stabled in an 1890s Oregon pine stable. *6 km W. Open daily. (08) 9646 1004.*

[i] *Aeronautical Museum, 139 Vincent St; (08) 9646 1555.* Website: www.beverleywa.com

BOULDER

See Historic Highlights, p. 188

BRIDGETOWN

Map ref. 342 D10

Bridgetown is a quiet settlement in the lush, undulating timber-rich countryside of WA's south-west, where the land was first taken up by pastoralists in the 1850s. The town site was officially proclaimed in 1868.

Bridgedale Established in the late 1850s, Bridgedale remained in the Blechynden family until 1950. The house, with a sweeping roof of timber shingles, was centre to the family's farming and pastoral operations and base for their Bridgetown–Bunbury freight business. The parlour housed the district's first school for several years, from 1868. Once surrounded by outbuildings, Bridgedale now sits amongst attractive gardens on the banks of the Blackwood River. *Hampton St. Open Fri.–Sun.* $ *(08) 9761 1555 or (08) 9321 6088. NT.*

ALSO OF INTEREST The Old Gaol & Police Station, with its shingled roof. The police station opened in 1880, with two cells added in 1892. *Hampton St. Tours by appt. (08) 9761 1740.*

IN THE AREA Donnelly Timber Mill Museum is an historic steam-operated mill. *26 km SW. Tours by appt.* $ *(08) 9772 1244.*

[i] *Hampton St; (08) 9761 1740.*

BROOME

Map ref. 348 G9

See Historic Highlights, p. 184

BUNBURY

Map ref. 342 C8, 344 C10

A thriving port, originally called Port Leschenault, with beautiful sandy beaches and the Darling Ranges in the distance. It was settled in 1838, following favourable reports on the district by Lt HW St Pierre Bunbury. American whalers who sheltered in Koombana Bay provided markets for the pioneer farmers, but a more lucrative timber industry was soon established. Bunbury owes its continued existence to its fine natural harbour and is today one of the State's largest cities.

King Cottage Museum A characteristically colonial bungalow-style brick house, built by bricklayer Henry King c. 1870. Now a museum with artifacts from Bunbury's pioneer past. *77 Forrest Ave. Open Tues., Thurs. & Sun. afternoons, or by appt.* $ *(08) 9721 3929.*

ALSO OF INTEREST Bunbury has a range of heritage properties. Pick up a map from Visitor Information (in the old railway station, 1904) and explore areas such as the Stirling Street Historic Precinct. There are classic pubs, including the Rose Hotel (1865), with its delicate iron lacework and verandahs, added in 1897. *Cnr Victoria & Wellington sts.* Picturesque St Mark's Church, built of pit-sawn timber by the Rev. Wollaston, later Anglican Archdeacon of WA, is the State's second-oldest church (1842). *Charterhouse Close, Picton Junction. Open daily.*

[i] *Old Railway Station, Carmody Pl.; (08) 9721 7922.* Website: www.justsouth.com.au

BUSSELTON

Map ref. 342 B9, 344 C10

On the sweeping shores of Geographe Bay and the pleasant banks of the Vasse River, Busselton is one of WA's oldest established areas and a popular seaside resort. French explorer Nicholas Baudin named the river Vasse, and Geographe Bay after his ship. The pioneering Bussell family, after whom the town is named, took up land here in 1832. The town soon established itself as a port.

Busselton Historic Museum Located near the river, shaded by giant peppermint trees, this museum is housed in the old Butter Factory. Local history exhibits include historic dairy equipment and photographs. There's also a furnished house and a schoolhouse. *Peel Tce. Open Wed.–Mon. afternoons.* $ *(08) 9754 2166.*

St Mary's Anglican Church Said to be the oldest stone church in WA (1844) and one of the prettiest with its riverside setting, it was built of limestone and jarrah with a she-oak roof. The foundation stone was laid by Frances Bussell. The timber ceiling is especially notable. *Cnr Peel Tce & Bussell Highway. Open daily.*

ALSO OF INTEREST The Old Courthouse (1854–56) has also served as a gaol, stable, post office and bond store. It is now part of an historic complex of buildings converted to a gallery, craft studios and cafe. The original gaol cells can be inspected. *4 Queen St. Open daily. (08) 9752 1603.* The unusual Villa Carlotta (1896–97) has shuttered french windows, and a tower with beautiful bay views provides guesthouse accommodation. *110 Adelaide St. Not open for inspection. (08) 9754 2026.* In Victoria Park, the *Ballarat*, WA's first steam locomotive, built in 1871, was used to haul timber from Yoganup to Wonnerup. A marvellous timber jetty stretches 2 km into the Bay. Construction began in 1865 and continued over the next 90 years. A train takes a 40-min return trip along the jetty. There's a centre with historical information and a new underwater observatory on the jetty. Ⓢ *(08) 9754 3689.*

In the area Wonnerup was home to three generations of the Layman family, from 1837 to 1962. The complex now includes the c. 1837 house converted to a dairy and kitchen, an 1859 colonial homestead, and farm buildings including the stables with unique grass-tree floors. By the late 1800s Wonnerup was one of the best dairy farms in the south-west. From 1912 the property was managed by four unmarried Layman sisters. Today Wonnerup is furnished mainly in a late 19th-century manner. Opposite are the old schoolhouse (1873) and teacher's house (1885). *10 km NE, Layman Rd. Open daily.* Ⓢ *(08) 9752 2039 or (08) 9321 6088. NT.* Newtown House, a classic early colonial farmhouse and dairy (c. 1851), restored and surrounded by attractive gardens, serves lunches and teas and offers B&B accommodation. *10 km w. Cnr Bussell Hwy & Caves Rd, Vasse. Open Tues.–Sat. (08) 9755 4485.* Cape Naturaliste Lighthouse (1903) overlooks the sparkling waters of Geographe Bay and the wonderful Cape coastline; there is a maritime museum with guided tours and inspiring views (including whales if you're lucky). *38 km w, Cape Naturaliste Rd via Dunsborough. Open daily.* Ⓢ *(08) 9755 3955.*
🖪 *38 Peel Tce; (08) 9752 1288.* Website: www.downsouth.com.au
See also Margaret River

COOLGARDIE
Map ref. 344 I6

Prospectors Arthur Bayley and William Ford discovered gold in this semi-arid wasteland, around 550 km east of Perth, in 1892. Their very first sample of quartz yielded 15.7 kg of gold. The settlement that sprang up, almost within weeks, was known as Fly Flat. The town was officially named Coolgardie in August 1893, and by 1900 the population numbered 15 000, with 23 hotels, two stock exchanges, six banks and three daily newspapers. Life was primitive, water virtually non-existent and disease rife: between 1894 and 1899 typhoid claimed 1000 lives. But grand buildings were erected, the

railway reached town in 1896, and, more importantly, the lifesaving water pipeline from Perth was connected in 1903. As the surface gold petered out the diggers moved on, and the population dwindled. Today's town is small, but memories of the gold-rush days linger on.

Goldfields Exhibition A record of the 'rush to be rich' – the excitement and the hardship of life on the goldfields, told through historic photographs, life-like models and an interesting film. Don't miss the Aboriginal artifacts in the upstairs gallery. The exhibition is in the former Warden's Court building (1898), one of the finest buildings on the goldfields. *62 Bayley St. Open daily.* Ⓢ *(08) 9026 6090.*

Pharmaceutical & Dentist Display This quirky collection combines the 'tools of the trade' with the truth behind some old-fashioned 'cures' – pills that were no more than sugar-coated soap, cheap bourbon potions and baby medicine laced with cannabis and sugar. Housed in the former Drill Hall (1896). *60 Bayley St. Open daily.* Ⓢ *(08) 9026 7383.*

Warden Finnerty's House A substantial stone residence with shuttered french doors and windows, lofty rooms and an enormous gabled roof area, all devices to help cool the house. It was built in 1895 for Coolgardie's first mining warden and resident magistrate, John M Finnerty. *2 McKenzie St, off Hunt St. Open daily.* Ⓢ *(08) 9026 6090 or (08) 9321 6088. NT.*

Also of interest The once hectic railway station, opened in 1896, is now a transport museum. *Woodward St. Open Sat.–Thurs.* Ⓢ *(08) 9026 6388.* Ben Prior's Open Air Museum features goldfields equipment and machinery. *Bayley St. Open at all times. (08) 9026 6029.* Coolgardie has a wealth of boom-style architecture including classic, verandahed pubs, such as the Denver City Hotel (1898) in Bayley St. Historical markers with photographs offer a surprising then-and-now look at the town and help conjure the town's golden days. At Coolgardie Cemetery rows of weathered headstones reveal the heavy toll of goldfields life. *1 km w, Great Eastern Hwy.*
🖪 *62 Bayley St; (08) 9026 6090.* Website: www.kalgoorlieandwagoldfields.com.au
See also Kalgoorlie–Boulder

COSSACK
Map ref. 343 G1, 346 A1

Once a busy pearling port and the first port in the far north, Cossack is an historic town site with several carefully preserved stone buildings standing proudly in the rugged, red landscape. The port, originally known as Tien Tsin Harbour (after the barque *Tien Tsin*, which carried the first settler in 1863), was declared a town in 1872. Cossack was a service centre for **Roebourne**, about 12 km inland, until a jetty to service larger ships was established at Point Samson in 1904.

Social History Museum Housed in the imposing courthouse (1895) built

Marvel Bar Hotel, Coolgardie

when the population numbered just 250 (Asians and Aboriginal people weren't included in the count). The museum documents the town's colourful history and its pioneer settlers. *Main St. Open daily.* Ⓢ

ALSO OF INTEREST Cossack's first stone buildings are handsome and solid, designed to withstand tropical cyclones. The Cossack Backpackers' Accommodation is in the former post and telegraph building (1884–85). Also notable are the stone customs house and bonded store (1895), and the police quarters and gaol (1867). The cemetery has a Japanese section, a legacy of pearling days.

🛈 *Old Gaol, Queen St, Roebourne; (08) 9182 1060.* Website: www.pilbara.com
See also Roebourne

DERBY
Map ref. 349 J7

Derby, on King Sound in the State's far north, was settled in the 1880s after surveyor and explorer Alexander Forrest optimistically, if mysteriously, praised the district's pastoral potential. The isolated Kimberley region once relied heavily on this port, particularly during the 1880s gold rush to **Halls Creek**. English buccaneer William Dampier was the first recorded European to land in King Sound, in 1688.

OF INTEREST Wharfingers House, a tropical bungalow (1920s) built for the local harbour master, contains a small museum. Check at Visitor Information for opening times. Ⓢ *(donation).* Old Derby Gaol, built in 1906 exclusively for the detention of Aboriginal prisoners; later non-Aboriginal prisoners were held here also. The town's oldest surviving building, it is fully restored. *Open at all times. Loch St.* The sad tale of the Aboriginal outlaw Jandamarra, or 'Pigeon', in the 1890s, symbolises the often-disastrous relationship between black and white in Australia's history. Collect a Pigeon Heritage Trail brochure from Visitor Information.

IN THE AREA The huge old Boab Prison Tree, around 1500 years old, was used for many years as a staging point for prisoners being walked to Derby. It is a registered Aboriginal site, and visitors are requested not to climb into or approach close to the tree. *7 km s.*

🛈 *2 Clarendon St; (08) 9191 1426.* Website: www.derbytourism.com

DONGARA
Map ref. 344 B4

Dongara, a tiny village on the coast, around 360 km north of Perth, was at the heart of a flourishing wheat-growing district in the 1800s. Several historic buildings and some magnificent century-old Moreton Bay fig trees line the main street.

OF INTEREST The dramatic four-storey Royal Steamroller Flour Mill (1894) is one of WA's last remaining steam flour mills. The complex once had its own branch rail line. The building is being restored, but can be seen from Brand Hwy. Russ Cottage, a modest four-room stone cottage (1860s), built by pioneer settler Titus Russ, retains original family furnishings. The kitchen floor is said to be made from crushed anthills, a surprising example of colonial ingenuity. *Point Leander Dr. Open Sun. & by appt.* Ⓢ *(08) 9927 1617.* Priory Lodge (1881), built as an inn and owned at one time by Dominican nuns, is now a private hotel. *St Dominics Rd. (08) 9927 1090.* At the Church of St John the Baptist (1884) the pews are reputedly made from driftwood salvaged from shipwrecks. *Cnr Church & Waldeck sts. Open for Sunday service 10 a.m. (08) 9927 2107.* Pick up a heritage trail brochure from Visitor Information. Ⓢ

🛈 *Dongara Library, 7 Waldeck St; (08) 9927 1404.*
See also Greenough

FREMANTLE
Map ref. 338 B11, 342 C4, 344 C8

See Historic Highlights, p. 186

GERALDTON
Map ref. 344 A3

Geraldton's long maritime history began with the Dutch mutineers and shipwrecked seamen who unwillingly landed on these shores in the 1600s. The first officially recorded British visit was in 1822, led by Capt. Philip Parker King. Copper, lead and gold discoveries brought people to the district in the 1840s and '50s. The area was surveyed in 1849 and declared a town in 1872. Geraldton is now one of WA's largest cities.

Maritime Museum Unique displays include bronze cannons, earthenware pots and navigational equipment retrieved from Dutch ships, such as the *Batavia* and *Zuytdorp*, wrecked off the coast in the 17th and 18th centuries. Part of the WA Museum – Geraldton. *1 Museum Pl., Batavia Coast Marina. Open daily.* Ⓢ *(donation). (08) 9921 5080.*

St Francis Xavier's Cathedral A magnificent stone cathedral (1916–38), one of Australia's finest and most unusual, designed by English architect–priest Monsignor John Hawes in the Byzantine style. The interior is equally as dramatic. *Cathedral Ave. Open daily. Tours Mon. 10 a.m. & Fri. 2 p.m.*

ALSO OF INTEREST WA Museum – Geraldton features natural history exhibits and records the district's history. *1 Museum Pl., Batavia Coast Marina. Open daily.* Ⓢ *(donation). (08) 9921 5080.* The Hermitage (1937), designed by Monsignor John Hawes as a residence. *Onslow St. Not open for inspection.* Pick up the Monsignor Hawes Heritage Trail from Visitor Information for more about this fascinating character and his buildings in the district.

IN THE AREA The whitewashed Bluff Point Lighthouse Keeper's Cottage (1870) is home to the local historical society. *5 km N, Chapman Rd. Open Thurs.* Ⓢ 60 km offshore, the beautiful but treacherous Houtman Abrolhos Islands, discovered by Europeans in 1619, were the scene of the *Batavia* mutiny in 1629, when 125 men, women and children were murdered. The ruins of two small huts survive. Aerial and boat tours are available.

🛈 *Bill Sewell Complex, cnr Bayley St & Chapman Rd; (08) 9921 3999.* Website: www.geraldtontourist.com.au

GREENOUGH
Map ref. 344 B4

Situated in the valley of the Greenough River, in a strange landscape dotted with river gums twisted almost horizontal by the salt-laden coastal winds, this hamlet is a monument to pioneer determination and faith. The Front Flats, as they were known, were settled in the 1850s and flourished briefly as a wheat-growing area, but most farmers were eventually defeated by drought, crop rust and disastrous floods.

Greenough Hamlet A cluster of stone

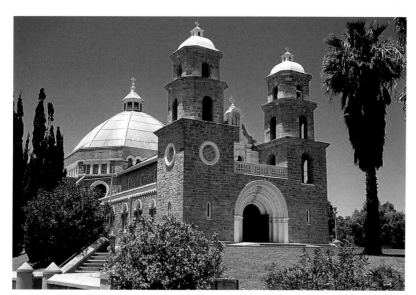
St Francis Xavier's Cathedral, Geraldton

buildings, which conjure the life of a small, 19th-century farming community. The sturdy buildings include a courthouse, general store (now a tea-room and visitors centre), lock-up, police quarters, post office and more, built 1860s–70s, and restored by the National Trust. A tour offers some worthwhile insights into Greenough's history. *Cnr Brand Hwy & McCartney Rd. Open daily.* Ⓢ *(08) 9926 1084.*
Pioneer Museum Built c. 1860 by John Stephen Maley as the 'home cottage' to the adjacent three-storey Victoria Flour Mill (sometimes known as Maley's Mill), this colonial house was once home to John, his wife and 14 children. It is now the setting for a folk museum. *Phillips Rd. Open Sat.–Thurs.* Ⓢ *(08) 9926 1058.*
ALSO OF INTEREST The three-storey Clinch's Mill, built c. 1856 but extended in 1891. *Not open for inspection.* The substantial Cliff Grange homestead, built c. 1870 to house the mill manager. *Brand Hwy. Not open for inspection.* Hampton Arms, an 1863 inn, is now a charming guesthouse and restaurant. *Company Rd. Open daily. (08) 9926 1057.*
IN THE AREA The Walkaway railway station, opened as part of Queen Victoria's jubilee celebrations in 1887, is now a museum. *7 km E. Padbury Rd, Walkaway. Open Tues.–Sun.* Ⓢ
🄸 *Greenough Hamlet, cnr Brand Hwy & McCartney Rd; (08) 9926 1160 or (08) 9926 1084.* Website: www. greenough.wa.gov.au
See also Dongara, Geraldton

GUILDFORD
Map ref. 341 O9

See Around Perth, p. 168

HALLS CREEK, (OLD)
Map ref. 349 P9

On the edge of the Great Sandy Desert, more than 2800 km north-east of Perth, Halls Creek was the site of WA's first gold rush, in 1885. Two thousand miners arrived within the first year, to find little gold, harsh conditions and hostile Aboriginal tribes. All that remains of the original town site is the crumbling ruins of the old mudbrick post office and cemetery. The new town site is 16 km to the west.
🄸 *Great Northern Hwy, Halls Creek; (08) 9168 6262.*

KALBARRI
Map ref. 343 C13, 344 A2

Kalbarri's spectacular red cliff coastline has witnessed numerous shipwrecks. The first white men believed to have landed permanently in Australia were two Dutchmen sent ashore for their part in the *Batavia* mutiny, which took place off the WA coast. They landed just south of Kalbarri in 1629. In 1712 the Dutch East Indiaman *Zuytdorp* was wrecked off the coast, and in 1839 English explorer Lt Grey struggled ashore after his ship was wrecked. Grey and his party had to walk more than 600 km south to Perth. Despite these early associations, the town was only set up in the 1950s. Today it is known as a holiday resort.

OF INTEREST At Wittecarra Creek, near Red Bluff, an historic cairn marks the possible landing site of the Dutch mutineers in 1629. *4 km S.* Relics of the *Batavia* and *Zuytdorp* are in the Maritime Museum at **Geraldton**.
🄸 *Grey St; (08) 9937 1104, freecall 1800 639 468.* Website: www.wn. com.au/kalbarrionline

KALGOORLIE–BOULDER
Map ref. 344 I6

See Historic Highlights, p. 188

KOJONUP
Map ref. 342 G9, 344 E11

A settlement grew up here after 1837, when Alfred Hillman was guided to the site of a 'never-failing spring' by the local Aboriginal people. The town takes its name from the Aboriginal word *kodja*, meaning 'stone axe'. It served as an outpost to protect the mail run and a convenient stop on the long Albany to York route. The small town is in the wheat-belt district, around 250 km south-east of Perth.
Military Barracks Museum A sturdy stone house (c. 1845), with huge old pepper trees. The massive walls and chimneys, small windows and steeply sloping roof are typical of many isolated, early WA dwellings. Built originally as a barracks for soldiers stationed in the district to protect the early settlers, it later served as a church, school and residence. Now a local history museum. *Spring St. Open Sun. afternoons or by appt.* Ⓢ *(donation). (08) 9831 1148.*
ALSO OF INTEREST Kodja Place, an interpretive centre incorporating Visitor Information, explores the town's history and culture, with a strong focus on the lives of its Indigenous inhabitants and the challenges faced by both Aboriginal people and Europeans trying to survive in the bush. *Open daily. (08) 9831 1686.*
🄸 *Albany Hwy; (08) 9831 1686.* Website: www.promaco.com.au/kojonup

KUNUNURRA
Map ref. 349 Q5

Kununurra is a modern town in the Kimberley, built when the Ord River Irrigation Scheme was being developed in the 1960s.
IN THE AREA Argyle Downs Homestead is the stone house built by members

of the famous pioneering Durack family in 1894. The family undertook an epic two-and-a-half-year journey from Qld, overlanding 7250 head of cattle. Despite many misadventures, they arrived with 3000 cattle to form the basis of the Kimberley beef industry. Their now legendary achievements are recorded in Dame Mary Durack's classic book *Kings in Grass Castles*. The house, moved to its present site in 1976, is now a museum, and a monument to pioneers such as the Durack family. *72 km s. Parker Rd, next to Lake Argyle Tourist Village. Open daily during the Dry season.* Ⓢ *(08) 9167 8088.*

🄸 *East Kimberley Tourism House, Coolibah Dr.; (08) 9168 1177.*

LEONORA–GWALIA Map ref. 344 I3

The twin towns of Leonora and Gwalia – the name is Celtic for Wales – were spawned in this vast, arid landscape by the discovery of gold in the 1890s. Leonora, with its small shops and spacious streets, has remained virtually unchanged since 1900. When the immensely rich and long-lasting Sons of Gwalia mine closed in 1963, Gwalia became almost a ghost town. In recent years, however, mining has resumed, breathing new life into the town.

Former Gwalia State Hotel Standing in splendid isolation, this grand, two-storey hotel (1903) epitomises the optimism and confidence of the gold era. It was the first WA State Hotel, built to try to reduce the 20-odd illegal alcohol suppliers operating in Gwalia. It is now used as accommodation for employees of the Sons of Gwalia mining company. Herbert Hoover, later President of the USA, was at one time manager of the mine.

Also of interest In Leonora, buildings such as the Grand Hotel (c. 1900), the post office (c. 1900), Barnes Federal Theatre (1901) and the White House Hotel, all in Tower St, suggest busier days. Gwalia has miners' cottages, a general store and guesthouse. The museum is a treasure trove of memorabilia dating back to 1898. The Oregon headframe, steam winding engine and original mine buildings commissioned by Herbert Hoover overlook today's mining area. *Tower St. Open daily.* Ⓢ *(08) 9037 7210.*

🄸 *Gwalia Historical Township & Museum; (08) 9037 7210.* Website: www.leonora.wa.gov.au

MANDURAH Map ref. 342 C5, 344 C9

An ambitious but unsuccessful settlement programme was attempted here in the 1830s by Thomas Peel, English entrepreneur and cousin of the British Home Secretary and future Prime Minister, Sir Robert Peel. Today, this coastal city at the mouth of the Peel Inlet retains few vestiges of its earliest days. Just 74 km south of Perth it is both holiday resort and busy commuter centre for the capital.

Hall's Cottage This limestone cottage with its narrow verandah and pit-sawn timber floors was built in 1832 by one of Mandurah's first settlers, Henry Hall. *Leighton Rd, Halls Head. Open Sun. afternoons.* Ⓢ *(08) 9535 8970.*

Also of interest Christ Church (c. 1871), cnr Scholl St & Pinjarra Rd, has hand-carved wooden pews. Thomas Peel and other pioneers of the district are buried in the graveyard. The charming old Cooper's Mill, the district's first flour mill, started in 1843 on Cullenup Island, can be visited.

🄸 *75 Mandurah Tce; (08) 9550 3999.*
See also Pinjarra

MANJIMUP Map ref. 342 D10, 344 D11

Manjimup, on the edge of majestic karri and jarrah forests, just over 300 km south of Perth, was first settled in the 1850s. Its history has been closely tied to the timber industry since the colony's earliest days, when the qualities of jarrah as a building timber were discovered. The first pit-sawn timber was shipped from the Swan River Colony in 1830.

Manjimup Regional Timber Park An impressive and engaging complex that details the importance of forests and the history of the timber industry. Within the park are the Age of Steam Museum, a timber museum, fire lookout tower, and a cluster of historic buildings including an early millhouse. Visitor Information is also based here. *Cnr Rose & Edward sts. Open daily.* Ⓢ *(08) 9771 1831.*

In the area This is tall timber country and the area's natural history outshines any man-made structures. Follow the winding logging roads to see some of the country's most magnificent and oldest trees. On Perup Rd is the King Jarrah, said to be 600 years old. *3 km NE.* At One Tree Bridge lies the remains of a single karri felled in 1904 to cross the Donnelly River. Signage here records the district's early European history. *23 km w.* A little further, on Graphite Rd, you can see the so-called Four Aces, four majestic karri specimens estimated at 300–400 years old, towering up to 79 m high. *24 km w.* At Dingup stands the pioneer church (c. 1896), built by early settler Thomas Giblett, and Giblett's home, Dingup House (1870), built of pit-sawn timber. *10 km N. Both open by appt. (08) 9772 4206.*

🄸 *Cnr Rose & Edwards sts; (08) 9771 1831.*
See also Bridgetown, Pemberton

MARBLE BAR Map ref. 346 D2

Marble Bar, reputedly Australia's hottest town, was at its peak after the discovery of alluvial gold in the Pilbara in the 1880s. More than 5000 people braved the desolation and searing heat in search of riches, but they soon moved on. The town takes its name from a distinctive bar of jasper, mistaken for marble, that crosses the nearby Coongan River.

Of interest Impressive government buildings, still in use, were built of locally quarried stone in 1895. At the time, Marble Bar obviously envisaged a big future. *Cnr Francis & Conquest sts. Open daily. (08) 9176 1166.*

🄸 *Marble Bar Travellers' Stop, Lot 232 Halse Rd; (08) 9176 1166.*

MARGARET RIVER Map ref. 342 A10

In the State's south-west, the Margaret River area is renowned for its vineyards and wineries. The town is a favourite holiday resort. There were pioneers in the district in the 1850s and timber-getters in the 1870s, but the town itself was not established until the government Group Settlement Scheme moved migrants into the district in the 1920s.

The Old Settlement A typical 1920s group settlement farm, with houses, a blacksmith's workshop, dairy and more. An informative tour reveals the history and the hardship of those early days. There's also an outstanding photographic museum. *Higgins St. Open daily.* $ *(08) 9757 2775.*

Also of interest Margaret River abounds with B&Bs, including the picturesque, heritage-listed Basildene Manor (1912). *Lot 100 Wallcliffe Rd. (08) 9757 3140.*

In the area Within the Leeuwin–Naturaliste National Park is Ellensbrook, a modest stone and timber house built by Alfred and Ellen Bussell in 1857, which became home to their 12 children. From the 1870s the property was managed by Bussell daughters Fanny and, later, Edith, who provided a home here for Aboriginal children. *12 km NW, Ellensbrook Rd. Open Sat.–Sun. Check for other times.* $ *(08) 9321 6088. NT. National Park (08) 9752 1677.*

[i] *Cnr Bussell Hwy & Tunbridge Rd; (08) 9757 2911.* Website: www.margaretriverwa.com

Moora
Map ref. 344 C6

The little township of Moora, north of Perth and in the foothills of the Darling Ranges, was declared a town in 1895.

In the area To the east is Berkshire Valley, a fascinating, well-preserved 19th-century homestead complex of a dozen major buildings, begun by James Clinch in 1847, and remarkably like an old English village. Erected over 25 years, the buildings show a wide range of techniques and materials. Pisé, adobe, random rubble and burnt bricks made by hand on the property combine in the solid, practical, well-planned group. The gatehouse features lanterns and an 1867 date plate. The Old Flour Mill (1847) contains a folk museum. *19 km E. Open every second Sun. in the month from Apr.–Nov. or by appt.* $ *(08) 9654 9040.*

[i] *Shire Offices, 34 Padbury St; (08) 9651 1401.*

Mount Barker
Map ref. 342 H12

Surrounded by gently undulating countryside, Mount Barker is 350 km south-east of Perth, on the edge of the ancient Porongurup Ranges. The district was first settled by Europeans in the 1830s and became a renowned agricultural region. Recently it has earned a reputation for its vineyards.

Old Police Station & Gaol Looking more like a country cottage than a gaol, this rustic building (1867–68) was convict-built of ironstone and jarrah, with a sweeping roof. Rooms are furnished to depict how they were used c. 1865–1910; other buildings in the complex contain local memorabilia. *Albany Hwy. Open Sat.–Sun. & school hols.* $ *(08) 9851 2505.*

Also of interest St Werburgh's Chapel (1872–73), sheltering beneath a steeply pitched roof, with encircling verandah and quaint stone and corrugated-iron bell-tower. The chapel is on private property, but visitors are welcome. The adjoining cemetery overlooks the Hay River Valley. The Mount Barker Heritage Trail is a 30-km drive highlighting the district's historic sites.

[i] *57 Lowood Rd; (08) 9851 1163.* Website: www.comswest.net.au/~mtbarkwa

Mundaring
Map ref. 342 D3, 344 C8

This small town in the Darling Ranges, today almost a suburb of Perth, really began in the late 1890s, when workers arrived to work on the Mundaring Weir and pipeline for the acclaimed Goldfields Water Supply Scheme. The pipeline carried water more than 500 km to arid Outback towns such as **Kalgoorlie**.

CY O'Connor Museum The former No. 1 Pumping Station, for the goldfields water pipeline, was opened in 1903 and named in honour of the Scheme's engineer. The surrounding parkland is popular for picnics. *Mundaring Weir, Mundaring Rd. Open Mon.–Fri.; also Sat.–Sun. afternoons.* $ *(08) 9295 2455.*

[i] *The Old School, 7225 Great Eastern Hwy; (08) 9295 0202.* Website: www.mundaringtourism.com.au

New Norcia
Map ref. 342 D1, 344 C6

New Norcia was founded in 1846 by Spanish Benedictine monks Dom Rosendo Salvado and Dom Joseph Serra as a mission for Aboriginal people. This exceptional town contains a unique heritage of Spanish colonial-style buildings. The town is still home to a community of Benedictine monks who own and administer the settlement.

Museum & Art Gallery The remarkable collection comprises paintings by 17th-century Italian and Spanish Old Masters, jewellery, rare manuscripts and a 16th-century Murillo bible. *Great Northern Hwy. Open daily.* $ *(08) 9654 8056.*

Also of interest New Norcia's buildings include the majestic Romanesque-style Holy Trinity Abbey Church (c. 1861), monastery guesthouse, giant flour mill (1879), the splendidly ornate St Gertrude's (1908) and St Ildephonsus' (1913) colleges and a hotel (originally a hostel), all built in the Mediterranean architectural tradition. Typically colonial vernacular cottages and a delightful octagonal apiary are just some of the other buildings. A guided tour is highly recommended, allowing visitors a glimpse 'behind closed doors'. There is also an informative heritage trail brochure. *Tours twice daily.* $

[i] *New Norcia Museum & Art Gallery, Great Northern Hwy; (08) 9654 8056.* Website: www.newnorcia.wa.edu.au

See also Moora

Northam
Map ref. 342 E3, 344 D7

Declared a town in 1833, Northam, in the gently undulating farmland of the Avon Valley, grew slowly until the 1850s but boomed with the discovery of the Eastern Goldfields and the coming of the railway in the 1880s. Today, just an hour's drive east of Perth, it is a major regional centre.

Morby Cottage A modest pioneer dwelling, built c. 1836 for Northam's first settler, John Morrell, the cottage served as the town's first school and church. It now houses a museum. *Avon Dr. Open Sun.* $ *(08) 9622 2100.*

Also of interest The Avon Valley Arts Centre is located in both the Jacobean-gabled former Girls' School (1877) and the unusual Old Post Office (1892). *33 Wellington St. Open daily. (08) 9622 2245.* The 1886 station was the headquarters of the eastern district of the Eastern Goldfields Railway for 80 years. It is now the Old Railway Station Museum. *Fitzgerald St. Open Sun.* $ *(08) 9622 2100.*

In the area Katrine Barn is a delightful 1858 stone barn now restored and in

use as a private museum and art and craft gallery. *16 km NW. Katrine Rd. Open by appt. (08) 9622 3790.*
🖪 *Minson Ave; (08) 9622 2100.* Website: www.avon.net.au/~northam
See also Toodyay, York

NUNGARIN   Map ref. 342 I1, 344 F7

A tiny town in the wheat belt northeast of Perth, in a district first settled by Europeans in the 1860s.
IN THE AREA Mangowine Homestead, built c. 1874, formed the centre of the Adams family's pastoral and sandalwood enterprise. After the 1880s, the family opened an inn for prospectors on their way to the Yilgarn Goldfields. The homestead features massively thick, random stone and mudbrick walls and huge chimneys. The interior has a spartan simplicity, with stone floors and unlined ceilings. The Adams family lived at Mangowine for almost a century. *14 km N, Karomin North Rd. Open daily.* Ⓢ *(08) 9046 5149 or (08) 9321 6088. NT.*
🖪 *Shire Offices, Railway Ave; (08) 9046 5006.*

PEMBERTON   Map ref. 342 D11, 344 C11

Edward Brockman, son of Perth's first mayor, settled in this quiet valley in the State's south-east in 1861 to begin breeding horses for export. Soon timber-getters moved in. They opened up the giant karri forests and established the timber industry, which is still a major part of Pemberton's economy.
Karri Forest Discovery Centre An introduction to the history and ecology of the karri forests. A museum documents some of the district's pioneering history. *Brockman St. Open daily.* Ⓢ *(donation). (08) 9776 1133.*
Pemberton Tramway A replica of a quaint 1907 red rattler crosses historic trestle bridges and winds through the magnificent forest country. *Trips daily.* Ⓢ There's also an historic steam train, which operates between Pemberton and Lyall Siding. *Trips Sat.–Sun., May–Nov. only.* Ⓢ *Trams and train depart Railway Cres. (08) 9776 1322.*
🖪 *Karri Visitors Centre, Brockman St; (08) 9776 1133.* Website: www.pembertontourist.com.au
See also Manjimup

Parlour at Mangowine Homestead, Nungarin

PERTH   Map ref. 338 H3, 342 C4, 344 C8

See p. 162–71

PINJARRA   Map ref. 342 C6, 344 C9

A small rural township near the banks of the Murray River, in one of the State's oldest established and most attractive farming districts. At the 'Battle of Pinjarra' in 1834, a confrontation between a local Aboriginal group and British troops, an estimated 15 Aboriginal people were shot in retaliation for the death of a soldier.
Edenvale Late Victorian brick villa (1888) with bay windows and belled verandah, built for Edward McLarty, whose parents were amongst the district's pioneers. Visitor Information is here, and a pleasant tearoom. Liveringa (1885), on the same property, was Edward's first home. There is a heritage rose garden within the grounds. Behind Edenvale is the Roger May Machinery Museum. The old schoolhouse (1896) across the road now houses a quilting craft shop. *Cnr George & Henry sts. Open daily. (08) 9531 1438.*
ALSO OF INTEREST The Heritage Trail is an easy walk which takes in some of Pinjarra's historic properties, including the mudbrick St John's Church (1860s) with an interesting old graveyard. *Cnr Henry St & South Western Hwy.* Hotham Valley Steam Train runs between Pinjarra and Dwellingup. *Details from Visitor Information.*
🖪 *Edenvale, cnr George & Henry sts; (08) 9531 1438.*
See also Australind, Busselton, Mandurah

ROEBOURNE   Map ref. 343 G1, 346 A2

Roebourne is the oldest town in the north-west of the State, established in 1866 and named after WA's first Surveyor-General, JS Roe. Several handsome buildings survive from the 1880s and 1890s. A horse-tramway was started in 1887, connecting Roebourne with the port of **Cossack**, 12 km away.
OF INTEREST Post office (1887), Sholl St, and courthouse (1887), Hampton St, both still in use. The police station and former gaol (1897) are built of local bluestone and bricks that arrived in the colony as ship's ballast. The old gaol now houses the local history museum, an arts and craft centre and Visitor Information. *Cnr Carnarvon Tce & Queen St. Open daily. (08) 9182 1060.* The former Union Bank (1889), Roe St, is now home to community groups. Holy Trinity Church (1894) is also of interest. *Cnr Fisher Dr. & Withnell St.*
IN THE AREA The Burrup Peninsula is one of the most prolific sites for ancient rock art in the world. The Yapurrara people who once lived here have left a rich cultural legacy, tens of thousands of rock engravings, now within Dampier Archipelago National Park. Ask at the Conservation & Land Management (CALM) office at Karratha. *(08) 9186 8288.*

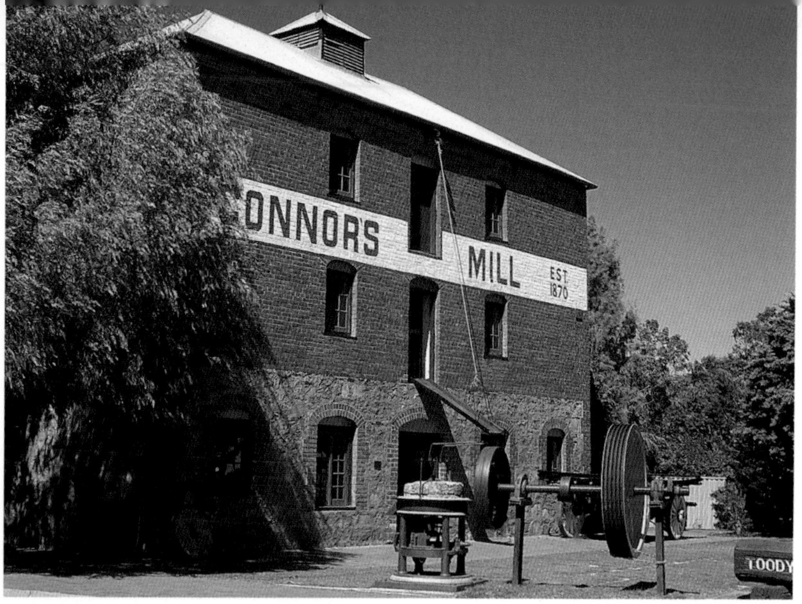

Connor's Mill, Toodyay

[i] *Old Gaol, Queen St; (08) 9182 1060.*
Website: www.pilbara.com
See also Cossack

Rottnest Island Map ref. 342 B4

Dutchman Willem de Vlamingh considered Rottnest a 'terrestrial paradise . . . delightful above all other Islands' when he landed there in 1696. Mistaking the small marsupials, or quokkas, for rats, he named the island Rottnest or Rat's Nest. In 1838 it became a penal colony for Aboriginal people, which it remained until 1903. In all 3700 Aboriginal men were imprisoned on the island. It is now a public reserve and wildlife sanctuary, a popular holiday destination just 19 km from Perth. Its historic buildings, amongst the oldest in the State, are a fascinating and surprisingly intact archive from the 1800s.

The Quod A convict-built, octagonal limestone building centred around a courtyard, erected in 1864. Accommodation is available in the restored cells and Boys' Reformatory (1888).

Rottnest Hotel Built in 1859 as the Governor of WA's summer residence. It provides meals and accommodation. *(08) 9292 5011.*

Rottnest Museum An excellent museum, highlighting the island's history and including relics from ships wrecked off the island's coast. The c. 1857–59 building was a haystore and grain crushing mill. *Digby Dr. Open daily. (08) 9372 9753.*

Salt Store Gallery & Exhibition Centre Originally built to store salt, this limestone building (1898) in Thomson Bay has since been used as a post office, a powerhouse, bank, library, museum and as offices. *Digby Dr. Open daily. (08) 9372 9752.*

ALSO OF INTEREST The clusters of historic limestone buildings were mainly built by Aboriginal labour in 1840–60. The free walking tours are highly recommended – there's plenty to explore. Details from Visitor Information. The guns at Oliver Hill Battery were installed in 1937 as part of Australia's coastal defences, but were quickly obsolete. A light rail takes trips to Oliver Hill, and there are daily tours. $ *Book at Visitor Information, (08) 9372 9752.* Wadjemup Lighthouse was built of the island's limestone in 1895 and Bathurst Lighthouse, on Bathurst Point, dates from 1900. *Not open for inspection.* Around Thomson Bay, the huge old Moreton Bay figs, gnarled olive trees and the cycling vistors – no private cars are allowed on the island – create a peaceful, village atmosphere.

[i] *Henderson Ave; (08) 9372 9752.*

Southern Cross Map ref. 344 G7

Southern Cross, almost 370 km east of Perth, was the site of the first major gold find on the Eastern Goldfields. Gold was discovered here in 1887 by prospectors Tom Risely and Mick Toomey, who followed the Southern Cross star constellation. The town was soon overshadowed by **Coolgardie**, **Kalgoorlie** and other rich fields, but the golden days are still evident in some wonderful old buildings. Gold is still mined here.

OF INTEREST The first courthouse on the Eastern Goldfields (c. 1892) is now home to the Yilgarn History Museum, focusing on the district's goldmining history and pioneer memorabilia. *Antares St. Open Mon.–Sat. & Sun afternoons.* $ *(08) 9047 5010.* Museum & Bottle Collection, in the handsome old Government Office Building (1892). Lisignoli's Store (1890s) has a distinctive lacework balcony. Headstones at the original cemetery attest to the number of typhoid victims on these goldfields. Like the town itself, many of the streets running east–west are named after constellations, while all north–south streets are named after stars.

[i] *Great Eastern Hwy; (08) 9049 1001.*

Toodyay Map ref. 342 E2, 344 D7

Cradled in the Avon Valley, the small hamlet of Toodyay has a legacy of 19th-century buildings with an old-world charm, providing a tangible link with its pioneering past. First settled in the early 1830s, it has been declared an historic town by the National Trust. Toodyay (pronounced too-jay) was originally called Newcastle.

Connor's Mill This handsome three-storey building, at first a steam flour mill and later the town's powerhouse, has been an intrinsic part of the streetscape since the 1870s. It contains a working flour mill display. *Stirling Tce. Open daily.* $ *(08) 9574 2435.*

ALSO OF INTEREST Old Newcastle Gaol Museum is a sturdy, random stone building, convict-built c. 1865. Originally a convict-hiring depot, it was later a prison until c. 1898. Now a colonial history museum. *Clinton St. Open Mon.–Fri.; also Sat.–Sun. & pub hol afternoons.* $ *(08) 9574 2435.*

IN THE AREA Coorinja Vineyard, begun in 1880, specialises in fortified wines. *4 km s on Toodyay Rd. Open Mon.–Sat. (08) 9574 2280.*

[i] *Connor's Mill, Stirling Tce; (08) 9574 2435.* Website: www.gidgenet.com.au/toodyay
See also Northam, York

Wonnerup Map ref. 342 B8

See Busselton

York Map ref. 342 F3, 344 D8

See Historic Highlights, p. 190

HISTORIC HIGHLIGHTS

Exchange Hotel, Kalgoorlie–Boulder

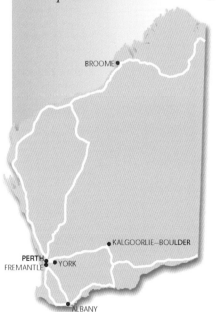

Western Australia is a vast state. Its climate and landscape vary enormously, and so too do its historic highlights. They range from the old whaling port of Albany in the south, and Fremantle with its rich architectural heritage, to the remote but historic pearling port of Broome. In the arid Outback, Kalgoorlie–Boulder has tangible links with its goldmining past, whilst in the fertile Avon Valley, York's colonial and Victorian buildings recall its 19th-century heyday.

ALBANY

Albany, Western Australia's first European settlement, spreads across the hills that fringe the sparkling waters of Princess Royal Harbour. Major Edmund Lockyer arrived from New South Wales on Christmas Day 1826, aboard the tiny brig *Amity*, to establish a military outpost and forestall any French territorial claims. Whaling developed, but the town's growth was slow until the 1850s when Albany became a coaling depot for the regular English mail steamers. Until Fremantle's harbour was enlarged in 1897, this was Western Australia's major port. Albany, declared a city in 1998, is a popular holiday resort.

Albany Visitor Information Centre
Old Railway Station, Proudlove Pde
(08) 9841 1088, freecall 1800 644 088
Website: www.albanytourist.com.au

Courthouse
Still serving its original purpose, this unusual 1895 building features bold stonework and distinctive recessed doorways. Note the elaborate British coat-of-arms beside the left-hand arch, at the main entrance. *Cnr Stirling Tce & Collie St. Not open for inspection.*

Queen Victoria Rotunda
The elegant rotunda (c. 1898), erected in commemoration of Queen Victoria's Diamond Jubilee, offers panoramic views of Princess Royal Harbour. *Stirling Tce.*

Patrick Taylor Cottage Museum
A wattle-and-daub cottage, possibly built about 1831 by the town's first harbour master, who sold it to Patrick Taylor, later a prominent Albany citizen. Now the Albany Historical Society museum. *31 Duke St. Open daily afternoons.* $ (08) 9841 6174.

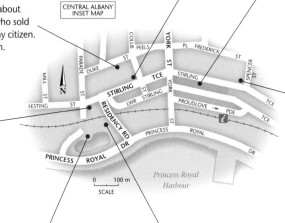

Old Gaol Museum
Originally a convict-hiring depot (c. 1851) and converted to the district gaol in 1872. Now a museum focusing on justice, convicts and law enforcement. *Cnr Parade St & Stirling Tce. Open daily.* $ (08) 9841 1401.

Old Post Office
This romantic red-brick building, begun in 1869, has a round, shingle-roofed tower and turret and a quaint, balustraded corner balcony added in 1896. The tower has a fine spiral stairway of Sydney bluestone. *Stirling Tce. Not open for inspection.*

Brig *Amity*
Full-scale replica of the *Amity*, which brought Major Lockyer, his sailors and convicts to King George Sound in 1826. The original was shipwrecked in Bass Strait in 1845. *Princess Royal Dr. Open daily.* $ (08) 9841 6885.

The Residency Museum
Near the site where Major Lockyer's party stepped ashore in 1826, the museum was built as stores and offices for the convict-hiring depot, in 1856. It later became the Government Resident's home. It is now a branch of the WA Museum. The collection includes silverware once owned by Major Lockyer. *Residency Rd. Open daily.* $ (08) 9841 4844.

ALSO OF INTEREST
On the summit of Mt Clarence, a fine bronze equestrian statue is a memorial to the Anzacs who fought in World War I. For many, Albany was their last Australian port of call. *Apex Dr.*

Albany Town Hall, c. 1900

Town Hall
A High Victorian building of granite, with a domed clock tower, built in 1888. Albany's first moving pictures were shown here in the early 1900s. It is now used as a theatre. *York St. Not open for inspection.*

The Old Farm, Strawberry Hill
A delightful stone cottage on part of the original 1827 government farm. Sir Richard Spencer bought the property when he became Albany's second Government Resident, in 1832. In 1836, Sir Richard and Lady Spencer built a two-storey granite extension for their family of nine children. Strawberry Hill, as it was known, became the centre of Albany's social life, and much of Spencer's official business was conducted here. The family retained the cottage until 1869. Strawberry Hill has late Georgian and Victorian furnishings.
Old Farm Rd, off Middleton Rd, Mira Mar. Open daily. Ⓢ *(08) 9841 3735. NT.*

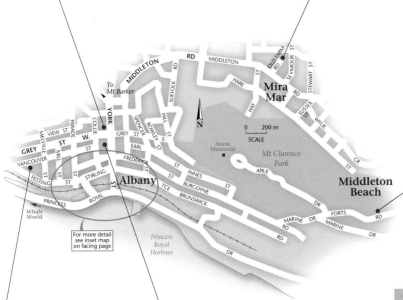

The Forts
Princess Royal Fortress was commissioned in 1893 to protect the port from enemy attack and was operational until 1956. The complex includes the Commanding Officer's Residence, stables and barracks. The former Military Institute houses a tearoom.
Forts Rd, Middleton Beach. Open daily. Ⓢ

Vancouver Arts Centre
The rather austere old Albany Hospital (1896) is now an arts centre.
85 Vancouver St. Open daily. (08) 9841 9260.

Church of St John the Evangelist
Consecrated in 1848, St John's is WA's first consecrated church. The handsome rectory in the gardens behind was built 1848–50, with the second floor added in 1875. The first resident was the Rev. J Wollaston, later the first Anglican Archdeacon of WA.
York St. Open daily. (08) 9841 5015.

IN THE AREA
At Frenchman Bay is **WHALE WORLD**, on the site of the former Cheynes Beach Whaling Co. Station, which only closed in 1978. At its busiest, 850 whales a season were brought to this station. The museum includes whale skeletons, the last of the whale-chasers, the *Cheynes IV*, and historic film footage. There's also an aircraft display. *20 km SE. Frenchman Bay Rd. Open daily. Tours hourly.* Ⓢ *(08) 9844 4021.*

BROOME

In the early 1900s Broome was the boisterous pearling capital of the world, with more than 350 luggers using the port, sea captains striding the streets in tropical suits and solar topees, and a flourishing Chinatown. The population, whose descendants make up today's multi-racial community, included Japanese, Chinese, Malays, Koepangers (Timorese), Europeans and Aboriginal people. Explorer John Forrest selected the site on Roebuck Bay and named it after Sir Frederick Broome, then Governor of Western Australia, in 1883. Today, Broome, with its unique history and tropical beaches, has become a popular resort.

Broome Visitor Information Centre
Cnr Bagot St & Broome Rd
(08) 9192 2222
Website: www.ebroome.com/tourism

An old deep-sea diving helmet

Cable Beach
The famed Cable Beach was named after the telegraph cable that linked Broome with Java in 1889.

Japanese Cemet[...]
Headstones hewn from sandstone, a[...] inscribed with Japanese characte[...] More than 900 pearling sailors an[...] divers are buried h[...]
Port Dr.

Pearling luggers, Roebuck Bay, 1912

Shinju Matsuri Festival
This colourful 'Festival of the Pearl', held in August or September, celebrates Broome's Japanese heritage and pearling history.

Chinese Cemetery
As well as Chinese headstones th[...] are Aboriginal, Muslim and Euro[...] graves, a reminder of Broome's ethnic diversity.
Port Dr.

HISTORY
The pearling industry flourished in Broome from the 1880s until the beginning of World War I. Contracts were cancelled, there was no money to buy the mother-of-pearl, and labour was short. After the war, recovery was slow. Markets had shrunk as plastics were replacing pearl shell to make products such as buttons. When World War II broke out, the town's entire Japanese population was interned. Broome was bombed, and the pearling business again ground to a halt. When the industry finally began again, it was based on farming cultured pearls rather than diving. It is again a lucrative business, although overshadowed by tourism.

Pearling lugger, Streeters Jetty

William Dampier
English buccaneer William Dampier sailed into the bay that now bears the name of his vessel, *Roebuck*, around 1699.

Matso's Cafe
Typical of Broome's distinctive architecture, this building was Broome's first Union Bank (1900). It is now a cafe and brewery.
Cnr Hamersley & Carnarvon sts. Open daily.
(08) 9193 5811.

Courthouse

A handsome tropical building of teak with wide verandahs, erected in 1889 as the Cable House containing the transmitter for the telegraphic cable linking Broome (and thus Australia) with England. One story claims that the prefabricated structure was intended for Kimberley in South Africa and that the windows were designed to resist attack by hostile African tribesmen. The building is still in use as a courthouse.
Cnr Frederick & Hamersley sts. Not open for inspection.

Sun Picture Gardens

A unique corrugated-iron clad indoor/outdoor theatre, which opened in 1916 showing silent movies. Miraculously, it has withstood tropical cyclones and wartime bombing. There's some great movie memorabilia in the theatre museum.
8 Carnarvon St. Open daily for historic tours at 11 a.m. and 2 p.m. Films shown nightly. $ (08) 9192 1077.

Chinatown

In Broome's pearling heyday this part of town in the old port area was home to many nationalities. Some original buildings have been reconstructed, though the tropical climate means not much that is truly original remains.

Pearl Luggers

The luggers were at the heart of the pearling industry. Visitors can inspect two restored luggers on guided tours.
44 Dampier Tce. Open daily. $ (08) 9192 2059.

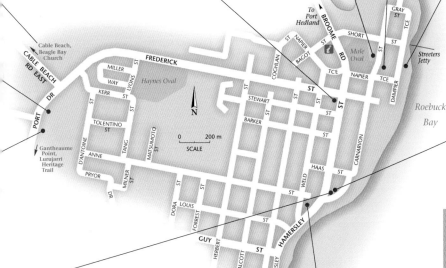

Captain Gregory's House

An elegant tropical bungalow, designed by Japanese architect Gurachi Hori and built in 1911 for Capt. A Gregory, who owned one of Broome's most successful pearling businesses. The house is jarrah timber with iron cladding, the timber being jointed without nails. It is now a gallery.
Cnr Hamersley & Carnarvon sts. Open daily. (08) 9193 5379.

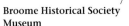

Broome Historical Society Museum

A fascinating regional museum, housed in the old customs house and containing a wealth of photographs and artifacts related to Broome's pearling and maritime history, and the 1942 Japanese bombing raids.
Cnr Hamersley & Saville sts. Open daily. $ (08) 9192 2075.

Bedford Park

The park contains a memorial to William Dampier, and the engine of a plane downed by a Japanese fighter plane in 1942. The wrecks of other planes bombed during the war can be seen at low tide in Roebuck Bay. An estimated 70 people were killed in the Japanese bombing raids.
Hamersley St.

IN THE AREA

At **GANTHEAUME POINT**, giant dinosaur footprints visible at low tide (1.5 m or less) are believed to be over 130 million years old. A plaster cast of the prints has been created at the top of the cliff, for visitors who miss the low tide. Nearby is Anastasia's Pool, a rockpool built by a former lighthouse keeper for his wife, who suffered from severe arthritis. *7 km sw.*
BEAGLE BAY CHURCH features magnificent pearl shell decorating the altar. The church, built by Pallottine monks, dates from 1918. *118 km N. $ (08) 9192 4913.*
The **LURUJARRI HERITAGE TRAIL**, prepared by Broome's Aboriginal community, follows an Aboriginal song cycle along the coast, north from Gantheaume Point. Ask for a map at Visitor Information.

FREMANTLE

Captain James Stirling chose Fremantle as the site for a town and port, in 1829. Unfortunately it proved to be unsuitable for most ships, and for several decades the settlement languished. But the introduction of convict labour, the gold rushes of the late 19th and early 20th centuries, and the expansion of the harbour, all saw Fremantle develop into a bustling port. Today, although Perth's urban areas are encroaching, Fremantle remains one of the world's best-preserved 19th-century ports, with a unique maritime personality and a rich architectural heritage.

Fremantle Visitor Information Centre
Town Hall, 8 William Street
(08) 9431 7878
Website: www.freofocus.com.au

Elders Building
This splendid corner building, with its round copper-clad turret, was erected in 1902 for Dalgety's, then a major shipping agent. The navy used it as an intelligence headquarters for shipping during World War II.
11 Cliff St. Not open for inspection.

Lionel Samson Building
Lionel Samson bought two lots at Fremantle's first sale of town lands in 1829 and established his merchant and import business, which operates to this day on the same site. The present building dates from 1898.
31–35 Cliff St. Not open for inspection.

CY O'Connor Statue
As well as enlarging Fremantle's harbour, Charles O'Connor also designed the ambitious Goldfields Water Scheme, a pipeline stretching more than 550 km to the arid goldfields.
Cliff St.

CENTRAL FREMANTLE INSET MAP

Round House
WA's first gaol and oldest surviving colonial building (1830–31), designed by WA's first Civil Engineer, Henry Reveley. Although actually 12-sided, the fort-like building soon became known as the Round House. The Colony's first hanging took place here in 1844. The tunnel below was excavated by a whaling company in 1837 to allow easier access between the landing jetty and High St. The Round House's cannon is fired daily.
High St (over railway line). Open daily. **$**
(08) 9336 6897.

Fremantle Aboriginal Walking Tour
Explore Fremantle's Aboriginal heritage and culture, before and after European settlement, through the eyes of a Nyoongar guide.
Tours depart from WA Maritime Museum, cnr Cliff St & Marine Tce. Wed., Fri., Sun. **$**
(08) 9431 8469.

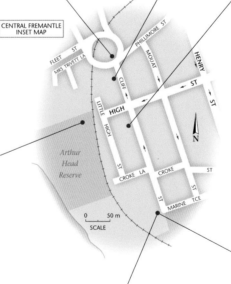

WA Maritime Museum
The museum building was constructed by convicts as the commissariat store and customs house (1850s). WA's fascinating maritime heritage is well explained here. Don't miss the remains of the Dutch East Indiaman *Batavia*, shipwrecked off the WA coast in 1629. Part of the *Batavia's* cargo was an arch of stone intended for a castle in Java. The reconstructed arch stands 7 m high. In 2002 this building will become the Shipwrecks Museum, and the Maritime Museum will open in dramatic new premises at Victoria Quay.
Cnr Cliff St & Marine Tce. Open daily. Tours available. **$** *(donation). (08) 9431 8444.*

Film & Television Institute (WA)
The Institute occupies one of WA's oldest and most unusual structures, the former Fremantle Boys' School, a pale sandstone building (c. 1855) with distinctive Dutch gables.
92 Adelaide St. Not open for inspection.

Fremantle History Museum
Convict-built in the 1860s, this majestic Colonial Gothic landmark was originally an asylum for the insane. Today it is a social history and heritage museum. Fremantle Arts Centre is also here.
Cnr Ord & Finnerty sts. Open daily Sun.–Fri. and Sat. afternoons. Ⓢ *(tours only). (08) 9430 7966.*

Samson House
An elegant limestone house, built 1888–1900 for a mayor of Fremantle, Michael Samson – son of pioneer merchant Lionel Samson.
Cnr Ellen & Ord sts. Open Sun. afternoons. Ⓢ *(08) 9430 7966.*

St John's Anglican Church
A pale sandstone church (1879–82) with elegant lancet windows. The surrounding flagstones arrived in the colony as ship's ballast.
Cnr Adelaide & Queen sts. Open daily.

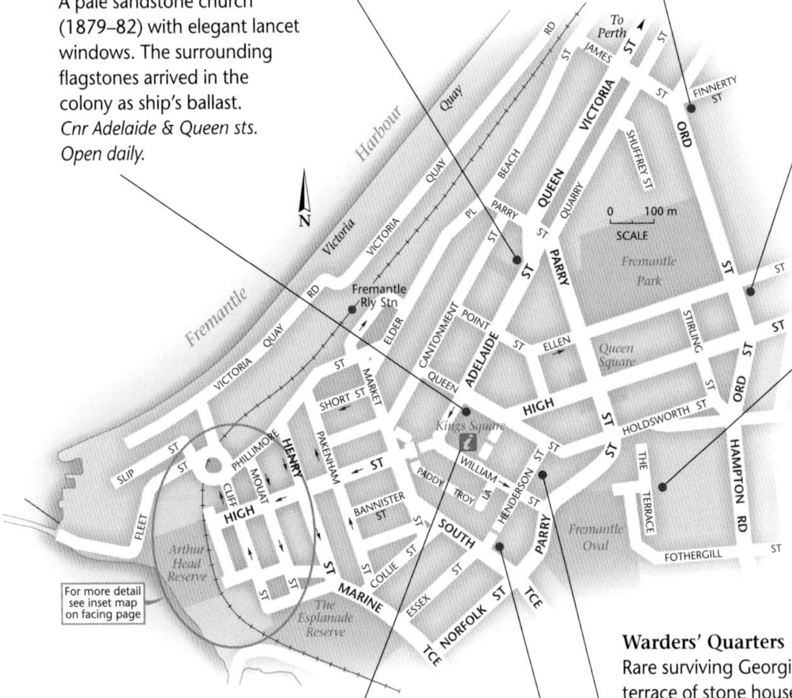

Fremantle Prison
This formidable stone edifice, built by convicts in 1851–59 from limestone quarried on the site, was in use as a prison 1855–1991. Within the walled compound are the silent punishment cells, gallows, chapel and the Women's Prison. Evening candlelight tours are fascinating, if eerie.
1 The Terrace. Open daily. Regular day tours; evening tours Wed. & Fri. (booking essential). Ⓢ *(tours only). (08) 9430 7177.*

Warders' Quarters
Rare surviving Georgian terrace of stone houses (1850), built for Fremantle Gaol warders.
Henderson St. Not open for inspection.

Town Hall
The grand late-Victorian town hall (1885–87) opened as part of Queen Victoria's jubilee celebrations. Fremantle's Visitor Information is on the ground floor.
8 William St. Open office hours. (08) 9431 7878.

Fremantle Markets
These spacious covered markets with distinctive facade and ornate iron gates opened in 1897. They have been restored to their original Victorian grandeur.
Cnr South Tce & Henderson St. Open Fri.–Sun. and Mon. pub hols. (08) 9335 3120.

HISTORY
For many years Fremantle was no more than 'a collection of low white houses scattered over the scarce whiter sand'. When transportation was introduced in 1850, however, convict labour provided the manpower to erect a number of handsome sandstone buildings. Some of these historic buildings are still standing, now open to the public as galleries and museums. In the late 19th century, with the gold rush, thousands of people arrived by ship, and trade increased dramatically. When the enlarged harbour, the masterpiece of Engineer-in-Chief CY O'Connor, was completed in 1897, Fremantle became an international port. Banks, warehouses, shipping company headquarters and flamboyant hotels testify to those years of expansion and optimism.

Map labels: To Perth, JAMES ST, BD, VICTORIA, FINNERTY ST, ORD, SHUFFREY ST, QUAY, QUAY, BEACH, QUEEN, QUARRY, PARRY, PL, PARRY, Harbour, Victoria, Fremantle Rly Stn, Fremantle Park, ELDER, CANTONMENT, POINT, ELLEN, Queen Square, STIRLING, ORD ST, ST, Victoria Quay, QUAY, SHORT ST, MARKET ST, ADELAIDE ST, Queen, HIGH, HOLDSWORTH ST, ORD ST, HAMPTON RD, Fremantle, SLIP ST, PHILLIMORE, HENRY, PAKENHAM ST, Kings Square, WILLIAM, HENDERSON ST, PARRY ST, THE TERRACE, FLEET, CLIFF, MOUAT, HIGH, BANNISTER ST, PADDY TROY, SOUTH, Fremantle Oval, FOTHERGILL, ST, Arthur Head Reserve, MARINE, COLLIE ST, ESSEX, NORFOLK ST, TCE, TCE, The Esplanade Reserve, 0 100 m SCALE, N

For more detail see inset map on facing page

KALGOORLIE-BOULDER

In 1893, in this strangely desolate landscape, almost 600 km east of Perth, Irishman Paddy Hannan found the first small nuggets of gold that led to the discovery of the Golden Mile, 'the richest square mile on earth'. In no time a huge shantytown sprang up at the furthest reaches of colonial civilisation and by 1895 Kalgoorlie was proclaimed a town. By then the 'twin city' of Boulder had also been declared, enabling workers to live closer to the mines. Other gold towns have faded, but Kalgoorlie has continued to prosper, with gold and nickel still mined today.

Kalgoorlie–Boulder Tourist Centre
250 Hannan St
(08) 9021 1966
Website: www.kalgoorlieandwagoldfields.com.au

Hotels
At its peak, Kalgoorlie–Boulder boasted a thirst-slaking 92 hotels. It is still well endowed with pubs. Amongst them are the York Hotel (1900), 259 Hannan St, with grand Edwardian staircase and gracious interiors; the Exchange Hotel (1900), 135 Hannan St, its timber-railed balconies and verandahs shading the footpaths. The young Herbert Hoover, later President of the USA, but then a mining engineer, stayed at the Exchange around 1900. The hotel is handsomely restored. *Both hotels open daily.*

Goldfields War Museum
Military memorabilia from the Boer War to Vietnam. Displays include tanks, artillery, radio equipment and photographs.
Burt St. Open daily and pub hols.
Ⓢ *(08) 9093 1083.*

Burt Street
This street, the heart of Boulder, still possesses a wealth of late-Victorian buildings. It once boasted 12 hotels, most of which were open 24 hours a day. The splendid late-Victorian Grand Hotel (1897) reflects those golden days.
Burt St. Open daily.

Courthouse
Classical arcaded courthouse, dated 1900–06.
Burt St. Not open for inspection.

Town Hall
A fine building (1908) with domed clock tower and a theatre with a mechanical sliding roof. Celebrations following the theatre's opening in 1908 continued for a week. The Hall contains a priceless, Victorian-era stage curtain hand-painted by renowned scenic artist Philip Goatcher. The curtain can be viewed each Wed.
Burt St. Open Mon.–Fri. (08) 9093 1087.

HISTORY
Living conditions around Kalgoorlie were harsh, the landscape barren and dwellings often made of no more than tin or hessian. Gold was there in plenty, but another precious commodity – water – was not. Hygiene was difficult, typhoid common. The solution was the Goldfields Water Scheme, masterminded by WA's Engineer-in-Chief, CY O'Connor. Water was carried by pipeline from the Darling Ranges just east of Perth over 550 km to the Eastern Goldfields. The pipeline reached Kalgoorlie in 1903 amid riotous celebrations, one official commenting that he had 'never seen so much talk about water and seen so little of it consumed'.

Golden Mile Loopline Railway
Leave from the 1897 Boulder Station on the Loopline, once the busiest railway in Australia. A commentary relates the highs and lows of the goldfields' history.
Boulder Station, Burt St. Train trips run daily on the hour. Ⓢ *(08) 9093 3055.*

Mining Hall of Fame
Located at Hannans North Reserve, the site of one of the Golden Mile's most lucrative mines, the various exhibitions are a tribute to the past, present and future of mining in Australia. Visitors can descend the shaft to inspect the underground workings, view heritage buildings and mining equipment, pan for gold and see gold being poured.
5 km N, Broadarrow Rd. Open daily. Regular tours.
Ⓢ *(08) 9091 4074.*

WA Museum – Kalgoorlie–Boulder
This engaging museum captures the history of gold in the district, and the lifestyles of the rich and the not-so-lucky. The collection includes a pub, a miner's cottage, dentist's surgery, and a bank. Gold bars, gold bullion, nuggets and jewellery are displayed in the underground vault. Highly recommended.
17 Hannan St. Open daily.
Ⓢ *(donation). (08) 9021 8533.*

Government Buildings
An impressive two-storey complex and an exceptional example of goldfields architecture (1897). The post office clock tower dominates the city's skyline.
Hannan St. Not open for inspection.

British Arms Hotel
Making no concession to the antipodean climate, the former British Arms Hotel (1899), just 4 m wide, was reputedly the world's narrowest hotel.
Part of the WA Museum.

Town Hall
A grand Edwardian building (1908) with Classical Revival facade, magnificent staircase and elaborate pressed metal ceilings inside. There is a gallery upstairs and historic photos on display.
Cnr Hannan & Wilson sts. Open Mon.–Fri.
(08) 9021 9808.

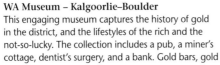

Ivanhoe Headframe
Headframes held the machinery for the cages that lowered miners. There used to be more than 100 of these structures towering over 'Kal'; this is the last. Climb to the top for views of the city.
Part of the WA Museum.

Kalgoorlie Cup, 1906

Kalgoorlie Racecourse
The racecourse has long been part of the city's life. The red-brick buildings (1900–20) feature corrugated iron roofs with gables and towering finials. The Kalgoorlie Cup has been run annually since 1895.
Charles St.

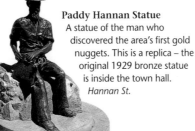

Paddy Hannan Statue
A statue of the man who discovered the area's first gold nuggets. This is a replica – the original 1929 bronze statue is inside the town hall.
Hannan St.

Palace Hotel
For many years the goldfields' best-known hotel, frequented by visiting celebrities. When opened in 1897 it was the town's first hotel with electricity.
Cnr Hannan & Maritana sts. Open daily.
(08) 9021 2788.

IN THE AREA
See Coolgardie, Leonora–Gwalia

YORK

York, Western Australia's oldest inland town, has a rare charm. Surrounded by the fertile Avon Valley, with a distinctive blend of colonial and Victorian architecture, its history dates back to the colony's earliest days. The well-watered valley was cultivated from the early 1830s in a bid to help feed the struggling Swan River Colony. The town itself was gazetted in 1836. Gold discovered in the area in 1889 briefly brought prosperity, but when the train line was extended to Northam in 1894, York was bypassed and settled into the peaceful existence it still enjoys today.

York Visitor Information Centre
York Town Hall, 81 Avon Tce
(08) 9641 1301
Website: www.yorkwa.com.au

Old Gaol, Courthouse & Police Station
The courthouse was designed by WA's respected Colonial Architect GT Poole and officially opened in 1895. It has been restored by the National Trust, with one room still used as a Court of Petty Sessions. Visitors can view the courtroom, the 1850s prison cells (one with ball and chain) and a trooper's cottage (1852).
Avon Tce. Open Tues.–Sun. afternoons. Ⓢ
(08) 9641 2072. NT.

Settlers' House
A two-storey mud-brick house built c. 1853 and extended in 1877 to house WA's first newspaper, the *York Chronicle*. French doors and delicately paned casement windows open on to the upstairs balcony, which overlooks a brick-paved courtyard. The building now provides B&B accommodation.
Rear 125–135 Avon Tce. (08) 9641 1096.

Castle Hotel
York's first licensed hotel, and the State's oldest remaining inland hotel, was started in 1842 as a coaching inn. The oldest part of the present building dates from 1853.
97 Avon Tce. Open daily.
(08) 9641 1007.

St Patrick's Church
The foundation stone was laid on St Patrick's Day 1875 and the church finished in 1886, complete with Italian stained-glass windows. The square tower figures prominently on York's skyline.
South St. Open daily.

ALSO OF INTEREST
BLANDSTOWN, one of the first settled areas in York, still retains its semi-rural character and has more than 30 heritage-listed properties. These include the picturesque colonial Albion Inn, first licensed in 1861, now a B&B. *19 Avon Tce. (08) 9641 1580.*
Further along is Wansbrough House, a single-storey residence of colonial Georgian style, c. 1859, also a B&B. *22 Avon Tce. (08) 9641 2887.*
In Newcastle St you can see the unique stone and iron **MARWICK'S BARN**, built for the Marwick family's coach and carriage business (1870). The high entrance was to allow laden camels to enter. *Not open for inspection.*
See also Northam, Toodyay

Town Hall
A splendid town hall (1911) in an unusual corner position. The magnificent arched entrance is surmounted by a wonderfully ornate pediment. The Visitor Information is located here.
81 Avon Tce. Open daily.
(08) 9641 1301.

Jah Roc Mill Gallery
The former York Flour Mill is a fine example of early Australian industrial architecture. The four-storey brick mill has been a local landmark since erected in 1892. Extensively renovated, it is now a fine furniture and art gallery, with artists-in-residence and a cafe.
7–15 Broome St. Open daily. (08) 9641 2522.

Faversham House

A grand colonial mansion and one of York's oldest residences, built as a single-storey house c. 1831, but substantially enlarged in the 1850s. The Monger family for whom it was built were sandalwood traders and merchants. Now a luxury B&B.
24–26 Grey St. (08) 9641 1366.

Post Office

Designed by Colonial Architect GT Poole, this building dates from 1893–95. The post office is still in use.
Avon Tce.

Church of the Holy Trinity

This is one of WA's first country churches, the oldest section dating from 1854, but the church has been enlarged several times. The square Norman-style tower, lowered following an earthquake in 1968, was restored in 1988.
Cnr Newcastle & Pool sts. Open daily.

York Motor Museum

Housed in an imposing late-Victorian building (1890s), complete with historic kerbside petrol bowser. The museum is a showcase for classic and vintage cars, racing cars and motorcycles.
116 Avon Tce. Open daily. Ⓢ
(08) 9641 1288.

Residency Museum

Built in 1853 this classic early-colonial bungalow, sheltering beneath a sweeping roof, with shuttered french windows, originally formed part of a convict-hiring depot. It was later the official residence of the York magistrates. There are period furnishings, historic photos and artifacts.
Brook St. Open Tues.–Sun. afternoons. Ⓢ
(08) 9641 1301.

Langsford House

A gracious two-storey residence with a high-pitched sweeping roof, and delightful gardens, built in 1873 in an area known as Blandstown. It is now classified by the National Trust and provides luxury B&B accommodation.
18 Avon Tce. (08) 9641 1440.

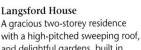

Balladong Farm

WA's oldest inland farm, settled in the 1830s, said to be named after an Aboriginal tribe of the district. The complex includes an 1850s brick granary, giant stone stables and a shearing shed. Balladong is a 'working museum', where traditional farming skills, such as blade-shearing, can be seen.
Parker Rd. Open daily. Ⓢ *(08) 9641 1389.*

NORTHERN TERRIT

*The Northern Territory is Australia's last frontier.
Its European history is short and its architectural
heritage limited, in many cases destroyed by the
intensity of the tropical climate. But here it is possible
to sense how ancient this country really is, and how
inextricably our history is entwined with the often
spectacular, sometimes haunting landscape. For
Aboriginal people, this has always been so.*

A Timeless Land

Alice Springs Telegraph Station Historical Reserve

Aboriginal people have lived in this country for tens of thousands of years. Theirs is the oldest living culture in the world, and it remains most evident in the Territory. Their history lies in the Dreamtime stories that have been passed down through generations, and is recorded in the thousands of rock-art galleries, in paintings and carvings, found throughout their ancestral lands.

The British tried several times in the 1800s to establish settlements along the northern coast. They hoped to claim the land for themselves, to pre-empt French settlement, and to create a trading port. Military outposts were set up at Fort Dundas on Melville Island,

HISTORIC HIGHLIGHTS

For a look around the Northern Territory's most interesting historic town and its surrounds, see the pages listed below.

Alice Springs Historic buildings and some fascinating museums capture the pioneer spirit of the Outback. This is also the place to learn a little about the Red Centre's unique natural history and its ancient Aboriginal heritage, before exploring the real thing. *See p. 208*

Around Alice Springs A little further out of Alice, visitors can see the first stone buildings in Central Australia, including the original Alice Springs Overland Station complex, started in the 1870s, and the old Stuart Town Gaol. *See p. 210*

Fort Wellington on Raffles Bay, and then in 1838, Victoria Settlement at Port Essington. All failed disastrously.

PORT DARWIN

In 1839 British Captain JC Wickham and John Lort Stokes, aboard HMS *Beagle*, sighted and named the expansive harbour of Port Darwin.

Renewed interest in the North was aroused after explorer John McDouall Stuart completed the first successful south–north crossing of the continent in 1862. In 1869, a site was chosen on Port Darwin, and gazetted as Palmerston. This isolated outpost was officially renamed Darwin in 1911.

COMMUNICATIONS BREAKTHROUGH

Perhaps the single most important development in the growth of the Territory was the establishment of the Overland Telegraph Line. The telegraph cable, linking Adelaide with Darwin, then by underwater cable to Java and on to Europe, stretched more than 3000 km across the Outback. When opened in 1872, it dramatically reduced communication time with Europe and the southern colonies.

Aboriginal art, Nourlangie Rock, Kakadu National Park

TIMELINE

1838 Victoria Settlement is established at Port Essington. The third attempt by the British to settle in northern Australia, it fails dismally and is abandoned in 1849.

1869 GW Goyder arrives at Port Darwin to survey the new town of Palmerston (renamed Darwin in 1911).

1870 Building starts on the Overland Telegraph Line, to link Palmerston (Darwin) and Adelaide.

1871 Gold is discovered at Pine Creek.

1911 The NT is formally transferred from the SA government to the Commonwealth of Australia.

1933 Gold is discovered at Tennant Creek and sparks Australia's last great goldrush.

1942 Darwin is bombed by the Japanese during World War II.

1978 The NT is granted self-government.

CHINESE MINE FOR GOLD

Gold discoveries boosted the population for a while, bringing eager diggers to places such as Pine Creek in the 1870s, but conditions here were isolated and tough. Chinese labourers were brought in to work the goldfields at Pine Creek and by the late 1880s there were about 8000 Chinese in the Top End, vastly outnumbering Europeans. White settlers feared that Asians would overrun the country, and legislation was introduced in 1888 to restrict their entry.

PASTORAL EXPANSION

More important than gold in opening up the Top End were the pastoralists. Their epic droving exploits, overlanding cattle in the 1870s and 1880s, have gone down in Australian legend. The stations established then laid the foundations for the cattle industry, which still plays a part in the Territory's economy.

In 1911 the administration of the Northern Territory was handed to the Commonwealth, and finally, in 1978, the Territory was formally granted self-government.

Darwin, 1870s

A TIMELESS LAND   195

DARWIN *Tropical Frontier*

Old Police Station

VISITOR INFORMATION

TOURISM TOP END
Cnr Mitchell & Knuckey sts
Darwin NT 0801
(08) 8936 2499
www.ntholidays.com/home.asp

NATIONAL TRUST OF AUSTRALIA (NT)
Burnett House, 4 Burnett Place
Myilly Point NT 0820
(08) 8981 2848
www.northernexposure.com.au/trust.
html

Darwin is the most modern of all Australian capitals, a tropical city on a far northern tip of the continent. Its easygoing atmosphere belies its tough beginnings. Darwin has been ravaged by the tropical climate, heavily bombed during World War II and almost entirely rebuilt after the devastation of Cyclone Tracy in 1974.

Despite cyclones and bombings, Darwin retains a sense of heritage and a small number of historic buildings recall its earlier days. Its excellent museums and galleries document the city's past but also emphasise the Territory's ancient Aboriginal heritage and more recent European and Asian history.

In 1839 Captain JC Wickham and John Lort Stokes, aboard the HMS *Beagle*, sighted the fine northern harbour Port Darwin, and named it after renowned naturalist Charles Darwin, who had made an earlier voyage aboard the *Beagle*. In 1869 South Australia's Surveyor-General, GW Goyder, chose and surveyed the townsite. It was formally named Palmerston, though it was generally referred to as Darwin or Port Darwin (a name which was not made official until 1911).

The first Government Resident arrived in 1870, and the tiny settlement celebrated the start of the Overland Telegraph Line that same year. Gold discovered at Pine Creek in the 1870s boosted Palmerston's economy and population, and, despite the climate and isolation, the outpost struggled valiantly on.

In 1884 pearl shell beds were discovered in the harbour, attracting Japanese, Malays and other nationalities to set up a pearling industry. In 1887, however, a major cyclone almost reduced the town to rubble, and it was back to struggling.

During World War II Darwin became a strategic naval, airforce and supply base, but it appears to have been ill-prepared for an air attack. In early 1942 the town was bombed by Japanese war planes in the first of more than 60 raids. In that first air raid hundreds of people were killed, three warships were sunk and 23 aircraft destroyed. Darwin suffered severely, but the precise extent of the damage and the toll were concealed from the rest of Australia for many years.

In 1974, disaster struck again when an estimated 80 per cent of the town was destroyed by Cyclone Tracy. Most of the city's historic buildings were demolished or severely damaged. But this is a city of remarkable resilience and Darwin was rebuilt yet again. Although there was little left, wherever possible, historic buildings were restored to provide a link with the town's pioneering past.

These days, as interest in Australia's environmental and cultural heritage – especially Aboriginal heritage – increases, growing numbers visit Darwin or use it as a base to explore some of the country's most fascinating history.

FIVE TOP SIGHTS

Australian Aviation Heritage Centre, *p. 201*
Australian Pearling Exhibition, *p. 198*
Fannie Bay Gaol, *p. 201*
Lyons Cottage (BAT House), *p. 200*
Museum & Art Gallery of the NT, *p. 201*

Museum & Art Gallery of the Northern Territory

Brown's Mart

INNER DARWIN

1 Admiralty House
One of the last of Darwin's 1930s houses, built for the naval officer commanding northern Australia, and admirably suited to the tropical climate. It features three-quarter high walls and open eaves to allow air to circulate.
Cnr Knuckey St & the Esplanade, City. Not open to the public.

2 Australian Pearling Exhibition
Commercial diving for pearl shells began off the NT coast in the 1850s. Once the cumbersome 'hard-hat' era of deep-sea diving began in the 1880s, it developed into a lucrative if dangerous trade. The pearling industry attracted many ethnic groups, but notably the Japanese. This imaginative exhibition covers the history of pearling, including more recent developments, such as farming cultured pearls.
Stokes Hill Wharf, The Wharf Precinct, City. Open daily. $ *(08) 8999 6573.*

■ BAT House
See Lyons Cottage

3 Brown's Mart
Darwin's oldest commercial building (1883), a sturdy stone structure built for Vaiben Solomon, a mayor of Darwin and later Premier of South Australia. EV Brown, also a mayor of Darwin, operated the Mercantile Mart and Mining Exchange here between 1887 and 1896. The building has also served as auction rooms, a steamship office, the Crown Law Office, police headquarters, a boarding house and even a brothel. Now home to the Darwin Theatre Company. A history of the building is available from the office in the adjoining administration building.
12 Smith St, City. (08) 8981 5522.

■ Burnett House
See Myilly Point Heritage Precinct

4 Christ Church Cathedral
Darwin's first Anglican church was built on this site in 1902. The stone porch was added in 1944 as a memorial to those who lost their lives in the Territory during WW II. After Cyclone Tracy, the porch was the only part remaining and has been incorporated into the new cathedral.
Smith St, City. Open daily.

5 Darwin Botanic Gardens
Several hundred varieties of lush tropical and sub-tropical flowers and trees flourish in this quiet oasis, thanks to the foresight of Dr Maurice Holtze, a Russian immigrant and botanist who established the garden on this site for the government in 1886. Holtze, with the aid of Chinese coolies, grew vegetables to supplement the meagre government rations. There are guided walks during the Dry season, on Wed. at 11.30 a.m. & Thurs. at 5.00 p.m.
Gardens Rd, The Gardens. Open daily. (08) 8981 1958.

6 Government House
This is one of the few buildings in Darwin to remain virtually unscathed by cyclones and war-time bombing, and is Darwin's oldest surviving building. The rambling white house (1879), standing in a luxuriant tropical garden, is a far cry from the first Government House – a log hut with a mud floor and unbleached calico windows. The design features steeply pitched gables topped by iron finials, and adjustable wooden louvres to provide shade and control the airflow. It is home to the Administrator of the NT.
The Esplanade, City. Not open for inspection.

7 Lyons Cottage (BAT House)
The Darwin Cable Company built

Darwin Botanic Gardens

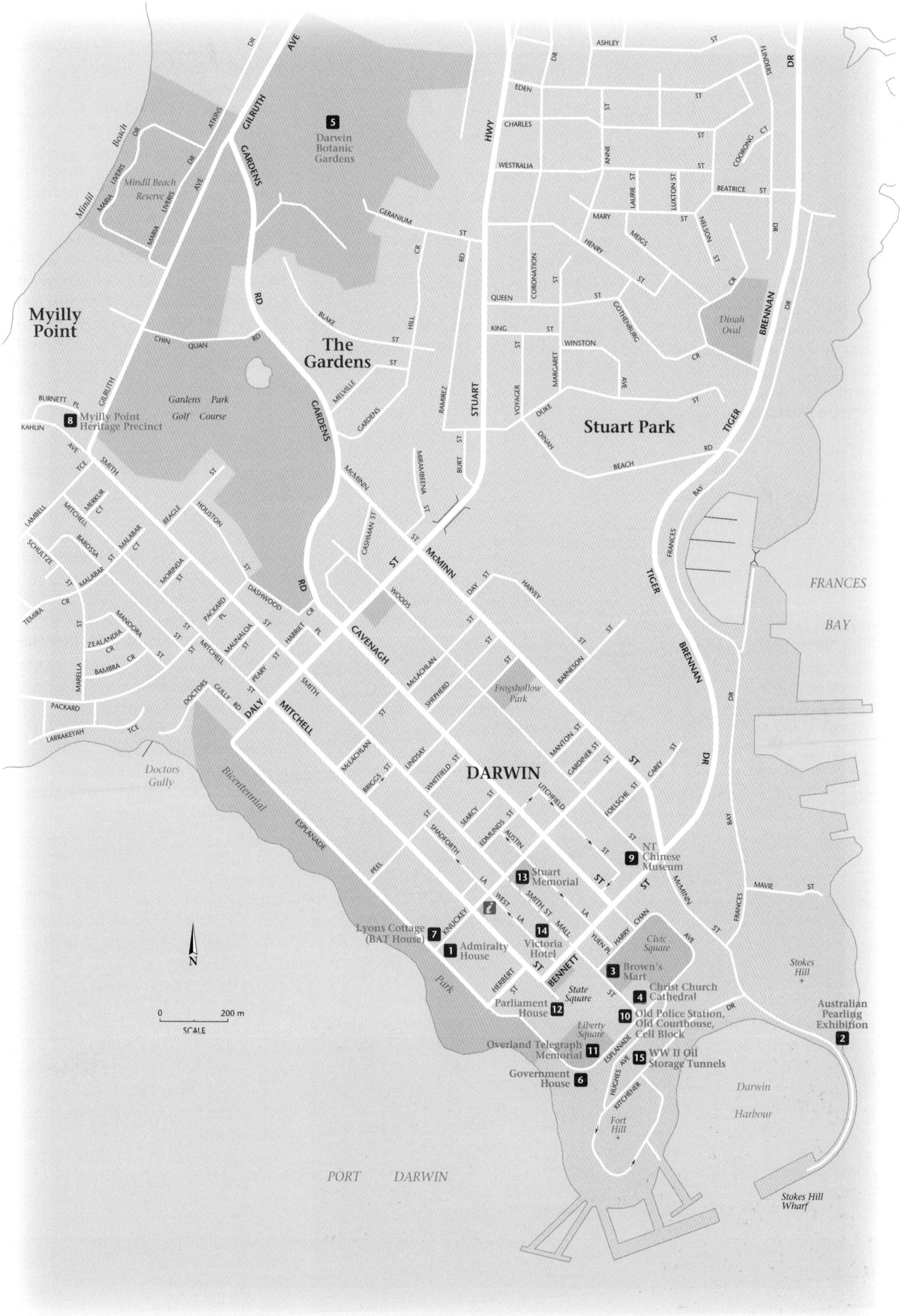
Myilly Point
The Gardens
Stuart Park
DARWIN
5 Darwin Botanic Gardens
Mindil Beach Reserve
Mindil Beach
Gardens Park Golf Course
8 Myilly Point Heritage Precinct
Dinah Oval
Frogshollow Park
Doctors Gully
Bicentennial Park
FRANCES BAY
PORT DARWIN
Darwin Harbour
Stokes Hill
Stokes Hill Wharf
Fort Hill
Civic Square
State Square
Liberty Square
1 Admiralty House
2 Australian Pearling Exhibition
3 Brown's Mart
4 Christ Church Cathedral
6 Government House
7 Lyons Cottage (BAT House)
9 NT Chinese Museum
10 Old Police Station, Old Courthouse, Cell Block
11 Overland Telegraph Memorial
12 Parliament House
13 Stuart Memorial
14 Victoria Hotel
15 WW II Oil Storage Tunnels
GILRUTH AVE
GARDENS RD
STUART HWY
TIGER BRENNAN DR
McMINN ST
CAVENAGH ST
MITCHELL ST
SMITH ST
DALY ST
ESPLANADE
BENNETT ST
KNUCKEY ST
FRANCES BAY DR
N
0 200 m
SCALE

this colonial bungalow (1925) for staff working on what was known commonly as the 'British Australia Telegraph' (BAT). The stone was quarried from the harbour beach cliff-faces, the original roof tiles were English, and much of the timber was imported from Asia. Lawyer John Lyons bought the cottage in 1952. Lyons became mayor of Darwin in 1959, and the cottage played an important part in the city's social and political life. Although damaged by Cyclone Tracy, it has been restored. The interiors reflect the era 1926–42. Displays here, including historic photographs of European and Aboriginal Larrakeyah people of the area, capture some of Darwin's early history.
74 The Esplanade, City. Open daily. (08) 8981 1750.

8 Myilly Point Heritage Precinct

Three kilometres from the historical area of the Darwin Peninsula is the 1938–39 tropical housing precinct at Myilly Point. The National Trust head office is located in the precinct. The four remaining houses, designed by Beni Burnett for senior public servants, have a high level of significance for the Northern Territory's architectural heritage. Myilly Point is a promontory of land; Myilly is an Aboriginal word meaning 'stone place'. *(08) 8981 2848.* **Burnett House**, located in the Myilly Point Heritage Precinct, is owned by the Commonwealth Government and leased to the National Trust. The house contains a museum, a shop and tea rooms. *Open Mon.–Fri. 10.00 a.m. to 1.00 p.m. High tea served in the gardens on Sundays from 3.30 p.m. until 6.00 p.m. Ⓢ (08) 8981 0165.*

9 NT Chinese Museum

Members of the first Chinese families arrived in the Top End in the 1870s to work on the goldfields. Those that stayed soon took up other jobs and Chinese people have played a significant role in the economic and social development of the city. This small museum includes some wonderful photographs and stories which reflect the experiences of Chinese individuals, families and groups in different historical, personal, social, economic and cultural settings. Adjacent is the Chung Wah Temple. The site on which the temple stands has been the focus for Chinese religious and social activity in Darwin since the 1880s.
25 Woods St, City. Museum open limited hours Wed.–Mon. Ⓢ (donation). (08) 8981 8461.

10 Old Police Station, Old Courthouse, Cell Block

These limestone buildings, erected in 1884, were used as the headquarters of the NT Mounted Police and then as a courthouse until 1942, when the Royal Australian Navy took over the premises. Although extensively damaged by Cyclone Tracy, reconstruction following the original designs has brought them back to life and they are now used as offices for the NT Administrator.
The Esplanade, City. Not open for inspection.

11 Overland Telegraph Memorial

A memorial to those who built the Overland Telegraph Line, a communications link crossing almost 3000 km from Adelaide to Darwin, through some of the most inhospitable

country in the world. In just one year and 11 months, these men cut and planted more than 36 000 poles and transported 2000 tonnes of equipment. The first message relayed from London to Adelaide on 22 October 1872 heralded a new era of communications for Australia.
The Esplanade, City.

12 Parliament House

This monumental contemporary building, opened in 1994, stands on a significant historic site. Just two years after European settlement, in 1871–72, a cable station, overland telegraph terminus and post office were built on the land. The stone buildings were destroyed during the Japanese air raids of 1942. The NT Library, also located here, holds a substantial collection with a special focus on NT history and culture.
State Sq., City. Parliament House: guided tours Sat. at 10 a.m. & 12 noon. Booking essential. (08) 8946 1509. Library open Mon.–Sat. (08) 8946 1521.

13 Stuart Memorial

Scotsman John McDouall Stuart was the first white man to cross the centre of the continent from south to north, completing the journey after several attempts when he reached a point just east of Darwin in July 1862.
Cnr Smith and Knuckey sts, City.

14 Victoria Hotel

A Darwin icon, the Vic has played a role in Darwin's social life since it was built in 1890. Although damaged by successive cyclones, it has been rebuilt using much of the original stone and manages to retain a distinctive character.
27 Smith St (The Mall), City. Open daily. (08) 8981 4011.

Government House

15 WW II Oil Storage Tunnels

A network of five concrete tunnels built 1942–45 to store oil for the navy after the above-ground tanks were destroyed by Japanese bombing. One tunnel, 171 m long, is open to the public and features photographs of the war years in and around Darwin.
Kitchener Dr., City. Open daily May–Oct. (except closed Mon. Nov.–Apr.); closed 10–27 Dec. & all Feb. Ⓢ (08) 8985 6333.

Old coastal battery, East Point Military Museum, Fannie Bay

AROUND DARWIN

① Australian Aviation Heritage Centre
Map ref. 351 I12

The dominant display is the massive B-52 bomber, but also worth a look are a Mk VIII Spitfire replica, a de Havilland Dove, a Tiger Moth, and the wreck of the Japanese Zero fighter shot down over Darwin in 1942. WW II footage of the bombing of Darwin brings to life just how extensive the damage was.
557 Stuart Hwy, Winnellie. Open daily. Ⓢ (08) 8947 2145.

② East Point Military Museum
Map ref. 350 B2

Darwin was the first city on the Australian mainland to be bombed by an enemy force. In February 1942 nearly 200 Japanese bombers attacked the port, where 47 Allied ships were anchored. In two days, more than 200 people were killed and hundreds more were wounded. The old coastal battery, command post, observation towers and gun emplacements remain. The museum houses an extensive array of army, navy and air force war relics.

East Point Rd, Fannie Bay. Open daily. Ⓢ (08) 8981 9702.

③ Fannie Bay Gaol
Map ref. 350 D5

The oldest section is the grim cell block, opened in 1883 with 31 prisoners and in use for nearly a century. In 1887, the stone infirmary was added. During World War II, the prisoners were all pardoned and released and the military took over the buildings. The gallows, copied from England's notorious Newgate Gallows, were built in 1952 for the last execution to take place in the NT. Fannie Bay Gaol has held all types of offenders, including political prisoners.
East Point Rd, Fannie Bay. Open daily. (08) 8999 8290.

④ Museum & Art Gallery of the NT
Map ref. 350 D7

This major gallery is a showcase for one of the country's finest collections of Aboriginal art and material culture, including work by the Tiwi people from Bathurst and Melville islands. As well, South-East Asian and Pacific art and artifacts are displayed, and maritime archaeology and the Territory's natural and social history are explored. The Cyclone Tracy Gallery is a favourite attraction. A vast boatshed houses the Maritime Gallery, with diverse craft, built using traditional skills. There's a Macassan *prau*, pearling luggers, a traditional Aboriginal wetlands canoe sewn from stringybark, and more. Changing exhibitions from interstate and overseas are also held.
19 Conacher St, Bullocky Point. Open daily. Ⓢ (08) 8999 8201.

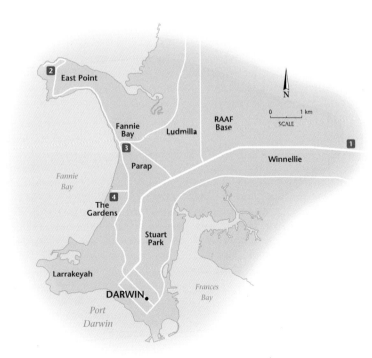

NORTHERN TERRITORY FROM A TO Z

Hermannsburg church

ADELAIDE RIVER Map ref. 352 E7

Around 114 km south of Darwin, this small town was first settled by workers on the Overland Telegraph Line in the 1870s. Adelaide River benefited from the gold discoveries at **Pine Creek** during the 1870s, and swelled during World War II when it became a major military centre. Today the town is a supply centre for the surrounding stations and a popular stop on the Stuart Hwy.

Adelaide River War Cemetery The orderly rows of headstones recall the more than 60 civilians killed in the 64 air raids on Darwin from 1942 to 1943, and the 434 service men and women who died in the Territory during World War II. *Memorial Dr. Open at all times. (08) 8976 7053.*

Railway Station Museum The first train steamed in to the station in 1888, after its five-hour journey from **Darwin** (or Palmerston, as it was still known). Today, railway memorabilia, Aboriginal artifacts and a World War II display can be viewed. *Stuart Hwy. Open daily.* Ⓢ *(donation, which includes refreshments). (08) 8976 7100.*

🄸 *Cnr Knuckey & Mitchell sts, Darwin; (08) 8981 4300.*

ALICE SPRINGS Map ref. 357 J8

For sights close to Alice Springs, see Historic Highlights, p. 208 & p. 210

IN THE AREA The landscape surrounding Alice Springs is rich in Aboriginal legend and lore. The spectacular scenery and the rare flora and fauna of the MacDonnell Ranges, the traditional home of the Arrernte people, are intimately linked with Aboriginal Dreamtime stories. The history in those stories is passed from generation to generation, and recorded in ancient rock carvings and paintings. *Note: some sites are on Aboriginal land and a permit is needed to visit them.* The Ochre Pits, 111 km w of Alice, is just one of many significant sites. The pits were long used by Aboriginal people as a source of ochre for their rock painting, body painting and medicinal purposes, while ochre was also valued as a trading commodity. At Wallace Rockhole the Western Arrernte community provides tours that offer an introduction into their culture and include a visit to the site of traditional petroglyphs, where the rock is chipped or pecked to create a pattern. *117 km sw. Booking essential.* Ⓢ *(08) 8956 7993.* On the Old South Rd, within a conservation park, the Ewaninga rock carvings can be seen on low sandstone outcrops. *39 km s.* Corroboree Rock is believed to have been the site of initiation ceremonies. *43 km E.* Past Ross River Station is N'Dhala Gorge, a site of special significance to the Eastern Arrernte culture. There are estimated to be more than 6000 prehistoric carvings or petroglyphs, the oldest dating back 10 000 years. The carvings are sheltered by the rugged walls of the gorge. *90 km E (the last 10 km is 4WD only).* Aboriginal-guided tours of the area offer the chance to learn about Indigenous history, and the history of white settlement, from another perspective. There are numerous guided tours available in Central Australia. Ask at Visitor Information or contact the NT Holiday Helpline, 133 068, for details.

🛈 *CATIA, Gregory Tce (south end of Todd Mall); (08) 8952 5800 or freecall 1800 645 199.* Website: www. centralaustraliantourism.com *See also Hermannsburg*

ARLTUNGA
Map ref. 357 L8

The ghost town of one of Australia's most isolated, most desolate goldfields, Arltunga lies 110 km E of Alice Springs and more than 1600 km from Adelaide, in the East MacDonnell Ranges. The first diggers arrived in 1887. Some had walked from the railhead at Oodnadatta, more than 600 km to the south, pushing their few possessions in wheelbarrows. The gold rush was brief – the alluvial gold was quickly won – but the government battery operated from 1898–1913. The last of the hopeful prospectors lingered on until 1980.

Arltunga Historical Reserve Skilfully worked but crumbling stone walls and rusting machinery are a stark reminder of pioneering hardship. The old police station and gaol have been restored and abandoned mine workings litter the landscape. The isolated cemetery records the poignant toll of gold fever. At the Visitor Centre, the historical museum has photographs and background on the gold-rush days. *Open daily. Tours twice weekly June–Sept. (08) 8956 9770.* 🛈 *Arltunga Historical Reserve; (08) 8956 9770.*

BORROLOOLA
Map ref. 355 O3

Borroloola is a small, isolated town in the Gulf Country, more than 950 km SE of Darwin. Explorer Ludwig Leichhardt was the first European to pass this way on his epic 5000-km trip from Moreton Bay (Brisbane) to Port Essington in 1844–45. In the 1870s–80s a small settlement grew up as a staging post for overlanders moving cattle on the long haul from Queensland to the NT and WA. Borroloola, declared a town in 1885, soon earned itself a wild reputation as a lawless outpost, attracting hard drinkers, cattle-duffers, rum smugglers and criminals. These days the small town, on Aboriginal land, is a service centre for the fishing, pastoral and mining industries.

Borroloola Old Police Station The old police station (1886) now houses photographs and memorabilia, and documents some of the town's colourful frontier history. Pick up a heritage trail brochure from here. *Off Robinson Rd. Open Mon.–Fri.* Ⓢ *(08) 8975 4149. NT.* 🛈 *McArthur River Caravan Park, Robinson Rd; (08) 8975 8734.*

DARWIN
Map ref. 350 E11, 352 O5

See pp. 196–201

HERMANNSBURG
Map ref. 356 H9

Hermannsburg Mission Station was established in 1877 by Lutheran missionaries, who overlanded from South Australia for 22 months to bring their faith to the Arrernte (Aranda) Aboriginal people. Whilst the missionaries in their zeal discouraged traditional Aboriginal customs, over time they recorded the language and many ancient customs. In 1982 the land was returned to its traditional owners and today Hermannsburg is an Aboriginal community. Visitors are welcome but are asked to respect the privacy of the residents. The Aboriginal name for the town is Ntaria.

OF INTEREST The stone-walled buildings with rough-dressed desert timbers and iron roofs, looking like German farm buildings, are amongst the oldest in Central Australia. The cluster of buildings, most listed on the National Estate Register, includes a

Borroloola Museum

Rock-art gallery, Kakadu National Park

smithy (1882), a church (1888) and a schoolhouse (1896). The old colonists' house (1885) is now a museum. $ *Open daily.* Strehlow's House (1897) contains work by local artists and the Kata-Anga Tearoom. *Open Tues.–Sun.* Aboriginal artist Albert Namatjira, born here in 1902, became famous for his classic watercolour landscapes of the area with its dramatic ghost gums. Works by Namatjira and other Hermannsburg artists can be viewed in the gallery. $ *Open daily, closed 24 Dec.–3 Jan.* (08) 8956 7402.

🇮 CATIA, Gregory Tce (south end of Todd Mall); (08) 8952 5800 or freecall 1800 645 199. Website: www. centralaustraliantourism.com

JABIRU
Map ref. 352 H6

Jabiru is a modern mining town established in Kakadu National Park in the 1970s.

Bowali Visitor Centre (Kakadu National Park Headquarters) The impressive display here provides an introduction to Kakadu, from both an Aboriginal and non-Aboriginal perspective. *2.5 km w on Kakadu Hwy. Open daily.* $ *(08) 8938 1120.*

Kakadu National Park Kakadu is famed for its ancient rock-art galleries, which reveal a range of artistic styles and techniques recording Aboriginal history. At Ubirr, Aboriginal people sheltered within the rock caves over thousands of years, and the art they left captures their daily activities as well as mythological beliefs, in a range of styles. In the main gallery, a painting of a thylacine, or Tasmanian tiger, which became extinct on the mainland 2000 years ago, gives some indication of the age of these paintings. *44 km NE of Jabiru. Open daily May–end Nov. Open 2 p.m.–sunset Dec.–end April (until road floods at Magela Crossing – usually Dec.–Mar.).* Another important site is Nourlangie Rock, where magnificent rock-art galleries can be viewed in shelters at the rock's base. Indigenous people lived in the main shelter, the Anbangbang shelter, during the Wet season, for more than 20 000 years. Some of the artwork was painted over in the 1960s, as is traditional, by a respected Aboriginal artist. *35 km s of Jabiru.* Further on is the peaceful and less-visited Nanguluwur Gallery, which includes 'contact' art. In these paintings Aboriginal artists chronicle the arrival of Macassans (from the Indonesian islands) and Europeans to these northern shores: for example, a European sailing ship is depicted. *36 km s of Jabiru.* Walking tracks lead to most of the rock-art sites. To protect and preserve the sites, stay on tracks and do not touch painted

surfaces. *Detailed maps and park notes from Kakadu Park Headquarters. Ranger-guided walks in the Dry season. (08) 8938 1120.*

Warradjan Aboriginal Cultural Centre This Centre offers an interpretation of the Creation Era, by the traditional owners of these lands, the Bininj. Displays explain the traditional culture and history of the Bininj. *50 km sw, 4.5 km off Kakadu Hwy. Open daily. (08) 8979 0051.*

🇮 *6 Tasman Plaza; (08) 8979 2548.*

KAKADU NATIONAL PARK
Map ref. 352 G5

Kakadu is one of the world's great wilderness areas, covering 19 000 sq km on the western edge of Arnhem Land near the Alligator River. It is classified on the World Heritage List, a cultural and ecological treasure. The ancient landscape is breathtakingly beautiful, the plant and animal life astonishingly rich and varied. The park contains some of the most impressive Aboriginal cave paintings in the world, ancient rock-art galleries, a legacy of the 50 000 years and more that Aboriginal people have lived in this area. Kakadu is of immense importance in the history of Aboriginal people, and is part of the heritage of all Australians.
See also Jabiru

KATHERINE
Map ref. 352 G10

Some of the finest pastoral land in the Territory surrounds Katherine. Explorer John McDouall Stuart named the Katherine River in 1862 and a repeater station, part of the Overland Telegraph Line, was established here in 1872. The town dates from the 1920s.

Katherine Museum Originally built as an air terminal in the 1940s, this museum houses artifacts, photographs, maps and more related to the region's pioneering history. An original Gypsy Moth aircraft, flown by the first flying doctor, Dr Clyde Fenton, is housed here. *Gorge Rd. Open daily (Mar.–Oct.); Mon.–Sat. mornings & Sun. afternoons (Nov.–Feb.).* $ *(08) 8972 3945.*

O'Keeffe House A rustic bush dwelling, erected as an Officers' Mess in 1942, is typical of old-fashioned bush

Springvale, near Katherine

ingenuity born of necessity. It features rustic slabs of bark off-cuts, flywire and corrugated iron. Pioneer families, including the O'Keeffe family, lived here. *Riverbank Dr. Open Mon.–Fri. afternoons (May–Sept.).* Ⓢ *(08) 8972 1686. NT.*

Railway Museum This spartan, prefabricated station building opened in 1926 when the railway was extended from **Pine Creek**, providing a crucial link with the outside world. During World War II it was the strategic headquarters of the Northern Australian Railway. There are displays on railway and wartime history. *Railway Tce. Open Mon.–Fri. afternoons (May–Sept.).* Ⓢ *(08) 8972 1686. NT.*

IN THE AREA Springvale, the Territory's first official pastoral station, was built in 1878 by pioneer Alfred Giles, on the banks of the Katherine River. Giles overlanded 12 000 sheep and 2500 cattle in an epic 19-month journey from South Australia, one of the longest droving trips in Australia's history. The sturdy sandstone homestead is the oldest remaining in the Territory. The Indian raintrees around the house were planted by Giles' wife Augusta, one for each of their children. *8 km w, Shadforth Rd, off Zimin Dr. Open daily. Free guided tours of the homestead Mon.–Fri. at 3 p.m. (May–Oct.). Accommodation & camping facilities available. (08) 8972 1355.* Ancient Aboriginal paintings form patterns along some of the spectacular gorges in Nitmiluk (Katherine Gorge) National Park. *29 km NE. Tours*

available – ask at the Katherine Visitor Centre or at the Visitor Centre within the Park, (08) 8972 1253.
🄸 *Cnr Stuart Hwy & Lindsay St; (08) 8972 2650.*

MATARANKA   Map ref. 352 I11

Located just over 100 km SE of Katherine, the small town of Mataranka is at the heart of the countryside immortalised in Jeannie (Mrs Aeneas) Gunn's classic tale *We of the Never Never*. Her evocative descriptions conjure the people and the places she experienced when she lived on nearby Elsey Station in the early 1900s. During World War II more than 100 military units were stationed in the district, including an Aboriginal Army Camp.

Elsey Homestead Replica The house is a meticulous reconstruction of the original homestead where author Jeannie Gunn lived, recreated for the 1980s film version of her book *We of the Never Never*. The house is within the Mataranka Homestead Tourist Resort. *Homestead Rd. Open daily. Walking tours May–Oct. (08) 8975 4544.*

ALSO OF INTEREST Capturing the essence of the Outback, the Never Never Museum includes a railway van used to carry freight and troops, an original Furphy water tank, stockman's hut and more. Signs and photographs document some of the area's tough pioneering and wartime history. *At rear of Council Chambers, Stuart Hwy.* There are life-size sculptures of

characters from *We of the Never Never* in Martin Park. *Cnr Martins Rd & Stuart Hwy.* Visitor Information has heritage trail brochures.

IN THE AREA At Elsey Cemetery, graves include those of Jeannie Gunn's husband Aeneas (Jeannie outlived her husband by more than 50 years), as well as characters depicted in her autobiographical book. *20 km s.*
🄸 *Stockyard Gallery, Roper Tce; (08) 8975 4530.*

NEWCASTLE WATERS   Map ref. 354 I6

Newcastle Waters, almost a ghost town, is synonymous with the drovers who pioneered stock routes across the Outback. The first cattle were driven along the Murranji Track, from Victoria River to Newcastle in 1886, guided by Nat Buchanan and members of the Mudbarra tribe. The track greatly shortened the east–west journey but, without permanent water, was a dangerous route. Some called the Murranji the 'ghost road of the drovers'. By 1924, the government had sunk bores along the track, and in 1930 a town site – Newcastle Waters – was chosen at the junction of the Murranji, Barkly and north–south stock routes. Cattle numbers increased but finally road trains replaced droving, and the town was virtually abandoned by the 1960s.

OF INTEREST The National Trust-owned Jones' Store (George Man Fong's

Monument to drovers, Newcastle Waters

House) is one of the town's oldest surviving buildings (c. 1936). The rustic store supplied provisions for drovers. *Drovers Dr. Open daily (unattended). (08) 8981 2848.* The old Junction Hotel (1930s) has memorabilia related to the town's droving history. *Open daily (unattended).*

[i] *Tennant Creek Visitor Information Centre, Battery Hill Mining Centre, Peko Rd, Tennant Creek; (08) 8962 3388.* Website: www.centralaustraliantourism.com

Pine Creek Map ref. 352 F8

Gold was discovered near Pine Creek in 1871 and a busy shantytown soon grew up. Goldfields were usually tough, but this was tougher than most: isolated, hot, with scarcely any water and few amenities. Chinese miners brought in as cheap labour coped with the conditions, however, and by the 1880s there were 2000 Chinese around Pine Creek. Fear of an Asian invasion soon put a stop to that, and legislation was introduced in 1888 to stop them entering the Territory. (Other colonies had already introduced similar legislation.) New technology in recent years has seen goldmining grow in importance once again. Pine Creek is around 230 km SE of Darwin.

Pine Creek Repeater Station Museum The old telegraph repeater station, built at Burrundie in 1889 but later moved to Pine Creek, is the oldest surviving prefabricated building in the Territory. In its day it has also been a clinic, a hospital, a post office and military communications centre. *Railway Tce. Opening hours vary seasonally, but usually open daily Apr.–Sept.* $ *(08) 8976 1391. NT.*

ALSO OF INTEREST Some rough and ready old buildings around town (often featuring corrugated iron) hark back to the pioneering and goldfield days. Pine Creek railway precinct, off Main Tce, includes the old railway station, goods shed and an 1877 Beyer Peacock steam-engine locomotive (which has been restored). The precinct was a focal point for the town for many years. Chinese, as well as other foreign workers, laboured on the Darwin to Pine Creek railway, which opened in 1889. This was to be part of the often-mooted transcontinental rail line, which more than a century later, is finally under construction again. *Railway station open daily in the Dry season.* $ *(donation). (08) 8976 1391. NT.* At Gun Alley Gold Mining there's a restored steam ore-crusher and other old equipment. You can hear the colourful history of goldmining days and try your hand panning for gold. *159 Gun Alley. Ring for opening times.* $ *(08) 8976 1221.* At Miners Park, just off Main Tce, you can see historic mining machinery and displays related to the region's goldmining. *Open at all times. NT.* A timeline alongside the Heritage Park footpath (starting at the railway station) traces the history of Pine Creek from its original Aboriginal tribes, through to the Overland Telegraph workers, gold miners, pastoralists, and up to the present day. *Heritage Park. Open at all times.*

[i] *Diggers Rest Motel, 32 Main Tce; (08) 8976 1442.* Website: www.pinecreek.nt.gov.au

Old overland telegraph station complex, Tennant Creek

Tennant Creek Map ref. 355 K10

A telegraph repeater station opened near here in 1872, but the town really came to life with Australia's last great goldrush, in 1933. Modern mining methods have seen mines in the area again yielding valuable deposits – the district still contains some of the Territory's richest mines. Tennant Creek is on the Stuart Hwy, 500 km N of **Alice Springs**.

Battery Hill Mining Centre A glimpse of the old and the new – the historic 140-year-old, 10-headed stamper, used to crush ore, is operated daily. You can see how the early miners used the mill to treat their gold. There are underground mine tours demonstrating mining technology from traditional to present-day techniques, a mining museum, a mineral museum and a small theatrette. Visitor Information is also located here. *Peko Rd. Open daily (May–Sept.); Mon.–Fri. & Sat. afternoons (Oct.–Apr.). Tours daily.* $ *(08) 8962 1281.*

ALSO OF INTEREST Tuxworth-Fullwood House, a National Trust museum in the old Army Camp Hospital (1942), houses a photographic display with local memorabilia illustrating the history of the region. *Schmidt St. Open afternoons Apr.–Sept.* $ *(08) 8962 4396.* Don't miss the uniquely Australian Catholic Church of Christ (1904), which includes corrugated iron in its construction, moved here by truck from Pine Creek in 1936. *Not open for inspection.* Take the heritage walk by following information plaques around the town. The headstones of pioneers at the Tennant Creek Cemetery tell their own story.

IN THE AREA The old overland telegraph station complex features historic buildings dating from 1874. *11 km N, Stuart Hwy. Open daily. (08) 8962 3388.*

[i] *Battery Hill Mining Centre, Peko Rd; (08) 8962 3388.* Website: www.centralaustraliantourism.com

Timber Creek

Map ref. 354 D2

There's not much to see at the tiny town of Timber Creek, but the area is closely linked to the earliest days of European exploration in the Territory. Explorer AC Gregory, who had sailed from Moreton Bay (Brisbane), brought his small boat up the Victoria River estuary in 1855 and set up a base camp at the site he named Timber Creek. The party spent several months exploring the district. In the 1880s a port grew up here as a depot for supplies headed for pastoral stations such as the vast Victoria River Downs, once the country's largest station.

Timber Creek Police Station This is a rare survivor of the early stations built for police in the Northern Territory. The station was built in 1908 from galvanised iron with rows of timber shutters. It served the region until the 1930s. Restored by the National Trust, it houses artifacts and historic photographs. *O'Keefe St. Open Mon.–Fri. mornings (May–Oct.). (08) 8975 0671.*

[i] *Timber Creek Tourist Park, Victoria Hwy; (08) 8975 0722.*

Uluru–Kata Tjuta National Park

Map ref. 356 D12

See Yulara

Yulara (Ayers Rock Resort)

Map ref. 356 D12

Yulara (Ayers Rock Resort) is a modern settlement, the base for most people visiting Uluru–Kata Tjuta National Park. The resort town has been developed to help minimise the impact of tourism on the surrounding countryside and its low-rise design blends into the desert environment.

In the area The Uluru–Kata Tjuta National Park, registered on the World Heritage List, is famed both for its natural and cultural heritage, and is on land owned by the Anangu Aboriginal people. Anangu have inhabited this area for more than 20 000 years and their knowledge and history are an integral part of any visit. The Uluru–Kata Tjuta Cultural Centre, situated 1 km from the base of Uluru, provides an excellent introduction to the complex spiritual significance of the area to the Anangu. Displays help explain the Tjukurpa (the Creation stories), which form the basis of Anangu law (also known as the Tjukurpa). *Open daily. (08) 8951 3138.* Just 1 km from the entrance looms the majestic Uluru, the 'magnificent pebble' of Aboriginal legend. Geologically it is ancient, an outcrop rearing 348 m above the spinifex plains, formed 500–600 million years ago. To the Anangu, Uluru is sacred, every cleft and ridge a mark created by ancient ancestors during the Creation Era. Around the base are cave paintings, carvings and sacred sites. Ernest Giles was the first white man to sight the rock in 1872. In 1873 it was named Ayers Rock, after the South Australian Premier, and was known by that name for many years. Although it is possible to climb Uluru, the Anangu request that visitors respect its spiritual importance and do not make the climb. There are many alternative activities, including walks around the base of the rock and Aboriginal guided tours. About 48 km w of Uluru are the astonishing mountains, once called The Olgas but now known as Kata Tjuta or 'the place of many heads'. When Giles sighted them in 1872 he described them as 'rounded minarets, giant cupolas and monstrous domes'. Their hues are as brilliant as Uluru and they too are an integral part of Aboriginal legend, and the Australian heritage. There are many tours available, including Anangu-guided tours. The Cultural Centre and the Visitor Information at Yulara (Ayers Rock Resort) have extensive information on this World Heritage site. *448 km sw of Alice Springs. Park open daily.* $ *(08) 8956 3138.*

[i] *Visitors Centre; (08) 8957 7888.*

Victoria Settlement

Map ref. 352 G2

In the far north of the Territory, on the Cobourg Peninsula, the crumbling ruins of Victoria Settlement in the Gurig National Park mark one of the earliest sites in the area's European history. The British had previously established and abandoned settlements at Melville Island (1824–28) and Raffles Bay (1826–29) and in 1838, determined to 'defend the North' from foreign invasion, they established a settlement on the edge of Port Essington. After 11 years struggling against the intense tropical climate, isolation, lack of food, and resistance from Aboriginal tribes protecting their lands, the British abandoned Victoria Settlement. In all, 56 men, women and children had died in the lonely outpost. *Gurig National Park, 550 km NE of Darwin, is on Aboriginal land and access is severely restricted. The park is accessible by 4WD only during the Dry season (May–Oct.) or by charter flight. A permit is needed. Contact Black Point Ranger Station (08) 8979 0244.*

Kata Tjuta, Uluru–Kata Tjuta National Park

ALICE SPRINGS

Alice Springs is almost the geographical centre of Australia, a young town in an ancient land. Running through it is the Todd River, a usually dry watercourse fringed by river gums. Around it are the barren, time-worn folds of the richly coloured MacDonnell Ranges – semi-desert, ancient hill and mountain country – the legendary landscape created during the Aboriginal Dreamtime. In recent years, intense interest in the Outback and Aboriginal culture has made the city a thriving base for tourists to explore the Red Centre.

Central Australian Tourism Industry Association (CATIA)
Gregory Tce (south end of Todd Mall)
(08) 8952 5800 or freecall 1800 645 199
Website: www.centralaustraliantourism.com

Old Stuart Town Gaol
Alice's second oldest building is a gaol built in 1907–09. Stone was quarried from the MacDonnell Ranges and the roofing hauled from Oodnadatta by pack camel. The gaol's first white prisoners were locked up for offences such as horse stealing and passing dud cheques. The last two prisoners were incarcerated for riding the 'Ghan' without tickets. The gaol closed in 1938.
8 Parsons St. Open daily Mon.–Fri. & Sat. mornings (Mar.–Dec.) Ⓢ *(08) 8962 4516. NT.*

Travel poster, 1930s

Royal Flying Doctor Service of Australia logo

Royal Flying Doctor Base Visitor Centre
This uniquely Australian service, begun in 1928 by the Rev. John Flynn, was to provide a 'mantle of safety' for the people living and working in the remote Outback. The base at Alice, opened in 1939, is fully operational.
8–10 Stuart Tce. Open Mon.–Sat.; also Sun. & pub hol afternoons. Tours every 30 mins. Ⓢ *(08) 8952 1129.*

FLYNN OF THE INLAND
The Rev. John Flynn, 'Flynn of the Inland', was a Presbyterian minister and a director of the Australian Inland Mission. He was also a visionary and the founder of the Royal Flying Doctor Service. In 1926, at Flynn's suggestion, Alfred Traeger, an electrical engineer, developed a pedal-operated radio transmitter capable of reaching remote properties. These pedal radios were used by the Royal Flying Doctor Service and the School of the Air, also conceived by Flynn.

Patient being moved from a Royal Flying Doctor Service plane, 1930s

National Pioneer Women's Hall of Fame

Housed in the restored courthouse (1928) the exhibitions here are devoted both to the women who helped pioneer Central Australia, and to Australia's pioneering women, in all fields and all endeavours. *Cnr Hartley & Parsons sts. Open daily (closed mid-Dec. to end Jan.).* Ⓢ *(08) 8952 9006.*

Marie Johannsen and daughter en route to Hermannsburg, 1909

HISTORY

Aboriginal people have lived in Central Australia for 20 000 years or more. White man's history here has been brief. Explorer John McDouall Stuart passed through Central Australia on his epic overland crossing in 1862. The Overland Telegraph Line, to link Adelaide and Darwin, followed this route almost a decade later. One of the repeater stations was named Alice Springs after the superintendent's wife, Alice Todd. The town of Stuart, which grew up nearby, was renamed Alice Springs in 1933. The 'town called Alice' remained a sleepy outpost for decades, but transport and communication have gradually eroded the tyranny of distance.

The Residency

Central Australia was briefly, in 1926–31, a separate territory of the Commonwealth. The Residency was built in 1927 to accommodate the first Government Resident. Historic displays document some of the region's European history. *29 Parsons St. Open daily. (08) 8951 5688.*

Adelaide House

This was Central Australia's first hospital, opened in 1926 and designed by the Rev. John Flynn. Today it's a museum documenting those early days and Flynn's achievements. Behind the house is a stone radio hut used by Alfred Traeger and Flynn for the first field radio transmission using a pedal-operated radio, in 1926. *Todd Mall. Open Mon.–Fri. (Mar.–Nov.)* Ⓢ *(08) 8952 1856.*

Hartley Street School

Alice Springs' first purpose-built school, constructed in 1930 with wide eaves and an open verandah, and extended in the 1940s. It is now the National Trust Museum. *37–43 Hartley St. Open limited hrs Mon.–Fri. (closed mid-Dec. to end Jan.). (08) 8952 4516. NT.*

Aboriginal Art & Cultural Centre

A modern art and craft gallery, but there is also a history display with Arrernte artifacts, historic photographs and traditional Aboriginal instruments. Enthusiasts can even learn to play the didjeridu. *86 Todd St. Open daily.* Ⓢ *(for tours only). (08) 8952 3408.*

IN THE AREA

For more about sites around Alice Springs see p. 210, and the Alice Springs entry in Northern Territory From A to Z, p. 202.

AROUND ALICE SPRINGS

One of the most remarkable features of Alice Springs is its extraordinary isolation. Common themes in its history have been the importance of communications and transport – the tools that have gradually linked Alice with the rest of the country and the world. The Overland Telegraph Line, camel trains, steam trains, road trains and aviation have played a key role in creating and sustaining this remote Outback town.

Central Australian Tourism Industry Association (CATIA)
Gregory Tce (south end of Todd Mall)
(08) 8952 5800 or freecall 1800 645 199
Website: www.centralaustraliantourism.com

Museum of Central Australia
An informative natural history museum, focusing on the Central Australian environment, landscape and the creatures that inhabit it. The museum also houses the Strehlow Research Centre display. Prof. Ted Strehlow, born and raised at **Hermannsburg**, devoted his life to helping the Arrernte people preserve their rich culture.
Cnr Larapinta Dr. & Memorial Ave. Open daily.
Ⓢ *(08) 8951 1122.*

Builders of the Telegraph, from left: J Little, engineer Robert Patterson, Charles Todd, surveyor AJ Mitchell

Flynn's Grave
A monument to the Rev. John Flynn, 'Flynn of the Inland', founder of the Australian Inland Mission, pioneer of the Royal Flying Doctor Service and School of the Outback.
5 km w. Larapinta Dr.

THE OVERLAND TELEGRAPH

In 1870 work began on the Overland Telegraph Line. This remarkable engineering and communications feat involved building a cable line from Adelaide to Darwin, almost 3000 km across some of the world's harshest country, with repeater stations at regular intervals. It was then linked to an underwater cable from Java to Darwin so that messages could be relayed via submarine cable to Europe. The massive project was completed in just two years. When the line opened in October 1872, it heralded a new era in communications in Australia. Charles Todd, South Australia's Postmaster-General, supervised the project.

Central Australian Aviation Museum
This museum acknowledges the pivotal role that aviation has played in opening up Central Australia and the NT. Housed in the original Connellan Airways hangar, on the site of Alice Springs' first aerodrome (1920s), exhibits include the remains of the infamous *Kookaburra*, whose pilot and engineer perished in the Tanami Desert in 1929, and other aviation memorabilia.
Cnr Larapinta Dr. & Memorial Ave. Open daily. Ⓢ
(08) 8951 5686.

Mecca Date Garden
Australia's oldest date plantation, established in 1950, though some of the transplanted palms were up to 95 years old. In the 1800s, botanist Baron von Mueller encouraged explorers to plant the seeds of dates around waterholes for future travellers. Camel drivers also planted the palms in the Outback.
Lot 340, Palm Circuit. Open daily.
(08) 8952 8493.

Alice Springs Telegraph Station Historical Reserve

This is where Alice started – in the first stone buildings erected in Central Australia, built in 1871 as a station for the Overland Telegraph Line. The complex includes the barracks and residence, telegraph office, a working blacksmith shop and various outbuildings. Tours available.
2 km N, off Stuart Hwy. Open daily. Ⓢ *for historic precinct; picnic grounds free. (08) 8952 3993.*

Memorial Cemetery

The first recorded burial here took place in 1888, but only a few weathered tombstones remain. Just inside the gate is the grave of Harold Lasseter, who died in 1931 searching for the now fabled Lasseter's gold reef. Renowned Aboriginal artist Albert Namatjira (1902–59) is also buried here.
Memorial Ave.

Albert Namatjira by Sir William Dargie, 1957

For more detail see map on page 209

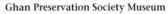

Old Timers Traeger Museum

A tribute to those stalwart early settlers who pioneered the Outback. Photographs and exhibits dating back to the 1890s are a vivid reminder of their spartan lifestyles.
Old Timers Village, 446 South Stuart Hwy. Open daily afternoons or by appt. Closed Nov.–Feb. Ⓢ *(08) 8952 2844.*

Ghan Preservation Society Museum

The legendary train known as the 'Ghan' travelled its narrow-gauge track from Adelaide to Alice for 50 years, from 1929. Named in honour of the Territory's early Afghan camel drivers, it is now part of the museum.
MacDonnell Siding, Norris Bell Ave. Open daily. Ⓢ *(08) 8955 5047.*

National Road Transport Hall of Fame

A remarkable collection of meticulously presented vehicles, from vintage cars and army jeeps to the world's first motorised road train. Tours available.
MacDonnell Siding, Norris Bell Ave. Open daily. Ⓢ *(08) 8952 7161.*

QUEENSLAND

Colonial He

From its lush tropical fringe to the rugged Outback, Queensland has a unique history and a style all its own. Its cities boast grand buildings from their river-port and gold heydays. Legendary names, such as Birdsville and the Diamantina River, conjure the pioneering era. There are rare and ancient treasures, too – magnificent galleries of Aboriginal rock art, and fossil fields dating back millions of years.

e

Anzac Memorial Park, Townsville

The first European known to have sighted the Australian mainland was Willem Jansz, who sailed down the west coast of Cape York aboard the small three-master *Duyfken*, or 'Little Dove', in 1606.

In 1770 Captain James Cook's vessel HMS *Endeavour*, severely damaged by a jagged reef, was careened for several weeks on the Endeavour River, near present-day Cooktown, whilst being repaired. Cook and famed botanist Joseph Banks made some of the first European observations of Australia's unique flora and fauna here, including sighting their first kangaroo 'of a Mouse Colour, very slender made and swift of foot'.

HISTORIC HIGHLIGHTS

For a look around some of Queensland's most interesting historic towns, see the following entries.

Charters Towers   Charters Towers' grand buildings – many restored – testify to the aspirations of this gold-rich town in the 1880s and 1890s. The fascinating old Venus Gold Battery can be inspected. *See p. 238*

Maryborough   A treasure trove of Queensland architectural styles, from formal buildings to timber houses wrapped in a cocoon of latticework, sheltered behind verandahs. Maryborough presents its history in some excellent museums. *See p. 240*

Rockhampton   One of Australia's finest customs houses and elaborate buildings line Quay Street, reflecting its era as a major river port. The city still thrives and its historic buildings are well preserved. *See p. 242*

Townsville   North Queensland's largest city boasts heritage buildings, funded by gold in the late 1800s. Impressive two-storey pubs epitomise the State's tropical architecture. Don't miss the Museum of Tropical Queensland. *See p. 244*

PENAL BEGINNINGS

It was not until 1824, however, that European settlement took place in Queensland. Surveyor-General John Oxley, under instruction from New South Wales' Governor Sir Thomas Brisbane, chose a site for a penal settlement near Moreton Bay. Later that year a military party and about thirty convicts set up camp at Redcliffe. Aboriginal people defending their traditional land, and a severe shortage of water, forced the group to move to the present site of Brisbane the following year.

Within a few years Moreton Bay was self-sufficient, though it remained off limits to free settlers, who were clamouring for new lands. Opposition to transportation was also on the increase. In response, the government reduced the convict numbers and then closed the penal colony in 1839.

The Moreton Bay district was officially thrown open to free settlement in 1842, but land-hungry squatters had not waited. Explorer Allan Cunningham discovered the magnificent Darling Downs west of the Great Dividing Range in 1827, and by 1840 Patrick Leslie and others were already grazing this fine pastoral country.

Wolston House, Wacol

TIMELINE

1606   Dutchman Willem Jansz makes the first recorded sighting of Australia – the west coast of Cape York.

1770   Capt. Cook spends several weeks near present-day Cooktown whilst his crew repairs the HMS *Endeavour*.

1824   A penal settlement is established at Moreton Bay. It moves to Brisbane the following year, but is closed by 1839.

1842   The Moreton Bay district is opened to free settlers.

1859   Queensland is declared a separate colony with Sir George Bowen as first Governor.

1867   The colony's first major gold find is made near the Mary River, leading to the settlement of Gympie.

1873   Gold is discovered on the Palmer River in North Queensland – diggers, including thousands of Chinese, flock to the goldfields.

1891   Shearers' strike near Barcaldine leads to the founding of the Australian Labor Party.

1901   Queensland joins the new Commonwealth of Australia.

QUEENSLAND IS BORN

During the 1850s, frustrated by Sydney's lack of interest, a shortage of funds and distance from the government, those in Brisbane, as well as the Darling Downs pastoralists, began to press for independence. Despite intense opposition from Sydney, Queen Victoria decreed that there would be a new colony. In 1859, Queensland was born.

Vast distance, an often desolate, arid interior, and in the far north, a tropical climate that brought debilitating heat, cyclones and devastation, made settlement difficult and even dangerous. But there was also the richly fertile Darling Downs, fine ports along the coast, and a wealth of minerals.

The colony soon matured. Cattle farms fanned out across the State. The coastal lands proved ideal for sugarcane, and dairying and agriculture slowly began to play a role in the colony's growth.

The discovery of gold in the 1880s provided the much-needed catalyst to swell the population and government finances. Railway lines were built and ports thrived, while Queensland's towns shook off their makeshift appearance for one of solidity, permanence and sometimes even grandeur.

Parliament House, Brisbane, 1870s

Old Windmill

BRISBANE *City on the River*

VISITOR INFORMATION

BRISBANE VISITOR INFORMATION CENTRE
Queen St Mall
Brisbane QLD 4000
(07) 3006 6290
www.brisbanetourism.com.au

TOURISM QUEENSLAND
(07) 3535 3535
www.tq.com.au

THE NATIONAL TRUST OF QUEENSLAND
Old Government House, George St
Brisbane QLD 4000
(07) 3229 1788
www.nationaltrustqld.org

Brisbane sprawls over low hills, the city centre cradled in a loop of the wide Brisbane River. High-rise buildings dominate the skyline, but the nineteenth-century buildings that remain rank among Australia's finest. Spreading Moreton Bay figs, the brilliance of jacaranda trees in bloom and the subtropical sun give Brisbane its own unique character.

Brisbane began as a penal colony in 1825, an outpost of New South Wales, a small huddle of convicts guarded by soldiers of the British regiments. For the first four and a half years the colony was under the command of Captain Patrick Logan, a brutal and hated leader, who was responsible for the first buildings and for Moreton Bay's reputation as a place of cruel punishment.

The Indigenous people who lived in the Brisbane area, which was well supplied with food and water, were quickly pushed off their traditional hunting and fishing grounds, including the peninsula known as Min-an-jin, on which the City Botanic Gardens stand today.

Two buildings remain from those earliest days. The Old Windmill, built at Spring Hill c. 1828, was part of Logan's plan to make the settlement self-sufficient. The other structure still standing, and open today as a museum, is the Commissariat Store, built between 1828 and 1829 to store provisions. Convicts in chains laboured in Brisbane's often searing temperatures to level the site above the river and build a retaining wall before erecting the building.

By 1829, with almost a thousand convicts, Moreton Bay was the largest convict settlement on the mainland. Within three years, however, as opposition to transportation increased, the authorities began to consider closing the settlement. The number of convicts was gradually reduced, and in 1839 the penal colony was effectively closed.

In 1859, amidst immense pomp and splendour, and with just sevenpence-halfpenny in the government coffers, Queensland was declared a separate colony. At first there was some lobbying for Ipswich to become the capital, and still others felt that Cleveland should be the port and capital, but Brisbane won the day.

The colony was blessed with vast areas of land, and land sales brought money flowing into the new capital. Brisbane experienced a building boom in the late 1860s and another period of affluence in the 1870s and 1880s when gold was discovered. Although private houses – raised on stilts, shuttered and screened from the sun – reflected a sensible understanding of the subtropical climate, public buildings were more often built to dazzle the onlooker. Grand in scale and frequently ornate, they proclaimed the optimism of the day. Those that remain, such as the former Treasury, now a casino, and the elegant Parliament House, still serving its original purpose, are a legacy of Brisbane's past.

FIVE TOP SIGHTS

Commissariat Store, *p. 218*
The Naval Stores, *p. 220*
Newstead House, *p. 222*
Parliament House, *p. 221*
Wolston House, *p. 223*

Customs House

Commissariat Store

INNER BRISBANE

1 Anzac Square War Memorial

Running between Ann and Adelaide sts, Anzac Sq. is a popular inner city park and a dignified space affording views of the GPO (1871–79) and the Central Railway Station (1900). The Shrine of Remembrance with its Eternal Flame forms the focal point. The design and plantings are symbolic – the three radial pathways represent the Navy, Army and Air Force and the six bottle trees represent the six contingents of Queensland Light Horse Regiments that served in South Africa. The water fountains represent renewed life and cleansing. Beside Anzac Sq. in the pedestrian tunnel is the World War II Shrine of Memories, which includes a mosaic containing over 140 000 hand-cut Venetian glass enamel tiles and soils from official World War II cemeteries. *Adelaide St, City. Open daily. Shrine of Memories open Mon.–Fri. 9 a.m.–2.15 p.m. (07) 3221 0722.*

2 The Cathedral of St Stephen

A neo-Gothic stone cathedral built 1863–74 to replace the modest church adjacent (now **St Stephen's Chapel**). The majestic western end, distinguished by unusual twin spires and an exceptional collection of 19th- and 20th-century stained-glass windows, is a prominent feature of the inner city streetscape. The cathedral was renovated in 1989. Guided tours reveal the cathedral's history and its collection of religious art (booking essential). *249 Elizabeth St, City. Open Mon.–Fri. mid morning, Sun. after masses, other times by appt. (07) 3224 3111.*

3 City Botanic Gardens

This magnificent subtropical garden, notable for its tall bunya pines, majestic Moreton Bay figs, palm trees and exotic flowers, is situated on part of the original government farm, selected in 1828 to supply food for the penal settlement. When Walter Hill became the first Director of the Botanical Reserve in 1855, the garden covered only 2.4 ha, but was later extended to include a river frontage, now one of its finest features. Hill built the sandstone and marble fountain (1867) to provide the first pure drinking water for visitors. *Alice St, City. Open daily. Free tours daily except Sun. (07) 3403 8888.*
See also A Walk Around the George Street Precinct, p. 225

4 City Hall & Brisbane City Gallery

The Corinthian portico and monumental 90-m tower of this building preside over King George Sq. Although somewhat overshadowed by more modern buildings, the tower remains a distinctive landmark. The heritage-listed building (1920–30), faced with sandstone, features a carved central pediment by sculptor Daphne Mayo, depicting Queensland's pioneer settlers. Visitors can take the lift and then stairs to the glassed-in clock tower for views of Brisbane. Performances are held regularly in the grand circular Concert Hall. The gallery located on the ground floor presents visual arts, social history, contemporary craft and design exhibitions. *King George Sq., City. City Hall & gallery open daily. Clock tower Mon.–Sat. (07) 3403 8888.*

5 Commissariat Store

A fascinating link with colonial days, this remarkably solid structure was built by convicts in 1828–29 and was originally the office of the much-hated administrator of the penal settlement, Capt. Patrick Logan. The freestone walls are more than half a metre thick, and pit-sawn and hand-adzed timbers and hand-cut sandstone can be seen. Grain was stored on the second floor

Anzac Square War Memorial

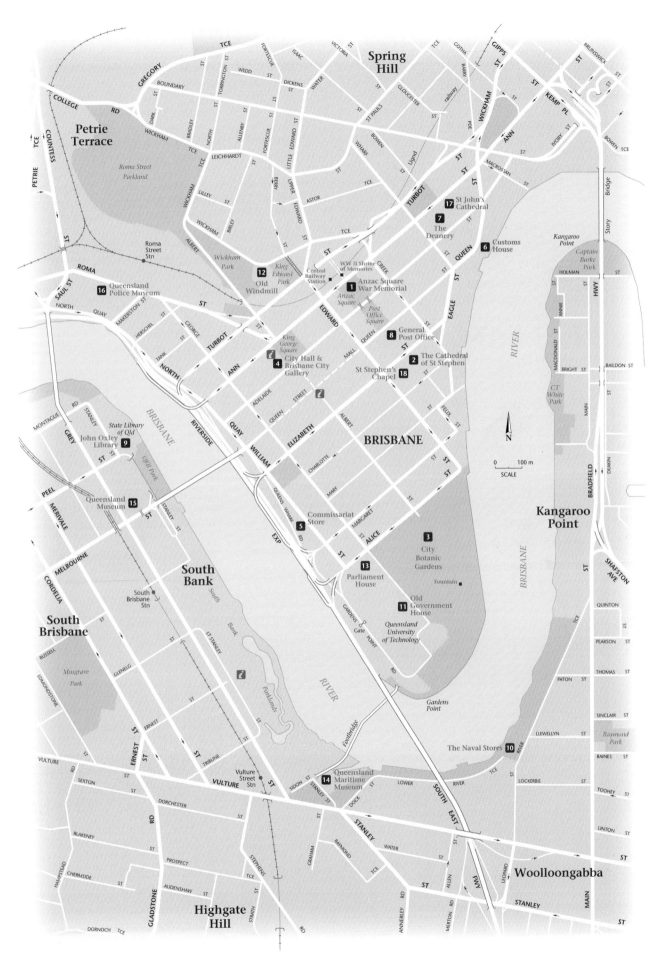

Spring Hill

Petrie Terrace

Roma Street Parkland

17 St John's Cathedral

7 The Deanery

6 Customs House

Kangaroo Point

Captain Burke Park

12 Old Windmill

WW II Shrine of Memories

1 Anzac Square War Memorial

Anzac Square

Post Office Square

16 Queensland Police Museum

Wickham Park

King Edward Park

Central Railway Station

Roma Street Stn

8 General Post Office

2 The Cathedral of St Stephen

18 St Stephen's Chapel

4 City Hall & Brisbane City Gallery

King George Square

RIVER

BRISBANE

CT White Park

State Library of Qld

9 John Oxley Library

15 Queensland Museum

Brisbane

5 Commissariat Store

3 City Botanic Gardens

Fountain

13 Parliament House

11 Old Government House

Queensland University of Technology

Kangaroo Point

South Bank

South Brisbane

South Brisbane Stn

Musgrave Park

Gardens Point

RIVER

Raymond Park

10 The Naval Stores

14 Queensland Maritime Museum

Vulture Street Stn

Woolloongabba

Highgate Hill

N

0   100 m
SCALE

during the convict era. The third storey – added in 1913 – bears the original 1829 date-plate. After the penal settlement was closed the building was used to house immigrants and later to store archives. Meticulously restored, it is now a museum and the headquarters of the Royal Historical Society of Queensland. Guided tours reveal the building's long history.

115 William St, City. Open Tues.–Sun. Ⓢ *(07) 3221 4198.*
See also A Walk Around the George Street Precinct, p. 224

6 Customs House

The stately, copper-domed Customs House is imposing, particularly when seen from the waterfront. Constructed in 1886–89, it served its original purpose for more than a century. Internally the Customs House is distinguished by exceptional craftsmanship and joinery. The restored building is now a cultural, educational and heritage facility of the University of Queensland. There is a brasserie and art gallery, a university information office and the magnificent Long Room, overlooking the river, is a venue for fine music concerts.

399 Queen St, City. Open daily. Tours Sun. (07) 3365 8999.

7 The Deanery

John Petrie built this handsome two-storey residence for Dr William Hobbs in 1853. It was considered the finest house in Brisbane and was rented as the residence for Queensland's first Governor, Sir George Bowen, from 1859 until the official Government House was completed in 1862. In December 1859, the eagerly awaited proclamation declaring Queensland separate from NSW was read from the balcony of this building. Since 1910 the Deanery, as it is now known, has been the residence of the Anglican Dean of Brisbane.

417 Ann St. City. Not open for inspection.

8 General Post Office

The Classical Revival building, erected as the post office in 1871–72 but later substantially extended, is built on the site originally occupied by the first female factory prison and subsequently by a gaol. An annual distribution of blankets to the area's dispossessed Aboriginal people also took place here in the 1800s. 'Gaol Hill', as it was called, was levelled to build the post office. Overlooking Anzac Sq., this forms part of one of Brisbane's most historic precincts.

261 Queen St, City.

9 John Oxley Library

Within the modern State Library, the John Oxley Library of Queensland History is a special treasure trove, a repository of information about Queensland's history and heritage, providing an outstanding resource for researchers as well as the casual browser. The collection embraces not just books but maps, artworks, diaries, rare Australiana and one of the country's most important historical photographic collections.

4th Level, State Library of Queensland, Cnr Peel & Stanley sts, South Brisbane. Open Sun.–Fri. (07) 3840 7880.

10 The Naval Stores

In the prosperous 1880s, the isolated colony feared a Russian invasion and prepared to defend itself. The Naval Stores, built in 1887 as part of Brisbane's marine defence strategy, were initially home to the Queensland Marine Defence Force, the early colony's very own navy. The Stores, used to house weapons and ammunition and service the colony's defence vessels, were in use for almost a century. The restored building is now a historical discovery centre, with naval defence and the Brisbane River as special themes.

Off Lower River Tce, Kangaroo Point. Open Mon., Sat.– Sun. (07) 3403 8888.

11 Old Government House

A splendid Classical Revival sandstone mansion, built 1860–62 for Brisbane's first Governor, Sir George Bowen, and designed by Colonial Architect Charles Tiffin. Projecting curved bays, Classical columns, arcaded loggias and restrained but excellent detailing make it outstanding for its time in the infant colony. Bowen praised it as 'handsome and commodious'. Later additions include the billiard room (1899) and balcony on the south-west side (1906). Although unfurnished, the graciousness and scale of the mansion, overlooking the **City Botanic Gardens**, provide a glimpse into the lifestyle of the privileged in the colonial era. It remained as a government residence until 1910 and is now headquarters of the National Trust (Qld). The interior is being restored.

QUT Gardens Point Campus, George St, City. Open Mon.–Fri. Tours by appt. Ⓢ *(tours only). (07) 3229 1788. NT.*
See also A Walk Around the George Street Precinct, p. 224

12 Old Windmill

Built by convicts in 1828–29, this is one of only two buildings from the

Old Government House

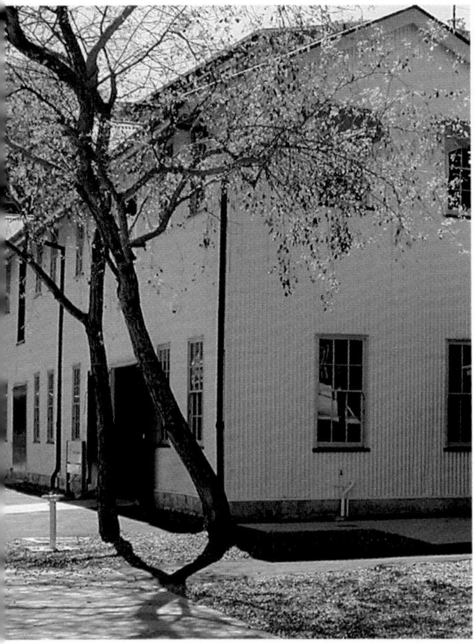

The Naval Stores, Kangaroo Point

convict era remaining in Brisbane (the other is the **Commissariat Store**). It proved unsuccessful as a windmill, and a treadmill was installed to grind grain and as a punishment for convicts. In 1840 two Aboriginal people convicted of murdering a government surveyor were hanged from the windmill sails. After the penal settlement closed, the mill fell into disuse. It later became a shipping signal station and fire brigade lookout, and in 1894 a time-ball (still in place) was installed. Although sometimes referred to as the observatory, it was never used for this purpose.
Wickham Tce, City. Not open for inspection.

[13] Parliament House
Overlooking the leafy environs of the Botanic Gardens, this wonderful French Renaissance-style building was built in stages between 1865 and 1895, though the first sitting of Parliament took place here in 1868. Sweeping cedar staircases, ceilings highlighted with gold leaf, glittering Waterford crystal chandeliers and original painted and leadlight windows create a rich interior. This is one of the few buildings in Brisbane still used for its original purpose.
Cnr George & Alice sts, City. Gallery open when Parliament is sitting. Tours Mon.–Fri. & Sun. (07) 3406 7562.
See also A Walk Around the George Street Precinct, p. 225

[14] Queensland Maritime Museum
Located on the south bank of the Brisbane River at the end of the pedestrian bridge, this museum incorporates the original 1880s Dry Dock, built to service sailing and steam ships. Two of the most prominent exhibits are the World War II frigate HMAS *Diamantina* and an historic pearling lugger. Visitors can also take a trip on the 1925 steam tug, SS *Forceful*, during the 'steaming season'.
Cnr Sidon & Stanley sts, South Brisbane. Open daily. Steam tug trips Good Friday to June & early Sept.–Dec. $ (07) 3844 5361.

[15] Queensland Museum
The museum's South Bank campus is located in a modern building, but its extensive collection was begun in 1862. Diverse displays cover social, technological and natural history. Don't miss the small plane in which Queensland pioneer aviator Bert Hinkler made the first England–Australia solo flight in 1928.
Cnr Grey & Melbourne sts, South Bank, South Brisbane. Open daily. (07) 3840 7555.

[16] Queensland Police Museum
An intriguing insight into the history and responsibilities of Queensland's constabulary since it commenced operations in 1864. In its early days the 'Force' was divided into the Metropolitan, Rural, Water and Native Police divisions. Infamous Brisbane crimes, murder cases and other subjects are covered and displays range from an elegant colonial-era police baton and a modern motorcycle to a voodoo doll.
200 Roma St, City. Open Mon.–Fri. (07) 3364 6425.

[17] St John's Cathedral
The Anglican cathedral's foundation stone was laid in 1901 and was built in three stages, the first being finished in 1910. Almost a century later, the third stage of the cathedral is finally nearing completion – the last Gothic Revival cathedral in the world to be built to original designs, which are from c. 1888. The interior is superb, with a soaring space dominated by the only fully vaulted stone ceiling in Australia. Wood carvings in Queensland timbers, stained-glass lights and specimens of 350-million-year-old fossiliferous limestone are other highlights.
373 Ann St, City. Open daily. Regular guided tours. $ (donation). (07) 3835 2248.

[18] St Stephen's Chapel
St Stephen's is Brisbane's oldest church, a modest Gothic structure built of sandstone in 1847–49 by A Gould and was the main Roman Catholic place of worship until 1874. It is sometimes referred to as the Pugin Chapel, as the design is attributed to noted architect AW Pugin, one of the designers of the Houses of Parliament in London, as well as a number of churches and cathedrals in Australia. The small chapel has a quiet dignity. The apse space has been devoted to a shrine of Blessed Mary MacKillop.
249 Elizabeth St. Open Mon.–Fri. mid morning, Sun. after Masses, other times by appt. (07) 3224 3111.

Also of interest
Brisbane's Living Heritage Network is a Brisbane City Council initiative to raise awareness of the city's heritage. A heritage trails brochure, website (www.brisbanelivingheritage.org) and events calendar provide information about current and forthcoming heritage venues and activities.

St John's Cathedral

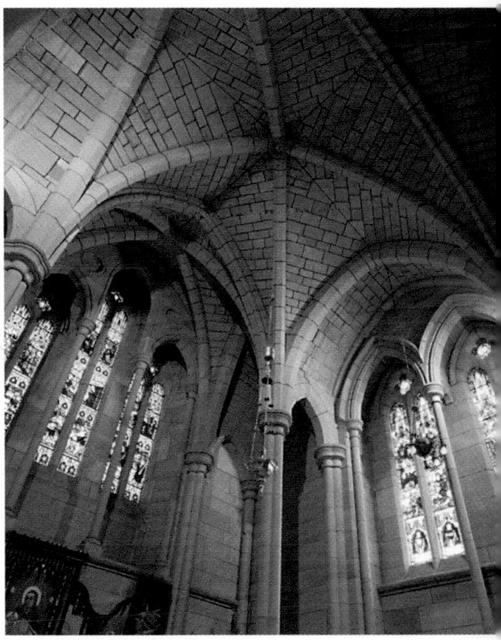

Newstead House

AROUND BRISBANE

1 Boggo Road Gaol
Map ref. 358 F9

Opened in 1903, Queensland's oldest surviving prison building, and undoubtedly its most notorious, has been preserved as a museum, to provide a visual record of the State's penal system. Visitors can step into the steel-doored cells and imagine the isolation of life behind bars. Guided tours by former prison guards give an inside perspective on the gaol's history (booking essential). For those who enjoy an extra thrill there are ghost tours and haunted 'sleepovers'.
150–160 Annerley Rd, Dutton Park. Open Mon.–Fri. 9 a.m.–2 p.m. $ *(07) 3846 7423. Ghost tours (07) 3844 6606.*

2 Brisbane Tramway Museum
Map ref. 358 B4

Well stocked with classic tram cars and tramway memorabilia, this museum also offers a trip back in time, when you can ride the rails on a restored tramcar.
50 Tramway St, Ferny Grove. Open Sun. afternoons. $ *(07) 3351 1776.*

3 The Court House Restaurant
Map ref. 359 R6

Cleveland's original sandstone and brick courthouse (1853) was built when Cleveland was being considered as a possibility for the new colony's main port. The walls are handmade brick and the window sills are of sandstone brought out from England as ballast on sailing ships. The new wing incorporates sandstone and porphyry from the foundations of Brisbane's 1875 Supreme Courthouse, which was demolished in 1978. Cleveland is said to have a resident ghost (but a happy one).
1 Paxton St, Cleveland. Restaurant open daily. (07) 3286 1386.

4 Fort Lytton
Map ref. 359 M4

This defence complex was built in the 1880s when the isolated colonies feared a Russian invasion. The fortress is near the mouth of the Brisbane River, and is surrounded by a water-filled moat. A museum interprets aspects of Queensland's early military and social history.
South St, Lytton. Open Sun. $ *(07) 3393 4647.*

5 Government House
Map ref. 358 D7

'Fernberg', as it was originally known, was built by German settler and wealthy Brisbane merchant Johann Heussler in 1864–65. It was substantially extended and altered in the 1880s and the towered facade bears all the hallmarks of the Victorian Italianate style. It was taken over as a 'temporary' Government House in 1911, but remains a vice-regal residence to this day. Overlooking the city, and surrounded by formal gardens and native bush, the house is a significant part of Brisbane's history. *Fernberg Rd, Paddington. Open twice a year, usually 26 Jan. & in Sept. (07) 3858 5700.*

6 Miegunyah
Map ref. 358 G6

A gracious colonial residence, built in 1886 for businessman and politician William Perry and reflecting the Victorian era's love of ornamentation. It is constructed of timber and graced by intricate lacework balustrading, columns and valances. The interiors are richly Victorian. Miegunyah has been restored and furnished by the Queensland Women's Historical Association as a tribute to the State's pioneer women. Devonshire teas are served on the wide verandah overlooking the shaded garden.
35 Jordan Tce, Bowen Hills. Open Wed., Sat.–Sun. Tours available. $ *(07) 3252 2979.*

7 Newstead House
Map ref. 358 G6

This outstanding heritage property, the oldest private residence in Brisbane, is set in parkland, with a commanding view of the Brisbane River and Breakfast Creek. It was built in 1846 for Patrick Leslie, the first pastoralist to settle on the Darling Downs, who sold it the following year to his brother-in-law Capt. John Wickham, the NSW Government Resident. Newstead became the unofficial Government House, renowned for its gracious balls, parties and soirees, and was extended during the 1850s to cope with the lavish scale of entertainment. The house has been described as

the quintessential Australian homestead. The colonial Georgian style is simple but elegant with an encircling verandah and distinctive balustrading. It is furnished as a colonial gentleman's residence, and glows with the rich patina of well-polished timbers. Concerts are held regularly on the western lawn.
Breakfast Creek Rd, Newstead. Open Mon.–Fri.; also Sun. & pub hol afternoons. $ *(07) 3216 1846.*

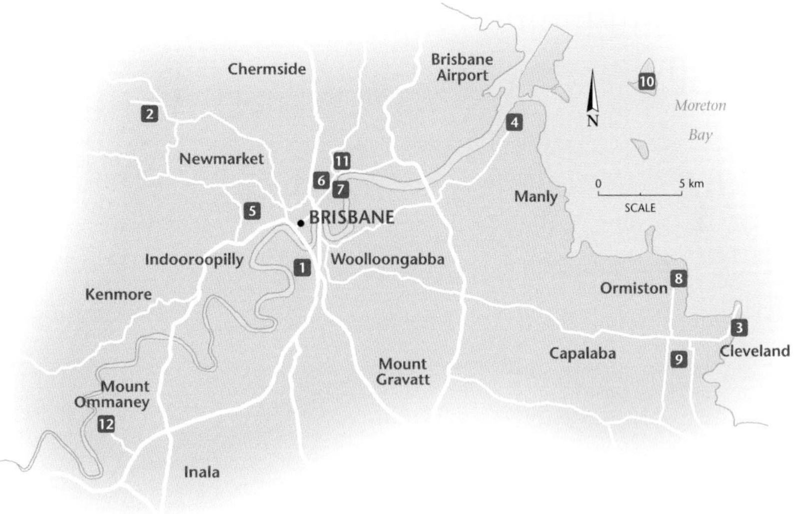

[8] Ormiston House
Map ref. 359 R10

Looking across Moreton Bay, the 17-room Ormiston House was built of handmade bricks c. 1862 by Capt. Louis Hope, one of the pioneers of the Queensland sugar industry. Hope, a former captain in the Coldstream Guards, produced the colony's first commercial sugar crop in 1863. The house, with its steeply hipped roof, paired Doric columns, broad verandah and shuttered windows, shows traces of the colonial Georgian style. The magnificent gardens have an old-world charm.
Wellington St, Ormiston. Open most Sun. afternoons (Mar.–Nov. only). $ *(07) 3286 1425.*

[9] Redland Museum
Map ref. 359 P7

An eclectic but well-presented display documenting the history of the Redlands area, which was settled in the 1840s. Its main town, Cleveland, was surveyed in 1850 and was for a number of years considered as a possibility for the new colony's main port. A series of local shipping mishaps finally put paid to this idea.
60 Smith St, Cleveland. Open Mon.–Fri. 11 a.m.–3 p.m.; Sat.–Sun. afternoons. $ *(07) 3286 3494.*

[10] St Helena Island
Map ref. 359 Q3

From 1867 until the 1920s Queensland's main prison was located on this small offshore island, which was first settled by Europeans as a quarantine station in the 1860s. At one time sugarcane was grown and milled here, and various other trades practised, but the island was abandoned in the 1930s and the buildings are largely in ruins. The oldest structures (1860s) were built of stone quarried on the island and locally made bricks and mortar. Portrayals of prison life by actors take visitors back in time.
Moreton Bay Marine Park. Day & evening tours, including meals. Vessel departs Manly. Booking essential. $ *(07) 3893 1240.*

[11] Temple of the Holy Triad
Map ref. 358 G6

The only Chinese temple in Brisbane and one of the few left in the entire State. Small and delicately proportioned, with a double-gabled roof highlighted by elaborate ridge details, it was built in 1884 by Chinese market gardeners. It has been restored by the Chinese community.
Cnr Higgs & Park sts, Breakfast Creek. Open daily. (07) 3262 5588.

[12] Wolston House
Map ref. 360 B2

Massive Moreton Bay figs shade this charming but modest 1850s sandstone and brick country residence, designed by William Pettigrew, later a mayor of Brisbane, and built in 1852 for Dr Stephen Simpson, Commissioner of Crown Lands for the Moreton Bay settlement. The kitchen, originally separate but joined to the main house at a later date, has rough, whitewashed walls and a hessian-lined ceiling. The other rooms possess a colonial refinement with their elegant half-glazed french doors, casement windows and handsome joinery. Wolston is surrounded by gently rolling countryside.
349 Grindle Rd, Wacol. Open Sat.–Sun. $ *(07) 3271 1734.*

Also of interest
The flamboyant Breakfast Creek Hotel (1889), 2 Kingsford Smith Dr., Breakfast Creek, is renowned for its beer garden. At Brisbane Airport, the *Southern Cross*, the aeroplane in which Charles Kingsford Smith made the first air crossing of the Pacific in 1928, is on permanent display.

Miegunyah, Bowen Hills

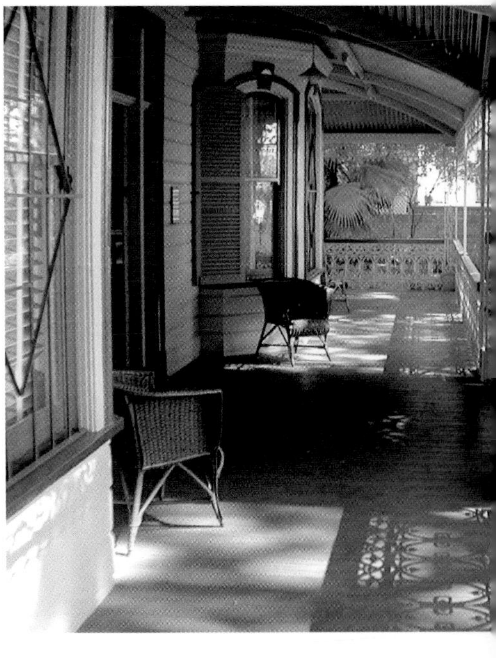

A Walk Around the George Street Precinct

Astroll from the lush City Botanic Gardens to the formal Queens Gardens encompasses some of the oldest and most prestigious sites in Brisbane. From the modest, convict-built Commissariat Store, to magnificent Victorian buildings which exemplify the immense optimism of the late-19th century, much is revealed about Brisbane's heritage.

Brisbane Visitor Information Centre
Queen St Mall
(07) 3006 6290
www.brisbanetourism.com.au

Old Treasury Building
This vast and impressive Italian Renaissance-style building, erected in stages between 1885 and 1928, was designed by Colonial Architect JJ Clark. The design is said to have been conceived as 'a palace with sun-drenched white walls'. The site was formerly occupied by the penal settlement's first guardhouses and military barracks. A casino now occupies the building.
Cnr George & Queen sts.

Land Administration Building
Similar in style to the Old Treasury, this extravagant former government building (1901–05) is on the site occupied by the penal colony's Commandant's residence. The building has been refurbished as a prestigious hotel, the Conrad International.
130 William St.

Commissariat Store
Built in 1828–29 by convicts labouring in chains, this is one of only two remaining convict structures in Brisbane. A third floor was added in 1913. The building, which has served many purposes, has been carefully preserved and is now a museum and headquarters of the Royal Historical Society of Queensland.
115 William St. Open Tues.–Sun. (S)
(07) 3221 4198.
See also p. 218

Convict leg irons at the Commissariat Store

The Mansions
This unusual red-brick terrace of six houses (c.1890) features deep, shaded loggias well suited to the subtropical climate. The stone cats at the corners of the parapet are sculpted from New Zealand limestone. Distinguished early occupants of The Mansions included physicians, surgeons and dentists. Boutique shops, including a National Trust gift shop, and offices now occupy the restored buildings.
Cnr George & Margaret sts. (07) 3221 9365.

Old Government House
An exceptionally fine early colonial mansion, built overlooking the Botanic Gardens in 1860–62 as the official home for the first Governor of Queensland, Sir George Bowen and his wife, Lady Roma Diamantina. It is now headquarters of the National Trust (Qld).
QUT Gardens Point Campus, George St. Open Mon.–Fri. Tours by appt. (S) *(tours only). (07) 3229 1788. NT.*
See also p. 220

Lady Roma Diamantina Bowen, an Italian countess and wife of Queensland's first Governor.

Old Treasury Building

The Queensland Club
The Queensland Club, Brisbane's most exclusive club, was formed just four days before the colony's separation from NSW in 1859. This palatial, tropical building, completed in 1884, was designed by FD Stanley, a member of the club, who was also the architect of Brisbane's GPO. The Club provided a home away from home for colonial gentlemen.
1–19 Alice St. Not open for inspection.

Queensland Club, c. 1880s

Queens Gardens
St John's pro-Cathedral (1854) was demolished in 1904 to create this inner city park. The bronze statue of Queen Victoria, unveiled in 1906, is a replica of an original in England.
George St.

City Botanic Gardens
The Gardens occupy part of a site known to the traditional Aboriginal owners as 'Min-an-jin', which was part of their hunting and fishing grounds. In 1828 convicts were put to work here to grow vegetables for the colony. By 1855 the area had been set aside as botanic gardens. The lush grounds include a magnificent avenue of bunya pines, planted in the 1850s by the first Director, Walter Hill.
Alice St. Open daily. Free tours daily except Sun.
(07) 3403 8888. See also p. 218

Parliament House
The first elected Queensland Parliament convened in the old convict barracks in Queen Street from 1860 until 1868, when the first part of the grand French Renaissance-style Parliament House was completed. Colonial Architect Charles Tiffin won an Australia-wide competition with his impressive design. The interiors have been lavishly restored.
Cnr George & Alice sts.
See p. 221 for opening details.

Stained-glass window of
Queen Victoria, Parliament House

QUEENSLAND FROM A TO Z

Blackall Historical Woolscour

BARCALDINE Map ref. 366 C11, 373 Q11

Barcaldine, in the cattle country of Queensland's central west, was established in 1886 on Charles Cameron's Barcaldine Downs station. The town figured prominently in the 1891 shearers' strike, when 400 shearers camped on the fringes of Barcaldine for several months, protesting the use of non-union labour. The strike was finally broken, but it gave birth to the political Labor movement. The following year Thomas Ryan, a member of the strike committee, became the first endorsed Labor candidate in the Australian parliament. The locals pronounce the name Bar-CALL-din.

Australian Workers Heritage Centre This unique centre celebrates the contribution that workers have made in pioneering and building Australia, through re-created settings, photographs and audio-visual displays. *Ash St. Open daily.* Ⓢ *(07) 4651 2422.*

ALSO OF INTEREST Housed in one of the town's oldest bank buildings, the eclectic display of local memorabilia at the Folk Museum is both quirky and fascinating. *Cnr Gidyea & Beech sts.* Ⓢ

Open daily. (07) 4651 2223. The Tree of Knowledge is an old ghost gum opposite the railway station, where the striking shearers of 1891 held meetings. A plaque commemorates 'the loyalty, courage and sacrifice of these stalwart men and women of the west'. (The camp site was about 5 km NE of town.) *Oak St.* The Masonic Temple (1901), a two-storey building of iron and timber with Classical facade, is perched, Queensland-fashion, on low timber stumps. It was originally a bank. *39 Beech St. Ask at Visitor Information to see inside.*

Oak St; (07) 4651 1724. Website: www.outbackholidays.tq.com.au/barcaldine.htm

BEAUDESERT

Map ref. 365 P10

Beaudesert lies in the rich Logan and Albert river valleys in southern Queensland, behind the Gold Coast. The area was explored by Capt. Patrick Logan, commander of the Moreton Bay penal settlement, in 1826–27 and opened up for settlement in the 1840s.

Historical Museum This authentic slab hut (1875) with shingled roof, peeled-log verandah posts and timber-clad chimney, typical of the earliest pioneer building techniques, has colonial furnishings. An 1885 timber house, historic machinery and farm implements are also displayed. *Jubilee Park. Open daily.* Ⓢ *(07) 5541 1284.*

54 Brisbane St; (07) 5541 3740.

BEENLEIGH

Map ref. 361 P11, 365 Q9

Less than 40 km south-east of Brisbane, the town of Beenleigh was once the business centre of the sugar industry. At its peak, in the 1880s, there were around 30 sugar mills operating in the district.

Beenleigh Rum Distillery Australia's oldest working distillery was founded in 1884. Englishman Francis Gooding and his brother-in-law John Davy started Queensland's second sugarcane plantation in 1865 and opened the Beenleigh Sugar Mill five years later. In 1884 they bought a copper still from James 'Bosun' Stewart, who had been producing moonshine aboard the riverboat SS *Walrus*, and the Beenleigh Rum Distillery was born. There are rum tastings, tours and a museum. *Distillery Rd. Open Mon.–Fri.* Ⓢ *(07) 3807 2307.*

Cavill Walk, Surfers Paradise, (07) 5538 4419.

BIRDSVILLE

Map ref. 374 E5

Birdsville sits in isolation on the fringe of the desolate Simpson Desert and the gibber stones of the Sturt Stony Desert in the State's far south-west corner. It began as the Diamantina Crossing in 1879, a customs depot where tolls were collected on stock and supplies crossing the border from SA. At its peak the township boasted three hotels, several stores, offices, two blacksmiths and a doctor and was the starting point for cattle drives along the lonely Birdsville Track. Federation in 1901 brought free trade, and Birdsville's fortunes – if not its frontier spirit – waned.

Birdsville Hotel The town's only remaining hotel, the weathered, well-worn stone pub is a welcome sight at the end of the rough 486-km trip along the 'Track' from Maree, SA. It has withstood fire, cyclones and floods since c. 1884. *Adelaide St. Open daily. (07) 4656 3244.*

ALSO OF INTEREST Pioneer artifacts, old droving kit and a Cobb & Co. coach are part of the acclaimed Birdsville Working Museum's collection. *Waddi Dr. Open daily (April–Oct.).* Ⓢ *(07) 4656 3259.* The crumbling shell of the rudely constructed old Royal Hotel (c. 1882), Adelaide St, where John Flynn (of the Royal Flying Doctor Service) established the Australian Inland Mission Station in 1923, still stands. The colourful annual Birdsville Races, first held in 1882, attract thousands of spectators each September.

Wirrari Centre, Billabong Blvd; (07) 4656 3300. Website: www.outbackholidays.tq.com.au/birdsville.htm

BLACKALL

Map ref. 364 A1, 366 D13, 373 R13, 375 R1

At the heart of excellent sheep and cattle country in central Queensland, the small township of Blackall, on the banks of the Barcoo, was surveyed in 1868.

OF INTEREST Queensland's first artesian bore was sunk on the corner of Aqua & Garden sts in 1885. Legendary gun shearer Jackie Howe sheared 321 sheep in 7 hours 40 minutes, using blade shears, at nearby Alice Downs station in 1892 and earned his place in Australian history. The record was finally beaten, using machine shears, in 1950 (the blade-shearing record stands).

IN THE AREA Blackall Historical Woolscour, built in 1908, is the State's only steam-powered woolscour (where wool is washed after shearing). The hot water from an artesian bore was converted into steam to drive the engines and enormous wool dryers. The original pumps, presses and pulleys, in use until the 1970s, are still intact. *4 km N, Evora Rd. Open daily. Regular tours.* Ⓢ *(07) 4657 4637.*

Short St; (07) 4657 4637. Website: www.outbackholidays.tq.com.au/blackall.htm

BRISBANE

Map ref. 358 F7, 365 P9

BUDERIM

Map ref. 365 Q7

In the lush mountain country behind the Sunshine Coast, the district around Buderim was settled in the 1870s. Sugarcane, bananas, coffee and now ginger have been farmed in the richly fertile soil.

Buderim Pioneer Cottage One of Buderim's earliest houses, a cottage of pit-sawn cedar and beech (1876) with french doors opening on to a

Birdsville Hotel

verandah and a lush garden, is now a local history museum. The house retains some of its original furnishings, providing a glimpse of home life in this farming district in the 1880s, and many photos. *Ballinger Cres. Open daily.* Ⓢ *(07) 5445 8005.*
🛈 *Old Post Office, Burnett St; (07) 5477 0944.*

BUNDABERG　　　　Map ref. 365 O2

Bundaberg, a gracious coastal town, lies around 370 km north of Brisbane. First settled in 1867, it is surrounded by the source of its prosperity, the fertile Burnett River plains, planted with spreading fields of sugarcane. Bert Hinkler, the city's most famous son, made the first solo flight from England to Australia in 1928. Several museums have been moved to the Bundaberg Botanic Gardens on the north edge of the town.

Fairymead House Sugar Museum A magnificent 1890s plantation homestead is now the venue for a museum documenting the local sugar industry and paying tribute to its pioneers. *Mt Perry Rd, Bundaberg North. Open daily.* Ⓢ *(07) 4153 6786.*

Hinkler Glider Museum A replica of Hinkler's glider and models of his aircraft can be viewed. Visitor Information is also located here. *271 Bourbong St (at the southern end of Tallon Bridge). Open daily. (07) 4152 2333.*

Hinkler House Memorial Museum The home of pioneer aviator Bert Hinkler, designed by Hinkler and moved from Southhampton (UK) to Bundaberg in 1984. The interior is classic 1920s, with a wealth of photographs and memorabilia. *Mt Perry Rd, Bundaberg North. Open daily.* Ⓢ *(07) 4152 0222.*

Historical Museum Photographs, period costumes and pioneer artifacts help trace the city and district's history in this well-presented folk museum. *Mt Perry Rd, Bundaberg North. Open daily.* Ⓢ *(07) 4152 0101.*

ALSO OF INTEREST A genuine coal-fired cane train takes visitors on a track through the Botanic Gardens. *Mt Perry Rd, Bundaberg North. Sun. (also Wed. in Queensland school hols).* Ⓢ *(07) 4152 6609.* Buildings of note in Bourbong St include the 1889 School of Arts building, now an art gallery. *Open daily.* Opposite is the Italianate post office (1880s), with its soaring

30-m clock tower. *Open business hours.* The two-storey former Commercial Bank (1891), cnr Maryborough & Bourbong sts, features elegant columns, wide verandahs and a delicately etched fanlight above the main entrance. Bundaberg is famed for its rum, distilled from locally produced sugarcane molasses. Tours of the Bundaberg Distillery, and historical artifacts in a relocated 'Queenslander', introduce the technology and history of this 'Queensland spirit'. *Avenue St. Open daily.* Ⓢ *(07) 4131 2999.*

IN THE AREA At Mon Repos Beach and Conservation Park there are stone walls built by Kanakas, the South Sea Islanders who were brought to Australia ('duped or induced', as one historian comments) to work the sugarcane fields. By the 1890s, thousands of Kanakas had arrived. The Pacific Island Labourers Act, passed in 1901, prohibited the importation of Kanakas. Most returned to their homeland but some remained, and their descendants are an active part of the community today. *14 km E.*

🛈 *186 Bourbong St; (07) 4152 9289.* Website: www.bundaberg.qld.gov.au
See also Childers

CAIRNS　　　　Map ref. 369 N6

Cairns lies on the shores of Trinity Bay, which was discovered and named by Capt. James Cook on Trinity Sunday, 1770. The town began as a port in the 1870s after the discovery of the Hodgkinson goldfield, but the oldest buildings date from around 1900. Although Cairns has grown into something of a luxurious modern resort town, some heritage buildings remain, a tangible link with the past.

Cairns Museum An old-fashioned Queensland corner building, sheltered by deep timber verandahs, the former School of Arts (1907) is home to a notable regional museum, which highlights northern Queensland's diverse history, from the Aboriginal and Islander culture, to Chinese immigration, goldmining and more. There are wonderful photographs and interesting Aboriginal artifacts. *Cnr Lake & Shields sts, City Place. Open Mon.–Sat.* Ⓢ *(07) 4051 5582.*

Cairns Regional Gallery Grand both without and within, the historic

Historic House, Charleville

former State Government Insurance Office, built in the neo-Classical style in the 1930s, now accommodates the innovative Regional Gallery. The building is classified by the National Trust. *Cnr Abbott & Shields sts. Open Mon.–Fri.; also Sat.–Sun. afternoons.* Ⓢ *(07) 4031 6865.*

Flecker Botanic Gardens A lush tropical garden, established in 1886, with more than 10 000 plant species and 100 varieties of palm trees. An Aboriginal Plant Use garden contains species traditionally used for food, medicine and weapons. *94 Collins Ave, Edge Hill. Open daily. (07) 4044 3398.*

ALSO OF INTEREST The 'Barbary Coast' precinct, Lower Abbott St, Wharf St and the lower end of Lake St, where big old hotels, capacious warehouses, and other late-19th and early-20th century buildings combine with towering palms to remind the visitor that this was once the hub of a thriving shipping district.

IN THE AREA Not to be missed is the rail trip to Kuranda aboard beautifully preserved, old-fashioned carriages. The train wends its way through magnificent gorges and past crashing waterfalls to Kuranda's much-photographed 1915 railway station, festooned with tropical plants. It took hundreds of men four years to hack their way through the dense jungle and to tunnel through rock to complete this track to the Herberton tin mines in 1881. Twenty men died working on the project. Kuranda is a small town surrounded by lush tropical growth. *Train leaves Cairns Railway Station at 9.30 a.m. Sun.–Fri., and 8.30 a.m. Sat.* $ *Booking (07) 4031 3636 or 1800 620 324.*

[i] *51 The Esplanade; (07) 4051 3588.* Website: www.cairns.qld.gov. au

See also Chillagoe, Cooktown, Herberton

CHARLEVILLE Map ref. 364 B6

Charleville, in the arid mulga country of Queensland's south-west, was surveyed in 1868 and quickly became important as a stopping place on the overland stock route from NSW to western Queensland. In the 1890s it had 500 registered bullock teams, its own brewery and 10 pubs to keep the bullockies content. In 1893 Cobb & Co. established a factory at Charleville, and soon all the company's Australian coaches were built here. But Cobb & Co.'s fortunes declined as the railway extended into the west and the factory closed in 1920. Charleville is now an important agricultural centre.

Historic House The former Queensland National Bank and bank residence (1881), a timber building with elaborate timber pediment, retains its original marble fireplaces and handsome cedar joinery. Exhibits document Charleville's history and include a rail ambulance and replica Cobb & Co. coach. *Alfred St. Open daily.* $ *(07) 4654 3349.*

ALSO OF INTEREST The restored Corones Hotel (c. 1929), built by Greek migrant Harry (Poppa) Corones, features a grand stairway and splendid dance hall. Aviator Amy Johnson was just one of many famous guests. Tours are followed by afternoon tea. *Wills St. Open daily.* $ *(07) 4654 1022.* The Steiger Vortex Rainmaking Gun was one of 10 guns fired into the air in 1902 in a desperate attempt to break a six-year drought. The bizarre experiment proved unsuccessful. *Bicentennial Park, Stuart St.* Heritage trail brochures are available from the railway station. A plaque at the airport commemorates Qantas's first regular air service, from Charleville to Cloncurry, which began on 2 November 1922. (By way of contrast, Cobb & Co.'s last Australian coach service, from Surat to Yuleba in southern Queensland, was in August 1924.)

IN THE AREA A cairn marks the site where Ross and Keith Smith made an emergency landing on their epic London–Sydney flight in 1919. *19 km N.*

[i] *Cunnamulla Rd; (07) 4654 3057.* Website: www.outbackholidays.tq.com.au/charleville.htm

CHARTERS TOWERS Map ref. 366 E2

See Historic Highlights, p. 238

CHILDERS Map ref. 365 O3

Set on rolling hills, and the rich red soil of sugarcane country, Childers, 53 km south of Bundaberg, owed its initial wealth to sugar. The town was almost razed by fire in 1902, but enough remained – and has been carefully preserved – to earn Childers a reputation for its heritage buildings.

Pharmaceutical Museum & Art Gallery An award-winning museum centred around the original red-cedar fittings and ground glass bottles of the old pharmacy. There's an art gallery in the former dentist's surgery upstairs. Visitor Information is also located here. *90 Churchill St. Open Mon.–Fri. & Sat. mornings.* $ *(07) 4126 1994.*

ALSO OF INTEREST A cottage (c. 1890), a sugarcane locomotive imported from the UK in 1916, and a wealth of local memorabilia can be viewed at the Historical Society Complex. *Taylor St. Open Mon.–Fri. mornings.* $ *(07) 4126 1640.* Churchill St has a rich legacy of late-Victorian buildings with an extravagant array of urns, pediments and deep verandahs stretching across the footpaths. Notable are the Grand Hotel, moved to Childers in the 1880s, and the Federal Hotel (1907) with its 'Wild West' swinging doors. The Royal Hotel, North St, dates from the 1890s. A memorial in Millennium Park acknowledges the South Sea Islanders (Kanakas) brought to Queensland to work the sugarcane fields.

[i] *90 Churchill St; (07) 4126 1994.*

See also Bundaberg, Maryborough

CHILLAGOE Map ref. 369 K7

An isolated outback town in the Far North, which was a significant mining centre for copper, silver, lead and gold from the 1890s until the 1940s. At its peak more than 1000 men worked at the smelter. Marble and gold are mined here today.

OF INTEREST Relics of the district's mining heyday and Aboriginal artifacts are displayed at the Heritage Museum. Visitor Information is also located here. *7 Hill St. Open daily.* $ *(07) 4094 7109.* The abandoned flues, copper smelters, derelict furnaces and slag heaps that dominate the landscape are important reminders of Queensland's mining history. Around 15 km NW, past the old settlement of Mungana, traditional Aboriginal paintings can be found in the limestone caves. Maps from Visitor Information.

[i] *7 Hill St; (07) 4094 7109.* Website: www.athertontableland.com

Pharmaceutical Museum, Childers

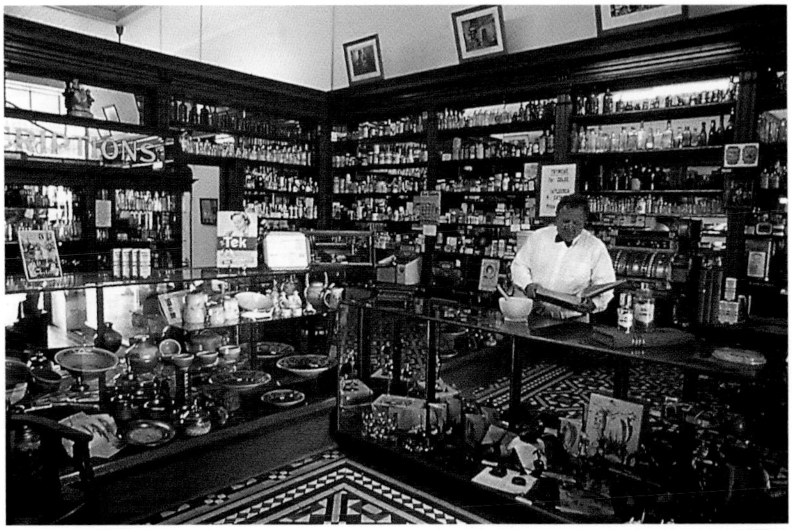

CLONCURRY

Map ref. 372 G4

Explorer John McKinlay detected signs of copper while searching for Burke and Wills in this arid north-west countryside in 1861. Pioneer pastoralist Ernest Henry discovered the copper lodes six years later. The Great Australian mine was established, Cloncurry was born and the boom lasted until after World War I. The first Royal Flying Doctor Service base was established here by the Rev. John Flynn in 1928. The pastoral industry and mining have kept Cloncurry prosperous.

John Flynn Place An informative museum which traces the history of the Royal Flying Doctor Service, and the personal story of its founder, the remarkable and visionary John Flynn. *Daintree St. Open daily May–Oct.; Mon.–Fri. only Nov.–April; closed mid-Dec.–Jan.* Ⓢ *(07) 4742 4125.*

Mary Kathleen Memorial Museum & Park Historic relics and buildings from the abandoned uranium mining town of Mary Kathleen. A favourite exhibit is one of explorer Robert O'Hara Burke's water bottles. *McIlwraith St. Open daily May–Oct.; Mon.–Fri. only Nov.–April; closed mid-Dec.–Jan.* Ⓢ *(07) 4742 1361.*

ALSO OF INTEREST On the road to the airport, the Afghan Cemetery contains the graves of Afghans, who came with camel teams to haul ore from the mines. Only one has a headstone (facing Mecca).

IN THE AREA The rugged Selwyn Ranges to the west of Cloncurry are littered with abandoned mine workings. Where the Barkly Hwy crosses the Corella River is a memorial to Burke and Wills, the first white men in the district. *43 km w.* Battle Mountain, where determined Kalkadoon warriors fought a pitched – and futile – battle in 1884 against mounted troopers armed with carbines, in a bid to defend their land, is 100 km N.
🛈 *Mary Kathleen Memorial Museum & Park, McIlwraith St; (07) 4742 1361. Website: www.outbackholidays.tq. com.au/cloncurry.htm*

COOKTOWN

Map ref. 369 L3

Cooktown was the site of the first, if transient, European settlement on Australia's east coast. Capt. James Cook was forced ashore in 1770 when his barque the *Endeavour* was damaged on the coral reef, and he and his party spent 48 days camped here. In 1873, gold was discovered on the Palmer River. Within two years 'Cook's Town' was a gold-rush port with 65 hotels and a main street 3 km long. By the mid-1880s nearly 30 000 people depended on the settlement, and it was the second largest town in Queensland. By 1900 the gold was gone, and Cooktown was left to fade into near obscurity. Sleepy Cooktown is a hidden treasure and one of Australia's most historic towns.

James Cook Museum A first-rate regional museum with exhibits relating to Cook's life and voyages, a Chinese temple in memory of the 18 000 or so Chinese who came to the goldfields, traditional Aboriginal tools and weapons. The gracious building (1887–89) was originally the Convent of St Mary School. The original anchor and a cannon from the *Endeavour*, jettisoned by Cook when his ship struck the reef, are prized possessions. *Cnr Helen & Furneaux sts. Open daily (closed Feb.–Mar.).* Ⓢ *(07) 4069 5386. NT.*

ALSO OF INTEREST A number of buildings epitomise the tremendous optimism of this isolated gold-rush outpost in the 1800s. The grand, two-storey former Queensland National Bank (1889) has its fine cedar joinery and old counters still intact. *Charlotte St. Not open for inspection.* The elegant, weatherboard Cooktown Hospital, an outstanding example of Queensland's early colonial architecture, served the community from 1879 to 1986. *May St. Not open for inspection.* Cooktown Motor Inn is located in a two-storeyed, verandahed building erected by former Cooktown mayor, PE Seagren, in 1880 as a store. A Gothic monument (1888) to Mrs Watson commemorates the heroine who perished in 1881 while fleeing with her child from Lizard Island following an attack by hostile Aboriginal people. It is now believed the Watsons' cottage was built on a sacred Aboriginal burial site. *Charlotte St.* Mrs Watson's grave can also be seen. There are various monuments to Capt. Cook and a re-enactment of Cook's landing is held each Queen's Birthday long weekend in June. A wander through the Cooktown Cemetery reveals how tough life was in these remote parts. A shrine (1887) here recalls the thousands of Chinese who came to the diggings, but there is just a solitary Chinese headstone.
🛈 *101 Charlotte St; (07) 4069 5446 or freecall 1800 001 770.*
See also Cairns, Laura

COOMINYA

Map ref. 365 D9

Bellevue Homestead A fine specimen of Queensland vernacular architecture, this rambling house is important for its long association with the region's pastoral and social life. It was built c. 1870s, though damaged by floods in 1893. Bellevue Station was part of the original Wivenhoe run established in the early 1840s. George Taylor and his wife Edith lived here after 1884, entertaining such guests as HRH the Prince of Wales (later King Edward VIII). Bellevue is really two houses joined by a 'breezeway' extended around a courtyard, with deep verandahs. Inside, cedar panelling, pressed metal ceilings and ruby glass create a period charm. *Opposite Bellevue Hotel. Open Mon.–Wed., Sat.–Sun. Closed Dec.* Ⓢ *(07) 5426 4209. NT.*
🛈 *Esk Shire Offices, 2 Redbank St, Esk; (07) 5424 1200.*
See also Ipswich

CROYDON

Map ref. 368 F10

The last of the great Queensland gold rushes started here in 1885, in the heart of Queensland's Gulf Country. The goldfield was dry – barren sand and stunted scrub. Water was virtually non-existent and white ants a constant plague, yet by 1887 there were 7000 hopefuls and 36 thirst-quenching hotels in Croydon. Around 21 tonnes of gold was extracted in all, but by 1926 few miners were left on the field. Today the town is a living, working museum of gold-rush history.

OF INTEREST The town's historic buildings are clues to a busier past. The functional timber and tin courthouse, dating from 1887, has been classified by the National Trust. *Open Mon.–Fri.* The surgeon's house (1887) is now a bottle museum. The friendly general store has been trading since 1894. The Croydon Shire Hall (1892) is now home to Visitor Information and regular tours of the historic precinct depart from here. *Samwell St. (07) 4745 6125.* The historic Gulflander train, built to carry gold and people to the port of **Normanton** more than a century ago, now takes tourists on a nostalgic trip. *Gulflander departs Croydon each Thurs. for Normanton. (07) 4745 1391.*

🚊 *Samwell St; (07) 4745 6125.* Website: www.gulf-savannah.com.au *See also Normanton*

DALBY
Map ref. 365 M8

Originally known as 'Myall Creek', Dalby lies around 200 km west of Brisbane on Queensland's Darling Downs, surrounded by the State's richest grain-growing country and wealthy pastoral lands. Dalby was declared a town in 1854 and is today a substantial regional centre.

OF INTEREST Dalby Pioneer Park Museum features working machinery, pioneer tools, and many historic buildings that have been re-erected on site. *3 Black St. Open daily.* Ⓢ *(07) 4662 4760.*

IN THE AREA On the Dalby–Jandowae road is Jimbour House, one of Queensland's finest homesteads, a lofty two-storey sandstone mansion built in 1874 by Joshua Bell, on one of the first runs taken upon the Darling Downs in the early 1840s. Bell's 'mansion in the wilds' was a sophisticated design, with Tuscan colonnades, french doors, bowed verandahs and Welsh slate-tiled roof. There were 24 rooms, and the cost was estimated at £30 000. Original buildings in the grounds include a four-storey timber water-tower (which contains a dwelling) and a tiny timber chapel. Jimbour is carefully preserved. The gardens are extensive, magnificently planned and maintained. *29 km N. Gardens open daily (except in wet weather). House open occasionally for special events.*

🚊 *Thomas Jack Park, cnr Drayton & Condamine sts; (07) 4662 1066.* Website: www.dalbytown.com

GYMPIE
Map ref. 365 P6

James Nash's discovery of gold here in 1867 started Queensland's first great gold rush and helped save the young colony from bankruptcy. Within months 25 000 people had arrived to try their luck. In all, about 114 tonnes of gold was extracted before the last mine closed in the 1920s. Gympie, 160 km north of Brisbane, retains interesting buildings from its golden days.

Gold Mining & Historical Museum An extensive and engaging museum, on the site of one of Gympie's richest goldmines. The showpiece is a modest timber house (1880s), one-time home of Andrew Fisher, the first Queenslander to become Australia's Prime Minister (1908–15). *215 Brisbane Rd. Open daily.* Ⓢ *(07) 5482 3995.*

Woodworks Forestry & Timber Museum Cross-cut saws, pit-saws, bullock wagons, drays, a timber-getter's bark hut and demonstrations by 'old time timbermen' provide an insight into this traditional industry. *Cnr Fraser Rd & Bruce Hwy. Open Mon.–Fri. & Sun. afternoons. Demonstrations Wed. at 10 a.m. & 1 p.m.* Ⓢ *(07) 5483 7691.*

ALSO OF INTEREST The winding main street, Mary St, began as a bullock track in the hectic early days of the gold diggings. Dominating the sky-line is the tower of the courthouse (1900–02), cnr Channon & King sts, though there are a number of buildings from the late Victorian era. Heritage trail brochures from Visitor Information. The Valley Rattler Steam Train, a restored 1923 C-17 steam engine, runs the 40-km journey from Gympie to Imbil. *Tozer St. Sun. & Wed.* Ⓢ *(07) 5482 2750.*

🚊 *Cooloola Regional Information Centre, Bruce Hwy (near Lake Alford); 1800 444 222.* Website: www.cooloola. org.au

HERBERTON
Map ref. 369 M8

An old tin-mining town on the Atherton Tablelands, Herberton got its start when prospectors Willie Jack and John Newell discovered a rich tin lode in this remote, hilly country in 1880. There's not much action these days, though a few timber buildings from the late 1800s are a link with the past.

Herberton Historical Village A slab hut, butcher, colonial cottage, old school-house, coach and livery stable – in fact over 30 buildings in all – reveal aspects of the pioneer lifestyle. *6 Broadway. Open daily.* Ⓢ *(07) 4096 2271.*

ALSO OF INTEREST The battery of the Northern Freehold Mining Co. was hauled through almost impenetrable scrub from Port Douglas by a team of 81 bullocks in November 1880. Substantial remains of the tin-mining equipment and shafts are scattered around the town's outskirts.

🚊 *Old Post Office Gallery, Herberton Rd, Atherton; (07) 4091 4222.* Website: www.athertontableland.com.

IPSWICH
Map ref. 363 C8, 365 P9

Ipswich, south-west of Brisbane on the edge of the Bremer River, is a large provincial city. It began in 1827 as a convict-manned quarry to

Jimbour House, Dalby

supply urgently needed limestone for Brisbane buildings. After the area was opened to free settlers in 1842, Ipswich developed rapidly as a busy river port linking the rich Darling Downs pastoral stations and Brisbane. The discovery of extensive coal deposits in the 1860s (still being mined) and the coming of the railway in that decade hastened the town's growth. Ipswich is well endowed with historic buildings, including many private residences in the traditional Queensland style.

Claremont A honey-coloured sandstone villa, set in a lush garden, Claremont was built by parliamentarian John Panton in 1858. In 1863 Panton sold the house to George Thorn, Ipswich's first free settler, who became a successful merchant and later entered parliament. Claremont embodies the restrained colonial Georgian style, with shuttered french doors opening on to a spacious verandah. *1a Milford St. Not open for inspection.*

Courthouse Designed by Charles Tiffin, later Colonial Architect of Queensland, and erected in 1859 (the verandahed wings added c. 1880s), this is one of the few buildings in the State built before Queensland was declared a separate colony. *East St. Not open for inspection.*

St Paul's Church The oldest Anglican church in the State (1858), built just before Queensland's separation from NSW in 1859 and described that year as 'one of the nicest churches in New South Wales'. *Cnr Nicholas & Brisbane sts. Open daily.*

ALSO OF INTEREST A Classical Revival facade was added in 1864 to the school of arts (1861) to make it sufficiently imposing to be the town hall. Now an art gallery. *Brisbane St. Entry via D'Arcy Doyle Pl. Open daily.* Close by is the redbrick tower of the post office (1900). Ipswich has a significant legacy of houses from the 1800s and early 1900s. Although not open for inspection, the following are of interest: Ginn Cottage, cnr Ginn St & Meredith Lane, built by merchant W Ginn c. 1857 and one of the town's oldest cottages; the splendidly elegant Gooloowan (1862–64), Quarry St, set amidst a garden of giant camphor laurel trees, built for a prominent merchant family; and Garowie (1887),

59 Whitehall St, a two-storey Victorian mansion built for James Cribb, who became a local politician. The Queensland Country Women's Association Hostel (1890), Darling St, epitomises Queensland's domestic architecture, shuttered and shrouded in latticework and lacework and flanked by palm trees. St Mary's Church (1904) has the grandeur of a cathedral. *Mary St. Open daily.* Queensland's first railway line, from Ipswich to Grandchester, opened in 1865. The present station dates from 1892. *Bell St.* Picturesque Queens Park, Milford St, has lovely views over Ipswich. Opposite the park is Cunningham's Knoll. Explorer Allan Cunningham looked west from this point (marked by a cairn) in 1828 and sighted the gap in the Great Dividing Range that led to the discovery of the rich pastoral country to the west.

IN THE AREA At Grandchester, the timber railway station, the oldest in the State, opened in 1865 as the terminus for Queensland's first rail line (from Ipswich). *46 km w.* Also worth visiting are Wolston House at Wacol (see **Brisbane***)* and Bellevue Homestead at **Coominya**.

🖪 *Cnr D'Arcy Doyle Pl. & Brisbane St; (07) 3281 0555.* Website: www.ipswichtourism.com.au

JONDARYAN
Map ref. 365 M8

Jondaryan is not much more than a few buildings on the Warrego Highway, 175 km west of Brisbane, surrounded by sheep country in the State's 'Golden West'.

Jondaryan Woolshed Historical Museum & Park The 56-stand woolshed on Jondaryan station was Queensland's largest when it was built of ironbark slabs and red cedar in 1859. The massive ceiling beams, imported from England, were so long that they were reputedly lashed to the side of the ship. Jondaryan was one of the first free selections taken up on the legendary Darling Downs in 1842. By the 1860s the station extended over 62 775 ha and ran 150 000 sheep. The first of the great shearers' strikes in Queensland took place here in 1890. Jondaryan is now part of a 'working museum', including a grand former bank, a century-old schoolroom, smithy shop and boundary rider's hut. Demonstrations such as

shearing and butter making are an added attraction and a major heritage festival is held annually in August. Accommodation is available in the old Shearers' Quarters. *Evanslea Rd. Open daily. Regular tours.* Ⓢ *(07) 4692 2229.*

🖪 *Dalby Visitor Information Centre, Thomas Jack Park, cnr Drayton & Condamine sts, Dalby; (07) 4662 1066.* Website: www.dalbytown.com *See also Dalby, Toowoomba*

LAURA
Map ref. 369 K3

Laura grew up in the 1870s as a stop en route to the Palmer River goldfields and became the main railhead for the fields, at one period handling 20 000 passengers a year. Today the population, predominantly Aboriginal, is about 90.

OF INTEREST Laura is the heart of 'Quinkan country', where there are numerous Aboriginal rock paintings and 'pounded' rock designs, diverse in style and treatment, but vivid and immensely important to Aboriginal culture. This is one of the largest collections of prehistoric art in the world. In Aboriginal mythology, the Quinkans are spirits that haunt the hills and cliffs. Rock painting has flourished here for over 1000 years, though some works may be much earlier. Aboriginal people painted the rock surfaces while camping in the sandstone escarpments during the wet season. At Quinkan Reserve, walking tracks lead to the magnificent rock galleries at Split Rock (30 min) and Gu Gu Yalangi (2 hrs).

Blacksmith, Jondaryan Woolshed

12 km SE. The Aboriginal-run Ang Gnarra Visitor Centre at Laura can arrange guided tours. $ *Open Mon.–Thurs. (07) 4060 3200.* The Laura Aboriginal Dance and Cultural Festival, a four-day festival, is staged biennially in June.

[i] *Ang Gnarra Information Centre, Peninsula Development Rd. Open Mon.–Thurs. (07) 4060 3200.*

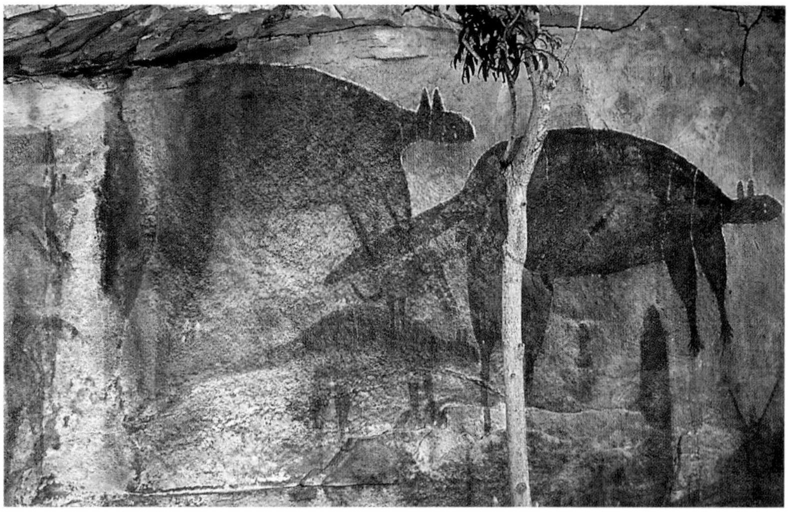

Aboriginal art, Laura

LONGREACH Map ref. 366 A11, 373 O11

Longreach, settled in the 1870s, is the largest town in Queensland's far west, located 700 km inland from Rockhampton. Cattle stations stretch out on all sides to the dusty horizon.

Australian Stockman's Hall of Fame & Outback Heritage Centre A remarkable tribute to those men and women who have shaped the history and lifestyle of Outback Australia. The collection is extensive, diverse and thorough, touching on many themes. As well as larger-scale displays – such as wagons and an 1860s slab hut – diaries, letters and an ongoing oral history project record the personal, often poignant, story of life in the Outback. *Sir James Walker Dr. Open daily.* $ *(07) 4658 2166.*

Qantas Founders Outback Museum & Qantas Hangar The Queensland and Northern Territory Aerial Services Ltd (QANTAS) was registered on 16 November 1920, the brainchild of two ex-Flying Corps officers, W Hudson Fysh and PJ McGinness. It was financed by a group of graziers. The original iron hangar (1921) was also Australia's first aircraft factory (1926–30). Qantas airlines had its headquarters in Longreach from 1922–34. An audio-visual display, documents and a full-size replica of the first type of passenger aircraft flown by the airline are amongst the exhibits. *Sir Hudson Fysh Memorial Dr. Open daily.* $ *(07) 4658 3737.*

ALSO OF INTEREST The building which supplied electricity to Longreach and district from 1921–85 is now the Powerhouse Museum. *Swan St. Open afternoons (April–Oct.)* $ *(07) 4658 3933.* Visitor Information is in a replica of the original Qantas booking office.

IN THE AREA Starlight's Lookout offers excellent views of the countryside. It was in this area that Harry Redford, alias Capt. Starlight, masterminded one of Australia's great robberies. With four friends he stole 1000 cattle from Mt Cornish Station, overlanded them across treacherous country into SA and sold them. He was arrested in Adelaide, brought back to Queensland and tried, but acquitted. Rolf Boldrewood's classic novel *Robbery Under Arms* is based on Starlight's exploits. *55 km* NE.

[i] *Eagle St; (07) 4658 3555.* Website: www.longreach.qld.gov.au

See also Winton

MACKAY Map ref. 367 L5

Mackay is known as the 'sugar capital' of Australia, a prosperous city on the northern coast. The first crop was planted here in 1865, the first sugar produced two years later, and by 1874, one third of all Queensland's sugar crop was grown in Mackay's well-watered valleys. For many years the industry was dependent on Kanakas, South Sea Islanders who were brought, often under force, to work the plantations and in many cases treated as little more than slave labour.

OF INTEREST Pick up a heritage walk brochure from Visitor Information and explore some of the town's magnificent 19th-century buildings along the broad, palm-lined streets of the city centre. The courthouse (c. 1880) and Commonwealth Bank (c. 1880), are two of the finest. *Victoria St.* The imposing National Bank (1922) dominates the corner of Victoria & Wood sts, and further along is the monumental Classical Revival Masonic temple (1927). The old town hall (1912) features shaded arcades and a squat tower. *Not open for inspection.* Historic guided tours are available. *(07) 4957 8994.*

IN THE AREA General Gordon Hotel, situated in the middle of the cane fields, is one of the region's last original country pubs, and was built in 1886. *20 km* SE. *Homebush Rd, Homebush. Open daily. (07) 4959 7324.* Greenmount Historical Homestead (1912), a spacious timber Queenslander complete with original furnishings, offers a tantalising glimpse into a bygone lifestyle. It was built by Albert Cook, whose family were the first pioneers in the district. The Cooks lived at Greenmount for three generations. The homestead, surrounded by a lush tropical garden with sprawling fig trees, overlooks sugarcane fields. *18 km* W. *Greenmount Rd, Walkerston, off Peak Downs Hwy. Open Mon.–Fri. mornings & Sun.* $ *(07) 4959 2250.*

[i] *The Mill, 320 Nebo Rd; (07) 4952 2677 or 1300 130 001.* Website: www.mackayregion.com

MARYBOROUGH Map ref. 365 P4

See Historic Highlights, p. 240

MOUNT ISA Map ref. 372 E4

Stony red hills surround Mount Isa, a mining town whose buoyant economy is based on some of the world's richest deposits of silver, lead, copper and zinc ore found deep beneath the ground. The Outback city only began in the 1920s, but the surrounding countryside is ancient – fossils found at Riversleigh date back 30 million years.

Kalkadoon Tribal Centre & Cultural Keeping Place The Kalkadoon people, a proud and warlike tribe who lived along the Leichhardt and Cloncurry rivers, fought valiantly in the 1800s to defend their land from white settlers. Their rich cultural heritage has been retained by their descendants. *Riversleigh Fossils Centre, 19 Marian St. Open Mon.–Fri.* Ⓢ *(adults). (07) 4749 1555.*

Riversleigh Fossils Centre This award-winning Centre is devoted to the World Heritage-listed Riversleigh fossil sites, north-west of Mount Isa. A documentary film, dioramas and interactive displays present an outstanding introduction to these remarkable prehistoric finds. *19 Marian St. Open daily (shorter hours off season).* Ⓢ *(07) 4749 1555.*

ALSO OF INTEREST The Tent House, with a canvas roof beneath a free-standing iron roof, is typical of houses built in Mount Isa in the 1930s and '40s. The ingenious design provided ventilation and some relief from the harsh climate. *In the grounds of the Fourth Ave Motor Inn. Open limited hours April–end Sept. (07) 4743 3853. NT.* John Midlin Mining Museum, located close to the world's largest silver–lead mine, offers an insight into the history and workings of the gigantic mine. *Church St. Open daily (shorter hours off season).* Ⓢ *(07) 4749 1558.* Frank Aston Underground Mine has 90 metres of tunnels with displays as well as outdoor exhibits. *Shackleton St. Open daily.* Ⓢ *(07) 7443 0601.*

IN THE AREA On the edge of Lawn Hill National Park, the limestone at Riversleigh Fossil Fields has yielded unique fossil finds of previously unknown birds, reptiles and mammals, millions of years old. Access is difficult but tours are available. *250 km NW. Contact Queensland National Parks & Wildlife Service, (07) 7443 2055.*

🄸 *Riversleigh Fossils Centre, Marian St; (07) 4749 1555. Website: www. riversleigh.qld.gov.au*

MOUNT MORGAN   Map ref. 367 N11

In 1882 the Morgan brothers realised the potential of Ironstone Mountain, which became known as the mountain of gold. They formed a company but by 1886 had sold their shares to four astute businessmen who began mining in earnest. By 1900 Mount Morgan was proclaimed a town, the population was 4000, and more than 80 tonnes of refined gold had been won. The mountain of gold then turned into a mine of copper, when it was discovered that rich copper deposits lay beneath the gold. Prices slumped after World War I, but in the 1930s open-cut mining was introduced and smelting began. Located 38 km south-west of Rockhampton, Mount Morgan is still a mining town.

Mt Morgan Gold and Copper Mine What began as a mountain is now one of the biggest man-made holes in the world – a crater 2.5 km long and 325 m deep – which has yielded more than 13 979 kg of gold and huge quantities of copper ore. *East St.*

Old Mine Site The towering octagonal chimney, mines office, the treatment plant and mining relics scattered across the site are an integral part of Queensland's mining history. Guided tours explore the mine site, as well as caves with dinosaur footprints, and the town. *Tours twice daily.* Ⓢ *Book at Visitor Information, (07) 4938 2312 or (07) 4938 1081.*

ALSO OF INTEREST Most of Mount Morgan's wealth was spent elsewhere, but a few historic buildings remain. The old Queensland National Hotel (1890s) with its quirky gazebo tower, and the Grand Hotel (1901), also with a decorative tower, preside over Morgan St. The surprisingly formal Classical courthouse (1899), Hall St, standing in a prominent hilltop position and the substantial Masonic hall (1903), Gordon St, both hint at the town's busier days. *Neither open for inspection.* Displays at the Historical Museum capture the town's early years. *87 Morgan St. Open Mon.–Sat. mornings & Sun.* Ⓢ *(07) 4938 2122.* The railway station (1898), with its delicately scaled porticos, now houses Visitor Information. A restored steam locomotive departs from here (Sun. only); visitors can also ride a fettler's trolley. *Mon.–Fri.* Ⓢ *(07) 4938 2312.* Until 1952 a 'rack railway', one of only two in Australia, allowed extra traction so that trains could cope with the steep Razorback Range ascent. The swing bridge (1890s) that spans the Dee River, at the end of Morgan St, was one of six erected to allow workers easy access to the mine. The Mafeking Bell, cast in 1900 from pennies donated by local schoolchildren and made from melted watch cases, marked the time for townspeople when the mine was closed in the late 1920s and there was no mine hooter. It also rang for peace celebrations at the end of both World Wars. *Dee St (in front of Boy Scout Building).*

🄸 *Railway Station; (07) 4938 2312.* See also Rockhampton

NORMANTON   Map ref. 368 C8, 371 I8

An Outback town in the vast, sparsely populated Gulf country of northern Queensland, Normanton was established in 1868 as a port and boomed briefly during the 1880s and 1890s gold rush at Croydon, when a busy train service linked the towns, but then faded just as quickly.

The Gulflander A quaint 'tin hare' rail motor, introduced in 1922 on the historic 1891 rail line, the Gulflander makes the 151-km trip from Normanton to **Croydon** weekly. Both the rails and sleepers used in this line are steel, to prevent the ravages of white ants. The station's distinctive barrel-vaulted platform shelter of corrugated iron dates from 1891. *Gulflander departs Normanton Wed. a.m., returns from Croydon Thurs. a.m. (07) 4745 1391.*

ALSO OF INTEREST Corrugated iron is a mainstay here, though the National Trust-classified Bank of NSW (1896) is timber with exposed timber cross-bracing, in the Queensland vernacular style. *Cnr Landsborough & Little Brown sts.* You can still see the original cast-iron gas street lights and, in Landsborough St, the town's original well.

IN THE AREA 38 km SW, just over the Little Bynoe River, then about 2 km off the road, is Camp 119, Burke and Wills' most northerly camp on their tragic 1860–61 expedition.

🄸 *Carpentaria Shire Offices, Landsborough St; (07) 4745 1166. Website: www.gulf-savannah.com.au*

RAVENSWOOD   Map ref. 366 G2

Ravenswood is a shadow of its former self, a faded but fascinating old gold-mining town inland from Townsville, retaining just enough grand buildings to hint at its glory days. The first gold was discovered here in 1869. Intense activity was followed by a lull and then, in the late 1890s, by another boom. But by 1914 Ravenswood had been left to languish. A few residents keep the old town alive.

Imperial Hotel Epitomising one-time prosperity, the Imperial (1902) rises proudly from its slender verandah posts and lavishly decorated balconies to its extravagant parapet. Inside, the rooms are steeped in Edwardian character. *Macrossan St. Open daily. (07) 4770 2131.*

ALSO OF INTEREST The main street, Macrossan St, weaves, with slight bumps and curves, through the township, testifying to its hurried beginnings. Along its way are the handsome Railway Hotel (1902), with its restored facade, Thorp's Building (1880s), some stone steps (all that remains of Browne's Ravenswood Hotel), the old School of Arts (c. 1876) and several small, weathered shops. St Patrick's Church (1871), Deighton St, is also of interest.

IN THE AREA Poppet heads and tall Cornish flues are silhouetted against the skyline, while China apple trees and rubber vines, planted by miners, run riot over abandoned mines and the landscape. The land is scarred by mullock heaps and old diggings.

🛈 *74 Mosman St, Charters Towers; (07) 4752 0314. Website: www. charterstowers.qld.gov.au*
See also Charters Towers

ROCKHAMPTON   Map ref. 367 N11

See Historic Highlights, p. 242

ROMA   Map ref. 361 H6

Roma, in the western Darling Downs, was the first town to be officially gazetted after Queensland's separation from NSW in 1859. The town was named after Lady Roma Diamantina Bowen, the wife of the colony's first Governor, Sir George Bowen. Australia's earliest natural gas strike was made at Hospital Hill in 1900, and for a time the gas was used to light the town. The first vines were planted in the district in 1863 by Samuel Symons Bassett.

Railway station, Normanton

Romavilla Winery Queensland's oldest winery, established in 1863. The lofty timber winery, built in 1878, is still in use. There are cellar door tastings and sales. *Northern Rd. Open Mon.–Sat. & pub hol mornings. ⓢ (for tours). (07) 4622 1822.*

ALSO OF INTEREST In 1872 the infamous Capt. Starlight (Harry Redford) was tried in the Roma courthouse for cattle-rustling, and although undoubtedly guilty, he was acquitted – his daring escapade and superior bush skills having earned the admiration of the jury. Visitors are welcome to inspect the new courthouse (1901) when court is not in session. *McDowall St.* Magnificent stained-glass and leadlight windows, some dating back to 1875, enhance St Paul's Church (1915). *Cnr Arthur & Bunjil sts.* A series of plaques, starting at the corner of Bowen & Whip sts, relate the history of oil and gas exploration in Roma from 1900.

IN THE AREA Meadowbank Museum, in an old two-storey hayloft on a cattle property, is filled with an astonishing array of horse-drawn vehicles, antiquated machinery, a doll display and other artifacts. *15 km w, Warrego Hwy. Open by appt only. Closed Feb. ⓢ (07) 4622 3836.*

🛈 *71 Arthur St; (07) 4622 1416. Website: www.romatourism.asn.au*

TOOWOOMBA   Map ref. 365 N9

Toowoomba's strategic position on the edge of the fertile Darling Downs has

ensured its continuing prosperity since the 1840s, when the first squatters and teamsters made this their meeting place on the long haul between the coast and the great stations of the 'golden west'. The first settlement was at Drayton, now a Toowoomba suburb, but shortage of water forced the townspeople to move. Toowoomba is Queensland's largest inland city, cloaked in magnificent gardens and flowering trees, which have earned it the title Garden City.

Cobb & Co. Museum (part of the Queensland Museum) A superb collection of original horse-drawn vehicles, including the Cobb & Co. coach that ran the great staging company's last trip in 1924. Other vehicles range from weathered timber farm drays and wagons, to the elaborate and elegant phaetons and landau carriages of the well-to-do. An Indigenous display is also part of the museum. *27 Lindsay St. Open daily. ⓢ (07) 4639 1971.*

Royal Bull's Head Inn William Horton opened the first inn, a rough slab hut, on this site c. 1847, when it was a popular meeting place for squatters and teamsters. The first church service on the Downs was held here in 1848. The inn, extended in 1859, became a private residence, and for over 50 years served as Drayton's post office. The vertical-slab kitchen is thought to be part of Will Horton's original inn. *Brisbane St, Drayton. Open Thurs.–Mon. ⓢ (07) 4630 1869. NT.*

ALSO OF INTEREST In a city of parks, Queens Park, Hume St, set aside as a

public garden in 1865, is one of the prettiest. The Italian Renaissance facade of the post office (1878), a dominant element in Margaret St, is complemented by the impressive courthouse (1870s), which stands adjacent. The town hall (1900), notable for its square clock tower and Dutch-gabled parapet, houses the Regional Art Gallery. *531 Ruthven St. Open Tues.–Sat. & Sun. afternoons. (07) 4688 6652.* Toowoomba has many fine private houses, for example Vacy Hall (1888), a handsome Victorian residence set in formal grounds, which is now a B&B. *135 Russell St. (07) 4639 2055.* Across the road, the distinguished Clifford House (1860) is now a restaurant. *120 Russell St.* Queensland's first brewery was established in Toowoomba in 1869 by Patrick Perkins. The 1870s malt house is an intriguing Victorian-era industrial building, although beer is no longer brewed there. *Not open for inspection (but can be seen from Mort St).*
[i] *Cnr James & Kitchener sts; (07) 4639 3797 or freecall 1800 331 155.* Website: www.toowoomba.qld.gov.au
See also Jondaryan, Warwick

TOWNSVILLE

Map ref. 369 P12

See Historic Highlights, p. 244

WARWICK

Map ref. 365 N11

Warwick was the first town on the rolling Darling Downs, established in the 1840s on the banks of the Condamine River. Its importance as a supply centre for the huge pastoral runs was overshadowed by the growth of other, more strategically placed towns, but Warwick possesses a remarkable collection of grand heritage buildings, hinting at its Victorian and Federation-era prosperity.

Pringle Cottage John McCulloch, a Scottish stonemason, erected this quaint stone building, reminiscent of a crofter's cottage, c. 1870s. A Mrs F Pringle and her daughter ran a school here from 1898–1905. The restored cottage is used as a folk and local museum. *81 Dragon St. Open Wed.–Sun. $ (07) 4661 2028.*

ALSO OF INTEREST Old St Mary's (1864), a modest, low, sandstone building, became a school when the imposing late Gothic Revival St Mary's Church, with its soaring tower, opened next door in 1926. *Palmerin St. Open daily.* The two-storey Italianate sandstone town hall, opened in 1888, is one of the grandest public buildings in regional Queensland. Other buildings of note are the prominent post office with arcaded verandahs (1898), cnr Palmerin & Grafton sts, and the monumental Masonic Lodge (1886), Guy St. *Not open for inspection.* An excellent heritage trail brochure is available.

IN THE AREA Talgai Homestead is a classic colonial sandstone residence of elegant proportions, built c. 1868 at the heart of a flourishing pastoral property. It is set in spacious grounds. *40 km N. Dalrymple Creek Rd, Allora. Heritage accommodation; afternoon teas & meals, booking essential. (07) 4666 3444.* It's worth exploring other towns in the area, such as Allora, Yangan and Stanthorpe – their histories reach back to Queensland's early colonial days.
[i] *49 Albion St; (07) 4661 3401.* Website: www.qldsoutherndowns.org.au
See also Toowoomba

Talgai Homestead, near Warwick

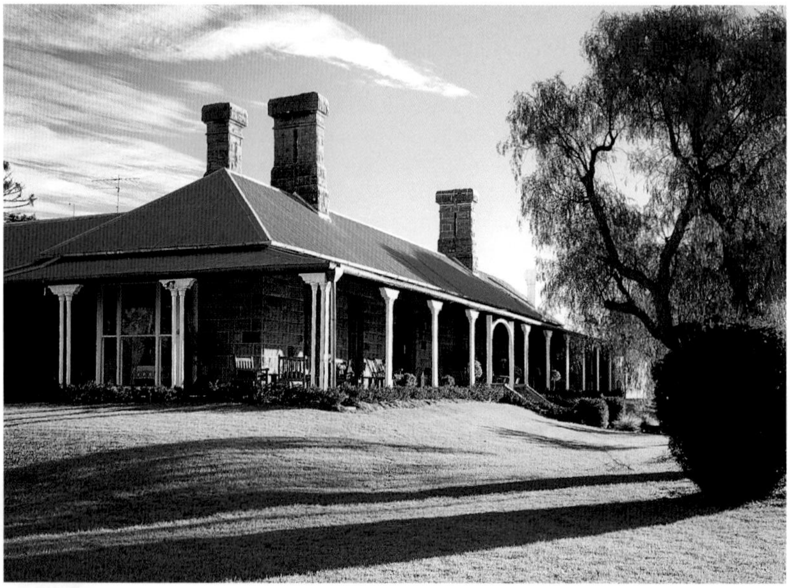

WINTON

Map ref. 373 M8

Winton, established in 1875, is surrounded by vast sheep and cattle stations. *Waltzing Matilda* was composed by Banjo Paterson on Dagworth Station near Winton in 1895 and reputedly sung at the North Gregory Hotel in town a few days later. Qantas had its beginnings here when the first meeting of directors took place in 1921. During the 1891 shearers' strike, one of the biggest and most bitter in Queensland's history, more than 500 striking shearers camped just south of town (*see* **Barcaldine**).

OF INTEREST The Waltzing Matilda Centre presents history and legend through interactive displays. Qantilda Pioneer Place, located at the Centre, highlights the region's past and its association with Qantas and also has Aboriginal artifacts. *Elderslie St. Open daily. $ (07) 4657 1466.* Corfield & Fitzmaurice, established as general merchants in Winton in 1878, are still in business; their stylish general store in the main street dates from 1916. Today the store features fossil displays, a dinosaur diorama and gemstones. *Elderslie St. Open Mon.–Fri. & Sat. mornings. (07) 4657 1486.* The Royal Theatre, opened 1918, is one of Australia's last two open-air picture theatres (the other is at **Broome, WA**). *Elderslie St. Open Wed. p.m. April–Nov. $ (07) 4657 1296.*

IN THE AREA Lark Quarry Conservation Park has footprints, estimated at 93 million years old, which record the world's only known dinosaur stampede. *111 km SW. (07) 4652 7333.*
[i] *Waltzing Matilda Centre, Elderslie St; (07) 4657 1466.* Website: www.outbackholidays.tq.com.au/winton.htm
See also Longreach

HISTORIC HIGHLIGHTS

Brennan & Geraghty's Store Museum, Maryborough

Since Queensland's earliest days, its regional towns have developed a certain self-sufficiency, isolated from the capital, Brisbane. Three of the highlight towns are ports, historically vital in the days when there were few roads in the State, and the fastest route was often by river or sea. In the 1800s, Maryborough, Rockhampton and Townsville all flourished as the ports for inland goldfields, and they have the fine heritage architecture to prove it. Charters Towers was itself a gold town. Today, a perfect time-capsule, its lovingly restored buildings are a reminder of a bygone era.

CHARTERS TOWERS

Charters Towers, in the State's far north, was Queensland's premier gold town, surrounded by the 'fabulously wealthy' Burdekin River flats. The first nuggets were found in 1871. By 1890 Charters Towers was a city of 30 000, 'superior in wealth and equal in commerce, culture and refinement to any city of the same population in Europe'. When gold yields finally dwindled after 1910, however, so too did the population. Today, Charters Towers once again benefits from gold mining, though it's also a busy service town for the surrounding cattle properties. Its heritage buildings are a vivid reminder of the great gold-rush days.

Charters Towers Visitor Information Centre
74 Mosman St
(07) 4752 0314
Website: www.charterstowers.qld.gov.au

City Hall
The Queensland National Bank built this grandiose bank for its gold-wealthy customers in 1891. It is now used as offices.
Cnr Gill & Mosman sts. Foyer open for inspection.

Stock Exchange, c. 1905

Stock Exchange Arcade
Built in 1878, the arcade became the pulse of Charters Towers when the stock exchange rented an office here in 1890. The exchange operated 24 hours a day, seven days a week. Distinctive features are the lofty, glazed roof and the vaulted canopy filled with richly coloured glass. It is now restored and used as a shopping arcade. The National Trust has an office, there's a cafe, art gallery, mining memorabilia and a museum.
76 Mosman St. Arcade, assay room & museum open daily. $\text{\textcircled{\$}}$
(07) 4787 2374. NT.

HISTORY

Three prospectors and a young Aboriginal boy, Jupiter, found gold in the district's hills on Christmas Day, 1871. Within a year the first gold battery could be heard thumping, and 28 others soon followed. As the alluvial gold yield fell in the 1880s, cyanide processing and diamond drilling were introduced – production more than doubled and the boom continued. Between 1872 and 1916, more than £25 million worth of ore was mined. On a tide of enthusiasm, grand Victorian buildings were erected and the local citizens proudly referred to their town as 'The World'. Gold production eventually fell and many people moved on.

Former Australian Bank of Commerce
A grand building (1891), with a robust, neo-Classical facade, built by the Australian Joint Stock Bank, which failed the following year. The elegant rooms now form part of the World Theatre complex. Tours daily.
Mosman St. Open daily. (07) 4787 8472.

Lyall's Jewellery Store
Lovely bowed windows add a touch of big city sophistication to this delightful, diminutive Victorian shop (c. 1889). David Lyall, a Scottish jeweller, who built the shop, sold fine jewel made in London from Charter Towers gold.
90 Mosman St. Not open for inspection.

Zara Clark Folk Museum

Last used by Bartlam's, general merchants, these 19th-century shop buildings feature showy pediments and bullnose verandah awnings. The folk museum is run by the National Trust.
Cnr Mosman & Mary sts. Open daily. Ⓢ
(08) 4787 4161. NT.

Boer War Veterans Memorial Kiosk

A charming late-Victorian rotunda, built in 1910 to honour the city's own regiment. Quaint ventilators punctuate the bell-cast roof. Lissner Park was established in 1891.
Lissner Park.

Civic Club

A gentlemen's club built in 1886, in the manner of a spacious Queensland residence, handsomely fitted out for genteel recreation. The interiors remain virtually unaltered. Visitors are welcome.
Ryan St. Open Mon.–Sat. (07) 4787 1096.

Ay-Ot Lookout

An elaborate two-storey residence (1886), Ay-Ot is well suited to the tropical climate with its timber fretwork bargeboards, latticework panels and deep verandahs. The house is furnished with period pieces.
Cnr Hodgkinson & High sts. Open Mon.–Fri. Ⓢ
(07) 4787 2799.

Post Office

The post office was built in 1892, although the four-storey clock tower which dominates the town's skyline was added in 1898.
Cnr Gill & Bow sts.

The Day Dawn Mining Co. Claim

In the Area

Venus Gold Battery, the first complete battery (1872) at Charters Towers, is an outstanding 19th-century industrial structure, which operated for 100 years. The huge old wooden leaching vats, part of the cyanide extraction works, are possibly the oldest relics. The battery has been restored to working order.
Millchester Rd, Millchester. Open daily. Tours twice a day. Ⓢ *(07) 4787 2222. NT.*
See also Ravenswood, Townsville

Pfeiffer House

German miner William Pfeiffer, who established the Day Dawn Mining Co., built this splendid timber mansion with more than 20 rooms in 1879, directly across the road from his mine. The restored house is now a Mormon chapel.
Paull St. Not open for inspection.

MARYBOROUGH

Maryborough, on the State's south-east coast, grew steadily from the 1840s, its early prosperity closely tied to the Mary River. The busy port handled cedar, pine and wool from the hinterland. Gold, discovered at Gympie in 1867, provided a further stimulus to growth. Sugarcane farms sprang up along the riverbanks, a sugar refinery and engineering works were set up. By the 1890s the town was well established. The wharves are now gone, but 19th-century civic buildings, leafy parks and a fascinating collection of Queensland-style timber houses provide the backdrop to Maryborough's life today as a busy regional centre.

Maryborough/Fraser Island Visitor Information Centre
BP South, Bruce Hwy
(07) 4121 4111
Website: www.maryborough.qld.gov.au

Post office, 1870s

Wharf Street Precinct
Although the wharves are long gone, some wonderful old buildings, such as the Italianate post office (1869), are a reminder of the city's 19th-century prosperity. The Maryborough Heritage Gateway Project incorporates the original Federation-style Customs House (1901) and Bond Store Museum in this precinct, and illustrates the importance of the port to development in the region.
Customs House, cnr Wharf & Richmond sts. Open daily. Ⓢ *(07) 4190 5800.*

Courthouse
Overlooking the leafy environs of Queens Park, a fine Italianate building with timber balustrading.
Richmond St. Not open for inspection.

Original Maryborough Site
From c. 1847–55, the town was located about 7 km upstream on the Mary River, but was relocated so that deep-water wharves could be built. Little evidence of the old town remains, but you can follow the heritage signs along the river to learn about Maryborough's beginnings.
Cnr Alice & Aldridge sts. Open at all times.

Rosehill Homestead & Tea Gardens
The homestead, overlooking the Mary River, was built of handmade bricks in 1859 for pioneer John Eaton.
30 Rosehill Rd, Tinana. Open Thurs.–Fri. & Sun. afternoons. Ⓢ *(07) 4122 1093.*

Maryborough Heritage Centre
During the Gympie gold rush, four million ounces of gold passed through Maryborough's three banks, including the former Bank of New South Wales (1878). It now houses genealogy and family history records.
Cnr Wharf & Richmond sts. Open Mon.–Fri. & Thurs. evenings. Ⓢ *(07) 4123 1620.*

CENTRAL
MARYBOROUGH
INSET MAP

Queens
Park   Rotunda

Post
Office

KENT

WHARF

ST

BAZAAR

Customs
House

Mary

River

RICHMOND

0   50 m

SCALE

ST

N

Bond Store Museum
The oldest wing of the bond store dates from 1864. The Port of Maryborough's excellent museum captures various aspects of the district's history. It includes information about the South Sea Islanders, known as Kanakas, who were brought into Australia to labour on the sugar plantations in the 1800s.
101 Wharf St. Open daily. Ⓢ
(07) 4190 5730.

JE Brown Warehouse
James Brown opened his Provisions and Victuals merchant business in 1857, and had this three-storey warehouse built in 1879. It was also used for dances, balls and boxing tournaments. It is now a restaurant.
Wharf St. (07) 4123 1000.

Time Cannon
A brass cannon, possibly used by the Dutch East India Company in the 17th century, and presented to the people of Maryborough, is on display in the Bond Store Museum. A replica of the cannon is fired at 1 p.m. every Thurs. – market day – and for special occasions.

Mortuary Chapel

The arched timber chapel, built 1883–84, was used as a shelter whilst mourners waited for the horse-drawn hearse to arrive. *Maryborough Cemetery.*

Maryborough Historical Society

The Society displays historic photographs and memorabilia in the impressive School of Arts building (1887). Note the keystone of Minerva, the Roman goddess of wisdom. *Kent St (opp. City Hall). Open Wed.–Fri. mornings. (07) 4122 2376.*

Queens Park

Established in the 1860s, this serene park is shaded by majestic overhanging trees. The band rotunda was imported from Glasgow and erected in 1890. The last Sunday of every month is 'Picnic in the Park' day with steam-train rides and brass bands playing in the rotunda. *Sussex St. Open daily. (07) 4123 8888.*

City Hall

The imposing red-brick town hall, funded by a local citizen, GA White, was built in 1908 to replace a more modest timber town hall. *388 Kent St. Open Mon.–Fri. (07) 4190 5800.*

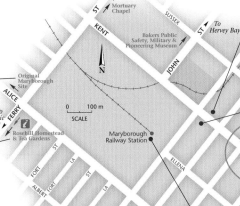

Railway Museum

A fully restored steam locomotive is at the heart of this small museum. The Victorian-era railway station dates from the 1870s. *Lennox St. Open by appt. (07) 4123 9261.*

One of Maryborough's 'Queenslanders'

Brennan & Geraghty's Store Museum

A true time capsule, this general store was run by the same family from 1871 to 1972 and has been preserved intact by the National Trust. Inside, shelves are stacked with old-fashioned provisions. *64 Lennox St. Open daily. $ (07) 4121 2250. NT.*

ALSO OF INTEREST

Maryborough has many fine examples of Queensland's unique traditional domestic architecture, which evolved in response to the tropical climate. Timber houses, many raised on stilts, shelter behind broad verandahs, often with intricate screens of timber fretwork and iron lacework. Bakers Public Safety, Military & Pioneering Museum houses a huge display from over 140 countries with thousands of exhibits, including military items from 1853. *20 Gallipoli St. Open Tues. & Fri.; also Mon., Thurs. & Sat. afternoons & pub hols. $ (donation). (07) 4122 4990.*

ROCKHAMPTON

Rockhampton is one of Queensland's largest cities, with a swag of outstanding 19th-century architectural gems strung along Quay Street, a legacy of its hectic era as a river port. The town was established in 1855 but became a major port when gold was discovered inland at nearby Cannona and later Mount Morgan. By the early 1900s, however, the railway had replaced the river in importance and commercial enterprise moved closer to the station. The imposing riverfront buildings were left to languish, but the rich countryside ensured Rockhampton's future – today the city is known as the 'beef cattle capital' of Australia.

Customs House, Quay Street, c. 1906

Rockhampton Visitor Information Centre
Customs House, 208 Quay St
(07) 4922 5339
Website: www.rockhampton.qld.gov.au

Archer Park Station & Steam Tram Museum

A small, quaint, timber building, the station (1899) has spandrels of iron lacework and a delicately glazed fanlight. Visitors can inspect the museum or ride the restored Purrey Steam Tram, made in France and believed to be one of only two of its kind left in the world.
Denison St. Open Tues.–Sun. $ *(07) 4922 2774.*

IN THE AREA

GLENMORE HOMESTEAD is an unusual complex comprising a rudimentary slab house (1858), originally a goldminers' inn; a rustic 1859 log cabin; and a stone and adobe-brick house built by a Mexican stonemason in 1862. Glenmore has been owned by the Birbeck family since 1861. Regular bush dances are held here.
8 km N, Belmont Rd, Parkhurst. Open Sun. $ *(07) 4936 1033.*

Off the Capricorn Hwy, 11 km SW, is **GRACEMERE HOMESTEAD**, a fine slab homestead, built in 1858 by Colin Archer (whose brothers discovered the Fitzroy River), and still owned by the Archers. One of Australia's biggest cattle auctions is held in the town of Gracemere every Mon. from 7.30 a.m. (open to public). *House not open for inspection.*

ROCKHAMPTON HERITAGE VILLAGE An outdoor museum with slab cottages, vintage machinery, horse-drawn coaches and vintage vehicles evoking days gone by. Every Sun. there are blacksmithing demonstrations, carriage rides and more.
11 km N, cnr Bruce Hwy & Boundary Rd, Parkhurst. Open daily. $ *(07) 4936 1026.*
See also Mount Morgan

Glenmore Homestead

Post Office

The exceptionally grand post office (1892) has deep arcades and a clock tower culminating in a highly decorative belfry.
Cnr East & Denham sts.

Wiseman's Cottage

A tiny, single-room cottage of rough, random rubble stone, all that remains of a 16-room house built in 1859 for William Wiseman, Commissioner of Crown Lands for the district. Wiseman chose the site for Rockhampton.
Laverack St. Not open for inspection.

Rockhampton Heritage Village

t Aubin's

his old-fashioned brick residence
vas probably built by a German
ettler named Rodekirchen in the
870s. It is surrounded by several
mall historic buildings, a fragrant
erb farm, small cottage shop and
working blacksmith's shop.
Canoona Rd. Open Mon., Wed.–Sun.
Ⓢ *(07) 4922 0302.*

Supreme Court

Tropical palms flank the
facade of the Classical pale
sandstone courthouse,
dating from 1887. The
wrought-iron gates are
especially fine. Now owned
by the Central Queensland
University.
*East St. Not open for
inspection.*

Criterion Hotel

The first hotel on this site was the Bush Inn,
built by Robert Parker in 1857. In 1889 his
daughter commissioned the grandiose,
three-storey, towered Criterion.
Cnr Quay & Fitzroy sts. (07) 4922 1225.

Quay Street

Quay St, overlooking the Fitzroy River, retains
one of the finest 19th-century commercial
streetscapes in Australia. More than 20
buildings, stretching from the Fitzroy Bridge
to Derby St, are outstanding. Pick up a
walking tour brochure from Visitor
Information.

Heritage Tavern

This was originally the Commercial
Hotel (1898). The lavish iron
lacework across the lengthy three-
storey facade is believed to have
been designed and cast locally.
*Cnr Quay & William sts. Open daily.
(07) 4927 6996.*

Customs House

One of Australia's most impressive customs
houses, this building is a testament to
Rockhampton's early importance as a port.
Started in 1898, it features a Corinthian
colonnade and a magnificent copper dome.
Visitor Information is located here.
208 Quay St. Open daily. (07) 4922 5339.

Botanic Gardens

Established in 1869, a haven of
luxuriant tropical growth, this is
renowned as one of the world's
finest subtropical botanic gardens.
*Spencer St. Open daily.
(07) 4922 1654.*

ALSO OF INTEREST

The gracious Borough Chambers, built in
1885, served as the town hall until 1919.
It is now home to the Rockhampton &
District Historical Society. *Stapleton Park,
North Rockhampton. Open Tues. & Thurs.
10 a.m.–2 p.m. or by appt.* Ⓢ *(07) 4927
8431.* Many of Rockhampton's historic
buildings were established with the
wealth generated by mining. Typical are
the old Harbour Board Building, Quay St
(not open for inspection) and in Bolsover
St, the decorative facade of Schotia
Place, built in 1888 as the City Markets.
Not open for inspection. Churches of
special interest include St Andrew's
Church (1893), cnr Bolsover & Derby sts,
St Paul's Cathedral (1879–83), cnr Alma
& William sts, and St Joseph's Cathedral
(1899), William St, with its distinctive
towering spires.

TOWNSVILLE

Townsville is Queensland's largest tropical city, with the massive bulk of craggy Castle Hill looming up behind and the sparkling blue waters of Cleveland Bay lapping its shores. The settlement began as a straggling line of bark huts and canvas tents, a port for pastoral lands. But wharves and wool stores were soon set up, and by 1866 the first town land sales had taken place. Pastoral stations gave birth to Townsville, but it was the lucrative goldfields of Ravenswood and Charters Towers that nurtured the town. In the 1880s, Townsville's harbour was enlarged and the railway was extended inland. Agriculture and industry expanded, and Townsville has continued to prosper.

Townsville Visitor Information Centre
303 Flinders Mall
(07) 4721 3660 or freecall 1800 801 902
Website: www.townsvilleonline.com.au

Hotels
Townsville possesses a generous selection of 19th-century hotels, almost all two-storey, often on a corner, shaded by verandahs. Tattersall's Hotel (1889), Wickham St, noted for its iron lacework; Lang's Hotel (1880s), Flinders St; the restored Shamrock Hotel (1889), Palmer St; and Townsville's oldest, the Exchange Hotel (1881), Flinders St, built for Andrew Ball, one of the men who chose the town site, are just a few examples.

The Shamrock Hotel

CENTRAL TOWNSVILLE
INSET MAP

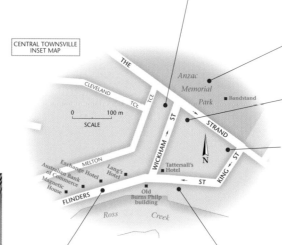

Flinders St Precinct
At 169 Flinders St, the grandiose former Australian Bank of Commerce (1888) with its richly decorated facade, is now a nightclub. The Old Burns Philp building (1895), at no. 108, now also a nightclub, was the headquarters of this trading company, established in Townsville in 1875 and now known throughout the South Pacific.

Customs House
Commanding a superb view of Cleveland Bay, this fine building (1900–02) features a distinctive curved portico, echoed by the lookout tower.
Cnr Wickham St & The Strand. Not open for inspection.

Customs House, c. 1902

Anzac Memorial Park & Bandstand
Anzac Park's distinctive and elegant bandstand (1913) is shaded by spreading fig trees – the first of them planted in the 1880s – and tall palms.
The Strand.

Criterion Hotel
Former stockman WA Ross, after whom Ross River and Ross Creek were named, opened the first Criterion Hotel on this site in 1865. The present pub, sheltered by a wide verandah, was built in 1904.
10 The Strand. (07) 4721 5777.

Museum of Tropical Queensland
At the heart of this spectacular new museum are the fascinating relics and history of the HMS *Pandora*, the British ship which was carrying mutineers from HMS *Bounty* back to England for trial in 1791 when it was wrecked on the Great Barrier Reef. Natural history displays and excellent exhibits focusing on Aboriginal and Torres Strait Islander cultures can also be viewed.
70–102 Flinders St East. Open daily. Ⓢ (07) 4726 0600.

Townsville Museum

One of Townsville's oldest public buildings, the rather severe former Magistrate's Courthouse (1877), now houses a collection highlighting the city's pioneer past.
Cnr Sturt & Stokes sts. Open Mon.–Fri. & Sun. Ⓢ *(07) 4772 5725.*

Army Museum

Townsville has a long military history and today has a substantial Army and RAAF presence. The city was a strategic base for Australian and US military during World War II and was bombed three times by Japanese aircraft.
Jezzine Barracks, Kissing Point, North Ward. Open Mon.–Fri. mornings; Sat.–Sun. & pub hols 10 a.m.–2 p.m. (07) 4777 1007.

Former Queen's Hotel

Once the largest hotel in Queensland and a popular meeting place for graziers visiting the port, this gracious red-brick building (1900–20) features deep, shaded arcades.
The Strand. Not open for inspection.

Maritime Museum

The former pier master's office moved to this site, and the 1866 Bay Rock lighthouse, which originally overlooked Cleveland Bay, are part of this maritime museum.
42–68 Palmer St. Open Mon.–Fri.; also Sat.–Sun. afternoons. Ⓢ *(07) 4721 5251.*

Sacred Heart Cathedral

A striking, red-brick Gothic-style cathedral (1902), built at the base of rocky Castle Hill, to replace a church destroyed by a cyclone in the 1890s.
266 Stanley St. Open daily.

Heritage Centre

A c. 1884 miner's cottage, an 1888 gentleman's villa, and a c. 1920 farmhouse, all moved to this site, demonstrate the housing styles that evolved to suit Queensland's tropical heat and lifestyle.
5 Castling St, West End. Open Wed. 10 a.m.– 2 p.m. & Sat.–Sun. afternoons. Closed Dec. & Jan. Ⓢ *(07) 4772 5195. NT.*

Victoria Bridge

One of only two such bridges in Australia, the steel swing bridge was constructed in 1889 by HC Royce of Rolls-Royce fame. The swing section allowed ships to pass.
Stokes St.

For more detail see inset map on facing page

ALSO OF INTEREST

The original tall clock tower of the old post office (1886) was considered a vulnerable target during World War II and was dismantled. The copper-domed tower dates from the 1960s. *Cnr Flinders & Denham sts. Not open for inspection.* Queens Park, Warburton St, one of the city's earliest parks, was the site of Townsville's first agricultural show in 1880. Adjacent is Queens Gardens, Paxton St, well endowed with exotic and native trees and established as the first botanic gardens in 1870. *Both open daily.*

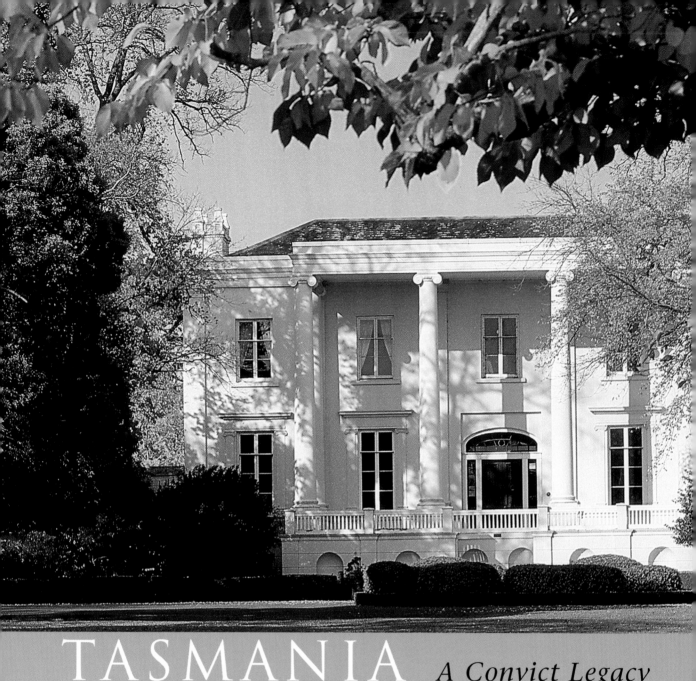

TASMANIA — *A Convict Legacy*

A legacy of fine colonial buildings, country mansions and quaint rural villages makes Tasmania a living museum of early Australian settlement. But what is picturesque and so well preserved today was built largely by the sweat of convict labour and at the expense of the Aboriginal Tasmanians, whose rich past is still evident in many places.

Clarendon House, Evandale

Discovered by the Dutch explorer Abel Janszoon Tasman in 1642, the island was left to its Aboriginal residents for a further 130 years before white settlement began. Tasman called it Van Diemen's Land in honour of the Governor-General of the Dutch East Indies, Anthony van Diemen, who commissioned his journey.

Towards the end of the eighteenth century both the French and English dropped anchor, but it was not until the voyage of Matthew Flinders and George Bass in 1798 that Van Diemen's Land was discovered to be an island. Finally, fearful that the French might take action, the British authorities claimed the island for the Crown.

HISTORIC HIGHLIGHTS

For a look around some of Tasmania's most interesting historic sites, see the pages listed below:

Launceston   Australia's third-oldest city, founded in 1805 and bearing many signs of its colonial beginnings. Grand Victorian buildings, including a splendid customs house, attest to Launceston's late 19th century importance as a major river port. *See p. 278*

Port Arthur   Port Arthur is a unique legacy of Tasmania's convict era. The haunting remains of the asylum, the Gothic-style church, guardhouse tower and more stand silently around the isolated bay. *See p. 280*

Richmond   A delightful village in the valley of the Coal River, declared a town in 1825. Its convict-built bridge is Australia's oldest remaining, and Richmond boasts many fine early colonial buildings. *See p. 282*

FIRST SETTLEMENT

The first white settlers arrived in 1803 and made their base at Risdon Cove on the Derwent estuary, although the site was abandoned five months later in favour of the site where Hobart now stands.

Van Diemen's Land was seen primarily by the British government as a dumping ground for prisoners and in the first 50 years of settlement, it became the repository for 74 000 convicts. Many of them were first offenders and were given reasonably responsible jobs.

Under Governor Lachlan Macquarie's policy, convicts could become emancipated – admitted back into society and granted privileges like free settlers. These emancipists played an important role in establishing the colony.

Recalcitrant convicts and further offenders were isolated in penal stations, such as those at Macquarie Harbour and Maria Island, and later the infamous Port Arthur.

EXPLORATION

As exploration into the hinterland proceeded, the colony attracted many free settlers to its rich agricultural lands and so

Maria Island

TIMELINE

1642   Dutch sailor Abel Tasman discovers part of Tasmania, which he names Van Diemen's Land.

1803–4 The British start a settlement at Risdon Cove. Aborigines approach and are fired on – 50 are killed, and the colony's 'Black War' begins. The settlement is moved and Hobart Town established.

1853   The last convicts are transported to the colony.

1856   The name Tasmania is officially adopted for the colony.

1871   One of the world's richest tin deposits is discovered at Mt Bischoff.

1876   Truganini, the last full-blooded Aboriginal Tasmanian, dies.

1877   Port Arthur Gaol is closed.

1895   Tasmania is the first colony to introduce hydro-electricity, harnessing water to produce electricity for Launceston.

1901   The Commonwealth of Australia is declared, with Tasmania one of the six new States.

began to prosper and develop. Exploiting the vast natural resources of stone and timber and the equally vast resource of convict labour, pockets of the Tasmanian countryside quickly began to resemble the settlers' English homeland, with comforting Georgian houses, stone churches, intricate bridges and miles and miles of hawthorn hedges.

THE TRADITIONAL OWNERS

The Aboriginal Tasmanians, who had lived on the island for more than 20 000 years, lost all their land within 30 years. The 200 or so survivors of European disease and decades of war with the settlers were shipped to Flinders Island in the 1830s. By 1847, they were no longer considered a threat and the 47 remaining were allowed back to mainland Tasmania, to a settlement at Oyster Cove.

SELF-GOVERNMENT

Separation from New South Wales was granted in 1825, and the transportation of convicts ceased in 1853. By 1856 the colony had been granted responsible government and became known officially as Tasmania.

Hobart, 1880s

Government House

HOBART *Historic Seaport*

VISITOR INFORMATION

TASMANIAN TRAVEL & INFORMATION CENTRE
Cnr Elizabeth & Davey sts
Hobart, TAS 7000
(03) 6230 8233
www.discovertasmania.com.au

NATIONAL TRUST OF AUSTRALIA
(TASMANIA)
413 Hobart Rd
Franklin Village, TAS 7249
(03) 6344 6233
www.tased.edu.au/tasonline/nattrust/

Tasmania's capital was originally intended to be at Risdon Cove, about 8 kilometres further up the Derwent River from where Hobart now stands. A British settlement was founded there in 1803, but due to the lack of fresh water it was soon abandoned in favour of Sullivans Cove. The new settlement was named after Lord Hobart, the Secretary of State for the Colonies.

Indeed, it was not a bad choice on the part of Lieutenant-Colonel David Collins and his party of 300, who arrived on 21 February 1804, for Hobart's fortunes have centred ever since on the Derwent estuary, one of the world's finest deep-water harbours.

Hobart's first few years were slow, and when Governor Lachlan Macquarie arrived in 1811 he was unimpressed by the straggle of makeshift huts and general disorder. He issued instructions for the town to be surveyed and initiated building regulations, as he had done in Sydney. The plan of the city centre today remains much as it was when the streets were laid out at Macquarie's request.

Begun as a port for landing free settlers, convicts and supplies, Hobart soon became a base for South Seas whalers. By 1827 the population had reached 5000, and the following decades saw the port develop as a major ship-building centre for the colonies. The heart of this activity was Battery Point, so called because of the gun emplacements installed to defend the town against the French. The district gained an abundance of port pubs, ships' chandlers and a colourful reputation.

As the colony began to grow, so too did Hobart, becoming a busy seaport for the export of wool, wheat and corn. Other industries emerged, and grand Victorian buildings took their place alongside the city's impressive colonial architecture.

Hobart is Australia's second oldest city and retains more of its historic heritage than any other capital. This owes something, no doubt, to the fact that it has not developed as rapidly as the mainland capitals. But it is also because care has been taken to preserve historic buildings. Many of Hobart's CBD buildings are classified by the National Trust – 60 in Davey and Macquarie streets alone. Much of the architecture, both public and residential, is in the simple Georgian style, with brick and sandstone the favoured materials. It is Hobart's special charm to offer history not merely on every corner but in whole blocks of city and residential streets, which – but for obvious modern touches – remain much as they were in the nineteenth century.

Though now a city of some 220 000 inhabitants and sprawling along both banks of the Derwent, reaching to the base of Mt Wellington, Hobart's fascinating colonial past is still within reach.

FIVE TOP SIGHTS

Cascade Brewery *p. 256*
Narryna Heritage Museum *p. 258*
Runnymede *p. 257*
Salamanca Place *p. 254*
Tasmanian Museum & Art Gallery *p. 255*

Theatre Royal

Allport Library & Museum of Fine Arts

INNER HOBART

Allport Library & Museum of Fine Arts
See State Library of Tasmania

1 Anglesea Barracks & Military Museum of Tasmania
Building began in 1814 on what is now the oldest military establishment in Australia still used by the Army. Two impressive bronze cannons dating from some time before 1774 are mounted in the grounds. One theory has it that they were souvenired from the brig HMS *Sirius* by a detachment of the 73rd Regiment, which served in Hobart from 1810–14. The Barracks also contains the original officers' quarters and mess, the old drill hall, and gaol.
Davey St, City. Open Tues. for guided tours at 11 a.m. & by appt. $ *(03) 6237 7160.*

2 Battery Point
See p. 258

3 Government House
Built of sandstone in the Gothic Revival style in 1855–58, this is considered by many to be the most splendid building in Tasmania, described by English novelist Anthony Trollope in the 1800s as 'the best belonging to any British colony . . . it lacks nothing necessary for a perfect English residence'.
Lower Domain Rd, City. Gardens & main house open once a year. (03) 6234 2611.

4 Hobart Rivulet
Running from Mt Wellington to the River Derwent, this constant supply of fresh water was the reason Lt-Gov. David Collins chose Sullivans Cove for his new settlement in 1804. However, it quickly turned into an open sewer, due in part to its over-use by flour mills and other light industries of the time. Its proximity to the hospital, whose staff is said to have dumped body parts directly into the rivulet, did not help. The original water supply for the **Cascade Brewery** and **Female Factory**, it now runs under the city. Weekly tours take participants beneath the CBD, where a fascinating aspect of Hobart's history is revealed.
Hobart Rivulet Tours, cnr Elizabeth & Davey sts, City. $ *(03) 6238 2711.*

5 Hydro-Electric Headquarters
The 1938 design brief for the new Hydro-Electric Commission headquarters asked for a building that 'expressed electricity'. The Art Deco edifice has illumination praised at the time as the 'finest in Australia, probably not equalled in the world'. The building is now the administrative centre of the Hobart City Council.
Cnr Elizabeth & Davey sts, City. Not open for inspection.

6 *Lady Nelson* replica
This full-sized replica of the *Lady Nelson* was built in Woodbridge, near Hobart, in 1988 and is used for sail training, charters and historical re-enactments. The original brig, built in 1799, was involved in Tasmania's first three white settlements – Risdon Cove in 1803, George Town on the Tamar River in 1804, and Sullivans Cove (now Hobart) also in 1804. It was also among the vessels sent to Victoria to retrieve Lt-Gov. Collins and the other settlers from the failed settlement of Sorrento. In 1811 the *Lady Nelson* conveyed Gov. Macquarie on his tour of the State.
Elizabeth St Pier, City. Office open Mon.–Fri. $ *(03) 6234 3348.*

7 Maritime Museum of Tasmania
The museum brings to life Tasmania's rich maritime history, with displays of pictures and equipment from the whaling era, models of various ships, and relics from sunken

Lady Nelson replica

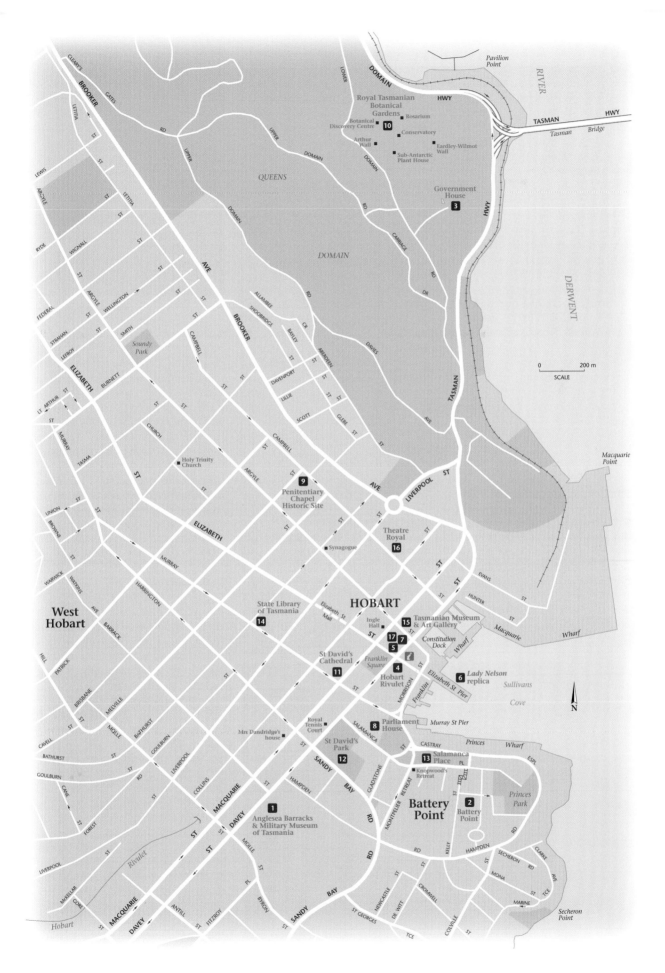

River

Pavilion
Point

TASMAN

DOMAIN

HWY

RIVER

TASMAN HWY

Tasman
Bridge

Royal Tasmanian
Botanical
Gardens

Botanical
Discovery Centre **10** Rosarium

Conservatory

Arthur
Wall

Eardley-Wilmot
Wall

Sub-Antarctic
Plant House

QUEENS

DOMAIN

Government
House **3**

DERWENT

SCALE

0   200 m

Macquarie
Point

Soundy
Park

Holy Trinity
Church

Penitentiary
Chapel
Historic Site **9**

Theatre
Royal **16**

Synagogue

HOBART

West
Hobart

State Library
of Tasmania **14**

Ingle
Hall

Tasmanian Museum
& Art Gallery **15**

17 7

Constitution
Dock

Macquarie   Wharf

St David's
Cathedral **11**

Franklin
Square **4**

Hobart
Rivulet

5

6 Lady Nelson
replica

Sullivans
Cove

Elizabeth St Pier

Mrs Dandridge's
house

Royal
Tennis
Court

Parliament
House **8**

Murray St Pier

N

St David's
Park **12**

Salamanca **13**
Place

Knopwood's
Retreat

Princes   Wharf

Castray

1

Anglesea Barracks
& Military Museum
of Tasmania

Battery
Point

2
Battery
Point

Princes
Park

Rivulet

Hobart

Secheron
Point

vessels. It is housed adjacent to historic Constitution Dock in the impressive neo-Classical Carnegie Building, constructed in the early 20th century as the Tasmanian Public Library.

Cnr Argyle & Davey sts, City. Open daily. Guided tours of museum and port area Mon., Wed., Fri. at 11 a.m. Ⓢ *(03) 6234 1427.*

8 Parliament House

The seat of government in Tasmania has seen many alterations and additions since it was built by convicts between 1835 and 1840 as Hobart's first customs house and bond store. Constructed of stone quarried from what is now a lake in the grounds of **Government House**, to a design by John Lee Archer, it was converted to Parliament House when the colony became self governing in 1856. Amid all the changes, the tiny Legislative Council Chamber has remained exactly as it was, dominated by a massive portrait of a young Queen Victoria.

Murray St, adjacent to Salamanca Pl., City. Visitors gallery open on sitting days. Tours by appt. 1300 135 513.

9 Penitentiary Chapel Historic Site

Designed by John Lee Archer in 1831 as a chapel for the adjacent Prisoners' Barracks (which were demolished in 1966), it is one of the few examples of Georgian ecclesiastical architecture in the Commonwealth. Two wings of the building were converted

for criminal courts in 1860. The chapel continued in use until 1961 while the courts were used until 1983. There are underground passages, solitary cells and an execution yard. It is now the Hobart office of the National Trust.

Cnr Brisbane & Campbell sts, City. Open daily. Ⓢ *Day tours (03) 6231 0911. Ghost tours 0417 361 392. NT.*

10 Royal Tasmanian Botanical Gardens

The development of these beautiful gardens, spread over 13.5 ha in the Queens Domain, goes back to 1818. The 280 m Eardley-Wilmot Wall between the gardens and **Government House** is said to be the longest convict-built wall in Australia still standing. Another brick wall, the Arthur Wall, built at Gov. Arthur's behest in 1829, can be heated from internally situated fireplaces to help the growth of exotics. Buildings include a conservatory, a rosarium, the Botanical Discovery Centre and the Sub-Antarctic Plant House. Tours available.

Queens Domain, City. Open daily. Ⓢ *for Conservatory & Botanical Discovery Centre. (03) 6234 6299.*

11 St David's Cathedral

This sandstone church, built in the Gothic Revival style (1868), boasts several treasures. The altar vessels include five solid silver pieces presented by King George III in 1803 for the new settlement, and there is a collection of stones from many

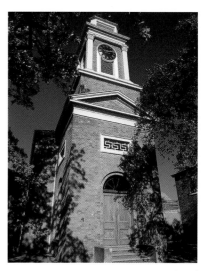

Penitentiary Chapel

well-known English abbeys and cathedrals. The organ, comprising 3000 pipes, is considered one of the finest in Australia. It was installed in Old St David's in 1858, replacing a 1823 organ, which is still used in St Matthew's Church, **Rokeby**, on Hobart's Eastern Shore. Architecturally, St David's is particularly noted for its carved oak screen and magnificent stained-glass windows, including the famous East Window, above the high altar, best seen in the early morning or evening light.

125 Macquarie St, City. Open daily. (03) 6234 4900.

12 St David's Park

The tombs and monuments to one side of this pleasant inner city park are a reminder that it started off as Hobart's first cemetery. Gravestones date from 1804. Particularly interesting are the graves of mariner Capt. James Kelly, after whom Kelly Steps, linking Salamanca Place and Battery Point, is named, and those of two Lieutenant-Governors, Collins and Eardley-Wilmot.

Cnr Davey St & Sandy Bay Rd, City.

13 Salamanca Place

The sandstone buildings along the waterfront in Salamanca Place are the finest early warehouses in Australia, remaining almost as they were when built between 1835 and 1860. The area was an international whaling centre in the 1850s and 1860s, later servicing cargo ships carrying Tasmanian apples to Europe, Japanese and other international fishing boats,

Parliament House

as well as visiting naval vessels, among others. While the whole waterfront area has been restored and the warehouses now house art and craft galleries, bookshops, restaurants, cafes and theatres, the adjacent docks continue to supply both visiting and home-port vessels, including Australia's Antarctic ships. Knopwood's Retreat, named after the original owner of the land and Van Diemen's Land's first parson, Rev. 'Bobby' Knopwood, was the first public house in Salamanca, originally trading under the name Whalers Return. A brass plate, about 2 m from the building's north-west corner, marks the original high-water mark. There is a large outdoor market at Salamanca Place on Saturday mornings.

Salamanca Place

14 State Library of Tasmania

The State Library's Heritage Collections include many treasures for both browsers and researchers. The Allport Library and Museum of Fine Arts contains one of Australia's best collections of colonial art, English antique furniture, decorative arts and rare books. The WL Crowther Library has rich collections on many subjects (especially whaling and medical history) as well as some fine colonial works of art. The Tasmaniana Library is the premier collection of published material relating to Tasmania.
91 Murray St (cnr Bathurst St). Open Mon.–Fri., & last Sat. each month. Tours by appt. (03) 6233 7511.

Soldier's coat, Tasmanian Museum & Art Gallery

15 Tasmanian Museum & Art Gallery

A section of this building is itself a museum piece, since it includes Hobart's oldest structure – the 1808 Commissariat building. The complex also includes the Private Secretary's Residence, the convict-built Bond Store, and the waterfront Customs House (1902), a heavily embellished late-Victorian Classical building. The art gallery has a fine collection of colonial art, watercolours and prints, including the works of John Glover and Benjamin Duterrau. The museum collection includes Aboriginal artifacts and convict relics, as well as intriguing whaling and shipping displays.
40 Macquarie St, City. Open daily. Guided tours Wed.–Sun. Ⓢ (for selected exhibitions). (03) 6235 0777.

16 Theatre Royal

A thousand people attended the laying of the foundation stone in 1834, every ship in the harbour showed its colours, and 'those suitably equipped fired away all afternoon'. This small theatre, opened in 1837, is renowned worldwide for its beautiful interior and is the oldest theatre in Australia still in use. Lord Olivier called it 'the best little theatre in the world' and Dame Sybil Thorndike also praised it highly. The theatre was devastated by fire in 1984, but has been restored to its former glory.
29 Campbell St, City. Open Mon.–Sat. Tours by appt. Ⓢ (03) 6233 2026.

17 Town Hall

Henry Hunter, Tasmania's most prolific architect in the Victorian style, designed this Classical Revival building, with many Italianate flourishes, in 1864. It stands on the site where David Collins pitched the first marquee on 21 February 1804 after moving the settlement across the River Derwent from Risdon Cove.
Cnr Macquarie & Elizabeth sts, City. Upstairs rooms usually open business hours (free). Tours Tues. afternoons & Thurs. mornings. Ⓢ (03) 6238 2711.

Also of interest

Holy Trinity Church, 17 Church St, North Hobart, has Australia's oldest peal of bells, first rung in 1847 to usher in Regatta Day and still rung annually on that occasion. *17 Church St, North Hobart. Key from rectory next door. (03) 6234 6535.* Hobart's Synagogue (1843), built in the Egyptian style, is the oldest in the country. *59 Argyle St, City. Inspection by appt. (03) 6234 4720.* Ingle Hall (1814) in Macquarie St is one of Australia's oldest buildings. It now houses the Mercury Print Museum. *89 Macquarie St, City. Open Mon.–Fri. Ⓢ (03) 6230 0623.* Truganini spent the last years of her life at Mrs Dandridge's house. *167 Macquarie St, City. Not open for inspection.* The Royal Tennis Court was built in 1875 in an 1831 brewery complex. It is still in use and visitors are welcome to watch. *45 Davey St, City. Open daily. (03) 6231 1781.*

Cascade Brewery, South Hobart

AROUND HOBART

1 Austins Ferry
Map ref. 379 L8

An early commercial River Derwent crossing, used among others by Gov. Macquarie during his 1821 journey through the Midlands. Austins Ferry is also the site of Australia's oldest Congregational church, Hestercombe Chapel. Built in 1833 by wealthy Hobart merchant Henry Hopkins, the church is tiny but charming, with a fireplace (still used on wintry Sundays), a doll-like organ and rings on the back wall for securing horses. The cemetery has many graves of convicts who died building nearby **Bridgewater** Causeway. *Open by appt. (03) 6249 1014.* The freestone Black Snake Inn (1833) was also built by convicts. Its licence lapsed in 1860. *Not open for inspection.*

2 Cascade Brewery
Map ref. 376 D9

Hop vines were brought to Hobart as early as 1822, and the cultivation of hops and brewing have been two of Tasmania's important industries. Cascade is synonymous with commercial brewing in Tasmania, and the

Cascade Company is the second oldest public company still in existence in Australia. The brewery was established in 1824 by Peter Degraves, the stone building erected c. 1832 and extended in 1927. The Cascade Museum traces the history of brewing in the State.
140 Cascade Rd, South Hobart. Tours Mon.–Fri. at 9.30 a.m. & 1.00 p.m. Booking essential. $ *(03) 6221 8300 or (03) 6235 4353.*

3 Female Factory Site
Map ref. 376 E9

The women's prison, or Female Factory, which housed female convicts transported to Van Diemen's Land from 1828 until its closure in 1877, is the site of a major conservation and archaeological program. This was the female equivalent of Port Arthur. Most of the women were poor, young and single, transported for petty crime. Children of the prisoners were also kept there, and suffered a high death rate. All profits from a modern fudge factory on site go towards the conservation works.

16 Degraves St, South Hobart. Open Mon.–Fri. Tours at 10.30 a.m. $ *(03) 6223 3233.*

4 Lady Franklin Gallery
Map ref. 376 D7

Australia's first public museum, styled like a Greek temple, was intended to bring an appreciation of the classical arts to the culturally deprived colonials. It was built in 1842 at the initiative of Lady Jane Franklin, the wife of the governor, who did much to redress the poor social conditions and lack of educational opportunities she found in the colony. Unfortunately, the completion of this particular project coincided with her departure. The building was neglected, and the valuable collection of books, works of art and statues was dispersed. It was used for many years as a fruit warehouse. Restored, it is now a gallery and headquarters of the Art Society of Tasmania.
268 Lenah Valley Rd, Lenah Valley. Open Sat. & Sun. afternoons. (03) 6228 0076.

5 Mount Nelson Signal Station
Map ref. 376 G12

In 1811 Mt Nelson, with its expansive views of the River Derwent and D'Entrecasteaux Channel, was chosen by Gov. Macquarie as the site for a signal station to inform Hobart Town of ships entering the river. In 1836, it became a part of the complex semaphore system of communications between Hobart and Port Arthur. It took two minutes for news of a convict escape to reach Hobart. Mt Nelson continued as a base for shipping communications, using Hobart's first telephone service and then radio, until 1969. The original signal station and mast have been restored and the 1897 signalman's quarters is now a restaurant.
700 Nelson Rd, Mount Nelson. Open daily. (03) 6223 3407.

Female Factory Site, South Hobart

6 New Town

Map ref. 376 E7

One of the first villages to grow up around Hobart, New Town is now an inner suburb. It contains a number of buildings of historic interest, including two notable churches. The former Congregational (now Uniting) Church was designed by James Blackburn in the Romanesque Revival style and built in 1842. *New Town Rd. Open by appt. (03) 6228 1068 or (03) 6228 6643.* The Gothic Revival St John's Church, built by convicts in 1835, was designed by John Lee Archer. *St John's Ave. Open daily. (03) 6228 1131.* Next door to the Congregational Church is Mr Galloway's Cottage, where bushranger Martin Cash in his later years dictated the entertaining account of his exploits. *Not open for inspection. See also Runnymede*

7 Risdon Cove Historic Site

Map ref. 376 G3

Now owned by the Aboriginal community, this is the site of Tasmania's first European settlement in September 1803, and the colony's intended capital. Soon after arrival, the English massacred a group of Aboriginal men, women and children who came running towards the camp while chasing kangaroos. Lt-Gov. David Collins arrived several months later from Victoria and insisted on moving the settlement to Sullivans Cove, now Hobart. As such, it is the only site for an Australian capital remaining in anything like its original form. Excavations have turned up some of the original buildings, including the store (Tasmania's oldest stone building) and several huts. Some have been rebuilt. *Bowen Park, East Derwent Hwy, Risdon. Open daily.*

8 Runnymede

Map ref. 376 F6

This single-storey Georgian stone villa was built c. 1836 for Robert Pitcairn, the first lawyer to qualify in Tasmania and a leading advocate of the abolition of transportation. In 1850 the house passed to Francis Nixon, the colony's first Anglican bishop, who sold it c. 1864 to Capt. Charles Bayley. Bayley renamed the house Runnymede, after his favourite ship, and it remained in his family until 1967. It has been restored and furnished as an example of an 1860s mansion; each previous owner is remembered in a 'memorial room'. *61 Bay Rd, New Town. Open daily, closed July. $ (03) 6278 1269. NT.*

9 Shot Tower

Map ref. 379 L9

An outstanding example of its kind, this 48-m high tower was designed, engineered and built (with the help of two stonemasons) by Joseph Moir in just nine months. It was completed in 1870 and in operation until 1904. All grades of shot were produced, from fine dustshot to buckshot, the secrets of which Moir had to set about learning once he had mastered the construction of the tower. Apart from the tower, which can be climbed, there is a tearoom and an adjoining museum. *Channel Hwy, Taroona. Open daily. $ (03) 6227 8885.*

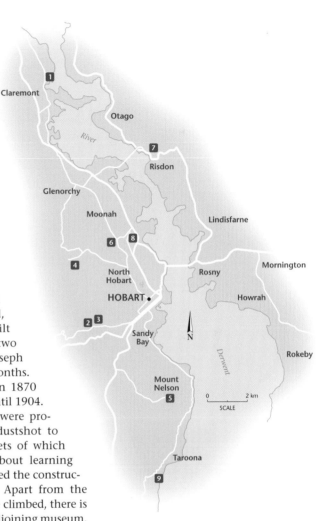

The library at Runnymede, New Town

A WALK AROUND BATTERY POINT

Considered to be Australia's most complete colonial village, Battery Point has changed little since the 1830s and 1840s, when it was settled by fishermen and seafarers. With its dramatic glimpses of sea and mountain, narrow, hilly streets, corner pubs and quaint cottages, the modern-day visitor will find much to enjoy here.

Montpelier Retreat (Battery Point)
by Harry Buckie, 1950

HISTORY

Named after the battery of guns established here in 1818, Battery Point was first settled by early Hobart identity, Rev. 'Bobby' Knopwood, who was granted 12 ha of land bordering Sullivans Cove. He began selling off parcels of land in 1816 when he ran into financial troubles. The area began to transform from farmland to residential in the 1830s. The grand houses Stowell and Secheron date from 1831, while Narryna (now a museum) was built in 1833–36. With Sullivans Cove on one side and ship yards on another, Battery Point evolved into a mariners' village. Residents of 1852 included master mariners and mariners, merchants, shipwrights, coopers, boat builders, boatmen, seamen, fishermen and the harbour master. It is this Battery Point which has been preserved so well.

Kelly Steps
Built in 1839 on land owned by Capt. James Kelly, famous for his 1815–16 voyage around Tasmania in a whale boat, the steps were a convenient link between residential Battery Point and the wharf area. *Between Kelly St & Salamanca Pl.*

Arthur Circus
A rare example of an authentic Georgian streetscape, Arthur Circus is a circle of 16 cottages (1847–52) built around a village green. The cottages are privately owned. *Off Runnymede St.*

Narryna Heritage Museum
Built in 1833–36 this substantial sandstone Georgian residence retains all its original features. Narryna has been furnished to reflect the lifestyle of early settlers. Of special interest are the Huon pine bedroom and the outbuildings, with their fine collection of vehicles and tools.
103 Hampden Rd. Open daily Mon.–Fri., & Sat.–Sun. afternoons. Ⓢ *(03) 6234 2791.*

St George's Anglican Church
Australia's finest Classical Revival church. Built by two noted Colonial Architects – the body in 1836–38 by John Lee Archer, and the spire, in 1847, by James Blackburn. The portico was added in 1888.
28 Cromwell St. Open daily. (03) 6223 3393.

Lenna
An elaborate Italianate mansion (1874–80).
Once a private residence, now an elegant hotel
and restaurant.
20 Runnymede St. Open daily. (03) 6232 3900.

Signal Station
The village's oldest surviving building, dating
from 1818. Built to accompany the original
battery of guns, it was later used as a signal
station, part of the communications system
between Hobart and Port Arthur.
Princes Park. Not open for inspection.

Andrew Inglis Clark

Rosebank
Designed in 1870 by Andrew Inglis
Clark, Supreme Court judge and
an author of the Australian
Constitution. Said to have housed
one of Australia's finest private
libraries, which was donated to the
University of Tasmania, where
Clark served as vice-chancellor.
*11 Hampden Rd. Not open for
inspection.*

Victorian Town Houses
Lovely examples of red-brick houses built
cheaply around 1850 to pattern designs.
The worn front steps in the Colville St
house are most likely the result of
overzealous cleaning with pumice stone.
*Cnr Colville & Sloane sts and 48 & 50
Hampden Rd. Not open for inspection.*

Secheron
Built by the Surveyor-General of Van
Diemen's Land, George Frankland, in 1831.
It was sold in 1838 to John Cameron who
gave it to his niece as a wedding present.
Secheron was a maritime museum for some
time, but is again privately owned.
21 Secheron Rd. Not open for inspection.

Historic re-enactments recall
a bygone era

Shipwright's Arms Hotel
Built in 1843 and licensed in 1846, the hotel
is one of the few to trade continuously under
the same name and in the same premises.
It has a fine display of photographs of vessels
that have sailed on the Derwent.
*29 Trumpeter St. Open daily.
(03) 6223 5551.*

Mr Watson's Cottages
6–12 Napoleon St are simple Georgian houses
built (c. 1850) by shipbuilder John Watson. His
whaling captain brother lived in one. Opposite
is the Star of Tasmania, a hotel from 1850–60.
*Cnr Napoleon & Trumpeter sts.
Not open for inspection.*

Mariners Cottages
Two cottages (c. 1840) thought
to have been once owned by
master mariner James Kelly and
subsequently by shipbuilder John
Watson, who owned one of the
adjacent slipways. Extensively
restored.
*42 & 44 Napoleon St. Open for
special NT events. (03) 6223 5200.*

ALSO OF INTEREST
The National Trust conducts walking
tours of Battery Point on Sat. mornings,
leaving from the Wishing Well in
Franklin Square, Macquarie St. Ⓢ
(03) 6223 7570.

TASMANIA FROM A TO Z

Grubb Shaft Gold & Heritage Museum, Beaconsfield

AVOCA
Map ref. 379 N1, 381 O11

On the junction of the South Esk and St Pauls rivers, Avoca is a small town at the centre of an extensive farming district. Settlers who took up land grants here in the 1820s included Simeon Lord, a former convict who rose to become one of Sydney's richest men.

Bona Vista The home built in 1848 by Simeon Lord's son, also Simeon, is considered one of Tasmania's most attractive colonial houses. Built like a fortress around a courtyard, it was nevertheless robbed by bushrangers Dalton and Kelly, who, after shooting a constable, used Lord's carriage to carry away his silver. *Rossarden Rd. Not open for inspection.*

St Thomas' Anglican Church This local landmark (1842), built of freestone in the Romanesque Revival style, is attributed to Colonial Architect James Blackburn, who was transported to Tasmania in 1833. The sandstone was quarried on the Bona Vista estate. *Main St. (See notice on door for opening details.)*

ALSO OF INTEREST The Parish Hall, built from local stone in 1850 as a storehouse, was given to the church in 1937. It is now the post office. *Cnr Blenheim St & Esk Main Rd. Open during office hours.* Blenheim Hall, known also as Marlborough House, was also built in 1850. It was originally meant to be a hotel but it was thought to be too close to the church so instead became a boys' grammar school in 1856. Now a private house. *Blenheim St. Not open for inspection.*

🛈 *Avoca Roadhouse, 4 Falmouth St; (03) 6384 2157.*

BEACONSFIELD

Map ref. 381 K7

First settled in the 1860s, Beaconsfield quickly developed into a rich mining area, with an iron smelter operating here in the 1870s. With the discovery of gold in 1877, it temporarily became Tasmania's third biggest town. The Tasmania Gold Mine yielded more than 26 tonnes of gold from the Tasman Reef before water seepage caused it to close in 1914. The mine was reopened in 1980.

Grubb Shaft Gold & Heritage Museum The museum is housed in the restored Grubb Shaft building, built in 1905, with magnificent Romanesque arches, to house steam-driven winding equipment for the mine. Similarly magnificent buildings were constructed to house the pump engines and other mine equipment and offices – most have been at least partially restored. Other exhibits relate to goldfields life, early telecommunications and the apple industry. Across the road is a replica of a miner's hut and a school of 100 years ago, moved here from Flowery Gully. *West St. Open daily.* $ *(03) 6383 1473.*

York Town Nothing but a plaque on the road off the West Tamar Hwy 10 km N marks the site of the 1804 European settlement of northern Tasmania. Water shortages and other difficulties forced settlers back across the Tamar River to found what is now **George Town** in 1807.

ALSO OF INTEREST The old weatherboard post office (1875) is now a newsagency. *Cnr West & Weld sts.* One of Tasmania's earliest picture theatres, Alicia Hall (c. 1901), is now a charity shop. *Weld St.*

[i] *Cnr Main & Winkleigh rds, Exeter; (03) 6394 4454.* Website: www.wtc.tas.gov.au

BOTHWELL

Map ref. 379 K5

At the southern gateway to the rugged Central Highlands lies the quiet rural township of Bothwell, classified on the National Estate Register as an historic town. The Scottish name Bothwell was bestowed by Gov. George Arthur in 1824 after Mary Queen of Scots' last husband, the Earl of Bothwell. Settlement began in 1821, with its lovely wide streets laid out within four years. Some of the Scottish settlers brought golf clubs with them, and the first golf game in Australia was played in 1830 at nearby Ratho. Bothwell has more than 50 heritage-listed buildings.

Australasian Golf Museum The museum, in a Gothic Revival sandstone schoolhouse, is an annexe of the Tasmanian Museum and Art Gallery in Hobart. It has Australia's only display of golfing memorabilia, of local, national and international significance. *Market Pl. Open daily.* $ *(03) 6259 4033.*

Bothwell Grange Built in 1836 as a country pub and horse exchange for the highlands, the Grange is now a guesthouse. *Alexander St. Open daily. (03) 6259 5556.*

Castle Hotel A good example of early hotel architecture in the colony. The oldest section dates from 1829, while the single-storey red-brick building adjoining the hotel was built as a hall c. 1860. The Castle is the only licensed hotel remaining in Bothwell. *Patrick St. Open daily. (03) 6259 5502.*

Fort Wentworth Sandstone barracks with extensive verandahs, built in 1832 to house a military detachment under the command of Capt. D'Arcy Wentworth. Later a watchhouse, and now a private residence. *Wentworth St. Not open for inspection.*

Ratho & Golf Course Alexander Reid, from Ratho Banks near Edinburgh, most likely brought golf clubs with him when he came to Van Diemen's Land and took up his grant at Bothwell in 1822. The nine-hole course he established on his property Ratho – Australia's first – still exists, complete with fences around the greens to keep off the sheep. Visiting golfers welcome (green fees apply). *Lake Hwy. Open daily. Inq. Australasian Golf Museum. (03) 6259 4033. House not open for inspection.*

St Luke's Uniting Church Australia's second oldest Presbyterian church, designed by Colonial Architect John Lee Archer in 1828 and completed three years later. For 60 years it served both the Presbyterian and Anglican communities. The stone heads of a Celtic god and goddess above the door are attributed to convict sculptor Daniel Herbert, who received a pardon for his fine stone carving on the Ross Bridge. *Alexander St. Open daily. (03) 6259 5577.*

St Luke's Uniting Church, Bothwell

Slate Cottage A typical Georgian brick cottage of great charm, complete with a fanlight over the front entrance, tiny attic rooms and a slate roof, built in 1835 by Edward Bowden Snr. *High St. Not open for inspection.*

Thorpe Water Mill English settler Thomas Axford, who took up land here in 1822, built a very fine brick flour mill on his property, Thorpe, soon after. Wheat grown on the farm was ground for flour until the 1890s. Today visitors can see the restored water mill, one of the last in the country still operating, being used to grind grain. *2 km NE, on Interlaken Rd. Open by appt.* $ *(03) 6259 5678.*

Wentworth House Originally known as Inverhall, this restrained Palladian-style mansion (1833) was built by Capt. D'Arcy Wentworth, brother of the famous William Charles Wentworth, who was in the first European party to cross the Blue Mountains. Capt. Wentworth began building a sandstone villa when he was police magistrate in Bothwell. He sold it c. 1833 to his successor, Major Charles Schaw, who enlarged it into a grand mansion. *Wentworth St. House not open for inspection. Gardens occasionally open as part of Open Garden Scheme.* $

ALSO OF INTEREST Local stone was another popular building material, and a good example of its use can be seen in St Michael and All Angels' Anglican Church (1891) in Market Pl. Particularly noteworthy are the porch's solid stone seats, the circular staircase leading to the belfry, a fireplace in the west wall and the sandstone high altar. *Open daily. (03) 6259 5698.* Also in Market Pl. is a rare vertical sundial, a memorial to the 110 men who fought – of whom 29 died – in World War I. Alexander St, named after Alexander Reid of Ratho, has several early buildings of note. The simple whitewashed Literary Society Building was the site of Tasmania's first public library, founded in 1834. Now council offices. *Open during office hours.* Further along the street is the two-storey Fealy's building (c. 1850), with its flagstone footpath; the post office (1891), formerly Commercial Bank of Tasmania; and two cottages that are typical of Bothwell materials and craftsmanship, including bricks laid in the popular chequerboard pattern. The Bootmaker's Shop, originally next to Elizabeth House but relocated, houses a complete bootmaker's shop, still as it was in the 1930s. *High St. Open by appt. (03) 6259 5649.*

IN THE AREA All that remains of the once important market town of Melton Mowbray is a large hotel and a few houses. The Melton Mowbray Hotel, licensed since 1846, stands at the junction of the Midland and Lake hwys. The horse trough outside the hotel was carved from a single piece of stone. *21 km SE. Blackwell Rd. Open daily. (03) 6259 1122.*

Australasian Golf Museum, Market Pl.; (03) 6259 4033. Website: www. bothwell.tco.asn.au/about.html

BREADALBANE
Map ref. 381 M9

Originally called Brumby's Plains, after a local settler, but Gov. Macquarie renamed the area in 1821, again invoking Scotland. The district was notorious for sheep stealing and a place where bushranger Matthew Brady found much support. It was at an inn here that the bushranger shot dead a constable, even though the unfortunate constable had been recently gaoled for letting Brady escape. Breadalbane is now just minutes from Launceston airport.

Woolpack Inn Built in 1839, this Georgian inn was a staging post on the Launceston–Hobart route until 1920. In 1847 a trotting match took place from Launceston to the inn but ended when the contestants were arrested for dangerous driving. Now a private residence. *Midland Hwy. Not open for inspection.*

Tourism & History Centre, 18 High St, Evandale; (03) 6391 8128. Website: www.gatewaytas.com.au
See also Evandale, Longford

BRIDGEWATER
Map ref. 379 L7

At the Midland Hwy crossing of the River Derwent, just 19 km N of Hobart, Bridgewater was once an important market town. The township, first known as Green Point, is on the north bank, although the original site chosen was on the opposite shore. OF INTEREST The causeway, some 1.3 km long, was begun in the 1830s by 200 convicts sentenced to secondary punishment – good conduct men had longer chains suspended between ankle and waist, petty offenders had their chains shortened, causing chafing and restricting movement. They barrowed 2 million tonnes of stone and clay from a nearby quarry. The watchhouse (1838), at the southern end of the causeway, is all that is left of the convict station. A bridge, co-designed by James Blackburn, was finally opened in 1849; the current opening bridge was completed in 1946.

Council Offices, Tivoli Rd, Gagebrook; (03) 6263 0333.

BRUNY ISLAND
Map ref. 379 M11

This rugged island off the south-east coast is one of Tasmania's most historically significant places. Truganini and Woorrady were members of the Nuenonne tribe, which called the island home for thousands of years until European violence and disease destroyed them. Many middens still exist on Bruny's beaches. The island was a favourite resting place for early explorers. Tasman sheltered offshore in 1642. Furneaux followed in 1773, Cook in 1777, Cox in 1789 and Bligh in 1788 and 1792. Matthew Flinders' first Australian landing was also on the island. The French Admiral Bruni d'Entrecasteaux made the first accurate survey of the channel separating the island from the mainland in 1792, and so the island bears his name. Tasmania's first apple trees were planted here during Bligh's second visit. From 1820 to 1850, Bruny had a thriving whaling industry, centred on Adventure Bay.

Bligh Museum Built of convict-made bricks left over from the building of St Peter's Church, the museum documents the island's early history and Pacific exploration. It is located in Adventure Bay, where there are also several memorials to early explorers. *Adventure Bay. Open daily; closed Tues. in winter.* Ⓢ *(03) 6293 1117.*

Wentworth House, Bothwell

Truganini memorial, Bruny Island

Also of interest Convict-built Cape Bruny lighthouse (1836), on South Bruny, is the second oldest lighthouse in Australia. The grounds are open to the public (a National Parks Pass is required to visit). *(03) 6298 3114.* The remains of the convict-built St Peter's Church (1846) are on private property near the airstrip at Variety Bay, North Bruny. *Open by appt. (03) 6260 6366.* The Local History Room, attached to the council chambers at Alonnah, focuses on the island's European settlers. *Open daily. (03) 6293 1139.* Cemetery Beach is the site of the earliest known European burials on South Bruny, dating back to 1856. The headstones are sandstone, possibly quarried by convicts across the bay at Ventenat Point. *Cemetery Rd, Lunawanna.* A vehicular ferry operates throughout the day to Bruny Island, from Kettering, 34 km from Hobart.

ℹ *Bruny D'Entrecasteaux Visitor Centre, 81 Ferry Rd, Kettering; (03) 6267 4494, freecall 1800 676 740.* Website: www.bruny.tco.asn.au/visitor.html

Buckland

Map ref. 379 N7

A small town 66 km NE of Hobart, famous for its beautiful colonial church (c. 1846) and, more specifically, for a window in the church. The east-facing sanctuary window in the Church of St John the Baptist dates from the 13th or 14th century and was originally designed for Battle Abbey in England, built on the site of the Battle of Hastings. To preserve it from Cromwell in the 17th century, the window was buried at a nearby residence for over 200 years. The Abbey was badly damaged and never restored, and the window was eventually given by the Marquis of Salisbury to the first rector of Buckland, Rev. Fox, and installed in 1849. *Tasman Hwy. Open daily. (03) 6257 3321.*

ℹ *Ye Olde Buckland Inn, Kent St; (03) 6257 5114.*

See also Colebrook, Richmond

Burnie

Map ref. 380 G6

Built around the shores of Emu Bay, on Tasmania's north coast, the industrial city of Burnie was first settled by Europeans in 1827. The densely wooded countryside provided the basis for a timber industry, although the town grew slowly until it became an important port for mineral exports in the 1880s. Burnie has been a major paper manufacturing centre since the 1930s.

Australian Paper Mill Paper production continues in the 1930s industrial complex that dominates Burnie. *Marine Tce. Tours Mon.–Fri. (no children under 10). (03) 6430 7777.* A disused pulp mill has been turned over to traditional handmade paper-making methods and visitors are welcome to participate. *Creative Paper Mill, East Mill, Old Surrey Rd. Open Mon.–Fri. & by appt.* $ *(03) 6430 7717.*

Pioneer Village Museum A reconstruction of typical early Burnie buildings – from an old-fashioned dentist's surgery to a newspaper printery, shops and dwellings, plus a good collection of artifacts and memorabilia. *Visitors' Complex, Civic Centre Plaza, off Little Alexander St. Open Mon.–Fri. & Sat.–Sun. afternoons.* $ *(03) 6430 5746.*

Also of interest The town's oldest building, Burnie Inn, built and licensed in the 1840s, can be seen in Burnie Park, York St. *Not open for inspection.* The imposing, two-storey, police station (c. 1908) began life as a dentist's house and surgery. *88 Wilson St. Not open for inspection.*

ℹ *Civic Centre Plaza, off Little Alexander St; (03) 6434 6111.* Website: www.burnie.net

Campbell Town

Map ref. 379 M2, 381 N12

Named by Gov. Macquarie after his wife, Elizabeth Campbell, Campbell Town began life in 1821 as a garrison post, one of a chain between Hobart and Launceston. It soon became a prosperous rural centre, yet retains many well-preserved links with its fascinating colonial past.

Churches Campbell Town has a number of lovely early churches. The oldest is Kirklands (c. 1829), 12 km W of the town, which is still in use. A small Scottish-style country church, with a graveyard which is older than the church itself. In later years, poet AD Hope, whose father was minister at Kirklands, lived here as a boy. *Valleyfield Rd, via Macquarie Rd. Open by appt. (03) 6381 1194.* The Anglican St Luke's Church was completed in 1839, with John Lee Archer the supervising architect. Archer is reported to have insisted that parts of several walls be pulled down and rebuilt by another contractor. *Cnr Pedder & Bridge sts. Open daily.* On the south-east wall of St Michael's Catholic Church are engraved the initials WW and the coat of arms of Bishop Willson, Bishop of Tasmania when the church was built in 1857. It was built to designs sent by the Bishop's friend, London architect Augustus Pugin. *King St. Open by appt. (03) 6381 1122.* St Andrew's Presbyterian Church, now the Uniting Church, at the north end of town, was also built in 1857, for Rev. Dr Adam Turnbull, who held several official positions in Hobart, including Colonial Treasurer, before falling out with Gov. Sir William Denison over transportation. It cost him his position and pension, so he turned to the Church. The church organ originally belonged to Bishop Nixon, the first Anglican Bishop of Tasmania. *High St. Open by appt. (03) 6381 1332.*

The Grange Designed by James Blackburn with a gabled roofline reminiscent of a 17th-century English farmhouse. The house was built in 1847 by Dr William Valentine, a devotee of the sciences who was involved in the first telephone call in the Southern Hemisphere in 1875. With a telescope installed for the occasion, The Grange also played host to a

Red Bridge, Campbell Town

group of American astronomers who watched the transit of Venus in 1874. Now a B&B and conference centre. *High St. (03) 6381 1686.*

Heritage Highway Museum Located in the courthouse (1905), which is still a working court four times a year, the museum exhibits include the telephones used for the historic phone call. *103 High St. Open Mon.–Sat. (03) 6381 1353.*

Hotels The Campbell Town Inn, which opened for business as The Beehive in 1840, has an unusual carved stone staircase. *Cnr High & Queen sts. (03) 6381 1171.* It has a ledger from the original Campbell Town Inn (1823), a wooden building that was replaced by brick in 1828. This 1828 structure is believed to be the oldest existing house in Campbell Town. *170 Bridge St. Not open for inspection.* The Campbell Town Motel and Bistro opened as the Caledonian in 1834. *High St. (03) 6381 1158.* Closer to the bridge in High St is the Foxhunter's Return (c. 1838), an old coaching inn that has been restored and operates as a B&B. *(03) 6381 1602.* The original Foxhunter's Return opened in Bridge St in 1829, which until the Red Bridge opened in 1838 was Campbell Town's main street.

Red Bridge Built by convicts in 1836–38 using an estimated 1.5 million bricks, this bridge over the Elizabeth River, also named by Macquarie for his wife, has the broad arrow denoting convicts stamped on the heavy iron staples on the parapets.

ALSO OF INTEREST Howley Lodge (1845) was built for Campbell Town's first Anglican rector. *Bridge St. Not open for inspection.* Hugh Kean's brewery (1839), a freestone building, which was built following the opening of the bridge, is now an antique store. *Midland Hwy. Open daily. (03) 6381 1198.* There is a signposted historic town walk.

Heritage Highway Museum, 103 High St; (03) 6381 1353. Website: www. tasmaniacentral.tas.gov.au/towns/ campbelltown/index.asp
See also Cleveland

CLEVELAND   Map ref. 379 M1, 381 M11

Poor soil and lack of water put paid to an early proposal that Cleveland become the main town of the northern Midlands. Hundreds of convicts were put to work clearing a square mile, but although at times a coaching stop and a probationary depot for ticket-of-leave men, it remained a small village. Evidence of the original grand plan, however, can be seen in Cleveland's fine Georgian buildings.

Cleveland House Opened (c. 1830) as the Bald Faced Stag, this was another inn popular among bushrangers. Visitors recalled how the door would be opened by a frightened, well-armed publican. It is now the home of The Stables Gallery. *12787 Midland Hwy. Open Thurs.–Sun. (03) 6391 5705.*
Cleveland Union Chapel This small church (1855), used by Anglicans

and Methodists, has a curved ceiling and windows on only one side. It also has a fascinating graveyard. *Midland Hwy. Open by appt. (03) 6391 5525.*

St Andrew's Inn Built in 1845 to serve the increasingly heavy traffic between Hobart and Launceston, this inn was a well-known haunt of bushrangers seeking potential victims. Once derelict, it is again open to travellers as a restaurant, B&B and conference centre. It overlooks the ruins of the old probationary depot. *Midland Hwy. Open for lunch Wed.–Sun., dinner Tues.–Sat. (03) 6391 5525.*

IN THE AREA A local landmark at Conara is the Georgian house Smithvale, a former inn now commonly known as the Disappearing House for the way it disappears behind rises as travellers from the south move towards it. *5 km s on Midland Hwy. Not open for inspection.*

Heritage Highway Museum, 103 High St, Campbell Town; (03) 6381 1353. Website: www.tasmaniacentral.tas. gov.au/towns/cleveland/index.asp
See also Campbell Town

COLEBROOK   Map ref. 379 M6

Between Richmond and Oatlands in the southern Midlands, Colebrook was originally called Jerusalem. It was settled soon after 1824, when Lt. Grimes and ex-convict Const. Jorgen Jorgensen discovered the fertile valley at the head of the Coal River while searching for cattle. Colebrook lay on the main road from Hobart to Oatlands until the Bridgewater bridge over the River Derwent opened in the late 1840s. Even so it remained the most popular route for some time because of the poor condition of the new road.

Jerusalem Probation Station This is the best preserved convict station in Tasmania, with a number of the buildings intact, including the courthouse, the officers' and overseer's quarters, the infirmary and the supervisor's cottage. The prison church was burnt in the massive 1967 bushfires. The probation station opened in 1837, and about 300 convicts were stationed here at any one time. They worked on the main road, in the coal mines and on the prison farm and were hired out to local settlers.

The station closed in 1854. All of the buildings are now on private property. *Richmond St. Tours including afternoon tea on the first Sun. of each month.* Ⓢ *(03) 6259 7263.*

Nicholls Store A mixture of Colonial and Georgian architecture, this convict brick building (1840) is now an art and craft gallery and tearoom. *34 Richmond St. Open daily, closed Fri. afternoons. (03) 6259 7263.*

St Patrick's Catholic Church Tasmania has the largest number of works by architect Augustus Pugin outside the UK. The designer of the Houses of Westminster in London agreed to design several churches for his friend, Bishop Willson, the Catholic Bishop of Tasmania. He sent plans and models, with which local architects were briefed. Churches were built at **Oatlands**, **Campbell Town** and Colebrook (1857), and major alterations were undertaken at Richmond. The cemetery contains the grave of Father William Dunne, the first priest to be chaplain to Catholic convicts. *Yarlington Rd. Open by appt. (03) 6259 7263.*

Also of interest St James' Anglican Church, built in 1885 by public subscription, is known for its stained-glass window dedicated to those who served in World War I. *Open by appt. (03) 6259 7114.* Hardwick House, on Jerusalem Creek to the south of town, was built as a mill in 1884. Now a private home. *Not open for inspection.* The Colebrook History Room was built from sandstone salvaged when Colebrook Park (1831) was demolished in 1986 to make way for the Craigbourne Irrigation Dam. The History Room has a collection of local memorabilia. *20 Richmond St. Open by appt. (03) 6259 7263 or (03) 6259 7114.*

🛈 *Nicholls Store, 34 Richmond St; (03) 6259 7263.*

DELORAINE　　Map ref. 381 J9

Beautifully located on the banks of the Meander River with the spectacular Western Tiers in the distance, Deloraine grew from a village in the 1840s to a thriving agricultural centre, its prosperity reflected in fine civic buildings and country homesteads.

Arcoona Designed in 1892 by the local doctor to take full advantage of

Calstock, Deloraine

the views, this late Victorian home has beautiful stained-glass windows, original Victorian stencilling and carved blackwood mantles. Now a guesthouse. *East Barrack St. Gardens open daily. (03) 6362 3443.*

Bonney's Inn This Georgian inn, built in 1831 by John Bonney, the son of a convict, has been faithfully restored, complete with cedar mantles, panelled joinery and period furnishings and colours. It is now a traditional English-style B&B. *19 West Pde. (03) 6362 2974.*

Bowerbank Mill Designed by Tasmania's first native-born architect, William Archer, and built c. 1853 in the Georgian style, this whitewashed brick mill features a slate gabled roof. Note the handsome windows divided by glazing bars and set in arched openings. The original machinery here was water driven but as this wasn't very successful, the mill was converted to steam in 1871. Now an art and craft gallery, with self-contained accommodation. *4455 Meander Valley Hwy. Open daily. (03) 6362 2628.*

Calstock An elegant homestead and property where Australia's finest racehorses were once bred, it is now a guesthouse. Just south of Deloraine, on the road to the Great Lake, the house and stables were begun c. 1830 and the main part of the house was built in grand style in the 1850s. *Lake Hwy. (03) 6362 2642.*

Deloraine Folk Museum This single-storey brick building, erected in 1864, was originally the Family and

Commercial Inn. The building has attics and dormers and a splay corner entrance typical of the era. There is also a local and family history room. *98 Emu Bay Rd. Open daily.* Ⓢ *(03) 6362 3471.*

St Mark's Anglican Church This prominent Gothic Revival church (1859) has a three-level tower with a spire. Inside are some noted woodcarvings and stained-glass windows. *East Westbury Pl. Open daily. (03) 6362 2010.*

Also of interest The Bush Inn (1848) is still in business. *7 Bass Hwy. (03) 6362 2365.*

🛈 *Deloraine Folk Museum, 98 Emu Bay Rd; (03) 6362 3471. Website: www. meandervalley.com*
See also Westbury

DERBY　　Map ref. 381 O7

Now classified as an historic town, Derby, in the north-east of the State, was an important and flourishing mining town in the late 1800s. In appearance it has changed little, although farming has replaced tin production as the town's main source of income. Derby is also the only place in Australia where a dam collapse has led to the loss of life. During heavy flooding in 1929 the Cascade Dam failed, killing 14 people.

Derby Tin Mine Centre Incorporating a number of the old mine buildings and the old Derby school, the museum complex features a shanty town with miner's cottage, general store, butcher's shop, mine office

and blacksmith's shed. *Main Rd. Open daily.* $ *(03) 6354 2262.*
ⓘ *Derby Tin Mine Centre, Main Rd; (03) 6354 2262.*

DEVONPORT

Map ref. 380 I6

Settled from the 1830s on, Devonport did not officially come into existence until 1890, when the towns of Formby and Torquay on either side of the Mersey River united. Like many settlements in north-west Tasmania, early buildings were mainly constructed using timber from the thick forests that covered the coastal plains. As such, many have long since been replaced. However, fine examples of houses from the late 19th and early 20th centuries survive.

Devonport Maritime & Local History Museum In the old harbour master's residence and pilot station (1920) at the mouth of the Mersey River, the museum has model ships from the days of sail and steam and features many items associated with the still busy Port of Devonport. *Victoria Pde & Gloucester Ave. Open Tues.–Sun.* $ *(03) 6424 7100.*

Don River Railway Begun in 1854 to bring timber out of the Don Valley, the original tramway was replaced by a rail line in 1916. The new line brought limestone from quarries worked by BHP, until the limestone too was exhausted. Despite declining traffic, it stayed open until 1963. Now restored and revived by the Van Diemen Light Railway Society, it runs vintage passenger trains to Coles Beach. *Don Rd. Open daily.* $ *(03) 6424 6335.*

Home Hill The family home of former Prime Minister Joseph Lyons and his wife, Dame Enid, was built in 1916, a year after their marriage. Carefully preserved, the house has some fine Queen Anne furniture and many unusual artifacts given to the couple during their careers. He was Premier of Tasmania 1923–28 and Prime Minister 1932–39. In 1943 Dame Enid became the first woman elected to the House of Representatives. *77 Middle Rd. Open Tues.–Thurs. & Sat.–Sun. afternoons.* $ *(03) 6424 3028 or (03) 6428 6289. NT.*

Tiagarra Aboriginal Cultural Centre & Museum A fascinating and wide-ranging display documenting the culture of Tasmanian Aboriginal people. Built on the Mersey Bluff headland, the centre is run by the local Aboriginal community. *Bluff Rd. Open daily.* $ *(03) 6424 8250.*

ALSO OF INTEREST There are many historic homes in the city, particularly in the vicinity of the river, and in the nearby villages of Don and Forth. Mt Pleasant (1859) has recently been restored. *Mary St, East Devonport. Not open for inspection.* Malunnah (1887), off Victoria Pde, was home of the Lane family for 80 years. *Not open for inspection.* In Forth, the Bridge Hotel (1871) is still a favourite with locals. *Main Rd, Forth. Open daily. (03) 6428 2239.* Nearby is Lenna (c. 1860), home of first settler James Fenton, whose *Bush Life in Tasmania* is an important record of pioneering days. *Grove St. Not open for inspection.*
ⓘ *Tasmanian Travel & Information Centre, 92 Formby Rd; (03) 6424 4466.* Website: www.devonport.tco.asn.au/ tourist.htm

EVANDALE

Map ref. 381 M9

Evandale is one of the best-preserved historic towns in Australia, with its mostly single-storeyed Georgian architecture. But links with the past reach beyond the architecture – Ned Kelly's father, John, worked in the town as a prisoner, while John Batman, the founder of Melbourne, and John Glover, a noted landscape painter, both lived in the area. For many years Evandale was an important sheep and cattle market.

Clarendon Arms Hotel Built in 1847 and featuring interesting murals of the district's history, this hotel is still in business. Convicts once paraded on the common behind the hotel. *11 Russell St. (03) 6391 8181.*

High Street Worth a leisurely stroll to appreciate the mix of Georgian and Victorian architecture, including the old headmaster's house (not open for inspection) and, next door, the earliest brick state school in Tasmania (1889), which is now the History & Tourism Centre. The Centre houses a display on the history of the town and Henry William Murray, Victoria Cross winner. *18 High St. Open daily. (03) 6391 8128.* At no. 13 is The Laurels (1835), one of the oldest homes in Evandale. *Not open for inspection.* Further along at no. 7 is the Evandale Library (1885), now an antique store. Nearby is the Victorian post office (1888), and opposite is the two-storey, whitewashed Solomon House, built in 1836 as the Clarendon Stores by Joseph Solomon, whose son Albert became Premier of Tasmania (1912–14). Now a guesthouse and cafe. *1 High St. (03) 6391 8331.*

St Andrew's Anglican Church The Bishop's chair in this local landmark (1871), with its 300-m steeple, is made of oak from Australia's first warship, HMS *Nelson*. Some 300 convicts are buried in the graveyard. *High St. Open by appt. (03) 6398 6215.*

St Andrew's Uniting Church Completed in 1840, its Doric columns, Classical bell-tower and Venetian chandelier

St Andrew's Uniting Church, Evandale

make this one of Australia's most outstanding rural churches. Many noted first settlers are buried in the churchyard. *High St. Open by appt. (03) 6391 8431.*

ALSO OF INTEREST 2 km SW on Leighlands Rd, Pleasant Banks is Australia's oldest superfine merino stud. The property was granted to David Gibson in 1809, but the Georgian homestead was not built until 1838. The owners still run a small flock of Saxon Merinos descended from sheep brought to the property in 1823. *Not open for inspection.* The Evandale Village Fair and National Penny Farthing Championships takes place on the last weekend in Feb. each year. *(03) 6391 8223.* Fallgrove is a fine Georgian house built in 1826 by Kennedy Murray, who not only married twice and fathered 19 children, but owned much of the land on which Evandale was built. *1 Logan Rd. Not open for inspection.* Strathmore has an early convict-built mill and homestead (1826), which now offers accommodation. *868 Nile Rd. (03) 6398 6213.*

IN THE AREA Clarendon House, set amid parklands and formal gardens and framed by overhanging elms, is one of the great colonial Georgian mansions. The two-storey facade is graced by a lofty portico, creating an impression of grandeur possibly unequalled by any private house built in Australia in the 19th century. The residence was completed in 1838 for wealthy merchant and wool-grower James Cox, whose father, William Cox, built the first road across the Blue Mountains. The network of outbuildings is diverse, revealing the self-sufficiency of a typical colonial country estate. The homestead has been restored by the National Trust. *8 km S, off Nile Rd. Open daily.* $ *(03) 6398 6220. NT.* On the Nile River, the village of Deddington has important links with the well-known English landscape painter John Glover, who settled here in 1832. *20 km SE.* Glover, his wife and two of his sons are buried in a family crypt in the Nile Chapel cemetery. The simple brick chapel (c. 1842) is on Deddington Rd, Deddington. *Open by appt. (03) 6398 6287.* The property Kingston, at Nile, includes a three-room convict-built cottage, lock-up and storeroom

Entally House, Hadspen

(1825). John Batman lived in the cottage for eight years before setting off for Port Phillip, where he founded Melbourne. He and Glover were friends and neighbours, and, with a small group, became the first white men to reach the summit of Ben Lomond, in 1833. *10 km SE. Open by appt. (03) 6391 5518.* The town of Perth, a former coaching stop, has many historic buildings, including several early inns. *8 km W.*

🛈 *Tourism & History Centre, 18 High St; (03) 6391 8128.*

See also Breadalbane, Longford

FLINDERS ISLAND Map ref. 378 C9, 381 R1

The largest in the Furneaux group of 70 islands discovered by Tobias Furneaux, the captain of Cook's support ship, the *Adventure*, the island is named after the explorer Matthew Flinders, who charted the area. It was a sealing ground in the late 18th and early 19th centuries and was settled formally in the 1830s, when the last Tasmanian Aboriginal people on the mainland were sent to Settlement Point (1835–47). Most died here. However, descendants of a number of Aboriginal women who lived with sealers on these islands eventually returned to mainland Tasmania, helping to rebuild the Tasmanian Aboriginal community.

Wybalenna The Aboriginal name for the island was Wybalenna, meaning Blackman's Houses. A chapel built for the Aboriginal settlement and

later used as a woolshed has been restored by the National Trust. The site is now owned by the Aboriginal community. *Settlement Point (22 km NW of Whitemark). Open by appt. (03) 6359 3532.*

🛈 *7 Lagoon Rd, Whitemark; (03) 6359 2380.* Website: www.flinders.tco. asn.au/

FRANKLIN Map ref. 379 K10

Stretching along the banks of the Huon River 45 km S of Hobart, Franklin is the oldest village in the Huon Valley, founded in 1804 and later named after Gov. Sir John Franklin. Much of Franklin was built by river traders, with timber milling an important early industry. Huon pine, Tasmania's coveted softwood, was found in the district. Wooden boats are still built in a number of Huon River towns.

OF INTEREST Franklin Tavern, the former Franklin Hotel, was built in 1851. *Main Rd. (03) 6266 3205.*

IN THE AREA Set in a former apple-packing shed, the Huon Valley Apple & Heritage Museum has displays of up to 500 different apples in season and restored working machines. *14 km NE on Huon Hwy, Grove. Open daily. (03) 6266 4345.*

🛈 *Huon River Jet Boats, Esplanade, Huonville; (03) 6264 1838.*

FRANKLIN VILLAGE Map ref. 381 M9

At first called Longmeadows, the village – now on the outskirts of

Launceston – was renamed in honour of Gov. Sir John Franklin.

Franklin House Once called The Hollies, this grand, two-storey, porticoed dwelling houses the National Trust's State headquarters. It was originally owned by Britton Jones, a Launceston brewer and innkeeper. From 1882 until 1922 it was the WK Hawkes School for Boys, one of Tasmania's finest, which housed and educated boys for 45 pounds a year. The house is an excellent example of early colonial Georgian architecture. *6 km s on Hobart Rd (Old Midland Hwy), via Kings Meadows. Open daily.* Ⓢ *(03) 6344 7824. NT.*

 Gateway Tasmania Travel Centre, cnr Paterson & St John sts, Launceston; (03) 6336 3133. Website: www. gatewaytas.com.au

GEORGE TOWN   Map ref. 381 K6

This northern settlement, named for King George III, got off to a false start when Col. William Patterson ran aground here in 1804, running up the colours and firing a salute nonetheless, before moving across the Tamar River to York Town. A permanent settlement was established three years later, but lost prominence as the colony's northern headquarters when that honour passed to Launceston.

The Grove An elegant Georgian house built c. 1827 for the port officer and magistrate, Lt Matthew Curling Friend. It has been carefully restored and is open for inspection. There is accommodation available and a licensed restaurant. Lunch and teas are served. *25 Cimitiere St. Open daily mid Sept.–mid May; Mon.–Fri. mid May–mid Sept.* Ⓢ *(03) 6382 1336.*

IN THE AREA Low Head Pilot Station is Australia's oldest continuously operating pilot station. Established in 1805, the surviving station buildings (c. 1835) now house a maritime museum, gallery and accommodation. The lighthouse was built in 1888 to replace the original 1830 structure. Displays in the museum include old diving equipment and items salvaged from shipwrecks. The station continues to guide ships into the Tamar. *5 km NW via Low Head Rd. Open daily.* Ⓢ *(03) 6382 1143 or (03) 6382 0111.*

 Cnr Main Rd & Victoria St; (03) 6382 1700. Website: www.georgetown. tas.gov.au

HADSPEN   Map ref. 381 L9

Now a popular residential district 12 km SW of Launceston on the banks of the South Esk River, the village retains an attractive row of Georgian buildings in Main Rd.

Entally House On the opposite bank of the river is Entally, one of Tasmania's most outstanding historic houses and one of its most picturesque. The pretty house, with its shady verandahs, scalloped bargeboards and shuttered windows, was built c. 1819 by Thomas Reibey II, whose mother, Mary, a successful businesswoman in Sydney, had arrived in the colony as a 13-year-old convict. Reibey's son, also called Thomas, became Premier of Tasmania (1876–77). The outbuildings at Entally House include a bluestone church, a two-storey coach-house and a glasshouse. The gardens are a delight. *Old Bass Hwy. Open daily.* Ⓢ *(03) 6393 6201. NT.*

Red Feather Inn This former coaching house, built in 1845, once provided a welcoming ale and homemade bread at the end of the uphill haul into town. Complete with all original buildings and fittings, it has been meticulously restored and is now a restaurant. *Main Rd. Open daily. (03) 6393 6331.*

 Gateway Tasmania Travel Centre, cnr Paterson & St John sts, Launceston; (03) 6336 3133. Website: www. gatewaytas.com.au
See also Launceston

HAMILTON   Map ref. 379 J6

Hamilton has seen little development since its initial period of spectacular growth in the early 1830s, when the availability of cheap labour provided by 300 or so convicts led to a building boom which can still be seen today in the town's many fine sandstone buildings. Today this small town is classified for its historic significance, and is just one hour from Hobart on the Lyell Hwy.

Glen Clyde House Convict-built in 1840 as a private home but licensed at various times, Glen Clyde House is now a craft gallery with tearooms and lovely gardens. *Lyell Hwy. Open daily. (03) 6286 3276.*

Heritage Centre & Museum Run by the Hamilton Historic Society, the museum is housed in the old Warder's Cottage (1840), used by gaolers. When not open, keys are available from Glen Clyde House or the Hamilton Inn. *Tarleton St. See door for opening times.*

Old School House One of the most impressive buildings in the Derwent Valley, the sandstone schoolhouse was built in 1858 at a cost of 751 pounds to house 80 pupils. Now renovated and offering B&B accommodation. *Franklin Pl. (03) 6286 3292.*

Old School House, Hamilton

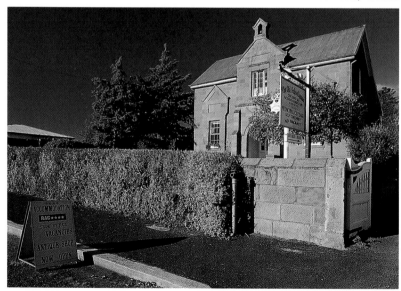

Prospect Villa & Gardens This house, c. 1824, which once belonged to the local surgeon, has been extensively restored and both it and its magnificent gardens are open to the public. *Plains Rd. Open daily Sept.–May.* Ⓢ *(03) 6286 3233.*

St Peter's Anglican Church Built when Van Diemen's Land was still included in the Diocese of Calcutta, India, St Peter's (1835) is a prominent sandstone church with square bell-tower. Its most famous feature is its single door, believed to be an attempt to prevent convicts escaping during services. *Ponsonby St. Open daily. (03) 6286 3205.*

ALSO OF INTEREST Many buildings date from the 1830s and 1840s, including a number of cottages available for accommodation; Blanch's Store (1830), which now houses the town bakery, in Maid Rd, (03) 6286 3206; and the Hamilton Inn (1830), the town's only licensed hotel, Tarleton St, (03) 6286 3204. A brochure produced by the Hamilton Historical Society provides information on the town and is available at most business outlets. ⓘ *Council Offices, Tarleton St; (03) 6286 3202.* Website: www.tasmaniacentral. tas.gov.au

HOBART
Map ref. 376 G8, 379 L8

See pp. 250–9

JERICHO
Map ref. 379 L5

Dating from 1816, Jericho is an early settlement in the southern Midlands, with many convict constructions, stone walls, bridges and culverts lining the road. The town was named prior to 1811 by Hugh Germain, who is said to have travelled through the area with a Bible and a copy of *The Arabian Nights*.

Jericho Probation Station Evocative ruins of the pisé (rammed-earth) walls just off the Midland Hwy, about 1 km from town. Plans of the probation station, which operated from 1840 and housed 200 convicts, are on display at the site. *Old Jericho Rd.*

ALSO OF INTEREST Opposite the Probation Station, known as the Fourteen Tree Plains, was the site of the first horse race in the State – in April 1826 – which gave birth to the Tasmanian Turf Club. The former Superintendent's Cottage, now known as Park Farm, built in 1842, offers colonial accommodation. *Old Jericho Rd. Open by appt. (03) 6254 4115.* St James' Anglican Church (1883), the second church on this site, contains records and memorabilia of the district's pioneering families and the grave of Australia's first VC soldier, Col. JH Bisdee. *Old Jericho Rd. (03) 6254 4115.* Many Georgian sandstone farmhouses can be seen from the Old Jericho Road. A fine sandstone bridge built in 1841 spans the River Jordan. ⓘ *85 High St, Oatlands; (03) 6254 1212.* Website: www.oatlands.tco.asn.au

KEMPTON
Map ref. 379 L6

A classified historic town 50 km from Hobart on the Midlands Hwy, Kempton dates from 1817 and is notable for its Georgian and Victorian buildings and cottages.

St Mary's Anglican Church Attributed to Colonial Architect James Blackburn, the church dates from 1844 and the adjoining cemetery includes graves of early pioneers from as early as 1828. *Main Rd. Open by appt. (03) 6265 8720.*

Wilmot Arms Inn Dating from 1843, when Kempton was a popular coaching stop, this Georgian inn has been restored and is now a B&B. *Main Rd. (03) 6259 1272.*

ALSO OF INTEREST Dysart House, a two-storey Georgian house built as a hotel in 1842. *Midland Hwy. Not open for inspection.* At the north end of town is Royal Farm, once the Royal Oak Inn, where in 1825 bushranger Matthew Brady hung his famous notice expressing his concern that Gov. Arthur 'is at large' and offering 20 gallons of rum to anyone 'who will deliver this person to me'. *Not open for inspection.* ⓘ *85 High St, Oatlands; (03) 6254 1212.* Website: www.tasmaniacentral.tas. gov.au

LATROBE
Map ref. 380 I7

Upstream of Devonport on the Mersey River, Latrobe was established in the 1850s and for a period was the most important town in the north-west. It once had its own shipyards and in the 1880s boasted three newspapers. A reminder of this prosperous past is the row of Victorian shopfronts in the main street.

Courthouse Museum Housed in the restored courthouse (1883), displays include a photographic history of the district, minute books of various organisations and a collection of early domestic, communications, agricultural and firefighting equipment. *Gilbert St. Open Fri. & Sun. afternoons or by appt.* Ⓢ *(03) 6428 6413.*

Frogmore A two-storey, towered brick villa (1880) in the Classical style. Inside, original wallpaper and stencilling have been retained. The estate was first settled by Miss Lucinda Moriarty, who arrived in the district in 1836. *Cnr Railton & Latrobe rds. Not open for inspection.*

Sherwood Hall Recently relocated to Bells Pde and fully restored and furnished in period style, this wooden building (1850) was home to early pioneers, ex-convict Thomas Johnson and his Aboriginal wife Dolly Dalrymple Briggs. Both died in the mid-1860s, respected citizens, and were buried under a laurel tree near their home's original site on the bank of the Mersey River, near the Railton Rd. *Bells Pde. Open Tues., Thurs., Sat. & Sun. or by appt. (03) 6426 2888.*

ALSO OF INTEREST Kenworthy's, now an antique store, has retained the wonderful shopfront and internal fittings from its early days as a clothing and haberdashery store. *84 Gilbert St. (03) 6426 2599.* Lucinda (c. 1891) is perched on a hillside overlooking the town and has cornice and ceiling work of a quality rarely seen in private homes. Now a guesthouse. *17 Forth St. (03) 6426 2285.*

IN THE AREA Port Sorell, the earliest settlement on the north-west coast, named after Gov. William Sorell in 1822. While a succession of fires destroyed all early buildings, historic markers give an indication of the town's original layout. *20 km NE.* There are also some historic wooden boats to be seen at Muddy Creek, to the south of Port Sorell. Nearby, at Hawley Beach, the area's oldest homes Larooma (1875) and Hawley House (1878) now both provide accommodation in a glorious coastal setting. *3 km N. Larooma (03) 6428 754. Hawley House (03) 648 6221.* ⓘ *70 Gilbert St; (03) 6426 2693.*

See Historic Highlights, p. 278

LONGFORD   Map ref. 381 L9

When the settlement at Norfolk Island in 1807 failed, many of the evacuated settlers received land grants around Longford. The town itself was established in 1814 when Newman Williat built a hotel. Many grew rich on agriculture, as can be seen by the heritage buildings in and around the town. Longford is classified as an historic town.

Bowthorpe Farm & Gardens This thoroughbred horse stud and pastoral estate includes an avenue of English oaks and elms planted in 1825, leading to the convict-built Georgian homestead (1835). *Pateena Rd. Open daily.* Ⓢ *(03) 6391 1253.*

Brickendon Historic Farming Village One of four homesteads in the district built by the pioneering Archer brothers, Brickendon (1826) belonged to William Archer and is a handsome, two-storey Georgian house of white-washed brick. The delicate portico, having unusual columns with iron tracery and beautiful detailing of the fanlight, is especially distinctive. Archer's descendants still live and farm there today. The Georgian homestead, European trees and 28-km hedge of white, pink and rose hawthorn are strongly reminiscent of rural England. The gardens contain a Gothic chapel, Dutch barns and a

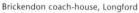

Brickendon coach-house, Longford

coach-house. The property is now open as a colonial farming village, with accommodation in cottages, some of which date from the 1820s. *Wellington St. Open Tues.–Sun. Closed Aug.* Ⓢ *(03) 6391 1251.*

Christ Church A showpiece among Longford's many fine buildings, this sandstone church was built by convicts and completed in 1839. Set in parkland enhanced by 100 varieties of pine donated by WHD Archer (son of Brickendon's founder), it features a magnificent stained-glass window and a tower with a clock bestowed by King George IV. Many noted pioneers are buried in the churchyard. *Wellington St. Open by appt. (03) 6391 1307.*

Woolmers One of Tasmania's historic treasures, Woolmers (1817) was opened to the public by the Archer Historical Foundation following the death in 1994 of the last of six Thomas Archers to live on the property. Woolmers is a time capsule, with generations of Archer belongings decorating the rooms and filling the outbuildings. Accommodation and meals are available in the workers' cottages. *5 km s. Woolmers La. Open daily.* Ⓢ *(03) 6391 2230.*

ALSO OF INTEREST Originally another Archer property, Panshangar Estate is a stately Georgian home set among beautiful English parks and gardens. A nine-square wing of the home has been turned into an apartment for guest accommodation. *Panshangar Rd. (03) 6397 6500.* Last century Longford had many inns and hotels.

Dining room at Woolmers, Longford

Most of them have long since been converted to other uses but are still recognisable from the street. Kilgour's Cottage, Archer St, is an outstanding example and was built by Thomas Archer as a wedding gift to his daughter. *Not open for inspection.* Rows of Georgian cottages can be seen in Burghley and Wellington sts. *Not open for inspection.*

IN THE AREA Artist Tom Roberts is buried in the graveyard of the picturesque 1840 Christ Church, Illawarra Rd, Illawarra. *Church open by appt. (03) 6391 1307.*

🏛 *Brickendon Historic Farming Village, Woolmers La.; (03) 6391 1251.*Website: www.longford.tco.asn.au

MARIA ISLAND   Map ref. 379 P7

This beautiful island off the east coast was established as Tasmania's second penal settlement in 1825. The convict settlement was in the north, at Darlington, and buildings included a penitentiary, a commissariat store and a jetty. It was closed in 1832 in favour of Port Arthur but re-opened 10 years later as a probation settlement. Further buildings were added, until the penal settlements were finally abandoned in 1850–51. In 1884 the island was leased to AGD Bernacchi to set up silk and winemaking industries. Buildings from this period include a Coffee Palace and the remains of cement works Bernacchi established in 1887. The island is now a national park. Basic accommodation is available in the old penitentiary, and there are extensive camping grounds, but no provisions or equipment are available. *Access by ferry from East Coaster Resort, Louisville, near Orford.* $ *(03) 6257 1589.*

🖫 *Maria Island Ranger Station; (03) 6257 1420.*

NEW NORFOLK
Map ref. 379 K8

Situated along the banks of the Derwent, New Norfolk is classified as an historic town, first known as 'The Hills'. Its name and beginnings result from the relocation of settlers from Norfolk Island after the settlement there closed in 1807. Gov. Macquarie later attempted to change its name to Elizabeth Town, after his wife, but New Norfolk stuck.

Bush Inn This two-storey inn has long played a part in New Norfolk community life. Town worthies met here to discuss major projects, and the local Methodists held their services here before a church was built. The building dates from 1815, and a licence was first granted in 1825, making this one of the oldest continuously licensed premises in Australia. *Montagu St. Open daily. (03) 6261 2256.*

Old Colony Inn Built in 1835, the inn is furnished with beautiful antiques and interesting items from early penal times, and now provides meals and accommodation. *Montagu St. Open daily. (03) 6261 2731.*

St Matthew's Anglican Church Tasmania's oldest worshipping Anglican church and probably oldest church outright (1823), although only the walls and floor of the nave are original. St Matthew's Close in the church grounds, built as a Sunday school (1866), is now a folk and craft shop. *Bathurst St. Open daily. (03) 6261 2223.*

Tynwald Willow Bend Estate A magnificent colonial mansion, complete with a tower, gabled roof, wide bay windows and an English country garden, built in 1830 and remodelled in the grand style around 1900. Fully restored, it now offers B&B and self-contained accommodation. *Hobart Rd. (03) 6261 2667.*

ALSO OF INTEREST Willow Court, Burnett St, was the first mental institution established in Australia, built in 1831. It consists of a large barrack square surrounded by wards. *Square open at all times.* Glen Derwent is an early Georgian homestead and outbuildings (1820), now providing colonial accommodation. *44 Hamilton Rd. (03) 6261 3244.* The New Norfolk area is well known for its hops, many of which were dried in the Oast House's three kilns from 1867 until 1969. *Off Hobart Rd, through Tynwald Park. Open Sat.–Sun.* The brown and rainbow trout that now stock Australian and New Zealand rivers are bred from those first raised at Plenty Salmon Ponds in 1864. The ponds are now a tourist attraction incorporating a museum and kiosk. *Open daily.* $ *(03) 6261 2583 or (03) 6261 1076.*

🖫 *Circle St; (03) 6261 0700.*

OATLANDS
Map ref. 379 M5

Oatlands has the largest collection of Georgian architecture in Australia, with 87 sandstone buildings located in High St and 138 within the town boundaries. It developed rapidly after 1832 when it was properly surveyed and proposed as the capital of the Midlands. Oatlands is listed on the National Estate Register as an historic town.

Callington Mill Oatlands was built on brewing and milling, and the 16-m high Callington Mill (1837) is a local landmark. Also known as the Oatlands Flour Mill, it now houses doll and agricultural museums. *Old Mill Lane. Open daily.* $ *(03) 6254 0039 or (03) 6254 1212.*

Courthouse Oatlands' oldest building (1829) is also the oldest Supreme Courthouse in Australia (sittings began in 1841). It took two convicts in irons only four months to complete. *The Esplanade. Open by appt. (03) 6254 1212.*

Holyrood House Once the home of Samuel Page, who ran the Royal Mail Stage Coach Line, this 1840 house has also been a doctor's residence and, for eight months in 1852, Oatlands Grammar School. A heritage garden surrounds the house. *40 High St. Not open for inspection.*

ALSO OF INTEREST St Paul's Catholic Church (1850) is one of four Tasmanian churches designed by Houses of Westminster architect, Augustus Pugin, for his friend, Bishop

Oast House, New Norfolk

Willson. *Gay St. Open by appt. (03) 6254 1212.* St Peter's Anglican Church was designed by John Lee Archer and Robert De Little in the traditional English style. Building commenced in 1838, using local sandstone. St Peter's square belfry is a dominant feature from the Midland Hwy. *Church St. Open by appt. (03) 6254 1111 or (03) 6254 1835.* Amelia Cottage and Forget-me-not Cottage (1838) offer colonial style accommodation. *104 High St. 0408 125 049.* The 1859 Campbell Memorial Church (Uniting) replaced a church that had opened in 1856, but was largely destroyed by a storm just two years later. *High St. Open by appt. (03) 6254 1358.* The attractive two-storeyed stone manse next to the church dates from 1860. *Not open for inspection.*

ℹ️ *85 High St. (03) 6254 1212.* Website: www.oatlands.tco.asn.au

PENGUIN Map ref. 380 H6

Magnificently sited overlooking Bass Strait, Penguin was the last of Tasmania's coastal towns to be settled, officially proclaimed in 1861. It is named for the little penguins still to be found in rookeries along the coast. The gold rush in Victoria in the 1850s was followed by a building boom, and the Penguin district, with its plentiful supply of timber, prospered.
Railway The relocated and restored railway station (1901) was opened

Callington Mill, Oatlands

to mark the station's centenary. Trains from the Don River Railway at Devonport pass through twice a month. *Main St. (03) 6424 6335.*
ALSO OF INTEREST Penguin boasts some lovely buildings, including the tiny library and Neptune Hotel, both in Main St. St Stephen's Anglican Church, built c. 1874, was enlarged in 1895 and is noted for its timber shingle roof, blackwood walls and lovely windows. *Main St. (03) 6437 1421.* Penguin's cemetery, high on the hill at the western end of Main St, includes the graves of many early pioneers as well as that of noted historian Lloyd Robson. The Uniting Church (1903) is built of wood with keyhole windows and highly decorative flourishes. *Main St. Open by appt. (03) 6437 2157.*

ℹ️ *Main St. (03) 6437 1421.* Website: www.penguin.tco.asn.au

PONTVILLE Map ref. 379 L7

Pontville, set on the banks of the Jordan River, was founded in 1830 as an extension of earlier Brighton but remains better preserved. It was built largely of freestone (sandstone) from the local quarries, which supplied most of the stone for buildings throughout Tasmania last century.
Lithgo's Row Built c. 1850 as a store and workers' cottages by former convict, William Lithgo. It now provides colonial accommodation. *Midland Hwy. (03) 6268 1665.*
Old Post Office Today known as Stace House, this stone building (c. 1840) was used as the post office from 1860–1973. The timber verandah was added in the 1850s. *Midland Hwy. Not open for inspection.*
St Mark's Anglican Church This small church was designed by talented architect James Blackburn in an unusual blend of Romanesque and Italianate styles and built 1839–41 in the district's creamy white stone. The front entrance, with its zig-zag detailed arch and Tuscan columns, is striking. *Midland Hwy. Open daily. (03) 6268 1221.*
ALSO OF INTEREST Parts of the sandstone bridge across the Jordan River date from 1842. The Crown Inn, still operating as a hotel, was established in 1835. *256 Midland Hwy. (03) 6268 1235.*

ℹ️ *Brighton Council, Tivoli Rd, Gagebrook; (03) 6268 7000.* Website: www. brighton.tas.gov.au

PORT ARTHUR Map ref. 379 N10

See Historic Highlights, p. 280

QUEENSTOWN Map ref. 378 E3, 380 E12

Although Queenstown's halcyon days are long past, it remains a mining town. The wide streets lined with old buildings amid the towering mountains of the rugged west coast give the classified historic town a unique atmosphere. While a little vegetation is returning to the surrounding hills, they are still largely bare of trees, which were killed at the turn of the century by a combination of logging, smelting and heavy rain. Gold was discovered in 1883 but was soon surpassed in riches by copper. Around the turn of the century, Queenstown and its copper mines were booming, with 5000 inhabitants and 14 hotels. These days operations are scaled to the fluctuating world copper market, and only a few hotels remain.
Abt Railway One of the largest tourism developments to take place in Tasmania is the $30 million redevelopment of this railway, which wound its way through 34 km of thick forests, up and down steep mountains, and over 40 bridges from 1896 until it closed in 1963. While its main purpose was to carry ore from the Mt Lyell Mine to the port at Strahan, it was especially famous for carrying most of Queenstown's residents to the coast for the annual company picnic and then, rowdily, home again. Restored Abt locomotives, specially designed to cope with steep gradients, and carriages now carry passengers. *Driffield St. Open daily.* 💲 *(03) 6471 1700.*
Empire Hotel Completed in 1901, the hotel is a reminder of Queenstown's boom-time glory, with a magnificent handmade blackwood staircase. *2 Orr St. Open daily. (03) 6471 1699.*
Eric Thomas Galley Museum A display of over 1000 historical photographs of the west coast, housed in the former Imperial Hotel (1897), Queenstown's first brick hotel. *Cnr Driffield & Sticht sts. Open daily.* 💲 *(03) 6471 1483.*
Mt Lyell Mine Tours of the mine surface and underground are conducted

daily. The mine, still operating, opened in 1883. *1 Driffield St. Open daily.* Ⓢ *(03) 6471 2388.*

Penghana Formerly the mine's general manager's home, this late Victorian mansion (1898) overlooks the town. It is now a B&B. *32 Esplanade. (03) 6471 2560.*

ALSO OF INTEREST The Queenstown cemetery, on the southern edge of town, has graves of early miners, many with headstones cut from Huon pine. It also contains the graves of the 42 men who died underground during the 1912 mine fire. *Conlan St.* Gormanston, the original mine town, was a thriving community with, among other grand buildings, eight hotels. Only a handful of families continue to live on in the town's old mine houses. *6 km W.*

🅘 *Mt Lyell Mine Tour Office, 1 Driffield St; (03) 6471 2388.* Website: www. queenstown.tco.asn.au

RICHMOND
Map ref. 379 M7

See Historic Highlights, p. 282

ROKEBY
Map ref. 379 M8

The town of Rokeby dates from 1809 and boasts one of Tasmania's few village greens. It was here that the first export apples were grown in 1828, and the first wheat ever grown in Tasmania was also reaped in Rokeby.

OF INTEREST St Matthew's Church, completed in 1843, contains some notable items. The organ is the first keyboard brought to Australia, in 1823. It and the handsome pulpit were relocated from old St David's, Hobart. Some of the chancel chairs were carved in timber from ships in Nelson's fleet. One of Tasmania's most colourful figures, the first chaplain of Van Diemen's Land, the Rev. Robert 'Bobby' Knopwood, is buried in the churchyard. *Cnr King St & North Pde. Key required. (03) 6247 7527.*

🅘 *Council Offices, 12 Somerville St, Sorell; (03) 6265 2201.*

ROSS
Map ref. 379 M3, 381 N12

Founded in 1812, Ross was important as a military post, stock market and coaching stop between Hobart and Launceston; it became the business centre for the surrounding farmlands,

and the area has long been famous for the quality of its wool. A classified historic town, Ross retains an unmistakable Georgian village quality with its arrow-straight, tree-lined main street flanked by simple colonial buildings and the blend of warm-brown stonework, old-fashioned gardens and English elms.

The Barracks This simple, single-storey Georgian building (1836) once housed the English soldiers who were responsible for maintaining law and order in the village during the settlement period. Now a private residence. *Bridge St. Not open for inspection.*

Man O'Ross Hotel First opened in 1817 and rebuilt and panelled in Tasmanian oak 14 years later, this is the village's only licensed hotel today. It stands on a corner of the main crossroads known locally as Temptation. The other three corners are Recreation (the town hall), Salvation (the Catholic church) and Damnation (the old gaol, now a private residence). *Cnr Bridge & Church sts. Open daily. (03) 6381 5240.*

Ross Bridge The village's pride is the beautiful three-arched sandstone bridge that spans the Macquarie River. It was built between 1833 and 1836 and replaced an earlier timber structure. Although designed by Government Architect John Lee Archer, the real credit is due to convict Daniel Herbert, who, with stonemason James Colbeck, was responsible for the almost 200 beautifully carved Celtic symbols, animals, faces and other motifs decorating the arches. Herbert was granted a pardon for his fine work. (He is buried in Ross's original burial ground, off Park St, under a magnificent tombstone of his own design.)

Ross Memorial Library & Recreation Room Originally the headquarters of the 50th Ordinance Corps, whose regimental coat of arms together with the date 1836 is carved above the door. *Bridge St. (03) 6381 5466.*

Scotch Thistle Inn Built as a coaching inn in the 1840s, this two-storey building has served as a boarding house and a private home. Across the lovely old courtyard, paved with convict-made bricks, stands the original coach-house and, behind it, the blacksmith's shop. It is now a B&B. *Church St. (03) 6381 5213.*

Detail of Ross Bridge, Ross

Tasmanian Wool Centre Incorporating Visitor Information, a heritage museum and wool exhibition area, the centre also runs guided tours of the village on request, booking essential. *Church St. Open daily.* Ⓢ *(03) 6381 5466.*

ALSO OF INTEREST The post office, built in 1896, has a charming Victorian quality, domestic in scale. *Church St. Open Mon.–Fri.* The oldest church remaining is St John's Anglican Church, a handsome design built using stone from the first St John's and opened in 1869. *Church St. Open daily.* The Methodist Church, now Uniting, was largely financed by Capt. Horton of Somercotes, in 1882. It is built in the traditional Gothic style on a hill overlooking the town. *Church St. Open daily.* The Female Factory Site, or women's prison, operated from 1848–54. The only building remaining on the 3-ha site is the commandant's cottage, in which can be found a site model and other displays. *Off Bond St. Open daily. (03) 6381 5466.*

IN THE AREA South of Ross is Somercotes, which was settled in 1823 by Capt. Samuel Horton and has been in the same family ever since. All buildings on the property are classified, including the single-storey Georgian homestead, and the estate workers' cottages, which are now used for colonial accommodation. Bushranger Martin Cash paid a visit to the property in 1843, firing off a shot to intimidate his captives. The bullet is still buried in an architrave. Tours for groups, booking essential. *4 km s, Mona Vale Rd. (03) 6381 5231.*

Tasmanian Wool Centre, Church St; (03) 6381 5466. Website: www. taswoolcentre.com.au

SHEFFIELD

Map ref. 380 I8

A farming town situated at the base of spectacular Mt Roland in the island's north-west, Sheffield has become famous for the many murals by local artists depicting its pioneering past.

Slaters Country Store This department store was established in 1899, selling everything from tailor-made clothing to early radios. Still run by the same family, the store contains the only flying-fox cash register system left in Tasmania. *52 Main St. (03) 6491 1121.*

IN THE AREA Waldheim Chalet (1912) was the home of Cradle Mountain legend Gustav Weindorfer, who brought the first tourists to the valley in his bid to have the area protected. He was successful in 1922, when 158 000 ha between Cradle Mountain and Lake St Clair were declared a scenic reserve. Today they form part of Tasmania's Wilderness World Heritage Area. Weindorfer lived here until his death in 1932 (he is buried at Waldheim). The chalet houses a history display and audio presentation. Accommodation is available

Man O'Ross Hotel, Ross

at Waldheim Cabins. *60 km sw on Connells Ave. Open daily. (03) 6492 1110.*

Pioneer Cres.; (03) 6491 1036. Website: www.sheffield.tco.asn.au

STANLEY

Map ref. 380 D3

Physically, Stanley is dominated by The Nut, a huge volcanic outcrop, around the base of which the village straggles. Historically it is the oldest and most interesting settlement in Tasmania's north-west, founded in 1826 as the headquarters of the Van Diemen's Land Company, which was formed in London to cultivate land and breed fine-wool sheep in the colony. In the gold-boom years, it became significant as a port for shipping goods to the Victorian goldfields. Stanley is a classified historic town.

Highfield Historic Site Designed by company surveyor and noted explorer Henry Hellyer, Highfield is a sandstone house built in 1835 for the Chief Agent of the Van Diemen's Land Company. Restored by the National Parks and Wildlife Service, its outbuildings include a chapel, servants' quarters, stables and barns. *Highfield La. (off Scenic Dr.). Open daily. $ (03) 6458 1100.*

Lyons Cottage Stanley was the birthplace of Joseph Lyons, the only Tasmanian to become Prime Minister (1932–39). His family's weatherboard cottage (1840s) has been furnished in period style. *14 Alexander Tce. Open daily. $ (03) 6458 1145.*

Stanley Discovery Museum & Genealogy Centre A folk museum and art centre with a collection of shell work and items of historical interest, including ships' relics. *Church St. Open daily, closed June–July. $ (03) 6458 1145.*

Union Hotel Built in 1847, with a handsome stone arched cellar and maze of narrow staircases. *21 Church St. Open daily. (03) 6458 1161.*

ALSO OF INTEREST St James' Presbyterian Church is one of Australia's early prefabricated buildings. The weatherboard sections arrived from England in 1853. *Fletcher St. Open by appt. (03) 6458 1449.* Bluestone stores near the harbour are reminders of Stanley's 19th century importance as a port. Some were designed by Colonial Architect John Lee Archer, whose

home, Poet's Cottage, was here. He is buried in the picturesque local cemetery, as is Henry Hellyer. *Browns Rd.*

IN THE AREA Woolnorth, one of Tasmania's most fascinating properties, is still owned and operated by the London-based Van Diemen's Land Company, although its size has shrunk to 22 200 ha, or one-seventh of the original 1825 grant. Now farming cattle and sheep, the property contains a number of historic buildings, including the oldest building in the north-west, the 1831 cookhouse cottage. Tours and accommodation are available at Woolnorth, booking essential. *75 km w, via Smithton & West Montagu. Open daily. $ (03) 6452 1493.* While the exact details are still disputed, Woolnorth was the site of an 1827 massacre – company shepherds killed a group of Aboriginal people at Cape Grim. Further south is Tasmania's best-known Aboriginal rock-art site, Mt Cameron West, which has been recently returned to Aboriginal ownership. *80 km w, via Marrawah.*

The Nut Chairlift, Browns Rd; (03) 6458 1286.

STRAHAN

Map ref. 378 D3, 380 D12

Still the only port on Tasmania's west coast, Strahan handled more cargo than any other Tasmanian port in its heyday, when it was the outlet for ore mined in Queenstown and also for Huon pine logs, floated down the Gordon River. From a peak of 2000, the population dwindled to about 460, until the dispute over plans to dam the Franklin River threw Strahan into the international spotlight in the early 1980s. These days it is one of Tasmania's busiest tourist centres, with many of its notable historic buildings renovated. Strahan is also at the end of the Abt railway line.

Morrisons Huon Pine Mill Operated by the third generations of well-known pining families, this mill has been treating Huon pine and other Tasmanian timbers using traditional methods since 1940. Both the Morrison and Bradshaw families, which run this and a more modern mill in Queenstown, began pining in the region in the early 20th century.

The waterfront, Strahan

Nowadays, the Huon pine is salvaged from the forest floor and flooded rivers under government supervision, not felled. *The Esplanade. Open daily. (03) 6471 7235.*

Sarah Island From Strahan one can take trips up the Gordon River and around Macquarie Harbour. Of special interest is the trip to Sarah Island, the site of Tasmania's first penal settlement in 1822, mentioned in Marcus Clark's classic novel *For the Term of His Natural Life*. The settlement was abandoned after 12 years (and revived briefly in 1846). Ruins of some of the major buildings and shipyard are all that remain. *World Heritage Cruises (03) 6471 7174. Gordon River Cruises (03) 6471 4300.*

Strahan Visitors Centre This award-winning centre is a fascinating retelling of the region's past, with displays on the history of Aboriginal people, convicts, hydro development and conservation. The play, *The Ship That Never Never Was*, tells the story of the last ship built on Sarah Island, and is performed daily at the centre's amphitheatre. *The Esplanade. Open daily.* Ⓢ *(03) 6471 7622.*

ALSO OF INTEREST On the Esplanade is the impressive former Customs and Telegraph Office (1901), now the post office and the National Parks and Wildlife Service office (open office hours) and the 1897 former Union Steamship Co. (not open for inspection). Two of Strahan's grand

mansions, Franklin Manor (1896) and Ormiston House (1899), provide colonial accommodation and dining. *Franklin Manor, The Esplanade, (03) 6471 7311. Ormiston House, The Esplanade, (03) 6471 7077.* At Regatta Point, the original Abt railway station building (1899) is the terminus for the reconstructed Abt railway running from **Queenstown**. *(03) 6471 1700.* The Piners Festival, which includes traditional piners' punt races, is held in March each year. *(03) 6471 7017.*

🛈 *The Esplanade; (03) 6471 7622.* Website: www.strahan.tco.asn.au/ visitorinfo.htm

SWANSEA   Map ref. 379 P4, 381 P13

Swansea developed during the 1820s and 1830s, growing to the point where it became the administrative centre of Glamorgan, Australia's oldest municipality, proclaimed in 1860. The original council chambers are still used. A classified historic town, Swansea is nestled on Great Oyster Bay overlooking magnificent Freycinet Peninsula.

Bark Mill & East Coast Museum Australia's only restored and fully operative bark mill dates from the 1880s. Black wattle bark was used in the tanning of skins, and many examples are displayed. There is also an excellent museum of local memorabilia dating from early settlement

days. *96 Tasman Hwy. Open daily.* Ⓢ *(03) 6257 8382.*

Glamorgan Community Centre This building started life as a school in 1860. It has since served as a War Memorial Institute and now incorporates a museum of local history. *22 Franklin St. Open Mon.–Sat. afternoons and evenings.* Ⓢ *(03) 6257 8215.*

Morris's General Store A substantial three-storey store dating from 1838 and still in business. A small museum displays items connected with the store's history. *13 Franklin St. Open shop hours. (03) 6257 8101.*

Spiky Bridge About 8 km s on the Tasman Hwy is a convict-built bridge (1843), commonly known as Spiky Bridge because of the spikes made of fieldstones.

ALSO OF INTEREST The Swan Inn (formerly Bay View Hotel), built 1841, has undergone many changes, but the original two-storey brick and stone building is still discernible. *Franklin St. Open daily. (03) 6257 8899.* The imposing Meredith Inn (1853) has been converted to a B&B. *Noyes St. (03) 6257 8119.*

IN THE AREA The town of Triabunna was an important whaling port early last century and a garrison town in the 1820s, and retains many early buildings. *51 km sw on Tasman Hwy.*

🛈 *Swansea Bark Mill & East Coast Museum, 96 Tasman Hwy; (03) 6257 8382.*

TUNBRIDGE   Map ref. 379 M4, 381 M13

Established in 1809, when it was called Tunbridge Wells, Tunbridge became the central coaching stop between Hobart and Launceston and was the site of much-prized salt plains at a time when salt had to be imported from Europe. The plains can still be seen east of the village.

Tunbridge Wells Inn The oldest standing building in the region, the inn was built as a residence in 1825. When the main highway came through Tunbridge a few years later, the building was converted to an inn and remained licensed until 1838. Now a B&B. *Victoria St. (03) 6255 2126.*

Victoria Inn The sandstone mounting steps outside this former Georgian coaching inn (1843) are thought to have been originally outside the Tunbridge Wells Inn. Also outside the

Victoria, today known as Tunbridge Manor and a private home, is a roller cut from a single block of sandstone, part of the convict road- and bridge-building equipment used in the area. *Main Rd. Not open for inspection.*

ALSO OF INTEREST The stone bridge on Old Main Rd that spans the Blackman River was built by convicts in 1848. The former 'Blind Chapel', late 1800s, is so called because the wall of the chapel overlooking the Victoria Inn is windowless. The local explanation is that this was to prevent parishioners gazing upon temptation. *Old Main Rd. Not open for inspection.*

🛈 *85 High St, Oatlands; (03) 6254 1212.* Website: www.oatlands.tco.asn.au

WADDAMANA Map ref. 379 J3, 381 J13

South of the Great Lake in central Tasmania is the Waddamana Power Station (1916), which provided the first hydro-electric power to Hobart. The workers' quarters have been converted into tourist accommodation and a field study centre.

Waddamana Power Station Museum A tribute to the beginning of hydro-electric development in Tasmania, which had a profound impact physically, socially and culturally on the island throughout the 20th century. Run by Hydro Tasmania, the museum features an array of machinery, photographs, artifacts and other memorabilia. *On the C178, 37 km NW of Bothwell. Open daily. Tours available.* Ⓢ *(03) 6259 6158.*

🛈 *Great Lake Hotel, Great Lake Hwy, Miena; (03) 6259 8163.*

WESTBURY Map ref. 381 K9

Life still centres around the village green in Westbury, and today it is used for fetes, fairs and picnics. The classified historic town was surveyed in 1823 and laid out in 1828 on a bold scale but never fulfilled the early intention to make it a gateway city to Tasmania's north-west.

Fitzpatrick's Inn An attractive, two-storey Georgian inn, originally called the Commercial Hotel (1833) and later the Olde English Inn, this was the first licensed inn in Westbury. Now an antique gallery and B&B. *56 Bass Hwy. Open daily. (03) 6393 1153.*

Pearns Steam World An extensive collection of steam-driven machinery, dating back to 1900. *65 Bass Hwy. Open daily.* Ⓢ *(03) 6393 1414.*

White House This square of buildings enclosing a courtyard started life c. 1840 as White's Token Store. Later additions include a coach depot, a Methodist meeting place, a bakery and a flour mill. Today the complex provides a veritable feast of history for the visitor. In the old store or White House is an excellent collection of 17th and 18th century furniture and memorabilia. The Old Mill House houses a toy museum with items from 1850–1950. The bake-house oven has been restored to working order, and there is an early ice-cream vending machine.

Waddamana Power Station Museum, Waddamana

170 King St. Open Tues.–Sun. Closed July. Ⓢ *(03) 6393 1171. NT.*

IN THE AREA Culzean is an intriguing Anglo-Indian style house built (1835–40) for Capt. Edward Martin. The house is surrounded by magnificent gardens and a huge lake. *1 km N, William St. House not open for inspection. Gardens open daily Oct.–June.* Ⓢ *(03) 6393 1132.*

🛈 *Clarke's Antiques and Gingerbread Cottages, 52 William St; (03) 6393 1140.* Website: www.meandervalley.com

ZEEHAN Map ref. 378 D1, 380 D11

Abel Tasman in 1642 was the first white man to lay eyes on what is today known as Mt Zeehan. But it was Bass and Flinders, during their circumnavigation of Tasmania, who named it and Mt Heemskirk after Tasman's two ships. It took the discovery of silver-lead more than a century later for a settlement to develop. By 1900 Zeehan had become Tasmania's third largest city. The mining boom continued until 1908 and with it came the embellishment of Zeehan's main street with several impressive buildings. Zeehan is a classified historic town.

Former Grand Hotel Grand in both name and Victorian design, this hotel (1898) has long since ceased to entertain the famous, but is still in business. *Main St. (03) 6471 6225.*

Gaiety Theatre This lavish theatre, which seated 1000 people, is actually part of the Grand Hotel. It opened in 1898 and in its heyday featured the best of local and visiting talent, including Lola Montez, Enrico Caruso and Dame Nellie Melba. It is sometimes used for community events. *Main St. (03) 6471 6225.*

West Coast Pioneers Memorial Museum Housed in the old Zeehan School of Mines (1893), this is said to be the finest mining museum in Australia. Certainly its mineral collection is one of the world's best. There is a wide-ranging display of early mining equipment and memorabilia, locomotives, and a small display of Tasmanian animals and birds, as well as Aboriginal artifacts. *Main Rd. Open daily.* Ⓢ *(03) 6471 6225.*

🛈 *West Coast Pioneers Memorial Museum, Main Rd; (03) 6471 6225.* Website: www.zeehan.tco.asn.au/out. html

HISTORIC HIGHLIGHTS

Convict-built bridge, Richmond

Tasmania has a wealth of small, charming villages nestled in idyllic settings, as well as historic sites linked to its settlement days. Launceston is of special note, the third oldest city in Australia. Richmond retains the quiet charm of a small Georgian village. The haunting ruins of Port Arthur are a fascinating time capsule, recalling the country's convict origins.

LAUNCESTON

Tasmania's second – and Australia's third – oldest city was founded in 1805. Bass and Flinders sighted the Tamar Estuary, on which Launceston stands, during their voyage of 1798, but it was six years before the area was settled. The settlement was initially called Patersonia, after expedition leader Lieutenant-Colonel William Paterson, but he soon changed the name to Launceston in honour of Governor King, who was born at a town of that name in Cornwall. By 1825 Launceston, with its growing wealth as an industrial and rural centre and as a major river port, was the official northern headquarters of the colony.

Launceston post office, early 1900

Post Office
This robust building represents the full flowering of the Victorian style. Rising at one corner is a lofty, round tower, described at one time as a pepper-pot. The post office was completed in 1889, the tower in 1903.
Cnr St John & Cameron sts.

Gateway Tasmania Travel Centre
cnr Paterson & St John sts
(03) 6336 3133
Website: www.gatewaytas.com.au

Macquarie House
This substantial, three-storey building, erected in 1830 as a warehouse for merchant Henry Reed, served as a military barracks in the 1840s. Most famously, the Batman and Fawkner expeditions to establish Melbourne were supplied from here. It is now a gallery and restaurant.
Charles St, Civic Sq. Open daily.
(03) 6334 6558.

Old Umbrella Shop
Small in scale and beautifully detailed, this elegant Victorian shop has survived virtually unaltered since it was built in the 1860s. The plate-glass windows were among the first used in the town. The National Trust maintains this gem as a gift shop and information centre.
60 George St. Open Mon.–Fri. & Sat. mornings.
(03) 6331 9248. NT.

Queen Victoria Museum & Art Gallery
A splendid example of late-19th century public architecture to celebrate Queen Victoria's jubilee, opened in 1891. It is a showcase for the Museum's natural history collections and also houses a richly decorated Chinese temple.
Wellington St. Open Mon.–Sat. & Sun. afternoons.
(03) 6323 3777.

Penny Royal World
This huge complex features an 1825 corn mill moved stone by stone from Barton, near Cressy. There is also a wheelwright and blacksmith shops, a museum, tavern and water mill. A restored tramway runs to the old Cataract quarry site, and there is a paddle-steamer, *Lady Stelfox.* Accommodation is available in the old Barton water mill.
147 Paterson St. Open daily.
(03) 6331 6699.

Customs House

The imposing customs house (1885), built in the Classical Revival style, is a reminder of how prosperous the port was during the 19th century.
Esplanade. Not open for inspection.

Queen Victoria Museum – Inveresk

At the former Launceston Railway workshops, a unique industrial heritage site, the museum presents contemporary and heritage cultural collections and Tasmanian history. A feature is the industrial blacksmith shop.
Invermay Rd, Inveresk. Open daily. (03) 6323 3777.

Albert Hall

The scene of many concerts, exhibitions and other cultural activities since it was built in 1891 for the Tasmanian International Exhibition.
Tamar St (bordering City Park). (03) 6331 7433.

City Park

A magnificent 12-ha retreat with enormous oaks and elms that date back to when the gardens were laid out in the 1820s. It features a small monkey enclosure, established late in the 19th century, a conservatory and an ornamental fountain.
Cimitiere, Tamar, Brisbane & Lawrence sts. (03) 6323 3610.

Colonial Motor Inn

The main wing of the motel complex is a spacious two-storey brick building erected in 1847 for the prestigious Launceston Grammar School. Part of the motel is in the former St John's Parish Hall, a charming brick building (1842) with steep gables and soaring timber finials.
Cnr Elizabeth & George sts. (03) 6331 6588.

ALSO OF INTEREST

At the Batman Fawkner Inn one can stay in an establishment dating from c. 1824. The first landlord was John Pascoe Fawkner, renowned as one of Melbourne's earliest settlers. *35 Cameron St. (03) 6331 7222.* St John St contains a distinguished array of commercial buildings and several churches, as well as late colonial and Victorian residences, including the Regency house Nelumie at no. 159, built in 1842 for Dr W Russ Pugh, who performed the first operation with an anaesthetic in the Southern Hemisphere in 1847. *Not open for inspection.* About 5 km from the city centre is Australia's oldest woollen mill, Waverley Woollen Mills, dating from 1874. Tours available. *Waverley Rd, Waverley. Open Mon.–Fri.* Ⓢ *(03) 6339 1106.* The synagogue, the second oldest in Australia, was built in 1844 in the Regency Egyptian style. *126 St John St. Not open for inspection.*

Christ Church Baptist

Overlooking Princes Sq., this church (1883–85), with a wealth of Gothic detailing, replaced a sober Greek Revival chapel (1842), known as Milton Hall, that stands adjacent.
Frederick St. Open by appt. (03) 6331 4900.

St John's Anglican Church

Building started on this striking church in 1824, though the nave was finally added in 1938. The Georgian tower has a clock and weathervane. John Batman, famous as the founder of Melbourne, was married here.
157 St John St. Open daily. (03) 6331 4896.

PORT ARTHUR

The best known of Tasmania's penal settlements, Port Arthur was established in September 1830 when the Lieutenant-Governor of Van Diemen's Land, Colonel George Arthur, decided to concentrate the colony's penal stations in one area. Macquarie Harbour and Maria Island, which had served as secondary punishment centres for convicts who had committed further crimes in the colony, were closed and their inmates transferred to Port Arthur. It closed in 1877, 24 years after transportation ceased. By then, an estimated 12 500 sentences had been served at Port Arthur.

Port Arthur Historic Site
Port Arthur
Freecall 1800 659 101
Website: www.portarthur.org.au

Gov. George Arthur by Benjamin
Duterrau, c. 1832

Separate Prison
When corporal punishment ceased here in 1848, this prison was built to allow incorrigibles to reflect in silence on their sins. Even in the chapel, convicts sat in cubicles from which they could see only the chaplain, and they entered singly to avoid contact with each other. Any prisoner who persisted in abusing the rule of silence was locked away in total isolation. From the late 1860s on, every convict sent to Port Arthur served time here before joining the general prison population.

A re-enactment of Port Arthur's convict days

Interpretation Gallery
Within the Visitor Centre, this gallery lets you trace a convict's story, from the reason for the sentence to the transport ship and his time at Port Arthur, through the 'Lottery of Life'. The Visitor Centre also runs evening ghost tours.

Asylum
One of the last buildings erected at Port Arthur, after transportation had ended, the asylum (1867) housed those convicts deemed to be insane. Extensively damaged in the 1895 and 1897 bushfires, it was rebuilt and used as a town hall for Carnarvon, the name given to Port Arthur once the gaol closed. Now a museum and coffee shop.

IN THE AREA
THE COAL MINES SETTLEMENT, in the peninsula's far north, was known as 'hell on earth' to the convicts sent there from Port Arthur. Ruins of the warders' quarters, barracks and chapel remain, and an underground cell block is open daily for inspection. *30 km NW*. Australia's first railway carried passengers and supplies (shipped from Hobart) from Taranna to the penal settlement at Port Arthur, avoiding the rough sea journey around Cape Raoul. Carriages carrying up to half a tonne were pushed by four convicts. A replica of the railway can be seen in the grounds of **NORFOLK BAY CONVICT STATION** (1838), which also provides accommodation. *12 km N. 5862 Arthur Hwy, Taranna. (03) 6250 3487.*

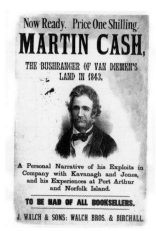

Now Ready. Price One Shilling.
MARTIN CASH,
THE BUSHRANGER OF VAN DIEMEN'S LAND IN 1843.

A Personal Narrative of his Exploits in Company with Kavanagh and Jones, and his Experiences at Port Arthur and Norfolk Island.

TO BE HAD OF ALL BOOKSELLERS.

J. WALCH & SONS: WALCH BROS. & BIRCHALL.

Bushranger Martin Cash, who spent time at Port Arthur, published a book about his experiences

Hospital
Little but the crumbling stone facade of the hospital remains. It was built in 1842 to replace an earlier wooden building and was well equipped for its day. It was badly damaged by the 1895 and 1897 bushfires.

Memorial Garden & Reflecting Pool

Behind the remains of the Broad Arrow Cafe is a memorial to the 35 people who were killed in a random shooting attack at Port Arthur on 28 April 1996.

Isle of the Dead

Those who ended their days at Port Arthur were buried on this island in the middle of the bay. It was the final resting place for about 1100 convicts, civilians, prison officers and soldiers. Convicts were buried in unmarked graves, while decorative headstones, carved by convicts of varying stonemasonry skill, marked the other graves. *Ferry operates daily Sept.–June.* $

Church

Completed in the Gothic style in 1837, this building is an impressive sight, even without a roof and windows. The church has 13 spires representing Christ and the apostles, but no name. Nor has it been consecrated, as it was always used by several denominations. A wooden steeple was blown down in 1875, and the church was gutted when sparks from a fire set it alight in 1884.

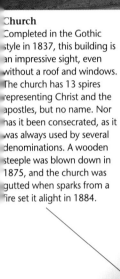

Point Puer Boys' Prison

Established about 1 km across the bay from the main prison at Port Arthur, Point Puer operated 1834–49 as a type of reform school, where 9- to 18-year-olds could be separated from adult convicts. It was the first time in the British penal system that boys and men were separated.

Map labels: To Hobart; Norfolk Bay Convict Station; ARTHUR HWY; Coal Mines Settlement; Gate; SCALE 0 — 100 m; N; CHURCH ST; JETTY RD; CHAMP ST; TRAMWAY ST; BOND ST; Radcliffe; Creek; TARLETON ST; Visitor Car Park; ST; Ferry; Isle of the Dead; Point Puer Boys' Prison; Mason Cove; Commandants Point

Penitentiary

Built in 1844, this was one of the largest grain mills in Australia until it was converted in 1855–57 to a penitentiary housing 484 convicts. The first and second floors were taken up with cells about 2 m x 1.5 m, in which the prisoners in leg irons slept. The mess-room, Catholic chapel and library occupied the third floor; the fourth floor was for better-behaved prisoners, who slept in dormitories. A cook-house, bake-house and wash-house block adjoin the main building.

The Guard Tower

This well-preserved stone building (1835) was a lookout post and lock-up for prisoners awaiting transportation to Hobart for trial for serious crimes and possible execution.

Commandant's House

Built in the 1830s for Capt. Charles O'Hara Booth, Commandant 1833–44, who, by all accounts, ruled the settlement justly but with little compassion. The house, away from the main penal settlement, stood in a large, private garden. It has been restored; the front to reflect Booth's period, the rear in turn-of-the-20th-century style, when it served as the Hotel Carnarvon.

PORT ARTHUR HISTORIC SITE

The convict ruins and restored buildings are set in 40 ha of landscaped grounds. A day ticket entitles visitors access to the historic site walking tours and harbour cruises.
Open daily. $ *Freecall 1800 659 101.*

RICHMOND

Richmond takes pride of place in a state renowned for its many colonial villages. The area was explored by Europeans in 1803 and, with the discovery of coal soon after, the district became known as Coal River. When Lieutenant-Governor Sorell proclaimed a township in 1824, he named it Richmond. The town soon developed as an important granary, becoming the colony's major wheat centre, and its strategic position also made it suitable as a military post and convict station. When the Sorell Causeway was built in 1872, Richmond was no longer on the main thoroughfare between Hobart and Port Arthur and settled down to the leisurely pace that remains part of its charm to this day.

Richmond Arms Hotel
This fine hotel, built in 1888 and noted for its beautiful cast-iron lace balconies, replaced the Lennox Arms (1827), which was destroyed by fire. A restored stable is all that remains of the original inn. Accommodation available.
42 Bridge St. (03) 6260 2109.

Old Hobart Town
21a Bridge St
(03) 6260 2502
Website: www.richmondvillage.com.au

Anglican church graveyard

Old Hobart Town
A unique model village of Hobart as it was in the 1820s. It was largely constructed using original plans and drawings from the era, some from the State Archives. There are more than 60 buildings and 400 period figurines.
Cnr Bridge & Henry sts. Open daily. Ⓢ
(03) 6260 2502.

ALSO OF INTEREST

The rear section of Mrs Currie's House was the original Prince of Wales Inn (1820), while the Georgian front was added c. 1850. It is now a B&B. *4 Franklin St. (03) 6260 2766.* The Millhouse on the Bridge, also a B&B, was built in 1853 by convicts as a steam mill. *2 Wellington St. (03) 6260 2428.* The original courthouse and council chambers (1825) are still council owned. *Bridge St. Not open for inspection.* The Anglican church graveyard across the Coal River makes for interesting browsing, the oldest tombstone dating from 1823. The former Richmond Hotel dates from the early 1830s and still bears the name of the 1838 licensee – Lawrence Cotham – above its door. *Cnr Henry & Bathurst sts. Not open for inspection.* Historical walks around Richmond are offered most days by appt. Ⓢ *(03) 6248 5510.*

Prospect House
This grand Georgian mansion on 10 ha of grounds was built by James Buscombe in 1830 and is now owned by his great-great-grandson, Mike Buscombe. It is a licensed restaurant offering specialities of Tasmanian produce, served in front of roaring log fires in winter. Visitors can inspect the old cellars, and accommodation is available in the original convict-built barn and hayloft.
Off the Hobart rd, just outside town. Open for dinner daily & lunch Wed.–Sun. (03) 6260 2207.

Richmond Bridge
Tasmania is known for its convict-built bridges, and the Richmond Bridge enjoys the distinction of being the oldest surviving in Australia. It was built of stone between 1823 and 1825 and, unlike the richly carved Ross Bridge, is functional rather than decorative. According to local legend the bridge is haunted by several ghosts, including that of a particularly harsh overseer who was murdered by the convict workers and disposed of under the bridge.

St John's Catholic Church
Built by convict architect Frederick Thomas, this Gothic Revival stone church opened for worship in 1837, at which stage only the nave was built, and is the oldest Catholic church in Australia still in use. It was completed in 1859, to models by Houses of Westminster architect Augustus Pugin. The copper-covered spire was added in the mid-1900s.
St John's Circle. Open daily. (03) 6260 2189.

Bridge Inn
One of Richmond's oldest inns, with a part of the building dating from c. 1817, it was licensed as a hotel from 1834 until 1975. It has been restored and today houses a complex of shops including an antique store and bakery.
Bridge St. Open daily.

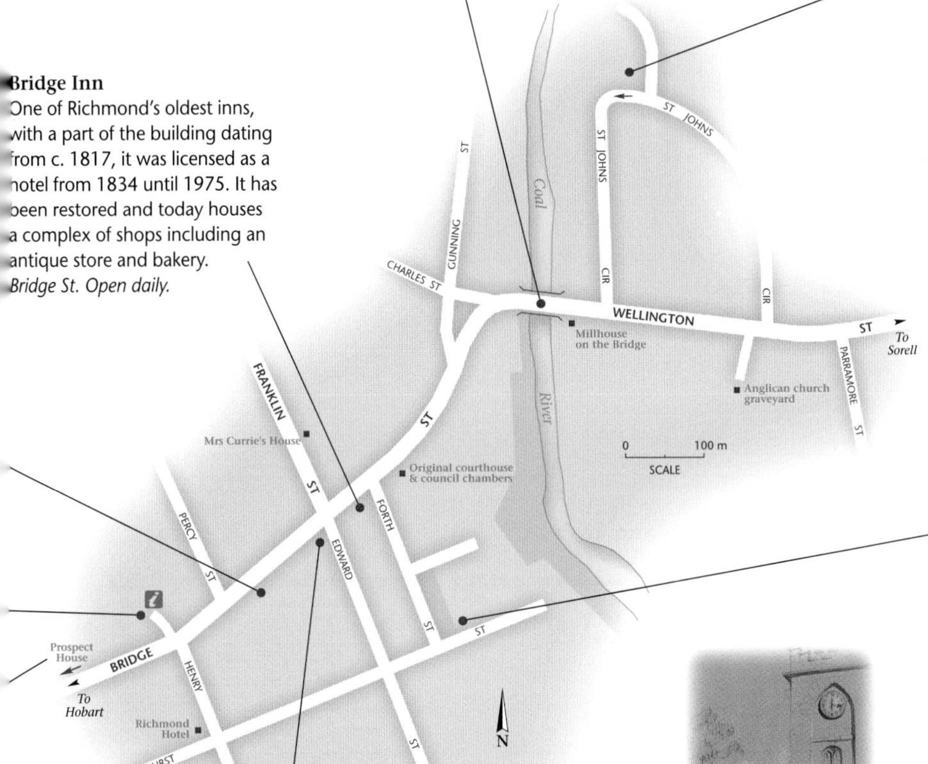

ST JOHNS CIR
ST JOHNS
GUNNING ST
CHARLES ST
Coal River
WELLINGTON ST
To Sorell
Millhouse on the Bridge
Anglican church graveyard
PARRAMORE ST
FRANKLIN ST
Mrs Currie's House
Original courthouse & council chambers
0 100 m
SCALE
FORTH ST
EDWARD ST
PERCY ST
Prospect House
BRIDGE ST
To Hobart
HENRY ST
Richmond Hotel
BATHURST ST
TORRENS ST
CHURCH ST
N

1825 AD

Richmond Gaol
As a penal settlement, Richmond predates Port Arthur by five years. The gaol (1825) is the oldest in Australia and is one of the best-preserved convict gaols, with original cells and locks. Originally only five small rooms, it was extended over the next 15 years, the stone wall surrounding the gaol being built last. Early inmates were bushrangers, Aboriginal prisoners and convicts working on road gangs. The old almond tree outside is believed to have been planted by an injured Aboriginal boy brought here for treatment. There is also a two-storey gaoler's house.
37 Bathurst St. Open daily. (S) (03) 6260 2127.

St Luke's Anglican Church
Designed by Colonial Architect John Lee Archer and built by convicts, this stone church (1834–36) is noted for its beautiful timbered ceiling, a complex web of struts and joints that earned the convict carpenter responsible his freedom. The lectern and the clock (1828) were both brought from England for old St David's in Hobart and relocated to Richmond in 1922.
Torrens St. Open by appt. (03) 6265 2445.

Saddler's Court

Saddler's Court
The handsome two-storey Georgian building (1848) once belonged to the Bridge Inn and was a saddlery for many years. Tasmanian art and craftwork, including sculpture and jewellery, can be viewed here.
48 Bridge St. Open daily. (03) 6260 2132.

ROAD MAPS OF AUSTRALIA

MAP SYMBOLS

Freeway; freeway under construction	
Highway, sealed	
Highway, unsealed	
Main road, sealed	
Main road, unsealed	
Secondary road, sealed, (suburbs maps only)	
Secondary road, unsealed, (suburbs maps only)	
Other road, sealed, with traffic direction arrow	
Other road, unsealed	
Mall	
Vehicle track	
Railway, with station	Paratoo
Total kilometres between two points	114
Intermediate kilometres	45
State border	
State capital city	○ **SYDNEY**
Town, over 50 000 inhabitants	○ **GEELONG**
Town, 10 000–50 000 inhabitants	○ **Bundaberg**
Town, 5 000–10 000 inhabitants	○ **Katherine**
Town, 1 000–5 000 inhabitants	○ Narrogin
Town, 200–1 000 inhabitants	○ Robe
Town, under 200 inhabitants	○ Miena
Suburb, on state and region maps	○ BELCONNEN
Suburb, on suburban maps	**Belconnen**
Locality (area name)	Williamsford
Pastoral station homestead	□ *Alroy Downs*
Major Aboriginal community	○ Borroloola
Aboriginal community	○ Murgenella
Roadhouse	Fortesque Roadhouse
Commercial airport	✈
Historical place of interest	■
Landmark feature	•
Adjoining map page number	304
National park	
Other reserve	
Aboriginal / Torres Strait Islander land	
Prohibited area	
Town listed in A to Z section	🏛

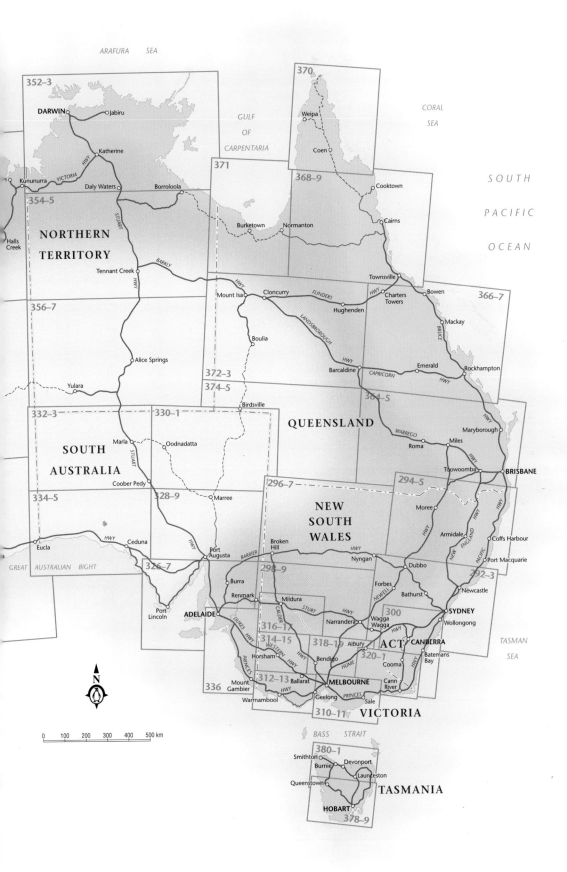

ARAFURA SEA

352–3

DARWIN ○——Jabiru

GULF

CORAL

OF

SEA

Katherine ○

CARPENTARIA

Weipa ○

370

Kununurra ○

VICTORIA HWY

Daly Waters ○——Borroloola ○

371

Coen ○

354–5

STUART HWY

368–9

Cooktown ○

SOUTH

Halls
Creek ○

NORTHERN
TERRITORY

BARKLY

Burketown ○ Normanton ○

Cairns ○

PACIFIC

OCEAN

Tennant Creek ○

HWY

Mount Isa ○ Cloncurry ○

FLINDERS

Townsville ○

356–7

Hughenden ○

Charters
Towers ○

Bowen ○

366–7

LANDSBOROUGH

HWY

Mackay ○

BRUCE

Alice Springs ○

Boulia ○

372–3

HWY

Emerald ○

CAPRICORN HWY

Rockhampton ○

332–3

374–5

Barcaldine ○

364–5

Marla ○

Oodnadatta ○

330–1

Birdsville ○

QUEENSLAND

WARREGO HWY

Maryborough ○

Yulara ○

STUART

SOUTH

AUSTRALIA

Coober Pedy ○

328–9

Roma ○

Miles ○

HWY

334–5

Marree ○

Toowoomba ○

BRISBANE ●

296–7

294–5

Eucla ○ Ceduna ○

HWY

Port
Augusta ○

BARRIER

NEW
SOUTH
WALES

Broken
Hill ○

Moree ○

NEW ENGLAND HWY

PACIFIC HWY

Armidale ○

Coffs Harbour ○

GREAT AUSTRALIAN BIGHT

326–7

Port
Lincoln ○

Burra ○

Renmark ○

298–9

HWY

Nyngan ○

Dubbo ○

Forbes ○

Port Macquarie ○

292–3

Newcastle ○

Mildura ○

STURT

Bathurst ○

DUKES HWY

316–17

Narrandera ○

Wagga
Wagga ○

300

SYDNEY ●

Wollongong ○

ADELAIDE ●

314–15

WESTERN HWY

318–19

Albury ○

Bendigo ○

ACT

320–1

CANBERRA ●

TASMAN

SEA

Horsham ○

HUME HWY

Cooma ○

Batemans
Bay ○

PRINCES HWY

336

312–13

Ballarat ○

MELBOURNE ●

Cann
River ○

Mount
Gambier ○

Geelong ○

PRINCES

Sale ○

HWY

Warrnambool ○

310–11

VICTORIA

N

0 100 200 300 400 500 km

BASS STRAIT

380–1

Smithton ○

Devonport ○

Burnie ○

Launceston ○

Queenstown ○

TASMANIA

HOBART ●

378–9

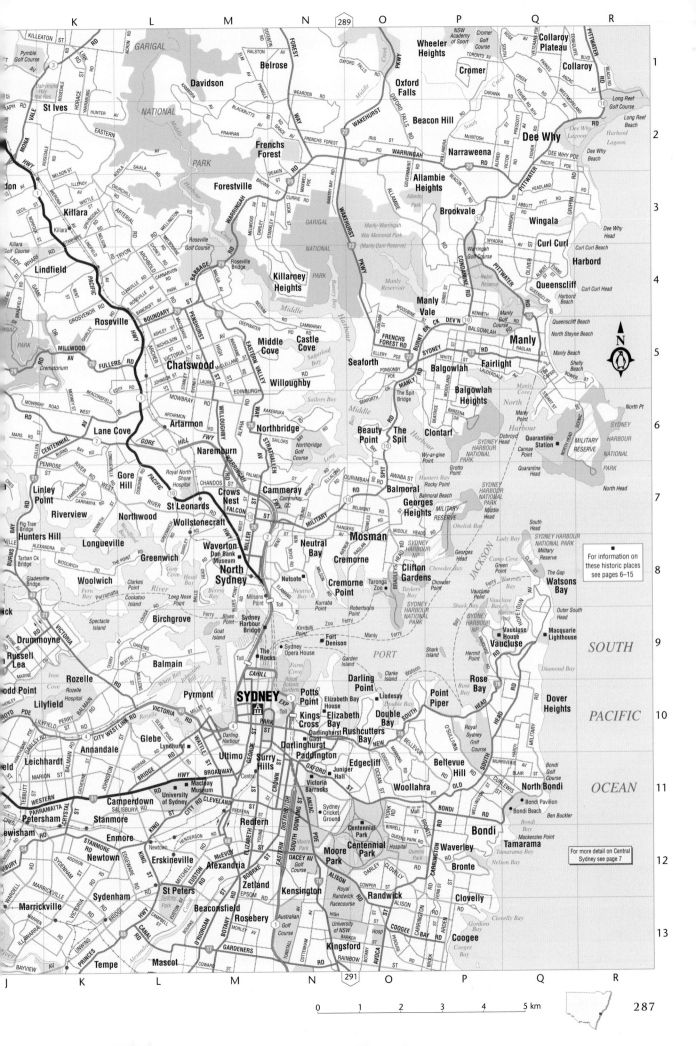

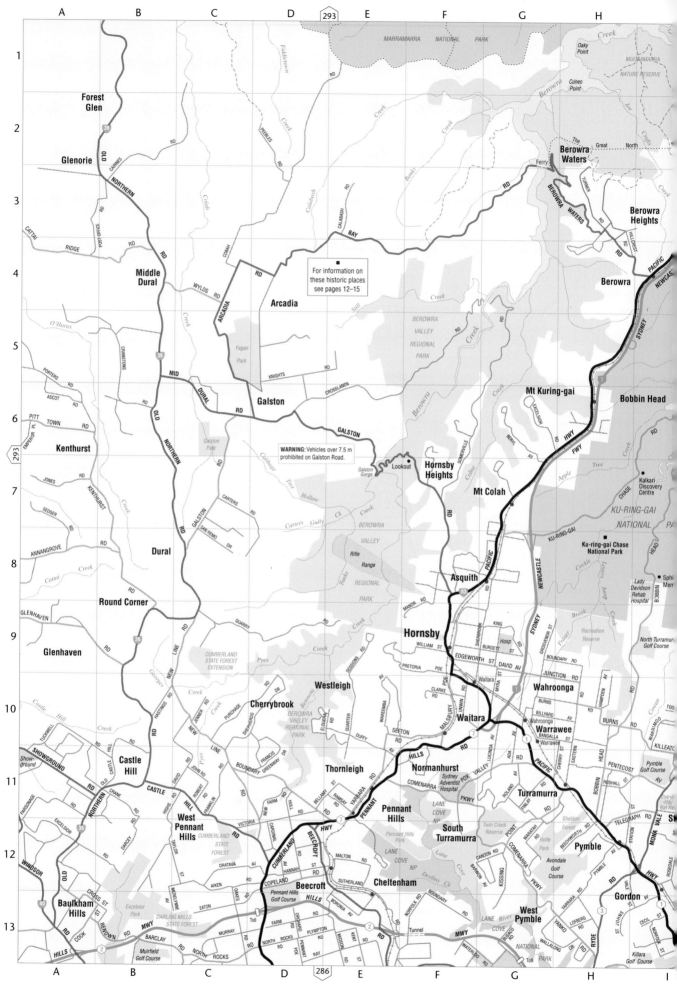

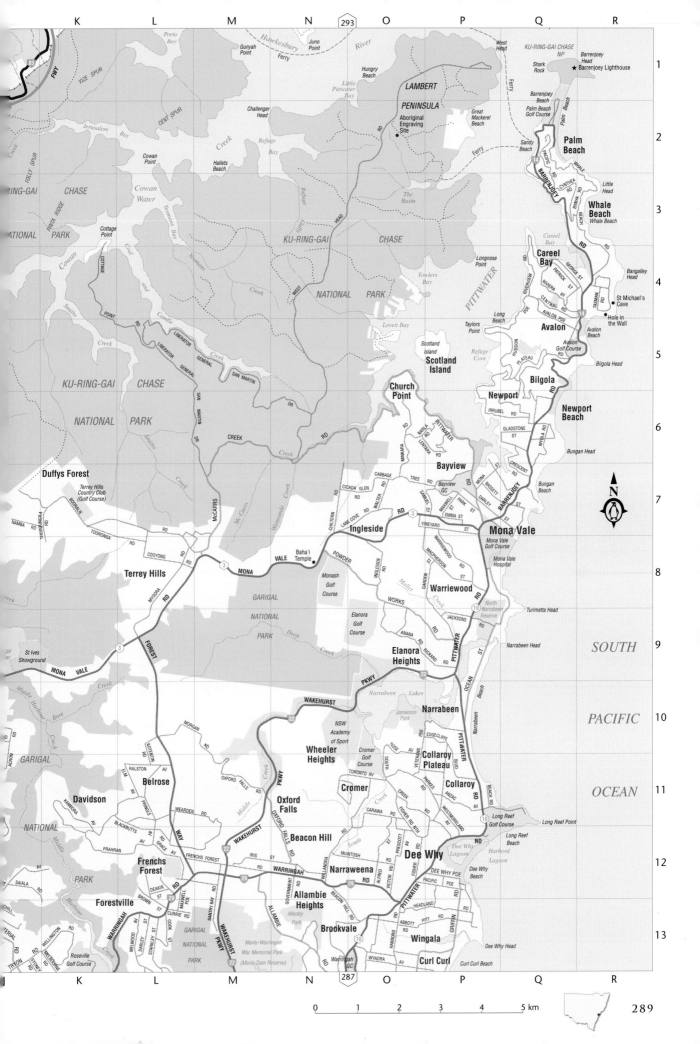

Hawkesbury River

Porto Bay

Gunyah Point

Juno Point

Challenger Head

Hungry Beach

Little Pittwater Bay

LAMBERT
PENINSULA

Aboriginal Engraving Site

Great Mackerel Beach

West Head

KU-RING-GAI CHASE NP

Barrenjoey Head

★ Barrenjoey Lighthouse

1

VIZE SPUR

CENT SPUR

Jerusalem Bay

Cowan Creek

Refuge Bay

Ferry

Barrenjoey Beach

Palm Beach Golf Course

Sandy Beach

Palm Beach

2

FOLLY SPUR

CHASE

Cowan Point

Hallets Beach

The Basin

PACIFIC

BARRENJOEY

CYNTHEA RD

Whale Beach

Whale Beach

3

PINTA RIDGE

NATIONAL

PARK

Cowan Water

Cowan

Yeomans Bay

KU-RING-GAI

CHASE

Towlers Bay

PITTWATER

Careel Bay

RIVERVIEW

GEORGE ST

PATRICK

RIVIERA AV

CENTRAL RD

AVALON PDE

Bangalley Head

TASMAN

St Michael's Cave

Hole in the Wall

4

Cottage Point

COTTAGE

POINT

RD

LIBERATOR

GENERAL

San Martin

SAN MARTIN

DR

Lovett Bay

Scotland Island

Scotland Island

Refuge Cove

Avalon

Avalon Beach

Avalon Golf Course

HUDSON

PLATEAU

PDE

5

Smiths Creek

Castle and Cowan Creek

LIBERATOR GENERAL

SAN MARTIN DR

Church Point

PITTWATER

MINKARA

NARLA

LENTARA RD

Newport

IRRUBEL RD

GLADSTONE ST

Bilgola

RD

Newport Beach

MYOLA RD

Bungan Head

6

KU-RING-GAI CHASE

NATIONAL PARK

CREEK

CREEK RD

RD

Bayview

Bayview GC

TREE

CABBAGE

PARK

MONA

BASSETT

DARLEY

ST

CRESCENT

BARRENJOEY

Bungan Beach

N

7

Duffys Forest

Terrey Hills Country Club (Golf Course)

BOORALIE

NAMBA

THUNDUNGRA

TOORONGA RD

MCCARRS

Mc Carrs Creek

Warrandin Creek

CICADA GLEN RD

CHILTERN

LANE COVE RD

WALTER RD

Ingleside

VALE RD

SAMUEL

VINEYARD

MAXWELL

EMMA ST

Mona Vale

Mona Vale Golf Course

Mona Vale Hospital

8

COOYONG RD

Terrey Hills

MYOORA RD

MONA

VALE

POWDER

Baha'i Temple

Monash Golf Course

INGLESIDE RD

Muller Creek

GARDEN ST

MACPHERSON ST

WARRIEWOOD RD

Warriewood

PITTWATER RD

North Narrabeen Reserve

Turimetta Head

9

St Ives Showground

MONA VALE

FOREST

GARIGAL

NATIONAL

PARK

Deep Creek

Elanora Golf Course

WORKS

ANANA

RICKARD RD

JACKSONS RD

Elanora Heights

PITTWATER

OCEAN ST

Narrabeen Head

SOUTH

9

Middle Harbour

Bore Creek

PKWY

WAKEHURST

Narrabeen Lakes

Jamieson Park

Narrabeen

Narrabeen Beach

PACIFIC

10

GARIGAL

MORGAN RD

KOTTERN

NSW Academy of Sport

Cromer Golf Course

ROSE AV

EDGECLIFFE

VETERANS PDE

PITTWATER BLVD

Collaroy Plateau

OCEAN

11

NATIONAL

Davidson

RALSTON AV

ELM AV

Belrose

OXFORD FALLS RD

Wheeler Heights

TORONTO AV

Cromer

HILDA

PARKES RD

ANZAC AV

Collaroy

WESTMORELAND

BEACH RD

Long Reef Golf Course

Long Reef Point

11

PRINGLE

BLACKBUTTS

WEARDEN RD

WAY

Oxford Falls

FISHER RD STH

Long Reef Beach

PRAHRAN

KAMBORA AV

GRACE AV

Middle Creek

Beacon Hill

McINTOSH RD

PRESCOTT AV

Dee Why

Dee Why Lagoon

Harbord Lagoon

12

Frenchs Forest

WAKEHURST PKWY

OXFORD FALLS RD

Narraweena

ALFRED

VICTOR RD

Dee Why Beach

12

SAIALA RD

Forestville

DEAKIN

BROWN ST

CURRIE RD

MAXWELL PDE

IRIS ST

FRENCHS FOREST

WARRINGAH

Allambie Heights

Allenby Park

GOVERNMENT RD

ALLAMBIE RD

WILLANDRA

BEACON HILL RD

PITTWATER

HEADLAND RD

HARBORD RD

PITT

Wingala

13

WARRINGAH RD

WELLINGTON ST

Roseville Golf Course

MELBOURNE RD

STANLEY ST

DARLEY ST

Middle Creek

GARIGAL NATIONAL PARK

Manly-Warringah War Memorial Park (Manly Dam Reserve)

WAKEHURST PKWY

Brookvale

Warringah GC

WYADRA AV

Curl Curl

Curl Curl Beach

Dee Why Head

13

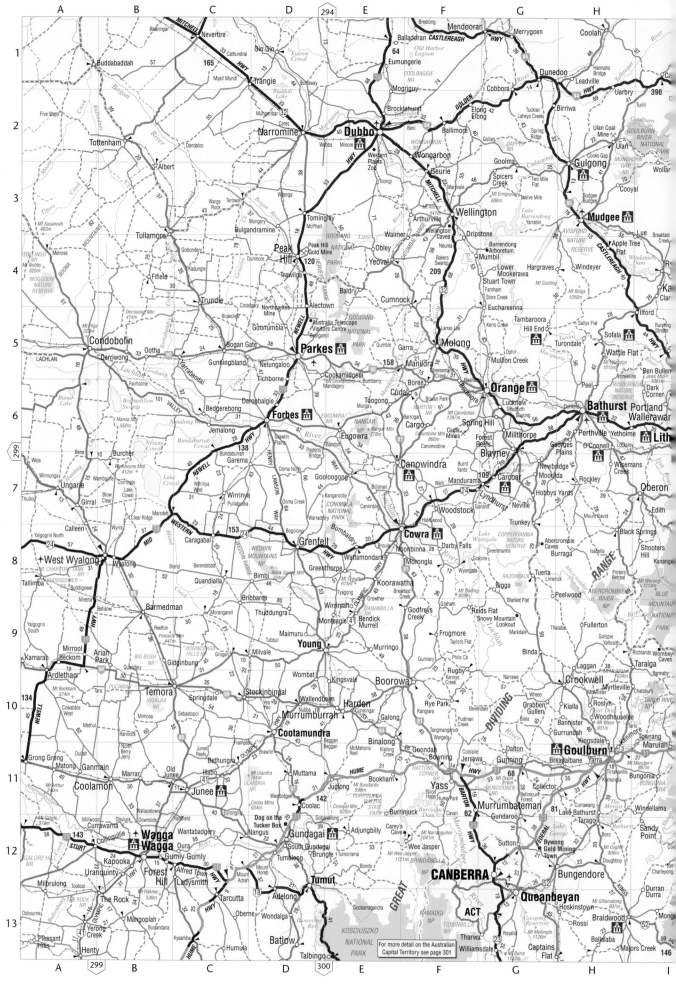

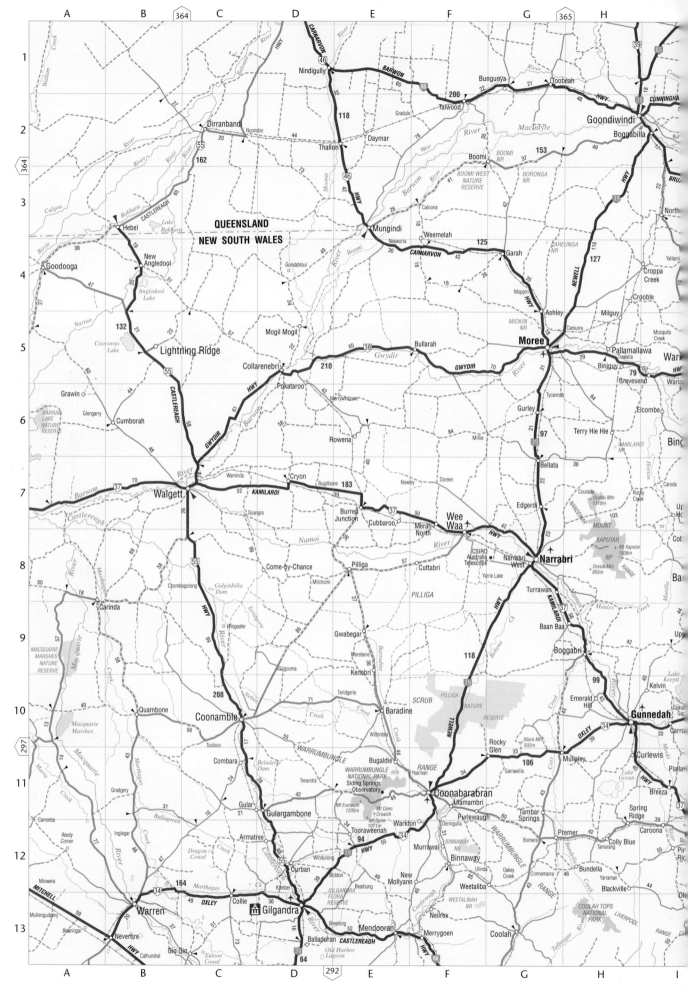

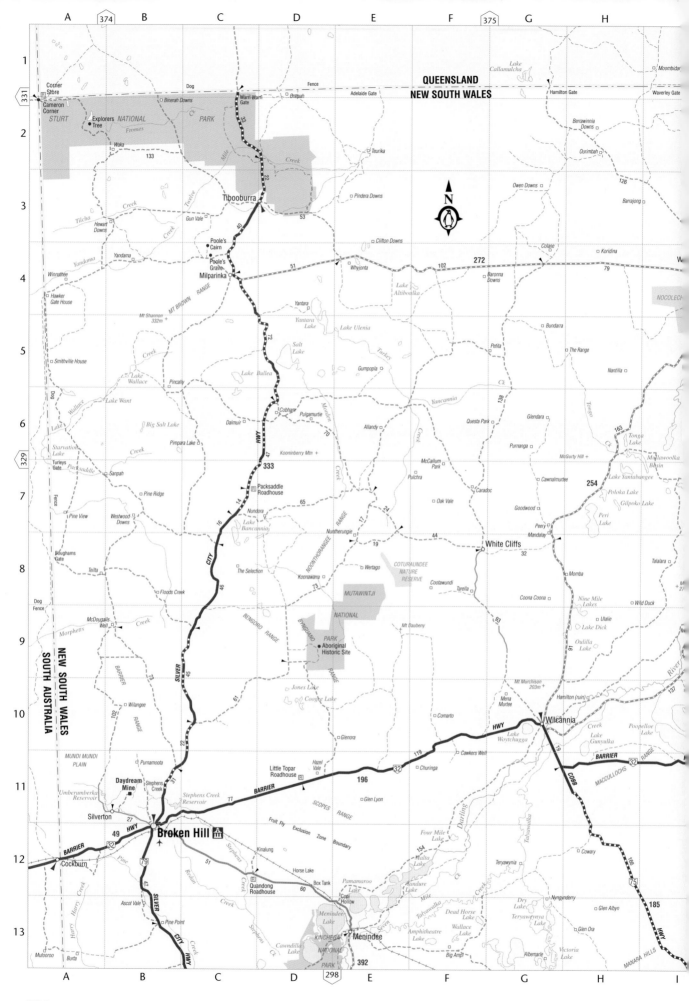

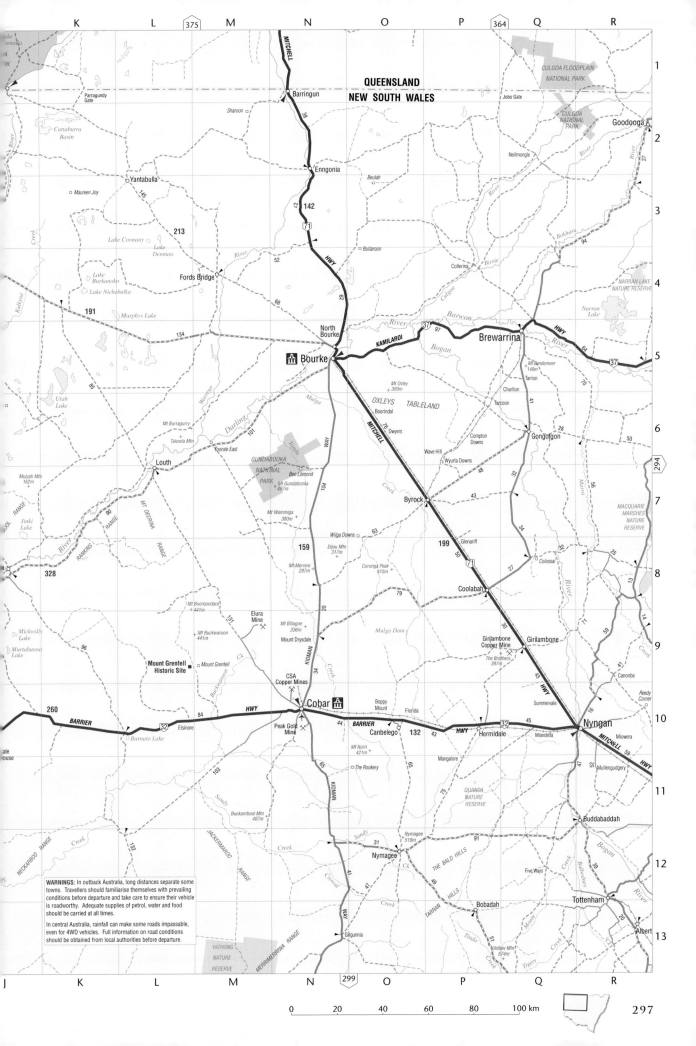

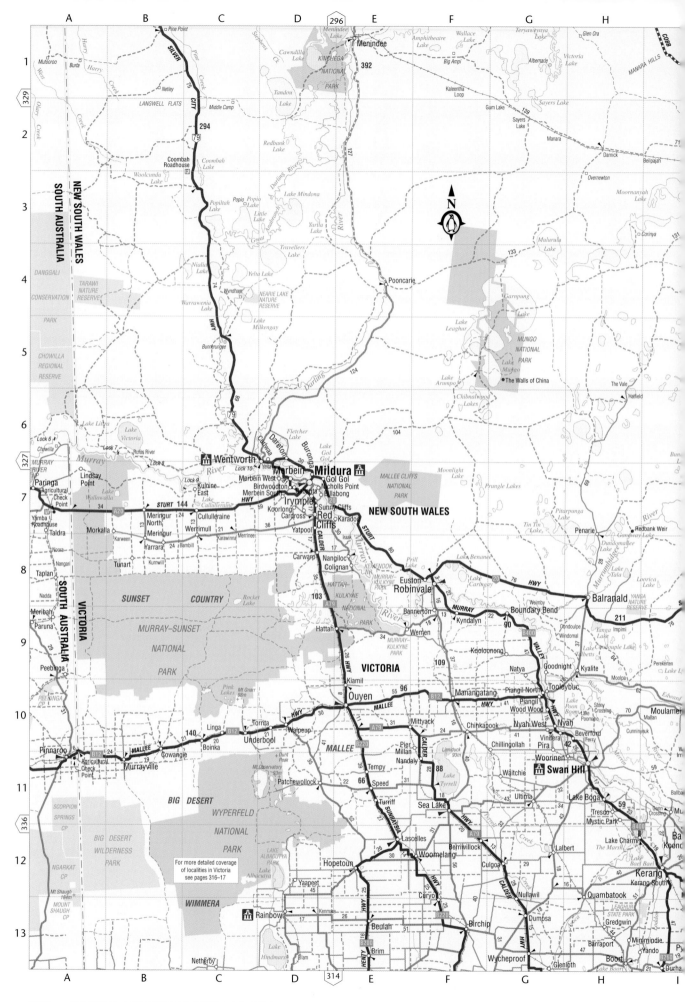

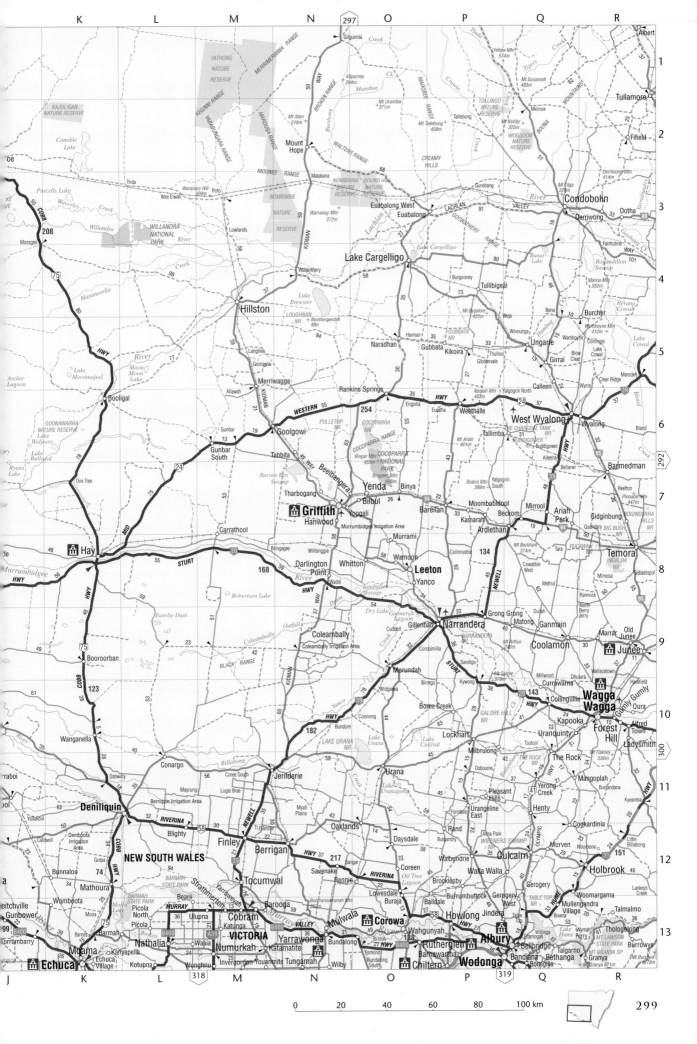

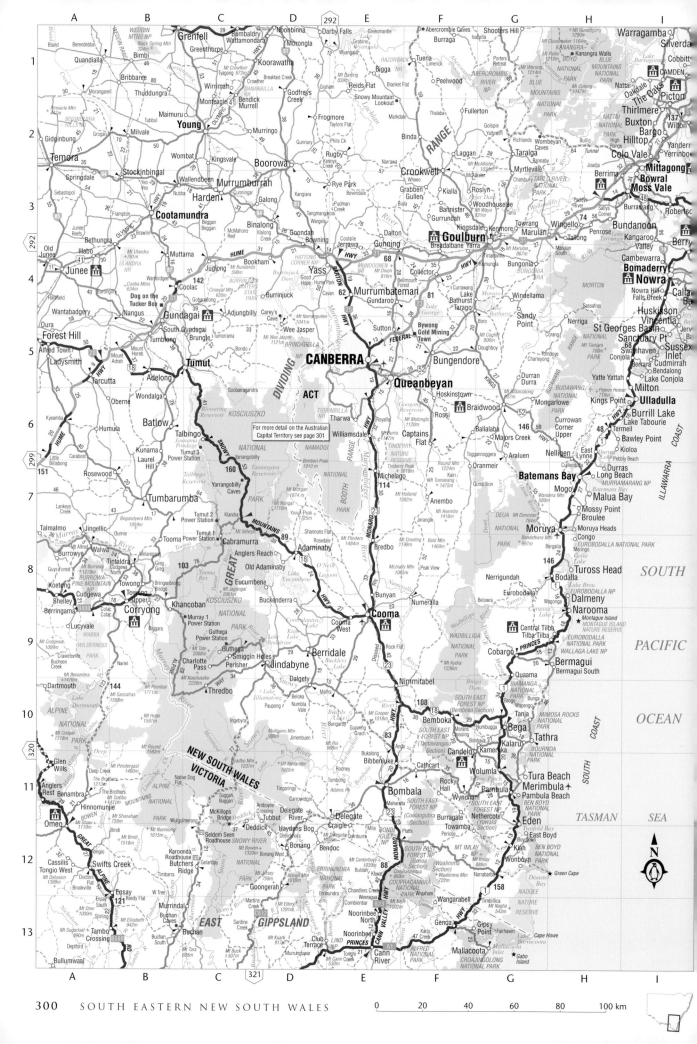

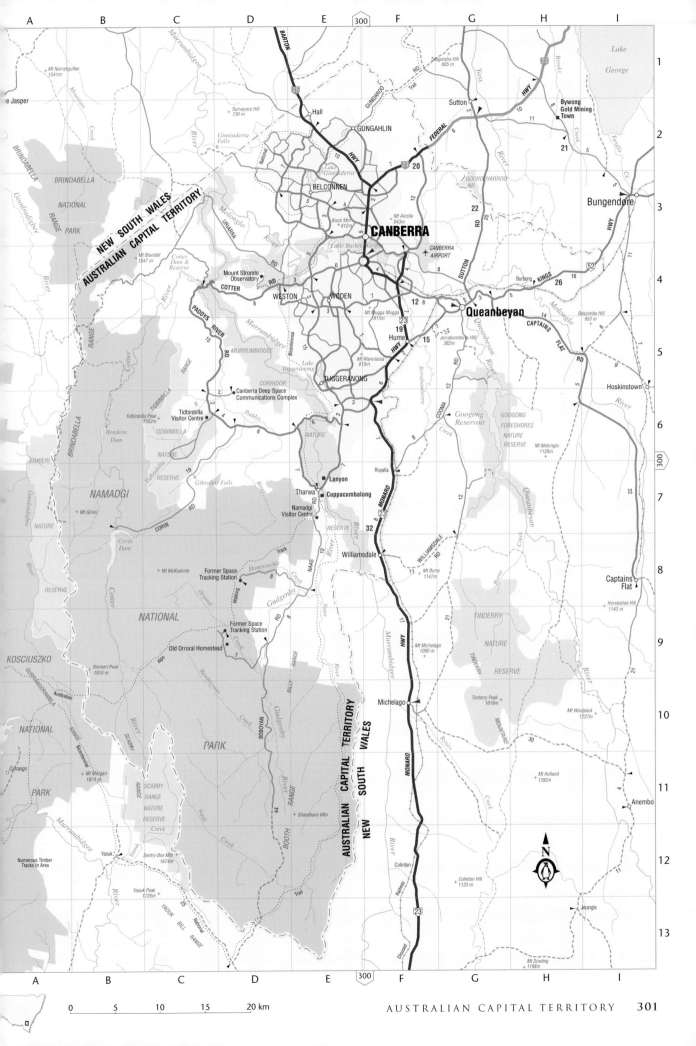

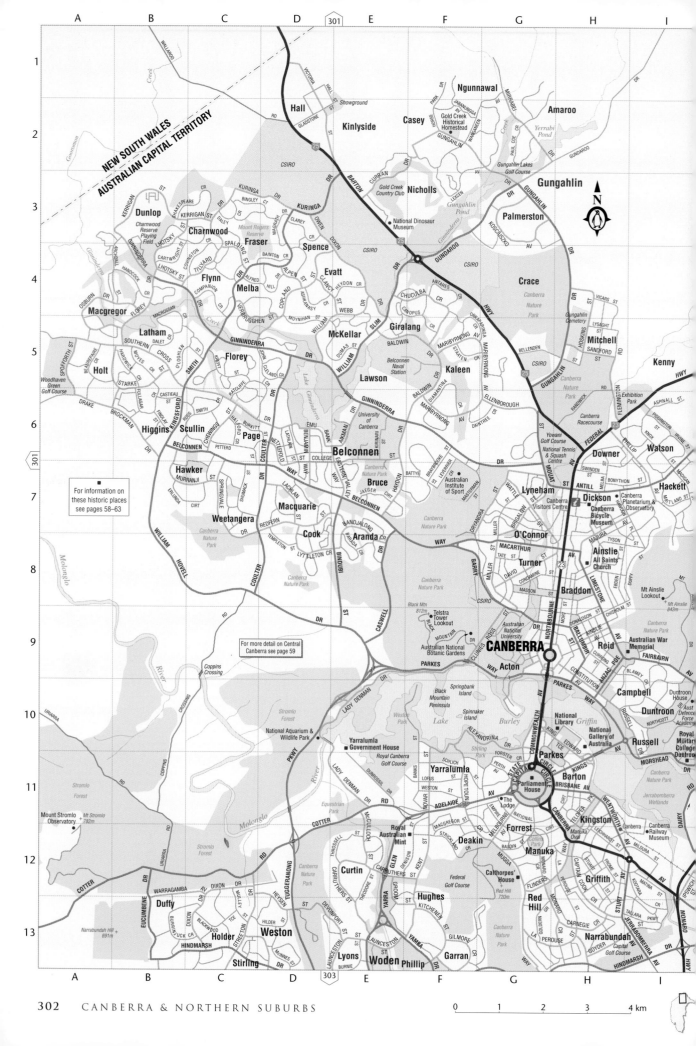

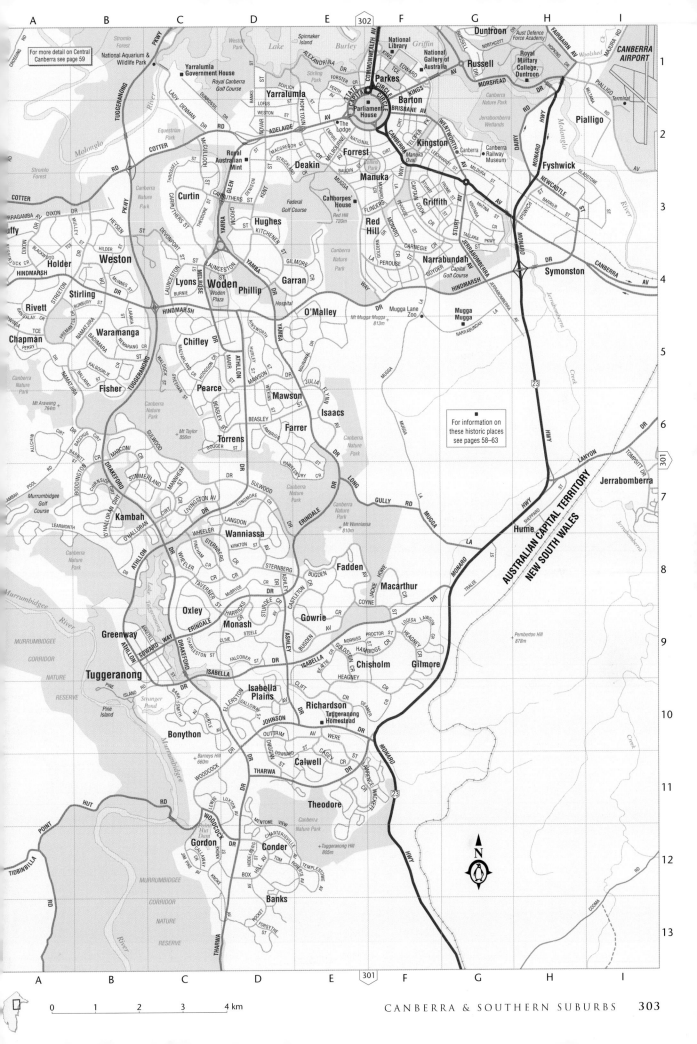

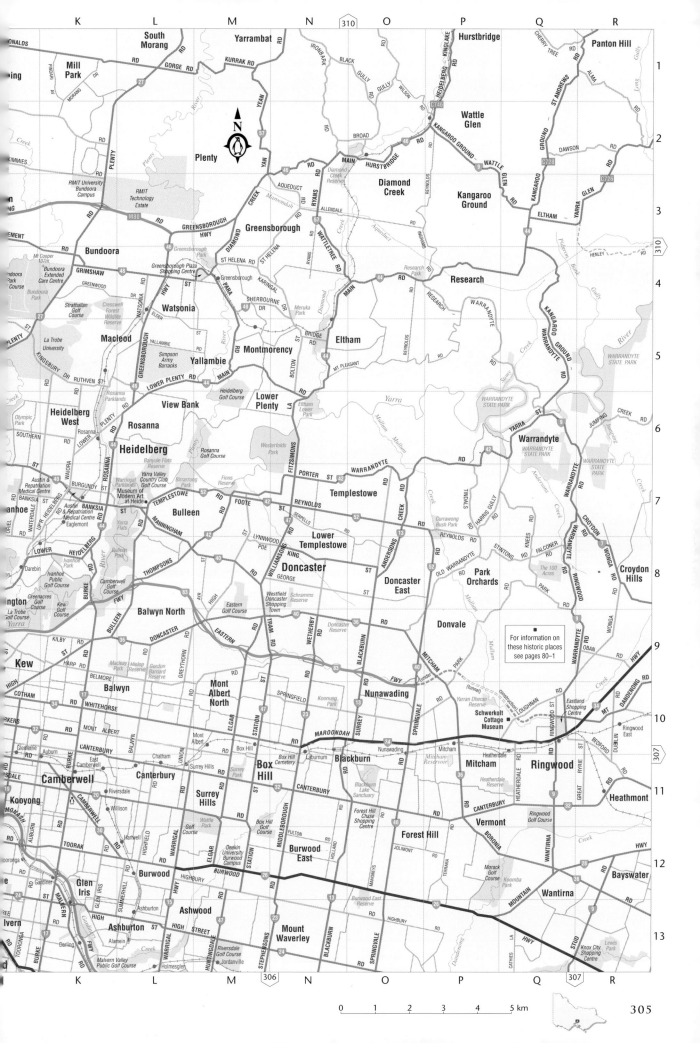

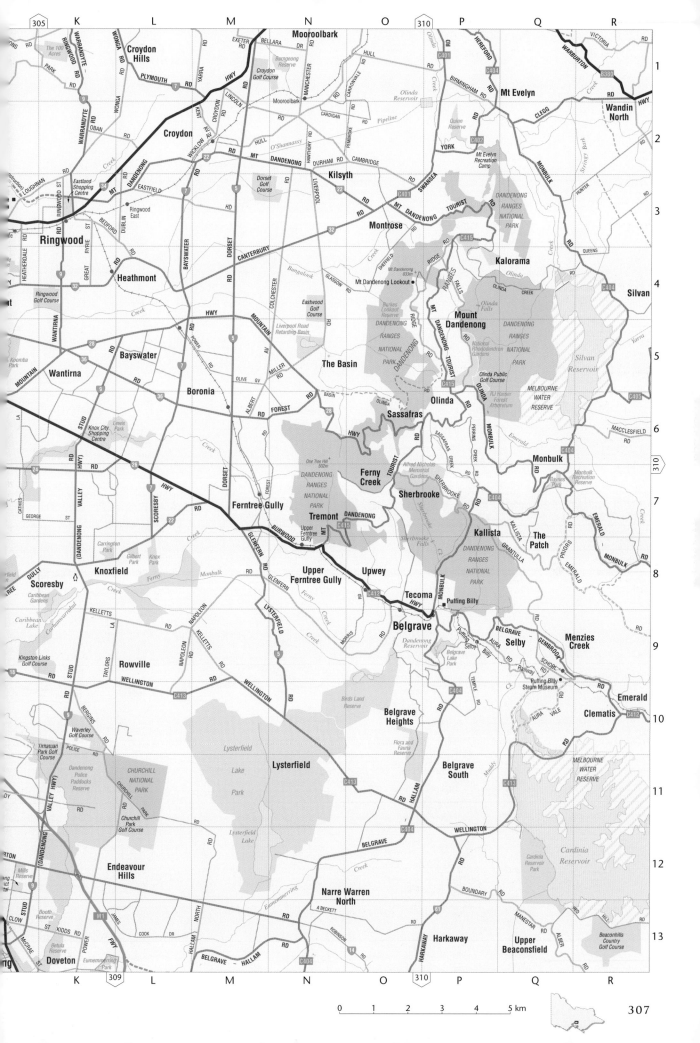

K L M N O P Q R

1
2
3
4
5
7
8
9
10
11
12
13

Mooroolbark

Croydon Hills

Croydon

Kilsyth

Mt Evelyn

Wandin North

Montrose

Ringwood

Heathmont

Kalorama

Silvan

Bayswater

Mount Dandenong

Wantirna

The Basin

Boronia

Olinda

Sassafras

Monbulk

Ferny Creek

Sherbrooke

Ferntree Gully

Tremont

Kallista

The Patch

Scoresby

Knoxfield

Upper Ferntree Gully

Upwey

Tecoma

Belgrave

Selby

Menzies Creek

Rowville

Emerald

Clematis

Belgrave Heights

Belgrave South

Lysterfield

Endeavour Hills

Narre Warren North

Harkaway

Upper Beaconsfield

Doveton

K L M N O P Q R

0 1 2 3 4 5 km

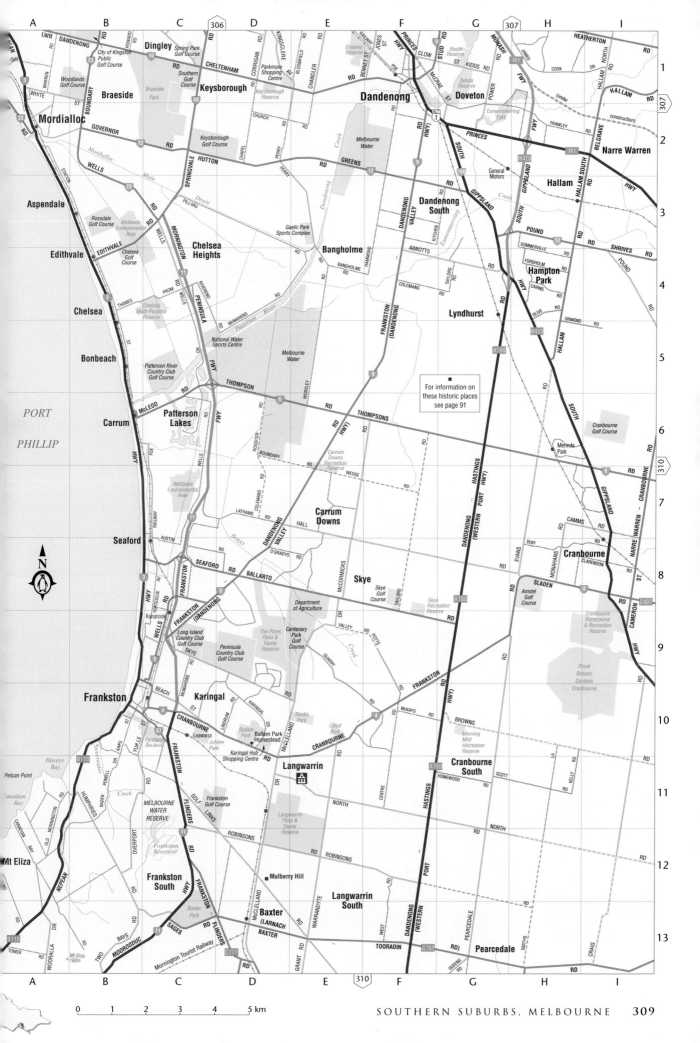

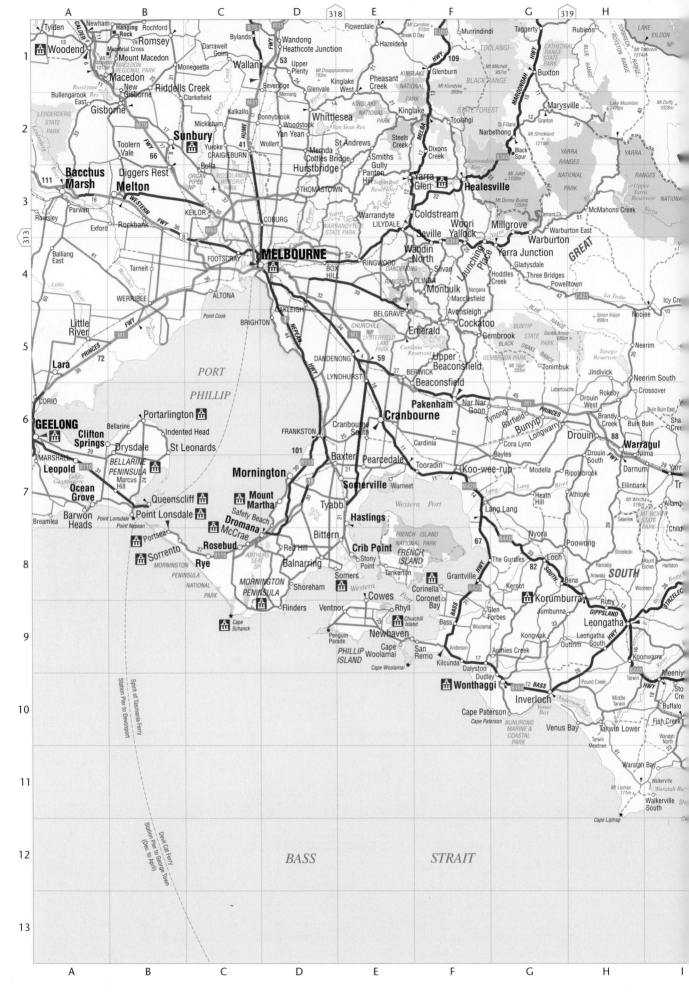

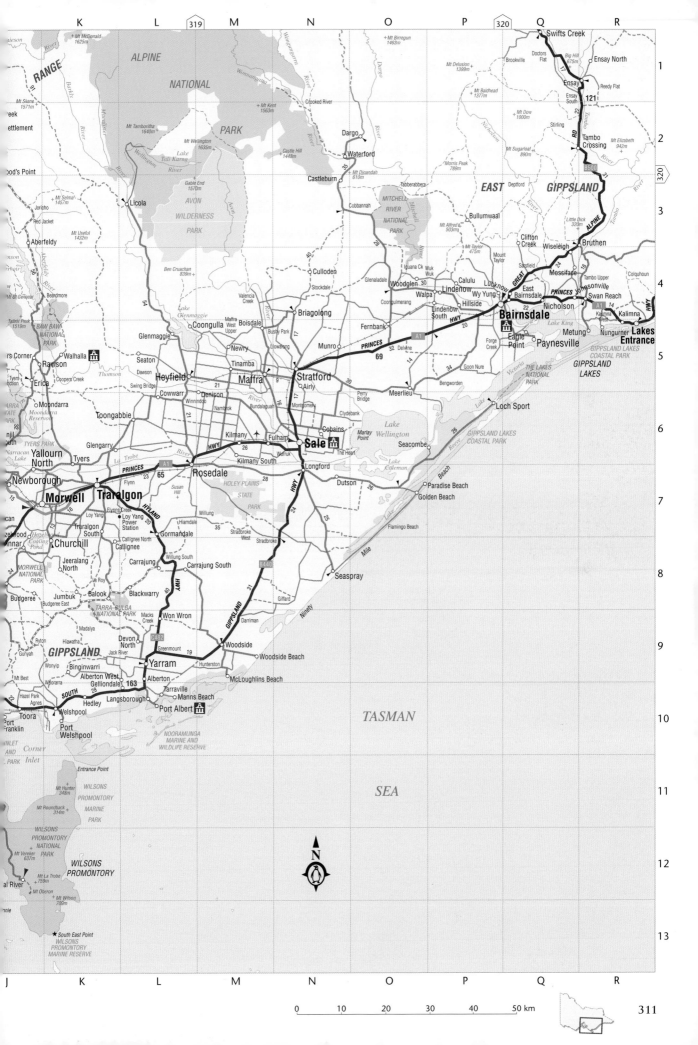

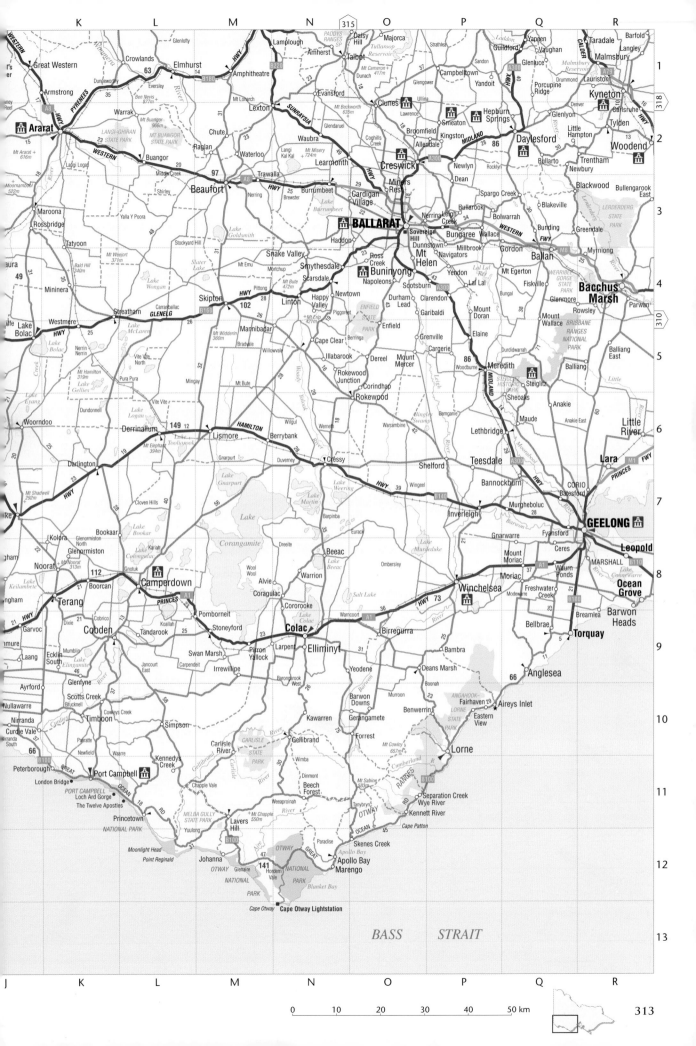

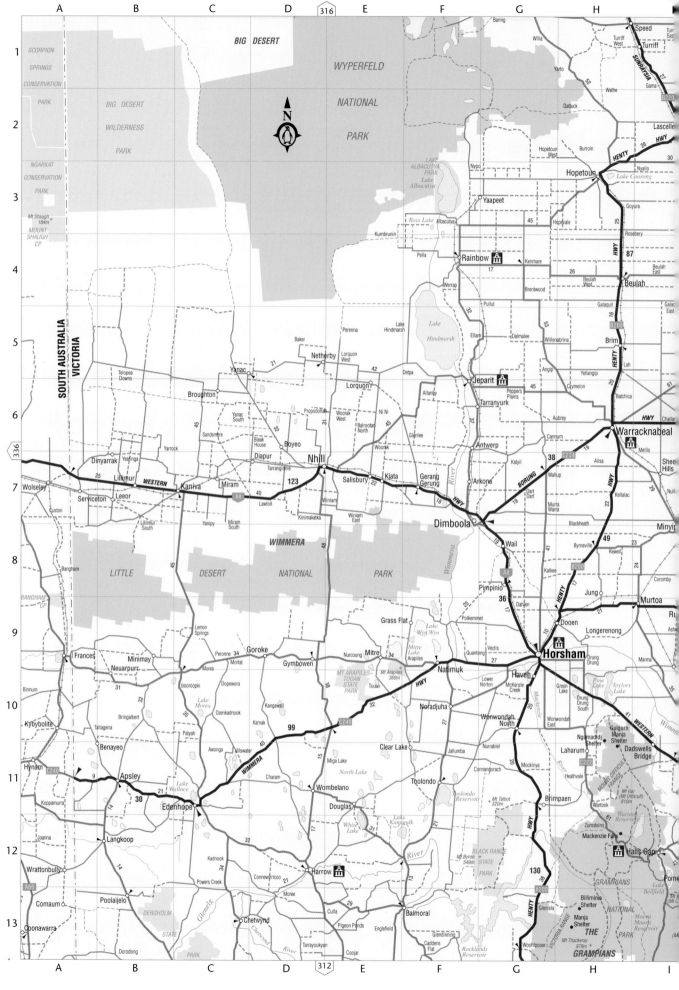

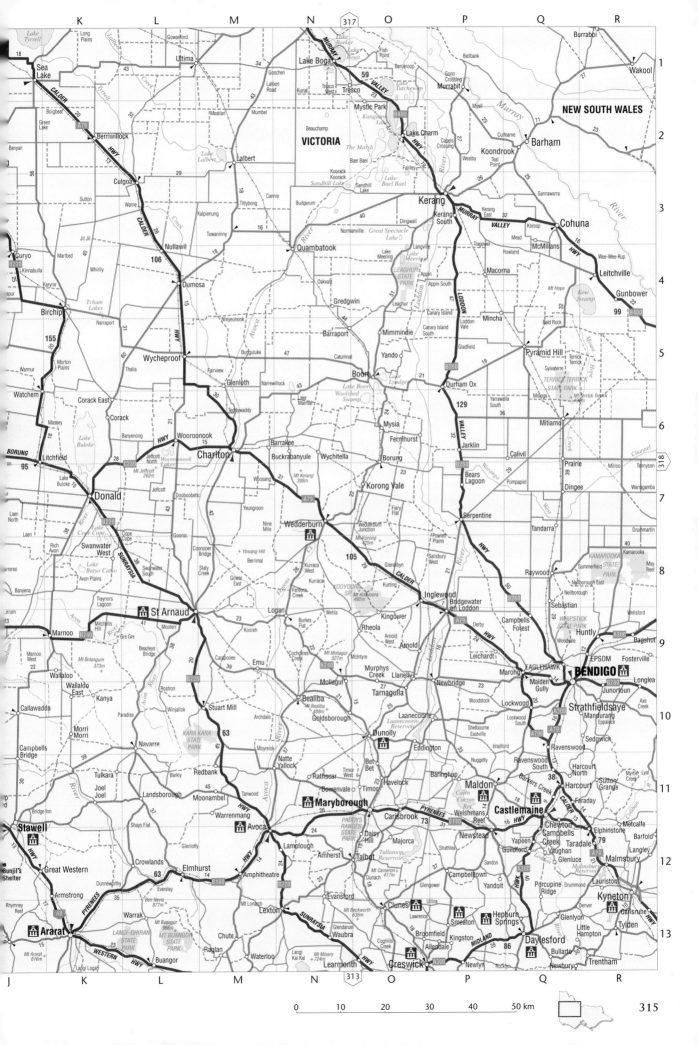

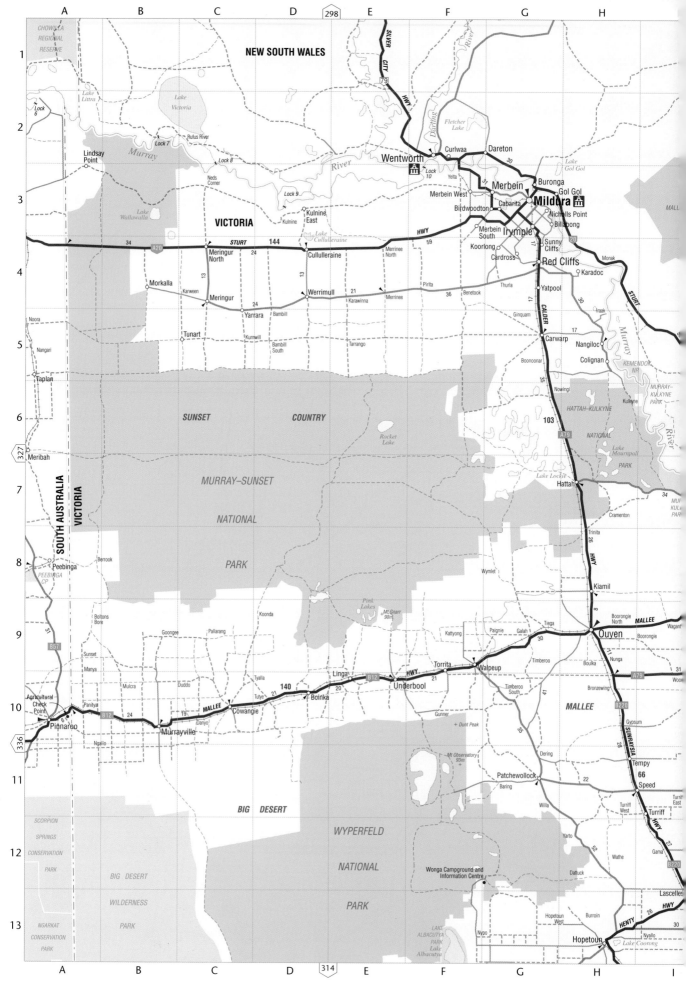

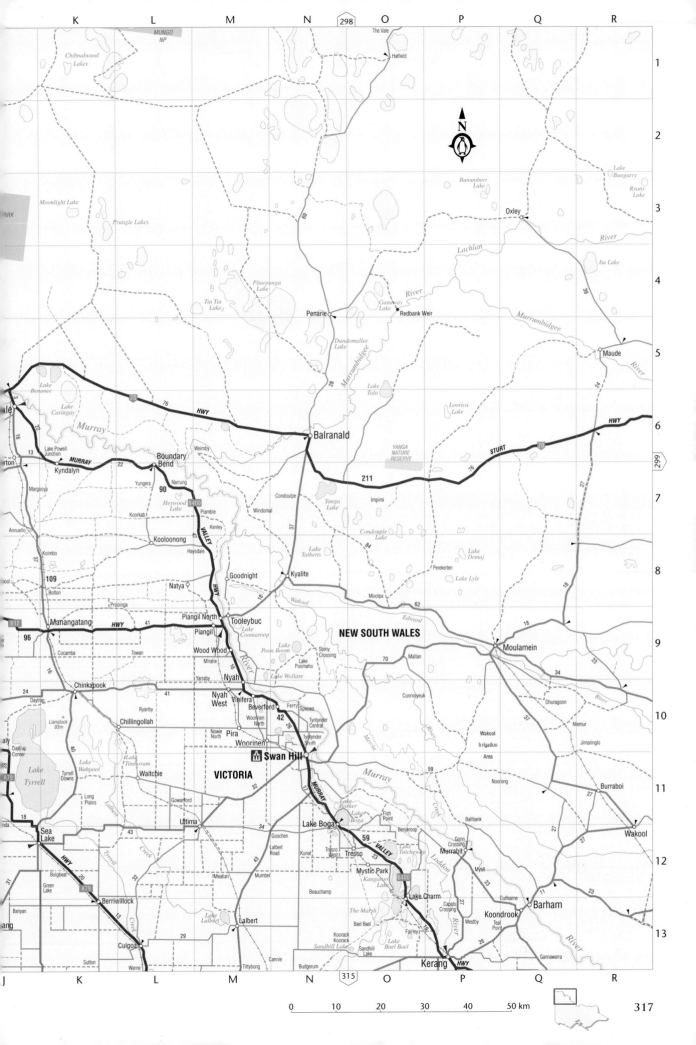

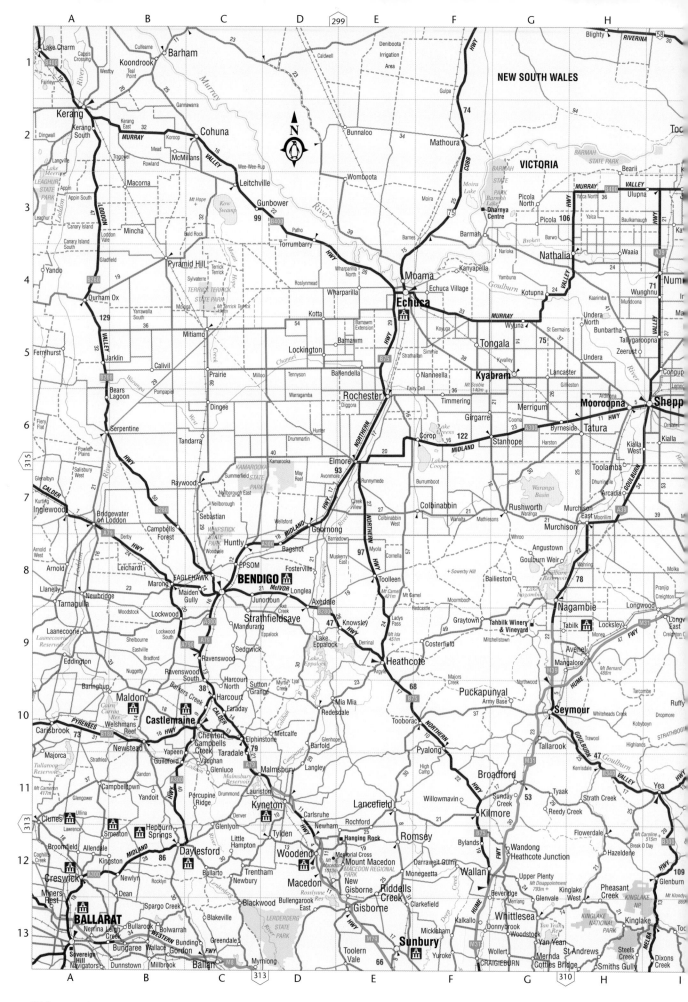

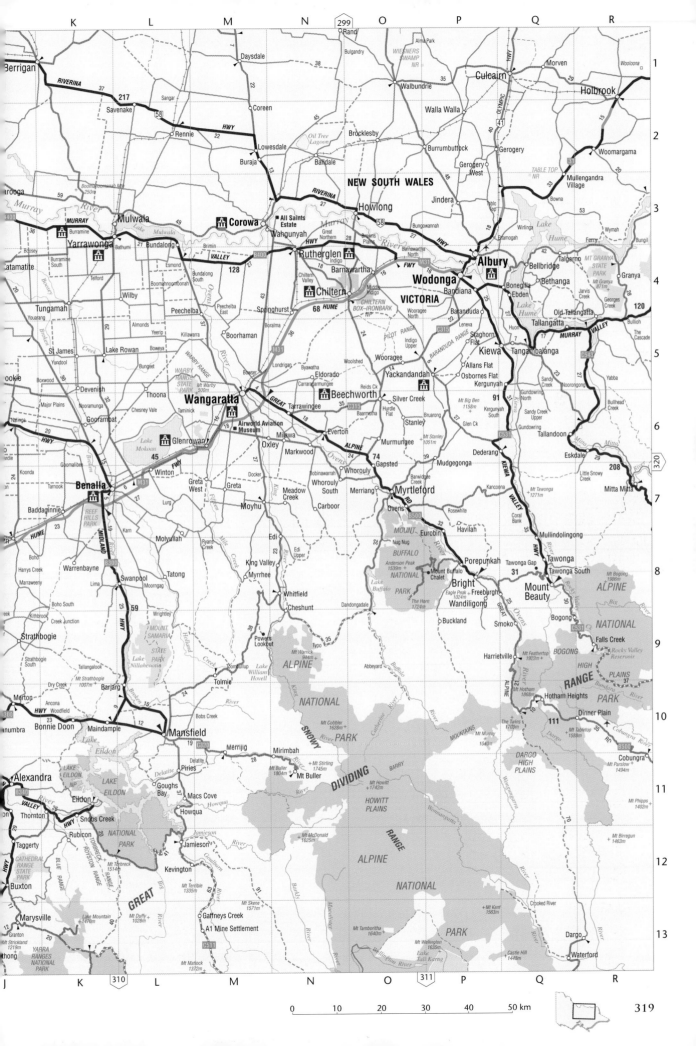

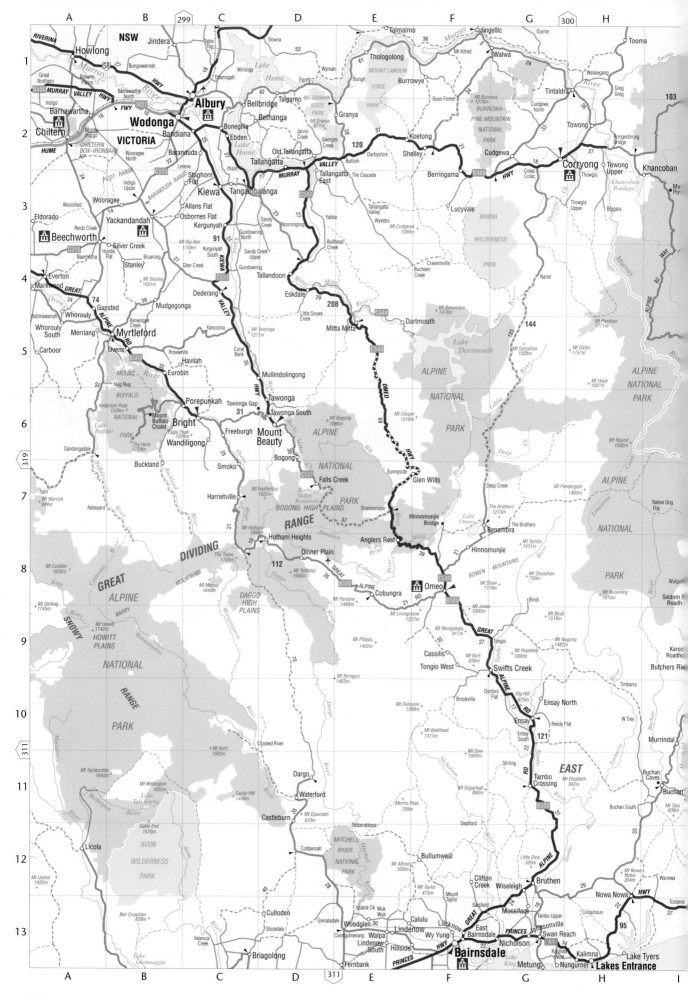

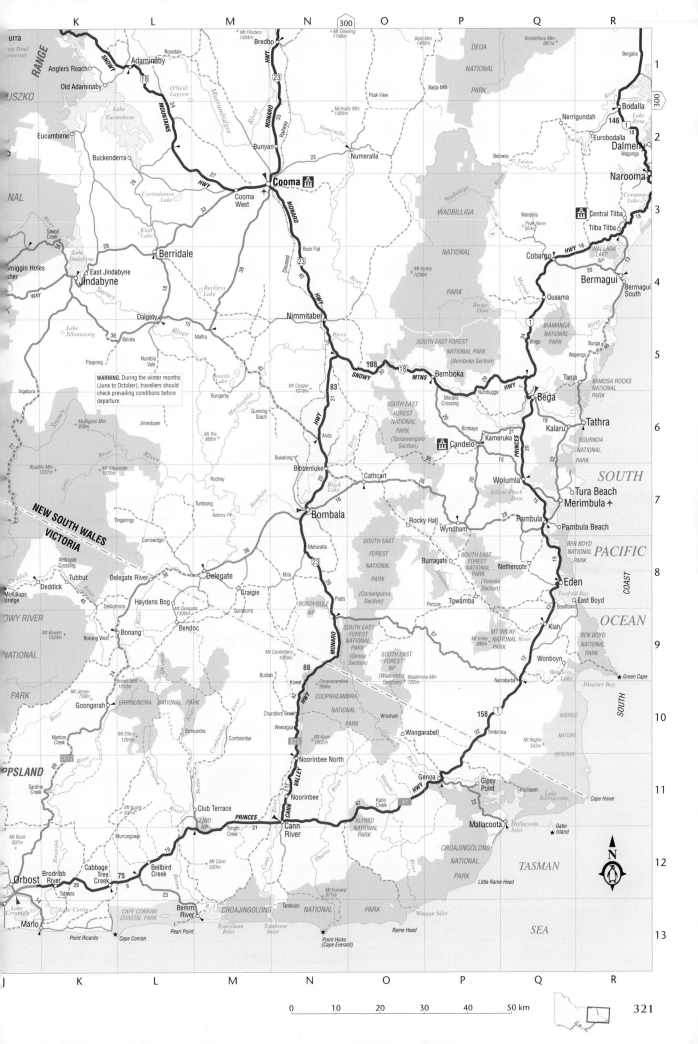

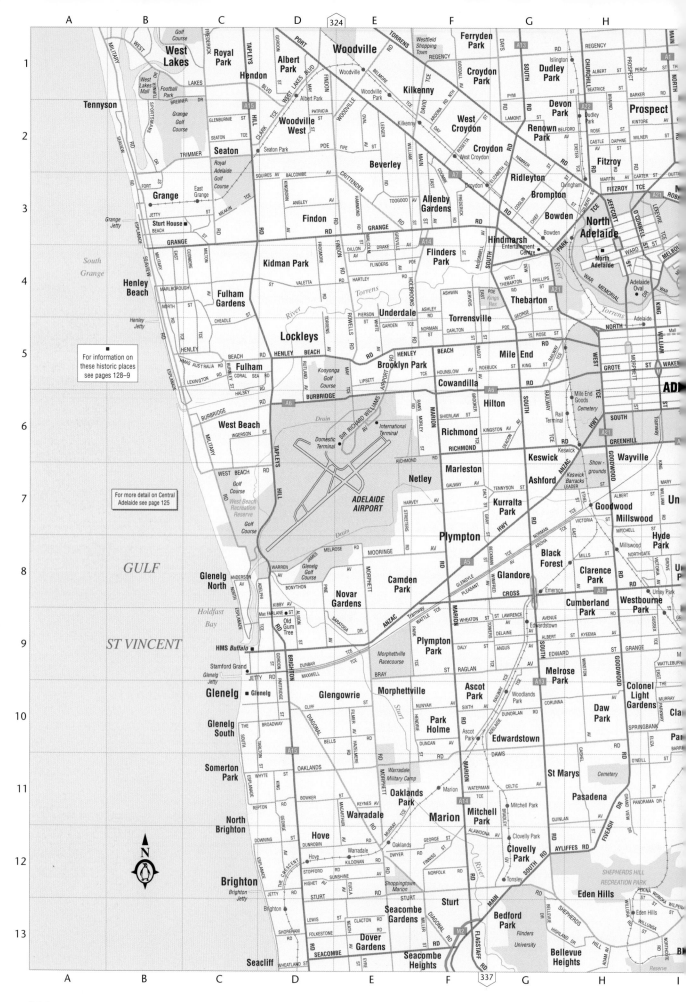

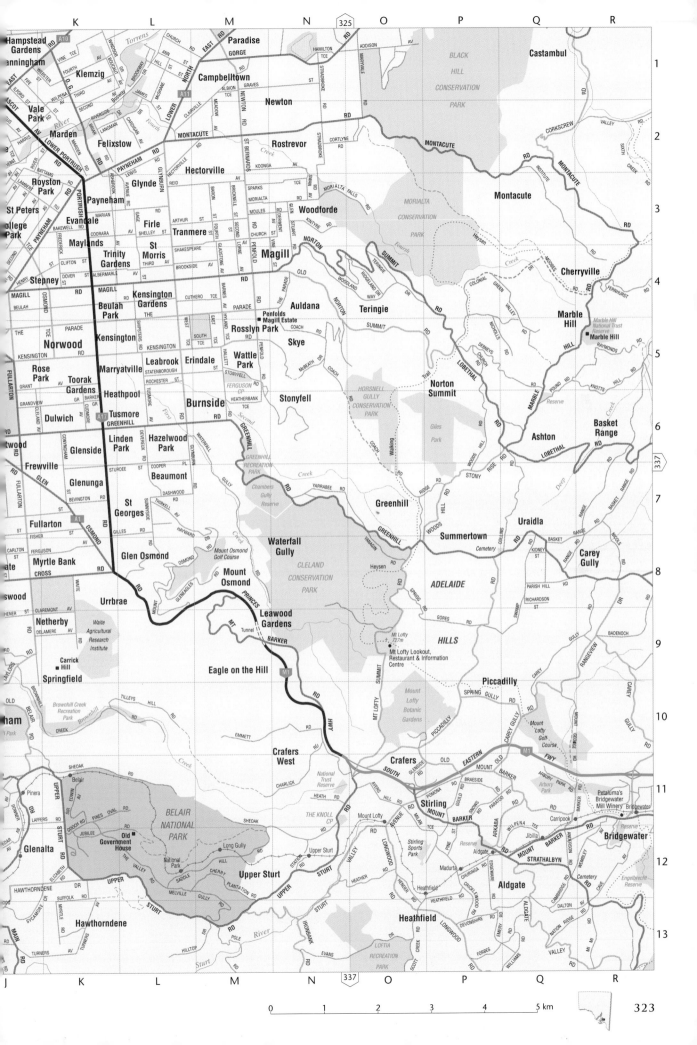

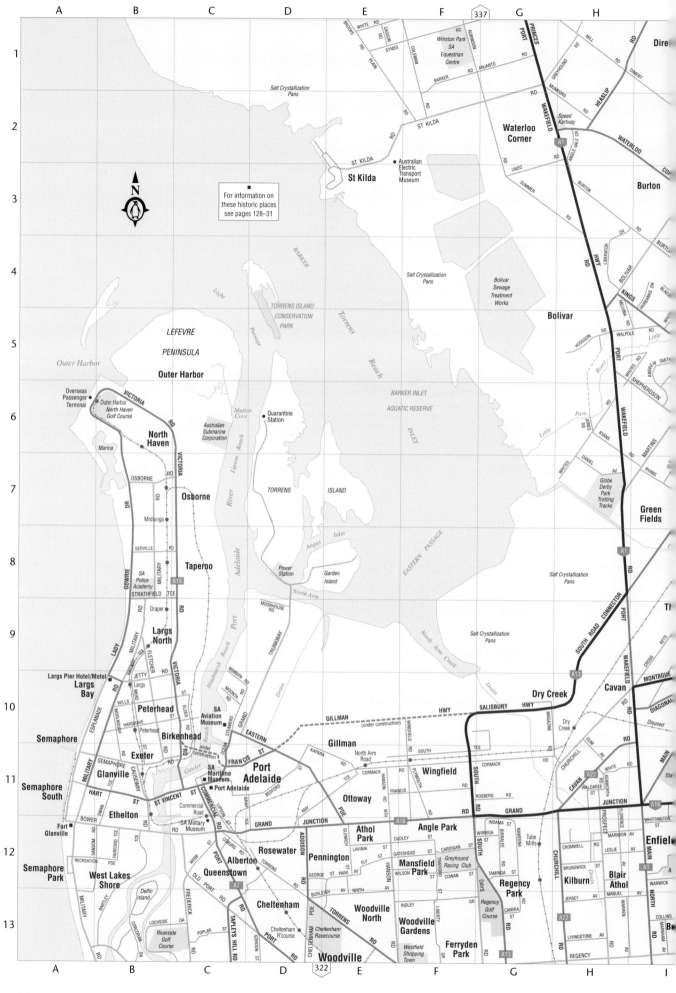

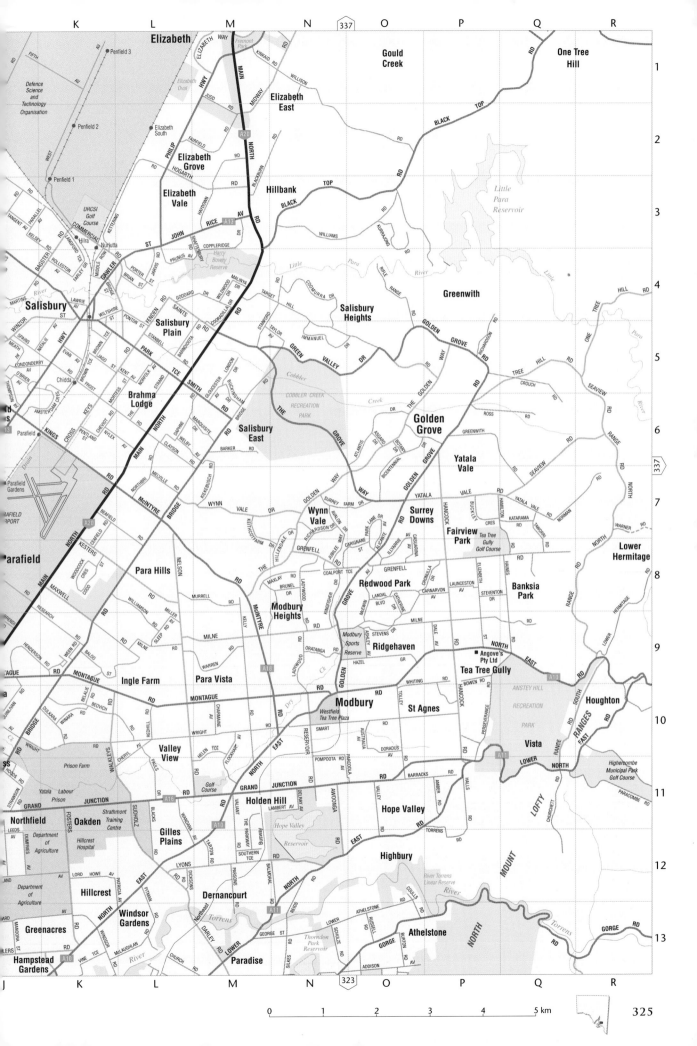

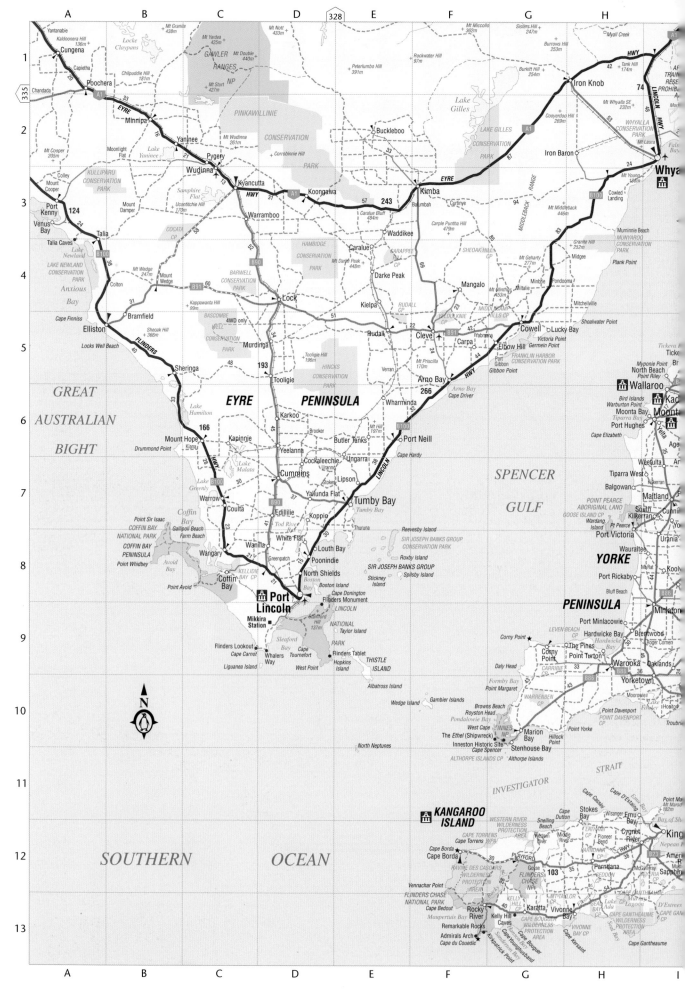

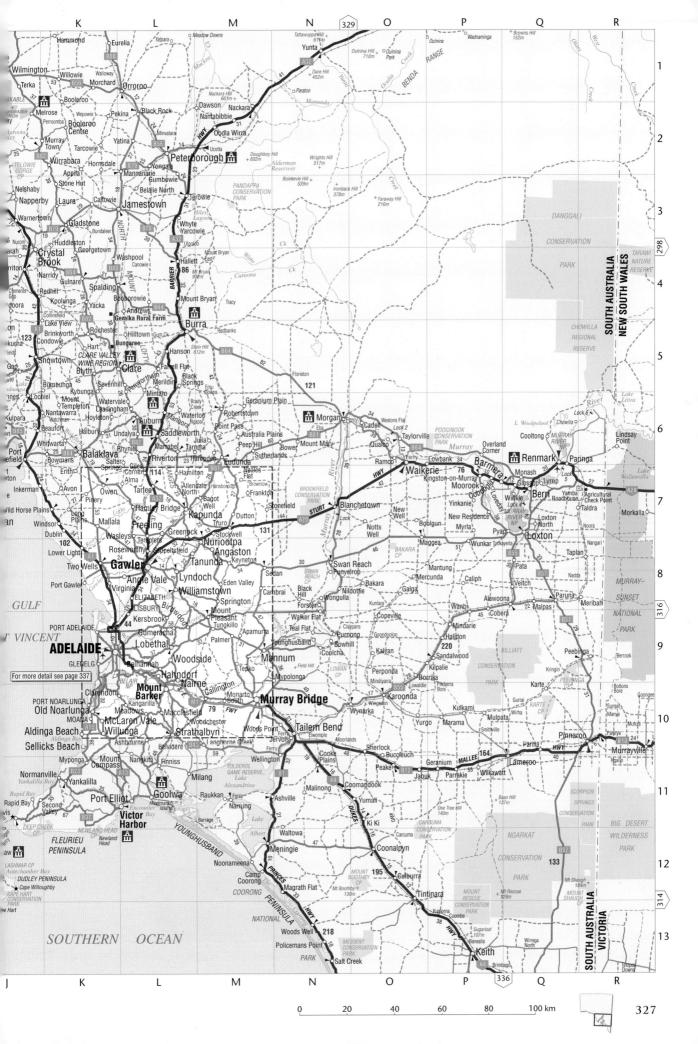

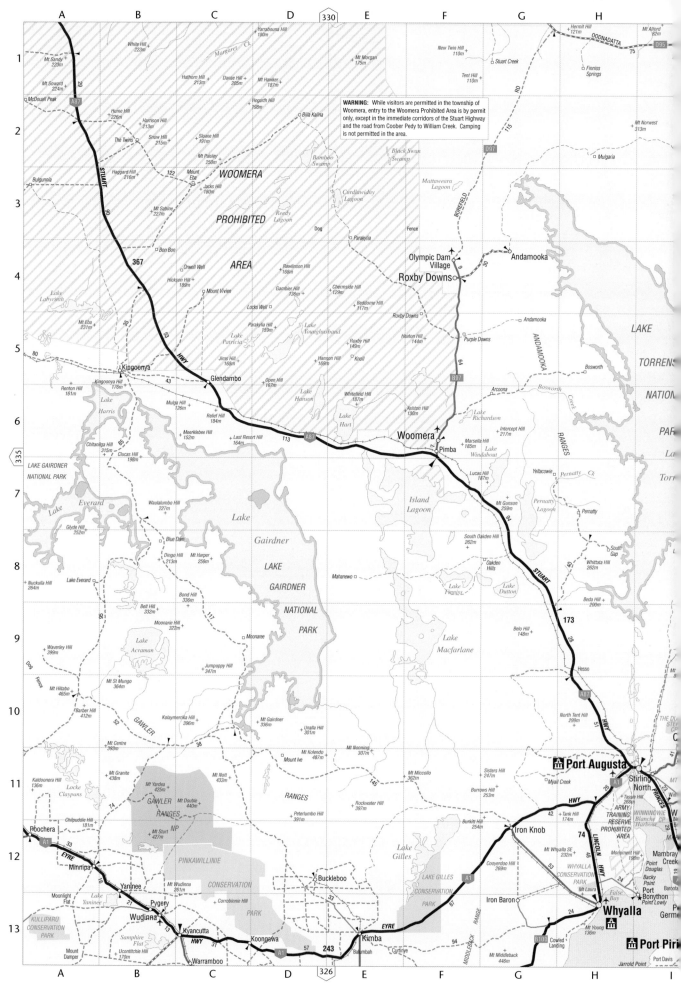

WARNING: While visitors are permitted in the township of Woomera, entry to the Woomera Prohibited Area is by permit only, except in the immediate corridors of the Stuart Highway and the road from Coober Pedy to William Creek. Camping is not permitted in the area.

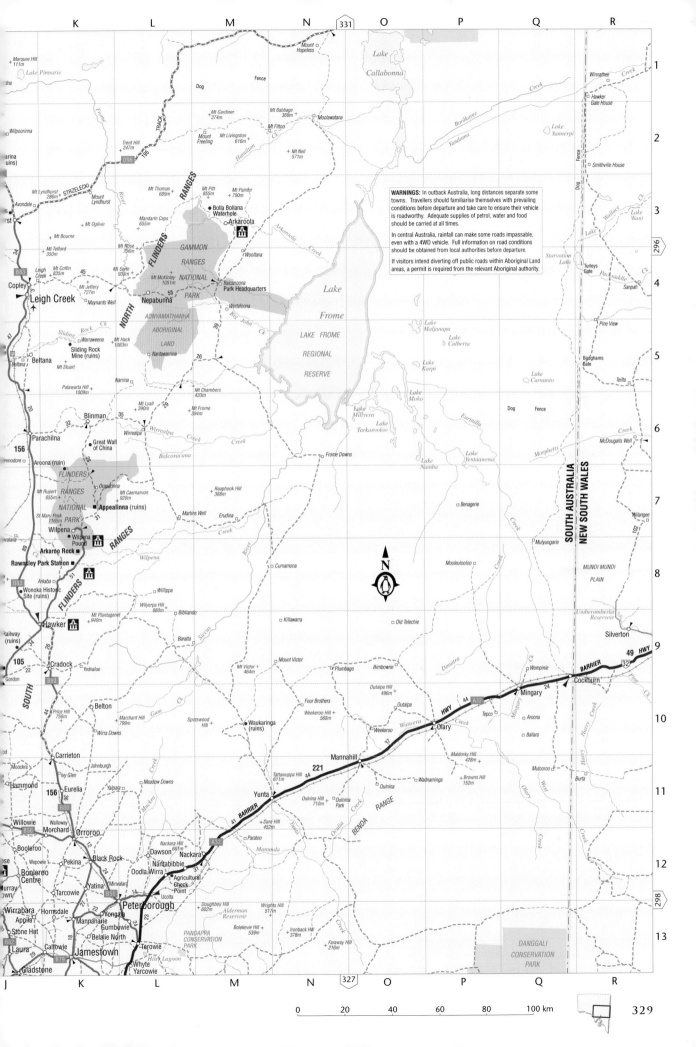

329

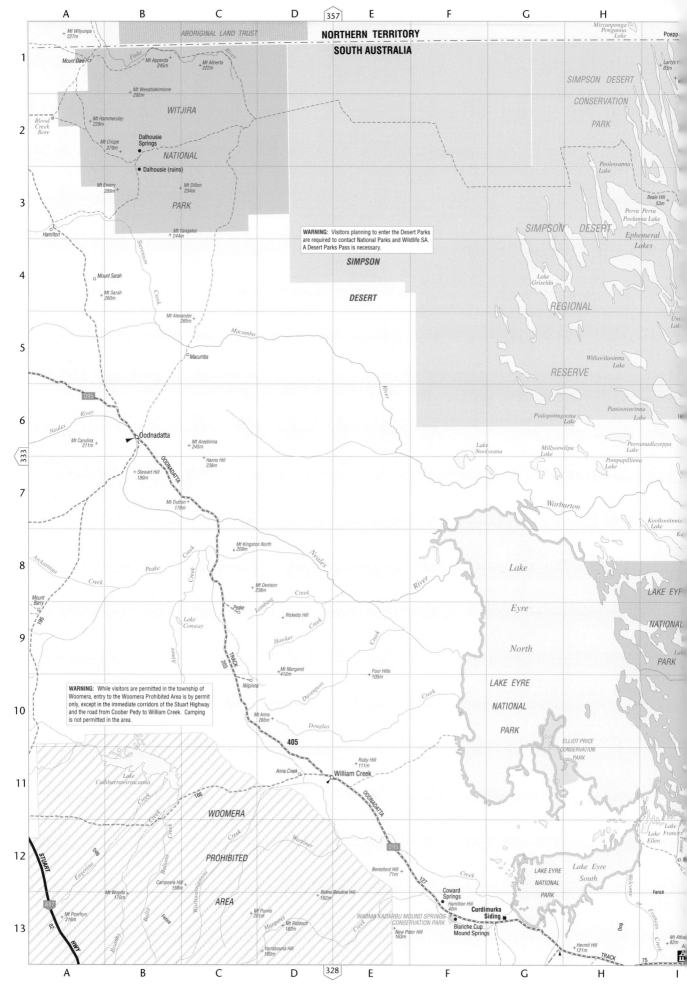

WARNING: Visitors planning to enter the Desert Parks are required to contact National Parks and Wildlife SA. A Desert Parks Pass is necessary.

WARNING: While visitors are permitted in the township of Woomera, entry to the Woomera Prohibited Area is by permit only, except in the immediate corridors of the Stuart Highway and the road from Coober Pedy to William Creek. Camping is not permitted in the area.

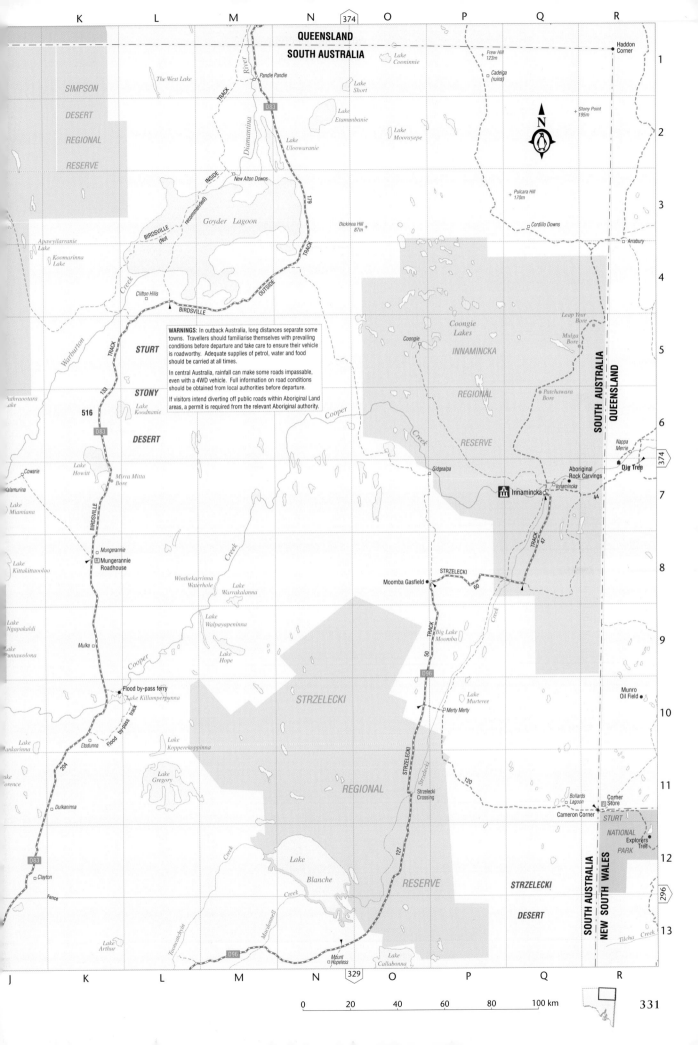

QUEENSLAND
SOUTH AUSTRALIA

Haddon
Corner

The West Lake

Pandie Pandie

*Lake
Cooninnie*

Frew Hill
123m

Stony Point
195m

*Lake
Short*

Cadelga
(ruins)

SIMPSON

DESERT

*Lake
Etamunbanie*

REGIONAL

*Lake
Moorayepe*

RESERVE

*Lake
Uloowaranie*

Pulcara Hill
170m

New Alton Downs

Cordillo Downs

Goyder Lagoon

Dickinna Hill
87m

Arrabury

Apawyilarranie
Lake

Clifton Hills

Koomarinna
Lake

BIRDSVILLE

BIRDSVILLE

WARNINGS: In outback Australia, long distances separate some
towns. Travellers should familiarise themselves with prevailing
conditions before departure and take care to ensure their vehicle
is roadworthy. Adequate supplies of petrol, water and food
should be carried at all times.

In central Australia, rainfall can make some roads impassable,
even with a 4WD vehicle. Full information on road conditions
should be obtained from local authorities before departure.

If visitors intend diverting off public roads within Aboriginal Land
areas, a permit is required from the relevant Aboriginal authority.

Coongie
Lakes

Leap Year
Bore

Mulga
Bore

Coongie

INNAMINCKA

Warburton

STURT

133

REGIONAL

Patchawarra
Bore

516

STONY

*Lake
Koodnanie*

RESERVE

Pathraootara
Lake

Cooper

Creek

DESERT

Gidgealpa

Nappa
Merrie

Cowarie

*Lake
Howitt*

Mirra Mitta
Bore

Aboriginal
Rock Carvings

Dig Tree

Kalamurina

Innamincka

Innamincka

*Lake
Miamiana*

44

Creek

Mungerannie

*Lake
Kittakittaooloo*

Mungerannie
Roadhouse

Winthekarrinna
Waterhole

*Lake
Warrakalanna*

STRZELECKI

*Lake
Ngapakaldi*

Moomba Gasfield

60

*Lake
Puntawolona*

Mulka

Cooper

Creek

*Lake
Walpayapeninna*

*Lake
Hope*

Big Lake
Moomba

Munro
Oil Field

Flood by-pass ferry

Lake Killamperpunna

STRZELECKI

*Lake
Murteree*

Merty Merty

*Lake
Bankarinna*

Etadunna

*Lake
Kopperekoppinna*

REGIONAL

120

Bollards
Lagoon

Corner
Store

*Lake
Florence*

204

Dulkaninna

*Lake
Gregory*

Strzelecki
Crossing

Cameron Corner

STURT

NATIONAL

PARK

Explorers
Tree

Creek

RESERVE

127

*Lake
Arthur*

Clayton

Lake
Blanche

STRZELECKI

Fence

Creek

DESERT

Mount
Hopeless

*Lake
Callabonna*

329

SOUTH AUSTRALIA
QUEENSLAND

SOUTH AUSTRALIA
NEW SOUTH WALES

374

296

Tilcha *Creek*

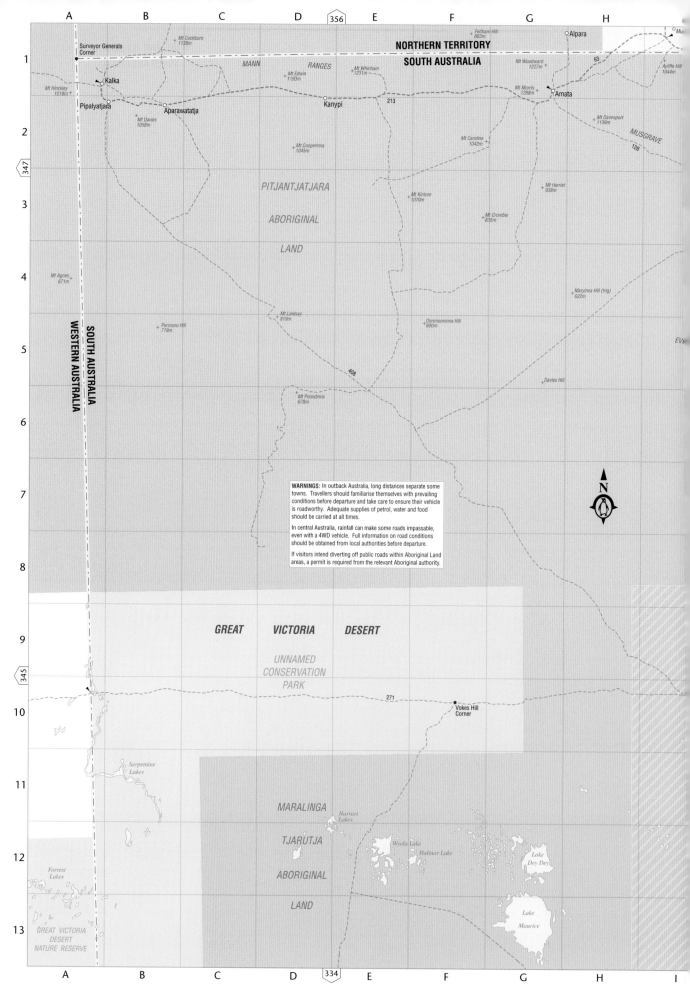

NORTHERN TERRITORY

SOUTH AUSTRALIA

A B C D E F G H

1

+ Mt Cockburn
1138m

MANN   RANGES   + Mt Whinham
1231m

+ Mt Edwin
1193m

Feltham Hill
863m

○ Alpara

Surveyor Generals
Corner

Mt Hinckley
1018m +

▲ Kalka

Pipalyatjara ○

Kanypi ○

213

Mt Woodward
1227m +

Mt Morris
1288m +

▲ Amata

63

Ayliffe Hill
1044m

○ Aparawatatja

+ Mt Davies
1058m

Mt Davenport
1139m +

2

+ Mt Cooperinna
1045m

Mt Caroline
1042m +

MUSGRAVE

128

347

PITJANTJATJARA

+ Mt Kintore
1070m

Mt Harriet
938m +

3

ABORIGINAL

+ Mt Crombie
835m

LAND

4

+ Mt Agnes
671m

Maryinna Hill (trig)
622m +

+ Mt Lindsay
819m

Donmooninna Hill
600m +

5

SOUTH AUSTRALIA

WESTERN AUSTRALIA

+ Permano Hill
719m

406

Davies Hill +

EV

6

+ Mt Poondinna
678m

7

WARNINGS: In outback Australia, long distances separate some towns. Travellers should familiarise themselves with prevailing conditions before departure and take care to ensure their vehicle is roadworthy. Adequate supplies of petrol, water and food should be carried at all times.

In central Australia, rainfall can make some roads impassable, even with a 4WD vehicle. Full information on road conditions should be obtained from local authorities before departure.

If visitors intend diverting off public roads within Aboriginal Land areas, a permit is required from the relevant Aboriginal authority.

N

8

9

GREAT   VICTORIA   DESERT

UNNAMED
CONSERVATION
PARK

345

271

● Vokes Hill
Corner

10

Serpentine
Lakes

11

MARALINGA

Nurrari
Lakes

TJARUTJA

Wyola Lake

Halinor Lake

Lake
Dey Dey

12

Forrest
Lakes

ABORIGINAL

LAND

GREAT VICTORIA
DESERT
NATURE RESERVE

Lake
Maurice

13

A B C D E F G H I

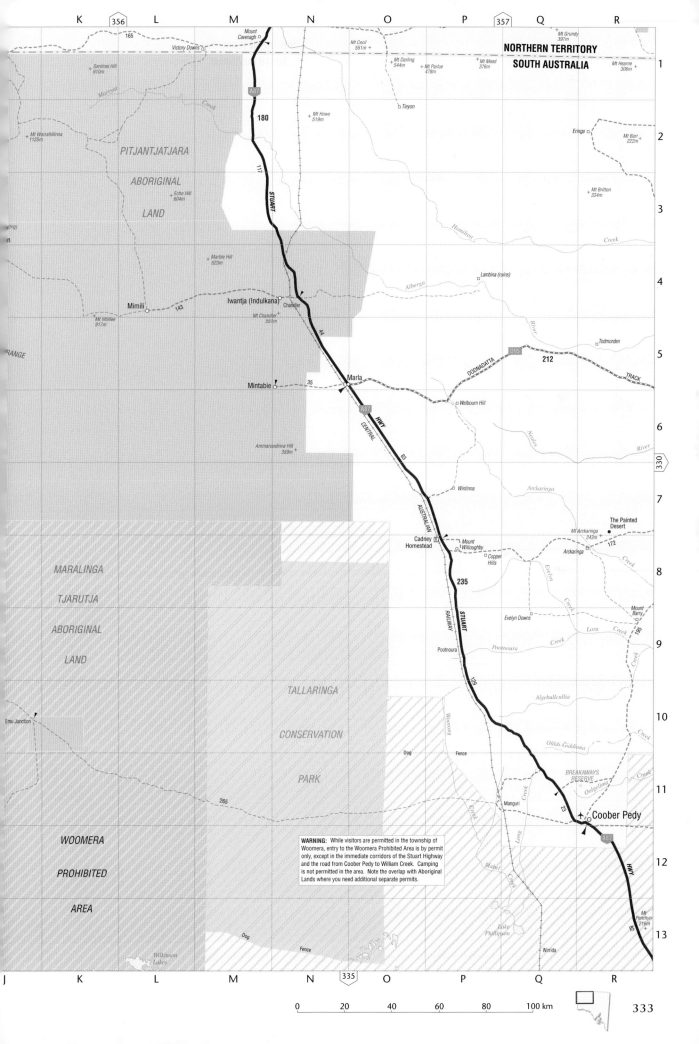

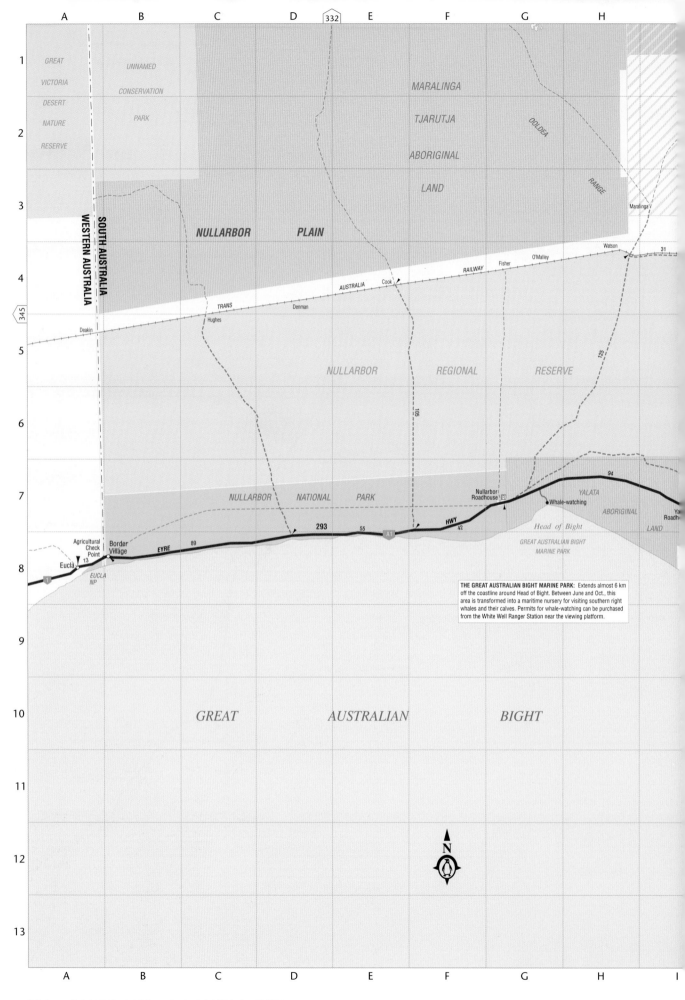

THE GREAT AUSTRALIAN BIGHT MARINE PARK: Extends almost 6 km off the coastline around Head of Bight. Between June and Oct., this area is transformed into a maritime nursery for visiting southern right whales and their calves. Permits for whale-watching can be purchased from the White Well Ranger Station near the viewing platform.

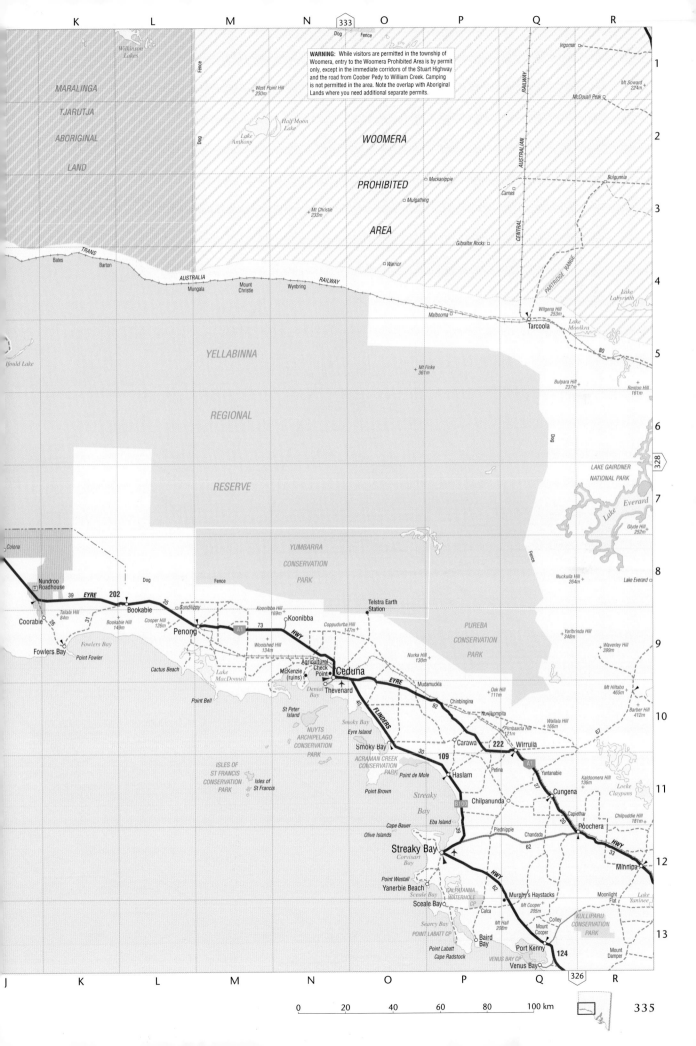

WARNING: While visitors are permitted in the township of Woomera, entry to the Woomera Prohibited Area is by permit only, except in the immediate corridors of the Stuart Highway and the road from Coober Pedy to William Creek. Camping is not permitted in the area. Note the overlap with Aboriginal Lands where you need additional separate permits.

MARALINGA

TJARUTJA

ABORIGINAL

LAND

Wilkinson Lakes

Dog Fence

West Point Hill 230m

Lake Anthony

Half Moon Lake

WOOMERA

PROHIBITED

AREA

Muckanippie

Mulgathing

Mt Christie 233m

Carnes

Ingomar

Mt Soward 224m

McDouall Peak

Bulgunnia

Gibraltar Rocks

Warrior

Bates

Barton

TRANS

AUSTRALIA

Mungala

Mount Christie

Wynbring

RAILWAY

Malboona

Tarcoola

Wilgena Hill 253m

Lake Labyrinth

Lake Moolka

YELLABINNA

Ifould Lake

Mt Finke 361m

Bulpara Hill 237m

Renton Hill 161m

REGIONAL

RESERVE

Dog Fence

LAKE GAIRDNER NATIONAL PARK

Lake Everard

Nuckulla Hill 264m

Lake Everard

Glyde Hill 252m

Colona

Nundroo Roadhouse

39 EYRE 202

Dog Fence

YUMBARRA CONSERVATION PARK

Telstra Earth Station

Yarlbrinda Hill 348m

Waverley Hill 399m

Coorabie

Talisla Hill 84m

29 31

Bookabie

Bookabie Hill 149m

35

Gundilippy

Cooper Hill 126m

Koonibba Hill 169m

Koonibba

Coppudurba Hill 147m

PUREBA CONSERVATION PARK

Mt Hiltaba 465m

Fowlers Bay

Point Fowler

Penong

73

A1

Woolshed Hill 134m

HWY

Nurka Hill 130m

Barber Hill 412m

Cactus Beach

Lake MacDonnell

McKenzie (ruins)

Agricultural Check Point

Ceduna

EYRE

Mudamuckla

92

Oak Hill 111m

Point Bell

Thevenard

Denial Bay

40

FLINDERS

Chinbingina

Wallala Hill 166m

67

St Peter Island

Smoky Bay

Eyre Island

Nunnikompita

Pimbaacla Hill 121m

NUYTS ARCHIPELAGO CONSERVATION PARK

ISLES OF ST FRANCIS CONSERVATION PARK

Isles of St Francis

Point de Mole

30

109

Haslam

Carawa

222

Wirrulla

Yantanabie

Kaldoonera Hill 136m

Locke Claypans

Point Brown

Streaky Bay

Petina

A1

Chilpanunda

Cungena

Chilpuddie Hill 181m

Cape Bauer

Eba Island

B100

39

Piednippie

Chandada

Capiethar

Poochera

Olive Islands

Streaky Bay

Corvisart Bay

62

HWY

33

Minnipa

Point Westall

Yanerbie Beach

Sceale Bay

Sceale Bay

SALPATANNA WATERHOLE CP

62

Murphy's Haystacks

Mt Cooper 205m

Moonlight Flat

Lake Yaninee

Calca

Searcy Bay

POINT LABATT CP

Mt Hall 208m

Colley

Mount Cooper

KULLIPARU CONSERVATION PARK

Baird Bay

Point Labatt

Cape Radstock

Port Kenny

124

Mount Damper

VENUS BAY CP

Venus Bay

326

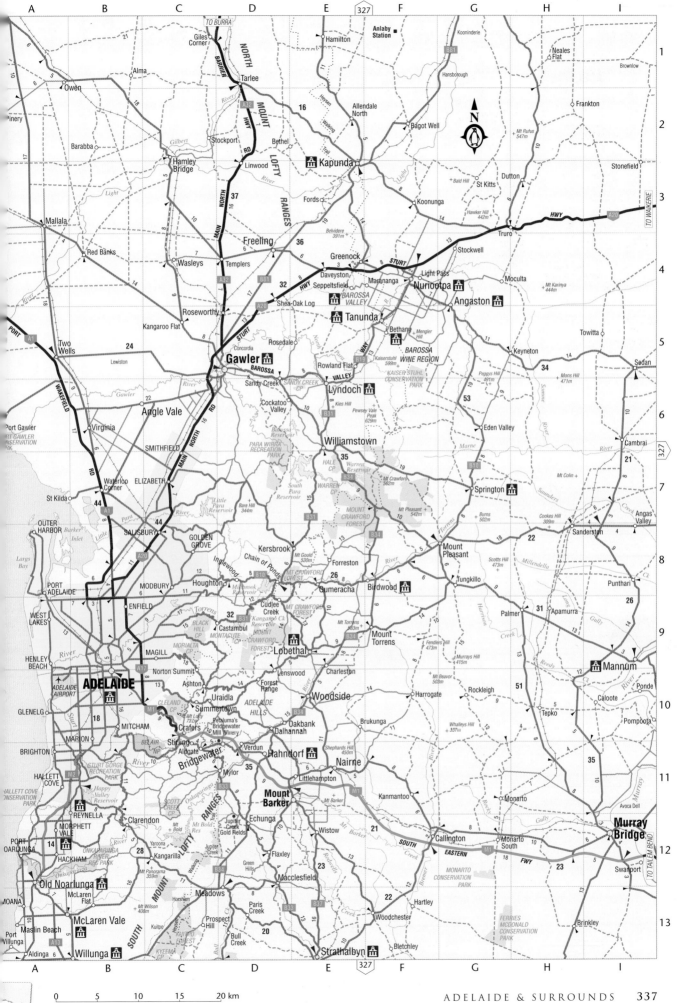

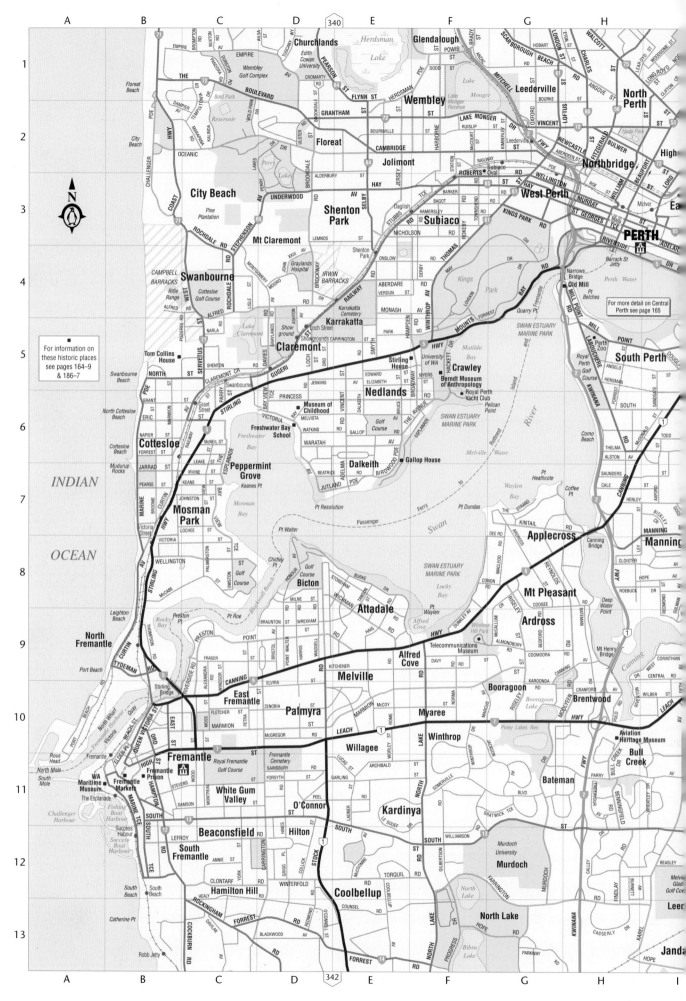

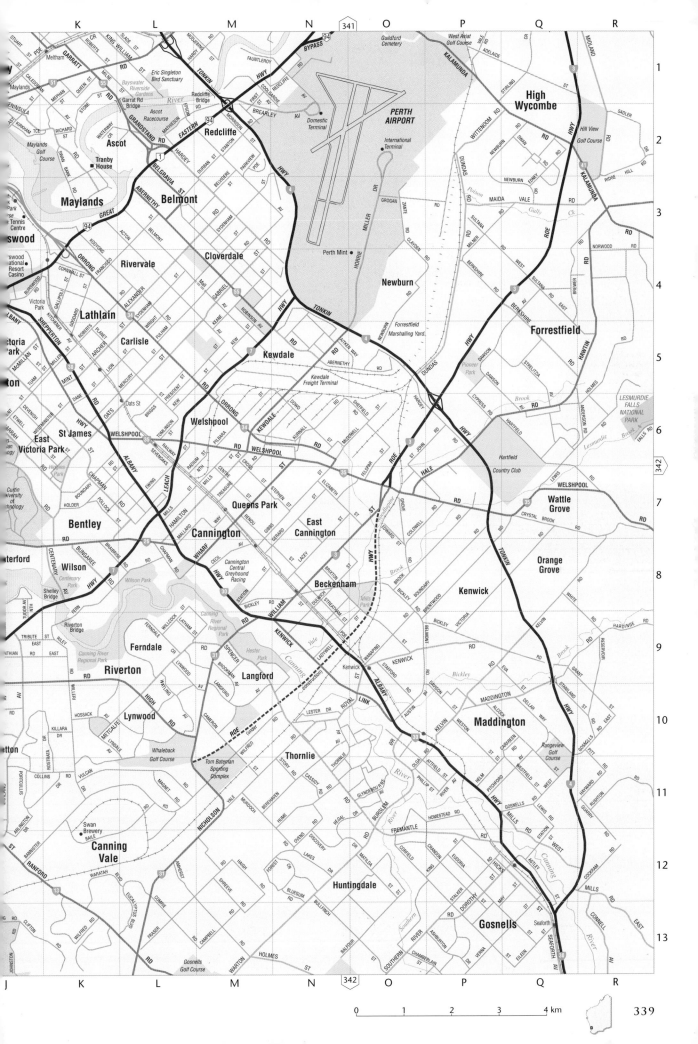

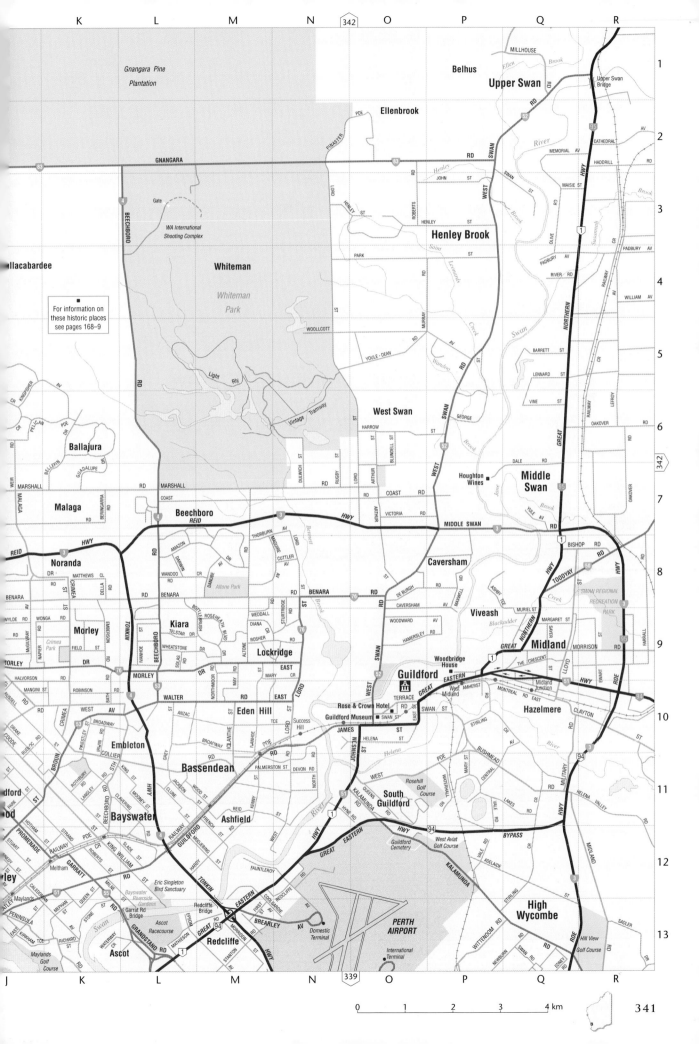

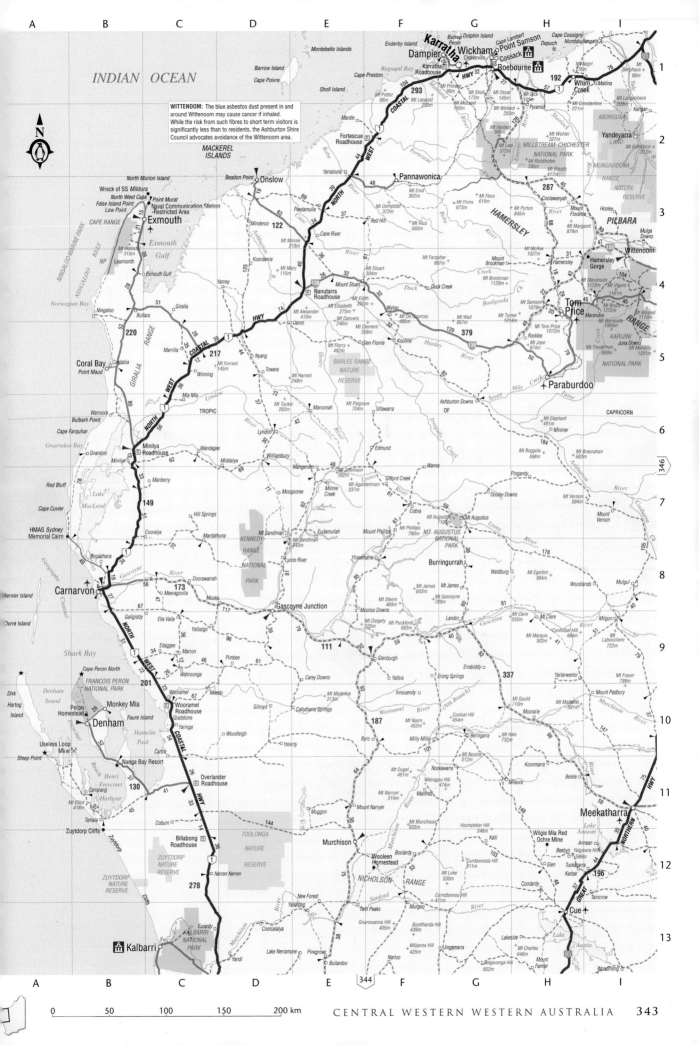

WITTENOOM: The blue asbestos dust present in and around Wittenoom may cause cancer if inhaled. While the risk from such fibres to short term visitors is significantly less than to residents, the Ashburton Shire Council advocates avoidance of the Wittenoom area.

INDIAN OCEAN

MACKEREL ISLANDS

N

CAPE RANGE NP

NINGALOO MARINE PARK

Exmouth

Exmouth Gulf

TROPIC OF CAPRICORN

Carnarvon

Shark Bay

FRANCOIS PERON NATIONAL PARK

Monkey Mia

Denham

Useless Loop Mine

Coral Bay

GIRALIA RANGE

HAMERSLEY RANGE

Tom Price

Paraburdoo

KARIJINI NATIONAL PARK

Wittenoom

Hamersley Gorge

PILBARA

MILLSTREAM-CHICHESTER NATIONAL PARK

Karratha
Dampier
Wickham
Point Samson
Cossack
Roebourne
Whim Creek

Onslow

Pannawonica

Fortescue Roadhouse

Nanutarra Roadhouse

Minilya Roadhouse

MT AUGUSTUS NATIONAL PARK

Mount Augustus

Burringurrah

Gascoyne Junction

KENNEDY RANGE NATIONAL PARK

Wooramel Roadhouse

Overlander Roadhouse

Billabong Roadhouse

Meekatharra

Murchison

TOOLONGA NATURE RESERVE

NICHOLSON RANGE

Cue

ZUYTDORP NATURE RESERVE

KALBARRI NATIONAL PARK

Kalbarri

0   50   100   150   200 km

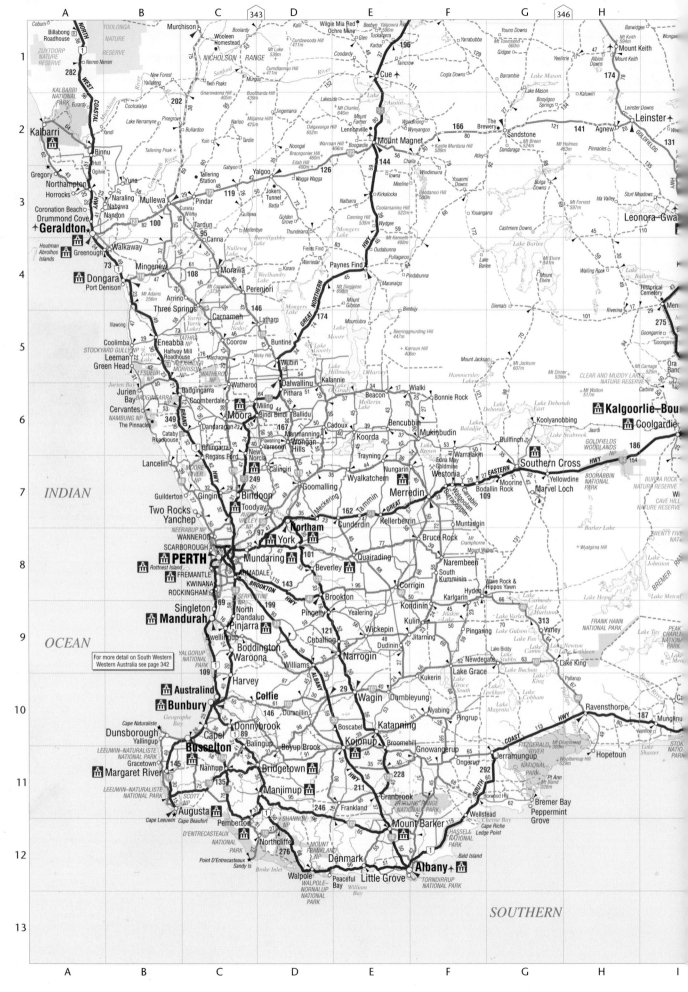

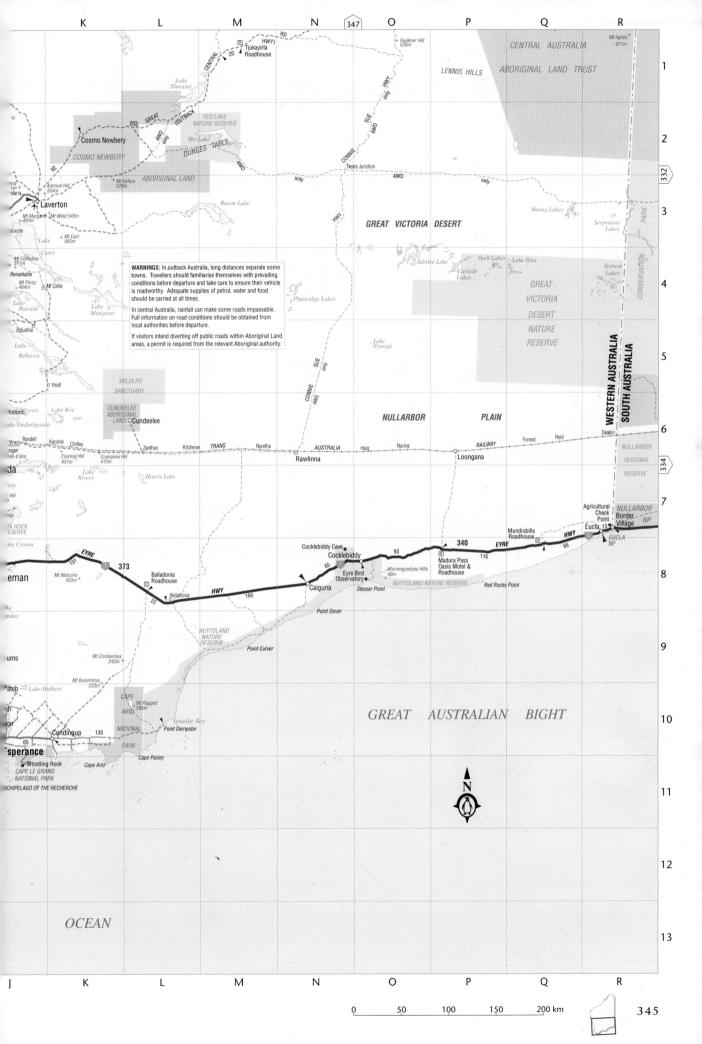

K L M N O P Q R

RD

Mt Agnes
671m

CENTRAL AUSTRALIA

ABORIGINAL LAND TRUST

LENNIS HILLS

Faulkner Hill
536m

Tjukayirla
Roadhouse

20

HWY

CENTRAL

Lake
Throssel

1

203

GREAT

OUTBACK

YEO LAKE
NATURE
RESERVE

4WD
only

Yeo Lake

DUNGES TABLE

4WD

SUE
4WD

Neale Junction

only

2

COSMO NEWBERY

Cosmo Newbery

CONNIE

92

Mt Selton
529m

4WD

only

Wanna Lakes

ABORIGINAL LAND

4WD

3

Admiral Hill
554m

Laverton

Rason Lake

GREAT VICTORIA DESERT

Serpentine
Lakes

Mt Margaret
+493m

Mt Weld 540m

PARK

Mt East
565m

Mt Collindina
511m

Lake
Carey

Jubilee Lake

Shell Lakes

Lake Ilma

GREAT

Forrest
Lakes

4

Mt Percy
464m

Mt Celia

Lake
Minigwai

Plumridge Lakes

Carlisle
Lakes

VICTORIA

CONSERVATION

Lake
Raeside

Lake
Nyanga

DESERT

Edjudina

SUE

NATURE

5

Lake
Rebecca

Yindi

WILDLIFE
SANCTUARY

CONNIE

only

RESERVE

WESTERN AUSTRALIA

SOUTH AUSTRALIA

4WD

Historic

Lake Yindarlgooda

CUNDEELEE
ABORIGINAL
LAND

Cundeelee

6

Karonie

Chifley

NULLARBOR

PLAIN

Deakin

Randell

Zanthus

Kitchener

TRANS

Naretha

AUSTRALIA

Haig

Nurina

RAILWAY

Forrest

Reid

NULLARBOR

ngar
Hill 416m

Erayinia Hill
431m

Coonanna Hill
415m

Rawlinna

Loongana

REGIONAL

7

Lake
Rivers

Harris Lake

RESERVE

Agricultural
Check
Point

NULLARBOR
NP

Border
Village

Eucla 13

A ROCK
RESERVE

Mundrabilla
Roadhouse

EUCLA
NP

Lake Cowan

EYRE

340

EYRE

HWY

66

8

197

373

Cocklebiddy Cave

93

116

Madura Pass
Oasis Motel &
Roadhouse

Mt Malcolm
455m

Balladonia
Roadhouse

Cocklebiddy

eman

65

HWY

Eyre Bird
Observatory

Wurrengoodyea Hills
90m

Red Rocks Point

andas

22

Balladonia

160

Caiguna

Slessar Point

NUYTSLAND NATURE RESERVE

Point Dover

9

NUYTSLAND
NATURE
RESERVE

Point Culver

Mt Coobaninya
243m

ums

Lake Hulbert

Mt Buraminya
233m

atch

CAPE
ARID

Mt Ragged
585m

Israelite Bay

10

h

NATIONAL

Point Dempster

GREAT   AUSTRALIAN   BIGHT

65

135

Condingup

PARK

Cape Pasley

sperance

Whistling Rock

Cape Arid

11

CAPE LE GRAND
NATIONAL PARK

N

ARCHIPELAGO OF THE RECHERCHE

12

OCEAN

13

J K L M N O P Q R

WARNINGS: In outback Australia, long distances separate some towns. Travellers should familiarise themselves with prevailing conditions before departure and take care to ensure their vehicle is roadworthy. Adequate supplies of petrol, water and food should be carried at all times.

In central Australia, rainfall can make some roads impassable. Full information on road conditions should be obtained from local authorities before departure.

If visitors intend diverting off public roads within Aboriginal Land areas, a permit is required from the relevant Aboriginal authority.

0   50   100   150   200 km

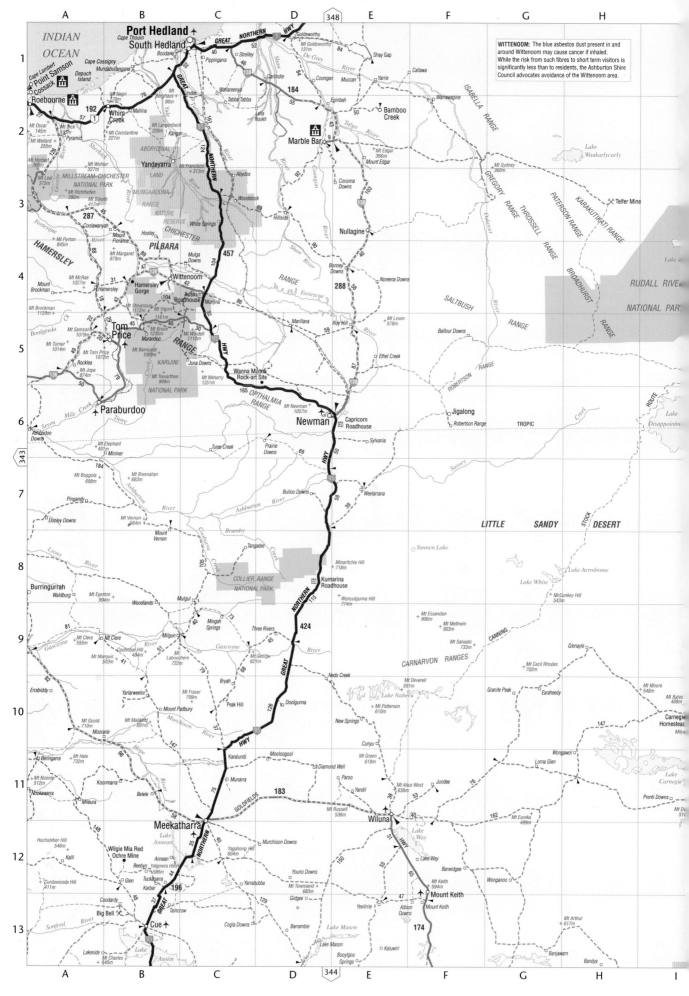

WITTENOOM: The blue asbestos dust present in and around Wittenoom may cause cancer if inhaled. While the risk from such fibres to short term visitors is significantly less than to residents, the Ashburton Shire Council advocates avoidance of the Wittenoom area.

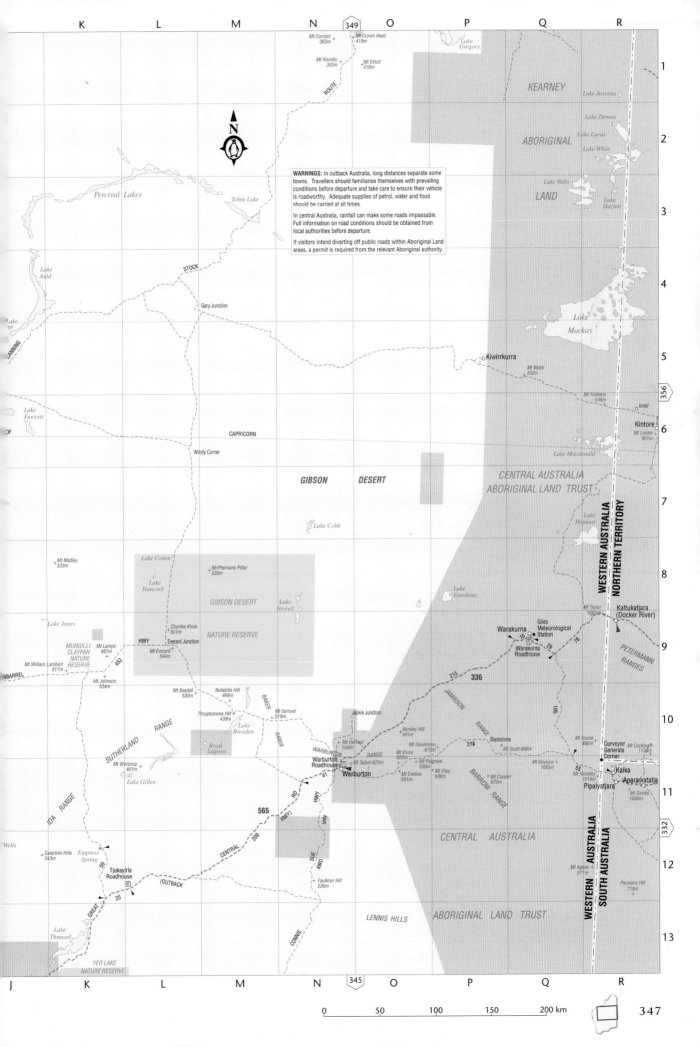

Mt Cornish
363m
Mt Crown Head
419m

Mt Romilly
353m
Mt Elliott
418m

Lake
Gregory

KEARNEY

Lake Jeavons

ABORIGINAL

Lake Dennis

Lake Lucas

Lake White

Percival Lakes

Tobin Lake

Lake Wills

LAND

Lake Hazlett

STOCK

Lake
Auld

ROUTE

Gary Junction

Lake
Mackay

LANNING

Lake
Fawcett

Kiwirrkurra

Mt Webb
532m

356

Mt Tietkens
546m

Ininti

Kintore

OF

CAPRICORN

Mt Leisler
901m

Windy Corner

Lake Macdonald

6

GIBSON   DESERT

CENTRAL AUSTRALIA
ABORIGINAL LAND TRUST

7

Lake Cobb

Lake
Hopkins

WESTERN AUSTRALIA
NORTHERN TERRITORY

Mt Madley
533m

Lake Cohen

McPhersons Pillar
530m

Lake
Hancock

GIBSON DESERT

Lake
Earnham

Kaltukatjara
(Docker River)

8

Lake Jones

Charles Knob
551m

Lake
Newell

Mt Taylor
1092m

Warakurna

Giles
Meteorological
Station

NATURE RESERVE

PETERMANN

MUNGILLI
CLAYPAN
NATURE
RESERVE

Mt Lampe
497m

452

HWY

Everard Junction

Mt Everard
544m

Warakurna
Roadhouse

29

76

RANGES

9

BARREL

Mt William Lambert
517m

Mt Johnson
534m

Mt Beadell
530m

Notabilis Hill
468m

BAKER

Mt Samuel
519m

JAMIESON

336

215

Jackie Junction

Mt Goosse
588m

105

Surveyor
Generals
Corner

Mt Cockburn
1135m

10

Thryptomene Hill
439m

Lake
Breaden

RANGE

Mt Halleast
555m

Bentley Hill
581m

Blackstone

Mt Scott 668m

RANGE

Mt Aloysius
1085m

55

SUTHERLAND

RANGE

Royd
Lagoon

WARBURTON

RANGE

Mt Elvira
603m

Mt Rawlinson
670m

249

RANGE

Kalka

Mt Worsnop
461m

Warburton
Roadhouse

Mt Talbot 623m

Mt Palgrave
539m

BARROW

Mt Hinckley
1018m

Aparawatatja

IDA   RANGE

Lake Gillen

Warburton

Mt Eveline
631m

Mt Eliza
646m

Mt Cooper
670m

Pipalyatjara

Mt Davies
1058m

11

565

RD

HWY

332

WESTERN AUSTRALIA
SOUTH AUSTRALIA

CENTRAL AUSTRALIA

CENTRAL

209

SUE
4WD
only

Wells

Calachini Hills
543m

Empress
Spring

59

Tjukayirla
Roadhouse

Mt Agnes
671m

12

20

(OUTBACK

Faulkner Hill
536m

Permano Hill
719m

GREAT

CONNIE

LENNIS HILLS

ABORIGINAL LAND TRUST

13

Lake
Throssel

YEO LAKE
NATURE RESERVE

WARNINGS: In outback Australia, long distances separate some towns. Travellers should familiarise themselves with prevailing conditions before departure and take care to ensure their vehicle is roadworthy. Adequate supplies of petrol, water and food should be carried at all times.

In central Australia, rainfall can make some roads impassable. Full information on road conditions should be obtained from local authorities before departure.

If visitors intend diverting off public roads within Aboriginal Land areas, a permit is required from the relevant Aboriginal authority.

0   50   100   150   200 km

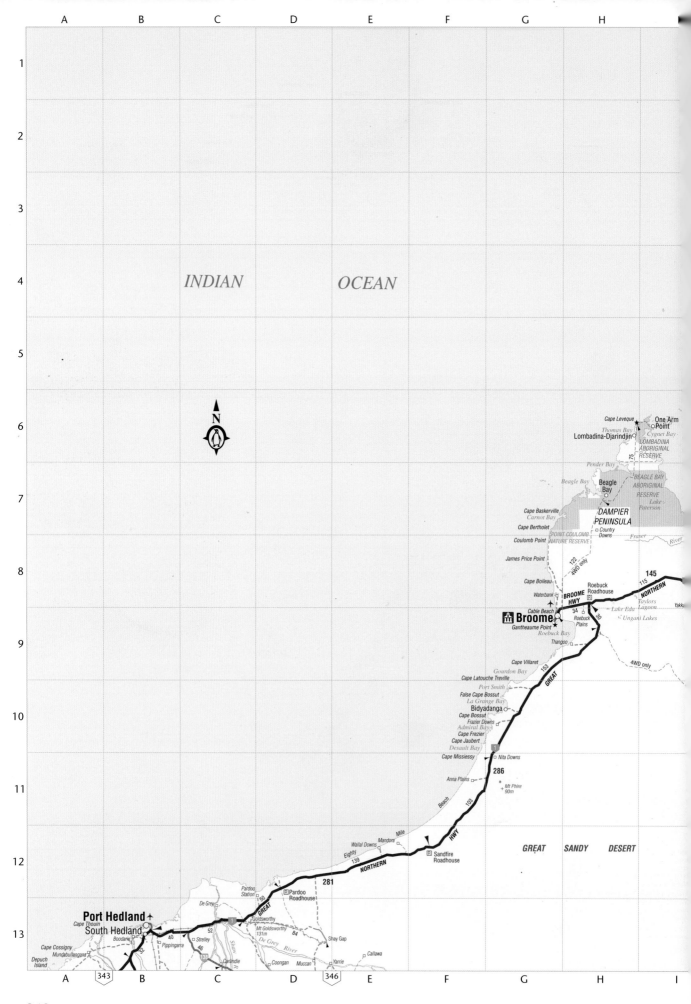

INDIAN OCEAN

N

One Arm
Point
Cape Leveque
Thomas Bay
Lombadina-Djarindjin
Cygnet Bay
LOMBADINA
ABORIGINAL
RESERVE
75
Pender Bay
Beagle Bay
Beagle
Bay
BEAGLE BAY
ABORIGINAL
RESERVE
Lake
Paterson
DAMPIER
PENINSULA
Cape Baskerville
Carnot Bay
Cape Bertholet
POINT COULOMB
NATURE RESERVE
Country
Downs
Fraser
River
Coulomb Point
James Price Point
122
4WD only
NORTHERN
145
115
Cape Boileau
Waterbank
BROOME
HWY
Roebuck
Roadhouse
Taylors
Lagoon
Yakka
Cable Beach
Broome
34
Lake Eda
30
Roebuck
Gantheaume Point
Plains
Ungani Lakes
Roebuck Bay
Thangoo
Cape Villaret
133
4WD only
Gourdon Bay
Cape Latouche Treville
GREAT
Port Smith
False Cape Bossut
La Grange Bay
Bidyadanga
Cape Bossut
Frazier Downs
Admiral Bay
Cape Frezier
Cape Jaubert
Desault Bay
Nita Downs
Cape Missiessy
286
Anna Plains
Mt Phire
90m
GREAT SANDY DESERT
Mile
Wallal Downs
Mandora
Beach
HWY
Eighty
139
Sandfire
Roadhouse
NORTHERN
281
GREAT
50
Pardoo
Station
Pardoo
Roadhouse
De Grey
Port Hedland
Goldsworthy
Cape Thouin
Mt Goldsworthy
131m
84
South Hedland
52
Shay Gap
Boodarie
Stelley
De Grey River
Cape Cossigny
Mundabullangana
40
Pippingarta
Callawa
46
Coongan
Muccan
Yarrie
Depuch
Island
Cariindie
Shaw R.
192

343

346

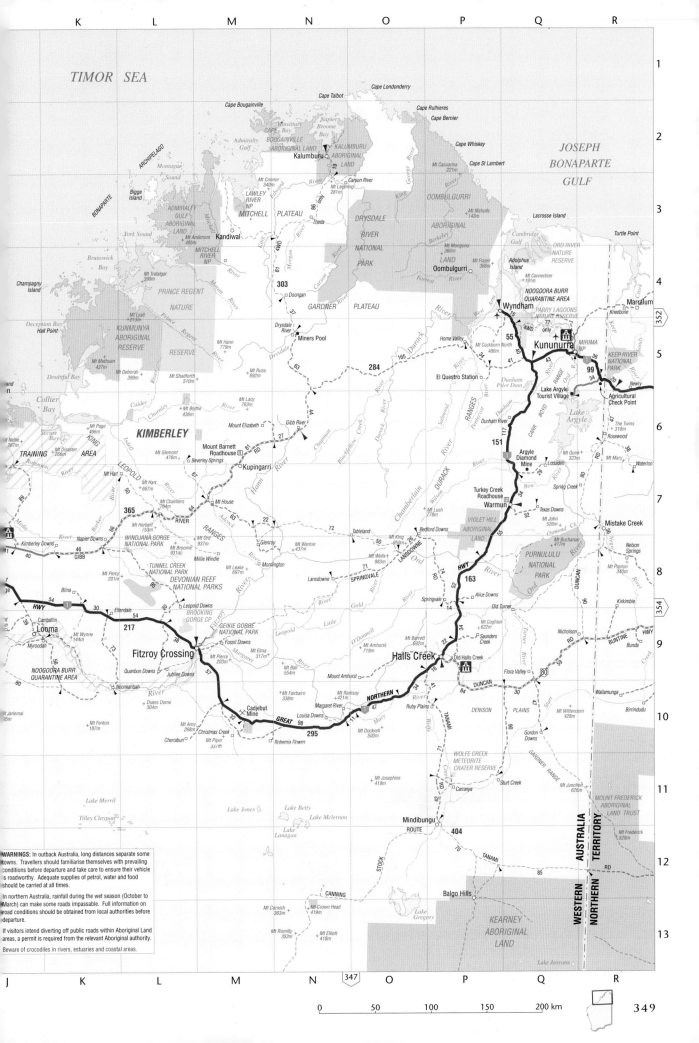

TIMOR SEA

1

JOSEPH BONAPARTE GULF

2

Cape Londonderry
Cape Talbot
Cape Bougainville
Vansittart Bay
Napier Broome Bay
Cape Rulhieres
Cape Bernier
Admiralty Gulf
Cape Whiskey
Cape St Lambert

BONAPARTE ARCHIPELAGO

Montague Sound
CAPE BAY
BOUGAINVILLE ABORIGINAL LAND
KALUMBURU ABORIGINAL LAND

Bigge Island

Kalumburu

Mt Connor 340m
Carson River
Mt Leeming 281m

OOMBULGURRI ABORIGINAL LAND

3

York Sound

ADMIRALTY GULF ABORIGINAL LAND
Mt Anderson +485m

Kandiwal

MITCHELL RIVER NP

LAWLEY RIVER NP
MITCHELL PLATEAU

4WD only
303
Doongan
Theda

DRYSDALE RIVER NATIONAL PARK

Mt Nicholls 143m

Lacrosse Island

Turtle Point

4

Brunswick Bay

Mt Trafalgar 390m

PRINCE REGENT NATURE RESERVE

37
GARDNER PLATEAU

Mt Mongona 366m
Mt Fraser 366m

Oombulgurri

ORD RIVER NATURE RESERVE

Mt Connection +191m
Adolphus Island

NOOGOORA BURR QUARANTINE AREA

Marralum
Kneeboone

352

Champagny Island

Mt Lyall +213m

KUNMUNYA ABORIGINAL RESERVE

Mt Methuen 427m
Mt Deborah 399m
Mt Shadforth 510m

Miners Pool
Drysdale River

Mt Russ 692m

284
165

Home Valley
Mt Cockburn North 486m

Wyndham
15
4WD only

Kununurra
55
MIRIMA NP
77
36

PARRY LAGOONS NATURE RESERVE

Agricultural Check Point
Newry
20

KEEP RIVER NATIONAL PARK

5

Deception Bay
Hall Point
Doubtful Bay

Calder River
Charnley River

KING LEOPOLD AREA
TRAINING

Mt Page +466m
Mt Disaster 266m

Mt Blythe +436m

Mount Elizabeth
Gibb River
44

27

41
43
El Questro Station
Dunham Pilot Dam
Lake Argyle Tourist Village
Lake Argyle

Rosewood
The Twins +318m

6

Collier Bay
Secure Bay

Nellie +267m

ROBINSON River

Mt Hart +667m

50
KIMBERLEY
LEOPOLD

Mt Glemont 478m
Mount Barnett Roadhouse
81
Beverley Springs
RD
63
Kupingarri

151
Argyle Diamond Mine
Lissadell
29
Spring Creek

Mt Quirk +323m
Waterloo
Mt Mary
80

RANGES

7

Meda River

Mt Herbert 753m
66
67
64
Mt Chalmers +764m
Mt House
RIVER
365
Mt Hart

Hann River
62
22

72
Tableland
Mt King +950m
26
Bedford Downs
50

Turkey Creek Roadhouse
Warmun
32
Texas Downs
Mt Lush 778m

Mt John +526m
59
Mistake Creek
Nelson Springs

PURNULULU NATIONAL PARK

8

Kimberley Downs
Napier Downs
GIBB
40
46

WINDJANA GORGE NATIONAL PARK

Mt Broome 931m
Mt Ord 937m
Glenroy
Millie Windie

Mt Warton +437m

Mt Wells 983m

LANSDOWNE
71
Springvale
74

VIOLET HILL ABORIGINAL LAND

HWY
163
Alice Downs
Old Turner

Mt Buchanan +417m
DUNCAN RD
Mt Panton 340m

Kirkimbie

354

Blina
HWY
54
30
Ellendale
Leopold Downs
54
30

TUNNEL CREEK NATIONAL PARK
DEVONIAN REEF NATIONAL PARKS
98

Mt Leake +697m

Lansdowne
SPRINGVALE
Gold River
Little River

52
14
Springvale
34
22
Saunders Creek

Mt Coghlan +622m
RD
BUNTINE HWY

Nicholson
Bunda

9

Looma
Camballin
39
56
Myroodah

Mt Wynne 144m
217
38

BROOKING GORGE CP
GEIKIE GORGE NATIONAL PARK

Fossil Downs

Mt Pierre 203m

Mt Barnett 692m

Halls Creek
Old Halls Creek
84
DUNCAN RD
30

Flora Valley
80
59
Wallamunga
Birrindudu

Noonkanbah

Fitzroy Crossing
Quanbun Downs
Jubilee Downs
57

Mt Elima 317m
Mt Ball 554m

O'Donnell River

Mt Amhurst 719m
Mount Amhurst
Margaret River

16
Ruby Plains
34
DENISON PLAINS
Mt Wittenoom 428m

10

Jarlemai 75m

NOOGOORA BURR QUARANTINE AREA
80

Dukes Dome 304m
River

Cadjebut Mine
98
Louisa Downs
295
Christmas Creek
Cherrabun
Mt Piper 331m
Mt Fairbank 338m
Mt Amy 268m
Mt Fenton 187m

NORTHERN
47
11
Mt Dockrell 500m
Mary River

TANAMI RD
Gordon Downs
06
Sturt Creek

Mt Josephine 419m
WOLFE CREEK METEORITE CRATER RESERVE
Carranya
Sturt Creek
71
42

Mt Junction 626m
GARDNER RANGE

MOUNT FREDERICK ABORIGINAL LAND TRUST
Mt Frederick 529m

11

Lake Merril
Tilley Claypan
Lake Jones
Lake Betty
Lake Mclernon
Lake Lanagan

Mindibungu
ROUTE
404

AUSTRALIA
NORTHERN
WESTERN
TERRITORY
RD
85

12

WARNINGS: In outback Australia, long distances separate some towns. Travellers should familiarise themselves with prevailing conditions before departure and take care to ensure their vehicle is roadworthy. Adequate supplies of petrol, water and food should be carried at all times.

In northern Australia, rainfall during the wet season (October to March) can make some roads impassable. Full information on road conditions should be obtained from local authorities before departure.

If visitors intend diverting off public roads within Aboriginal Land areas, a permit is required from the relevant Aboriginal authority.

Beware of crocodiles in rivers, estuaries and coastal areas.

CANNING STOCK ROUTE
Mt Carnish 363m
Mt Crown Head 419m
Lake Gregory
Balgo Hills
KEARNEY ABORIGINAL LAND
Mt Romilly 353m
Mt Elliott 418m
Lake Jeavons

13

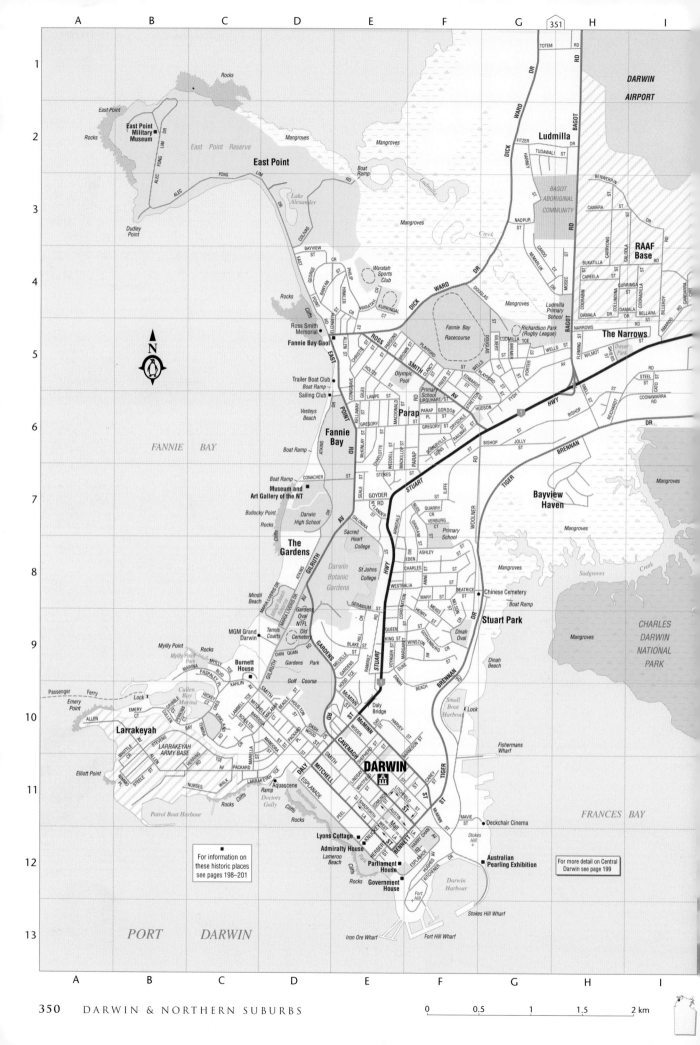

Map labels

DARWIN AIRPORT

TOTEM RD

Ludmilla
FITZER
TUDAWALI
HARNEY
DICK WARD DR
BAGOT RD

BAGOT ABORIGINAL COMMUNITY
NADPUR ST
CARDO
NEMARLUK
MOSEC

BENWERRIN ST
CAMARA ST
CALDOLA
RAAF Base
BUKATILLA ST
CARRYONG
CAREELA ST
CURRINGA
OODRABIN
COLUMDIRA
CURRIDILLA
CORADILLA
DAMALA
BELLARA
DAMALA
BILLEROY
GANDARRA CRT

The Narrows
NARROWS
FLEMING ST
WILMOT ST
SHEILS ST
AMAROO RD

DWYER PARK
STEEL ST
CATO ST
COONAWARRA RD
RICHARDT ST
BISHOP ST

Mangroves

CHARLES DARWIN NATIONAL PARK

DARWIN AIRPORT

Rocks
East Point
East Point Military Museum
ALEC FONG LIM DR
COLVAS
East Point Reserve
Mangroves
East Point
Rocks
FONG LIM
Lake Alexander
Dudley Point
ALEC FONG
BAYVIEW CR
GEORGE
PHILIP ST
Waratah Sports Club
RD
Boat Ramp
Mangroves
Mangroves

EAST POINT RD
RAMLAN
HINKLER CR
WARATAH
KURRINGAL CT
PARSONS ST
DICK WARD DR
DOUGLAS ST
Fannie Bay Racecourse
Creek
DOUGLAS
GILBERT
Mangroves
Ludmilla Primary School
Richardson Park (Rugby League)
WELLS ST
NARROWS
PORTER

Rocks
CLIFFS
Ross Smith Memorial
Fannie Bay Gaol
EAST POINT RD
ELIZABETH ST
ALLEN ST
CHRISTIE ST
ROSS ST
HOLTZE
SMITH
BROWNS
PLAYFORD
CLANCY
BREEF
WELLS
PLAYFORD
EDWARDS
STRETTON
HUDSON
FISH

Trailer Boat Club
Boat Ramp
Sailing Club
Vesteys Beach
Boat Ramp
POINT RD
KELLAWAY
LAMPE
GILES ST
GREGORY
MACDONALD ST
Parap
Olympic Pool
Primary School
URQUHART ST
AV
PARAP PL
GORDON
GREGORY
DRYSDALE
RAILWAY
SMITH AV
HWY
BISHOP ST
JOLLY ST
BISHOP
Bayview Haven
BRENNAN
Mangroves

ATKINS
CONACHER ST
Museum and Art Gallery of the NT
SEALE ST
STOKES ST
GOYDER RD
SALONIKA
FLINDERS
JOHNSTONE
GINS
SOMERVILLE
Fannie Bay
McKINLAY ST
CHARLOTTE ST
MACKILLOP ST
PARAP
STUART HWY
ILIFFE
QUARRY CR
VERBURG CT
Primary School
ARMIDALE
GRAHAM
WOOLNER RD
TIGER

FANNIE BAY
Boat Ramp
Bullocky Point
Rocks
Darwin High School
GILRUTH AV
Sacred Heart College
St Johns College
GERANIUM ST
WESTRALIA ST
EDEN ST
CHARLES ST
ANNE ST
ASHLEY
MARY ST
NELSON
MEIGS
BEATRICE
Chinese Cemetery
Boat Ramp
Sadgroves Creek
Mangroves

The Gardens
Darwin Botanic Gardens
Mindil Beach
MARINA LIVENS DR
Gardens Oval NTFL
Old Cemetery
MGM Grand Darwin
Tennis Courts
CR
CORONATION
HENRY ST
GOTTENBURG
WINSTON CR
Dinah Oval
Stuart Park
Dinah Beach
Mangroves

Myilly Point
Myilly Point Park
Rocks
Cullen Bay Marina
MYILLY
PASPALEY PL
Burnett House
CHIN QUAN
Gardens Park
Golf Course
MELVILLE
GARDENS
BLAKE ST
QUEEN ST
KING ST
MARGARET
DUKE
WINNELLIE
Small Boat Harbour
X Lock

Passenger Ferry
Lock
Emery Point
ALLEN
EMERY CT
GRIBBLE ST
CULLEN BAY
KAHLIN
HICKEYS
LAMBELL TCE
MITCHELL
SMITH
BEAGLE ST
HOUSTON
DASHWOOD
McMINN
GARDENS
HOOD TCE
STUART
VOYAGER ST
HARVEY
BARNESON ST
Fishermans Wharf
BRENNAN RD

Larrakeyah
WHITTLE CR
NIMMO PL
STEELE ST
HEERING
ALLEN
STEVENS
Larrakeyah Army Base
PACKARD
MARTELLA ST
HANDORA
MANTON
LINDSAY ST
WHITTEN
SMITH ST
SHEPHERD
CAVENAGH ST
TIGER ST

Elliott Point
NURSES WALK
LARRAKEYAH TCE
Aquascene
Ramp
Doctors Gully
DALY ST
MITCHELL ST
ESPLANADE
PEEL
SHADFORTH
WEST LA
EDMUNDS
AUSTIN
BENNETT
LITCHFIELD
McMINN ST
CAREY ST
MAVIE ST
Deckchair Cinema

Rocks
Cliffs
Lyons Cottage
Admiralty House
Lameroo Beach
Cliffs
Rocks
Parliament House
Government House
Fort Hill
KNUCKEY
HERBERT
BENNETT
HARRY CHAN AV
ESPLANADE
HUGHES AV
KITCHENER
Stokes Hill
Australian Pearling Exhibition
Darwin Harbour

DARWIN

Patrol Boat Harbour
Cliffs
PORT DARWIN
Iron Ore Wharf
Fort Hill Wharf
Stokes Hill Wharf

FRANCES BAY

FANNIE BAY

N

For information on these historic places see pages 198–201

For more detail on Central Darwin see page 199

0   0.5   1   1.5   2 km

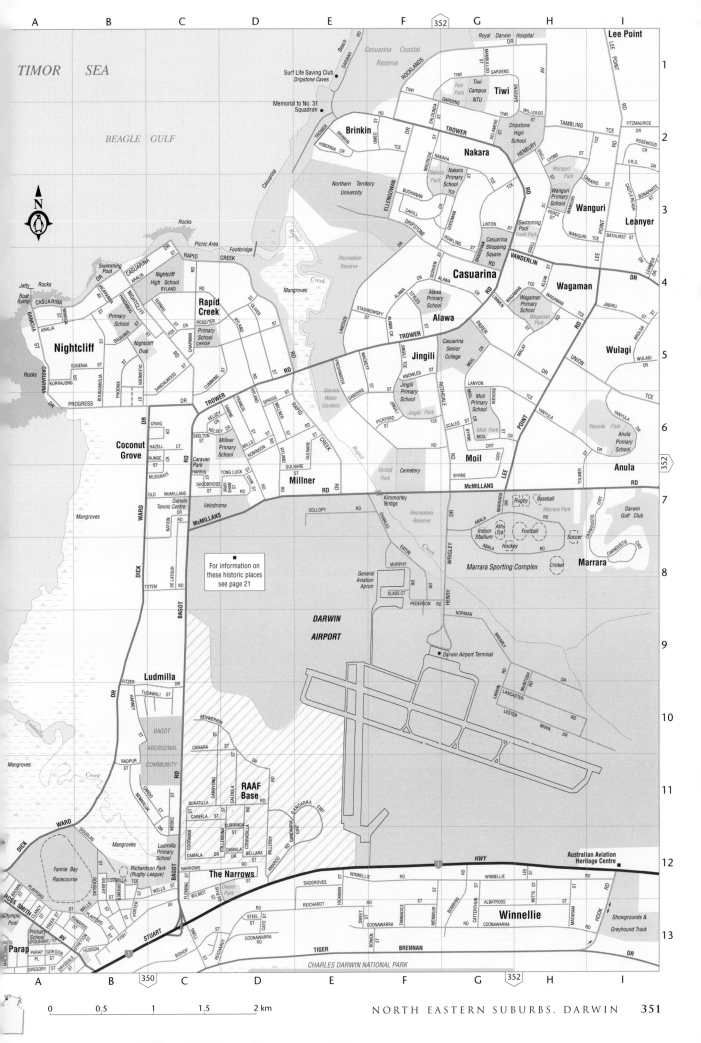

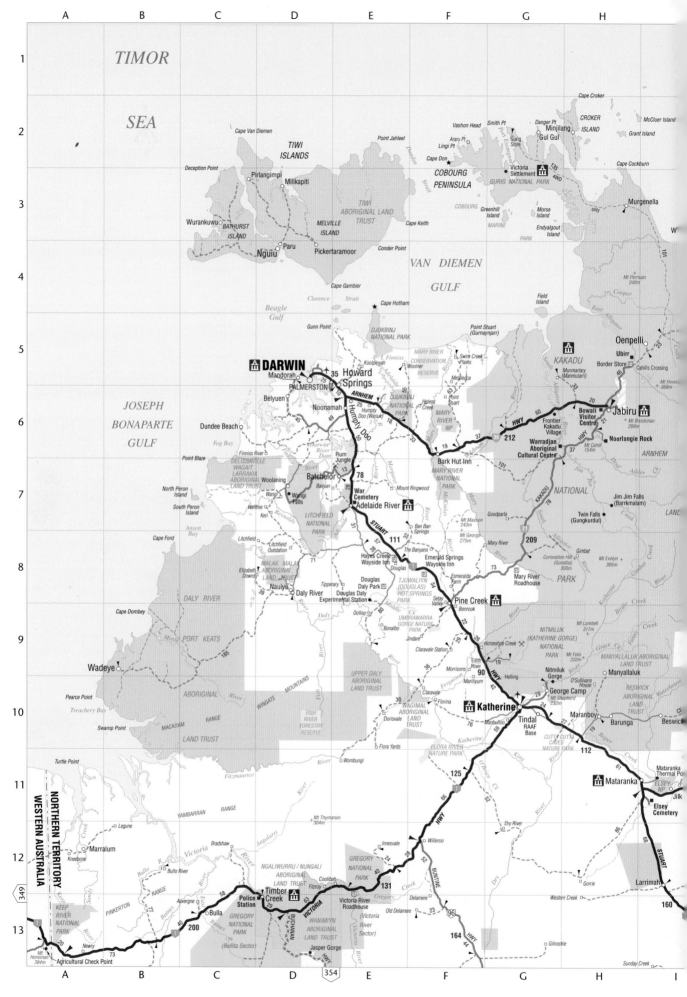

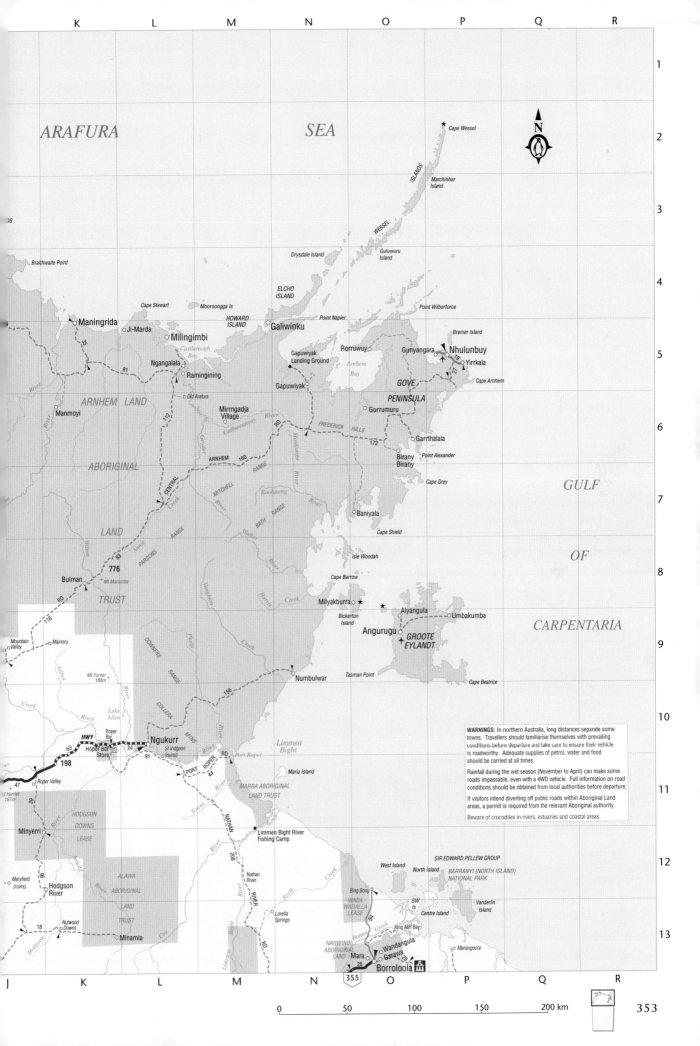

1

ARAFURA   *SEA*

★ Cape Wessel

2

Marchinbar
Island

WESSEL

3

ISLANDS

Braithwaite Point

Drysdale Island   Guluwuru
Island

4

ELCHO
ISLAND   Point Wilberforce

Cape Stewart   Mooroongga Is   Point Napier

■ Maningrida   *HOWARD*
                     ISLAND   Bremer Island
   ○ Ji-Marda   ○ Galiwinku   Rorruwuy ○   Gunyangara ○ ◣ Nhulunbuy

5

    ○ Milingimbi   ◣ Yirrkala
Castlereagh   Cape Arnhem
Bay   Gapuwiyak   *Arnhem*
○ Ngangalala   Landing Ground ● *Bay*   *GOVE*
  ○ Ramingining   *PENINSULA*

ARNHEM LAND   ○ Old Arafura   Gapuwiyak

6

■ Manmoyi   ○ Mirrngadja   *River*   ○ Gurrumuru
               Village   *FREDERICK*   ○ Garrthalala
ABORIGINAL   *ARNHEM* 160   *HILLS* 172   Point Alexander
                   RANGE   ○ Birany
               MITCHELL   Birany   *GULF*

7

LAND   *RANGE*   *Koolatong*   Cape Grey
                    BATH *River* ○ Baniyala
                     RANGE   Cape Shield   *OF*

8

83   *PARSONS*   Isle Woodah
776   Cape Barrow
■ Bulman   Milyakburra ○ ★   ★ ○ Alyangula
         + Mt Marumba   *Bickerton*   ○ Umbakumba
TRUST   *Island*   Angurugu ○   *CARPENTARIA*

9

Mountain ○ Mainoru   ★ *GROOTE*
Valley   *EYLANDT*
        + Mt Furner   Cape Beatrice
          188m   156   Tasman Point   ● Numbulwar

10

      116   *DOWNERS*   *Limmen*
                 RANGE   *Bight*
                Roper Bar   *COLLERA*
        HWY   ○   *MTNS*   Maria Island
     63   Roper Bar   ■ Ngukurr   St Vidgeon
        Store 24   (ruins)   *ROPER* *RD*
  198   91   *PORT*   Port Roper

11

47   ○ Roper Valley   44
 + Mt Harriet   *MARRA ABORIGINAL*
  187m   39   *LAND TRUST*
■ Minyerri

12

   HODGSON   *NATHAN*   ● Limmen Bight River
   DOWNS   Fishing Camp
   LEASE   208   Nathan River

Maryfield   *SIR EDWARD PELLEW GROUP*
(ruins)   *RIVER*   West Island North Island *BÁRRANYI (NORTH ISLAND)*
■ Hodgson   *ALAWA*   *NATIONAL PARK*
 River   *ABORIGINAL*   Bing Bong
        LAND   *SW*   Vanderlin

13

  18 ○ Nutwood   *TRUST*   *WADA*   *Is* Centre Island   Island
     Downs   *WADALLA*
                 ○ Lorella   *LEASE* King Ash Bay
                Springs   *NARWINBI*   Manangoora
■ Minamia   *ABORIGINAL*   ● Wandangula
                  LAND TRUST Mara ● Garawa
                    26   🏛
               355   ■ Borroloola

WARNINGS: In northern Australia, long distances separate some towns. Travellers should familiarise themselves with prevailing conditions before departure and take care to ensure their vehicle is roadworthy. Adequate supplies of petrol, water and food should be carried at all times.

Rainfall during the wet season (November to April) can make some roads impassable, even with a 4WD vehicle. Full information on road conditions should be obtained from local authorities before departure.

If visitors intend diverting off public roads within Aboriginal Land areas, a permit is required from the relevant Aboriginal authority.

Beware of crocodiles in rivers, estuaries and coastal areas.

0   50   100   150   200 km

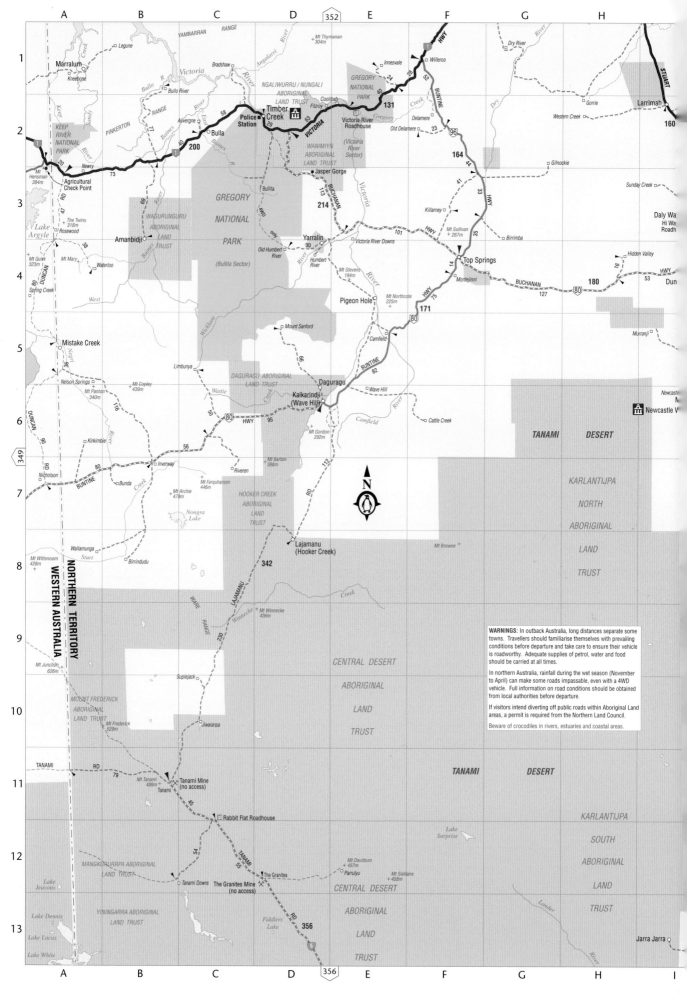

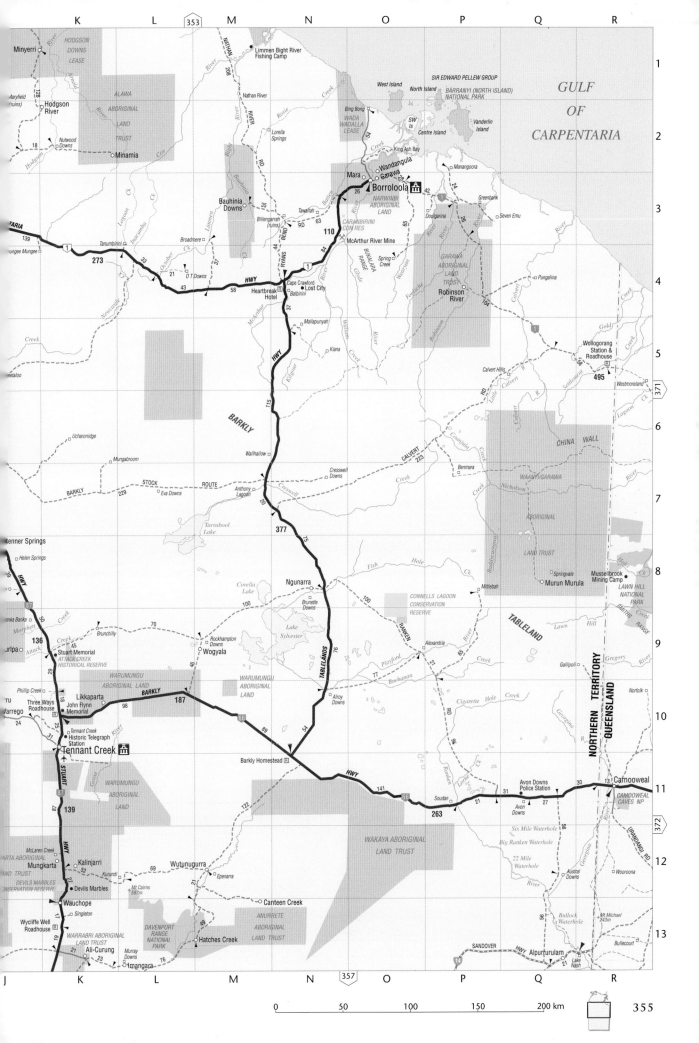

| K | L | M | N | O | P | Q | R |

GULF
OF
CARPENTARIA

SIR EDWARD PELLEW GROUP

BARRANYI (NORTH ISLAND)
NATIONAL PARK

West Island
North Island

Minyerri

HODGSON
DOWNS
LEASE

Maryfield
(ruins)
128

Hodgson
River

ALAWA

ABORIGINAL

LAND

TRUST

Nutwood
Downs
18

Minamia

Bauhinia
Downs

Limmen Bight River
Fishing Camp

Nathan River

Lorella
Springs

Bing Bong
Centre Island

Vanderlin
Island

King Ash Bay

SW
Is

Manangoora

Billengarrah
(ruins)

Tawallah

Mara
Garawa
Wandangula

Borroloola

Greenbank

NARWINBI
ABORIGINAL
LAND

Doolgarina

Seven Emu

Broadmere

CARANBIRINI
CON RES

McArthur River Mine

BUKALARA
RANGE

Pungalina

Robinson
River

Tanumbirini
273

139

TARIA

33

21
O T Downs

43

58

Heartbreak
Hotel

Cape Crawford
Lost City

Balbirini

Mallapunyah

Kiana

Spring
Creek

Calvert Hills

Wollogorang
Station &
Roadhouse
58
495

Westmoreland

371

BARKLY

115

HWY

Wallhallow

Anthony
Lagoon

Cresswell
Downs

CALVERT
223

Benmara

CHINA WALL

WAANYI/GARAWA

ABORIGINAL

LAND TRUST

STOCK
229
Eva Downs

ROUTE

20

377

75

Tarrabool
Lake

Fish

Hole

Ck

Springvale

Musselbrook
Mining Camp

LAWN HILL
NATIONAL
PARK

Ucharonidge

Mungabroom

Ngunarra

Brunette
Downs

100

Lake
Sylvester

100

CONNELLS LAGOON
CONSERVATION
RESERVE

Mittiebah

Murun Murula

TABLELAND

Lawn
Hill

SMITHS
RANGE

enner Springs

Helen Springs

HWY

87

136

rlpa

Banka Banka
50

45

Brunchilly

70

Rockhampton
Downs
Wogyala

46

TABLELANDS
76

Alexandria

Gallipoli

Gregory
River

NORTHERN TERRITORY
QUEENSLAND

Norfolk

WARUMUNGU
ABORIGINAL LAND

WARUMUNGU
ABORIGINAL
LAND

Playford

Buchanan

Cigarette Hole

Creek

Stuart Memorial
ATTACK CREEK
HISTORICAL RESERVE

62

Phillip Creek

Likkaparta
John Flynn
Memorial

BARKLY

187

66

89

54

Alroy
Downs

65

77

21

Three Ways
Roadhouse

98

RANKEN

RD

96

Camooweal

warrego

24

25

31

Tennant Creek

Historic Telegraph
Station

Barkly Homestead

HWY

141

66

263

Avon Downs
Police Station
31

Soudan
21

Avon
Downs

30

27

13

Camooweal

CAMOOWEAL
CAVES NP

372

STUART

87

139

HWY

122

WAKAYA ABORIGINAL

LAND TRUST

Six Mile Waterhole

Big Ranken Waterhole

22 Mile
Waterhole

56

URANDANGI RD

ARTA ABORIGINAL

AND TRUST

McLaren Creek

Mungkarta

Kalinjarri

52

Kunundi

Epenarra

69

21

Wutunugurra

Austral
Downs

Wooroona

DEVILS MARBLES
CONSERVATION RESERVE

Devils Marbles

Mt Cairns
597m

Wauchope

Singleton

Canteen Creek

ANURRETE

ABORIGINAL

LAND TRUST

56

Bullock
Waterhole

Mt Michael
243m

Bullecourt

Wycliffe Well
Roadhouse

11

61

WARRABRI ABORIGINAL
LAND TRUST

DAVENPORT
RANGE
NATIONAL
PARK

49

Hatches Creek

SANDOVER

HWY

Alpururulam

Lake
Nash

14

Ali-Curung

21
23

Murray
Downs
Imangara

76

357

| J | K | L | M | N | O | P | Q | R |

0   50   100   150   200 km

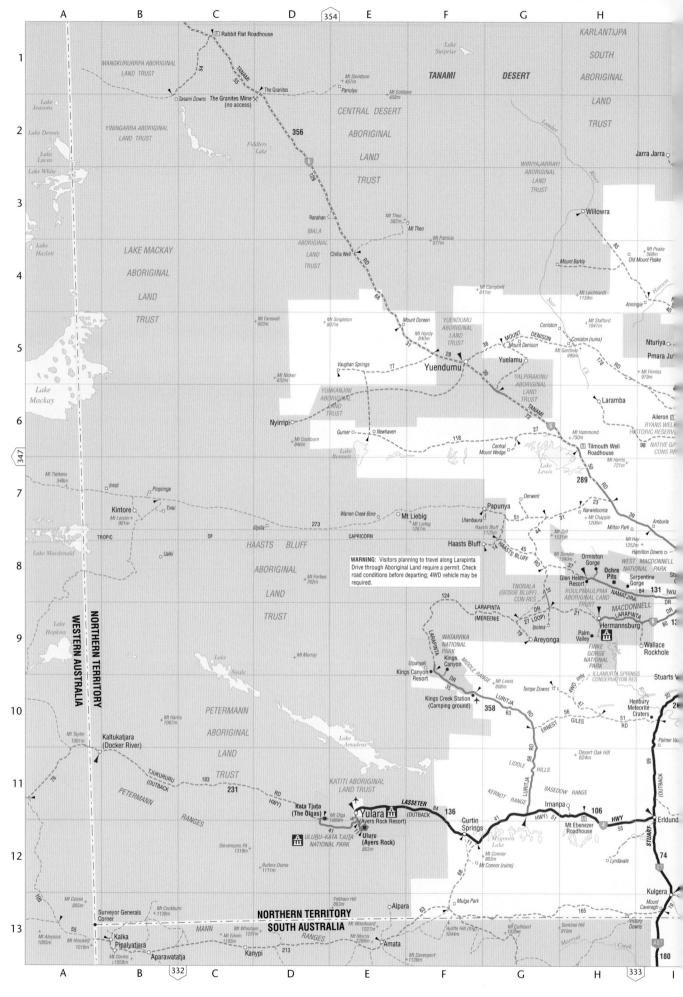

| | A | B | C | D | E | F | G | H | |

KARLANTIJPA

SOUTH

Rabbit Flat Roadhouse

1

MANGKURURRPA ABORIGINAL
LAND TRUST

54

Lake
Jeavons

Lake Surprise

Mt Davidson
+457m

Parrulyu

TANAMI DESERT

ABORIGINAL

55

The Granites

Tanami Downs

The Granites Mine
(no access)

Mt Solitaire
458m

LAND

2

Lake Dennis

YININGARRA ABORIGINAL
LAND TRUST

356

CENTRAL DESERT

ABORIGINAL

Jarra Jarra

TRUST

Lake
Lucas

Lake White

Fiddlers
Lake

729

LAND

Lander River

3

Lake
Hazlett

Ranahan

MALA

Mt Theo
582m

Mt Theo

Mt Patricia
577m

Willowra

TRUST

LAKE MACKAY

ABORIGINAL

Chilla Well

ABORIGINAL

RD

WIRIYAJARRAYI
ABORIGINAL
LAND
TRUST

85

Mt Peake
568m

Old Mount Peake

4

ABORIGINAL

LAND

68

Mt Campbell
+611m

Mt Leichhardt
+1139m

Anningie

40

Hanson

LAND

Mt Farewell
603m

Mt Singleton
+807m

Mount Doreen

YUENDUMU
ABORIGINAL
LAND TRUST

Mt Stafford
1047m

Stuart

5

TRUST

Mt Hardy
840m

MOUNT

DENISON

Coniston

Coniston (ruins)

Nturiya

Mt Gardiner
999m

Pmara Ju

31

Mount Denison

178

RD

Mt Finniss
979m

Vaughan Springs

77

28

38

178

Mt Nicker
+632m

Yuendumu

Yuelamu

Laramba

Aileron

30

RYANS WELL
HISTORIC RESERVE

6

Nyirripi

YUNKANJINI
ABORIGINAL
LAND
TRUST

YALPIRAKINU
ABORIGINAL
LAND
TRUST

TANAMI

72

NATIVE GA
CONS RE

Mt Cockburn
846m

Gurner

Newhaven

118

27

Mt Hammond
+750m

5

Tilmouth Well
Roadhouse

98

Lake
Bennett

Central
Mount Wedge

Lake
Lewis

50

RD

289

Mt Harris
721m

7

347

Mt Tietkens
546m

Ininti

Pinpimga

Tinki

Derwent

Papunya

51

23

31

Narwietooma

Mt Chapple
1206m

Milton Park

39

Amburla

Kintore

Mt Leisler
901m

Ulamhaura

Ulpanyali

Mt Zell
1531m

44

Mt Hay
1252m +

Hamilton Downs

TROPIC

OF

Warren Creek Bore

Mt Liebig

CAPRICORN

Mt Liebig
1267m

Haasts Bluff
1125m

45

Mt Sonder
1380m

Ormiston
Gorge

WEST MACDONNELL
NATIONAL
PARK

Illpilla

273

Ulaki

HAASTS BLUFF

Haasts Bluff

HAASTS BLUFF

RD

37

Glen Helen
Resort

Ochre
Pits

Serpentine
Gorge

84 131 Iwu

Mt Forbes
762m

ABORIGINAL

TNORALA
(GOSSE BLUFF)
CON RES

ROULPMAULPMA
ABORIGINAL LAND
TRUST

NAMATJIRA

MACDONNELL

DR

8

Lake
Hopkins

LAND

LARAPINTA
(MEREENIE)

27

21

LARAPINTA

Hermannsburg

6

80

13

9

Mt Murray

LARAPINTA

WATARRKA
NATIONAL
PARK

124

LOOP)

19

Ipolera

DR

Areyonga

Palm
Valley

FINKE
GORGE
NATIONAL
PARK

Wallace
Rockhole

TRUST

Kings
Canyon

MIDDLE RANGE

Mt Lewis
808m

ILLAMURTA SPRINGS
CONSERVATION RES

Stuarts V

Lake
Neale

Lake
Amadeus

Kings Canyon
Resort

35

Tempe Downs

4WD
only

River

Henbury
Meteorite
Craters

2

10

Mt Harris
1067m

PETERMANN

ABORIGINAL

Kings Creek Station
(Camping ground)

358

63

LURITJA

ERNEST

RD

GILES

56

51

RD

Palmer Va

Mt Taylor
1001m

Kaltukatjara
(Docker River)

TJUKURURU
(OUTBACK

LAND

RD

LIDDLE

68

Desert Oak Hill
+624m

RD

89

(OUTBACK

11

76

183

231

RD
HWY)

TRUST

KERNOT

RANGE

BASEDOW RANGE

Imanpa

106

HWY

Erldund

PETERMANN

KATITI ABORIGINAL
LAND TRUST

Kata Tjuta
(The Olgas)

Mt Olga
1069m

LASSETER

Yulara
Ayers Rock Resort)

84 136

41

Curtin
Springs

Mt Ebenezer
Roadhouse

4

55

RANGES

Stevensons Pk
1319m

41

ULURU–KATA TJUTA
NATIONAL PARK

Uluru
(Ayers Rock)
863m

11

Mygoora
Lake

74

12

Mt Gosse
885m

Butlers Dome
1111m

Mt Connor
863m

Mt Connor (ruins)

Lyndavale

STUART

Surveyor Generals
Corner

Mt Cockburn
+1138m

Feltham Hill
863m

Alpara

69

Mulga Park

165

Kulgera

Mount
Cavenagh

13

Mt Aloysius
1085m

55

Kalka

Pipalyatjara

MANN

Mt Whittburn
1291m

Mt Edwin
1193m

NORTHERN TERRITORY

SOUTH AUSTRALIA

Mt Woodward
1227m

Ayliffe Hill (tnd)
1044m

Mt Cuthbert
1035m

Sentinel Hill
910m

Victory Downs

A87

180

Mt Hinckley
1018m

Mt Davies
1058m

Aparawatatja

Kanypi

213

RANGES

Amata

Mt Morris
1288m

Mt Davenport
1139m

Marryat

Creek

WARNING: Visitors planning to travel along Larapinta
Drive through Aboriginal Land require a permit. Check
road conditions before departing; 4WD vehicle may be
required.

NORTHERN TERRITORY

WESTERN AUSTRALIA

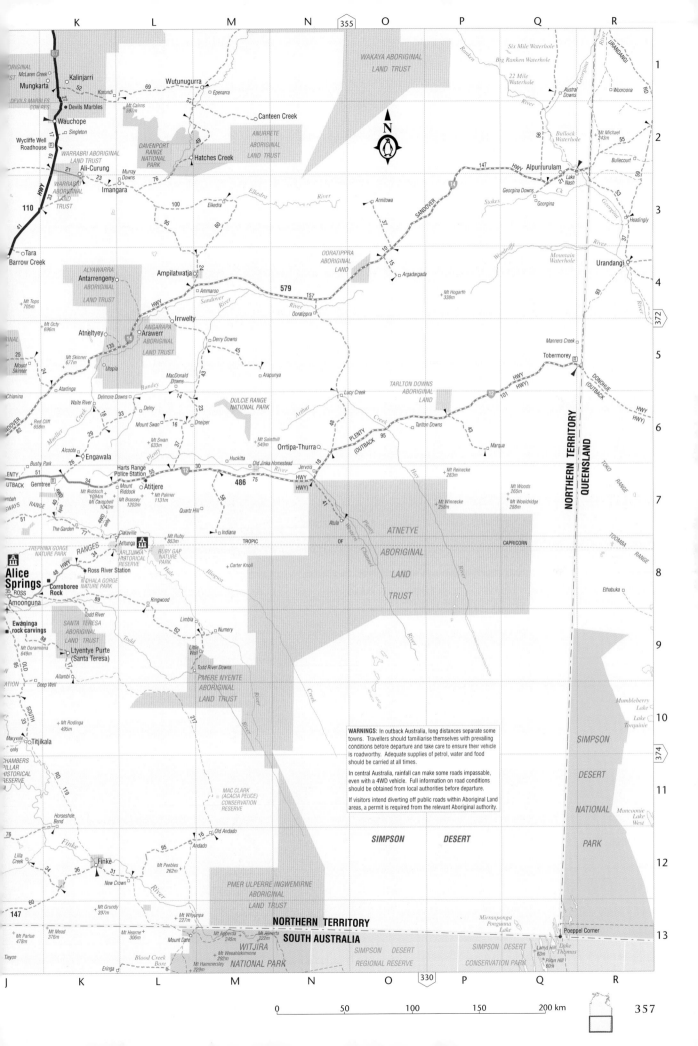

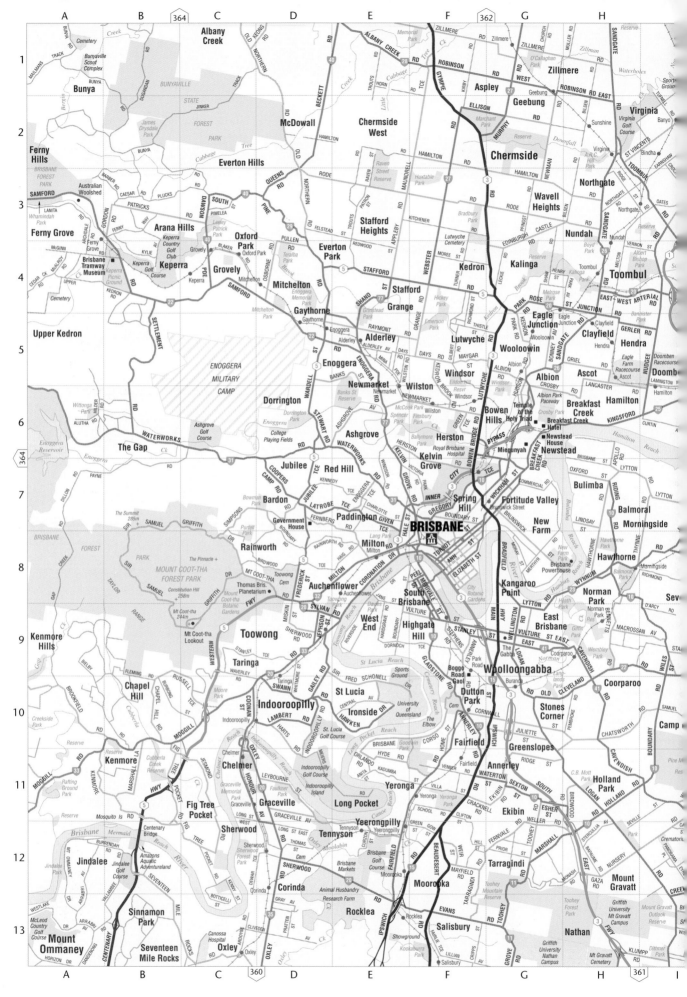

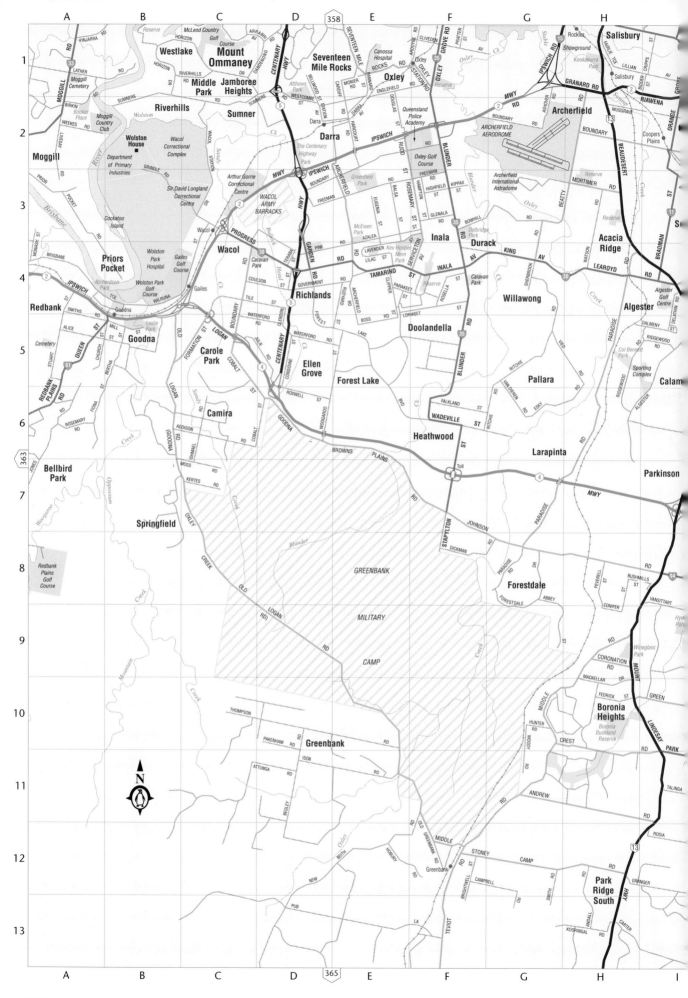

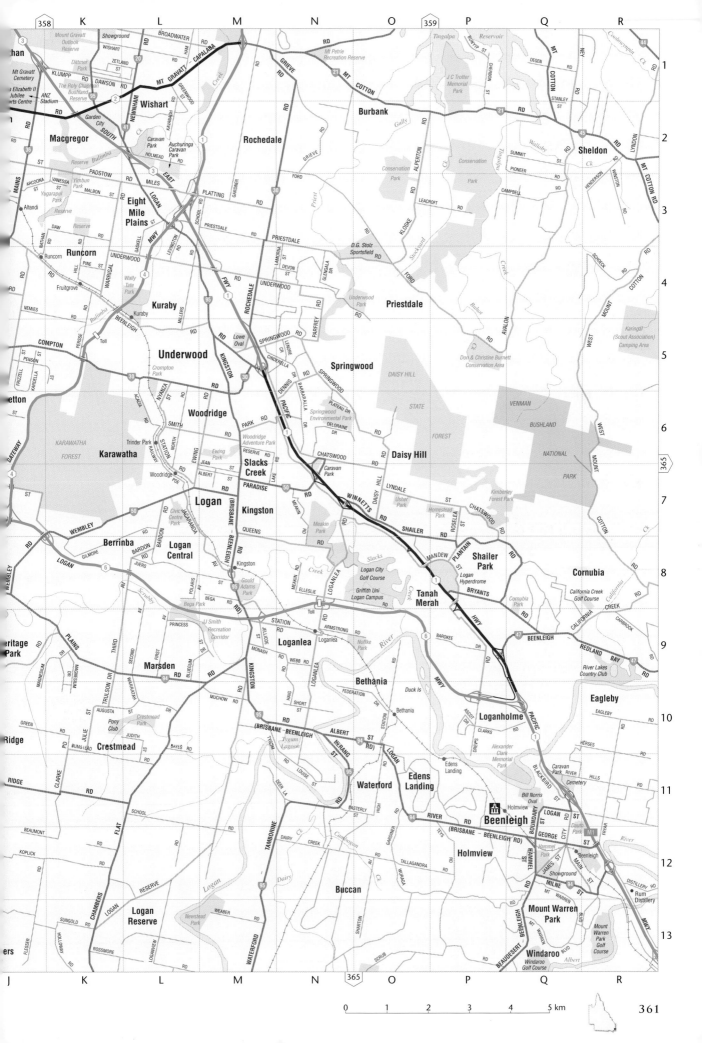

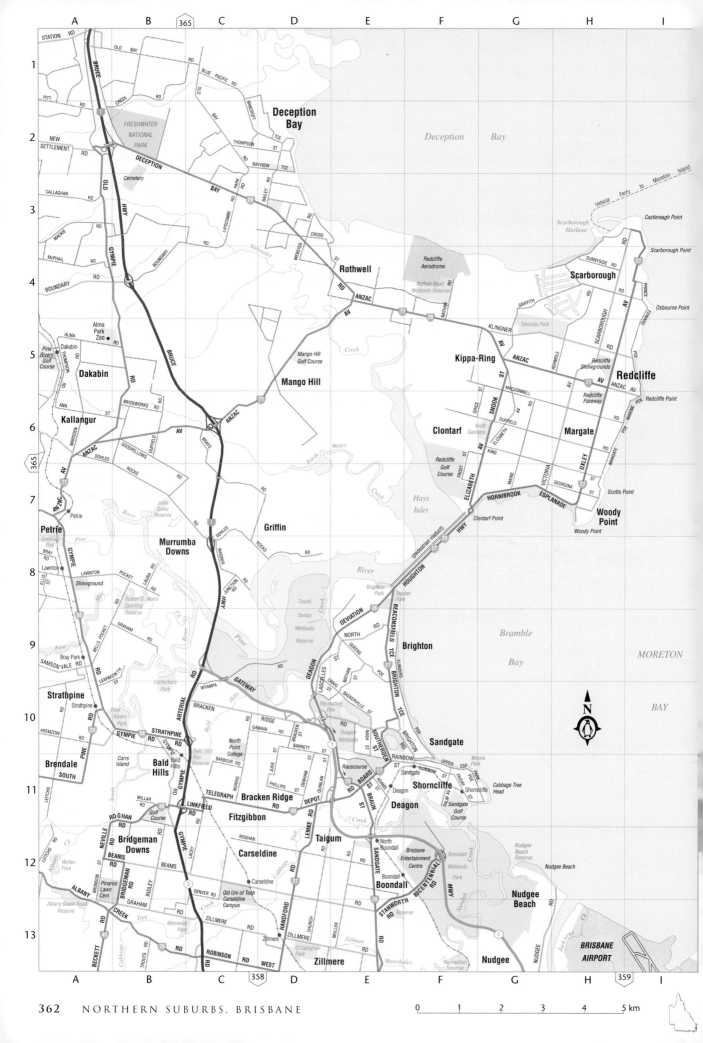

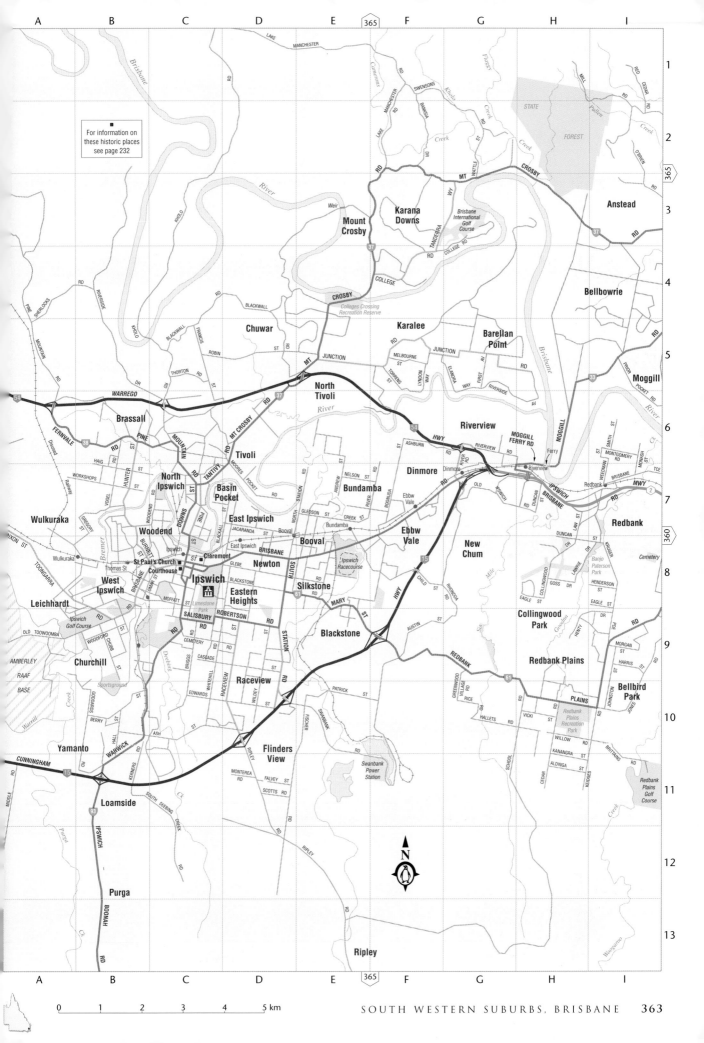

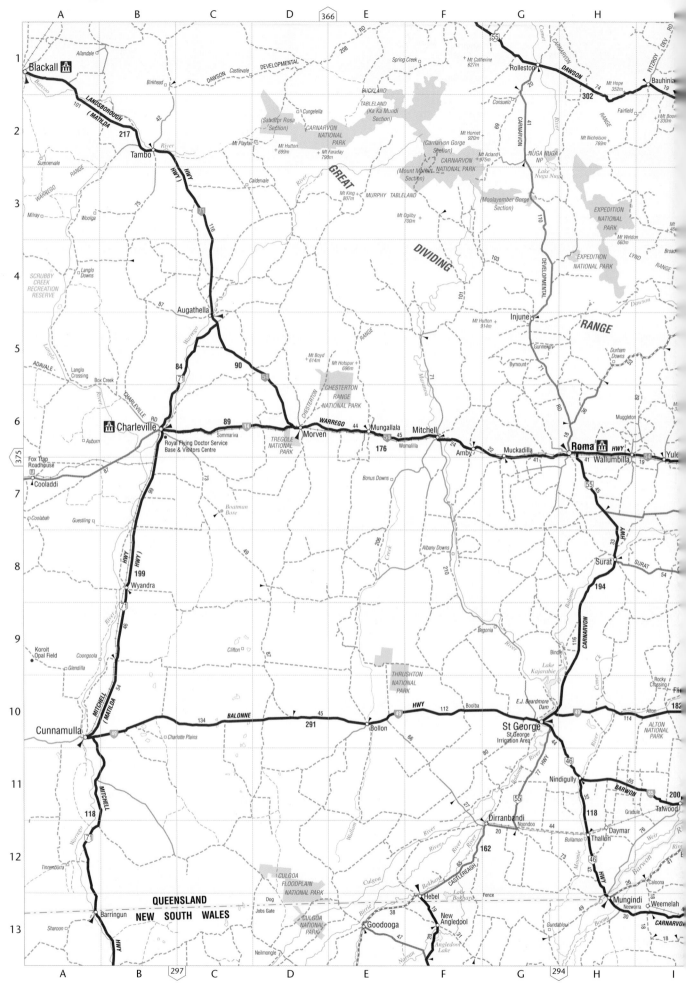

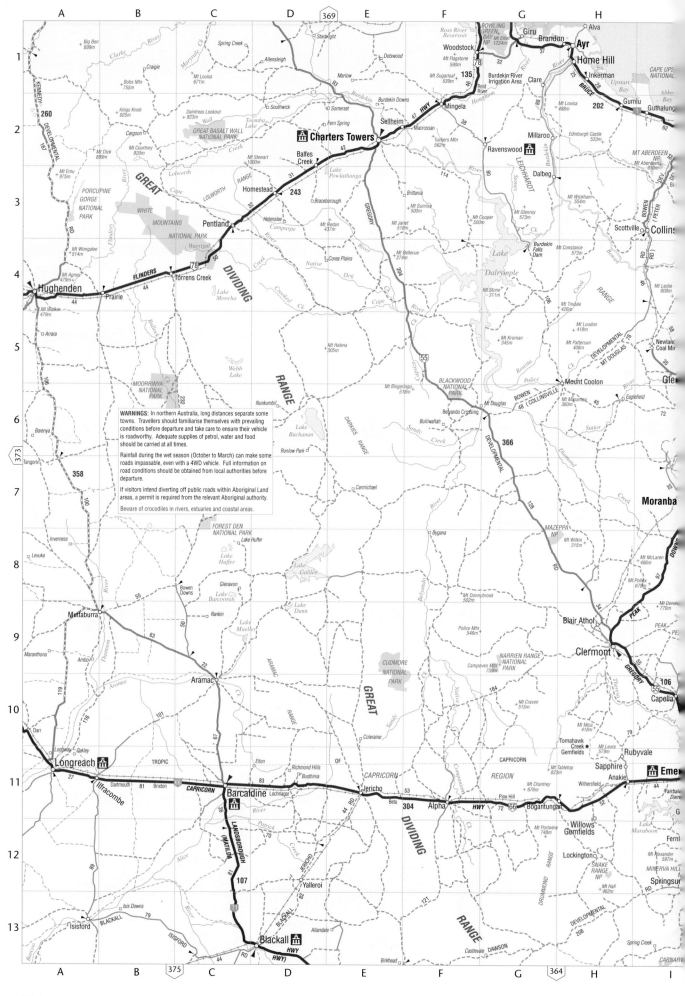

WARNINGS: In northern Australia, long distances separate some towns. Travellers should familiarise themselves with prevailing conditions before departure and take care to ensure their vehicle is roadworthy. Adequate supplies of petrol, water and food should be carried at all times.

Rainfall during the wet season (October to March) can make some roads impassable, even with a 4WD vehicle. Full information on road conditions should be obtained from local authorities before departure.

If visitors intend diverting off public roads within Aboriginal Land areas, a permit is required from the relevant Aboriginal authority.

Beware of crocodiles in rivers, estuaries and coastal areas.

CORAL SOUTH

GREAT SEA PACIFIC

OCEAN

Gloucester Island
GLOUCESTER ISLAND NP
Dingo
Beach
Earlando
Airlie
Beach
onvale
Shute
Harbour
pine
CONWAY
NP

THE WHITSUNDAYS
Hayman Island
Hook Island
Whitsunday Island
WHITSUNDAY ISLANDS NP
North Molle Is
Daydream Is
South Molle Is
Hamilton Island
Long Island
Lindeman
Island
Shaw Island

BARRIER

184
nsbury
Elaroo
Yalboroo
BRUCE
Seaforth Ball Bay
Calen
Kuttabul
Eungella
Walkerston
Finch
Hatton
HOMEVALE
NATIONAL
PARK
Homevale
creek

Repulse
Bay
Midge Point

SMITH ISLANDS
NATIONAL PARK
SOUTH CUMBERLAND ISLANDS
NATIONAL PARK
Brampton Island
Keswick Is
Scawfell Island
St Bees
Island

REEF

23
Hibiscus Coast
CAPE HILLSBOROUGH
Cape Hillsborough NP
Shoal Point
Mount
JUKES NP
Bucasia Eimeo
Slade Point
Mackay
Bakers Creek
Hector
Hoffbush Half Tide
Grasstree
Campwin Beach
Sarina Sarina Beach
Armstrong Beach
Eton

MARINE

NP

Blue Mtn
625m
Nebo
Mt White
594m
29
Koumala
Ilbilbie
Mt Scott
852m
CAPE PALMERSTON
NATIONAL PARK

Middle Island

South Island

NORTHUMBERLAND

73
abella
DIPPERU
NATIONAL
PARK
14
Carmila
Flaggy Rock
WEST HILL NP

ISLES

Quail Island
Stanage
Townshend Is

CAPRICORN

50
Cooper
588m
Saltbush Park
White Bluff Mtn
526m Clairview
334
St Lawrence
Mt Edward
171m
Broad
Sound
Mt Price
164m

MARLBOROUGH
102
Mt Joss
421m
Mt Buffalo
518m
Ogmore
SARINA
RD
Mt Phillip
393m
Mt Wellington
528m
Glenprairie
Mt Mulgrave
655m
BRUCE
74
Mt Wostall
550m

Pine Mtn
375m
Double Mtn
747m
Mt Atherton
438m

8

FITZROY
111
River
Balfesston
Bar Mtn
308m
Mt Bora
350m
DOWNS
72
Manly
Junee
82
Marlborough
RD
30
Kunwarara
Merimal
SHOALWATER
Bay
MILITARY
TRAINING
AREA
BYFIELD
NATIONAL
PARK
CHANNEL

9

ddlemount
24
Oaky Creek
Mine
Fairhill
119
DEVELOPMENTAL
Mt Gardiner
450m
Royles
Apis Creek
Clifton
Arizona
Burkan
Junee
Glen
Geddes
19
30
Milman
Farnborough
Yeppoon
Mulambin
Kinka Beach
Emu Park
Keppel Sands
Joskeleigh
KEPPEL BAY ISLANDS
NATIONAL PARK
Great Keppel Island
CAPRICORN COAST
North West
Island

10

Ensham
Mine
Telson
Round Mtn
66m
Yaamba
South Yaamba
Ridgelands
Dalma
ROCKHAMPTON
Gracemere
Kabra
The Caves
Parkhurst
Tungamull
FOLEYVALE
ABORIGINAL
COMMUNITY
Fitzroy
River
Mackenzie
RD

TROPIC OF CAPRICORN
Broadmount
600m
Curtis Island NP
Heron Island

CURTIS

Comet
CAPRICORN
35
19 Bluff
Blackwater
Blackwater
Mine
South
Blackwater
Mine
92
BLACKDOWN
TABLELAND
NATIONAL
PARK
Mt Success
490m
29
Dingo
Godwarri
36 270
Duaringa
61
66
Wallaroo
Namol
Hills
Coomooboolaroo
RD
Warren
Wycarbah
Westwood
Gogango
LEICHHARDT
Mt Battery
486m
Stanwell
Midgee
Bouldercombe
Bajool
Mount
Morgan
Raglan
Dululu
Mt Wheal
606m
107
Mt Hope
458m
Mount Larcom
Yarwun
Port
Alma
Mt Barker
161m
CURTIS
ISLAND
Scrubby Mtn
333m
Southend
BRUCE
Ambrose
Gladstone
Boyne Island
Tannum Sands

CHANNEL

CAPRICORNIA CAYS
NATIONAL PARK

Lady Musgrave Island

11

12

rt
Stephens
MAY
Cr
50
DEVELOPMENTAL
RANGE
EXPEDITION
CARNARVON RANGE
RD
WOORABINDA
ABORIGINAL
COMMUNITY
Mt Dawson
317m
33
Baralaba
Brackenly
Struan
94
Coomooboolaroo
Rannes
40
Goovigen
Jambin
17
Argoon
BANANA
Mt Ramsay
445m
145
Wowan
Dululu
BURNETT
RANGE
Cedric Mtn
707m
Lancefield
Mt Redshirt
597m
102
39
Calliope
Specimen Hill
671m
Calliope Coal Mine
& Power Station
Callide Dam
KROOMBIT TOPS
NATIONAL PARK
Mt Graarbi
800m
Nagoorin
Ubobo
River
Benaraby
CASTLE
TOWER
NP
EURIMBULA NP
Turkey
Beach
EURIMBULA
NP
Bustard
Bay
Seventeen Seventy
Agnes Water
Bororen
Mt Dromedary
477m
Miriam
Vale
DEEPWATER
NATIONAL PARK

DAWSON
HWY
Rolleston
364
46
Biloela
Banana
Thangool
DAWSON
365
HWY

13

0 25 50 75 100 km

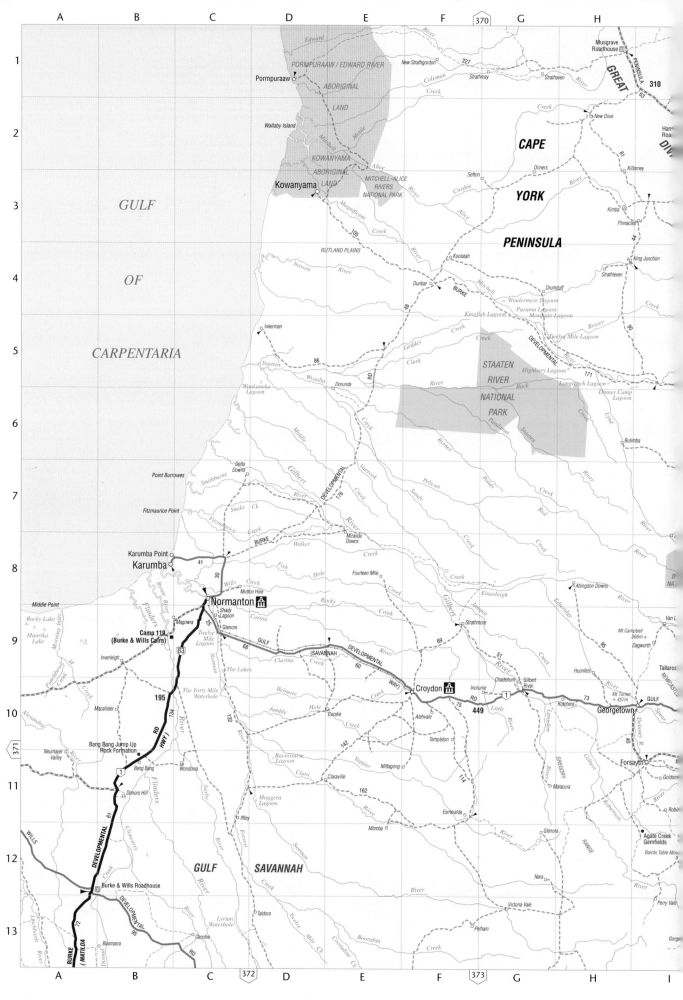

K L M N O P Q R

1

WARNINGS: In northern Australia, long distances separate some
towns. Travellers should familiarise themselves with prevailing
conditions before departure and take care to ensure their vehicle
is roadworthy. Adequate supplies of petrol, water and food
should be carried at all times.

Rainfall during the wet season (October to March) can make some
roads impassable, even with a 4WD vehicle. Full information on
road conditions should be obtained from local authorities before
departure.

If visitors intend diverting off public roads within Aboriginal Land
areas, a permit is required from the relevant Aboriginal authority.

Beware of crocodiles in rivers, estuaries and coastal areas.

LIZARD
ISLAND
NP
Lizard Island

Cape Flattery

Saddle Hill
508m
Mt Stuckey (Numbargulme)
479m
STARCKE NP
MT WEBB NP

Flat Top Hill
120m

Mt Jack
213m

Normanby River

2

PARK
Old Laura
Homestead

Mitchell River

Cape Bedford

Hope Vale
Mt Piebald
417m

ENDEAVOUR RIVER
NATIONAL PARK
Cooktown
MT COOK NP

GREAT

3

Fairview

Laura

Split Rock &
Gu Gu Yalanji
Rock-art Site

Mt McCormack
518m
Byerley Hill
445m
Black Mtn
465m

Glenrock

Helenvale
Rossville
Lion's Den
Historic
Hotel
CEDAR BAY NP

GREAT

Mt Hann
686m

Maytown

Lakeland
Mt Eykin
595m
Mt Amy
869m

Mt Misery 869m
Mt Finnigan
1148m

Wujal
Wujal
Ayton

4

Maitland
Downs

Palmer River
Roadhouse

Mt McDowall
South 543m
Mt Halycon
872m

DAINTREE
NATIONAL
PARK

Cape Tribulation
Mt Hemmant
1065m
Noah Beach

260

Groganville

Mt Elephant
1046m
Mt Spurgeon
1341m

DAINTREE

NATIONAL

PARK

Daintree

Wonga
Miallo
Cooya Beach

Cow Bay
Mt Alexandra
482m

CORAL

5

Mitchell

Mossman
Port Douglas
Craiglie
Oak Beach

Mount Carbine
Mt Frazer
1155m
Maryfarms
Mount
Molloy
Julatten

Trinity
Bay
Ellis Beach

BARRIER

GREAT
Mount Mulligan

Hermit Hill
885m

Kings borough
Thornborough
Mareeba-Dimbulah
Irrigation Area
Mt McLeod
808m
Mt White
764m

HANN
TABLELAND
NP

Palm Cove
Smithfield
CAIRNS
Kuranda
Biboohra
BARRON
GORGE
NP

Green Island
GREEN ISLAND NP

SEA

6

Chillagoe

Kays Mtn
759m

Black Mtn
530m

Arringunna Mtn
599m

Mareeba
Walkamin
Edmonton
Gordonvale
Aloomba

Fitzroy Island
FITZROY ISLAND
NATIONAL PARK

Mungana

Mt Arthur
450m
Mt Beatty
498m

CHILLAGOE-
MUNGANA
CAVES NP

Almaden

Dimbulah
Mutchilba
Tinaroo Falls
Tolga
Kairi
Atherton
Herberton
Watsonville
Timaburra
Yungaburra

Dobree Hill
610m
Mt Alexander
760m

Petford

Fishery Falls
Deeral
High Is

FRANKLAND
ISLANDS NP

RUSSELL RIVER

7

Two Mile
Dam

Mt McDevitt
551m

Oomann

Irvinebank

135

Malanda
Mt Bartle Frere
1622m
Babinda
Bramston Beach

Miriwinni

NATIONAL

RUSSELL RIVER
REEF

Round Mtn
493m

Bullock Creek

Geebung Hill
897m
MT HYPIPAMEE
NP

Tumoulin

Topaz

Flying Fish Point

EUBENAGEE SWAMP NP

8

DIVIDING

Mt Petty
587m

Mundera

Nymbool

Millaa
Millaa

79
PALMERSTON

Innisfail
South Johnstone
Mourilyan

PARK

HWY

Mt Eliza
557m

Mt Poole
710m

Mount Garnet
Innot Hot
Springs

Seven Mile
Hill 707m

RAVENSHOE

MILLSTREAM FALLS NP
Mt Koolmoon
1117m
Mt Pandanus
1103m

Mena
Creek

Cowley Beach

Silkwood
El Arish
Kurrimine Beach
Bingil Bay

HWY

RANGE

Mt Firth
774m

128

Mt Bear
841m

Wongaling Beach
Mission Beach
South Mission Beach

Dunk Island
FAMILY ISLANDS NP
Bedarra Island

9

Mt McDevitt

Greys Hill
619m

Mt Eliza
557m

Silent Hill
952m

Mt McBride
911m

Mt Sharpless
810m

Glen Ruth

Koombooloomba
Reservoir

Tiger Hill
868m

Tully

Euramo

HULL
RIVER
NP

Tully Heads

Bilyana

MARINE

Mt Tabletop
637m

Mt Misery
782m

FORTY MILE
SCRUB NP

Commissioners Gap
1028m

Princess Hills
795m

G W Knob
764m

Mt Carruchan
681m

148

Kennedy

Cape Richards
Cape Sandwich

EDMUND KENNEDY NP
Rockingham Bay

Cape Pitt
722m

10

Mount
Surprise

92

UNDARA VOLCANIC
NATIONAL PARK

Mt Tabletop
1002m

Walters Plains
Lake
Wairuna

Blencoe Falls
LUMHOLTZ
NATIONAL
PARK

Cardwell

Mt Graham
834m

HINCHINBROOK
Mt Bowen
1119m
ISLAND

Mt Diamantina
1000m

HINCHINBROOK ISLAND NP

REEF

Mt Juliet
637m

Rosella Plains

KENNEDY

Khirala

Oak Hills

Abergowrie

BRUCE

Lucinda

Pelorus Island (Yanooa)
Orpheus Island (Goolboddi)
ORPHEUS ISLAND NP

11

sleigh

The Lynd

RD

Mt Jordan
615m

Oasis
Roadhouse

Greenvale
Nickel Mine

52

Conjuboy

Lake
Lucy

Saltern Lagoon

Camel Creek

Mt Farquharson
548m
Lannercost
Trebonne
Toobanna

Mt Lee
829m

Michael
Creek

Halifax
Taylors
Beach

Ingham

Forrest
Beach

Great Palm Island

PALM
ISLANDS

Knob

Kidston

RD

Greys Hill
619m

RANGE

GREGORY

Greenvale
107

PALUMA RANGE
NATIONAL PARK

Douglas Creek

Mt Fox
811m

Bambaroo

Great Palm
Island

PARK

12

Mt Devlin
860m

Mt Teddy
864m

Mt Remarkable
820m

Pandanus Creek

252

Blue Water Springs
Roadhouse

HERVEYS

Runmut Creek

Taravale

CRYSTAL CREEK NP

Mt Spec
990m
Mutarnee

Balgal

Rollingstone
109

Halloonda

Bluewater

Mt Halifax
1063m

Magnetic
Island
MAGNETIC ISLAND NP
Horseshoe Bay
Nelly Bay
Picnic Bay
Pallarenda

Cape Cleveland
Cape Ferguson

13

54
DEVELOPMENTAL

Big Ben
899m

KENNEDY

RD

DEVELOPMENTAL

Clarke River

Spring Creek

Allensleigh

Craigie

Mt Louisa
671m

Starbright

Dotswood

136

RANGE

DEVELOPMENTAL

THURINGOWA

Mt Cataract
873m

Mt Zero
1036m

Round Mtn
375m

Woodstock

Mt Flagstone
590m

Mt Stuart
582m

TOWNSVILLE
Alligator Creek

BOWLING
GREEN
BAY
NP

Mt Elliot
1234m

Cungulla
Giru
Brandon

Cape Bowling Green
BOWLING GREEN BAY
NATIONAL PARK

Alva

Ayr

Home Hill

J K L M N O P Q R

0   25   50   75   100 km

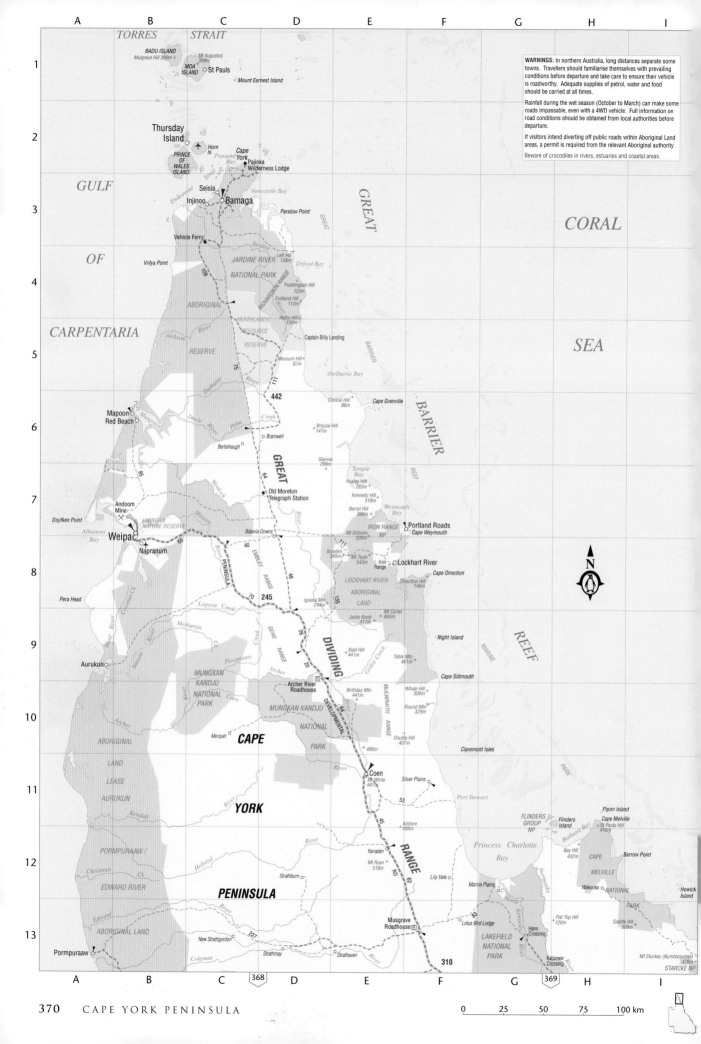

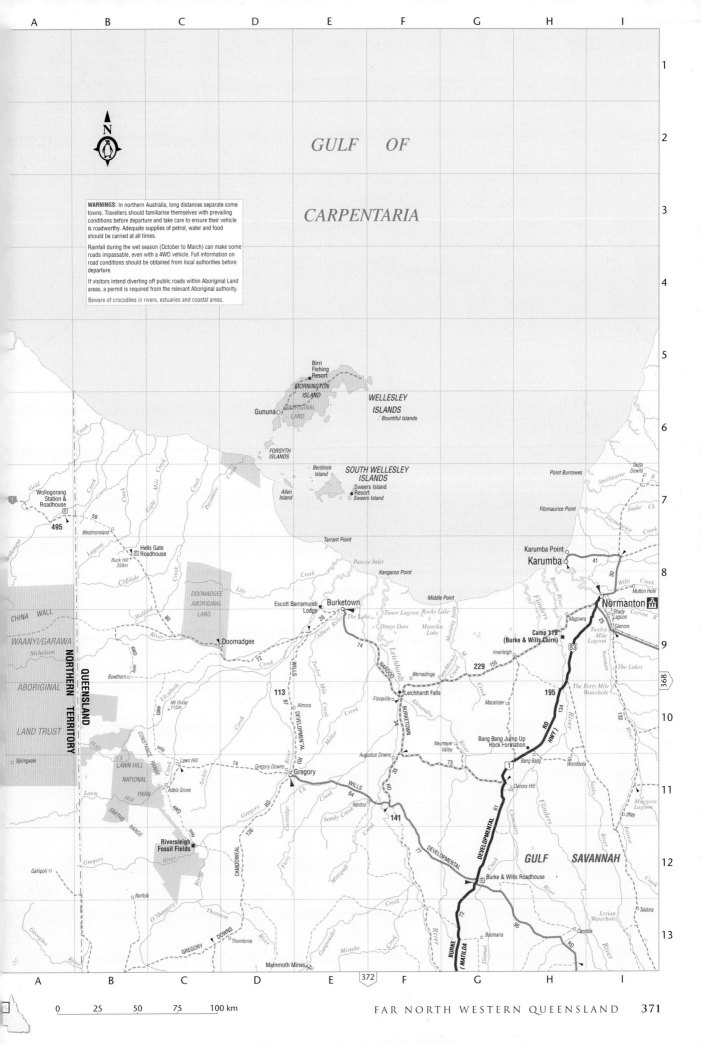

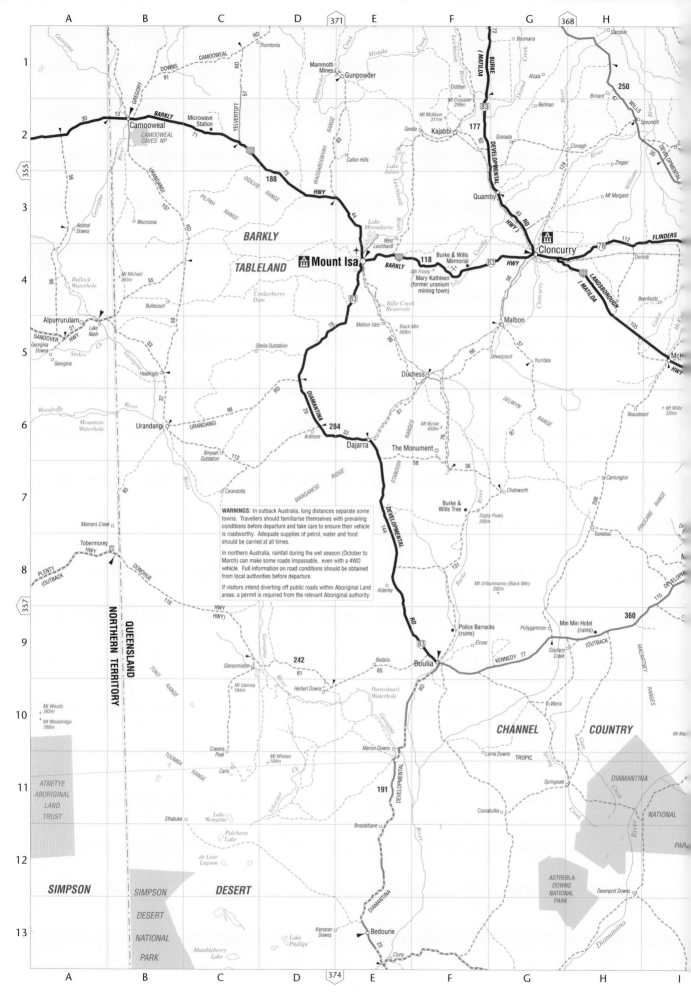

WARNINGS: In outback Australia, long distances separate some towns. Travellers should familiarise themselves with prevailing conditions before departure and take care to ensure their vehicle is roadworthy. Adequate supplies of petrol, water and food should be carried at all times.

In northern Australia, rainfall during the wet season (October to March) can make some roads impassable, even with a 4WD vehicle. Full information on road conditions should be obtained from local authorities before departure.

If visitors intend diverting off public roads within Aboriginal Land areas, a permit is required from the relevant Aboriginal authority.

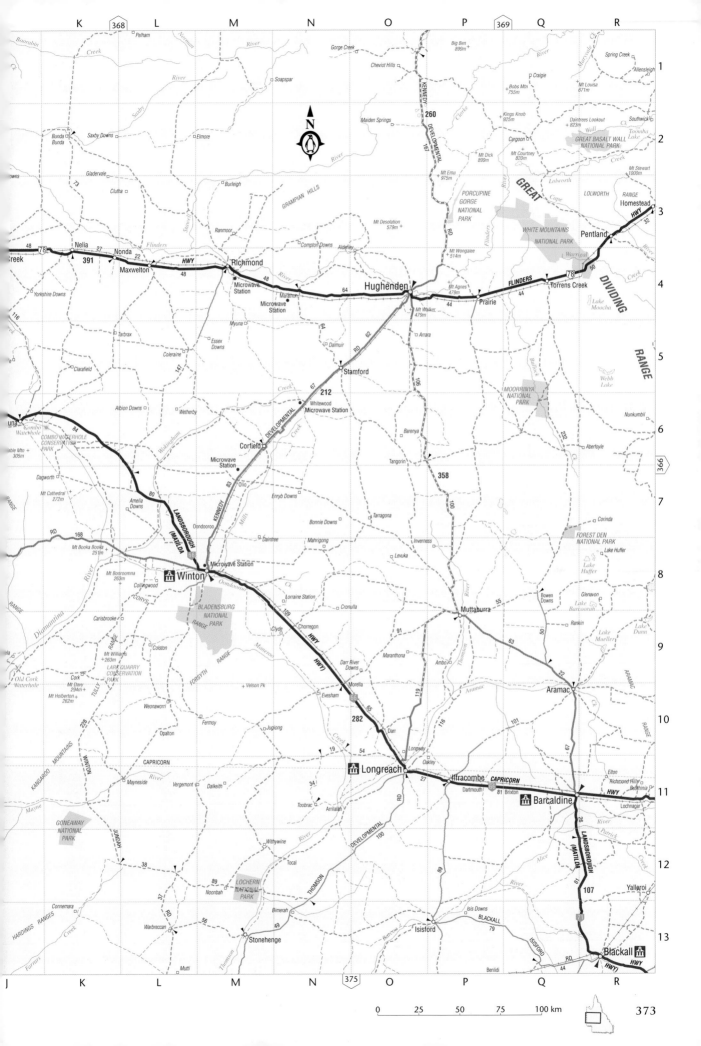

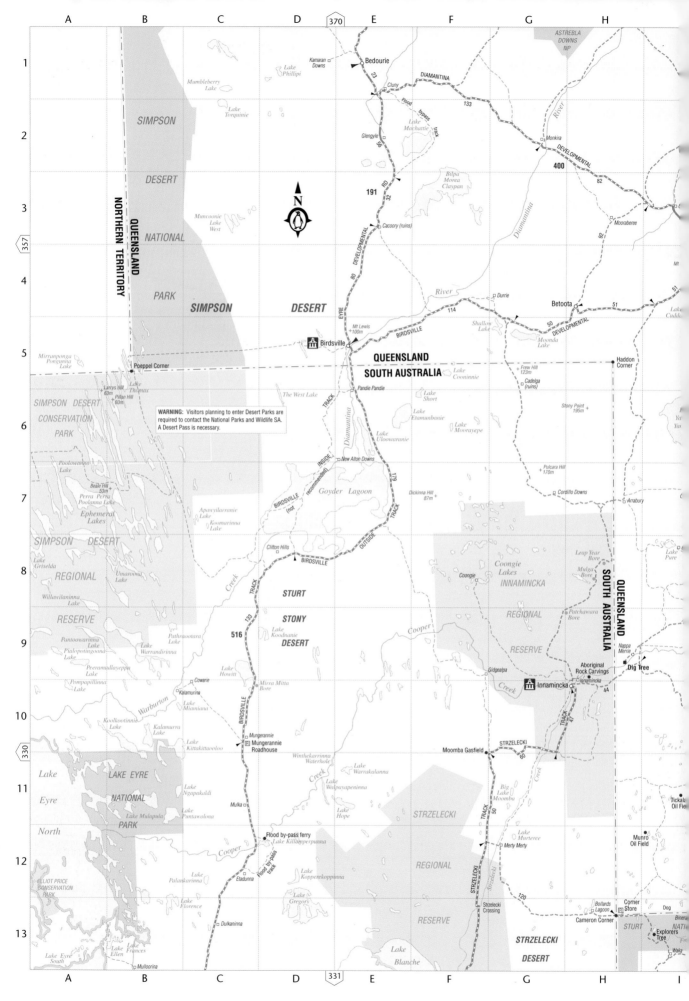

WARNING: Visitors planning to enter Desert Parks are required to contact the National Parks and Wildlife SA. A Desert Pass is necessary.

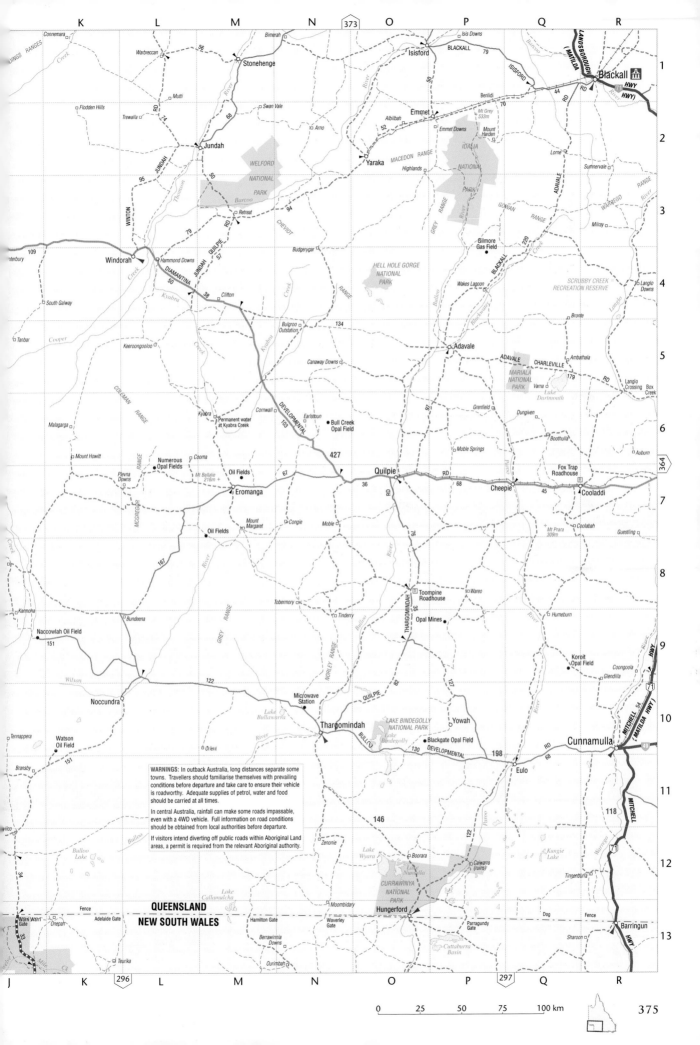

K L M N O P Q R

Connemara
BOODINGS RANGES
Creek
Warbreccan
Stonehenge
Bimerah
56
Mutti
Flodden Hills
Swan Vale
Trewalla
74
68
Jundah
River
WINTON RD
JUNDAH
95
50
WELFORD NATIONAL PARK
Thomson
Barcoo
94
Retreat
79
DIAMANTINA QUILPIE RD
57
Hammond Downs
Windorah
109
50
Clifton
38
Kyabra
CHEVIOT RANGE
Creek
South Galway
Kyabra
Bulgroo Outstation
134
Tanbar
Cooper
Keeroongooloo
Canaway Downs
Malagarga
COLEMAN RANGE
Kyabra
Permanent water at Kyabra Creek
Cornwall
Earlstoun
DEVELOPMENTAL
103
Bull Creek Opal Field
Mount Howitt
Cooma
Numerous Opal Fields
Mt Bellalie 216m
Plevna Downs
Oil Fields
67
427
Quilpie
Eromanga
36
RD
Kannoha
Mount Margaret
Congie
Moble
Oil Fields
167
Mount Margaret
Tobermory
Tinderry
GREY RANGE
MCGREGOR RANGE
Bundeena
76
Naccowlah Oil Field
151
Wilson
122
Noccundra
Microwave Station
Lake Bullawarra
Thargomindah
Orlerii
Tennappera
Watson Oil Field
151
Bransby
River
Lake Bindegolly
BULLOO
QUILPIE
82
127
DEVELOPMENTAL
130
198
34
Bulloo Lake
146
Zenonie
Lake Wyara
Boorara
Lake Callamulcha
QUEENSLAND
NEW SOUTH WALES
Fence
Adelaide Gate
Hamilton Gate
Waverley Gate
Moombidary
Hungerford
Warri Warri Gate
Onepah
Berrawinnia Downs
Teurika
Ourimbah
Cuttaburra Basin

J K L M N O P Q R

Isis Downs
Isisford
BLACKALL
79
Blackall
MATILDA HWY (MATILDA HWY)
LANDSBOROUGH
ISISFORD RD
44
Benlidi
70
Emmet
Albilbah
52
Emmet Downs
Mount Harden
Yaraka
Highlands
IDALIA NATIONAL PARK
MACEDON RANGE
Mt Grey 533m
Lorne
Sumnervale
WARREGO RANGE
ADAVALE
Milray
Budgerygar
GREY RANGE
HELL HOLE GORGE NATIONAL PARK
Gilmore Gas Field
Bullo
220
GOWAN RANGE
Wakes Lagoon
BLACKALL
Bronte
Langlo Downs
Adavale
ADAVALE
CHARLEVILLE
Ambathala
MARIALA NATIONAL PARK
179
RD
Langlo Crossing
Box Creek
Varna
Lake Dartmouth
Dungiven
Grenfield
Moble Springs
Boothulla
Auburn
River
364
RD
68
Fox Trap Roadhouse
Quilpie
Cheepie
45
Cooladdi
Warrego
Paroo
Mt Prara 309m
Coolabah
Guestling
Toompine Roadhouse
35
Wareo
Humeburn
THARGOMINDAH
Opal Mines
Koroit Opal Field
Coongoola
Glendilla
HWY
71
Yowah
Blackgate Opal Field
Cunnamulla
MITCHELL 54 (MATILDA HWY)
Eulo
68
RD
122
118
MITCHELL
71
Kungie Lake
Caiwarro (ruins)
Tinnenburra
NUMALLA
CURRAWINYA NATIONAL PARK
Hungerford
Parragundy Gate
Dog
Fence
Barringun
Sharoon
HWY

WARNINGS: In outback Australia, long distances separate some towns. Travellers should familiarise themselves with prevailing conditions before departure and take care to ensure their vehicle is roadworthy. Adequate supplies of petrol, water and food should be carried at all times.

In central Australia, rainfall can make some roads impassable, even with a 4WD vehicle. Full information on road conditions should be obtained from local authorities before departure.

If visitors intend diverting off public roads within Aboriginal Land areas, a permit is required from the relevant Aboriginal authority.

0 25 50 75 100 km

1
2
3
4
5
6
7
8
9
10
11
12
13

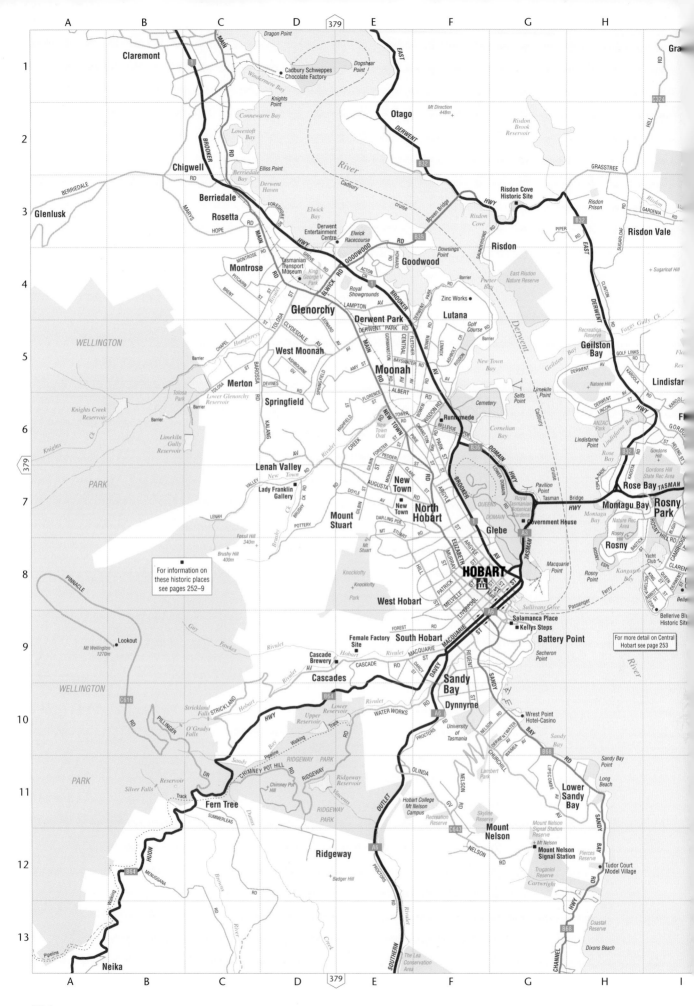

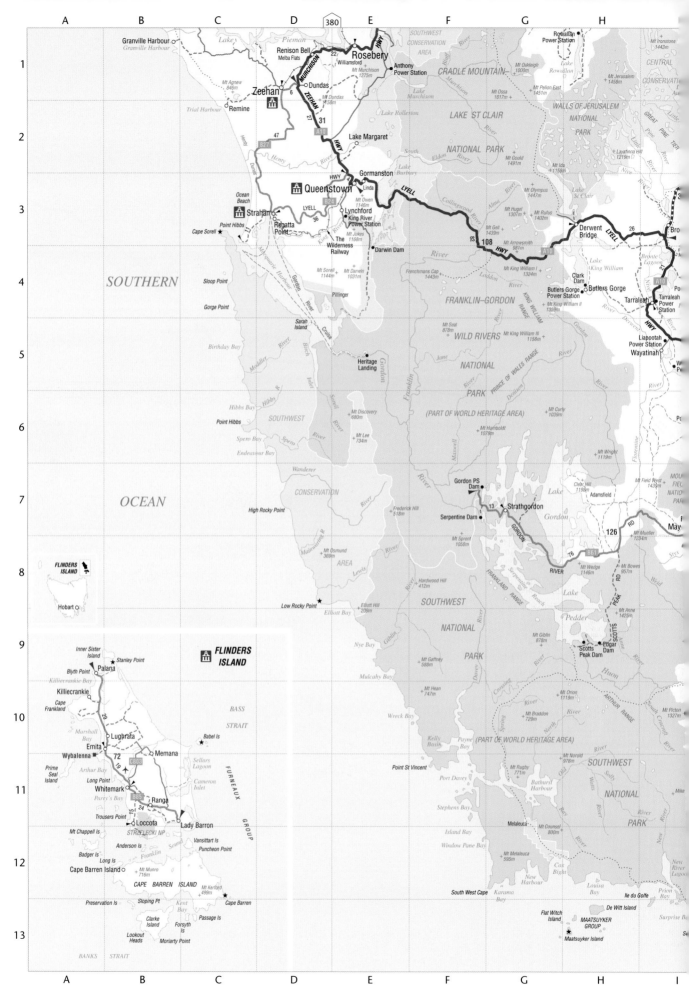

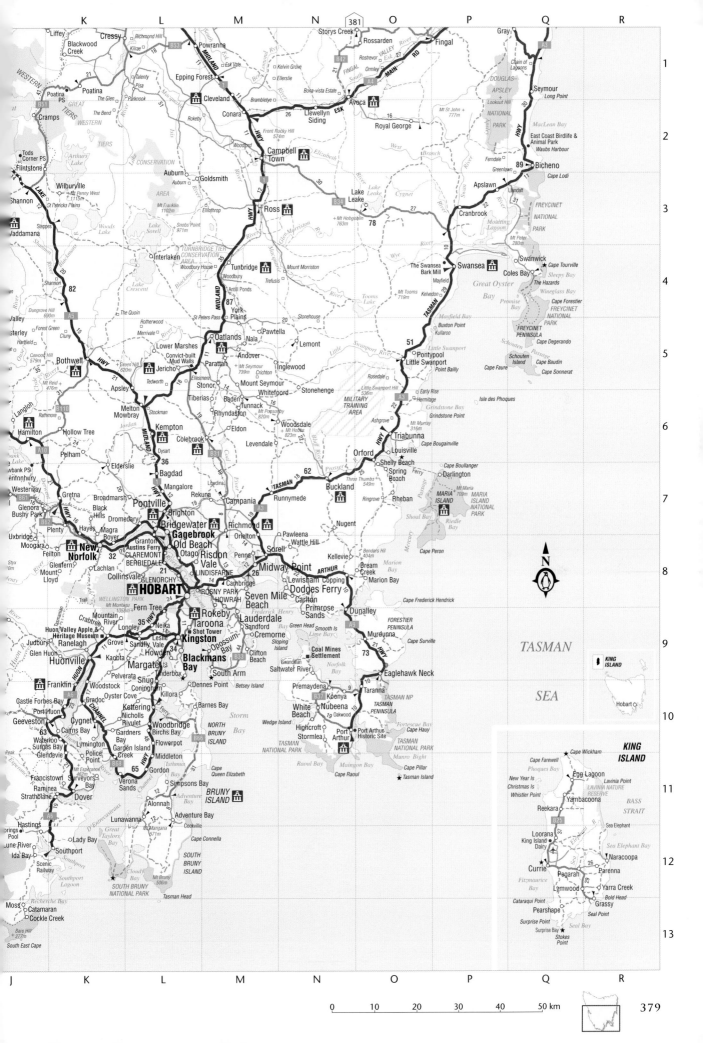

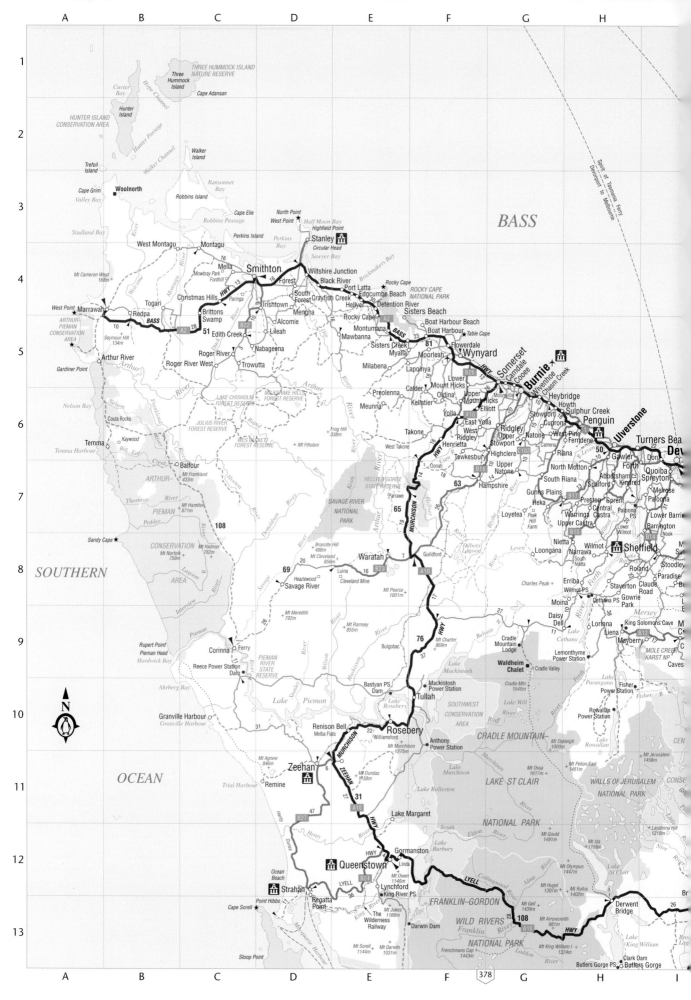

STRAIT

FLINDERS ISLAND

Ranga
Trousers Pt
Loccota
Lady Barron
Mt Chappell Is
STRZELECKI NATIONAL PARK
Adelaide Bay
Great Dog Is
FURNEAUX GROUP
Anderson Is
Badger Is
Vansittart Is
Long Is
Puncheon Pt
FRANKLIN SOUND

Cape Barren Island
Mt Munro 716m
CAPE BARREN ISLAND

Lesley Cove
Mt Kerford 499m
Kent Bay

Preservation Is
Sloping Pt
Clarke Island
Forsyth Is
Passage Is

BANKS STRAIT
Lookout Heads
Moriarty Point

Swan Island
Cape Portland
Vinegar Hill 52m
Lyme Regis
Waterhouse Island
Petal Point
Cape Portland
Musselroe Bay
Ninth Island
Waterhouse Point
Great Musselroe Bay
Cape Naturaliste

West Sandy Cape
Anderson Bay
Ringarooma Bay
Rushy Lagoon
Stony Head
East Sandy Cape
WATERHOUSE CONSERVATION AREA
Croppies Point
Tomahawk
Icena
MOUNT WILLIAM NATIONAL PARK
Lulworth
Noland Bay
Boobyalla
Five Mile Bluff
Waterhouse
Mt William 216m

Low Head
Beechford
Weymouth
Bellingham
Bridport
Mt Cameron 551m
Gladstone
Eddystone Point
George Town
Leura
Pipers River
Back Creek
B82
B84
Great Forester River
South Mount Cameron
B92
Eddystone Point
Lefroy
Pipers Brook
North Scottsdale
Forester
Ansons Bay

West Head
Greens Beach
Kelso
Rowella
Robigana
The Glen
Glen
Lebrina
Wyena
Nabowla
Lletinna
Scottsdale
Telita
Herrick
Moorina
Bay of Fires
Beauty Point
Bell Bay
Kayena
Springfield
Mt Stronach 497m
Kamona
Derby
The Gardens
Beaconsfield
Deviot
Tunnel
West Scottsdale
Branxholm
Weldborough
Exeter
Sidmouth
Lower Turners Marsh
North Lilydale
Lisle
Cuckoo
Tonganah
Talandeena
99
Lottah
Flowery Gully
Holwell
Gravelly Beach
Turners Marsh
Lilydale
Legerwood
Ringarooma
Goulds Country
Stewarts Hill
Mount Direction
Turners
Kongola
South Springfield
Cuckoo Hill
Goshen
Priory
Grants Point
Winkleigh
Exeter
Lanena
Rosevears
Underwood
SOUTH SPRINGFIELD FOREST PARK
Mt Maurice 1120m
Talawa
Alberton
Binalong Bay
Glengarry
Notley Hills
Dilston
Myrtle Bank
Targa
St Patricks River
Diddleum Plains
St Helens Point
Frankford
Legana
Patersonia
Trenah
Mt Victoria 1208m
Ryengana
ST HELENS POINT CONSERVATION AREA
Birralee
Rosevale
RIVERSIDE
TREVALLYN
MOWBRAY
Nunamara
Mt Barrow 1413m
Mt Young 903m
St Helens
Reedy Marsh
LAUNCESTON
Franklin Village
White Hills
Burns Creek
Musselboro
Upper Esk
Mt Saddleback 1277m
Parkside
Deloraine
Hadspen
ROSES TIER
Dianas Basin
Exton
Hagley
Carrick
Breadalbane
Blessington
Upper Blessington
Mathinna
Beaumaris
Westbury
Pateena
Alpine Village
Scamander
Osmaston
Glenore
Illawarra
Perth
Western Junction
Carr Villa
Legges Tor 1575m
Mt Nicholas 869m
Cornwall
37
Falmouth
Quamby Brook
Whitemore
Oaks
Toiberry
Evandale
Hampden
BEN LOMOND NATIONAL PARK
Tower Hill
Four Mile Creek
Golden Valley
Bishopsbourne
Longford
Nile
Deddington
English Town
St Marys
Bracknell
Cluan
Richmond Hill
Claremont
Mangana
Gray
Liffey
Cressy
Kilrae
Powranna
Storys Creek
Rossarden
Fingal
Blackwood Creek
Esk Vale
Kelvin Grove
Fingal
66
Breona
Epping Forest
Bona-vista Estate
Brambletye
Avoca
Pisa
Parknook
Ellerslie
Llewellyn Siding
Royal George
Seymour
Poatina
The Glen
Rokeby
Mt St John 777m
Long Point
Cramps
The Bend
Woodland
Front Rocky Hill 574m
Campbell Town
NATIONAL
Bicheno
Tods Corner PS
Auburn
Woodbury
Goldsmith
Conara
West
DOUGLAS-APSLEY NATIONAL PARK
Governor Island
Miena
Flintstone
Mt Franklin 1102m
Ross
Lake Leake
Ferndale
Greenlawn
Wilburville
St Patricks Plains
Snobs Point 971m
B34
Llandaff
Shannon
Steppes
Lake Sorell
Lake Leake
Apslawn
Waddamana
Woods Lake
Mt Hobgoblin 763m
Cranbrook
FREYCINET NATIONAL PARK
Lake Echo
Interlaken
TUNBRIDGE TIER CONSERVATION AREA
Woodbury House
Mt Morriston
78
The Swansea Bark Mill
Swansea
Swanwick
Glengowan
Tunbridge
Mayfield
Coles Bay
The Hazards

TASMAN

SEA

Great Oyster Bay

INDEX

This index includes all towns and roadhouses; major places of interest, landforms and water features are also included. National Parks mentioned in the text are also listed in the index.

As well, historic places included in the book have been grouped State-by-State under major headings to make them more accessible. For example, there are listings such as buildings, churches, gaols, gardens, goldfields, hotels and inns, museums and wineries.

Place names are followed by a map page number and grid reference and/or the text page on which that place name occurs. For example:

Bathurst NSW 292 H6, 42–3
Bathurst – place name
NSW – State
292 H6 – Bathurst appears on this map page
42–3 – Major entry for Bathurst appears on these pages

The alphabetical order followed in the index is that of 'word-by-word', where all entries under one word are grouped together. Where a place name consists of more than one word, the order is governed by the first and then the second word. For example:

Green Point
Greenbank
Greens Beach

Greenwoood
Greg Greg
Gregory

Names beginning with Mc are indexed as Mac and those beginning with St, as Saint.

The following abbreviations and contractions are used in the index:

ACT – Australian Capital Territory
JBT – Jervis Bay Territory
NSW – New South Wales
NT – Northern Territory
Qld – Queensland
SA – South Australia
St – Saint
Tas. – Tasmania
Vic. – Victoria
WA – Western Australia

ACKNOWLEDGEMENTS

Project Managers
Margaret Barca
Astrid Browne

Design
Cathy Larsen, Penguin Design Studio

Editor
Clare Coney

Additional writing
Sarah Dawson (South Australia), Libby Lester
(Tasmania)

Editorial assistance & checking
Saskia Adams, Susan McLeish,
Karin Niehs, Julie Sheridan

Picture research
Margaret Barca, Ingrid Ohlsson, Heidi Marfurt,
Julie Sheridan

Cartography
Julie Sheridan with assistance from Damien Demaj

Map checking & research
Michael Archer, Damien Demaj, Julie Sheridan

Paging
Post Pre-press Group, Brisbane

Index
Fay Donlevy

Production
Sue Van Velsen

This book could not have been produced without
the generous assistance of many organisations
and individuals around Australia. The author
and publisher wish to thank the following for
assistance with research, mapping and photos.

NEW SOUTH WALES
Antiquities Museum, University of New England
Armidale City Council
Armidale Folk Museum
Armidale Visitor Information Centre
Bathurst City Council
Bathurst Tourism
Berrima Courthouse
Berrima Information Centre
Blue Mountains Regional Tourism Organisation
Broken Hill City Council
Broken Hill Tourism
Goulburn City Council
Goulburn Tourism
Hawkesbury City Council (Windsor)
Hawkesbury Museum and Information Centre
Hero of Waterloo Hotel
Historic Houses Trust of NSW
Line of Lode Visitors Centre & Museum,
   Broken Hill
National Trust of Australia (NSW)
New England Regional Art Museum
Norman Lindsay Gallery & Museum/National
   Trust (NSW)
NSW National Parks and Wildlife Service
Parliament House
Parramatta City Council
Parramatta Heritage & Visitors Information Centre
Powerhouse Museum
Railway, Mineral & Train Museum, Broken Hill
Strand Arcade

Sydney Harbour Foreshore Authority
Sydney Visitor Information Centre
The Outback Regional Tourism Organisation
The Rocks Sydney Visitor Information Centre
Tourism NSW
Windsor Visitor Information Centre
Wingecarribee Shire Council (Berrima)

AUSTRALIAN CAPITAL TERRITORY
ACT Cultural Facilities Corporation
All Saints' Church
Australian Heritage Commission
Australian War Memorial
Canberra Tourism & Events Corporation
Canberra Visitors Centre
National Archives of Australia
National Library of Australia
National Museum of Australia
National Portrait Gallery
National Trust of Australia (ACT)
Old Parliament House
St John the Baptist Anglican Church

VICTORIA
All Saints Winery
Ballarat Visitor Information Centre
Beechworth Information Centre
Bendigo Visitor Information Centre
Burke Museum, Beechworth
Centre Management, The Block Arcade
Campaspe Shire Council (Echuca)
City of Ballarat
Coal Creek Heritage Village, Korumburra
Echuca Information Centre
Geelong Otway Tourism
Geelong Visitor Information Centre
Glenelg Shire Council (Portland)
Greater Bendigo City Council
Greater Geelong City Council
Indigo Shire Council
Indigo Shire Council (Beechworth)
Maldon Museum
Maldon Visitor Information Centre
Maritime Museum, Geelong
Marriner Theatres (Melbourne)
Mount Alexander Shire Council (Maldon)
Mt Alexander Shire (Marketing & Promotions)
National Trust of Australia (Vic.)
Old Parliament House/The Gold Museum
Portland Maritime Discovery & Visitors Centre
Queenscliff Visitor Information Centre
Sharp's Magic Movie House & Penny Arcade,
   Echuca
Sovereign Hill, Ballarat
The Briars, Mornington
Tourism Victoria

SOUTH AUSTRALIA
Barossa Wine & Tourism Association
Bungaree Station, Clare
Burra Visitor Information Centre
Corporation of the Town of Gawler
District Council of Mt Barker (Hahndorf)
District Council of Robe
Gawler Visitor Information Centre
Hahndorf Visitor Information Centre
Maritime Museum of South Australia
National Trust of Australia (SA)
Port Adelaide Visitor Information Centre
Regional Council of Goyder (Burra)
Robe Visitor Information Centre
South Australian Museum
South Australian Tourism Commission
Victor Harbor Visitor Centre

WESTERN AUSTRALIA
Albany Visitor Centre
Battye Picture Library/Library Services of Western
   Australia
Broome Historical Society Museum
Broome Tourist Bureau
City of Albany
City of Fremantle
City of Kalgoorlie–Boulder
Fremantle Chamber of Commerce
Fremantle Prison
Fremantle Tourist Bureau
Goldfields Tourism Association
Harvey District Tourist Bureau Inc.
Houghtons Winery
Kalgoorlie–Boulder Tourist Centre
Martin Peirson-Jones
Museum of Childhood
National Trust of Australia (WA)
Pearl Luggers, Broome
Perth Mint
Residency Museum, York
Rottnest Island Tourism
Shire of Broome
Shire of York
Swan Valley Tourism
West Australian Museum
Western Australian Tourism Commission
York Motor Museum
York Tourist Bureau

NORTHERN TERRITORY
Alice Springs Town Council
Central Australian Tourism Industry Association
Museum & Art Gallery of the Northern
   Territory
National Trust of Australia (NT)
Parks & Wildlife Commission of the Northern
   Territory
Royal Flying Doctor Service
Tennant Creek Regional Tourist Association
Tourism Top End

QUEENSLAND
Ay-Ot Lookout, Charters Towers
Brisbane City Council
Brisbane Marketing
Brisbane's Living Heritage Network
Bundaberg District Tourism & Development
   Board Ltd
Castling Street Heritage Centre, Townsville
Central Highlands Tourist Organisation
Charters Towers Tourist Information Centre
City of Charters Towers
City of Maryborough
City of Rockhampton
City of Townsville
Cooloola Regional Development Bureau
Fraser Coast South Burnett Regional Tourism
   Board
Mackay Tourism & Development Bureau Ltd
Museum of Tropical Queensland, Townsville
Newstead House, Brisbane
Queensland Art Gallery
Queensland's Southern Downs Tourist Association
   Inc.
Rockhampton Tourist Information Centre
Toadshow, Brisbane
Tourism Tropical North Queensland
Townsville Enterprise Ltd

TASMANIA
Central Tasmanian Tourism Centre
Clarence City Council (Richmond)

Government House
Launceston City Council
Launceston Tourism
Lenna, Battery Point
National Trust of Australia (Tas.)
Old Hobart Town Pty Ltd
Port Arthur Historic Site
Port Arthur Historic Site Management Authority
Queen Victoria Museum & Art Gallery
State Library of Tasmania
Tasmanian Museum & Art Gallery
Theatre Royal
Tourism Tasmania

Special thanks
All Hallows School, Brisbane, for permission to
   reproduce the portrait of Lady Roma Bowen
Yvonne O'Hara Close for permission to reproduce
   the portrait of Hans Heysen by Joshua Smith
Celestine Doyle, CDE Communications
David Gibson, Newstead House, Brisbane
Bill Foster, National Trust (Tasmania)

Historic Images
Particular thanks for assistance with historic
images from:
Image Library, State Library of New South Wales
J S Battye Library of Western Australian History
John Oxley Library, State Library of Queensland
La Trobe Collection, State Library of Victoria
National Library of Australia, Canberra
State Library of South Australia

PICTURE CREDITS

Abbreviations
AHC Australian Heritage Commission
APL Australian Picture Library
AWM Australian War Memorial
BLH Brisbane Living Heritage Network
BP Bruce Postle
CG Chris Groenhout
DS Dennis Sarson
GM Geoff Murray
GORM Great Ocean Road Marketing Inc.
HP Hellene Post
HHT Historic Houses Trust of New South Wales
JB JP & ES Baker
JL Jiri Lochman
JM John Meier
JOL John Oxley Library
KS Ken Stepnell
LS Len Stewart
LT Lochman Transparencies
NLA National Library of Australia
NR Nick Rains
NT National Trust of Australia
PAA Picturesque Atlas of Australia
PBA Penguin Books Australia
PI Photo Index
PM Peter McNeill
RE Rick Eaves
RJ Ray Joyce
SATC South Australian Tourism Commission
SLNSW State Library of New South Wales
SP Stock Photos
SS Steve Strike/Outback Photographics
TNSW Tourism New South Wales
TQ Tourism Queensland
TT Tourism Tasmania

IMAGE IDENTIFICATION

The following images are identified using alphabetical order reading from the top left-hand corner in a clockwise direction.

Cover & preliminary pages

Front cover and spine RJ (car pictured supplied courtesy of Avis Australia). *Front flap* Sovereign Hill Museums Association (a), SS (b), Sharp's Magic Movie House & Penny Arcade (c). *Back cover* PI (a), JM (b), RE (c), SS (d). *Back flap* SATC (a), NR (b), Tourism Victoria (c), Courtesy of Telstra/Arthur Mostead (d). *Half-title page* GM (a), CG (b), Goulburn Tourism (c). *Title page* PBA/ Andrew Gregory. *iv & v* JM. vi & vii CG. x SA Museum (a), National Portrait Gallery (b). *xi* Sydney Harbour Foreshore Authority (a), SLNSW (b), SS (c).

Chapters

1 NR. *2* JM. 3 PAA. *4* SP/Lance Nelson. *5* HHT/RJ. *6* PM (a), Australian National Maritime Museum (b). *8* HHT/RJ. *9* HHT/RJ (a), NSW Parliament House (b). *10* TNSW (a), Strand Arcade (b). *11* Powerhouse Museum (a), Ian Lever (b). *12* TNSW (a), HHT/Richard Gance (b). *13* PBA/NR. *14* Nutcote (a), NR (b). *15* HHT/RJ. *16* Hero of Waterloo Hotel (a), Sydney Harbour Foreshore Authority (b, d), PAA (c). *17* JM (a), PM (b), Sydney Harbour Foreshore Authority (c), HHT (d). *18* JB. *21* JM. *22* NR. *24* NT (NSW)/Norman Lindsay Gallery & Museum. *26* JM. *27* JB (a), JM (b). *28* NR. *29* NR. *30* CG. *31* JM. *32* TNSW. *33* HHT/RJ. *34* Cartoscope. *36* NR. *37* TNSW. *38* PBA/JB. *39* JM. *40* University of New England/ Museum of Antiquities (a), Armidale Visitor Information Centre (b, e), New England Regional Art Museum (oil on cardboard, gift of Howard Hinton 1946, the Howard Hinton Collection/c), TNSW (d). *41* Armidale Visitor Information Centre (a, b), Armidale Folk Museum (c, d). *42* Bathurst Visitor Information Centre (a, c, d, e), PAA (b). *43* JM (a), Bathurst Visitor Information Centre (b, c), NLA (Charles Meere, c. 1946, PIC R10684/d). *44* JM (a), Ian Lever (b), TNSW/ Robbi Newman (c), JB (d), SP/Lance Nelson (e). *45* Ian Lever (a), JB (b, c), NSW National Parks and Wildlife Service/Ford Kristo (d). *46* Broken Hill Visitor Information Centre (a), Railway, Mineral & Train Museum (b), PM (c), NLA (PIC R10309/d). *47* Broken Hill Visitor Information Centre (a), PM (b), Line of Lode Visitors Centre and Museum (c), NR (d). *48* JB (a, e), Goulburn Tourism (b), NLA (PIC T2848 NK6831/1-3/c), NLA (Auburn Street, Goulburn/d). *49* JM (a), JB (b, c), Goulburn Tourism (d). *50* Parramatta City Council (a, c), NLA (PIC R5103/b), SLNSW/ Mitchell Library (d). *51* Parramatta Heritage Centre (a), Parramatta Council/TNSW (b), SLNSW/Dixson Gallery (c), HHT/RJ (d), JM (e). *52* NLA (Terrace doorway, Dr Callaghan's House, Hardy Wilson, 1915, PIC R548/a), SLNSW/ Mitchell Library (b), Hawkesbury Museum & Visitor Information Centre/Alan Aldrich (c). *53* PBA/Kirstie Laffin (a, d, e, f), NLA (Hardy Wilson, 1912, PIC R659/b), Hawkesbury Museum & Visitor Information Centre/Alan Aldrich (c). *54* Canberra Tourism & Events Corporation. *56* JB. *57* NLA (Percy Trompf, Parliament House Canberra, c. 1930s, PIC poster Z150). *58* PBA/JB (a), National Archives of Australia (b). National Museum of Australia (a), National Portrait Gallery (John Weber (c. 1752-93), *Portrait of Captain James Cook RN* (1728-79), 1782, oil on canvas, purchased 2000 by Commonwealth Government with assistance of Robert Oatley and John Schaeffer, photo David Reid/b), PBA/JB (c). *61* PBA/JB (a), ACT Cultural Facilities Corporation (b). *62* JM (a), ACT Cultural Facilities Corporation (b). *63* Canberra Tourism & Events Corporation. *64* BP (a), AWM (George Lambert, *CEW Bean*, 1924, oil on canvas 90.7 x 71.7cm, ART07545/b; ARTV00332/c; d). *65* AWM (a, b, c, d, e). *66* JM. *68* Sovereign Hill Museums Association. *69* PAA. *70* BP. *71* CG. *72* JM (a), PBA/CG (b). *74* BP (a), PBA/CG (b). *75* BP (a), PBA/CG. *76* PBA/CG (a), KS (b). *77* Marriner Theatres. *78* CG. 79 PBA/CG (a, b). *80* PBA/Gary Lewis. *81* NT (Vic.). *82* ANZ Bank Archives (a), Block Arcade Management/John Kirby (b), CG (c). *83* PAA (a, d), Gold Museum (b), NLA (PIC 3292 CON 419/c). *84* JM. *85* APL/Douglass Baglin. *87* Mount Alexander Shire. *89* CG. *90* Coal Creek Heritage Village. *92* JM. *93* PBA/KS. *95* JM. *96* BP. *97* CG. *98* GORM. *99* JM. *100* NT (Vic.). *101* SP/Lance Nelson. *102* AHC (a), Ballarat Fine Art Gallery (b), JB (c), Ballarat Tourism (d). *103* NLA (Portrait of Adam Lindsay Gordon, c. 1865, PIC R10441/a), Ballarat Tourism (b), Sovereign Hill Museums Association (c, d). *104* Burke Museum (a, b, c), JB (d), CG (e). *105* Indigo Shire (a), JB (b), NLA (*Australasian Sketcher*, 1880, p. 134/c), SP/Lance Nelson (d). *106* JB (a), Central Deborah Goldmine (b), NLA (G. Pearce, The Myers Creek Rush, c. 1867, T2243/c), Bendigo Library (d), Tourism Victoria (e). *107* JM (a), JB (b), AHC (c), Tourism Victoria (d). *108* NLA (George French Angas, 'Sketches from an Artist's Travels', 1877, PIC R6460/a), PBA (b), Sharp's Magic Movie House & Penny Arcade (c), NLA (Raymond De Berquelle, Courthouse, 1994, PIC 952/1-40/d), PBA/Cathy Larsen (e). *109* JB (a, e), NLA (*Portrait of Henry Hopwood*, Dr John Phillips Collection, Plate No. 27932/b; Loading Wool, Echuca Wharf, 1874, *Australasian Sketcher*, 1874/c), PBA/Cathy Larsen (d), JB (e). *110* Geelong Otway Tourism (a, b). *111* Osborne House Naval and Maritime Museum (a), AHC (b), JM (c), NLA (PIC S723/d), NT (Vic.) (e). *112* JB (a, c), SP/Pauline Madden (b), NLA (Rupert Bunny, 1910, PIC R4000/d). *113* Maldon Historical Society (a, e), Mount Alexander Shire (b, c), APL/JB (d). *114* NLA (Fergusson & Mitchell, 1880, PIC U6661 NK 3321/a), AHC (b), PBA/CG (c). *115* NLA (*Admella* shipwreck, plate no. 26620/a), AHC (b, d), GORM. (c). *116* La Trobe Picture Collection, State Library of Victoria (a, d), BP (b), GORM (c), Borough of Queenscliffe (e). *117* BP (a), GORM (b), NLA (PIC R466/c). *118* JM. *120* JM. *121* NLA (PIC U974 NK3544-C). *122* NR. *123* BP. *124* SATC (a, b). *126* JM. *127* SA Museum (a), KS (b). *128* SATC (a, b). *129* BP. *130* BP (a), JB (b, d), PBA (c). *131* SATC (a, d), SA Maritime Museum (b), BP (c). *132* JM. *133* BP. *134* Bungaree Station. *135* NR. *136* SATC. *137* SATC. *138* SATC. *140* JM. *141* BP. *142* JM. *143* NR. *144* NR. *145* SATC. *146* KS. *147* SATC. *148* SATC. *149* JM. *150* BP (a, b, c, d). *151* SATC (a, c, d), BP (b), JM (e). *152* PBA/Paul Barnet (a, b, c, d), State Library of South Australia (e). *153* SATC (a), PBA/Paul Barnet (b, e), La Trobe Picture Collection, State Library of Victoria (c), BP (d). *154* NR (a), BP (b), SATC (c). *155* BP (a, e), NLA (PIC R4968/b), SATC (c, d), JM (f). *156* NR (a), State Library of South Australia (b), BP (c), JM (d). *157* BP (a, c, e), NLA (S.T. Gill, PIC S3737/b), JM (d). *158* PI/Greg Hocking. *160* PM. *161* PAA. *162* LT/DS. *163* Robert Garvey. *164* LT/DS (a), PI/ Paul Steel (b). 166 LT/Brian Downs (a), LT/LS (b). *167* WA Museum (a), JB (b). *168* KS. *169* Houghton Wines. *170* NLA (PIC R7617/a), LT/DS (b) LT/LS (c). *171* LT/LS (a, b), Perth Mint (c), LT/JL (d), WA Newspapers (e). *172* KS. 174 PI/Richard Woldendorp. *176* PBA/NR. *179* KS. *180* KS. *181* JB. *182* LT/LS (a), LT/Bill Belson (b), WA Museum (c), LT/JL (d). *183* Battye Library (9898P/a), KS (b), LT/Bill Belson (c), LT/DS (d). *184* LT/JL (a), SS (b), Martin Peirson-Jones (c), LT/Wade Hughes (d), Battye Library (001294D/e). *185* LT/DS (a), Pearl Luggers (b), Broome Historical Society (c), PM (d). *186* Fremantle Chamber of Commerce (a), WA Maritime Museum (b), KS (c). *187* WA Museum (a, b), Fremantle Prison (c), Fremantle Chamber of Commerce (d). *188* JB (a), Goldfields Tourism Association (b, c). *189* LT/DS (a, b), JB (c, e), LT/JL (d), WA Newspapers (f). *190* LT/Marie Lochman (a, d), LT/JL (b), PBA/Gary Lewis. *191* LT/JL (a, b, d, e), York Motor Museum (c). *192* JM. *193* Auscape International/John Shaw. *195* PAA. 196 LT/DS. *197* Museum & Art Gallery of the NT. *198* SS (a), James Braund (b). *200* KS. *201* SS. *202* GM. *203* SS. *204* BP. *205* SS (a, b). *206* SS. *207* PBA/JB. *208* SS (a, b), Royal Flying Doctor Service (c, e), NLA (Percy Trompf, *Winter Holidays by Rail to Central Australia*, c. 1930s, PIC Poster Z381/d). *209* National Pioneer Women's Hall of Fame (a), SS (b, c). *210* Alice Springs Cultural Precinct/SS (a, b), PBA (c), JB (d). *211* Auscape International/Jean-Paul Ferrero (a), Queensland Art Gallery (oil on canvas, 102.1 x 76.4 cm/b), SS (c). *212* NR. *214* JM. *215* PAA. *216* TQ. *217* BLH. *218* Commissariat Store (a), TQ (b). *220* SP/Lance Nelson. *221* BLH (a, b). *222* Newstead House. *223* BLH. *224* BP (a), JOL/All Hallows School (b), JB (c). *225* BP (a), PAA (b), BLH (c, d), City Botanic Gardens (e). *226* TQ. *227* SS. *228* TQ. *229* TQ. *231* TQ. *232* NR. *233* TQ. *235* SS. *236* JM. *237* JM. *238* JM (a, c), JOL (b), NR (d). *239* JM (a), Ay-Ot Lookout (b), PAA (c), TQ (d). *240* PAA (a), BP (b, c). *241* JM (a, c), BP (b), TQ (d, e). *242* JOL (a), SS (b), BP (c, e), TQ (d). *243* BP (a), TQ (b), SS (c). *244* JB (a), JOL (b), Museum of Tropical Queensland (c), SS (d). *245* Townsville Museum (a), NT (Qld) (b, c), TQ (d). *246* TT/RJ. *248* GM. *249* PAA. *250* Richard Bennett. *251* Theatre Royal. *252* State Library of Tasmania (a), GM (b). *254* TT/GM (a), TT (b). *255* TT/Nick Osborne (a), Tasmanian Museum & Art Gallery (b). *256* TT (a), RE (b). *257* RJ. *258* State Library of Tasmania (a), NLA (Trisha Dixon, c. 1990s, PIC P626/36/b), TT (c, d). *259* Lenna (a), AHC (b), NLA (Vandyck, c. 1909, PIC P2074/c), RE (d), RJ (e). *260* TT. *261* RJ. *262* NLA (Trisha Dixon, c. 1990s, PIC P626/30). *263* RE. *264* PBA/NR. *265* RJ. *266* HP. *267* RJ. *268* GM. *270* RJ (a), TT/RJ (b). *271* TT/GM. *272* TT/RJ. *273* RJ. *274* HP. *275* RE. *276* RE. *277* GM. *278* PAA (a), RE (b), TT/JB (c), Queen Victoria Museum & Art Gallery (d). *279* HP (a), TT/JB (b), HP (c), RE (d, e). *280* NLA (Benjamin Duterrau, c. 1832, PIC R15/a), JB (b), SLNSW (c), RE (d). *281* TT/George Apostolidis (a), JB (b, e), RJ (c), TT/GM (d). *282* JB (a), RE (b), KS (c), RE (d). *283* NR (a), GM (b), JB (c), NLA (Eirene Mort, 1933, PIC R5203/d), HP (e).

Viking

Published by the Penguin Group
Penguin Books Australia Ltd
250 Camberwell Road, Camberwell, Victoria 3124, Australia
Penguin Books Ltd
80 Strand, London WC2R 0RL, England
Penguin Putnam Inc.
375 Hudson Street, New York, New York 10014, USA
Penguin Books, a division of Pearson Canada
10 Alcorn Avenue, Toronto, Ontario, Canada M4V 3B2
Penguin Books (NZ) Ltd
Cnr Rosedale and Airborne Roads, Albany, Auckland, New Zealand
Penguin Books (South Africa) (Pty) Ltd
24 Sturdee Avenue, Rosebank, Johannesburg 2196, South Africa
Penguin Books India (P) Ltd
11, Community Centre, Panchsheel Park, New Delhi 110 017, India

First published by Penguin Books Australia Ltd, 2002

10 9 8 7 6 5 4 3 2 1

Copyright © Penguin Books Australia Ltd, 2002

The moral right of the author has been asserted

All rights reserved. Without limiting the rights under copyright reserved above, no part of this publication may be reproduced, stored in or introduced into a retrieval system, or transmitted, in any form or by any means (electronic, mechanical, photocopying, recording or otherwise), without the prior written permission of both the copyright owner and the above publisher of this book.

Printed in China by Midas Printing (Asia) Ltd

National Library of Australia Cataloguing-in-Publication data:

Barca, Margaret.
Explore historic Australia: your guide to Australia's fascinating past.

ISBN 0 670 90268 3.

1. Historic sites – Australia – Guidebooks.
2. Historic buildings – Australia – Guidebooks.
3. Australia – Guidebooks. I. Title.

919.404

Publisher's Note: Every effort has been made to ensure that the information in this book is accurate at the time of going to press. The publisher welcomes information and suggestions for correction or improvement.
Email: cartog@penguin.com.au

Disclaimers: Every effort has been made to trace copyright holders of historic images. The publisher cannot accept responsibility for any errors or omissions. The representation on the maps of any road or track is not necessarily evidence of public right of way.

www.penguin.com.au

Find out how
Telstra Country Wide™
can help you enjoy your holiday

Telstra Country Wide™ and Explore Australia

Telstra Country Wide provides communications services to three million regional and rural customers through a network of local managers and area offices across mainland Australia and Tasmania.

The Telstra Country Wide web site – **www.telstra.com/countrywide** – provides regional and rural Australians with relevant, local information, including an extensive online travel section provided by Explore Australia. The travel section includes detailed maps, comprehensive travel information, and online accommodation booking for locations Australia wide.

The Explore Australia CD-ROM contains tips on how Telstra Country Wide can help you enjoy your holiday – from planning your trip, staying in contact on the road and catching up with friends and family when you are back home.

Wherever you are in Australia, Telstra Country Wide has the information and services to help you enjoy your holiday.

Telstra
Country Wide

www.telstra.com/countrywide